ARIZONA

Where to Stay and Eat
for All Budgets

Must-See Sights
and Local Secrets

Ratings You Can Trust

Fodor's Travel Publications   New York, Toronto, London, Sydney, Auckland
www.fodors.com

FODOR'S ARIZONA 2005

Editor: Mary Beth Bohman

Editorial Production: David Downing
Editorial Contributors: Matt Baatz, Collin Campbell, Tom Carpenter, Andrew Collins, Janet Webb Farnsworth, Satu Hummasti, Mara Levin, Carrie Miner, Bob and Gloria Willis
Maps: David Lindroth, Inc.; Mark Stroud, Moon Street Cartography, *cartographers*; Bob Blake and Rebecca Baer, *map editors*
Design: Fabrizio La Rocca, *creative director*; Guido Caroti, *art director*; Melanie Marin, *senior picture editor*
Cover Design: Moon Sun Kim
Production/Manufacturing: Robert B. Shields
Cover Photo (tourists on horseback in the Grand Canyon): T. Gervis/Robert Harding World Imagery

ISBN 1–4000–1435–2

ISSN 1525–5026

SPECIAL SALES

This book is available for special discounts for bulk purchases for sales promotions or premiums. Special editions, including personalized covers, excerpts of existing books, and corporate imprints, can be created in large quantities for special needs. For more information, write to Special Markets/Premium Sales, 1745 Broadway, MD 6-2, New York, New York 10019, or e-mail specialmarkets@randomhouse.com.

AN IMPORTANT TIP & AN INVITATION

Although all prices, opening times, and other details in this book are based on information supplied to us at press time, changes occur all the time in the travel world, and Fodor's cannot accept responsibility for facts that become outdated or for inadvertent errors or omissions. So **always confirm information when it matters**, especially if you're making a detour to visit a specific place. Your experiences—positive and negative—matter to us. If we have missed or misstated something, **please write to us**. We follow up on all suggestions. Contact the Arizona editor at editors@fodors.com or c/o Fodor's at 1745 Broadway, New York, NY 10019.

PRINTED IN THE UNITED STATES OF AMERICA

10 9 8 7 6 5 4 3 2 1

DESTINATION ARIZONA

The splendor of Arizona's natural landmarks—from the vastness of the Grand Canyon to the 1,000-foot-high walls of Canyon de Chelly to the myriad shapes and spires of Monument Valley to Sedona's red rocks and the living Sonoran Desert—is reason enough to visit. But there is more to the state than beautiful vistas. Traces of a rich, layered history mark the awesome terrain and inspire artists, artisans, and the discerning shoppers who buy their work, from beautifully woven Navajo rugs to the cowboy paintings of the incomparable Lon Megargee. Arizona's cuisines are captivating, whether you enjoy spicy Sonoran Mexican or more sophisticated, contemporary Southwestern cuisine. Take time to absorb the calming lessons of the heat and the majestic landscape—on the still waters of a magnificent lake at sunset or beside a fountain on an awning-shaded patio over lunch—and a bit of Arizona will stay with you forever. Have a fabulous trip!

Tim Jarrell, Publisher

CONTENTS

On the Road with Fodor's F7
About This Book F8
What's Where F12
Great Itineraries F14
When to Go F16

On the Calendar F17
Pleasures & Pastimes F21
Fodor's Choice F23
Smart Travel Tips F29

① Phoenix, Scottsdale & the Valley of the Sun   1

Exploring the Valley
  of the Sun 4
Where to Eat 22
Where to Stay 42
Nightlife & the Arts 56

Sports & the Outdoors 61
Shopping 68
Side Trips near Phoenix 72
The Apache Trail 80
Valley of the Sun A to Z 86

② North-Central Arizona   91

The Verde Valley, Jerome &
  Prescott 95
Sedona & Oak Creek
  Canyon 109

Flagstaff 123
Side Trips near Flagstaff 135
North-Central Arizona
  A to Z 138

③ The Grand Canyon   142

Approaching the South Rim:
  Williams & Tusayan 146
Grand Canyon National Park:
  The South Rim 155
Grand Canyon:
  The West Rim 169

Approaching the North Rim:
  Lees Ferry & Jacob Lake 172
Grand Canyon National Park:
  The North Rim 179
The Grand Canyon A to Z 184

④ The Northeast   192

Navajo Nation East 194
The Hopi Mesas 205
Navajo Nation West 210
Navajo Nation North &
  Monument Valley 213

Glen Canyon Dam & Lake
  Powell 219
The Northeast A to Z 228

⑤ Eastern Arizona   231

The White Mountains 236
The Petrified Forest & the
  Painted Desert 256

Eastern Arizona A to Z 261

⑥ Tucson 264

Exploring Tucson 266
Where to Eat 285
Where to Stay 296
Nightlife & the Arts 306

Sports & the Outdoors 310
Shopping 315
Side Trips near Tucson 319
Tucson A to Z 322

⑦ Southern Arizona 327

Southeast Arizona 330
Southwest Arizona 355

Southern Arizona A to Z 365

⑧ Northwest Arizona & Southeast Nevada 368

Northwest Arizona 371
Southeast Nevada 380

Northwest Arizona & Southeast
Nevada A to Z 387

Understanding Arizona 389

Arizona at a Glance 390
The Native Southwest 392

Books & Movies 397

Index 400

Maps

Arizona F10–F11
Greater Phoenix 6
What to See in Downtown
Phoenix 8
What to See in Greater
Phoenix 10–11
What to See in Scottsdale 17
Where to Eat in the Valley of
the Sun 24–25
Where to Stay in the Valley of
the Sun 44–45
Side Trips near Phoenix 74
North-Central Arizona 96
Prescott 104
Sedona 110
Flagstaff 125
Grand Canyon South Rim 157
Grand Canyon North Rim 173

Northeast Arizona 198–199
Eastern Arizona 238
What to See in Downtown
Tucson 270
What to See at the University of
Arizona 274
What to See in Greater
Tucson 278
Where to Stay & Eat in
Tucson 286–287
Side Trips near Tucson 320
Southeast Arizona 332
Southwest Arizona 356
Northwest Arizona & Southeast
Nevada 374
Bullhead City & Laughlin,
Nevada 383

CloseUps

On the Mexican Menu 26
Baseball's Three Seasons 62
The Lost Dutchman Mine 81
Rodeo Lesson 107
Vortex Tour 111
Tips for Avoiding Canyon
    Crowds 148
Freebies at the Canyon 166
Grand Canyon Nature
    Primer 180

Reservation Rules 200
Reservation Realities 207
Traveling in Navajoland 214
The Writing on the Wall 247
The Desert's Fragile Giant 282
Where the West is Still
    Wild 304
A Tequila Snapshot 344
The Man Who Died Twice 376
General Jesup & the Camels 381

ON THE ROAD WITH FODOR'S

A trip takes you out of yourself. Concerns of life at home completely disappear, driven away by more immediate thoughts—about, say, what marvels will beguile the next day, or where you'll have dinner. That's where Fodor's comes in. We make sure that you know all your options, so that you don't miss something that's around the next bend just because you didn't know it was there. Because the best memories of your trip might well have nothing to do with what you came to Arizona to see, we guide you to sights large and small all over the region. You might set out to see the Grand Canyon, but back at home you find yourself unable to forget the sunset from atop one of the Hopi Mesas or that great Mexican restaurant on Tucson's South 4th Avenue. With Fodor's at your side, serendipitous discoveries are never far away.

Our success in showing you every corner of the Grand Canyon State is a credit to our extraordinary writers. Although there's no substitute for travel advice from a good friend who knows your style, our contributors are the next best thing—the kind of people you would poll for travel advice if you knew them.

Flagstaff resident Matt Baatz spends most free moments mountain biking and hiking the trails near Flagstaff and Sedona. He has traversed hundreds of miles of forest, desert, and canyon, but what remains unexplored may occupy him for years to come.

Newspaper columnist Tom Carpenter is a frequent contributor to *Arizona Highways* and *True West*. Tom has been poking around western Arizona and southern Nevada for over forty years. He still finds new and exciting places in the region to visit and explore.

Janet Webb Farnsworth is a true Native Arizonian; her family has been in the state for six generations. She's explored Arizona from one end to the other and is a frequent contributor to *Arizona Highways* and other southwestern travel magazines. She lives in Snowflake in Arizona's beautiful White Mountains.

Finland native Satu Hummasti came to Arizona almost eight years ago. She spent three years as an almost constant resident but now divides her time between Phoenix and New York City, where she works as a freelance writer and dancer.

Tucson updater Mara Levin divides her time among travel writing, social work, and her role as mom to two daughters. A native of California, Mara now lives in Tucson, where the grass may not be greener but the mountains, tranquility, and slower pace of desert life have their own appeal.

Carrie Miner first saw the Grand Canyon when she moved to Arizona at the age of 17. What she originally dismissed as a "big hole in the ground" soon became a challenge that she has now explored to its sublime depths. Carrie has written about her home state for Fodor's and for *Arizona Highways*.

Bob and Gloria Willis, a husband-and-wife freelance travel-writing and photography team, reside in Scottsdale. They spend time riding through, camping in, and four-wheeling through Arizona with their dog, who was adopted in one of their favorite places, Canyon de Chelly.

ABOUT THIS BOOK

The best source for travel advice is a like-minded friend who's just been where you're headed. But with or without that friend, you'll be in great shape to find your way around your destination once you learn to find your way around your Fodor's guide.

SELECTION

Our goal is to cover the best properties, sights, and activities in their category, as well as the most interesting communities to visit. We make a point of including local food-lovers' hot spots as well as neighborhood options, and we avoid all that's touristy unless it's really worth your time. You can go on the assumption that everything in this book is recommended wholeheartedly by our writers and editors. Flip to On the Road with Fodor's to learn more about who they are. It goes without saying that no property pays to be included.

RATINGS

Orange stars ★ denote sights and properties that our editors and writers consider the very best in the area covered by the entire book. These, the best of the best, are listed in the Fodor's Choice section in the front of the book. Black stars ★ highlight the sights and properties we deem Highly Recommended, the don't-miss sights within any region. In cities, sights pinpointed with numbered map bullets ❶ in the margins tend to be more important than those without bullets.

SPECIAL SPOTS

Pleasures & Pastimes and text on chapter-title pages focus on experiences that reveal the spirit of the destination. Also watch for Off the Beaten Path sights. Some are out of the way, some are quirky, and all are worthwhile. When the munchies hit, look for Need a Break? suggestions.

TIME IT RIGHT

Check On the Calendar up front and chapters' Timing sections for weather and crowd overviews and best days and times to visit.

SEE IT ALL

Use Fodor's exclusive Great Itineraries as a model for your trip. Either follow those that begin the book, or mix regional itineraries from several chapters. In cities, Good Walks guide you to important sights in each neighborhood; ▶ indicates the starting points of walks and itineraries in the text and on the map.

BUDGET WELL

Hotel and restaurant price categories from ¢ to $$$$ are defined in the opening pages of each chapter—expect to find a balanced selection for every budget. For attractions, we always give standard adult admission fees; reductions are usually available for children, students, and senior citizens. Look in Discounts & Deals in Smart Travel Tips for information on destination-wide ticket schemes. Want to pay with plastic? AE, D, DC, MC, V following restaurant and hotel listings indicate whether American Express, Discover, Diner's Club, MasterCard, or Visa is accepted.

BASIC INFO

Smart Travel Tips lists travel essentials for the entire area covered by the book; city- and region-specific basics end each chapter. To find the best way to get around, see the transportation section; see individual modes of travel ("Car Travel," "Train Travel") for details.

ON THE MAPS | Maps throughout the book show you what's where and help you find your way around. Black and orange numbered bullets ❻ ❻ in the text correlate to bullets on maps.

BACKGROUND | In general, we give background information within the chapters in the course of explaining sights as well as in CloseUp boxes and in Understanding Arizona at the end of the book. To get in the mood, review the suggestions in Books & Movies.

FIND IT FAST | Within the book, chapters are arranged in a roughly clockwise direction starting with Phoenix. Attractive routes and interesting places between towns are flagged as En Route. Heads at the top of each page help you find what you need within a chapter.

DON'T FORGET | Restaurants are open for lunch and dinner daily unless we state otherwise; we mention dress only when there's a specific requirement and reservations only when they're essential or not accepted—it's always best to book ahead. Hotels have private baths, phone, TVs, and air-conditioning and operate on the European Plan (a.k.a. EP, meaning without meals). We always list facilities but not whether you'll be charged extra to use them, so when pricing accommodations, find out what's included.

SYMBOLS

Many Listings

★ Fodor's Choice
★ Highly recommended
⊠ Physical address
✛ Directions
🕮 Mailing address
☏ Telephone
🖷 Fax
⊕ On the Web
✉ E-mail
🎟 Admission fee
☉ Open/closed times
▶ Start of walk/itinerary
⊟ Credit cards

Outdoors

⚠ Camping

Hotels & Restaurants

🏨 Hotel
🛏 Number of rooms
⟁ Facilities
¶◯¶ Meal plans
✕ Restaurant
⚑ Reservations
👗 Dress code
↘ Smoking
🕮 BYOB
✕🏨 Hotel with restaurant that warrants a visit

Other

🖐 Family-friendly
🛈 Contact information
⇨ See also
⊠ Branch address
☞ Take note

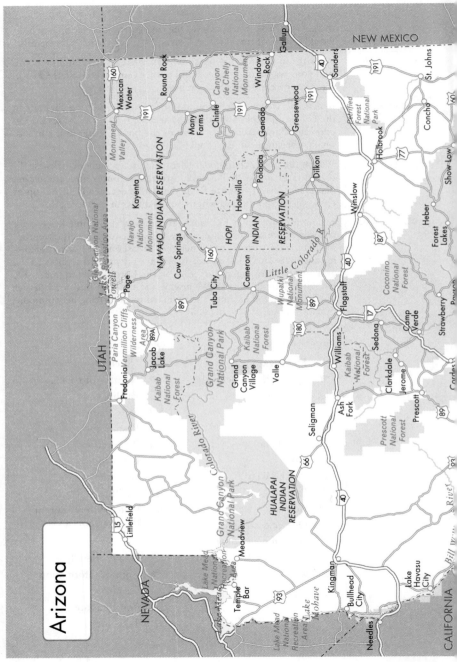

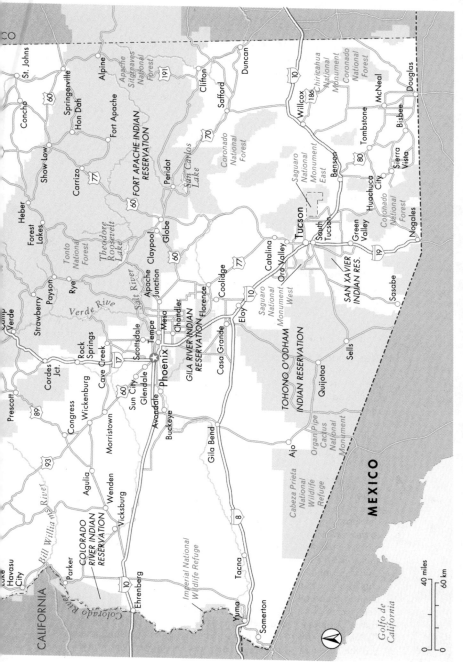

WHAT'S WHERE

(1) Phoenix, Scottsdale & the Valley of the Sun

Rising where the Sonoran Desert butts up against the Superstition Mountains, the Phoenix metropolitan area, known as the Valley of the Sun, is one of America's fastest growing communities. It includes Scottsdale, Tempe, and some 20 other communities surrounded by a landscape of stunning beauty. Frank Lloyd Wright was so taken with the area when he consulted on Phoenix's Biltmore resort in 1927 that he built a sprawling winter home, Taliesin West, on 600 rugged acres outside Scottsdale. Today, you can hike in the valley's superb desert parks, golf on championship courses, dine at some of the state's best restaurants, or luxuriate at pricey resorts and spas.

(2) North-Central Arizona

The laid-back towns of north-central Arizona are as bewitching as the landscape they inhabit. Phoenicians flee the summertime heat of the Valley to cool off in the mountains and to explore the territorial capital of Prescott and the copper camp of Jerome. Sedona's red rocks are the perfect backdrop for hiking and mountain biking, or for just relaxing at one of the many excellent B&Bs. The town's "vortices" may or may not concentrate the planet's energy and create a perfect environment for the nourishment and alignment of the soul, but they certainly have their draw. Young and outdoorsy Flagstaff is the hub of the entire region. North and south of Flagstaff are the cliff dwellings left by the Sinagua people who built prodigiously across this area in between the 8th and 15th centuries.

(3) The Grand Canyon

The Grand Canyon, one of nature's longest-running works in progress, both exalts and humbles the human spirit. Once you've seen the Canyon, you'll understand the true meaning of the word "grand." You can view the spectacle from the South Rim, but the North Rim is the rim less traveled, and its devotees don't mind a bit. They like the elbow room and willingly travel to see views that outdazzle even the stunners farther south. Don't just peer over the edge—take the plunge into the canyon on a mule train, on foot, or on a raft trip.

(4) The Northeast

Most residents of northeastern Arizona are Navajo and Hopi, and—although computers are part of their daily life now—traditions endure here that predate the conquistadors. Portions of high-desert country are holy to those who live here—almost all of this land is majestic. Wind and frost have created magical effects in stone, such as the petrified sand dunes in sunset-hued Antelope Canyon. Monument Valley is the starkly beautiful landscape made popular by Ansel Adams and countless Hollywood Westerns. Along with the living Navajo and Hopi communities, the White House Ruin in breathtaking Canyon de Chelly and the ruins at Betatakin and Keet Seel in Navajo National Monument are eloquent reminders of how ancient peoples wrested shelter from this fierce land. At Lake Powell, Glen Canyon Dam inverted the equation: here, humankind dominated nature, and the lake created is a spectacular meeting of earth and water.

5 Eastern Arizona

Eastern Arizona, by turns, is verdant or stark and haunting. The White Mountains, northeast of Phoenix, contain the world's largest stand of ponderosa pines, as well as alpine meadows decked with wildflowers and some of the cleanest air you'll ever breathe. If you love the outdoor life, you may well fall in love with this place. To the northeast, Homolovi Ruins State Park preserves five ancestral Hopi pueblos. The Painted Desert assumes hues from blood red to pink, then back again, as the sun rises, climbs, and sets. And Petrified Forest National Park protects a forest of trees that stood when dinosaurs walked the earth, the pieces of petrified logs looking deceptively like driftwood cast upon an oceanless beach.

6 Tucson

Claiming that Phoenix has paved over the desert in its sprawl, Tucsonans say the serenity of their mostly arid land imparts an easygoing personality to their city. A walk in verdant Sabino Canyon, a favorite of hikers that's within the city limits, does nothing to dispel that notion. Neither does a stroll among the towering cacti of Saguaro National Park. Colonial Spain and Mexico left a strong imprint on Tucson's art, architecture, cuisine, and culture. Traditional Mexican adobes and wide-porch Territorial homes underscore the city's Hispanic heritage. The residents of South 4th Avenue swear the best Mexican food north of the border is served here. A little farther out, city slickers enjoy daily horseback rides at some of the region's many guest ranches or luxury pampering at one of the local spas.

7 Southern Arizona

You might be tempted to dismiss southern Arizona as a desolate, empty landscape. You'd be wrong. Mountain-and-desert scenery as splendid as any in Arizona is one reason, including the remarkable fauna and rock formations at Chiricahua National Monument. Enduring pockets of the Old West in the form of ghost towns are another. Tombstone, not in the least ghostly, hums with commerce and reenactments of the shootout in the OK Corral. In southern Arizona, the old frontier is not the only frontier: at Kitt Peak National Observatory, astronomers gaze into the unexplored depths of the universe. And deep below the dry desert, near Benson, is Kartchner Caverns, one of the most spectacular wet cave systems in the world.

8 Northwest Arizona & Southeast Nevada

From pine-covered peaks and cacti-bedecked deserts, to the Colorado River and three long, enticing lakes, the under-explored northwest corner of Arizona is worth a closer look. Lake Havasu City offers a bit of Britannia in the form of London Bridge. Old-fashioned Americana reigns around Kingman, a hub on legendary Route 66, that pre-interstate icon of American restlessness and the call of the open road. Oatman is a ghost town with a main street straight out of a Western movie. Take a quick jaunt across the state line into Nevada for a look at the monumental Hoover Dam and a hand or two of blackjack in a riverside casino at Laughlin.

Highlights of Arizona
14 days

Ghostly Native American ruins, chamber music in Sedona, color-soaked canyons, shopping in Tucson: Arizona is full of history, culture, and good times. Start or end this survey with a few days in Phoenix.

PRESCOTT, JEROME & SEDONA
2 days. From Phoenix, head northwest to take a look around Prescott, "Everyone's Hometown," and its old-fashioned town square, Victorian homes, and pine-covered foothills. The near-ghost town of Jerome clings to the mountainside nearby. Surrounded by windswept sandstone, Sedona is breathtaking, as well.

GRAND CANYON
2 days. The Grand Canyon is truly one of the wonders of the world. Whether you raft the Colorado, ride a mule, tackle a hike, or gaze from the terrace of a rim-side hotel, time here is always an adventure.

NAVAJO NATIONAL MONUMENT & MONUMENT VALLEY
1 day. Tram tours led by Navajo guides roll past the sandstone mesas and spires of Monument Valley, where private cars can't go. At Navajo National Monument, linger among the cliff dwellings and ponder the lives of those who came before.

CANYON DE CHELLY
2 days. Journey into magical Canyon de Chelly on foot, on horseback, or in a guided four-wheel-drive vehicle to view Native American ruins and the magnificent sandstone landscape.

THE HOPI MESAS
2 days. Rising above the desert floor, the Hopi Mesas are home to some of the oldest inhabited villages in the United States.

PAINTED DESERT & PETRIFIED FOREST
1 day. If rocks could talk, those in Petrified Forest National Park and the Painted Desert would tell how eons of wind and rain polished the remains of a primeval swamp into gem-colored hills filled with fossils.

CORONADO TRAIL TO TUCSON
1 day. On the scenic Coronado Trail you will find treasure in abundance: aspen and fir forests, lakes stocked with trout, and wildlife.

TUCSON
2 days. While in Tucson, check out the beautiful San Xavier del Bac mission and the El Presidio Historic District surrounding the Museum of Art.

SAGUARO NATIONAL PARK
1 day. Both the east and the west sections of Saguaro National Park put you face to face with the eponymous cactus. Experience desert plants and animals at the Arizona-Sonora Desert Museum. At Old Tucson Studios, movies are still being filmed.

The Old West
12 days

Desperadoes, Indian warriors, galloping ponies, lawmen riding into the sunset: In Arizona, the Wild West is never far away. You can relive the romance at the state's historic locales, starting or ending with a stay in Tucson.

GHOST TOWNS
4 days. Guns still blaze and villains fall in Tombstone—but only during staged fights. Be sure to check out the OK Corral. Later, explore quaint Bisbee, now an artists' haven of restored Victorian homes and upscale bistros. After a morning in tumbledown Pearce, move on to Fort Bowie National Historic Site, where U.S. soldiers once skirmished with Cochise's Apaches. Downtown Willcox looks like the cow town it is and has two Western history museums.

SOUTH OF TUCSON
1 day. To appreciate the Spanish influence on small towns along the meandering Santa Cruz River, tour the mission at Tumacácori National Historic Park. Up the road is Tubac, site of Arizona's first European settlement and the Tubac Presidio State Historic Park and Museum.

PHOENIX
2 days. Downtown Phoenix preserves the city's first Anglo homes in Heritage Square and puts its Anglo history on display at the Phoenix Museum of History. Old Town Scottsdale preserves the Old West amid decidedly New West surroundings. And don't miss the rich Native American collection at the Heard Museum and Frank Lloyd Wright's Taliesin West.

NORTH OF PHOENIX
1 day. Catch a melodrama at the opera house or hop a buckboard to tour the re-created village at the Pioneer Arizona Living History Museum. In Wickenburg, home to many fine guest ranches, you'll find a tranquil site where justice was meted out: the Jail Tree.

THE VERDE VALLEY
2 days. Gold once lured folks to Prescott, giving rise to the former red-light district known as Whiskey Row; stop at Sharlott Hall Museum for a glimpse of the town's past. Old mine tunnels honeycomb the land around Jerome, where museums memorialize the local mining bonanza.

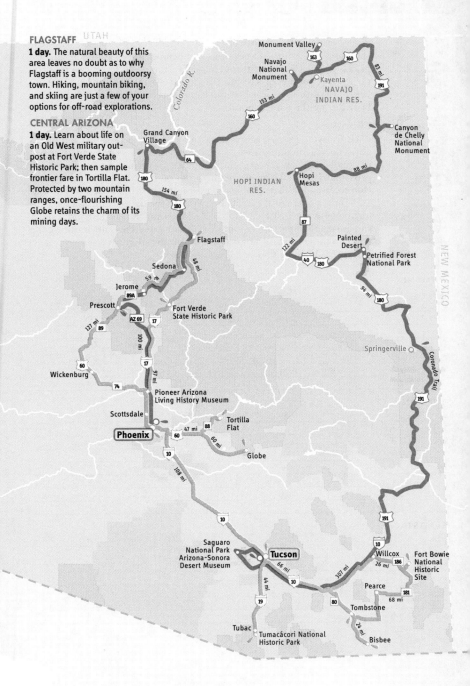

FLAGSTAFF

1 day. The natural beauty of this area leaves no doubt as to why Flagstaff is a booming outdoorsy town. Hiking, mountain biking, and skiing are just a few of your options for off-road explorations.

CENTRAL ARIZONA

1 day. Learn about life on an Old West military outpost at Fort Verde State Historic Park; then sample frontier fare in Tortilla Flat. Protected by two mountain ranges, once-flourishing Globe retains the charm of its mining days.

UTAH

Colorado R.

Monument Valley
163
160
83 mi
191

Navajo National Monument

Kayenta
NAVAJO INDIAN RES.

153 mi

160

Canyon de Chelly National Monument

Grand Canyon Village

64

88 mi

Hopi Mesas

HOPI INDIAN RES.

87

180

154 mi

180

122 mi

Painted Desert

40
180

Petrified Forest National Park

94 mi

180

Flagstaff

48 mi

Sedona

59 mi

Jerome
89A

Prescott

Fort Verde State Historic Park

17

127 mi
89

AZ 69

100 mi

Springerville

Colorado Trail

60

Wickenburg

74

17

97 mi

191

Pioneer Arizona Living History Museum

Scottsdale

Phoenix

60

47 mi

88

Tortilla Flat

60 mi

Globe

10

108 mi

191

10

Saguaro National Park Arizona-Sonora Desert Museum

10

Tucson

66 mi

Willcox

10

26 mi

186

Fort Bowie National Historic Site

307 mi

Pearce

181

44 mi

10

68 mi

19

80

Tombstone

24 mi

Tubac

Tumacácori National Historic Park

Bisbee

NEW MEXICO

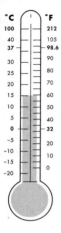

°C	°F
100	212
40	105
37	98.6
30	90
25	80
20	70
15	60
10	50
5	40
0	32
−5	20
−10	10
−15	0
−20	

High season at the resorts of Phoenix and Tucson is winter, when the snowbirds fly south. Expect the best temperatures—and the highest prices—from December through March; the posh desert resorts drop their prices—sometimes by more than half—from June through September. The South Rim of the Grand Canyon is busy year-round, but least busy during the winter months.

Climate

Phoenix averages 300 sunny days and 7 inches of precipitation annually. The high mountains see about 25 inches of rain. The Grand Canyon is usually cool on the rim and about 20°F warmer on the floor. Approximately 6 to 12 inches of snow fall on the North Rim; the South Rim receives half that amount. Temperatures in valley areas like Phoenix and Tucson average about 60°F to 70°F in the daytime during the winter and between 100°F and 115°F during summer. Flagstaff and Sedona stay much cooler, dropping into the 30s and 40s Fahrenheit during the winter and leveling off at 80°F to 90°F in the summer.

 Forecasts **Weather Channel** ⊕ www.weather.com.

PHOENIX

Jan.	65F	18C	May	93F	32C	Sept.	98F	36C
	38	3		57	14		69	20
Feb.	69F	20C	June	102F	37C	Oct.	88F	29C
	41	4		68	19		57	14
Mar.	75F	23C	July	105F	38C	Nov.	75F	23C
	45	7		78	23		45	7
Apr.	84F	28C	Aug.	102F	36C	Dec.	66F	19C
	52	11		76	24C		39	4

TUCSON

Jan.	64F	18C	May	89F	32C	Sept.	96F	36C
	37	3		57	14		68	20
Feb.	68F	20C	June	98F	37C	Oct.	84F	29C
	39	4		66	19		57	14
Mar.	73F	23C	July	101F	38C	Nov.	73F	23C
	44	7		73	23		44	7
Apr.	82F	28C	Aug.	96F	36C	Dec.	66F	19C
	51	11		71	22		39	4

FLAGSTAFF

Jan.	41F	5C	May	66F	19C	Sept.	71F	22C
	14	−10		33	1		41	5
Feb.	44F	7C	June	77F	25C	Oct.	62F	17C
	17	− 8		41	5		30	− 1
Mar.	48F	9C	July	80F	27C	Nov.	51F	11C
	23	− 5		50	10		21	− 6
Apr.	57F	14C	Aug.	78F	26C	Dec.	42F	6C
	28	− 2		48	9		15	− 9

Arizona's top seasonal events are listed below, and any one of them could provide the stuff of lasting memories. Contact local tourism authorities for exact dates and further information.

ONGOING

Jan. and Feb.

The **Parada del Sol Rodeo and Parade,** a popular state attraction on Scottsdale Road in Scottsdale, features lots of dressed-up cowboys and cowgirls, plus horses and floats.

May–Sept.

Flagstaff's Museum of Northern Arizona offers five **Hispanic, Hopi, Navajo, Pai,** and **Zuñi marketplaces** displaying the traditional and contemporary art of these significant Southwest cultures.

WINTER

Dec.

At the **Arizona Temple Gardens & Visitors Center Christmas Lighting,** in Mesa, more than 600,000 lights illuminate the walkways, reflection pool, trees, and plants.

Early Dec.

For the three days of **Old Town Tempe Fall Festival of the Arts,** the downtown area closes to traffic for art exhibits, food booths, music, and other entertainment.

Jan. 1

Tempe's nationally televised **Tostitos Fiesta Bowl Classic** kicks off the year with a match between two of the top college football teams in the nation.

Late Jan.

At the **FBR Open Golf Tournament** (formerly the Phoenix Open) in Scottsdale, top players compete at the Tournament Players Club.

The **Quartzsite Pow Wow Gem and Mineral Show** is a gigantic gem, mineral, and jewelry market, held the last Wednesday through Sunday of the month in Quartzsite, about 19 mi from the California border (take Interstate& 10 west of Phoenix, then Exit 17 or 19 in Quartzsite).

Early Feb.

The **Rodeo of Rodeos,** sponsored by the Phoenix Jaycees, opens with the Parada del Sol parade.

The **World Championship Hoop Dance Contest** at the Heard Museum in Phoenix attracts superbly skilled native hoop dancers from across the United States and Canada to compete for a world champion title.

Mid-Feb.

At **O'odham Tash** in Casa Grande, Native American tribes from around the country, and from Canada and Mexico, host parades, native dances, a rodeo, a powwow, costume displays, and food stands.

The huge **Tucson Gem and Mineral Show,** organized by the Tucson Gem and Mineral Society, attracts rock hounds—amateur and professional—from all over the world who come to buy, sell, and display their geological treasures and to attend lectures and competitive exhibits.

History comes to life during **Wickenburg Gold Rush Days,** when the Old West town puts on a parade, rodeo, dances, gold-panning demonstrations, a mineral show, and other activities.

La Fiesta de los Vaqueros features the world's longest "nonmechanized" parade—horses pull floats and carry dignitaries—launching a five-day rodeo at the Tucson Rodeo Grounds. An all-women's rodeo is included in the festivities.

SPRING

Early Mar.	In Phoenix, the **Heard Museum Guild Indian Fair and Market** is a prestigious juried show of Native American arts and crafts. Visitors can also enjoy Native American foods, music, and dance.
Mid-Mar.	For the **Lost Dutchman Gold Mine Superstition Mountain Trek** in Apache Junction, the Dons of Arizona search for the legendary lost mine, pan for gold, and eat lots of barbecue to keep up their strength. There are crafts demonstrations and fireworks, too.
Mid–Late Mar.	In March, women compete in the **Standard Register PING Tournament,** at the Moon Valley Country Club in Phoenix.
Mid–Late Mar.	In March, celebrate the Old West and the American cowboy at the **National Festival of the West,** at WestWorld in Scottsdale.
Late Apr.	Tucson hosts the **International Mariachi Conference,** four days of mariachi-music workshops and performances, along with cultural and educational exhibits.
	Bisbee's **La Vuelta de Bisbee** is one of Arizona's largest bicycle races and attracts top racers from around the country to the hills of the historic mining town.
	Yaqui Easter is celebrated in old Pasqua Village (Tucson) with various activities taking place during the Palm Sunday and Easter weekends. Visitors are welcome to watch traditional Yaqui dances and ceremonies.
Early May	During the **Route 66 Fun Run Weekend** from Seligman to Topock, the longest drivable stretch of the historic road between Chicago and Los Angeles, is feted with a Show-and-Shine car rally—anyone with a vehicle can join the ride—and various activities along the route, including entertainment, barbecues, and a Miss Route 66 beauty pageant.
Late May	During the **Rendezvous,** the townspeople of Williams set up an interpretive village and reenact the lives of 1800s mountain traders. Events include a steak fry and a Buckskinners black powder shoot.

SUMMER

Early June	Festivities of **Old West Day/Bucket of Blood Races,** in Holbrook, include arts and crafts, Western dress, and Native American song and dance, in addition to the 10-km (6-mi) fun run and 20-mi bike ride from Petrified Forest National Park to Holbrook.
First Week in July	**Prescott Frontier Days and Rodeo,** billed as the world's oldest rodeo, finds big crowds and an equally big party on downtown Whiskey Row.
Mid-July	The **Native American Arts & Crafts Festival** in Pinetop-Lakeside brings storytellers, dancers, musicians, and artists together for two days in the White Mountains east of Phoenix.
First Weekend in Aug.	Flagstaff's **SummerFest** is a gathering of painters, potters, musicians, and other artists from around the United States. They vie with carnival rides and food vendors for the crowd's attention.
Early Aug.	The **Southwest Wings Birding Festival,** held throughout Cochise County and in Bisbee, includes field trips to local canyons and forests, lectures by recognized Audubon authorities, and other avian-oriented events.
Mid-Aug.	The **Payson Rodeo,** known as the "World's Oldest Continuous Rodeo," draws top cowboys from around the country to compete in bull-riding and calf- and steer-roping contests.

FALL

Sept.	Each September the **Grand Canyon Chamber Music Festival** is held in the Shrine of the Ages auditorium at the South Rim. Call or write for schedule information and advance tickets.
Early Sept.	The **Navajo Nation Annual Tribal Fair** is the world's largest Native American fair. Held in Window Rock, it includes a rodeo, traditional Navajo music and dances, food booths, and an intertribal powwow.
Late Sept.	At the **Jazz on the Rocks Festival** in Sedona, four or five ensembles perform in a spectacular red-rock setting.
Early Oct.	**Rex Allen Days** in Willcox honors the local cowboy film star and narrator for Walt Disney productions with a parade, country fair, concerts, rodeo, dances, and more.
	Andy Devine Days, in Kingman, honors the film and television actor with a parade and rodeo.
Mid-Oct.	At **Tombstone's Helldorado Days,** this town relives the spirited Wyatt Earp era and the shoot-out at the OK Corral.
Mid–Late Oct.	A weeklong event, **London Bridge Days** includes a Renaissance festival, a parade, and British-theme contests in Lake Havasu City.
Late Oct.	In late October, you can join the celebration of traditional Navajo culture at the **Western Navajo Fair** in Tuba City.

Early Nov.	During the Thunderbird Hot-Air-Balloon Classic, 150 or more balloons participate in Scottsdale's colorful race.
Late Nov.	At 111 mi, El Tour de Tucson is the largest perimeter bicycling event in the world, attracting international celebrity cyclists.
Last Weekend in Nov.	The waters of Lake Powell alight with the Festival of Lights Boat Parade as dozens of illuminated boats glide from Lake Powell Resort to Glen Canyon Dam and back.

PLEASURES & PASTIMES

Ballooning Nothing is as thrilling as soaring over the desert and mountains in a hot-air balloon, and Arizona is a great location to do it. The ballooning season runs from September through May, when weather and temperatures are at their best. Several companies can take you soaring into the clouds, and there are also several competitive ballooning events during the season if being a spectator is more to your liking.

Baseball The Arizona Diamondbacks are the big draw come April, but many fans come in March to watch professional teams warm up for the season in spring-training Cactus League games, most of them in the Phoenix area. The teams start their training camps as early as February. Free drills—held in the morning before an exhibition game—are fun to watch, and there's a good chance you might be able to chat with the players before or after these sessions. And the best part is that these games are much more affordable than they are in the major-league season. In some cases, reserved seats sell out each fall before the upcoming season, but you can almost always get general admission seats on game days.

Boating & Water Sports You may be surprised to find so many lakes in a desert state. In fact, Arizonans own more boats per capita than residents of almost any other state. The two national recreational areas, Glen Canyon (Lake Powell), in north-central Arizona, and Lake Mead (including Lake Mohave), in the northwest, have marinas, launching ramps, and boat and ski rentals. At both lakes you can take a paddle-wheeler tour or take the wheel yourself in a fully equipped houseboat. Lake Havasu, fed by the Colorado River in the western part of the state, is another popular site for boating, waterskiing, windsurfing, and jet-skiing. London Bridge, which was moved block by block from England and reassembled here, is a surreal vision at this lakeside resort. Saguaro and Canyon lakes, just east of Scottsdale, offer good boating and waterskiing for those based in the Phoenix area looking for a convenient day trip.

Golf Your clubs certainly won't gather dust in Arizona. Aside from attending the big-draw FBR Open, golfers flock to this state to tee off at the myriad top-ranked private and municipal courses. Year-round desert courses offer cheaper greens fees during the summer, while those in the northern parts usually shut down for the winter. Just about every resort has its own course or is affiliated with a private club, and the state has some of the best courses in the country.

Hiking Throughout the state, hikers can choose from trails that wind through the desert, climb mountains, meander past supernal rock formations, delve deep into forests, or circumnavigate cities. Hiking is the best way to see Grand Canyon National Park, and a trip down to the canyon floor will reward you with a lifetime of memories. But all over the state, you'll find developed trails, in the cool mountains near Flagstaff, in the White Mountains of eastern Arizona, in Phoenix's massive park system, and in the parks and preserves of southern Arizona. Whether it's desert or mountain hiking you are looking for, you're sure to find it somewhere in the state.

Horseback Riding
Traveling by horseback through the somewhat wild West or the scenic high country is perhaps the most appropriate way to explore Arizona. Stables offer a selection of mountain- or desert-trail rides lasting a half day, two days, or as long as two weeks. In northern regions the season is from May through October. If riding is the focus of your Arizona holiday, you might consider staying at a dude ranch, where you can saddle up every day.

Native American Culture
Attending Native American festivals and exploring the remains of earlier settlements can be a rewarding part of a trip to Arizona. As is the case with traveling anywhere, any effort made to enhance your understanding of local culture and history will enrich all aspects of your visit. Keep in mind, too, that when you enter a reservation you are, in effect, entering another country, one governed by different laws and customs. Obey *all* posted signs (some signs on the reservations look less than official, but they mean what they say) and ask at the reservation visitor center or check with local authorities if you have any questions.

Shopping
Many tourists come to Arizona for no other reason than to purchase fine Native American jewelry and crafts. Collectibles include Navajo rugs and sand paintings, Hopi katsina dolls (intricately carved and colorful representations of Hopi spiritual beings) and pottery, Tohono O'odham (Papago) basketry, and Apache beadwork, as well as the highly prized silver and turquoise jewelry produced by several different tribes.

Skiing
Cross-country and downhill skiing are winter pastimes in Arizona, even if its mountains don't quite match the scale of the Rockies. Flagstaff Nordic Center north of Flagstaff, Mormon Lake Ski Touring Center southeast of Flagstaff, the Grand Canyon's North Rim Nordic Center, and miles of crisscrossing trails around Alpine are good places for cross-country skiing. The three peaks of Sunrise Park Resort in the White Mountains are owned and operated by the White Mountain Apache tribe and constitute the state's largest ski area. Other popular areas are Arizona Snowbowl near Flagstaff and Mt. Lemmon Ski Valley near Tucson, the continent's southernmost ski slope.

Fodor's Choice
★

The sights, restaurants, hotels, and other travel experiences on these pages are our editors' top picks—our Fodor's Choices. They're the best of their type in the area covered by the book—not to be missed and always worth your time. In the destination chapters that follow, you will find all the details.

LODGING

$$$$	**Arizona Biltmore**, Phoenix. Phoenix's first luxury resort has maintained its high standards since 1929, with low-key elegance that makes it one of the classiest places in the Southwest.
$$$$	**The Boulders**, Carefree. The Valley of the Sun's most serene and secluded luxury resort hides among hill-size granite boulders in the foothills town of Carefree.
$$$$	**White Stallion Ranch**, Tucson. Southern Arizona's best guest ranch is just a few miles from the heart of Tucson.
$$$–$$$$	**Hermosa Inn**, Paradise Valley. This small resort was once the home of cowboy artist Lon Margaree, and its understated sophistication is a welcome change from the big splashy Phoenix resorts.
$$–$$$$	**Briar Patch Inn**, Sedona. It may not be in the heart of Sedona, but its lovely location in Oak Creek Canyon sets it apart.
$$$	**Arizona Inn**, Tucson. With almost all that you would want from a landmark inn—period furnishings, fireplaces, quiet and friendly service, even a midtown location—you won't be disappointed.
$$–$$$	**Red Setter Inn**, Greer. The hand-hewn log inn is the best thing going in the White Mountains of eastern Arizona.
$$	**Casa Tierra**, Tucson. In an adobe building, this fine B&B outside town is great for a desert getaway.
$–$$	**Cameron Trading Post**, Cameron. With its trading-post charm, this may well be the best base for seeing both the North and South rims of the Grand Canyon, as well as nearby Navajo-Hopi country.
$–$$	**Canyon Rose Suites**, Bisbee. Suites in this downtown B&B have full kitchens; there's even a full-service spa.
$–$$	**Grand Canyon Lodge**, North Rim. On the North Rim you can avoid the crowds as you enjoy the mighty abyss. The historic, rustic Grand Canyon Lodge has spectacular canyon views.
$–$$	**Lake Powell Resort**, Wahweap, Lake Powell. Although rooms are standard, this central source for Lake Powell recreation has cruises, river excursions, boat rentals, waterskiing, and a good restaurant—it's a nearly all-in-one resort.

$-$$	**La Posada,** Winslow. Spanish hacienda charm, railroad hotel history, a guest book studded with silver- screen stars, and easy access to Homolovi Ruins State Park are among the many lures of Winslow's top attraction.
$	**Comfort Inn,** Scottsdale. A comfortable, clean room in a convenient, safe location costs a third less than the pricey resorts nearby.
$	**Hotel Congress,** Tucson. A Western take on art-deco design is the calling card for this downtown hotel. The ever popular Club Congress downstairs keeps the hipster quotient (and occasionally the noise levels) high.

BUDGET LODGING

¢–$	**Bright Angel Lodge,** Grand Canyon Village. Mary Jane Colter's log-and-stone lodge gives you every bit as much atmosphere as the El Tovar but for half the price.
¢–$	**School House Inn Bed & Breakfast,** Bisbee. Once a real schoolhouse, this atmospheric B&B is your best budget choice in this quaint Old West town.
¢	**Reed's Lodge,** Springerville. This welcoming motel and its owner, Roxanne Knight, can make your stay in the White Mountains an exceedingly pleasant one.

RESTAURANTS

$$$$	**Marquesa,** Scottsdale. Expertly prepared Catalonian cuisine is served in the elegant Fairmont Scottsdale Princess dining room.
$$$–$$$$	**Janos,** Tucson. The innovative Southwestern cuisine of chef Janos Wilder keeps the crowds coming year-round.
$$$	**Lon's at the Hermosa,** Paradise Valley. The setting may be rustic, but the menu spans the globe with ingredients as fresh and contemporary as any in town.
$$$	**Restaurant Hapa,** Scottsdale. Thai, Chinese, and other astonishingly flavorful Asian-hybrid entrées and desserts add up to one big-time dining experience.
$$–$$$	**El Tovar Dining Room,** Grand Canyon Village. A meal in this historic dining room at the canyon's edge is an elegant way to while away your evening.
$$	**Café Poca Cosa,** Tucson. Superb Moorish architecture that calls to mind the Alhambra in Granada makes this fine Spanish restaurant a sight in its own right.
$$	**Kramer's at the Manzanita,** Cornville. The sophistication of the continental fare here is unexpected, considering the remote location.

BUDGET RESTAURANTS

¢–$ | **Cruisers Café 66,** Williams. You might think it's still 1957 at this little diner, and it's a much cheaper and better alternative than the fast-food places at the canyon rim.

¢–$ | **Mi Nidito,** Tucson. This local favorite is the best choice for Mexican on South 4th Avenue.

¢–$ | **Rendezvous Diner,** Greer. Your best choice in the charming mountain town is this simply superb family restaurant.

¢–$ | **Thai Spices,** Sedona. The curries at this small, unadorned restaurant have inspired devotion among vegetarians and carnivores alike.

¢ | **Carolina's,** Phoenix. As the lines at this humble spot attest, one of the culinary pleasures of coming to Phoenix is the opportunity to find delicious, authentic Sonoran Mexican cooking.

¢ | **Ruiz's Mexican Food & Cantina,** Benson. A tiny, homey Mexican diner packs in the crowds all day. And it's pronounced "Reese."

ARCHAEOLOGY

Homolovi Ruins State Park, northeast of Winslow. Two of the well-preserved pueblos here have more than 1,000 rooms; the Hopi hold them sacred.

Montezuma Castle National Monument, Camp Verde. The five-story cliff dwelling is one of the best-preserved archaeological sites in North America.

Navajo National Monument, Black Mesa. Betatakin and Keet Seel, two 13th-century pueblos, are the largest ever found in Arizona and among the best preserved.

Pueblo Grande Museum and Cultural Park, Phoenix. Phoenix's only national landmark was once a Hohokam village; it's a great place for kids to learn about Native American culture.

Tusayan Ruin and Museum, Grand Canyon, South Rim. This museum on Desert View Drive is a good place to get up close and personal with some of the original canyon residents.

Wupatki National Monument, East of Flagstaff. This well-preserved Hopi tall house in the shadow of Sunset Crater has more than 100 rooms.

DRIVES

Apache Trail, southeast of Phoenix. President Theodore Roosevelt thought this route through the mountains southeast of Phoenix was the "most sublimely beautiful panorama nature ever created." He was right.

Coronado Trail, eastern Arizona, near Springerville. The steep 123-mi stretch of highway from Springerville to Clifton is dramatic as it winds from verdant meadows down into the Sonoran Desert.

Goosenecks Region, southern Utah. This twisting canyon is almost as breathtaking as the Grand Canyon, though on a smaller scale.

Historic Route 66, west of Flagstaff. The longest continuous section of "The Mother Road" stretches from Seligman to Topock and is the site of the annual "Route 66 Fun Run" held each May.

Oak Creek Canyon, Sedona. Another stunning canyon, this one is quiet and tree-lined on its low end near Flagstaff, towering and majestic as it looks toward Sedona.

Point Sublime, Grand Canyon, North Rim. The panorama along the dirt road leading out to the point is one of the most awesome views you'll ever witness from the comfort of your car.

Salt River Canyon, Fort Apache Indian Reservation. This scenic stretch of U.S. 60 goes through a mini–Grand Canyon of multicolored spires and buttes that you won't soon forget.

Texas Canyon, near Willcox. Is it possible to tire of canyons? Not when they are like this one—hung with massive boulders in astonishing formations apparently defying gravity.

GOLF

ASU Karsten Golf Course, Tempe. This top university course allows you to play in the footsteps of the pros for a less-than-top price.

Gold Canyon Golf Club, Gold Canyon. This resort east of Phoenix has two scenic, championship courses.

The Lodge at Ventana Canyon Golf Course, Tucson. Tom Fazio designed this challenging course.

Randolph Park Golf Courses, Tucson. These municipal golf courses are dirt-cheap and high-quality; the North courses hosts the LPGA each year.

Sedona Golf Resort, Sedona. You might find it difficult keeping your eye on the ball at this beautiful course set against Sedona's red rocks.

Silver Creek Golf Club, Show Low. The quality and setting of this well-maintained course make it one of the state's great values.

Troon North Golf Courses, Scottsdale. Though expensive, these two courses are both tops in terms of quality, with a nod going to the Monument Course.

HISTORY

Heard Museum, Phoenix. An amazing collection of Native American art and artifacts is only half the story at the Heard; the museum works to foster the careers of and display pieces by working Indian artists.

Hoover Dam, Boulder City, NV. Completed in 1935 to control flooding and generate electricity, the dam is 727 feet high and 660 feet thick at the base.

London Bridge, Lake Havasu City. This 294-foot-long stone bridge once crossed the River Thames but has been the centerpiece of Lake Havasu City since it was rebuilt here in 1971.

Mission San Xavier del Bac, Tucson. Built from native materials by Franciscan missionaries between 1777 and 1797, the White Dove of the Desert still serves the community.

Pipe Spring National Monument, near Fredonia. The strategically important fort in the 19th century protected one of the only reliable sources of water for miles around; the museum gives you a fascinating glimpse at how frontier life was lived.

Riordan State Historic Park, Flagstaff. A grand log-and-stone mansion designed by the same architect who built the El Tovar Hotel is furnished with original Stickley pieces.

Sharlot Hall Museum, Prescott. One of Arizona's most important history museums comprises three period homes and a transportation museum.

Taliesin West, Scottsdale. Architect Frank Lloyd Wright's winter residence ingeniously integrates indoor and outdoor space.

NATURE

Arizona-Sonora Desert Museum, Tucson. This great zoo and botanical garden focuses on the flora and fauna of the Sonoran Desert.

Canyon de Chelly National Monument, Chinle. Thousand-foot cliffs contain ancient dwellings, including the White House, that are in profound harmony with their natural surroundings.

Chiricahua National Monument, southeast of Willcox. The pinnacles and spires in these 12,000 acres are among the most haunting and beautiful sights in the state.

Desert Botanical Garden, Phoenix. This is simply one of the greatest collections of desert flora in the Southwest.

Hualapai Mountain Park, Kingman. The Hualapai Mountains are considered a "biological island" surrounded by high-desert terrain. The park offers 10 mi of excellent hiking trails as well as picnic areas, cabins, RV and camping areas on more than 2,300 wooded acres.

Kartchner Caverns State Park, Benson. One of the most spectacular wet cave systems in the entire world, the caverns were kept secret for 14 years while they were readied for visitors. But make reservations far in advance, because now the secret is out.

Lake Mead National Recreation Area, Boulder, NV. There's nothing quite like the sight of a lake in the desert. This is the largest national recreation area in the country covering almost 1.5 million acres and includes Lake Mohave and Lake Mead.

Monument Valley Navajo Tribal Park, Monument Valley. The cathedral-like sandstone spires will be instantly familiar if you've seen Ansel Adams's photos or John Ford's Hollywood Westerns.

North Rim, Grand Canyon. The only way to get to know the canyon is to hike or ride a mule down through the geological eras to the bottom of the chasm.

Petrified Forest National Park, near Holbrook. Millions of fossilized trees, as well as animal skeletons, are spread out over what was once a forested marshland—225 million years ago, that is.

Saguaro National Park West, Tucson. You'll see the world's largest stand of saguaro cacti here, as well as fascinating petroglyphs made by the Hohokam people.

SMART TRAVEL TIPS

Finding out about your destination before you leave home means you won't squander time organizing everyday minutiae once you've arrived. You'll be more streetwise when you hit the ground as well, better prepared to explore the aspects of Arizona that drew you here in the first place. The organizations in this section can provide information to supplement this guide; contact them for up-to-the-minute details, and consult the A to Z sections that end each chapter for facts on the various topics as they relate to Arizona's many regions. Happy landings!

AIR TRAVEL

BOOKING

When you book, look for nonstop flights and remember that "direct" flights stop at least once. Try to avoid connecting flights, which require a change of plane. Two airlines may operate a connecting flight jointly, so ask whether your airline operates every segment of the trip; you may find that the carrier you prefer flies you only part of the way. To find more booking tips and to check prices and make online flight reservations, log on to www.fodors.com.

CARRIERS

Phoenix is a hub for America West and Southwest Airlines. These carriers offer the most direct flights in and out of Phoenix. Most of the country's other major airlines fly into Phoenix and have a few flights into Tucson as well; US Airways flies only to Phoenix.

Among the smaller airlines, Aerocalifornia flies between Tucson and Mexico only. ATA flies only to Phoenix. Frontier connects Phoenix to Denver and points beyond. Great Lakes Airlines flies to Phoenix and Page. Midwest Express connects Phoenix and Milwaukee.

British Airways flies direct from London to Phoenix; other airlines offer connecting flights from continental Europe to Phoenix and Tucson through their major U.S. hubs. Nonstop flights to Canada, Mexico, and Costa Rica are also available from

Air Travel
Airports
Bus Travel
Cameras & Photography
Car Rental
Car Travel
Children in Arizona
Consumer Protection
Customs & Duties
Disabilities & Accessibility
Discounts & Deals
Eating & Drinking
Ecotourism
Gay & Lesbian Travel
Health
Holidays
Insurance
For International Travelers
Lodging
Media
Money Matters
National Parks
Packing
Senior-Citizen Travel
Shopping
Sports & Outdoors
State Parks
Students in Arizona
Taxes
Time   o
Tipping
Tours & Packages
Train Travel
Travel Agencies
Visitor Information
Web Sites

Phoenix. Within Arizona, America West Express/Mesa Airlines flies from Phoenix to Flagstaff, Prescott, Lake Havasu, Kingman, and Yuma. Great Lakes Airlines connects Phoenix and Page. Scenic Airlines flies from Las Vegas to the Grand Canyon.

⌨ Major Airlines Alaska Airlines ☎ 800/252-7522 ⊕ www.alaskaair.com. **America West** ☎ 800/235-9292 ⊕ www.americawest.com. **American** ☎ 800/433-7300, 0845/778-9789 in the U.K. ⊕ www.aa.com. **Continental** ☎ 800/525-0280, 0800/776-464 or 01293/776-464 in the U.K. ⊕ www.continental.com. **Delta** ☎ 800/221-1212, 0800/414-767 in the U.K. ⊕ www.delta.com. **Northwest** ☎ 800/225-2525 ⊕ www.nwa.com. **United** ☎ 800/241-6522, 0845/844-4777 in the U.K. ⊕ www.united.com. **Southwest** ☎ 800/435-9792 ⊕ www.southwest.com. **US Airways** ☎ 800/428-4322 ⊕ www.usairways.com.

⌨ Smaller Airlines Aerocalifornia ☎ 800/237-6225. **ATA** ☎ 800/225-2995 ⊕ www.ata.com. **Frontier Airlines** ☎ 800/432-1359 ⊕ www.frontierairlines.com. **Great Lakes Airlines** ☎ 800/554-5111 ⊕ www.greatlakesav.com. **Midwest Express** ☎ 800/452-2022 ⊕ www.midwestexpress.com.

⌨ From Europe British Airways ☎ 0870/850-9850 in the U.K., 800/247-9297 within the U.S. ⊕ www.britishairways.com.

⌨ Within Arizona America West Express/Mesa ☎ 800/235-9292 ⊕ www.americawest.com. **Scenic Airlines** ☎ 800/535-4448.

CHECK-IN & BOARDING

Always **find out your carrier's check-in policy.** Plan to arrive at the airport about two hours before your scheduled departure time for domestic flights and 2½ to 3 hours before international flights. You may need to arrive earlier if you're flying from one of the busier airports or during peak air-traffic times. Despite its daily passenger volume, lengthy lines at the check-in counters or security checkpoints at Phoenix Sky Harbor are rarely a problem. To avoid delays at airport-security checkpoints, try not to wear any metal. Jewelry, belt and other buckles, steel-toe shoes, barrettes, and underwire bras are among the items that can set off detectors.

Assuming that not everyone with a ticket will show up, airlines routinely overbook planes. When everyone does, airlines ask for volunteers to give up their seats. In re-

turn, these volunteers usually get a several-hundred-dollar flight voucher, which can be used toward the purchase of another ticket, and are rebooked on the next flight out. If there are not enough volunteers, the airline must choose who will be denied boarding. The first to get bumped are passengers who checked in late and those flying on discounted tickets, so get to the gate and check in as early as possible, especially during peak periods.

Always **bring a government-issued photo I.D.** to the airport; even when it's not required, a passport is best.

CUTTING COSTS

The least expensive airfares to Arizona are priced for round-trip travel and must usually be purchased in advance. Airlines generally allow you to change your return date for a fee; most low-fare tickets, however, are nonrefundable. It's smart to call a number of airlines and check the Internet; when you are quoted a good price, book it on the spot—the same fare may not be available the next day, or even the next hour. Always check different routings and look into using alternate airports. Also, price off-peak flights, which may be significantly less expensive than others. Travel agents, especially low-fare specialists (⇨ Discounts & Deals), are helpful.

Consolidators are another good source. They buy tickets for scheduled flights at reduced rates from the airlines, then sell them at prices that beat the best fare available directly from the airlines. Many also offer reduced car-rental and hotel rates. Sometimes you can even get your money back if you need to return the ticket. Carefully read the fine print detailing penalties for changes and cancellations, purchase the ticket with a credit card, and confirm your consolidator reservation with the airline.

⌨ Consolidators AirlineConsolidator.com ☎ 888/468-5385 ⊕ www.airlineconsolidator.com; for international tickets. **Best Fares** ☎ 800/880-1234 or 800/576-8255 ⊕ www.bestfares.com; $59.90 annual membership. **Cheap Tickets** ☎ 800/377-1000 or 800/652-4327 ⊕ www.cheaptickets.com. **Expedia** ☎ 800/397-3342 or 404/728-8787 ⊕ www.expedia.com. **Hotwire** ☎ 866/468-9473 or 920/330-9418 ⊕ www.hotwire.com. **Now Voyager Travel** ✉ 45 W.

21st St., Suite 5A, New York, NY 10010 ☎ 212/459–1616 🖷 212/243–2711 ⊕ www.nowvoyagertravel.com. **Onetravel.com** ⊕ www.onetravel.com. **Orbitz** ☎ 888/656–4546 ⊕ www.orbitz.com. **Priceline.com** ⊕ www.priceline.com. **Travelocity** ☎ 888/709–5983, 877/282–2925 in Canada, 0870/876–3876 in the U.K. ⊕ www.travelocity.com.

ENJOYING THE FLIGHT

State your seat preference when purchasing your ticket, and then repeat it when you confirm and when you check in. For more legroom, you can request one of the few emergency-aisle seats at check-in, if you're capable of moving obstacles comparable in weight to an airplane exit door (usually between 35 and 60 pounds)—a Federal Aviation Administration requirement of passengers in these seats. Seats behind a bulkhead also offer more legroom, but they don't have under-seat storage. Don't sit in the row in front of the emergency aisle or in front of a bulkhead, where seats may not recline.

Ask the airline whether a snack or meal is served on the flight. If you have dietary concerns, request special meals when booking. These can be vegetarian, low-cholesterol, or kosher, for example. It's a good idea to pack some healthful snacks and a small (plastic) bottle of water in your carry-on bag. On long flights, try to maintain a normal routine, to help fight jet lag. At night, get some sleep. By day, eat light meals, drink water (not alcohol), and **move around the cabin** to stretch your legs. For additional jet-lag tips consult *Fodor's FYI: Travel Fit & Healthy* (available at bookstores everywhere).

Smoking policies vary from carrier to carrier. Many airlines prohibit smoking on all of their flights; others allow smoking only on certain routes or certain departures. Ask your carrier about its policy.

FLYING TIMES

Flying time to Phoenix or Tucson is 5½ hours from New York, 3½ hours from Chicago, 1¼ hours from Los Angeles, and 11 hours from London.

HOW TO COMPLAIN

If your baggage goes astray or your flight goes awry, complain right away. Most car-riers require that you **file a claim immediately.** The Aviation Consumer Protection Division of the Department of Transportation publishes *Fly-Rights*, which discusses airlines and consumer issues and is available online. You can also find articles and information on mytravelrights.com, the Web site of the nonprofit Consumer Travel Rights Center.

🛈 Airline Complaints **Aviation Consumer Protection Division** ✉ U.S. Department of Transportation, Office of Aviation Enforcement and Proceedings, C-75, Room 4107, 400 7th St. SW, Washington, DC 20590 ☎ 202/366–2220 ⊕ airconsumer.ost.dot.gov. **Federal Aviation Administration Consumer Hotline** ✉ for inquiries: FAA, 800 Independence Ave. SW, Washington, DC 20591 ☎ 800/322–7873 ⊕ www.faa.gov.

RECONFIRMING

Check the status of your flight before you leave for the airport. You can do this on your carrier's Web site, by linking to a flight-status checker (many Web booking services offer these), or by calling your carrier or travel agent.

AIRPORTS

Major gateways to Arizona include **Phoenix Sky Harbor International (PHX),** about 3 mi east of Phoenix city center, and **Tucson International Air Terminal (TUS),** about 8½ mi south of the central business area.

Phoenix Sky Harbor International Airport is the fifth-busiest airport in the world for takeoffs and landings but rarely gives way to congestion or lengthy lines, and its spacious, modern terminals are easily navigable. Sky Harbor's three passenger terminals are connected by inter-terminal buses, which run regularly throughout the day. Tucson International Airport has one terminal, and although it services far fewer passengers per day than Sky Harbor, it does offer nonstop flights to major metropolitan areas around the country.

🛈 Airport Information **Phoenix Sky Harbor International** ✉ 3400 E. Sky Harbor Blvd., 24th and Buckeye Sts., off I-10, Exit 149 ☎ 602/273–3300 ⊕ www.phxskyharbor.com. **Tucson International Airport** ✉ 7250 S. Tucson Blvd., at Valencia Rd. between I-10 and I-19 ☎ 520/573–8000 ⊕ www.tucsonairport.org.

BUS TRAVEL

Greyhound serves many Arizona destinations from most parts of the United States but does not serve any destinations on the Navajo and Hopi reservations in northeastern Arizona.

🚌 Bus Information **Greyhound Lines** ☎ 800/231-2222 ⊕ www.greyhound.com.

CAMERAS & PHOTOGRAPHY

The wide-open vistas, bright sky, dramatic canyons, and desert expanses make for great pictures but call for a few extra considerations for the photographer. Even if you are keeping your equipment list minimal, consider bringing a wide-angle lens, good for capturing panoramas, and a polarizing filter, which reduces glare. Because the light in Arizona tends to be bright, and dramatic contrasts in light and shade can over- or under-expose the entire picture, try to base the light reading on a more neutrally lit area in the picture. The *Kodak Guide to Shooting Great Travel Pictures* (available at bookstores everywhere) is loaded with tips.

🚩 Photo Help **Kodak Information Center** ☎ 800/242-2424 ⊕ www.kodak.com.

EQUIPMENT PRECAUTIONS

When hiking, especially if your trip traverses the desert or rivers, consider bringing an older, less-valuable camera. In any case, it is a good idea to carry extra plastic bags, in case of an unexpected desert wind- or rainstorm, and lens cloths for dust. **Don't pack film or equipment in checked luggage,** where it is much more susceptible to damage. X-ray machines used to view checked luggage are extremely powerful and therefore are likely to ruin your film. Try to ask for hand inspection of film, which becomes clouded after repeated exposure to airport X-ray machines, and keep videotapes and computer disks away from metal detectors. Always keep film, tape, and computer disks out of the sun. Carry an extra supply of batteries, and be prepared to turn on your camera, camcorder, or laptop to prove to airport security personnel that the device is real.

CAR RENTAL

Rates in Phoenix begin around $25 a day and $165 a week for an economy car with air-conditioning, an automatic transmission, and unlimited mileage. This does not include taxes and fees on car rentals, which can range anywhere from 16% to 46%, depending on pickup location. The base tax rate at Sky Harbor is about 30%. When you add the daily fees (which are about $5 a day), the taxes and fees can add up to almost half the cost of the car rental. You may be able to save by taking a cab to a retail location nearby, where you avoid the airport tax and additional daily fees. Taxes outside of the airport are typically around 25% or less.

Rates in Phoenix may be higher during the winter months, which is considered the high tourist season. Check the Internet or local papers for discounts and deals, as they can significantly lower rental rates. Local rental agencies may also offer lower rates.

🚗 Major Agencies **Alamo** ☎ 800/327-9633 ⊕ www.alamo.com. **Avis** ☎ 800/331-1212, 800/879-2847 or 800/272-5871 in Canada, 0870/606-0100 in the U.K., 02/9353-9000 in Australia, 09/526-2847 in New Zealand ⊕ www.avis.com. **Budget** ☎ 800/527-0700, 0870/156-5656 in the U.K. ⊕ www.budget.com. **Dollar** ☎ 800/800-4000, 0800/085-4578 in the U.K. ⊕ www.dollar.com. **Hertz** ☎ 800/654-3131, 800/263-0600 in Canada, 0870/844-8844 in the U.K., 02/9669-2444 in Australia, 09/256-8690 in New Zealand ⊕ www.hertz.com. **National Car Rental** ☎ 800/227-7368, 0870/600-6666 in the U.K. ⊕ www.nationalcar.com.

CUTTING COSTS

For a good deal, book through a travel agent who will shop around. Also, price local car-rental companies—whose prices may be lower still, although their service and maintenance may not be as good as those of major rental agencies—and research rates on the Internet. Consolidators that specialize in air travel can offer good rates on cars as well (⇨ Air Travel). Remember to ask about required deposits, cancellation penalties, and drop-off charges if you're planning to pick up the car in one city and leave it in another. If you're traveling during a holiday period, also make sure that a confirmed reservation guarantees you a car.

📠 **Local Agencies ABC Rent-A-Car** ✉ 2532 E. Jefferson St., Phoenix 85034 ☎ 602/681–9000 or 888/899–9997 ⊕ www.abc-rentacar.com. **Airport Rent-A-Car** ✉ 2325 E. Washington St., Phoenix 85034 ☎ 602/267–9100 or 800/347–4030. **Arizona Auto Rental** ✉ 3301 S. 6th Ave., Tucson 85713 ☎ 520/624–4548. **Saban's Rent A Car** ✉ 2934 E. McDowell Rd., Phoenix 85008 ☎ 602/269–9310. **Tucson Auto Rental** ✉ 2431 E. 22nd St., Tucson 85713 ☎ 520/622–7700.

INSURANCE

When driving a rented car you are generally responsible for any damage to or loss of the vehicle. You also may be liable for any property damage or personal injury that you may cause while driving. Before you rent, see what coverage you already have under the terms of your personal auto-insurance policy and credit cards.

For about $9 to $25 a day, rental companies sell protection, known as a collision- or loss-damage waiver (CDW or LDW), that eliminates your liability for damage to the car; it's always optional and should never be automatically added to your bill. In Arizona the car-rental agency's insurance is primary; therefore, the company must pay for damage to third parties up to a preset legal limit, beyond which your own liability insurance kicks in. However, **make sure you have enough coverage to pay for the car.** If you do not have auto insurance or an umbrella policy that covers damage to third parties, purchasing liability insurance and a CDW or LDW is highly recommended.

REQUIREMENTS & RESTRICTIONS

In Arizona most agencies won't rent to you if you're under the age of 21, and several major agencies will not rent to anyone under 25.

SURCHARGES

Before you pick up a car in one city and leave it in another, ask about drop-off charges or one-way service fees, which can be substantial. Also inquire about early-return policies; some rental agencies charge extra if you return the car before the time specified in your contract, but others will give you a refund for the days not used. To avoid a hefty refueling fee, fill the tank just before you turn in the car, but be aware that gas stations near the rental outlet may overcharge. It's almost never a deal to buy the tank of gas that's in the car when you rent it; the understanding is that you'll return it empty, but some fuel usually remains. Surcharges may apply if you're under 25 or if you take the car outside the area approved by the rental agency. You'll pay extra for child seats (about $8 a day), which are compulsory for children under five, and usually for additional drivers ($5 to $25 a day, depending on location and agency).

CAR TRAVEL

EMERGENCY SERVICES

Dial 911 to report accidents on the road and to reach police, the Arizona Department of Public Safety (Highway Patrol), or fire department. Highway safety boxes and emergency phones are rare on Arizona interstates or highways; call the highway patrol for help in any non-emergency situation.

📠 **Arizona Department of Public Safety** ☎ 602/223–2000, 602/223–2163 Highway Patrol.

ROAD CONDITIONS

The highways in Arizona are well maintained, but there are some natural conditions to keep in mind.

Desert heat. Vehicles and passengers should be well equipped for searing summer heat in the low desert. If you're planning to drive through the desert, make sure you are well stocked with radiator coolant, and **carry plenty of water, a good spare tire, a jack, and emergency supplies.** If you get stranded, stay with your vehicle and wait for help to arrive.

Dust storms. These usually occur from May to mid-September, causing extremely low visibility. Dust storms are more common on the highways and interstates that traverse the open desert (Interstate 10 between Phoenix and Tucson, Interstate 10 between Benson and the New Mexico state line, and Interstate 8 between Casa Grande and Yuma). If you're on the highway, **pull as far off the road as possible,**

turn off your headlights to avoid being hit, and wait for the storm to subside.

Flash floods. Warnings about flash floods should not be taken lightly. Sudden downpours send torrents of water racing into low-lying areas so dry that they are unable to absorb such a huge quantity of water quickly. The result can be powerful walls of water suddenly descending upon these low-lying areas, devastating anything in their paths. If you see rain clouds or thunderstorms in the area, stay away from dry riverbeds (also called arroyos or washes). If you find yourself in one, get out quickly. If you're with a car in a long gully, leave your car and climb out of the gully. You simply won't be able to outdrive a speeding wave. The idea is to **get to higher ground immediately when it rains.** Major highways are mostly flood-proof, but some smaller roads dip through washes; most roads that traverse through these low-lying areas will have flood warning signs, which should be seriously heeded during rainstorms. Washes filled with water should not be crossed until you can see the bottom. By all means, don't camp in these areas at any time, interesting as they may seem.

Fragile desert life. The dry and easily desecrated desert floor takes centuries to overcome human damage. Consequently, it is illegal for four-wheel-drive and all-terrain vehicles and motorcycles to travel off established roadways.

🚗 **Arizona Department of Transportation** ☎ 511 Arizona road information from within Arizona, 888/ 411-7623 Arizona road information from outside the state ⊕ www.az511.com.

RULES OF THE ROAD

Many stretches on Arizona interstates have 75 mph speed limits. In cities, freeway limits are between 55 mph and 65 mph. Seat belts are required at all times. Tickets can be given for failing to comply. Driving with a blood-alcohol level higher than 0.08 will result in arrest and seizure of your driver's license. Fines are severe.

At some point you will probably pass through one or more of the state's 23 Indian reservations. Roads and other areas within reservation boundaries are under the jurisdiction of reservation police and governed by separate rules and regulations. **Observe all signs and respect Native Americans' privacy.** Be careful not to hit any animals, which often wander onto the roads; the penalties can be very high.

Always **strap children under age five into approved child-safety seats.** In Arizona, children must wear seat belts regardless of where they're seated. In Arizona, you may turn right at a red light after stopping if there is no oncoming traffic. When in doubt, wait for the green.

CHILDREN IN ARIZONA

Many large resorts and dude ranches have special half-day or daylong activities for children, and many offer baby-sitting services. Children of all ages are enthralled by the Wild West flavor around Tucson and the southeastern part of the state, with Tombstone ranking as a particular favorite. If you're driving on long desert stretches, take along plenty of games and snacks.

The monthly magazine *Raising Arizona Kids* focuses on Phoenix happenings but also includes a calendar of children-friendly events around the state. You can buy single copies for $3.95 each at chains like Borders, Barnes & Noble, and B. Dalton; at local bookshops; and at retail outlets in Phoenix and surrounding areas, or send $19.95 for a year's subscription.

If you are renting a car, don't forget to arrange for a car seat when you reserve. For general advice about traveling with children, consult *Fodor's FYI: Travel with Your Baby* (available in bookstores everywhere).

🚗 *Raising Arizona Kids* ✉ 4545 E. Shea Blvd., Suite 168, Phoenix 85028 ☎ 602/953-5437 ⎙ 602/ 953-3305 ⊕ www.raisingarizonakids.com

FLYING

If your children are two or older, ask about children's airfares. As a general rule, infants under two not occupying a seat fly at greatly reduced fares or even for free. But if you want to guarantee a seat for an infant, you have to pay full fare. Consider flying during off-peak days and times; most airlines will grant an infant a seat without a ticket if there are available seats.

Experts agree that it's a good idea to use safety seats aloft for children weighing less than 40 pounds. Airlines set their own policies: if you use a safety seat, U.S. carriers usually require that the child be ticketed, even if he or she is young enough to ride free, because the seats must be strapped into regular seats. And even if you pay the full adult fare for the seat, it may be worth it, especially on longer trips. Do **check your airline's policy about using safety seats during takeoff and landing.** Safety seats are not allowed everywhere in the plane, so get your seat assignments as early as possible.

When reserving, request children's meals or a freestanding bassinet (not available at all airlines) if you need them. But note that bulkhead seats, where you must sit to use the bassinet, may lack an overhead bin or storage space on the floor.

LODGING

Most hotels in Arizona allow children under a certain age to stay in their parents' room at no extra charge, but others charge for them as extra adults; be sure to **find out the cutoff age for children's discounts.**

All Holiday Inns allow children under age 19 to stay free when sharing a room with an adult. In the Phoenix area, the Pointe Hilton Resort at Squaw Peak runs its Southwestern-themed Coyote Camp for children ages 4 to 12 year-round. The Funicians Kids Club at the Phoenician Resort in Scottsdale offers activities for children 5 to 12 throughout the year; Scottsdale's Hyatt Regency at Gainey Ranch also offers a full range of supervised daytime activities (with an emphasis on Native American crafts and stories) through its Camp Hyatt program, geared for children 3 to 12. The Westin La Paloma Hotel in Tucson has supervised activities year-round for children ages 6 months to 12 years through its Cactus Kids Club, as well as junior tennis camps for children 5 to 14 years old in summer. The Tanque Verde Guest Ranch, also in Tucson, offers year-round activities for children 4 to 11, which include horseback riding, tennis, fishing, swimming, and arts and crafts. Most of the above resorts also have baby-sitting services or can direct you to a trusted local agency.

⁊ Best Choices Holiday Inn ☎ 800/465-4329 ⊕ www.ichotelsgroup.com. **Hyatt Regency Scottsdale at Gainey Ranch** ☎ 480/991-3388 or 800/233-1234 ⊕ www.hyatt.com. **Phoenician Resort** ☎ 800/888-8234 ⊕ www.thephoenician.com. **Pointe Hilton Resort at Squaw Peak** ☎ 602/997-2626 or 800/947-9784 ⊕ www.pointehilton.com. **Tanque Verde Ranch** ☎ 800/234-3833 ⊕ www.tanqueverderanch.com. **Westin La Paloma Hotel** ☎ 520/742-6000 or 800/228-3000 ⊕ www.westinlapalomaresort.com.

SIGHTS & ATTRACTIONS

Places that are especially appealing to children are indicated by a rubber-duckie icon (🐤) in the margin.

CONSUMER PROTECTION

Whether you're shopping for gifts or purchasing travel services, **pay with a major credit card** whenever possible, so you can cancel payment or get reimbursed if there's a problem (and you can provide documentation). If you're doing business with a particular company for the first time, contact your local Better Business Bureau and the attorney general's offices in your state and (for U.S. businesses) the company's home state as well. Have any complaints been filed? Finally, if you're buying a package or tour, always consider travel insurance that includes default coverage (⇨ Insurance).

⁊ BBBs Council of Better Business Bureaus ✉ 4200 Wilson Blvd., Suite 800, Arlington, VA 22203 ☎ 703/276-0100 🖷 703/525-8277 ⊕ www.bbb.org.

CUSTOMS & DUTIES

IN AUSTRALIA

Australian residents who are 18 or older may bring home A$400 worth of souvenirs and gifts (including jewelry), 250 cigarettes or 250 grams of cigars or other tobacco products, and 1,125 ml of alcohol (including wine, beer, and spirits). Residents under 18 may bring back A$200 worth of goods. Members of the same family traveling together may pool their allowances. Prohibited items include meat products. Seeds, plants, and fruits need to be declared upon arrival.

Australian Customs Service ⟨ Regional Director, Box 8, Sydney, NSW 2001 ☎ 02/9213-2000 or 1300/363263, 02/9364-7222 or 1800/020-504 quarantine-inquiry line 🖷 02/9213-4043 ⊕ www.customs.gov.au.

IN CANADA

Canadian residents who have been out of Canada for at least seven days may bring in C$750 worth of goods duty-free. If you've been away fewer than seven days but more than 48 hours, the duty-free allowance drops to C$200. If your trip lasts 24 to 48 hours, the allowance is C$50. You may not pool allowances with family members. Goods claimed under the C$750 exemption may follow you by mail; those claimed under the lesser exemptions must accompany you. Alcohol and tobacco products may be included in the seven-day and 48-hour exemptions but not in the 24-hour exemption. If you meet the age requirements of the province or territory through which you reenter Canada, you may bring in, duty-free, 1.5 liters of wine *or* 1.14 liters (40 imperial ounces) of liquor *or* 24 12-ounce cans or bottles of beer or ale. Also, if you meet the local age requirement for tobacco products, you may bring in, duty-free, 200 cigarettes and 50 cigars. Check ahead of time with the Canada Customs and Revenue Agency or the Department of Agriculture for policies regarding meat products, seeds, plants, and fruits.

You may send an unlimited number of gifts (only one gift per recipient, however) worth up to C$60 each duty-free to Canada. Label the package UNSOLICITED GIFT—VALUE UNDER $60. Alcohol and tobacco are excluded.

Canada Customs and Revenue Agency ✉ 2265 St. Laurent Blvd., Ottawa, Ontario K1G 4K3 ☎ 800/461-9999 in Canada, 204/983-3500, 506/636-5064 ⊕ www.ccra.gc.ca.

IN NEW ZEALAND

All homeward-bound residents may bring back NZ$700 worth of souvenirs and gifts; passengers may not pool their allowances, and children can claim only the concession on goods intended for their own use. For those 17 or older, the duty-free allowance also includes 4.5 liters of wine or beer; one 1,125-ml bottle of spirits; and either 200 cigarettes, 250 grams of tobacco, 50 cigars, *or* a combination of the three up to 250 grams. Meat products, seeds, plants, and fruits must be declared upon arrival to the Agricultural Services Department.

New Zealand Customs ✉ Head office: The Customhouse, 17-21 Whitmore St., Box 2218, Wellington ☎ 09/300-5399 or 0800/428-786 ⊕ www.customs.govt.nz.

IN THE U.K.

From countries outside the European Union, including the United States, you may bring home, duty-free, 200 cigarettes, 50 cigars, 100 cigarillos, or 250 grams of tobacco; 1 liter of spirits or 2 liters of fortified or sparkling wine or liqueurs; 2 liters of still table wine; 60 ml of perfume; 250 ml of toilet water; plus £145 worth of other goods, including gifts and souvenirs. Prohibited items include meat and dairy products, seeds, plants, and fruits.

HM Customs and Excise ✉ Portcullis House, 21 Cowbridge Rd. E, Cardiff CF11 9SS ☎ 0845/010-9000 or 0208/929-0152 advice service, 0208/929-6731 or 0208/910-3602 complaints ⊕ www.hmce.gov.uk.

DISABILITIES & ACCESSIBILITY

Local Resources Arizona Office for Americans with Disabilities ✉ 100 N. 15th Ave., Suite 170, Phoenix 85007 ☎ 602/542-6276 or 800/358-3617, 602/542-6686 TTY ⊕ www.know-the-ada.com. **Sun Sound Reading Service** ☎ 602/231-0500 in Phoenix, 520/296-2400 in Tucson, 928/779-1775 in Flagstaff.

LODGING

Despite the Americans with Disabilities Act, the definition of accessibility seems to differ from hotel to hotel. Some properties may be accessible by ADA standards for people with mobility problems but not for people with hearing or vision impairments, for example.

If you have mobility problems, ask for the lowest floor on which accessible services are offered. If you have a hearing impairment, check whether the hotel has devices to alert you visually to the ring of the telephone, a knock at the door, and a fire/

emergency alarm. Some hotels provide these devices without charge. Discuss your needs with hotel personnel if this equipment isn't available, so that a staff member can personally alert you in the event of an emergency.

If you're bringing a guide dog, get authorization ahead of time and write down the name of the person with whom you spoke.

RESERVATIONS

When discussing accessibility with an operator or reservations agent, ask hard questions. Are there any stairs, inside *or* out? Are there grab bars next to the toilet *and* in the shower/tub? How wide is the doorway to the room? To the bathroom? For the most extensive facilities meeting the latest legal specifications, opt for newer accommodations. If you reserve through a toll-free number, consider also calling the hotel's local number to confirm the information from the central reservations office. Get confirmation in writing when you can.

SIGHTS & ATTRACTIONS

Many of the well-visited museums, attractions, and parks in Arizona are ADA-accessible. Grand Canyon National Park accepts the Golden Access Passport, which allows a traveler with a disability into the park free of charge; wide walkways that are wheelchair-accessible skirt several stretches of the canyon. The Petrified Forest, which stands on an open plain, can be viewed quite well from a vehicle. Kartchner Caverns offer easy access to the main areas. Larger cities in Arizona offer plenty of accessible parking.

TRANSPORTATION

Amtrak advises that you request redcap service, special seats, or wheelchair assistance when you make reservations. Also note that not all stations are equipped to provide these services. All passengers with disabilities are entitled to a 15% discount on the lowest available fare, and there are special fares for children with disabilities as well. Contact Amtrak for a free brochure that outlines services for older travelers and people with disabilities. Greyhound bus lines, which provides ser-

vice to many destinations in Arizona, will assist persons with disabilities throughout their trip, with advance notice; in the case of certain disabilities, Greyhound offers a half-price companion fare for those who accompany a traveler with a disability. For those wishing to rent a car, Avis, Hertz, and National can provide cars with hand controls in some destinations with advance notice; call ahead to confirm that you can be accommodated at your destination.

Complaints Aviation Consumer Protection Division (⇨ Air Travel) for airline-related problems. **Departmental Office of Civil Rights** ✉ for general inquiries, U.S. Department of Transportation, S-30, 400 7th St. SW, Room 10215, Washington, DC 20590 ☎ 202/366-4648 ⊟ 202/366-9371 ⊕ www.dot. gov/ost/docr/index.htm. **Disability Rights Section** ✉ NYAV, U.S. Department of Justice, Civil Rights Division, 950 Pennsylvania Ave. NW, Washington, DC 20530 ☎ ADA information line 202/514-0301, 800/ 514-0301, 202/514-0383 TTY, 800/514-0383 TTY ⊕ www.ada.gov. **U.S. Department of Transportation Hotline** ☎ for disability-related air-travel problems, 800/778-4838 or 800/455-9880 TTY.

TRAVEL AGENCIES

In the United States, the Americans with Disabilities Act requires that travel firms serve the needs of all travelers. Some agencies specialize in working with people with disabilities.

Travelers with Mobility Problems Access Adventures/B. Roberts Travel ✉ 206 Chestnut Ridge Rd., Scottsville, NY 14624 ☎ 585/889-9096 ⊕ www.brobertstravel.com ✎ dltravel@prodigy. net, run by a former physical-rehabilitation counselor. **Accessible Vans of America** ✉ 9 Spielman Rd., Fairfield, NJ 07004 ☎ 877/282-8267, 888/282-8267, 973/808-9709 reservations ⊟ 973/808-9713 ⊕ www.accessiblevans.com. **CareVacations** ✉ No. 5, 5110-50 Ave., Leduc, Alberta, Canada, T9E 6V4 ☎ 780/986-6404 or 877/478-7827 ⊟ 780/986-8332 ⊕ www.carevacations.com, for group tours and cruise vacations. **Flying Wheels Travel** ✉ 143 W. Bridge St., Box 382, Owatonna, MN 55060 ☎ 507/451-5005 ⊟ 507/451-1685 ⊕ www. flyingwheelstravel.com.

Travelers with Developmental Disabilities New Directions ✉ 5276 Hollister Ave., Suite 207, Santa Barbara, CA 93111 ☎ 805/967-2841 or 888/967-2841 ⊟ 805/964-7344 ⊕ www.newdirectionstravel.com.

DISCOUNTS & DEALS

Be a smart shopper and compare all your options before making decisions. A plane ticket bought with a promotional coupon from travel clubs, coupon books, and direct-mail offers or purchased on the Internet may not be cheaper than the least expensive fare from a discount ticket agency. And always keep in mind that what you get is just as important as what you save.

DISCOUNT RESERVATIONS

To save money, look into discount reservations services with Web sites and toll-free numbers, which use their buying power to get a better price on hotels, airline tickets (⇨ Air Travel), even car rentals. When booking a room, always **call the hotel's local toll-free number** (if one is available) rather than the central reservations number—you'll often get a better price. Always ask about special packages or corporate rates.

🛪 Airline Tickets **Air 4 Less** ☎ 800/AIR4LESS; low-fare specialist.

🛪 Hotel Rooms **Accommodations Express** ☎ 800/444-7666 or 800/277-1064 ⊕ www.acex. net. **Hotels.com** ☎ 800/246-8357 ⊕ www.hotels. com. **Quikbook** ☎ 800/789-9887 ⊕ www. quikbook.com. **Turbotrip.com** ☎ 800/473-7829 ⊕ www.turbotrip.com.

PACKAGE DEALS

Don't confuse packages and guided tours. When you buy a package, you travel on your own, just as though you had planned the trip yourself. Fly/drive packages, which combine airfare and car rental, are often a good deal. In cities, ask the local visitors bureau about hotel and local transportation packages that include tickets to major museum exhibits or other special events.

EATING & DRINKING

The restaurants we list are the cream of the crop in each price category. Properties indicated by an ✕⌂ are lodging establishments whose restaurant warrants a special trip. Unless otherwise noted, the restaurants listed in this guide are open daily for lunch and dinner.

In general, when you order a regular coffee, you get coffee with milk and sugar.

CATEGORY	COST*
$$$$	over $30
$$$	$20–$30
$$	$12–$20
$	$8–$12
¢	under $8

Prices are per person for a main course at dinner.

RESERVATIONS & DRESS

Reservations are always a good idea; we mention them only when they're essential or not accepted. Book as far ahead as you can, and reconfirm as soon as you arrive. (Large parties should always call ahead to check the reservations policy.) We mention dress only when men are required to wear a jacket or a jacket and tie.

SPECIALTIES

Two distinct cultures—Native American and Sonoran—have had the greatest influence on native Arizona cuisine. Chiles, beans, corn, tortillas, and squash are common ingredients for those restaurants that specialize in regional cuisine (cactus is just as tasty but less common). Mom-and-pop *taquerias* are abundant, especially in the southern part of the state.

WINE, BEER & SPIRITS

In Arizona, you must be 21 to buy any alcohol. Liquor stores are open daily, including Sunday, but must stop selling alcohol at 1 AM; bars also stop serving alcohol at this time. You will find beer, wine, and alcohol at most supermarkets. Possession and consumption of alcoholic beverages is illegal on Indian reservations.

ECOTOURISM

Arizona has some of the best-preserved prehistoric sites in the world. Both federal and state laws prohibit removal or destruction of artifacts from such sites. In Arizona, it is illegal to uproot or in any way harm a saguaro, and penalties are stiff. Whatever your activity, it is a good idea to tread lightly in natural settings. The Grand Canyon, Sedona, and numerous national forest, river, and canyon lands offer spectacular settings for group and self-guided backpacking and hiking trips. Remember to extinguish campfires and return the soil to its natural condition by mixing the ashes with dirt and water and covering the site with dirt.

GAY & LESBIAN TRAVEL

Arizona is a socially conservative state, but Phoenix has a large gay and lesbian population—one of the nation's largest—and Tucson has a visible gay scene as well. There are also small pockets of gay culture in Bisbee, Sedona, and Flagstaff. Although there are no statewide gay- and lesbian-oriented organizations in Arizona, the agencies listed below can help plan gay-friendly vacations. Information on gay establishments in specific cities can be found easily on the Internet. A good place to start is www.visitgayarizona.com, the official Arizona Travel and Tourism Web site for gay and lesbian travelers.

For details about the gay and lesbian scene in Bisbee, Flagstaff, Phoenix, Sedona, and Tucson, consult *Fodor's Gay Guide to the USA* (available in bookstores everywhere). *Echo* is a gay and lesbian news and entertainment magazine published biweekly that covers events throughout the state and is distributed all over Arizona. *HeatStroke News* is a Phoenix-based biweekly. The weekly *Observer* covers the Tucson area.

Local Publications *Echo* ☎ 602/266-0550. *HeatStroke News* ☎ 602/262-4328. *Observer* ☎ 520/622-7176.

Gay- & Lesbian-Friendly Travel Agencies Different Roads Travel ✉ 8383 Wilshire Blvd., Suite 520, Beverly Hills, CA 90211 ☎ 323/651-5557 or 800/429-8747 (Ext. 14 for both) 🖷 323/651-5454 ✉ lgernert@tzell.com. **Kennedy Travel** ✉ 130 W. 42nd St., Suite 401, New York, NY 10036 ☎ 212/840-8659 or 800/237-7433 🖷 212/730-2269 ⊕ www. kennedytravel.com. **Now, Voyager** ✉ 4406 18th St., San Francisco, CA 94114 ☎ 415/626-1169 or 800/255-6951 🖷 415/626-8626 ⊕ www.nowvoyager. com. **Skylink Travel and Tour/Flying Dutchmen Travel** ✉ 1455 N. Dutton Ave., Suite A, Santa Rosa, CA 95401 ☎ 707/546-9888 or 800/225-5759 🖷 707/636-0951; serving lesbian travelers.

HEALTH

ANIMAL BITES

Wherever you're walking in desert areas, particularly between April and October, **keep a lookout for rattlesnakes.** You're likely not to have any problems if you maintain distance from snakes that you see—they can strike only half of their length, so a 6-foot clearance should allow you to stay unharmed, especially if you don't provoke them. If you are bitten by a rattler, don't panic. Get to a hospital within two to three hours of the bite. Try to keep the area that has been bitten below heart level, and stay calm, as increased heart rate can spread venom more quickly. Keep in mind that 30% to 40% of bites are dry bites, where the snake uses no venom (still, get thee to a hospital). **Avoid night hikes without rangers,** when snakes are on the prowl and less visible.

Scorpions and Gila monsters are really less of a concern, since they strike only when provoked. To avoid scorpion encounters, don't put your hands where you can't see with your eyes, such as under rocks and in holes. Likewise, if you move a rock to sit down, make sure that scorpions haven't been exposed. Campers should shake out shoes in the morning, since scorpions like warm, moist places. If you are bitten, see a ranger about symptoms that may develop. Chances are good that you won't need to go to a hospital. Children are a different case, however: scorpion stings can be fatal for them. Always try to keep an eye on what they may be getting their hands into to avoid the scorpion's sting. Gila monsters are relatively rare and bites are even rarer, but bear in mind that the reptiles are most active between April and June, when they do most of their hunting. Should a member of your party be bitten, it is most important to release the Gila monster's jaws as soon as possible to minimize the amount of venom released. This can usually be achieved with a stick, an open flame, or immersion of the animal in water.

DEHYDRATION

This underestimated danger can be very serious, especially considering that one of the first major symptoms is the inability to swallow. It may be the easiest hazard to avoid, however; simply **drink every 10-15 minutes,** up to a gallon of water per day in summer. Always carry a water bottle, and replenish frequently, whether hiking, walking in the city, or at an outdoor sports or arts event.

HYPOTHERMIA

Temperatures in Arizona can vary widely from day to night—as much as 40°F. Be sure to **bring enough warm clothing for hiking and camping, along with wet-weather gear.** It is always a good idea to pack an extra set of clothes in a large, waterproof plastic bag (a large resealable bag will do) that would stay dry in any situation. Exposure to the degree that body temperature dips below 95°F produces the following symptoms: chills, tiredness, then uncontrollable shivering and irrational behavior, with the victim not always recognizing that he or she is cold. If someone in your party is suffering from any of this, wrap him or her in blankets and/or a warm sleeping bag immediately and try to keep him or her awake. The fastest way to raise body temperature is through skin-to-skin contact in a sleeping bag. Drinking warm liquids also helps.

SUN EXPOSURE

Wear a hat and sunglasses and put on sunblock to protect against the burning Arizona sun. And **watch out for heatstroke.** Symptoms include headache, dizziness, and fatigue, which can turn into convulsions and unconsciousness and can lead to death. If someone in your party develops any of these conditions, have one person seek emergency help while others move the victim into the shade and wrap him or her in wet clothing (is a stream nearby?) to cool him or her down.

HOLIDAYS

Major national holidays are New Year's Day (Jan. 1); Martin Luther King Day (3rd Mon. in Jan.); Presidents' Day (3rd Mon. in Feb.); Memorial Day (last Mon. in May); Independence Day (July 4); Labor Day (1st Mon. in Sept.); Columbus Day (2nd Mon. in Oct.); Thanksgiving Day (4th Thurs. in Nov.); Christmas Eve and Christmas Day (Dec. 24 and 25); and New Year's Eve (Dec. 31).

INSURANCE

The most useful travel-insurance plan is a comprehensive policy that includes coverage for trip cancellation and interruption, default, trip delay, and medical expenses (with a waiver for preexisting conditions).

Without insurance you'll lose all or most of your money if you cancel your trip, regardless of the reason. Default insurance covers you if your tour operator, airline, or cruise line goes out of business—the chances of which have been increasing. Trip-delay covers expenses that arise because of bad weather or mechanical delays. Study the fine print when comparing policies.

U.K. residents can buy a travel-insurance policy valid for most vacations taken during the year in which it's purchased (but check preexisting-condition coverage).

Always buy travel policies directly from the insurance company; if you buy them from a cruise line, airline, or tour operator that goes out of business you probably won't be covered for the agency or operator's default, a major risk. Before making any purchase, review your existing health and home-owner's policies to find what they cover away from home.

🛈 Travel Insurers In the U.S.: **Access America** ✉ 2805 N. Parham Rd., Richmond, VA 23294 ☎ 800/284-8300 🖷 804/673-1491 or 800/346-9265 ⊕ www.accessamerica.com. **Travel Guard International** ✉ 1145 Clark St., Stevens Point, WI 54481 ☎ 715/345-0505 or 800/826-1300 🖷 800/955-8785 ⊕ www.travelguard.com.

FOR INTERNATIONAL TRAVELERS

For information on customs restrictions, *see* Customs & Duties.

CAR RENTAL

When picking up a rental car, non-U.S. residents need a reservation voucher for any prepaid reservations that were made in the traveler's home country, a passport, a driver's license, and a travel policy that covers each driver.

CAR TRAVEL

Gas prices vary widely across Arizona, but stations are plentiful. Most stay open late (24 hours along large highways and in big cities), except in rural areas, where Sunday hours are limited and where you may drive long stretches without a refueling opportunity. Highways are well paved. Interstate highways—limited-access, multilane highways whose numbers are prefixed by "I–"—are the fastest routes. Interstates with three-digit numbers either encircle or spur from urban areas, which may have other limited-access expressways, freeways, and parkways as well. Tolls may be levied on limited-access highways. So-called U.S. highways and state highways are not necessarily limited-access but may have several lanes.

Along larger highways, roadside stops with restrooms, fast-food restaurants, and sundries stores are well spaced. State police and tow trucks patrol major highways and lend assistance. If your car breaks down on an interstate, pull onto the shoulder and wait for help, or have your passengers wait while you walk to an emergency phone (available in many states). If you carry a cell phone, dial *55, noting your location according to the small green roadside mileage markers.

Driving in the United States is on the right. Do obey speed limits posted along roads and highways. Watch for lower limits in small towns and on back roads. On weekdays between 6 and 10 AM and again between 4 and 7 PM expect heavy traffic. To encourage carpooling, some freeways have special lanes for so-called high-occupancy vehicles (HOV)—cars carrying more than one passenger.

Bookstores, gas stations, convenience stores, and rest stops sell maps (about $3) and multiregion road atlases (about $10).

CONSULATES & EMBASSIES

Australia Australian Consulate General & Trade Commission ⌧ 2049 Century Park E, Level 19, Los Angeles, CA 90067 ☎ 310/229-4800 🖷 310/277-5746 or 310/277-3462 ⊕ www.austemb.org/consulates/losangeles.htm.

Canada Canadian Consulate General ⌧ 550 S. Hope St., 9th floor, Los Angeles, CA 90071 ☎ 213/346-2700 🖷 213/620-8827 ⊕ www.losangeles.gc.ca.

New Zealand New Zealand Consulate General ⌧ 12400 Wilshire Blvd., Suite 1150, Los Angeles, CA 90025 ☎ 310/207-1605 🖷 310/207-3605 ⊕ www.nzcgla.com.

United Kingdom British Consulate General ⌧ 11766 Wilshire Blvd., Suite 1200, Los Angeles, CA 90025 ☎ 310/481-0031 🖷 310/481-2960 ⊕ www.britainusa.com/la.

CURRENCY

The dollar is the basic unit of U.S. currency. It has 100 cents. Coins are the copper penny (1¢); the silvery nickel (5¢), dime (10¢), quarter (25¢), and half-dollar (50¢); and the golden $1 coin, replacing a now-rare silver dollar. Bills are denominated $1, $5, $10, $20, $50, and $100, all mostly green and identical in size; designs and background tints vary. In addition, you may come across a $2 bill, but the chances are slim. The exchange rate at this writing is US$1.83 per British pound, US$1.20 per Euro, 75¢ per Canadian dollar, 76¢ per Australian dollar, and 68¢ per New Zealand dollar.

ELECTRICITY

The U.S. standard is AC, 110 volts/60 cycles. Plugs have two flat pins set parallel to each other.

EMERGENCIES

For police, fire, or ambulance, **dial 911** (0 in rural areas).

INSURANCE

Britons and Australians need extra medical coverage when traveling overseas.

Insurance Information In the U.K.: **Association of British Insurers** ⌧ 51 Gresham St., London EC2V 7HQ ☎ 020/7600-3333 🖷 020/7696-8999 ⊕ www.abi.org.uk. In Australia: **Insurance Council of Australia** ⌧ Insurance Enquiries and Complaints, Level 12, Box 561, Collins St. W, Melbourne, VIC 8007 ☎ 1300/780808 or 03/9629-4109 🖷 03/9621-2060 ⊕ www.iecltd.com.au. In Canada: **RBC Insurance** ⌧ 6880 Financial Dr., Mississauga, Ontario L5N 7Y5 ☎ 800/668-4342 or 905/816-2400 🖷 905/813-4704 ⊕ www.rbcinsurance.com. In New Zealand: **Insurance Council of New Zealand** ⌧ Level 7, 111-115 Customhouse Quay, Box 474, Wellington ☎ 04/472-5230 🖷 04/473-3011 ⊕ www.icnz.org.nz.

MAIL & SHIPPING

You can buy stamps and aerograms and send letters and parcels in post offices. Stamp-dispensing machines can occasionally be found in airports, bus and train stations, office buildings, drugstores, and the like. You can also deposit mail in the stout, dark blue, steel bins at strategic locations everywhere and in the mail chutes of large buildings; pickup schedules are posted. You can deposit packages at public collection boxes as long as the parcels are affixed with proper postage and weigh less than one pound. Packages weighing one or more pounds must be taken to a post office or handed to a postal carrier.

For mail sent within the United States, you need a 37¢ stamp for first-class letters weighing up to 1 ounce (23¢ for each additional ounce) and 23¢ for postcards. You pay 80¢ for 1-ounce airmail letters and 70¢ for airmail postcards to most other countries; to Canada and Mexico, you need a 60¢ stamp for a 1-ounce letter and 50¢ for a postcard. An aerogram—a single sheet of lightweight blue paper that folds into its own envelope, stamped for overseas airmail—costs 70¢.

To receive mail on the road, have it sent c/o General Delivery at your destination's main post office (use the correct five-digit ZIP code). You must pick up mail in person within 30 days and show a driver's license or passport.

PASSPORTS & VISAS
When traveling internationally, carry your passport even if you don't need one (it's always the best form of I.D.) and make two photocopies of the data page (one for someone at home and another for you, carried separately from your passport). If you lose your passport, promptly call the nearest embassy or consulate and the local police.

Visitor visas aren't necessary for Canadian or European Union citizens, or for citizens of Australia who are staying fewer than 90 days.

🚩 Australian Citizens **Passports Australia** ☎ 131–232 ⊕ www.passports.gov.au. **United States Consulate General** ✉ MLC Centre, Level 59, 19–29 Martin Pl., Sydney, NSW 2000 ☎ 02/9373–9200, 1902/941–641 fee-based visa-inquiry line ⊕ usembassy-australia.state.gov/sydney.

🚩 Canadian Citizens **Passport Office** ✉ to mail in applications: 200 Promenade du Portage, Hull, Québec J8X 4B7 ☎ 819/994–3500, 800/567–6868, 866/255–7655 TTY ⊕ www.ppt.gc.ca.

🚩 New Zealand Citizens **New Zealand Passports Office** ✉ For applications and information, Level 3, Boulcott House, 47 Boulcott St., Wellington ☎ 0800/22–5050 or 04/474–8100 ⊕ www.passports.govt.nz. **Embassy of the United States** ✉ 29 Fitzherbert Terr., Thorndon, Wellington ☎ 04/462–6000 ⊕ usembassy.org.nz. **U.S. Consulate General** ✉ Citibank Bldg., 3rd floor, 23 Customs St. E, Auckland ☎ 09/303–2724 ⊕ usembassy.org.nz.

🚩 U.K. Citizens **U.K. Passport Service** ☎ 0870/521–0410 ⊕ www.passport.gov.uk. **American Consulate General** ✉ Danesfort House, 223 Stranmillis Rd., Belfast, Northern Ireland BT9 5GR ☎ 028/9032–8239 ☎ 028/9024–8482 ⊕ usembassy.org.uk. **American Embassy** ✉ for visa and immigration information or to submit a visa application via mail (enclose an SASE), Consular Information Unit, 24 Grosvenor Sq., London W1 1AE ☎ 09055/444–546 for visa information (per-minute charges), 0207/499–9000 main switchboard ⊕ usembassy.org.uk.

TELEPHONES
All U.S. telephone numbers consist of a three-digit area code and a seven-digit local number. Within many local calling areas, you dial only the seven-digit number. Within some area codes, you must dial "1" first for calls outside the local area. To call between area-code regions, dial "1" then all 10 digits; the same goes for calls to numbers prefixed by "800," "888," "866," and "877"—all toll free. For calls to numbers preceded by "900" you must pay—usually dearly.

For international calls, dial "011" followed by the country code and the local number. For help, dial "0" and ask for an overseas operator. The country code is 61 for Australia, 64 for New Zealand, 44 for the United Kingdom. Calling Canada is the same as calling within the United States. Most local phone books list country codes and U.S. area codes. The country code for the United States is 1.

For operator assistance, dial "0." To obtain someone's phone number, call directory assistance at 555–1212 or occasionally 411 (free at some public phones). To have the person you're calling foot the bill, phone collect; dial "0" instead of "1" before the 10-digit number.

At pay phones, instructions often are posted. Usually you insert coins in a slot (usually 35¢–50¢ for local calls) and wait for a steady tone before dialing. When you call long-distance, the operator tells you how much to insert; prepaid phone cards, widely available in various denominations, are easier. Call the number on the back, punch in the card's personal identification number when prompted, then dial your number.

LODGING

Arizona's hotels and motels run the gamut from world-class resorts to budget chains and from historic inns, bed-and-breakfasts, and mountain lodges to dude ranches, campgrounds, and RV parks. **Make reservations well in advance for the high season**—winter in the desert south and summer in the high country. Tremendous bargains can be found off-season, when even the most exclusive establishments can cut their rates by half.

Phoenix and Tucson have the greatest variety of accommodations in the state. Resorts in Sedona and in some of the smaller, more exclusive desert communities can be pricey, but there are cheap chains in (or near) just about every resort-oriented destination in the state. Even the budget chains in these areas can have rates in the upper double-digits, however, especially on holidays and high-season weekends. The Grand Canyon area is equally pricey, but camping options, cabins, and dorm-style resorts on or near the national park grounds can be more affordable. If you plan to stay at the Grand Canyon, make lodging reservations far in advance. You might have a more relaxing visit, and find better prices, if you stay at one of the gateway cities; Tusayan, Williams, and Flagstaff to the south, and Jacob Lake, Fredonia, and Kanab, Utah, to the north.

The lodgings we list are the cream of the crop in each price category. We always list the facilities that are available, but we don't specify whether they cost extra; when pricing accommodations, always ask what's included and what costs extra. Properties are assigned price categories based on the range from their least-expensive standard double room at high season (excluding holidays) to the most expensive. Properties marked ✕⌨ are lodging establishments whose restaurants warrant a special trip.

Assume that hotels operate on the **European Plan** (EP, with no meals) unless we specify that they use the **Continental Plan** (CP, with a continental breakfast), **Breakfast Plan** (BP, with a full breakfast), **Modified American Plan** (MAP, with breakfast and dinner), or the **Full American Plan** (FAP, with all meals).

CATEGORY	COST*
$$$$	over $250
$$$	$175–$250
$$	$120–$175
$	$70–$120
¢	under $70

Prices are for two people in a double room during high season.

BED & BREAKFASTS

The Arizona Association of Bed and Breakfast Inns has member inns in most of the popular destinations in the state. The Arizona Trails Reservation Service has an extensive list of B&B and other lodging rentals throughout the state and can also help with vacation packages, tours, and golf vacations. Intimate lodgings in Arizona boast a range of styles, from Southwestern adobe haciendas in areas like Sedona and Tucson to pine cabins in the White Mountains. The Arizona Office of Tourism (⇨ Visitor Information) has a statewide list of B&Bs.

🛈 Reservation Services **Arizona Association of Bed and Breakfast Inns** 🏠 Box 22086, Flagstaff 86002 ☎ 800/284-2589 ⊕ www.arizona-bed-breakfast.com. **Arizona Trails Reservation Service** 🏠 Box 18998, Fountain Hills 85269 ☎ 480/837-4284 or 888/799-4284 ⊕ www.arizonatrails.com. **Mi Casa Su Casa** 🏠 Box 950, Tempe 85280 ☎ 480/990-0682 or 800/456-0682 🖷 480/990-3390 ⊕ www.azres.com.

CAMPING

You can choose from among federal, state, Native American, and private campgrounds in virtually all parts of the state. Most state parks have a 14-day maximum-stay limit. Camping is also permitted in

Arizona's seven national forests, but be forewarned that they often have no facilities whatsoever; in most cases, backcountry camping permits must be reserved.

Pack according to season, region, and length of trip. Basics include a sleeping bag, a tent (optional, and forbidden in some RV parks), a camp stove, cooking utensils, food and water supplies, a first-aid kit, insect repellent, sunscreen, a lantern, trash bags, a rope, and a tarp.

🔏 **Arizona State Parks Department** ✉ 1300 W. Washington St., Phoenix 85007 ☎ 602/542-4174 ⊕ www.azstateparks.com. **Apache Sitgreaves National Forest** ✉ 309 S. Mountain Ave., Springerville 85938 ☎ 928/333-4301 ⊕ www.fs. fed.us/r3/asnf. **Bureau of Land Management** ✉ 222 N. Central Ave., Phoenix 85004 ☎ 602/417-9528 ⊕ www.az.blm.gov. **Coconino National Forest** ✉ 1824 S. Thompson St., Flagstaff 86001 ☎ 928/527-3600 ⊕ www.fs.fed.us/r3/coconino. **Coronado National Forest** ✉ Federal Bldg., 300 W. Congress St., Tucson 85701 ☎ 520/670-4552 ⊕ www.fs.fed.us/r3/coronado. **National Park Service** ✉ 3115 N. 3rd Ave., Suite 101, Phoenix 85013 ☎ 602/640-5250 or 202/208-6843 🖷 602/640-5265 ⊕ www.nps.gov. **Prescott National Forest** ✉ 344 S. Cortez St., Prescott 86303 ☎ 928/443-8000 ⊕ www.fs.fed.us/r3/prescott. **Tonto National Forest** ✉ 2324 E. McDowell Rd., Phoenix 85006 ☎ 602/225-5200 ⊕ www.fs.fed.us/r3/tonto. **Williams-Forest Service Visitor Center** ✉ 200 W. Railroad Ave., Williams 86046 ☎ 928/635-4061 ⊕ www.williamschamber.com.

DUDE/GUEST RANCHES

Down-home Western lifestyle, cooking, and activities are the focus of guest ranches, situated primarily in Tucson and southern Arizona and Wickenburg northwest of Phoenix. Some are resortlike properties where guests are pampered, whereas smaller, family-run ranches expect *everyone* to join in the chores. Horseback riding and other outdoor recreational activities are emphasized. Most dude ranches are closed in summer. The Arizona Dude Ranch Association can give you the names and addresses of its member ranches and their facilities and policies. Contact the Arizona Office of Tourism (⇨ Visitor Information) for the names and addresses of dude ranches throughout the state.

🔏 **The Arizona Dude Ranch Association** ⌂ Box 603, Cortaro 85652 ☎ no phone ⊕ www.azdra.com.

HOME EXCHANGES

If you would like to exchange your home for someone else's, join a home-exchange organization, which will send you its updated listings of available exchanges for a year and will include your own listing in at least one of them. It's up to you to make specific arrangements.

🔏 **Exchange Clubs HomeLink International** ⌂ Box 47747, Tampa, FL 33647 ☎ 813/975-9825 or 800/638-3841 🖷 813/910-8144 ⊕ www.homelink. org; $110 yearly for a listing, online access, and catalog; $70 without catalog. **Intervac U.S.** ✉ 30 Corte San Fernando, Tiburon, CA 94920 ☎ 800/756-4663 🖷 415/435-7440 ⊕ www.intervacus.com; $125 yearly for a listing, online access, and a catalog; $65 without catalog.

HOSTELS

No matter what your age, you can save on lodging costs by staying at hostels. In some 4,500 locations in more than 70 countries around the world, Hostelling International (HI), the umbrella group for a number of national youth-hostel associations, offers single-sex, dorm-style beds and, at many hostels, rooms for couples and family accommodations. Membership in any HI national hostel association, open to travelers of all ages, allows you to stay in HI-affiliated hostels at member rates; one-year membership is about $28 for adults (C$35 for a two-year minimum membership in Canada, £14 in the U.K., A$52 in Australia, and NZ$40 in New Zealand); hostels charge about $10–$30 per night. Members have priority if the hostel is full; they're also eligible for discounts around the world, even on rail and bus travel in some countries.

🔏 **Hostels in Arizona Hostelling International Phoenix** ✉ 1026 N. 9th St., Phoenix, AZ 85006 ☎ 602/254-9803 ⊕ www.hiayh.org.

🔏 **Organizations Hostelling International–USA** ✉ 8401 Colesville Rd., Suite 600, Silver Spring, MD 20910 ☎ 301/495-1240 🖷 301/495-6697 ⊕ www. hiusa.org. **Hostelling International–Canada** ✉ 205 Catherine St., Suite 400, Ottawa, Ontario K2P 1C3 ☎ 613/237-7884 or 800/663-5777 🖷 613/237-7868 ⊕ www.hihostels.ca. **YHA England and**

Wales ✉ Trevelyan House, Dimple Rd., Matlock, Derbyshire DE4 3YH, U.K. ☎ 0870/870-8808, 0870/770-8868, 0162/959-2600 🖷 0870/770-6127 ⊕ www.yha.org.uk. **YHA Australia** ✉ 422 Kent St., Sydney, NSW 2001 ☎ 02/9261-1111 🖷 02/9261-1969 ⊕ www.yha.com.au. **YHA New Zealand** ✉ Level 1, Moorhouse City, 166 Moorhouse Ave., Box 436, Christchurch ☎ 03/379-9970 or 0800/278-299 🖷 03/365-4476 ⊕ www.yha.org.nz.

HOTELS

All hotels listed in this guide have private baths unless otherwise noted.

🔢 **Toll-Free Numbers Baymont Inns** ☎ 800/428-3438, 866/999-1111 ⊕ www.baymontinns.com. **Best Western** ☎ 800/528-1234 ⊕ www.bestwestern.com. **Choice** ☎ 800/424-6423 ⊕ www.choicehotels.com. **Clarion** ☎ 800/424-6423 ⊕ www.choicehotels.com. **Comfort Inn** ☎ 800/424-6423 ⊕ www.choicehotels.com. **Days Inn** ☎ 800/325-2525 ⊕ www.daysinn.com. **Doubletree Hotels** ☎ 800/222-8733 ⊕ www.doubletree.com. **Embassy Suites** ☎ 800/362-2779 ⊕ www.embassysuites.com. **Fairfield Inn** ☎ 800/228-2800 ⊕ www.marriott.com. **Four Seasons** ☎ 800/332-3442 ⊕ www.fourseasons.com. **Hilton** ☎ 800/445-8667 ⊕ www.hilton.com. **Holiday Inn** ☎ 800/465-4329 ⊕ www.ichotelsgroup.com. **Howard Johnson** ☎ 800/446-4656 ⊕ www.hojo.com. **Hyatt Hotels & Resorts** ☎ 800/233-1234 ⊕ www.hyatt.com. **La Quinta** ☎ 800/531-5900 ⊕ www.lq.com. **Marriott** ☎ 800/228-9290 ⊕ www.marriott.com. **Omni** ☎ 800/843-6664 ⊕ www.omnihotels.com. **Quality Inn** ☎ 800/424-6423 ⊕ www.choicehotels.com. **Radisson** ☎ 800/333-3333 ⊕ www.radisson.com. **Ramada** ☎ 800/228-2828, 800/854-7854 international reservations ⊕ www.ramada.com or www.ramadahotels.com. **Red Lion and WestCoast Hotels and Inns** ☎ 800/733-5466 ⊕ www.redlion.com. **Renaissance Hotels & Resorts** ☎ 800/468-3571 ⊕ www.renaissancehotels.com. **Ritz-Carlton** ☎ 800/241-3333 ⊕ www.ritzcarlton.com. **Sheraton** ☎ 800/325-3535 ⊕ www.starwood.com/sheraton. **Sleep Inn** ☎ 800/424-6423 ⊕ www.choicehotels.com. **Westin Hotels & Resorts** ☎ 800/228-3000 ⊕ www.starwood.com/westin. **Wyndham Hotels & Resorts** ☎ 800/822-4200 ⊕ www.wyndham.com.

MEDIA

NEWSPAPERS & MAGAZINES

Major Arizona-interest publications available statewide are *Arizona Business, Ari-*

zona Highways, and *Sunset Magazine. Phoenix Magazine, Metro,* and *Desert Living Magazine* focus on architecture, dining, style, arts, and events in the Phoenix area.

🔢 **Web sites Arizona Business** ⊕ www.azbusinessmagazine.com. **Arizona Highways** ⊕ www.arizhwys.com. **Metro** ⊕ www.metromagaz.com. **Sunset Magazine** ⊕ www.sunset.com.

TELEVISION

In Phoenix, Channel 12 (KPNX) is the NBC affiliate and a site for local news. Channel 15 (KNXV) and Channel 5 (KPHO) are, respectively, the ABC and CBS affiliates in Phoenix; both carry local and national news. The ABC affiliate in Tucson is Channel 9 (KGUN), and the CBS affiliate is Channel 13 (KOLD). PBS is broadcast through Arizona State University in Tempe on Channel 8 (KAET), and through the University of Arizona on Channel 6 (KUAT) in Tucson. COX, which can be found on Channel 9 or 52, broadcasts Phoenix Suns games and other sports events. Other major stations in the state include Channel 6 (KMOH) in Kingman, Channel 2 (KNAZ) in Flagstaff, and Channel 4 (KVOA) in Tucson, all NBC affiliates.

MONEY MATTERS

Prices throughout this guide are given for adults. Substantially reduced fees are almost always available for children, students, and senior citizens. For information on taxes, *see* Taxes.

ATMS

Most ATMs are on either the Cirrus (affiliated with MasterCard) or Plus system (affiliated with Visa).

🔢 **Cirrus** ☎ 800/424-7787 ⊕ www.mastercard.com. **Plus** ☎ 800/843-7587 ⊕ http://usa.visa.com.

CREDIT CARDS

Throughout this guide, the following abbreviations are used: **AE**, American Express; **D**, Discover; **DC**, Diners Club; **MC**, MasterCard; and **V**, Visa.

🔢 **Reporting Lost Cards American Express** ☎ 800/992-3404. **Diners Club** ☎ 800/234-6377. **Discover** ☎ 800/347-2683. **MasterCard** ☎ 800/622-7747. **Visa** ☎ 800/847-2911.

NATIONAL PARKS

Look into discount passes to save money on park entrance fees. For $50, the National Parks Pass admits you (and any passengers in your private vehicle) to all national parks, monuments, and recreation areas, as well as other sites run by the National Park Service, for a year. (In parks that charge per person, the pass admits you, your spouse and children, and your parents, when you arrive together.) Camping and parking are extra. The $15 Golden Eagle Pass, a hologram you affix to your National Parks Pass, functions as an upgrade, granting entry to all sites run by the NPS, the U.S. Fish and Wildlife Service, the U.S. Forest Service, and the Bureau of Land Management. The upgrade, which expires with the parks pass, is sold by most national-park, Fish-and-Wildlife, and BLM fee stations. A major percentage of the proceeds from pass sales funds National Parks projects.

Both the Golden Age Passport ($10), for U.S. citizens or permanent residents who are 62 and older, and the Golden Access Passport (free), for persons with disabilities, entitle holders (and any passengers in their private vehicles) to lifetime free entry to all national parks, plus 50% off fees for the use of many park facilities and services. (The discount doesn't always apply to companions.) To obtain them, you must show proof of age and of U.S. citizenship or permanent residency—such as a U.S. passport, driver's license, or birth certificate—and, if requesting Golden Access, proof of disability. The Golden Age and Golden Access passes are available only at NPS-run sites that charge an entrance fee. The National Parks Pass is also available by mail and via the Internet.

🏛 **National Park Foundation** ⊠ 11 Dupont Circle NW, 6th floor, Washington, DC 20036 ☎ 202/238–4200 ⊕ www.nationalparks.org. **National Park Service** ⊠ National Park Service/Department of Interior, 1849 C St. NW, Washington, DC 20240 ☎ 202/208–6843 ⊕ www.nps.gov. **National Parks Conservation Association** ⊠ 1300 19th St. NW, Suite 300, Washington, DC 20036 ☎ 202/223–6722 ⊕ www.npca.org. 🏛 **Passes by Mail & Online National Park Foundation** ⊕ www.nationalparks.org. **National Parks Pass** National Park Foundation ⊕ Box 34108, Washington, DC 20043 ☎ 888/467–2757 ⊕ www.nationalparks.org; include a check or money order payable to the National Park Service, plus $3.95 for shipping and handling (allow 8 to 13 business days from date of receipt for pass delivery), or call for passes.

PACKING

Pack casual clothing and resort wear for a trip to Arizona. Stay cool in cotton fabrics and light colors. T-shirts, polo shirts, sundresses, and lightweight shorts, trousers, skirts, and blouses are useful year-round in the south. Bring sun hats, swimsuits, sandals, and sunscreen—mandatory warm-weather items. Bring a sweater and a warm jacket in winter, necessary during December and January throughout the state, particularly in the high-country—anywhere around Flagstaff and north of it, and in the White Mountains east of Payson. And don't forget jeans and sneakers or sturdy walking shoes; they're important year-round.

In your carry-on luggage, pack an extra pair of eyeglasses or contact lenses and enough of any medication you take to last a few days longer than the entire trip. You may also ask your doctor to write a spare prescription using the drug's generic name, as brand names may vary from country to country. In luggage to be checked, **never pack prescription drugs, valuables, or undeveloped film.** And don't forget to carry with you the addresses of offices that handle refunds of lost traveler's checks. Check *Fodor's How to Pack* (available at online retailers and bookstores everywhere) for more tips.

To avoid customs and security delays, carry medications in their original packaging. Don't pack any sharp objects in your carry-on luggage, including knives of any size or material, scissors, nail clippers, and corkscrews, or anything else that might arouse suspicion.

To avoid having your checked luggage chosen for hand inspection, don't cram bags full. The U.S. Transportation Security Administration suggests packing shoes on top and placing personal items you don't want touched in clear plastic bags.

CHECKING LUGGAGE

You're allowed to carry aboard one bag and one personal article, such as a purse or a laptop computer. Make sure what you carry on fits under your seat or in the overhead bin. Get to the gate early, so you can board as soon as possible, before the overhead bins fill up.

Baggage allowances vary by carrier, destination, and ticket class. On international flights, you're usually allowed to check two bags weighing up to 70 pounds (32 kilograms) each, although a few airlines allow checked bags of up to 88 pounds (40 kilograms) in first class. Some international carriers don't allow more than 66 pounds (30 kilograms) per bag in business class and 44 pounds (20 kilograms) in economy. On domestic flights, the limit is usually 50 to 70 pounds (23 to 32 kilograms) per bag. In general, carry-on bags shouldn't exceed 40 pounds (18 kilograms). Most airlines won't accept bags that weigh more than 100 pounds (45 kilograms) on domestic or international flights. Expect to pay a fee for baggage that exceeds weight limits. Check baggage restrictions with your carrier before you pack.

Airline liability for baggage is limited to $2,500 per person on flights within the United States. On international flights it amounts to $9.07 per pound or $20 per kilogram for checked baggage (roughly $640 per 70-pound bag), with a maximum of $634.90 per piece, and $400 per passenger for unchecked baggage. You can buy additional coverage at check-in for about $10 per $1,000 of coverage, but it often excludes a rather extensive list of items, shown on your airline ticket.

Before departure, itemize your bags' contents and their worth, and label the bags with your name, address, and phone number. (If you use your home address, cover it so potential thieves can't see it readily.) Include a label inside each bag and **pack a copy of your itinerary.** At check-in, make sure each bag is correctly tagged with the destination airport's three-letter code. Because some checked bags will be opened for hand inspection, the U.S. Transportation Security Administration recommends that you leave luggage unlocked or use the plastic locks offered at check-in. TSA screeners place an inspection notice inside searched bags, which are re-sealed with a special lock.

If your bag has been searched and contents are missing or damaged, file a claim with the TSA Consumer Response Center as soon as possible. If your bags arrive damaged or fail to arrive at all, file a written report with the airline before leaving the airport.

 Complaints U.S. Transportation Security Administration Contact Center 866/289-9673 www.tsa.gov.

SENIOR-CITIZEN TRAVEL

Almost all museums, cultural centers, movie theaters, attractions, and national and state parks offer senior-citizen discounts with proper ID. Sun City, a suburb of Phoenix, is a major senior-citizen retirement community.

To qualify for age-related discounts, mention your senior-citizen status up front when booking hotel reservations (not when checking out) and before you're seated in restaurants (not when paying the bill). Be sure to have identification on hand. When renting a car, ask about promotional car-rental discounts, which can be cheaper than senior-citizen rates.

 Educational Programs Elderhostel 11 Ave. de Lafayette, Boston, MA 02111-1746 877/426-8056, 978/323-4141 international callers, 877/426-2167 TTY 877/426-2166 www.elderhostel.org. **Interhostel** University of New Hampshire, 6 Garrison Ave., Durham, NH 03824 603/862-1147 or 800/733-9753 603/862-1113 www.learn.unh.edu.

SHOPPING

If you are hunting for Native American or Mexican handiwork, avoid the tchotchkes sold in souvenir shops at the resorts or malls, and go for the real thing. Even if your travel plans don't include trips to a reservation or the border, you can find locally owned craft arts and crafts stores in major cities. Bargaining is acceptable in most antique and consignment shops, on the reservations, and in Mexico.

KEY DESTINATIONS

Scottsdale, one of the major resort destinations in the country, has attracted numerous designer department stores and boutiques in the past decade; Old Town Scottsdale, the former town center, is known for its art galleries and crafts stores, also pricey. Outdoor farmers markets in Scottsdale, Phoenix, and Tempe operate most of the year in the balmy Arizona sunshine. Markets are usually only open one or two days a week. Guadalupe, a township southeast of Phoenix, hosts a variety of Mexican markets and food shops. For tarot cards, healing crystals, handmade pottery, handwoven clothing, or anything out of the ordinary, head to Sedona. Bisbee and Jerome are also good bets for eclectic art and funky gifts. On the Hopi and Navajo reservations, look for small shopping centers, trading posts, and roadside stands, where you can find blankets, jewelry, dolls, leather items, and other traditional Native American work.

SPORTS & OUTDOORS

BICYCLING

The relatively flat terrain in the deserts and valleys, the mild winter weather, and spectacular vistas make for great biking in Arizona. Mountainous regions around Payson, Prescott, Sedona, and Tucson offer excellent mountain bike trails. If you plan on biking in the summer months, make sure you carry plenty of water and apply sunscreen regularly. Call the local or county Parks and Recreation Department in the area you're visiting for information on nearby bike paths. The Arizona Bicycle Club, Inc., publishes a schedule of the many bicycle races and tours that take place throughout the state.

🚲 **The Arizona Bicycle Club, Inc.** ✆ Box 7191, Phoenix, AZ 85011 ☎ 602/989-8740 ⊕ www.azbikeclub.com.

FISHING

Fishing license are required in Arizona and can be obtained in advance of your trip from the Arizona Game and Fish Department. For permission to fish on the San Carlos Apache or White Mountain Apache

reservation in eastern Arizona's White Mountains, contact the tribal office.

🚲 **Arizona Game and Fish Department** ⊠ 2222 W. Greenway Rd., Phoenix 85023 ☎ 602/942-3000, 866/462-0433 to purchase licenses by phone ⊕ www.gf.state.az.us. **San Carlos Apache Tribe** ✆ Box 0, San Carlos 85550 ☎ 928/475-2343 ⊕ www.itcaonline.com/tribes_sancarl.html. **White Mountain Apache Tribe** ✆ Wildlife and Outdoor Recreation Division: Box 220, Whiteriver 85941 ☎ 928/338-4385 ⊕ www.wmat.nsn.us.

GOLF

Arizona has some of the best and most popular golf courses in the United States. For a list of Arizona's many courses, contact the Arizona Golf Association.

🚲 **Arizona Golf Association** ⊠ 7226 N. 16th St., Suite 200, Phoenix 85020 ☎ 602/944-3035, 800/458-8484 in Arizona ⊕ www.azgolf.org.

HIKING

Never drink from any stream, no matter how clear it may be. Giardia organisms can turn your stomach inside out. The easiest way to purify water is to dissolve a water purification tablet in it. Camping-equipment stores also carry purification pumps. Boil water for 15 minutes, a reliable method, though time- and fuel-consuming. For more information about health concerns while hiking, see Health.

The Grand Canyon's Backcountry Office provides hikers with trail details, weather conditions, and packing suggestions for canyon hikes. For hikers who prefer to travel with a group, the Sierra Club leads a variety of wilderness treks. Contact the local chapters in Phoenix, Tucson, Kingman, Prescott, Sedona, and Flagstaff for information on guided hikes in these areas.

🚲 **Grand Canyon National Park Backcountry Office** ✆ Box 129, Grand Canyon 86023 ☎ 928/638-7875 🖷 928/638-2125 ⊕ www.nps.gov/grca. **Sierra Club Grand Canyon Chapter** ✆ 202 E. McDowell Rd., Suite 277, Phoenix 85004 ☎ 602/253-8633 ⊕ http://arizona.sierraclub.org.

RIVER RAFTING

The National Park Service maintains a list of outfitters that run white-water rafting trips on the Colorado. You can also contact the Grand Canyon River Permits Office for information on commercial and noncommercial river trips through the canyon. Mild to Wild Rafting and Wilderness Aware are outfitters based in Colorado that offer trips down the spectacular Salt River from March through May.

🏠 **Grand Canyon National Park** 🏠 Grand Canyon River Permits Office: Box 129, Grand Canyon 86023 ☎ 800/959-9164 or 928/638-7843 🖷 928/638-7844 ⊕ www.nps.gov/grca. **Mild to Wild Rafting** 🏠 53 Rio Vista Cir., Durango, CO 81301 ☎ 800/567-6745 🖷 970/382-0545 ⊕ www. mild2wildrafting.com. **Wilderness Aware Rafting** 🏠 Box 1550WS, Buena Vista, CO 81211 ☎ 800/462-7238 🖷 719/395-6716 ⊕ www.inaraft.com/salt.htm.

ROCKHOUNDING

The Department of Mines and Mineral Resources is an excellent source of information about specimens that can be found in each part of the state. There is also a small mining and mineral museum on the first floor of the building.

🏠 **Department of Mines and Mineral Resources** ✉ 1502 W. Washington St., Phoenix 85007 ☎ 602/255-3795 ⊕ www.admmr.state.az.us.

SKIING

Arizona has several ski areas in Flagstaff and the White Mountains. The resorts cater mostly to beginners and intermediate skiers (you won't find runs that match those in Colorado or Utah), and are popular with families. Sunrise Park Resort, in the White Mountains, is the largest in the state, with seven lifts, 65 runs, and a separate snowboarding area. Flagstaff, Williams, and Tucson area resorts have less variety, though the Arizona Snowbowl does offer a few advanced runs.

🏠 **Cross-country Skiing Contacts Flagstaff Nordic Center** ✉ U.S. 180, 16 mi north of Flagstaff, North Flagstaff ☎ 928/779-1951 ⊕ www. arizonasnowbowl.com. **Williams Valley Winter Sports Area** ✉ 1½ mi northwest of Alpine on U.S. 180, and 4½ mi west on Forest Service Rd. 249, Alpine ☎ 928/339-4384.

🏠 **Downhill Skiing Contacts Arizona Snowbowl** ✉ Snowbowl Rd., North Flagstaff ☎ 928/779-1951 ⊕ www.arizonasnowbowl.com. **Mt. Lemmon Ski Valley** ✉ 36 mi north of Tucson on Catalina Hwy., ☎ 520/749-8700, 520/547-7510 winter road conditions ⊕ www.fs.fed.us/r3/coronado/scrd. **Sunrise**

Park Resort ✉ AZ 273, 7 mi south of AZ 260 🏠 Box 117, Greer 85927 ☎ 928/735-7669, 800/772-7669 hotel reservations and snow reports ⊕ www. sunriseskipark.com.

STATE PARKS

Arizona state park day-use fees range from $5 to $8 per private vehicle. Campsites on park grounds range between $12 and $15, and are available on a first-come, first-served basis. If you plan on visiting several parks during your stay, consider the $45 Arizona State Parks Annual Pass. The pass admits you and the passengers in your vehicle (up to four adults) to most state parks in Arizona for a year; it also includes free museum admission for the holder of the pass. The pass does not include camping, nor does it include parks in the Colorado River area (Lake Havasu, Cattail Cove, Buckskin Mountain, and River Island, all of which are included in the $100 Colorado River State Parks Annual Pass). Passes can be purchased at any Arizona State Parks office.

🏠 **Arizona State Parks Department** ✉ 1300 W. Washington St., Phoenix 85007 ☎ 602/542-4174 ⊕ www.azstateparks.com.

STUDENTS IN ARIZONA

🏠 **I.D.s & Services STA Travel** ✉ 10 Downing St., New York, NY 10014 ☎ 212/627-3111, 800/777-0112 24-hr service center 🖷 212/627-3387 ⊕ www.sta. com. **Travel Cuts** ✉ 187 College St., Toronto, Ontario M5T 1P7, Canada ☎ 800/592-2887 in the U.S., 416/979-2406 or 866/246-9762 in Canada 🖷 416/979-8167 ⊕ www.travelcuts.com.

TAXES
SALES TAX

Arizona state sales tax (called a transaction privilege tax), which applies to all purchases except food in grocery stores, is 5.6%. Phoenix and Tucson levy city sales taxes of 1.8% and 2%, respectively, and Flagstaff taxes purchases at a rate of 1.51%. When added to county taxes, the total sales tax in Phoenix goes up to 8.1%; in Tucson, to 7.6%; and in Flagstaff, to 7.91%. Total sales taxes throughout the state range from 7.3% to 10.1%. Sales taxes do not apply on Indian reservations.

TIME

Arizona sets its clocks to mountain standard time—two hours earlier than Eastern standard, one hour later than Pacific standard. However, from April to October, when other states switch to daylight saving time, Arizona does *not* change its clocks; during this portion of the year, the mountain standard hour in Arizona is the same as the Pacific daylight hour in California. To complicate matters, the vast Navajo reservation in the northeastern section of the state *does* observe daylight saving time, so that from April to October it's an hour later on the reservation than it is in the rest of the state. Finally, the Hopi reservation, whose borders fall within those of the Navajo reservation, stays on the same non–Navajo, non–daylight saving clock as the remainder of the state.

TIPPING

At restaurants, a 15% tip is standard for waiters; up to 20% may be appropriate at more expensive establishments or for excellent service at any restaurant. The same goes for taxi drivers, bartenders, and hairdressers. Coat-check operators usually expect $1; bellhops and porters should get $1 per bag; hotel maids should get about $2 per day of your stay, and as much as $5 per day at some smaller, upscale B&Bs and inns. On package tours, conductors and drivers usually get $10 per day from the group as a whole; check whether this has already been figured into your cost. For local sightseeing tours, you may individually tip the driver-guide a few dollars if he or she has been helpful or informative. Ushers in theaters do not expect tips.

TOURS & PACKAGES

Because everything is prearranged on a prepackaged tour or independent vacation, you spend less time planning—and often get it all at a good price.

BOOKING WITH AN AGENT

Travel agents are excellent resources. But it's a good idea to collect brochures from several agencies, as some agents' suggestions may be influenced by relationships with tour and package firms that reward them for volume sales. If you have a special interest, find an agent with expertise in that area; the American Society of Travel Agents (ASTA; ⇨ Travel Agencies) has a database of specialists worldwide. You can log on to the group's Web site to find an ASTA travel agent in your neighborhood.

Make sure your travel agent knows the accommodations and other services of the place being recommended. Ask about the hotel's location, room size, beds, and whether it has a pool, room service, or programs for children, if you care about these. Has your agent been there in person or sent others whom you can contact?

Do some homework on your own, too: local tourism boards can provide information about lesser-known and small-niche operators, some of which may sell only direct.

BUYER BEWARE

Each year consumers are stranded or lose their money when tour operators—even large ones with excellent reputations—go out of business. So check out the operator. Ask several travel agents about its reputation, and try to **book with a company that has a consumer-protection program.** (Look for information in the company's brochure.) In the United States, members of the United States Tour Operators Association are required to set aside funds ($1 million) to help eligible customers cover payments and travel arrangements in the event that the company defaults. It's also a good idea to choose a company that participates in the American Society of Travel Agents' Tour Operator Program; ASTA will act as mediator in any disputes between you and your tour operator.

Remember that the more your package or tour includes, the better you can predict the ultimate cost of your vacation. Make sure you know exactly what is covered, and beware of hidden costs. Are taxes, tips, and transfers included? Entertainment and excursions? These can add up.

⁊ Tour-Operator Recommendations **American Society of Travel Agents** (⇨ Travel Agencies). **National Tour Association** (NTA) ✉ 546 E. Main St., Lexington, KY 40508 ☏ 859/226–4444 or 800/682–8886 🖷 859/226–4404 ⊕ www.ntaonline.com. **United States Tour Operators Association** (USTOA)

✉ 275 Madison Ave., Suite 2014, New York, NY 10016 ☎ 212/599-6699 🖷 212/599-6744 ⊕ www.ustoa.com.

PACKAGES

Like group tours, independent vacation packages are available from major tour operators and airlines. The companies listed below offer vacation packages in a broad price range.

🎇 Air/Hotel/Car **America West Vacations** ☎ 1920 W. University Dr., Tempe, AZ 85281 ☎ 800/356-6611 ⊕ www.americawestvacations.com. **Delta Vacations** ☎ 800/872-7786 ⊕ www.deltavacations.com. **Southwest Airlines Vacations** ☎ 800/243-8372 ⊕ www.swavacations.com. **United Vacations** ☎ 800/328-6877 ⊕ www.unitedvacations.com. **US Airways Vacations** ☎ 800/455-0123 ⊕ www.usairwaysvacations.com.

🎇 Custom Packages **Amtrak Vacations** ☎ 800/321-8684 ⊕ www.amtrak.com/savings/amtrakvacations.html.

THEME TRIPS

🎇 Archaeology **Archaeological Conservancy** ☎ 5301 Central Ave. NE, Suite 402, Albuquerque, NM 87108 ☎ 505/266-1540 ⊕ www.americanarchaeology.org. **Crow Canyon Archaeological Center** ☎ 23390 Rd. K, Cortez, CO 81321 ☎ 970/565-8975 or 800/422-8975 🖷 970/565-4859 ⊕ www.crowcanyon.org. **Southwest Ed-Ventures** ☎ Four Corners School of Outdoor Education, Box 1029, Monticello, UT 84535 ☎ 435/587-2156 or 800/525-4456 🖷 435/587-2193 ⊕ www.sw-adventures.org.

🎇 Environment **Earthwatch Institute** ✉ 3 Clock Tower Pl., Suite 100 ☎ Box 75, Maynard, MA 01754 ☎ 978/461-0081 or 800/776-0188 🖷 978/461-2332 ⊕ www.earthwatch.org.

🎇 Golf **Golfpac** ☎ Box 162366, Altamonte Springs, FL 32716-2366 ☎ 407/260-2288 or 800/327-0878 🖷 407/260-8989 ⊕ www.golfpactravel.com.

🎇 Motorcycling **Arizona Motorcycle Tours** ☎ 5253 E. Hilton Ave., Mesa, AZ 85206 ☎ 480/250-8685 ⊕ www.azmctours.com.

🎇 Native American History **Journeys into American Indian Territory** ☎ Box 575, East Port, NY 11941 ☎ 631/878-8655 or 800/458-2632 🖷 631/878-4518 ⊕ www.indianjourneys.com.

🎇 Natural History **Smithsonian Journeys** ☎ 1100 Jefferson Dr. SW, Room 3077, Washington, DC 20560 ☎ 202/357-4700 or 877/338-8687 🖷 202/633-9250 ⊕ www.smithsonianjourneys.org. **Victor Emanuel**

Nature Tours ☎ 2525 Wallingwood Dr., Suite 1003, Austin, TX 78746 ☎ 512/328-5221 or 800/328-8368 🖷 512/328-2919 ⊕ www.ventbird.com.

🎇 Self-Drive **Off the Beaten Path** ☎ 7 E. Beall St., Bozeman, MT 59715 ☎ 406/586-1311 or 800/445-2995 🖷 406/587-4147 ⊕ www.offthebeatenpath.com.

🎇 Spas **Spafinder** ✉ 91 5th Ave., 6th floor, New York, NY 10003-3039 ☎ 212/924-6800 or 800/255-7727 ⊕ www.spafinder.com represents numerous day and stay spas in Arizona.

TRAIN TRAVEL

Amtrak's *Southwest Chief* operates daily between Los Angeles and Chicago, stopping in Kingman, Flagstaff, and Winslow. The *Sunset Limited* travels three times each week between Los Angeles and Orlando, with stops at Yuma, Tucson, and Benson. There is a connecting bus (a 2½ hour trip) between Flagstaff and Phoenix.

🎇 Amtrak ☎ 800/872-7245 ⊕ www.amtrak.com.

TRAVEL AGENCIES

A good travel agent puts your needs first. Look for an agency that has been in business at least five years, emphasizes customer service, and has someone on staff who specializes in your destination. In addition, **make sure the agency belongs to a professional trade organization.** The American Society of Travel Agents (ASTA)—the largest and most influential in the field with more than 20,000 members in some 140 countries—maintains and enforces a strict code of ethics and will step in to help mediate any agent-client disputes involving ASTA members if necessary. ASTA (whose motto is "Without a travel agent, you're on your own") also maintains a Web site that includes a directory of agents. (If a travel agency is also acting as your tour operator, *see* Buyer Beware *in* Tours & Packages.)

🎇 Local Agent Referrals **American Society of Travel Agents (ASTA)** ✉ 1101 King St., Suite 200, Alexandria, VA 22314 ☎ 703/739-2782 or 800/965-2782 24-hr hotline 🖷 703/684-8319 ⊕ www.astanet.com. **Association of British Travel Agents** ✉ 68-71 Newman St., London W1T 3AH ☎ 020/7637-2444 🖷 020/7637-0713 ⊕ www.abta.com. **Association of Canadian Travel Agencies** ✉ 130 Albert St., Suite 1705, Ottawa, Ontario K1P 5G4 ☎ 613/

237-3657 ☎ 613/237-7052 ⊕ www.acta.ca. **Australian Federation of Travel Agents** ✉ Level 3, 309 Pitt St., Sydney, NSW 2000 ☎ 02/9264-3299 or 1300/363-416 ☎ 02/9264-1085 ⊕ www.afta.com. au. **Travel Agents' Association of New Zealand** ✉ Level 5, Tourism and Travel House, 79 Boulcott St., Box 1888, Wellington 6001 ☎ 04/499-0104 ☎ 04/499-0786 ⊕ www.taanz.org.nz.

VISITOR INFORMATION

Learn more about foreign destinations by checking government-issued travel advisories and country information. For a broader picture, consider information from more than one country.

◪ Tourist Information Arizona Office of Tourism ✉ 1110 W. Washington St., Suite 155, Phoenix 85007 ☎ 602/364-3700 or 866/298-3312 ☎ 602/364-3702 ⊕ www.arizonaguide.com.

◪ Native American Attractions Gila River Indian Community ⌖ Box 97, Sacaton, 85247 ☎ 520/562-6000 ☎ 520/562-6010 ⊕ www.gric.nsn.us. **Hopi Tribe Office of the Chairman** ⌖ Box 123, Kykotsmovi 86039 ☎ 928/734-2441 ☎ 928/734-2435 ⊕ www.hopi.nsn.us. **Navajo Nation Tourism Office** ⌖ Box 663, Window Rock 86515 ☎ 928/871-6436 or 928/871-7371 ☎ 928/810-8500 ⊕ www. discovernavajo.com. **Salt River Pima-Maricopa Indian Community** ⌖ 10005 E. Osborn Rd., Scottsdale, 85256 ☎ 480/850-8000 ☎ 480/850-8014 ⊕ www.saltriver.pima-maricopa.nsn.us. **Tohono O'odham Nation** ⌖ Box 837, Sells 85634 ☎ 520/383-2028 ☎ 520/383-3379 ⊕ www.itcaonline.com/ tribes_tohono.html. **White Mountain Apache Nation** ⌖ Box 700, Whiteriver 85941 ☎ 877/338-9628 ☎ 928/338-4778 ⊕ www.wmat.nsn.us.

◪ Government Advisories Consular Affairs Bureau of Canada ☎ 800/267-6788 or 613/944-6788 ⊕ www.voyage.gc.ca. **U.K. Foreign and Commonwealth Office** ✉ Travel Advice Unit, Consular Division, Old Admiralty Building, London SW1A 2PA ☎ 0870/606-0290 or 020/7008-1500 ⊕ www.fco. gov.uk/travel. **Australian Department of Foreign Affairs and Trade** ☎ 300/139-281 travel advice, 02/6261-1299 Consular Travel Advice Faxback Service ⊕ www.dfat.gov.au. **New Zealand Ministry of Foreign Affairs and Trade** ☎ 04/439-8000 ⊕ www.mft.govt.nz.

WEB SITES

Do check out the World Wide Web when planning your trip. You'll find everything from weather forecasts to virtual tours of famous cities. Be sure to visit Fodors.com (⊕ www.fodors.com), a complete travel-planning site. You can research prices and book plane tickets, hotel rooms, rental cars, vacation packages, and more. In addition, you can post your pressing questions in the Travel Talk section. Other planning tools include a currency converter and weather reports, and there are loads of links to travel resources.

For more specific information on Arizona, visit the following:

◪ Grand Canyon The Canyon ⊕ www. thecanyon.com. **Grand Canyon National Park** ⊕ www.nps.gov/grca.

◪ The Great Outdoors Arizona State Parks Web Site ⊕ www.azstateparks.com. **Great Outdoor Recreation Page** ⊕ www.gorp.com. **National Park Service Site** ⊕ www.nps.gov.

◪ Newsweeklies Phoenix New Times ⊕ www. phoenixnewtimes.com. **Tucson Weekly** ⊕ www. tucsonweekly.com.

PHOENIX, SCOTTSDALE & THE VALLEY OF THE SUN

1

MARVEL AT NATIVE AMERICAN ARTISTRY
at the prestigious Heard Museum ⇨*p.12*

GO ORGANIC
at Frank Lloyd Wright's Taliesin West ⇨*p.19*

SUCCUMB TO WESTERN ROMANCE
over dinner at Lon's at the Hermosa ⇨*p.32*

STAKE OUT THE PERFECT DECKCHAIR
by the Catalina Pool at the Biltmore ⇨*p.46*

KEEP YOUR EYE ON THE BALL
at a Cactus League spring-training game ⇨*p.62*

SPOIL A GOOD WALK IN THE DESERT
with 18 holes at Troon North ⇨*p.66*

TEST YOUR NERVE AND YOUR BRAKES
on the Apache Trail in the
Superstition Mountains ⇨*p.80*

Updated by
Bob and
Gloria Willis

PHOENIX RISES in the shimmering heat of the great Sonoran Desert in central Arizona. Here are some of the oldest human dwellings in the western hemisphere along with the homes of contemporary Native American tribes and one of America's fastest-growing major urban centers: metropolitan Phoenix, a melding of 22 communities, with a population of more than 3.4 million people.

The Valley of the Sun, a term synonymous with metro Phoenix, is named for its 325-plus days of sunshine each year. The Valley marks the northern tip of the Sonoran Desert, a prehistoric seabed that reaches from northwestern Mexico with a landscape offering much more than cacti. Palo verde and mesquite trees, creosote bushes, palms, and aloe dot the land, which is accustomed to being scorched by temperatures in excess of 100°F for weeks at a time. Late summer brings precious rain when monsoon storms illuminate the sky with brilliant lightning shows and the desert exudes the sweet scent of creosote. Spring sets the Valley blooming, from giant saguaros crowned in white flowers to masses of vibrantly painted wildflowers dotting desert crevices and mountain landscapes.

As the Hohokam discovered 2,300 years ago, the miracle of water in the desert can be augmented by human hands. Having migrated from northwestern Mexico, they cultivated cotton, corn, and beans in tilled, rowed, and irrigated fields for about 1,700 years, establishing more than 300 mi of canals—an engineering miracle, particularly when you consider the limited technology available. The Hohokam, whose name comes from the Piman word for "people who have gone before," constructed a great town upon whose ruins modern Phoenix is built, and then vanished. Drought, long winters, and other causes are suggested for their disappearance.

From the time the Hohokam left until the Civil War, the once fertile Salt River valley lay forgotten, used only by occasional small bands of Pima and Maricopa Indians. Then, in 1865, the U.S. Army established Fort McDowell in the mountains to the east, where the Verde River flows into the Salt River. To feed the men and the horses stationed there, a former Confederate Army officer reopened the Hohokam canals in 1867. Within a year, fields bright with barley and pumpkins earned the area the name Pumpkinville. By 1870, the 300 residents had decided that their new city would arise from the ancient Hohokam ruins, just as the mythical phoenix rose from its own ashes.

Phoenix would rise indeed. Within 20 years, it had become large enough—its population was about 3,000—to wrest the title of territorial capital from Prescott. By 1912, when Arizona was admitted as the 48th state, the area, irrigated by the brand-new Roosevelt Dam and Salt River Project, had a burgeoning cotton industry. Copper and cattle were mined and raised elsewhere but were banked and traded in Phoenix, and the cattle were slaughtered and packed here in the largest stockyards outside of Chicago.

Meanwhile, the climate, so long a crippling liability, became an asset. Desert air was the prescribed therapy for the respiratory ills rampant

If you have
3 days

See the **Heard Museum** ⑫ for its internationally acclaimed collection of Native American artifacts, and swing by the **Burton Barr Central Library** ⑩ on your way downtown to the **Arizona Science Center** ❷ and **Phoenix Museum of History** ❸. On day two, rise early and begin your day at Frank Lloyd Wright's **Taliesin West** ㉙; then head south into Scottsdale for a day of gallery browsing and a walk through **Old Town Scottsdale** ㉔. On your final day visit the stunning **Desert Botanical Garden** ⑲, and take a detour on your way home across Lincoln Drive in northeast Phoenix. This scenic route provides the best views of the Valley's beauty, so be sure to head west as the sun descends and the sky absorbs dozens of colors, introducing the evening.

If you have
5 days

Follow the tour above, and on the fourth day, consider some hiking: even inexperienced hikers will enjoy the walk up to **Papago Park**'s ⑱ Hole-in-the-Rock or the 1¼-mi trip to the top of Piestewa (formerly Squaw) Peak, whereas the more experienced may choose to ascend Camelback Mountain. **South Mountain Park** ⑮ has many trails for hikers of all abilities. Spend the afternoon exploring the stark beauty of the surrounding desert on horseback, in a jeep, or by hot-air balloon. On your fifth day, drive the loop of the **Apache Trail** ㊶–㊼, enjoying breathtaking views of Fish Creek Canyon—or head north to take a tour of **Arcosanti** ㊳ or explore the Old West town of **Wickenburg** ㊲.

If you have
7 days

Expand your drive of the **Apache Trail** ㊶–㊼ to include an overnight stay in 🅵 **Globe** ㊹. Along the way stop to enjoy the view of Weaver's Needle from the **Peralta Trail** ㊷, stroll through **Boyce Thompson Southwestern Arboretum** ㊸, or check out the ancient Hohokam ruins at **Casa Grande Ruins National Monument** ㊵ to the south of Phoenix.

If you'd like to plan your own driving tour, the Arizona Office of Tourism and *Arizona Highways* magazine have created a Web site ⊕ www.arizonascenicroads. com featuring 22 officially designated scenic routes.

in the sooty, factory-filled East; Scottsdale began in 1901 as "30-odd tents and a half dozen adobe houses" put up by health-seekers. By 1930, travelers looking for warm winter recreation as well as rejuvenating aridity filled the elegant San Marcos Hotel and Arizona Biltmore, first of the many luxury retreats for which the area is now known worldwide. The 1950s brought with them residential air-conditioning, an invention that made the summers bearable for the growing workforce of the burgeoning technology industry.

The Valley is very much a work still in progress; for better or worse, Phoenix is changing, and so quickly that even longtime residents have a difficult time keeping up. Historians are quick to point out that never in the world's history has a metropolis grown from "nothing" to attain the status of Phoenix in such a short period of time. But at the heart of all the bustle is a way of life that keeps its own pace: Phoenix is, after all, the world's largest small town—where people dress informally and where the rugged, Old West spirit lives on despite the sprawling growth. If the heat can be overwhelming at noon on a summer day, at least it has the restorative effect of slowing things down to an enjoyable pace.

EXPLORING THE VALLEY OF THE SUN

Phoenix has grown around what was once a cluster of independent towns in Maricopa County. Gaps between communities that were open spaces of desert a few short years ago have begun to close in and blend the entire Valley into one large, sprawling community. If it were not for the WELCOME signs of various municipalities on roadways, you would be hard-pressed to tell where one community ends and another begins. First-time visitors are often surprised to discover that some of the area's finest restaurants and shops are tucked into hotels and strip malls. Metro Phoenix, which occupies a large valley surrounded by desert hills and mountains ranges, retains a strong Western heritage.

Commuting through the region can be complex and exasperating unless you have a car of your own. From Sky Harbor airport, the one-way cab fare to the Four Seasons Resort in North Scottsdale (about 32 mi) can easily cost you more than the daily charge for a rental car. Public transit is here in varying degrees and is inexpensive, but services do not connect well within and between communities.

Getting Your Bearings

Phoenix is at the center of the Valley, with other communities radiating out from it. The East Valley includes Scottsdale, Tempe, Mesa, Fountain Hills, and Apache Junction, and just beyond the last is the southern edge of the Superstition Mountains. To the southeast are Gilbert, Guadalupe, Ahwatukee, Queen Creek, and Chandler. The West Valley includes Glendale, Peoria, Sun City, Avondale, Goodyear, and Litchfield Park.

Central Avenue, which runs north and south through the heart of downtown Phoenix, is the city's east-west dividing line. Everything east of Central is considered the East Valley and everything west of Central is the West Valley. One block east and parallel to Central Avenue is 1st Street. Avenues are on the west side of the Valley, and streets are on the east side. Street numbers increase as you drive farther from Central Avenue. Thus, 40th Street is 40 blocks east of Central, whereas 63rd Avenue is 63 blocks west of Central. North-south increments are taken from Washington Street in downtown Phoenix, so 4002 North 36th Street is 40 blocks north of Washington.

Downtown Phoenix

Growth in the Valley over the past two decades has created new demands on the downtown area. More spaces for large conventions and trade shows, rapid growth brought on by new business development, creation of new apartments and lofts, and new cultural and sports facilities have

1

Golf   The Valley of the Sun is among the top U.S. golf destinations, thanks to warm temperatures, azure skies, the scenic desert backdrop, and more than 200 challenging courses. The burgeoning growth of the area has brought with it an explosion of golf courses, many of them world-class in both quality and price. However, there are equally exciting yet more affordable courses to satisfy all levels of play and most every pocketbook. November through April is peak season; in summer, golf fees are a fraction of the cost, and many resorts offer packages combining resort stays with golf. Each January, thousands of golf aficionados descend upon the Valley to attend the prestigious FBR Open at the Tournament Player's Club in Scottsdale.

Mountains   The mountains surrounding the Valley of the Sun are among its greatest assets. Outdoors enthusiasts have plenty of ground to cover within the city limits on all of those sunny days in pursuit of their passions—be it hiking, bird-watching, or mountain biking. Piestewa (formerly Squaw) Peak, north of downtown, is popular with hikers. Camelback Mountain and the Papago Peaks are landmarks between Phoenix and Scottsdale. South of the city are the much less lofty peaks of South Mountain Park, which separates the Valley from the rest of the Sonoran Desert. East of the city, beyond Tempe and Mesa, the peaks of the Superstition Mountains—named for their eerie way of seeming just a few miles away—are the first of a range that stretches all the way into New Mexico. To the west, past Glendale and Litchfield Park, the formidable White Tank Mountains separate the Valley from the lands that slope steadily downward to the Mojave Desert of California. Finally, just an hour north of the Valley, the slopes of the Mogollon (pronounced *muh*-gee-on) Rim, all green with piñon, juniper, and Ponderosa pines, serve as a cool refuge for Valley dwellers, where Interstate 17 leads tens of thousands on exodus every weekend from May to September.

Spas   How do you define pleasure? If you answered "pampering," this is the place for you. Treatments involving smooth warm stones soaked in aromatic waters placed strategically up and down your back or quiet massages outside amid the blooming Sonoran Desert are only two options. Maybe it's a seaweed wrap or warm mineral bath. Whatever your fancy, the Valley has some of the best facilities in the world, from destination spas where you can buy weeklong packages to day spas where both locals and visitors relax and retreat. The newest include the Alzadora Spa at the Royal Palms Resort, Willow Springs Spa at the Fairmont Scottsdale Princess, the Golden Door Spa at the Boulders, the Sanctuary Spa at Sanctuary, and the Mist Spa at the Radisson. The Spas at Camelback Inn and the Arizona Biltmore continue to be old-time favorites.

---

helped create a more "real" downtown area. Downtown Phoenix is also known as Copper Square and is a mixture of Phoenix's past and present. Restored homes in Heritage Square, from the original town site, give you an idea of how far the city has come since its inception around the turn of the 20th century.

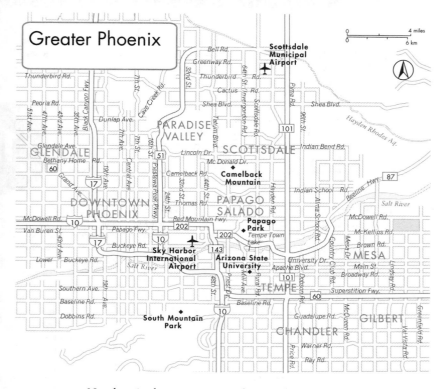

Numbers in the text correspond to numbers in the margin and on the What to See in Downtown Phoenix map.

a good walk

Park your car in the garage on the southeast corner of 5th and Monroe streets or at any of the many nearby public parking facilities (they're listed on the free map provided by Downtown Phoenix Partnership and available in local restaurants). Many of the sites on this walk, including Heritage and Science Park, the Arizona Center, and City Hall, are served by DASH (Downtown Area Shuttle), a free bus service. You can use DASH to get around or to get back to your car when you're finished.

Begin your tour in the blocks known as the Heritage and Science Park; the area from 5th to 7th streets between Monroe and Adams contains **Heritage Square ❶ ▶**, the **Arizona Science Center ❷**, and the **Phoenix Museum of History ❸**. From the corner of 5th and Monroe streets, walk two blocks west to **St. Mary's Basilica ❹**, Phoenix's first Catholic church. Head north one block to Van Buren Street. On the northeast corner of the intersection, you'll see two glass-clad office towers with a lane of royal palms between them. Follow the palm trees: they lead to the **Arizona Center ❺**, an open-air two-story mall. Leaving the Arizona Center, from the corner of 3rd and Van Buren streets, walk a block west to 2nd Street and then two blocks south, passing the 24-story Hyatt Regency hotel on your right, then another block and a half west on Adams Street to the **Museo Chicano** ◯. You can walk to Heritage and Science Park from here, catch a DASH shuttle back, or continue on two more blocks west toward the striking facade of the **Orpheum Theatre** ◯.

If you're really an indefatigable walker, continue south through the plaza on the Orpheum's east side to Washington Street; head east on Washington Street, passing Historic City Hall and the county courthouse on your right. At the intersection of Washington Street and 1st Avenue, you'll see Patriots Square Park on the southeast corner. Cross diagonally (southeast) through the park to the corner of Jefferson Street and Central Avenue. Another block east on Jefferson and then a block south on 1st Street will take you to the site of the **America West Arena** ◯. From the arena, follow Jefferson Street east for two blocks to South 4th Street and Phoenix's newest sports venue, **Bank One Ballpark** ◯. Afterward, catch the DASH shuttle back to your car.

TIMING In moderate weather, this walk is a pleasant daylong tour; from late May to mid-October, when the temperatures are at their hottest, it's best to break it up over two days. Be sure to take advantage of the free DASH.

What to See

❽ **America West Arena.** This 20,000-seat venue, known locally as the Purple Palace, is home to the Phoenix Suns NBA team, the Arizona Rattlers arena football team, and the Phoenix Mercury WNBA team. It's almost a mall in itself—with cafés and shops, it's interesting to see. Tour availability is determined by the day's schedule of events, and you must have a reservation. ✉ *201 E. Jefferson St., at 2nd St., Downtown Phoenix* ☎ *602/379–2000, 602/379–2060 tour reservations only* ⊕ *www.americawestarena.com* ✇ *Tours $3* ☉ *Tours weekdays by appointment only.*

❺ **Arizona Center.** Amid dramatic fountains, sunken gardens, and towering palm trees stands this two-tier, open-air structure, which is downtown's most attractive shopping venue. The center has about 50 shops and restaurants spread over two stories, open-air vendors, a large sports bar, and a multiplex cinema. ✉ *Van Buren St. between 3rd and 5th Sts., Downtown Phoenix* ☎ *602/271–4000 or 480/949–4386* ⊕ *www.arizonacenter.com.*

★ ✪ ❷ **Arizona Science Center.** With more than 300 hands-on exhibits, this is the venue for science-related exploration. You can pilot a simulated airplane flight, travel through the human body, navigate your way through the solar system in the Dorrance Planetarium, and watch a movie in the giant, five-story film theater. ✉ *600 E. Washington St., Downtown Phoenix* ☎ *602/716–2000* ⊕ *www.azscience.org* ✇ *Museum $9; combination museum, theater, and planetarium $19* ☉ *Daily 10–5.*

❾ **Bank One Ballpark.** Known affectionately as BOB, the Valley's major-league ballpark is home to the Arizona Diamondbacks. A retractable roof, natural-grass playing surface, family picnic area, and even a swimming pool let Phoenicians enjoy a day at the ballpark while escaping the summer heat. Tours are given Monday through Saturday. Call ahead as there are no tours on daytime game days. ✉ *401 E. Jefferson St., be-*

America West
Arena 8

Arizona
Center 5

Arizona
Science
Center 2

Bank One
Ballpark 9

Heritage
Square 1

Museo
Chicano 6

Orpheum
Theater 7

Phoenix
Museum of
History 3

St. Mary's
Basilica 4

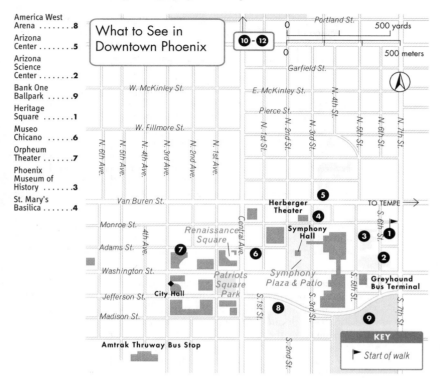

tween S. 4th and S. 7th Sts., Downtown Phoenix ☎ 602/462–6000, 888/
177–4664 tours only ⊕ www.diamondbacks.mlb.com ☒ Tours $6
⊙ Tours Mon.–Sat. 10:30, noon, 1:30, and 3 (10:30 and noon only on
evening-game days).

► ⟲ **❶** **Heritage Square.** In a parklike setting from 5th to 7th streets between
Monroe and Adams streets, this city-owned block contains the only remaining houses from the original Phoenix town site. On the south side
of the square, along Adams Street, stand several houses built between
1899 and 1901. The Teeter House contains a Victorian-style tearoom,
and the Thomas House and Baird Machine Shop is now Pizzeria Bianco
The one-story brick Stevens House holds the **Arizona Doll and Toy Museum** (⊠ 602 E. Adams St., Downtown Phoenix ☎ 602/253–9337), which
is open Tuesday through Saturday 10 to 4, Sunday noon to 4, and
closed in August; admission is $3.

The queen of Heritage Square is the **Rosson House,** an 1895 Victorian
in the Queen Anne style. Built by a physician who served a brief term
as mayor, it is the sole survivor among fewer than two dozen Victori-
ans erected in Phoenix. It was bought and restored by the city in 1974.
⊠ 6th and Monroe Sts., Downtown Phoenix ☎ 602/262–5029 ☒ $4
⊙ Wed.–Sat. 10–4, Sun. noon–4.

The Victorian-style tearoom in the **Teeter House** (✉ 622 E. Adams St., Downtown Phoenix ☎ 602/252–4682), which was built as a private home in 1899, serves authentic teatime fare; there are also heartier sandwiches and salads.

❻ Museo Chicano. Works of artists from the United States and Mexico are showcased here. Exhibits include art in many media from different periods, showing both classic and modern culture and making this site a premier center for enjoying Latin American art. ✉ *147 E. Adams St., Downtown Phoenix* ☎ *602/257–5536* ⊕ *www.museochicano.com* ☞ *$2* ☉ *Tues.–Sat. 10–4.*

❼ Orpheum Theatre. The Spanish colonial–revival architecture and exterior reliefs of this 1929 movie palace have long been admired. The eclectic ornamental details of the interior were meticulously restored as part of a 12-year, $14 million renovation project. Today, the Orpheum is a venue for live performances, from Broadway shows to ballet to lectures. Call for details on free guided tours and upcoming events. ✉ *203 W. Adams St., Downtown Phoenix* ☎ *602/534–5600* ☉ *Tours by appointment only.*

❸ Phoenix Museum of History. This striking glass-and-steel museum offers exhibits on regional history from the 1860s (when Anglo settlement began) through the 1930s. Interactive exhibits are designed to help you appreciate the city's multicultural heritage as well as witness its growth. ✉ *105 N. 5th St., Downtown Phoenix* ☎ *602/253–2734* ⊕ *www.pmoh.org* ☞ *$5* ☉ *Tues.–Sat. 10–5.*

❹ St. Mary's Basilica. The oldest standing church in Phoenix was founded in 1881. Inside the basilica (which Pope John Paul II visited in 1987) there's a magnificent stained-glass window designed in Munich. Mass is held daily, but call for visiting hours. ✉ *N. 3rd and Monroe Sts., Downtown Phoenix* ☎ *602/354–2100* ☞ *Free* ☉ *Hrs vary; call for opening times.*

The Cultural Center

The heart of Phoenix's downtown cultural center and renaissance is the Margaret T. Hance Park, also known as Deck Park. Built atop the Interstate 10 tunnel under Central Avenue, it spreads more than 1 mi from 3rd Avenue on the west to 3rd Street on the east, and ¼ mi from Portland Street north to Culver Street. It is the city's second-largest downtown park (the largest is half-century-old Encanto Park, 2 mi northwest). Deck Park is a good place from which to survey revitalized downtown neighborhoods and to appreciate the expansions and renovations of nearly all the area's museums.

Numbers in the text correspond to numbers in the margin and on the What to See in Greater Phoenix map.

Park free in the lot of the **Burton Barr Central Library** ❿ ► at the corner of Central Avenue and East Willetta Street. Two blocks north on Central, across McDowell Road, is the modern, green-quartz **Phoenix Art Museum** ⓫. North of the museum, a slight detour brings a brief respite from the noise and traffic of Central Avenue as well as a glimpse of some

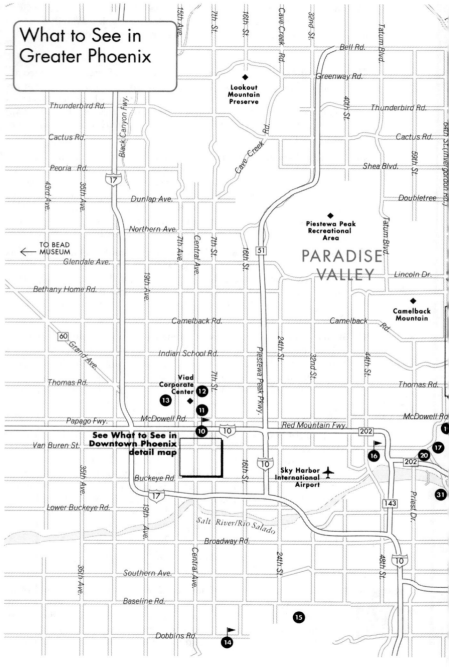

What to See in Greater Phoenix

Arizona State University **33**
Burton Barr Central Library .. **10**
La Casa Vieja **31**
Desert Botanical Garden **19**
Encanto Park **13**
Hall of Flame **20**
Heard Museum **12**
Mystery Castle **14**
Papago Park **18**
Phoenix Art Museum **11**
Phoenix Zoo **17**
Pueblo Grande Museum
and Cultural Park **16**
South Mountain Park **15**
Taliesin West **29**
Tempe City Hall **32**
Tempe Town Lake **30**

lovely residential architecture: head one block east on Coronado Road to Alvarado Road, and then follow Alvarado north for two longish blocks (zigzagging a few feet to the east at Palm Lane) to Monte Vista Road; turn left onto Monte Vista and proceed 50 yards west to the entrance of the **Heard Museum ⑫**. From the Heard, head south on Central Avenue toward the red-granite Viad Tower, with its refreshing fountains and intriguing sculpture garden. If you want to visit **Encanto Park ⑬**, which is west of 7th Avenue, you may wish to drive, since it's west of 7th Avenue and a bit far away to go on foot, particularly when the temperatures top 90°F.

TIMING   Seeing all the neighborhood's attractions makes a comfortable daylong tour in moderate weather; in the warm months, it is too much for one day. Valley Metro's Bus 0 runs up and down Central Avenue every 10 minutes on weekdays and every 20 minutes on Saturday.

What to See

▶ ⑩ **Burton Barr Central Library.** Architect Will Bruder's magnificent contribution to Phoenix has a copper exterior that evokes images of the mesas, buttes, and canyons of Monument Valley. Skylights, glass walls, and mirrors bathe the interior in natural light. The Crystal Canyon, a five-story glass atrium, is best appreciated on a swift ride in one of the glass elevators. On the top floor, a cable-suspended steel ceiling floats over the largest reading room in North America. Free one-hour tours are offered with advance reservations. ⊠ *1221 N. Central Ave., Downtown Phoenix* ☎ *602/262–4636, 602/262–6582 tour reservations* ⊕ *www.phxlib.org* ⊙ *Mon.–Thurs. 10–9, Fri.–Sat. 10–6, Sun. noon–6.*

need a
break?   Funky, friendly **Willow House** (⊠ 149 W. McDowell Rd., at 3rd Ave., Downtown Phoenix ☎ 602/252–0272) is a place to people-watch from an armchair or sofa and to grab a sandwich, dessert, or coffee. Check out the artwork on display, as well as the kaleidoscopic fish painted on the restroom walls.

ⓒ ⑬ **Encanto Park.** Urban Encanto (Spanish for "enchanted") Park covers 222 acres at the heart of one of Phoenix's oldest residential neighborhoods. There's a wide range of attractions here, including picnic areas, a lagoon when you can paddleboat and canoe, a municipal swimming pool, a nature trail, the Kiddieland/Enchanted Island amusement park, fishing in the park's lake, two public golf courses, and basketball and tennis courts. ⊠ *15th Ave. and Encanto Blvd.,* ☎ *602/261–8993* ☞ *Park free, Enchanted Island rides $1* ⊙ *Park daily 6 AM–midnight; Enchanted Island Wed.–Fri. 10–4, weekends 7–4.*

ⓒ ⑫ **Heard Museum.** Pioneer settlers Dwight and Maie Heard built a Spanish colonial–revival building on their property to house their impressive collection of Southwestern art. Today, the staggering collection of this museum includes such exhibits as a Navajo hogan, an Apache wickie-up (a temporary Native American structure, similar to a lean-to, constructed from branches, twigs, and leaves, sometimes covered with hides), and rooms filled with art, pottery, jewelry, katsinas, and textiles. The Heard also actively supports and displays pieces by working Indian

FodorsChoice
★

artists. Annual events include the Guild Indian Fair & Market and the World Championship Hoop Dance Contest. Children enjoy the interactive art-making exhibits. The museum has an incredible gift shop with authentic, high-quality goods purchased directly from native artists. There's a museum satellite branch in Scottsdale that has rotating exhibits. ☒ *2301 N. Central Ave., Downtown Phoenix* ☏ *602/252–8848 or 602/252–8840* ⊕ *www.heard.org* ⌑ *$7* ⊘ *Daily 9:30–5.*

⓫ Phoenix Art Museum. The green-quartz exterior of this modern museum is an eye-catching piece of architecture. The museum has 17,000 works of art from all over the world but is perhaps best known for its extensive and popular Western American Collection, which includes sculptures by Frederic Remington and paintings by Georgia O'Keeffe, Thomas Moran, and Maxfield Parrish. Since the museum hosts more than 20 significant exhibitions annually, there's usually something special to see. Tours of the collection are given at 2 PM daily. ☒ *1625 N. Central Ave., Downtown Phoenix* ☏ *602/257–1222* ⊕ *www.phxart.org* ⌑ *$7* ⊘ *Tues.–Sun. 10–5.*

off the beaten path

BEAD MUSEUM – In the historic district of downtown Glendale, this little museum attracts bead collectors from around the globe. Exhibits tell the intriguing story of international trade and intricate bead craft from 30,000 BC through today. There's a gift shop, and the 3,000-volume reference library can be perused by appointment. ☒ *5754 W. Glenn Dr., northwest corner of Glenn Dr. and 58th Ave., Glendale* ☏ *623/931–2737* ⌑ *$4, free Sun.* ⊕ *www.thebeadmuseum.com* ⊘ *Mon.–Wed. and Fri.–Sat. 10–5, Thurs. 10–8, Sun. 11–4.*

South Phoenix

A mostly residential area and home to much of Phoenix's substantial Hispanic population, South Phoenix—the area south of Buckeye Road—is worth a visit for two reasons: its family-style restaurants and roadside stands offer some of the best Mexican food in the city, plus South Mountain Park and one of the more unusual sights in the Valley—the Mystery Castle.

a good tour

From central Phoenix, take 7th Street south, past Baseline Road, to its junction with Mineral Road and **Mystery Castle ⓮** ►, a decidedly original home turned museum. After a tour, follow Mineral Road west for about ½ mi to Central Avenue and the entrance to **South Mountain Park ⓯**. Take any of several scenic drives through this 16,500-acre city-owned wilderness. Dobbins Lookout, 1,120 feet above Phoenix, has spectacular views of the city. Maps of all scenic drives as well as of hiking, mountain biking, and horseback trails are available at the Gatehouse Entrance just inside the park boundary.

TIMING Depending on how long you spend in the park, this tour can be accomplished in a couple of hours or can last an entire day. Leave about a half hour each way for driving, an hour to 90 minutes at the castle, and anywhere from a quick 20-minute drive to an all-day hike in South Mountain.

Sights to See

► ★ ⊕ ⓮ **Mystery Castle.** At the foot of South Mountain lies a curious dwelling built from desert rocks by Boyce Gulley, who came to Arizona to cure his tuberculosis. Boyce's daughter Mary Lou lives here now and leads tours on request. Full of fascinating oddities, the castle has 18 rooms with 13 fireplaces, a downstairs grotto tavern, and a roll-away bed with a mining railcar as its frame. The pump organ belonged to Elsie, the Widow of Tombstone, who buried six husbands under suspicious circumstances. ✉ *800 E. Mineral Rd., South Phoenix* ☎ *602/268–1581* ✍ *$5* ☉ *Oct.–June, Thurs.–Sun. 11–4.*

★ ⊕ ⓯ **South Mountain Park.** This desert wonderland, the world's largest city park (almost 17,000 acres), offers a wilderness of mountain-desert trails for hikers, bikers, and horseback riders—and a great place to view sunsets. The Environmental Center has a model of the park as well as displays detailing its history, from the time of the ancient Hohokam people to gold-seekers. Roads climb past picnic ramadas (shaded, open-air shelters) constructed by the Civilian Conservation Corps, winding through desert flora to the trailheads. Look for ancient petroglyphs, try to spot a desert cottontail rabbit or chuckwalla lizard, or simply stroll among the desert vegetation. ✉ *10919 S. Central Ave., South Phoenix* ☎ *602/ 495–0222* ✍ *Free* ☉ *Daily 5:30 AM–10:30 PM. Environmental Center Mon.–Sat. 9–5, Sun. noon–5.*

> **need a break?** **Carolina's** (✉ 1202 E. Mohave St., South Phoenix ☎ 602/252– 1503) makes the best flour tortillas for 100 mi, and the burritos are the best way to try them. You can eat at this small establishment or just pick up some carry-out, which you can enjoy as a picnic under one of the ramadas in South Mountain Park.

Papago Salado

The word Papago, meaning "bean eater," was a name given by 16th-century Spanish explorers to the Hohokam, a vanished native people of the Phoenix area. Farmers of the desert, the Hohokam grew corn, beans, squash, and cotton. They lived in central Arizona from about AD 1 to 1450, at which point their civilization abandoned the Salt River (Rio Salado) valley, leaving behind the remnants of their villages and a complex system of irrigation canals. The Papago Salado region is between Phoenix and Tempe and includes The Pueblo Grande ruins, the Desert Botanical Garden, the Phoenix Zoo, and Papago Park, which are all popular family attractions.

> **a good tour** From downtown Phoenix, take Washington Street east to the **Pueblo Grande Museum and Cultural Park** ⓰ ►, between 44th Street and the Hohokam Expressway (AZ 143). After a stop at the museum, follow Washington Street east 3½ mi to Priest Drive and turn north. Priest Drive becomes Galvin Parkway north of Van Buren Street; follow signs to entrances for the **Phoenix Zoo** ⓱ and **Papago Park** ⓲ or to the **Desert Botanical Garden** ⓳. Afterward, if you want to slide down the fire pole at the **Hall of Flame** ⓴, drive south on Galvin Parkway to Van Buren Street;

turn east and drive ⅛ mi, turning south onto Project Drive (at the buff-color stone marker that reads SALT RIVER PROJECT).

TIMING Seeing all the sights requires the better part of a day. You may want to save the Desert Botanical Garden for the end of your tour, as it stays open 8 AM to 8 PM year-round and is particularly lovely when lighted by the setting sun or by moonlight.

Sights to See

🌤 ⑲ **Desert Botanical Garden.** Opened in 1939 to conserve and showcase the
Fodor's Choice ecology of the desert, these 150 acres contain more than 4,000 differ-
★ ent species of cacti, succulents, trees, and flowers. A stroll along the ½-mi-long "Plants and People of the Sonoran Desert" trail is a fascinating lesson in environmental adaptations; children will enjoy playing the self-guiding game "Desert Detective." The Garden Shop is the place to purchase items associated with a green thumb. ☒ *1201 N. Galvin Pkwy., Papago Salado* ☎ *480/941–1225* ⊕ *www.dbg.org* ☒ *$9* ☉ *Oct.–Apr., daily 8–8; May–Sept., daily 7 AM–8 PM.*

> **need a break?** If you're headed to the Papago Salado region from downtown Phoenix, stop in **Kohnie's Coffee** (☒ 4225 E. Camelback Rd., Camelback Corridor ☎ 602/952–9948) for coffee, pastries, bagels, and scones. It's open at 7 AM (Sunday at 8 AM) and closed by 1 PM (noon on weekends and all day on Monday).

🌤 ⑳ **Hall of Flame.** Retired firefighters lead tours through more than 100 restored fire engines and tell harrowing tales of the "world's most dangerous profession." Children can climb on a 1916 engine, operate alarm systems, and learn fire safety lessons from the pros. Helmets, badges, and other firefighting-related articles are on display, dating from as far back as 1725. ☒ *6101 E. Van Buren St., Papago Salado* ☎ *602/275–3473* ⊕ *www.hallofflame.org* ☒ *$5.50* ☉ *Mon.–Sat. 9–5, Sun. noon–4.*

🌤 ⑱ **Papago Park.** An amalgam of hilly desert terrain, streams, and lagoons, this park has picnic ramadas, a golf course, a playground, hiking and biking trails, and even largemouth bass and trout fishing. (An urban fishing license is required for anglers age 15 and over.) The hike up to landmark **Hole-in-the-Rock** (a natural observatory used by the native Hohokam to devise a calendar system) is steep and rocky and a much easier climb up than down. **Governor Hunt's Tomb,** the white pyramid at the top of Ramada 16, commemorates the former Arizona leader and provides a lovely view. ☒ *625 N. Galvin Pkwy., Papago Salado* ☎ *602/256–3220* ☒ *Free* ☉ *Daily 6 AM–10 PM.*

🌤 ⑰ **Phoenix Zoo.** Four designated trails wind through this 125-acre zoo, replicating such habitats as an African savannah and a tropical rain forest. Meerkats, warthogs, desert bighorn sheep, and the endangered Arabian oryx are among the unusual sights. The Forest of Uco is home to the endangered spectacled bear from South America. Harmony Farm on the Discovery Trail introduces youngsters to small mammals, and a stop at the big red barn provides a chance to groom a horse or milk a cow. Make sure to save time to walk through the enchanting Butterfly Pavilion. The

30-minute narrated safari train tour costs $2 and provides a good orientation to the park. In December, the popular "Zoo Lights" exhibit transforms the area into an enchanted forest of more than 225 million twinkling lights, many in the shape of the zoo's residents. ⊠ *455 N. Galvin Pkwy., Papago Salado* ☎ *602/273–1341* ⊕ *www.phoenixzoo.org* ⊠ *$12* ☉ *Sept.–May, daily 9–5; June–Aug., daily 7 AM–8 PM.*

☾☉ **⑯** **Pueblo Grande Museum and Cultural Park.** Phoenix's only national land-
Fodor's Choice mark, this park was once the site of a 500-acre Hohokam village sup-
★ porting about 1,000 people and containing homes, storage rooms, cemeteries, and ball courts. Three exhibition galleries hold displays on the Hohokam culture and archaeological methods. View the 10-minute orientation video before heading out on the ½-mi Ruin Trail past excavated mounds and ruins that give a hint of Hohokam savvy: there's a building whose corner doorway was perfectly placed to watch the summer-solstice sunrise. Children will particularly like the hands-on, interactive learning center. ⊠ *4619 E. Washington St., Papago Salado,* ☎ *602/495–0901* ⊕ *www.pueblogrande.com* ⊠ *$2, free Sun.* ☉ *Mon.–Sat. 9–4:45, Sun. 1–4:45.*

Scottsdale

Historic sites, nationally known art galleries, and souvenir shops fill downtown Scottsdale; a quick walking tour can easily turn into an all-day excursion if you browse. Old Town Scottsdale has the look of the Old West, and 5th Avenue is known for shopping and Native American jewelry and crafts stores. Cross onto Main Street and enter a world frequented by the international art set (Scottsdale has the third-largest artist community in the United States). Discover more galleries and interior-design shops along Marshall Way.

Numbers in the text correspond to numbers in the margin and on the What to See in Scottsdale map.

**a good
tour**

Park in the free public lot on the corner of 2nd Street and Wells Fargo Avenue, east of Scottsdale Road.

Start your walk by exiting the parking structure from its northeast corner, where a short brick-paved sidewalk leads northward to the plaza of Scottsdale Mall. The **Scottsdale Center for the Arts** ㉑ ☞ is right there. Be sure to check out the **Scottsdale Museum of Contemporary Art** ㉒, right next door to the main center building. Stroll counterclockwise around the mall through its beautiful desert landscaping, fountains, and sculptures, passing Scottsdale's library and municipal buildings and ending up on the plaza's west side by **Scottsdale Historical Museum** ㉓. Continue west to the intersection of Brown Avenue and Main Street to reach the heart of **Old Town Scottsdale** ㉔, occupying four square blocks from Brown Avenue to Scottsdale Road, between Indian School Road and 2nd Street. From Main Street in Old Town, cross Scottsdale Road to the central drag of the **Main Street Arts District** ㉕. Turn north onto Goldwater Boulevard and gallery-stroll for another two blocks. At Indian School Road, head one block east to the **Marshall Way Arts District** ㉖. Continue two blocks north on Marshall Way to the fountain

Fifth
Avenue **27**

Main Street
Arts
District **25**

Marshall Way
Arts
District **26**

Old Town
Scottsdale . . . **24**

Scottsdale
Center for
the Arts **21**

Scottsdale
Convention
& Visitors
Bureau **28**

Scottsdale
Historical
Museum **23**

Scottsdale
Museum of
Contemporary
Art **22**

Taliesin
West **29**

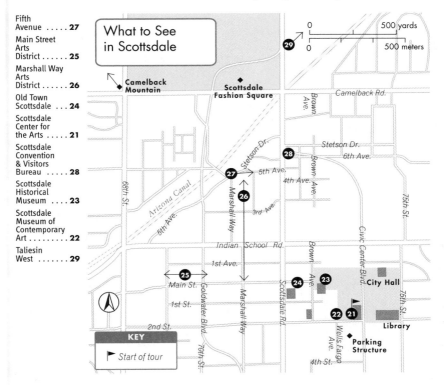

of prancing horses that marks **5th Avenue** ㉗. A couple of blocks north is the **Scottsdale Convention and Visitors Bureau** ㉘, on Scottsdale Road. If you return to 5th Avenue, you can catch the trolley back to Scottsdale Mall here, on the south side of the intersection of 5th Avenue and Stetson Drive, or walk the five blocks south on Scottsdale Road and one block east on Main Street.

It's a short but very worthwhile side trip from downtown Scottsdale to **Taliesin West** ㉙, Frank Lloyd Wright's winter home. Drive 20 minutes north on the 101 Freeway to Frank Lloyd Wright Boulevard. The entrance to Taliesin West is at the corner of Frank Lloyd Wright Boulevard and Cactus Road.

TIMING   You could easily spend a full day in downtown Scottsdale, browsing the countless galleries and shops. Most galleries on Main Street and Marshall Way are open Thursday evenings until 9. Although your tour of the downtown area can easily be completed on foot, a trolley runs through the area and out to several resorts: Ollie the Trolley charges $5 for an all-day pass, although service within downtown Scottsdale is free (☎ 480/970–8130 information). If you have a limited amount of time, spend a half-day in downtown Scottsdale and the rest of the day at Taliesin West.

What to See

㉗ 5th Avenue. For more than 40 years, this shopping stretch has been the location of boutiques and specialty shops. Whether you seek handmade Native American Arts and Crafts, casual clothing or cacti, you'll find it here—at such landmark shops as Adolfos Espoza, Kactus Jock, and Gilbert Ortega—plus colorful storefronts, friendly merchants, even an old "cigar-store" Indian. ⊠ *5th Ave. between Civic Center Rd. and Stetson Dr., Downtown Scottsdale.*

★ ㉕ Main Street Arts District. Gallery after gallery displays artwork of myriad styles—contemporary, Western realism, Native American, and traditional. Several antiques shops are also here; specialties include porcelains and china, jewelry, and Oriental rugs. ⊠ *Bounded by Main St. and 1st Ave., Scottsdale Rd. and 69th St., Downtown Scottsdale.*

㉖ Marshall Way Arts District. Galleries that exhibit predominantly contemporary art line the blocks of Marshall Way north of Indian School Road. Upscale gift and jewelry stores can be found here, too. Farther north on Marshall Way across 3rd Avenue, the street is filled with more art galleries and creative stores with a southwestern flair. ⊠ *Marshall Way, from Indian School Rd. to 5th Ave., Downtown Scottsdale.*

㉔ Old Town Scottsdale. Billed as "the West's Most Western Town," this area of Scottsdale has rustic storefronts and wooden sidewalks; it's touristy, but it's the closest you'll come to experiencing life here as it was 80 years ago. High-quality jewelry, pots, and Mexican imports are sold alongside the expected kitschy souvenirs. ⊠ *Main St. from Scottsdale Rd. to Brown Ave., Downtown Scottsdale.*

▶ ㉑ Scottsdale Center for the Arts. Galleries within this cultural and entertainment complex rotate exhibits frequently, but they typically emphasize contemporary art and artists. The airy and bright **Museum Store** (☎ 480/874–4464) has a great collection of unusual jewelry, as well as stationery, posters, and art books. ⊠ *7380 E. 2nd St., Downtown Scottsdale* ☎ *480/994–2787* ⊕ *www.scottsdalearts.org* ⊠ *Free* ☉ *Mon.–Wed. and Fri.–Sat. 10–5, Thurs. 10–8, Sun. noon–5; also during performance intermissions.*

㉘ Scottsdale Convention and Visitors Bureau. Pop inside to pick up some local maps, guidebooks, and brochures. Ask the helpful staff for a walking-tour map of Old Town Scottsdale's historic sites. ⊠ *4343 Scottsdale Rd., at Drinkwater Blvd., Suite 170, Downtown Scottsdale* ☎ *480/421–1004 or 800/782–1117* ⊕ *www.scottsdalecvb.com* ⊠ *Free* ☉ *Weekdays 8:30–6, Sat. 9–1.*

㉓ Scottsdale Historical Museum. Scottsdale's first schoolhouse, this redbrick building houses a version of the 1910 schoolroom, as well as photographs, original furniture from the city's founding fathers, and displays of other treasures from Scottsdale's early days. ⊠ *7333 Scottsdale Mall, Downtown Scottsdale* ☎ *480/945–4499* ⊕ *www.scottsdalemuseum. com* ⊠ *Free* ☉ *Sept.–June, Wed.–Sat. 10–5, Sun. noon–4.*

㉒ Scottsdale Museum of Contemporary Art. The spectacular Gerard L. Cafesjian Pavilion houses this museum. When you step through the immense glass entryway designed by artist James Fraser Carpenter and stroll through the spaces within the five galleries, you realize it's not just the spacious outdoor sculpture garden that makes this a "museum without walls." New installations are planned every few months, with an emphasis on contemporary art, architecture, and design. Free, docent-led tours are conducted on Thursday at 1:30. ⊠ *7380 E. 2nd St., Downtown Scotts-dale* ☎ *480/994–2787* ⊕ *www.scottsdalearts.org* ⌚ *$7, free Thurs.* ⊙ *Wed. noon–5, Thurs. 10–8, Fri. and Sat. 10–5, Sun. noon–5.*

need a break? The **Sugar Bowl Ice Cream Parlor** (⊠ 4005 N. Scottsdale Rd., Downtown Scottsdale ☎ 480/946–0051) transports you back in time to a 1950s malt shop. Doing business in the same building since 1958, the Sugar Bowl serves great burgers and lots of yummy ice-cream confections. Valley resident Bil Keane, creator of the comic strip "Family Circus," has often used this spot as inspiration for his cartoons, many of which are on display here.

㉙ **Taliesin West.** Ten years after visiting Arizona in 1927 to consult on de-
Fodor'sChoice signs for the Biltmore hotel, architect Frank Lloyd Wright chose 600
★ acres of rugged Sonoran Desert at the foothills of the McDowell Moun-tains as the site for his permanent winter residence. Today the site is a National Historic Landmark and still an active community of students and architects. Wright and apprentices constructed a desert camp here, using organic architecture to integrate the buildings with their natural surroundings. In addition to the living quarters, drafting studio, and small apartments of the Apprentice Court, Taliesin West also has two theaters, a music pavilion, and the Sun Trap—sleeping spaces surrounding an open patio and fireplace. Two guided tours cover different parts of the inte-rior, and a guided desert walk winds through the petroglyphs and land-scape from which Wright drew his vision. Five guided tours are offered, ranging from a one-hour "panorama" tour to a three-hour behind-the-scenes tour, with other tours offered seasonally. Times vary, so call ahead; all visitors must be accompanied by a guide. ⊠ *12621 Frank Lloyd Wright Blvd., North Scottsdale* ☎ *480/860–8810 or 480/860–2700* ⊕ *www.franklloydwright.org* ⌚ *$12.50–$45* ⊙ *Sept.–June, daily 8:30–5:30; July and Aug., Thurs.–Mon. 8:30–5:30.*

Tempe

In 1860, Charles Trumbell Hayden arrived on the east end of the Salt River, where he built a flour mill, warehouses, and a ferry across the river. This settlement and trade center became known as Hayden's Ferry. Other settlers soon arrived, including an English lord who felt—upon approaching the town from Phoenix and seeing the buttes, river, and fields of green mesquite—that the name should be changed to Tempe after the Vale of Tempe in Greece.

Today Tempe is home of Arizona State University's main campus and a thriving student population. A 20-minute drive from Phoenix, the tree- and brick-lined Mill Avenue (on which a flour mill at the site of Hay-den's original still stands) is the main drag, lined with student hangouts, bookstores, boutiques, eateries, and a repertory movie house.

The banks of the Rio Salado in Tempe are the future site of a commercial and entertainment district. Its first phase, Tempe Town Lake—a 2-mi-long waterway created by inflatable dams in a flood control channel—is open for boating. The lake is lined with biking and jogging paths, part of the project's design to encourage active recreation and promote development along the river over the next 10 years.

Numbers in the text correspond to numbers in the margin and on the What to See in Greater Phoenix map.

a good walk

Street parking is hard to find, but you can park in the public garage at Hayden Square, just north of 5th Street and west of Mill Avenue. Be sure to have your ticket stamped by local merchants to avoid paying parking fees. After parking, take a stroll a few minutes north to the shore of **Tempe Town Lake** ③⓪ ☞, where the new Tempe Arts Center, scheduled to open in 2006, is being built and where you can rent a boat, or you may wish to save the lake for a cool-down break later in the day. Continue south toward **La Casa Vieja** ③①, on the southwest corner of Mill Avenue and 1st Street. Continuing south on Mill Avenue you'll pass the old Hayden flour mill (which is no longer operating) and many specialty shops on the way to 5th Street; walk a block east to the inverted pyramid of **Tempe City Hall** ③②. Follow the pathway west through the grounds of City Hall and Plazita de Descanso, back to Mill Avenue. Head two blocks south on Mill to University Drive and proceed to Gammage Parkway, where you'll find the Grady Gammage Auditorium and ASU art museums and galleries on the southwest corner of the **Arizona State University** ③③ campus. You can walk back up Mill Avenue, catch the free FLASH shuttle northward (it stops on the north corner of Gammage Parkway and Mill Avenue), or wind your way northward through the university campus up toward ASU Sun Devil Stadium and "A" Mountain (so named by ASU students).

TIMING   If you're planning to shop as well as tour the campus and museums, allow four or five hours for exploring. Stop by the Town Lake for a break during the day so that you can take a boat ride or simply soak up some sunshine.

Sights to See

③③ **Arizona State University.** What began as the Tempe Normal School for Teachers—in 1886, a four-room red brick building and 20-acre cow pasture—is now the 750-acre campus of ASU, the largest university in the Southwest. The **ASU Visitor Information Center** (✉ 826 E. Apache Blvd., at Rural Rd. ☎ 480/965–0100) has maps of a self-guided walking tour (it's a long walk from Mill Avenue, so you might opt for the short version suggested here). You'll wind past public art and innovative architecture—including a music building that bears a strong resemblance to a wedding cake (designed by Taliesin students to echo Frank Lloyd Wright's Gammage Auditorium) and a law library shaped like an open book—and end up at the 74,000-seat ASU Sun Devil Stadium, home to the school's Sun Devils and home field for the NFL's Arizona Cardinals until 2006, when the Cardinals' new stadium in Glendale is slated to open. Admission to all ASU museums is free.

Heralded for its superior acoustics, the circular **Grady Gammage Auditorium** (⊠ Mill Ave. at Apache Blvd. ☎ 480/965–4050) was the last public structure completed by architect Frank Lloyd Wright, who detached the rear wall from grand tier and balcony sections in an effort to surround every patron with sound. The stage can accommodate a full symphony orchestra, and there's a 2,909-pipe organ. Artwork is exhibited in the lobby and in two on-site galleries. Free half-hour tours are offered weekdays between 1 and 3:30 during the school year.

While touring the west end of campus, stop into the **Arizona State University Art Museum** (⊠ Mill Ave. and 10th St. ☎ 480/965–2787 ⊕ asuartmuseum.asu.edu ☞ free ☉ Tues. 10–9, Wed.–Sat. 10–5, Sun. 1–5). It is in the gray-purple stucco Nelson Fine Arts Center, just north of the Gammage Auditorium. For a relatively small museum, it has an extensive collection, including 19th- and 20th-century painting and sculpture by masters such as Winslow Homer, Edward Hopper, Georgia O'Keeffe, and Rockwell Kent. Works by faculty and student artists are also on display, and there's a gift shop.

A short walk east of the Nelson Fine Arts Center, just north of the Hayden Library, ASU's experimental gallery and collection of crockery and ceramics are in the **Matthews Center** (⊠ Mill Ave. and 10th St. ☎ 480/965–2875 ☞ Free ☉ Sept.–May, Tues.–Sat. 10–5).

In Matthews Hall, the **Northlight Gallery** (⊠ Matthews Hall, Mill Ave., and 10th St. ☎ 480/965–6517 ☉ Mon.–Thurs. 10:30–4:30) exhibits works by both renowned and emerging photographers. There is no admission charge.

The **Edna Vihel Center for the Arts** (⊠ 3340 S. Rural Rd., ☎ 480/350–5287) is a short drive from downtown Tempe and a major arts venue, offering rotating exhibits of paintings and photography, as well as book signings, readings, and charity events. There's also a small theater for play and dance productions.

㉛ La Casa Vieja. In 1871, when Tempe was still known as Hayden's Ferry, this adobe hacienda was built as the home of Charles Hayden and was the town's first building. Now a restaurant called **Monti's La Casa Vieja,** the lobby and dining rooms display historical photographs and are a good choice for lunch or a steak dinner while visiting Tempe. ⊠ *1 W. Rio Salado Pkwy.* ☎ *480/967-7594* ⊕ *www.montis.com* ☉ *Sun.–Thurs. 11–10, Fri. and Sat. 11 AM–midnight.*

㉜ Tempe City Hall. Local architects Rolf Osland and Michael Goodwin constructed this inverted pyramid not just to win design awards (which they have) but also to shield city workers from the desert sun. The pyramid is constructed mainly of bronzed glass and stainless steel; the point disappears in a sunken courtyard lushly landscaped with jacaranda, ivy, and flowers, out of which the pyramid widens to the sky: stand underneath and gaze up for a weird fish-eye perspective. ⊠ *31 E. 5th St., 1 block east of Mill Ave.* ☎ *480/967-2001* ☞ *Free.*

▶ ℃ ㉚ **Tempe Town Lake.** The Town Lake is the newest addition to the growth of Tempe and attracts college students and Valley residents of all ages. Little ones enjoy the Splash Playground, and fishermen appreciate the rainbow trout–stocked lake. Call Rio Lago Cruises either to rent your own boat or take a Saturday sunset boat ride, which includes food, drinks, and music. Rio Lago's offices are north of 3rd Street between Mill and Ash avenues. A 13-acre marina completed in January 2004 is the latest addition to the Town Lake project. ✉ *990 W. Rio Salado Pkwy., between Mill and Rural Aves. north of Arizona State University* ☎ *480/517–4050 Rio Lago Cruises* ⊕ *www.tempe.gov/rio* 📠 *35-min Cruises $6, Sunset Cruises (Sat. only) $15* ☉ *Cruises Sun.–Thurs. 10–6, Fri.–Sat. 10–8.*

need a break? The outdoor patio of the **Coffee Plantation** (✉ 680 S. Mill Ave. ☎ 480/829–7878), a popular café near the ASU campus, is a lively scene—students cramming, local residents chatting over a cup of joe, and poets and musicians presenting their latest works.

WHERE TO EAT

Generations of Arizona schoolchildren have learned about the state's four Cs: copper, cattle, cotton, and climate. Today, a good argument could be made for adding a fifth in Phoenix: cuisine. New restaurants have proliferated dramatically in the Phoenix metropolitan area due to the Valley's rapid growth and the influence of the adventurous chefs who have emigrated here. An influx of Thai, Peruvian, Vietnamese, and Japanese restaurants have created a culinary scene of sophistication and diversity. Contemporary menus feature touches of the creator's homeland or ethnicity mixed with local recipes and ingredients. Pacific Rim or Latino foods are fused with spices native to the Southwest, such as Mexican coriander, fragrant Mexican oregano, *canela* sticks (Mexican cinnamon), and, of course, chiles from mild to explosive. Italian, Spanish, and even French favorites served in Phoenix might have a little more "bite" than elsewhere.

Many of the best restaurants in the Valley are in resorts, camouflaged behind courtyard walls, or tucked away in shopping malls. Newer, upscale eateries are clustered along Camelback Corridor and in Scottsdale. Great Mexican food can be found throughout the Valley, but the most authentic spots are in the Hispanic neighborhoods of South Phoenix.

Restaurants change hours, locations, chefs, prices, and menus frequently, so it's best to call ahead to confirm. Show up without a reservation during tourist season, and you may have to head for a fast-food drive-through window to avoid a two-hour wait for a table. All listed restaurants are open for lunch and dinner unless otherwise specified.

Prices

WHAT IT COSTS				
$$$$	**$$$**	**$$**	**$**	**¢**
AT DINNER over $30	$20–$30	$12–$20	$8–$12	under $8

Prices are per person for a main course. The final tab will include sales tax of 8.1% in Phoenix, 7.7% in Scottsdale.

Downtown Phoenix

American

$$–$$$$ ✕ **Durant's Fine Foods.** Durant's has endured since 1950 in the same lo-
cation, with the same menu, and even many of the original waitstaff, mak-
ing it one of Phoenix's legendary eating establishments. Steaks, chops,
and fresh seafood, including Florida stone crab, dominate here; when the
restaurant once tried to update its menu, regulars protested so furiously,
the idea was shelved. This was the first Valley restaurant to ban cell phones
in its dining room. Bravo! ✉ *2611 N. Central Ave., at Virginia, Down-
town Phoenix* ☎ *602/264–5967* ▭ *AE, D, DC, MC, V.*

$–$$ ✕ **Coronado Café.** You might miss this hidden treasure if it weren't for
the lines of customers waiting outside at lunchtime. This charming
1950s residence in the heart of Phoenix has a mere 30 seats and immediate parking for only three vehicles, but you'll be happy you stopped
by for such homemade favorites as chicken-corn chowder or a chicken
Caesar sandwich that you need to eat with a fork. The entrées change
daily, but on a hot summer day, be sure to order the homemade iced tea
(it's BYOB if you desire something with a little more kick). ✉ *2201 N.
7th St., Downtown Phoenix* ☎ *602/258–5149* ▭ *MC, V* ⊘ *Closed Sun.
No dinner Mon.*

¢–$ ✕ **Mrs. White's Golden Rule Café.** This downtown lunch spot is open only
until 5 PM, but it's the best place in town for true Southern cooking.
Every entrée—from fried chicken to pork chops—comes with corn
bread, and the peach cobbler is legendary. Catfish, black-eyed peas, and
collard greens are also on the menu. ✉ *808 E. Jefferson St., Downtown
Phoenix* ☎ *602/262–9256* ⬩ *Reservations not accepted* ▭ *No credit
cards* ⊘ *Closed weekends. No dinner.*

Chinese

¢–$$ ✕ **Gourmet House of Hong Kong.** Traditional Chinatown specialties, such
as *chow fun* (thick rice noodles), are excellent here. Try the assorted-
meat version, topped with chicken, shrimp, pork, and squid. Lobster
with black-bean sauce may be the world's messiest platter, but it's also
one of the tastiest. Along with an extensive seafood list, such adventurous
delights as five-flavor frogs' legs, duck feet with greens, and beef tripe
casserole are offered. ✉ *1438 E. McDowell Rd., Downtown Phoenix*
☎ *602/253–4859* ▭ *AE, D, DC, MC, V.*

Mexican

¢–$ ✕ **Oaxaca.** Mama's recipes for fresh tortillas, *calavasitas* (squash with
melted cheese), and excellent green-corn tamales have been drawing lo-
cals to this friendly establishment since 1976. The decor is dated and the
restaurant is not in the best neighborhood (just a few blocks from the
state capitol), but the food is authentic and freshly prepared in the restau-
rant's kitchen every day. Oaxaca attracts a crowd of local politicians and
men in blue. Guitarists entertain on weekends. ✉ *1516 W. Van Buren
St., Downtown Phoenix* ☎ *602/258–0804* ▭ *AE, D, MC, V.*

Pizza

★ $ ✕ **Pizzeria Bianco.** Brooklyn native Chris Bianco makes pizza with a pas-
sion in this small establishment in Heritage Square. He uses a wood-

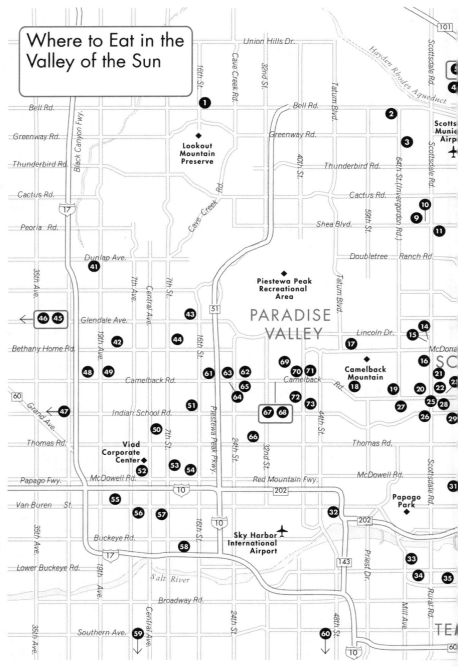

Where to Eat in the Valley of the Sun

Phoenix & Paradise Valley ▼
Avanti **66**
Carolina's **58**
China Chile **50**
Christo's
Ristorante **45**
Convivo **43**
Coronado Café **53**
Coup Des Tartes **51**
Durant's
Fine Foods **52**
elements **17**
Gourmet House
of Hong Kong **54**
Honey Bear's
BBQ **32**
La Fontanella **73**
La Grande Orange **72**
Lon's at the
Hermosa **69**
Los Dos Molinos **59**
Mediterranean
House **42**
Mrs. White's
Golden Rule Café **56**
Oaxaca **55**
Pizzeria Bianco **57**
Shinbay **60**
Taste of India **1**

Camelback Corridor ▼
Acqua E Sale **71**
Bistro 24 . . . . **65**
Christopher's Fermier
Brasserie &
Paola's Wine Bar **62**
Eddie Matney's **63**
Greekfest **64**
Original
Pancake House **20**
Tarbell's **68**
Tomaso's **67**
T. Cook's **18**
Tucchetti **61**
Vincent Guerithault
on Camelback **70**

Scottsdale ▼
Acacia **6**
AZ 88 . . . . **29**
Bandera **28**
Busters **13**
Carlsbad Tavern **30**
Cowboy Ciao **25**
Don & Charlie's **23**
Flat Wok **3**
The Grill at the TPC **4**

Havana Patio Cafe **2**
L'Academie Café **21**
La Hacienda **4**
L'Ecole **24**
Kashman's Place **7**
Los Sombreros
Mexican Cantina **16**
Malee's on
Main **27**
Maria's When in
Naples **10**
Marquesa **4**
Mary Elaine's **19**
Michael's
at the Citadel **5**
Morton's of Chicago **8**
Nello's **12**
Old Town
Tortilla Factory **26**
Rancho Pinot
Grill **14**
Razz's Restaurant
and Bar **11**
Restaurant Hapa **15**
Roaring Fork **22**
Salt Cellar **31**
Sushi on Shea **9**

Tempe, Mesa & Chandler ▼
C-Fu Gourmet **39**
Citrus Cafe **40**
Cyclo **38**
Four Peaks Brewing
Company **34**
House of Tricks **33**
Landmark **36**
Rosa's
Mexican Grill **37**
Tasty Kabob **35**

**West Phoenix, Glendale
& Litchfield Park** ▼
Arizona Kitchen **47**
Haus Murphy's **46**
Lily's Cafe **44**
Pepe's
Taco Villa **48**
Pho Bang **49**
Silver Dragon **41**

CloseUp

ON THE MEXICAN MENU

Although you'll find the largest concentration of good Mexican restaurants in Tucson, Phoenix has its fair share as well. Some menus are in Spanish only, so it's helpful to know the key words. The predominant cuisine is Sonoran, which is often accented with chiles, tamarind, cilantro, lime, and fresh native produce.

Aguas frescas: A fresh-fruit drink, sort of a smoothie
Albondigas: Meatball soup
Almendrado: An almond dessert, often the colors of the Mexican flag
Atole: A sweet drink made with corn masa, milk, and crushed fruit
Birria: Traditionally stewed goat, but often made with beef
Caldo de queso: Cheese-and-potato soup
Carne asada: Grilled marinated beef
Carne seca: Sun-dried, marinated beef
Carnitas: Stewed pork
Cazuela: Machaca soup
Chorizo: Spicy pork or pork-and-beef sausage

Enchiladas: Soft corn tortillas filled with meat or cheese, covered with sauce
Flautas: Rolled, deep-fried tacos
Horchata: Rice-milk and cinnamon drink
Machaca: Dried beef cooked with tomatoes, onions, chiles, and often egg
Mariscos: shellfish
Menudo: Hominy-and-tripe stew
Mole: A sauce made from chiles, spices, crushed seeds, and flavored with chocolate
Posole: Hominy-and-pork stew
Sopa Azteca: Soup, made with chicken, avocados, and tortillas in broth
Tacos: Tortillas, briefly heated, filled and wrapped into thin cylinders
Tamales: Pockets of corn dough, with savory fillings, which are wrapped in corn husks and steamed.
Tortas: Sandwich on a white bun
Tostadas: Lightly friend, open tortillas topped with meat, lettuce, etc.
Tripitas de leche: Tripe (the stomach) of a cow

fired brick oven imported from Italy and makes his own mozzarella cheese. Other toppings include homemade fennel sausage, wood-roasted cremini mushrooms, and the freshest herbs and spices. The wine bar next door is a good place to wait for your table, as the restaurant doesn't take reservations. ⊠ *623 E. Adams St., Downtown Phoenix* ☎ *602/ 258–8300* ⌦ *Reservations not accepted* ▭ *MC, V* ☉ *Closed Mon. No lunch weekends.*

Central Phoenix

Central Phoenix is bounded by Camelback Road on the north, Paradise Valley on the east, Interstate 17 on the west, and Buckeye Road (excluding Papago Salado) on the south.

American/Casual

¢–$ ✕ **La Grande Orange.** Craig and Kris DeMarco have created a wonderful gathering place in this small grocery store and fresh-food market in the heart of Arcadia, one of Phoenix's original neighborhoods. The store shelves are filled with gourmet cheese, bread, wine, fresh fruit and flowers, and decadent pastries supplied by local vendors. The small tables inside fill up quickly at breakfast and lunch and spill outside to patio seating. Valley residents drive for miles to feast on mouthwatering sandwiches, gourmet pizzas, and fruit smoothies. ⊠ *4410 N. 40th St., Central Phoenix* ☎ *602/840–7777* ▤ *AE, MC, V.*

Chinese

¢–$$ ✕ **China Chile.** You might drive past this place hundreds of times and never be tempted to stop, but beyond the bright pink facade and windowless storefront is a busy restaurant. Start with the plump, boiled wontons in a spicy Szechuan peanut sauce. The chicken in a phoenix nest is a crisp potato nest filled with succulent chicken, crunchy vegetables, and bean sauce garnished with quail eggs. Vegetable offerings, including the crispy Szechuan-style string beans in garlic sauce and spicy eggplant braised in chile paste, are a meal unto themselves. ⊠ *3501 N. Central Ave., Central Phoenix* ☎ *602/266–4463* ▤ *AE, DC, MC, V* ۞ *Closed Sun. No lunch Sat.*

Italian

$$–$$$ ✕ **Avanti.** Owners Angelo Livi and Benito Mellino have been welcoming guests to this classic Italian restaurant since 1974. Candlelight, a piano bar, and a dance floor are perfect for a special celebration. For starters, try one of the house specialties, light potato gnocchi paired with spinach ravioli. The veal dishes, such as saltimbocca or osso buco, are particularly memorable. Other entrées on the extensive menu include cioppino, paella, and a daily homemade pasta special. ⊠ *2728 E. Thomas Rd., Central Phoenix* ☎ *602/956–0900* ▤ *AE, D, DC, MC, V* ۞ *No lunch weekends.*

★ $$ ✕ **La Fontanella.** Quality and value add up to a winning combination at this outstanding neighborhood restaurant. The interior is reminiscent of an Italian villa, with antiques, crisp table linens, fresh flowers, and windows dressed in lace curtains. Chef-owner Isabelle Bertuccio turns out magnificent food, often using recipes from her Tuscan and Sicilian relatives. The escargot appetizer and herb-crusted rack of lamb entrée top the list. Homemade pasta is served with Sicilian semolina bread and homemade sausages or meatballs. For dessert, Isabelle's husband, Berto, creates sumptuous gelato, which he supplies to restaurants and resorts Valley-wide. ⊠ *4231 E. Indian School Rd., Central Phoenix* ☎ *602/955–1213* ⊕ *www.lafontanella.com* ▤ *AE, D, DC, MC, V* ۞ *No lunch weekends.*

Phoenix: Camelback Corridor

The Camelback Corridor, a veritable restaurant row, runs west to east from Phoenix to Scottsdale—the cities are divided by 64th Street.

American/Casual

¢–$ ✕ **Original Pancake House.** The flapjacks here inspire worship from local admirers, who wait patiently for a table on weekends. The signature apple pancake is made from homemade batter poured over sautéed apples, then baked to crispy perfection and glazed with cinnamon sugar. Other varieties, such as the Dutch Baby, an oven-baked confection served with whipped butter and powdered sugar, are also worth braving the crowds. Everything is made by hand, including oven-baked omelets, crepes, waffles, and egg dishes. ✉ *6840 E. Camelback Rd., Camelback Corridor* ☎ *480/946–4902* ⌖ *Reservations not accepted* ▭ *No credit cards* ☾ *No dinner.*

Contemporary

$$–$$$$ ✕ **Eddie Matney's.** A Phoenix star, chef Eddie Matney delights diners with traditional foods prepared in unexpected ways. You can order such creative and beautifully presented comfort foods as bacon- and basil-seasoned meat loaf with country mashed potatoes and wild mushroom gravy, or a macaroni casserole baked with goat cheese and topped with Dungeness crab. Desserts like the peanut butter, chocolate, and banana Boston cream pie are indulgent masterpieces. ✉ *2398 E. Camelback Rd., Camelback Corridor* ☎ *602/957–3214* ▭ *AE, D, DC, MC, V* ☾ *Closed Sun. No lunch weekends.*

$$–$$$ ✕ **Tarbell's.** Cutting-edge cuisine is the star at this sophisticated bistro. Grilled salmon served on a crispy potato cake and glazed with a molasses-lime sauce is a long-standing classic. The focaccia with red onion, Romano cheese, and roasted thyme is excellent, and imaginative designer pizzas are cooked in a wood-burning oven. Your sweet tooth won't be disappointed by Tarbell's warm, rich, chocolate cake topped with pistachio ice cream. Hardwood floors, copper accents, and a curving cherry-wood and maple bar create a sleek, cosmopolitan look. ✉ *3213 E. Camelback Rd., Camelback Corridor* ☎ *602/955–8100* ⌖ *Reservations essential* ▭ *AE, D, DC, MC, V* ☾ *No lunch.*

★ $$–$$$ ✕ **Tomaso's.** In a town where restaurants come and go overnight, Tomaso's has been a favorite since 1977, and for good reason. Chef Tomaso Maggiore learned to cook as a child at the family's restaurant in Palermo, Sicily, and honed his skills at the Culinary Institute of Rome. The result is authentic Italian cuisine that is consistently well prepared and delicious. The house specialty, *cuscinetto di vitella* (veal stuffed with prosciutto and mascarpone cheese) is outstanding. Other notables include *crostacei fradiavolo* (mounds of shellfish heaped over linguini), as well as risotto, osso buco, and cannelloni. ✉ *3225 E. Camelback Rd., Camelback Corridor* ☎ *602/956–0836* ▭ *AE, D, DC, MC, V* ☾ *No lunch weekends.*

French

$$–$$$ ✕ **Bistro 24.** Smart and stylish, with impeccable service, the Ritz's Bistro 24 has a parquet floor, colorful murals, an elegant bar, and an outdoor

patio. Stop here for a break from shopping and enjoy the largest Cobb salad in town and a cup of French-press coffee. For dinner, go with classic French steak au poivre with frites, cassoulet, bouillabaisse, or simply a well-prepared grilled salmon or crispy-skin whitefish. The bistro's Sunday brunch is a local favorite. ⊠ *Ritz-Carlton Hotel, 2401 E. Camelback Rd., Camelback Corridor* ☏ *602/952–2424* ⊟ *AE, D, DC, MC, V.*

$$–$$$ ✕ **Christopher's Fermier Brasserie & Paola's Wine Bar.** Chef Christopher Gross serves simple, delicious fare using the freshest ingredients and produce from local farmers. Foods are prepared in the brasserie tradition, and the salad with goat cheese, leek tart, lobster bisque, steak au poivre, and bouillabaisse are all of the highest order. Wine director Paola Gross offers more than 100 vintages by the glass in the wine bar and stocks an excellent selection of cigars. Thursday to Saturday from 10 PM to midnight, Gross dishes out "Leftovers from the Kitchen" for $9.95. ⊠ *Biltmore Fashion Park, 2584 E. Camelback Rd., Camelback Corridor* ☏ *602/522–2344* ⊟ *AE, D, DC, MC, V.*

Greek

$$–$$$ ✕ **Greekfest.** This informal but elegant restaurant is lovingly appointed with thick, arched, whitewashed walls; hardwood floors; and tasteful bric-a-brac. The food pleases as well. Search the menu's two pages of appetizers for *taramasalata* (mullet roe blended with lemon and olive oil) and *saganaki* (cheese flamed with brandy and extinguished with a squirt of lemon). Entrées, such as *exohiko* (succulent chunks of lamb with cheese and roasted vegetables baked in phyllo dough) or salmon *chios* (salmon fillet baked with feta cheese, kalamata olives, and pine nuts) are equally worth ordering. For dessert, the *galaktoboureko* (warm custard pie baked in phyllo) is a triumph of Western civilization. ⊠ *1940 E. Camelback Rd., Camelback Corridor* ☏ *602/265–2990* ⊟ *AE, D, DC, MC, V* ☺ *No lunch Sun.*

Italian

$$–$$$ ✕ **Acqua E Sale.** The veal dishes—like scallopini with white truffle and porcini-mushroom sauce—are wonderful at this quietly romantic spot. Chilean sea bass and ravioli stuffed with sweet butternut squash are also good choices. Appetizers include dishes that have come to be favorites of Americans: fried calamari, duck prosciutto, and buffalo-milk mozzarella and tomato salad. ⊠ *4225 E. Camelback Rd., Camelback Corridor* ☏ *602/952–1522* ⊟ *AE, MC, V* ☺ *Closed Sun. No lunch.*

☺ **$–$$** ✕ **Tucchetti.** Straw-clad Chianti bottles, red-checkered tablecloths, and strings of colorful lights are part of the festive, informal (and often loud) atmosphere here. The signature dish, a baked cube of spaghetti, is presented with dramatic fanfare by the upbeat staff. Hearty, home-style fare includes thin-crust pizzas, chicken Vesuvio, veal piccata, and several mix-and-match pastas and sauces. The endless salad bar has antipasti, homemade minestrone soup, and bread. On Monday, the kids' menu is free for those under 13, when they are accompanied by an adult. ⊠ *2135 E. Camelback Rd., Camelback Corridor* ☏ *602/957–0222* ⊟ *AE, D, MC, V.*

Mediterranean

★ **$$$–$$$$** ✕ **T. Cook's at the Royal Palms.** One of the finest restaurants in the Valley, T. Cook's oozes romance from its floor-to-ceiling windows with dramatic views of Camelback Mountain to its1930s-style decor. Rotisserie specialties are prepared in the restaurant's lodge-style fireplace. The Mediterranean-influenced menu includes lobster bisque with farm-raised Arizona shrimp, cream of spinach soup with nutmeg and spiced duck confit, osso buco, and spit-roasted chicken with baby corn. Desserts and pastries, prepared by famed pastry chef Pierino Jermonti, are nothing less than works of art. ⊠ *Royal Palms Resort & Spa, 5200 E. Camelback Rd., Camelback Corridor* ☎ *602/840–3610* ⚠ *Reservations essential* ⊟ *AE, D, MC, V.*

Southwestern

$$$ ✕ **Vincent Guerithault on Camelback.** Chef Guerithault is best known for creating French food with a Southwestern touch. You can make a meal of his famous appetizers, duck confit tamales and salmon quesadillas. His signature crème brûlée arrives in three thin pastry cups filled with vanilla, coffee, and coconut custard. On Saturday from 9 AM to 1 PM, exotic fruits, vegetables, and cheeses are sold at the Touch of Provence market held in the restaurant parking lot. ⊠ *3930 E. Camelback Rd., Camelback Corridor* ☎ *602/224–0225* ⚠ *Reservations essential* ⊟ *AE, DC, MC, V* ⊗ *No lunch weekends; closed Sun.*

North-Central Phoenix

North-central Phoenix is the area north of Camelback Road between Interstate 17 and Paradise Valley.

Contemporary

$$$–$$$$ ✕ **Convivo.** This is the closest you'll get to a Manhattan dining experience in the desert: a dozen tables, a tiny kitchen, and a rotating new American menu featuring fresh seasonal produce. American standards are combined with unexpected flavors in such dishes as the coconut-crusted ahi tuna topped with fried calamari and drizzled with plum-marigold-mint vinaigrette. The wine list is thoughtful and not overpriced. Save room for exciting desserts like the fudgy ancho-chile brownie. ⊠ *7000 N. 16th St., North-Central Phoenix* ☎ *602/997–7676* ⊟ *AE, D, MC, V* ⊗ *Closed Sun. and Mon. No lunch.*

French

★ **$$$–$$$$** ✕ **Coup Des Tartes.** Tables are scattered among three small rooms of an old house at this attractive, country French restaurant. It's BYOB, and there's an $8 corkage fee; however, all's forgiven when you taste the delicate cuisine prepared in the tiny kitchen. Chef-owner Natascha Ovando, a graduate of the French Culinary Institute in New York, changes the menu weekly, sometimes even daily. Offerings may include baked Brie, fennel-tinged sea bass, or lemon-herb chicken on a bed of spinach basil risotto. Ovando's signature dessert, a banana brûlée tart, is absolutely delectable. ⊠ *4626 N. 16th St., North-Central Phoenix* ☎ *602/212–1082* ⚠ *Reservations essential* ⊟ *AE, D, MC, V* ⛄ *BYOB* ⊗ *Closed Sun. and Mon. No lunch.*

Indian

$–$$ ✕ **Taste of India.** This perennial favorite in the Valley specializes in northern Indian cuisine. Breads here—*bhatura, naan, paratha*—are superb, and vegetarians enjoy wonderful meatless specialties, including *beng-han bhartha* fashioned from eggplant, and *bhindi masala*, a tempting okra dish. Just about every spice in the rack is used for the lamb and chicken dishes, so be prepared to guzzle extra water—or an English beer—if your server says an item is spicy. ✉ *1609 E. Bell Rd., North-Central Phoenix* ☎ *602/788–3190* ▭ *AE, D, MC, V.*

Italian

$$–$$$ ✕ **Christo's Ristorante.** Cozy and unassuming in a Phoenix strip mall, Christo's keeps its tables filled with loyal customers. Attentive servers ensure that your water glass never empties and that bread doesn't have enough time to cool. Folks rave about the roasted rack of lamb, the veal, and the tortellini alla papalina. All main courses come with soup and salad. ✉ *6327 N. 7th St., North-Central Phoenix* ☎ *602/264–1784* ▭ *AE, D, DC, MC, V* ☻ *Closed Sun.*

¢–$ ✕ **Mediterranean House.** The cuisine seems to cover an area between Greece and the Middle East, but the Korean owners still manage to dish out tasty and well-prepared Mediterranean food. The lentil soup is thick and spicy, and the Egyptian chicken—a huge plate of sliced chicken breast, battered and fried, is absolutely delicious. Vegetarians appreciate the combination plate piled with baba ghanouj, hummus, and falafel served with warm pita bread and a zesty yogurt sauce. ✉ *1588 E. Bethany Home Rd., North-Central Phoenix* ☎ *602/248–8460* ▭ *AE, MC, V* ☻ *Closed Sun. No lunch Sat.*

South Phoenix

South Phoenix is the area south of Buckeye Road, between 27th Avenue on the west and Tempe on the east.

Barbecue

¢   ✕ **Honey Bear's BBQ.** Honey Bear's motto—"You don't need no teeth to eat our meat"—may fall short on grammar, but this place isn't packed with folks looking to improve their language skills. This is Tennessee-style barbecue, which means smoky baby-back ribs basted in thick, zippy, slightly sweet sauce with a wonderful orange tang. The sausage-enhanced "cowbro" beans and scallion-studded potato salad are great sides. If a slab of ribs still leaves you hungry, finish up with the homemade sweet potato pie. ✉ *5012 E. Van Buren St., South Phoenix* ☎ *602/273–9148* ⌦ *Reservations not accepted* ▭ *AE, D, MC, V.*

Japanese

$–$$$ ✕ **Shinbay.** This small, serene spot is the perfect place to have a relaxing sushi meal, complete with flights of premium sake. The raw fish is the freshest in town, and the cooked dishes are also lovely. Three-course dinner specials change nightly. At lunch, the bento box is a good value. ✉ *15410 S. Mountain Pkwy., South Phoenix* ☎ *480/704–1422* ▭ *AE, MC, V* ☻ *No lunch weekends.*

Mexican

★ ¢–$$ ✕ **Los Dos Molinos.** In a hacienda that belonged to silent-era movie star Tom Mix, this entertaining restaurant focuses on New Mexican–style Mexican food. And that means *hot*. Hatch, New Mexico, chiles form the backbone of the dishes here, and the green-chile enchilada and beef taco are potentially lethal. The red salsa and the stacked enchiladas with an egg on top are so good you'll beg for more. There's also a funky courtyard where you can sip margaritas while waiting for a table. This is a must-do dining experience if you want some authentic New Mexican–style food, but come prepared to swig lots of water. ⊠ *8646 S. Central Ave., South Phoenix* ☎ *602/243–9113* ⚐ *Reservations not accepted* ⊟ *AE, D, MC, V* ⊘ *Closed Sun. and Mon.*

¢ ✕ **Carolina's.** This small, nondescript restaurant in south Phoenix makes
Fodor'sChoice the most delicious, thin-as-air, flour tortillas imaginable. In-the-know
★ locals and downtown working folks have been lining up at Carolina's for years to partake of its homey and downright cheap Mexican food. Tacos, tamales, burritos, flautas, and enchiladas are served on paper plates, and you can also purchase homemade chorizo and tamales by the dozen. Or, for a couple of dollars, you can buy a package of warm tortillas to take home, but chances are they'll be gone long before you arrive. ⊠ *1202 E. Mohave St., South Phoenix* ☎ *602/252–1503* ⊕ *www.carolinasmex.com* ⊟ *AE, D, DC, MC, V.*

Paradise Valley

Paradise Valley is a town that has been absorbed into the greater Phoenix area; it's bordered by McDonald Drive to the south, Scottsdale Road to the east, Shea Boulevard to the north, and the Phoenix Mountain Preserve to the west.

Contemporary

$$$ ✕ **elements.** Perched on the side of Camelback Mountain at the Sanctuary Resort, this is the spot for cocktails with breathtaking desert-sunset and city-light views. There's a cordial community table where you can sit and order such appetizers as duck spring rolls, chilled tiger shrimp with Asian slaw, and fried calamari with miso-scallion vinaigrette. Among the best main courses are rack of lamb and penne with wild mushrooms. ⊠ *Sanctuary on Camelback Mountain, 5700 E. McDonald Dr., Paradise Valley* ☎ *480/607–2300* ⊟ *AE, D, DC, MC, V.*

$$$ ✕ **Lon's at the Hermosa.** In an adobe hacienda hand-built by cowboy artist
Fodor'sChoice Lon Megargee, this romantic spot has sweeping vistas of Camelback
★ Mountain and the perfect patio for after-dinner drinks under the stars. Megargee's art and cowboy memorabilia decorate the dining room. The menu includes such appetizers as rock shrimp with roasted-corn sauce and juniper-smoked wild Chinook salmon. Wood-grilled, melt-in-your-mouth filet mignon over Gorgonzola-mashed potatoes and more exotic dishes like pecan-grilled antelope are main course options. Fresh vegetables and herbs are pulled from the property's own garden. Phoenicians love the Sunday brunch. ⊠ *Hermosa Inn, 5532 N. Palo Cristi Dr., Paradise Valley* ☎ *602/955–7878* ⊟ *AE, DC, MC, V* ⊘ *No lunch Sat.*

Scottsdale

Fast-growing Scottsdale can be broken down into roughly three neighborhoods. Downtown encompasses the small area bordered by Highland Avenue to the north, 56th Street to the west, Thomas Road to the south, and Scottsdale Road to the east; North Scottsdale includes everything north of Shea Boulevard; and Central Scottsdale is everything between Downtown and North Scottsdale. The Camelback Corridor restaurant row runs west–east from Phoenix to Scottsdale, with 64th Street the border between the two.

American

★ **$$$–$$$$** ✕ **The Grill at the TPC.** This is one clubhouse grill where everything is way over par, making it one of the better restaurants in Scottsdale. If you're hunting for a "melt-in-your-mouth steak," this might well be the place. There are prime steaks, both dry-aged and wet-aged beef. The "fish-market" style display offers different varieties of fresh fish flown in daily from the Pacific and Atlantic coasts. For proof, try the phenomenal sesame-crusted ahi tuna. ⊠ *Fairmont Scottsdale Princess Resort, 7575 E. Princess Dr., North Scottsdale, Scottsdale* ☎ *480/585–4848* ⌕ *Reservations essential* ☰ *AE, D, DC, MC, V.*

American/Casual

$–$$$ ✕ **Bandera.** For a tasty dinner before a night out on the town, try this casual, high-volume spot. The rotisserie chicken is wonderfully moist and meaty; you'll see the birds spinning in the big window before you even walk through the door. If you're not a poultry fan, rest assured that salads, fresh fish, prime rib, and meat loaf usually make it onto the weekly menu. The mashed potatoes are divine—you'll think Mom is in the kitchen peeling spuds. If you get here at prime eating hours, especially on weekends, be prepared to wait for a table. ⊠ *3821 N. Scottsdale Rd., Central Scottsdale* ☎ *480/994–3524* ⌕ *Reservations not accepted* ☰ *AE, D, MC, V* ⊘ *Closed Mon. No lunch.*

¢–$$ ✕ **Busters.** This local favorite in the Mercado del Lago Plaza is a casual, comfortable spot for good burgers, fresh oysters, build-your-own lavosh (Armenian pizza), wood-grilled steaks, and an impressive selection of imported beers. Choose patio seating overlooking Lake Margherite, where you can enjoy the setting sun splash color over the McDowell Mountains. ⊠ *8320 N. Hayden Rd., North Scottsdale* ☎ *480/951–5850* ☰ *AE, D, DC, MC, V.*

¢–$ ✕ **AZ 88.** A great spot for people-watching, this sleek, glassed-in restaurant serves huge martinis and great food at rock-bottom prices. Try the wonderful shrimp ceviche or a giant Cobb salad. Elsa's chicken, a grilled breast with pecans, peppers, and honey mustard, is among the inventive sandwiches, and sumptuous burgers are served with homemade waffle fries and chunks of fruit. The music is usually a bit too loud inside for casual conversation, so if the weather is good, ask to dine on the beautifully appointed patio overlooking Scottsdale Mall. ⊠ *7353 E. Scottsdale Mall, North Scottsdale* ☎ *480/994–5576* ☰ *AE, D, DC, MC, V* ⊘ *No lunch weekends.*

¢–$ ✕ **Kashman's Place.** To get a good feel for one North Scottsdale neighborhood, stop at Kashman's Place. Brooklyn transplants Nancy and Steve Kashman serve sumptuous omelets with crisp home fries, creatively blended salads, and piled-high sandwiches to a large following of locals. Their popularity is well earned, since everything here is deliciously fresh and portions are generous. The New York bagels are done the authentic way—boiled and baked on premises using filtered water they've duplicated from NYC water samples. The outside patio is dog friendly, so feel free to bring your favorite pooch. Expect lines on weekends. It's open from 6 AM to 3:30 PM daily. ⊠ *23425 N. Scottsdale Rd., at Pinnacle Peak Rd., North Scottsdale* ☎ *480/585–6221* ▤ *AE, D, DC, MC, V* ⊙ *No dinner.*

Chinese

♨ ¢–$ ✕ **Flat Wok.** You can be as decadent or calorie-conscious as you want at this all-you-can-eat Mongolian grill. Once you choose your own meat, seafood, vegetables, rice noodles, and sauces, the chef will wok what you build. A salad bar and pasta buffet round out the experience. ⊠ *6501 E. Greenway Pkwy., North Scottsdale* ☎ *480/948–5544* ▤ *AE, D, DC, MC, V.*

Contemporary

$$$–$$$$ ✕ **Acacia.** Worth the drive into the foothills of Pinnacle Peak, this restaurant is in the Four Seasons Hotel in far north Scottsdale. The menu includes some exotic offerings like spiced venison chops with potato hash, but most folks come for the steaks (try the 18-ounce bone-in rib eye) and the restaurant's chilled Seafood Pinnacle (a seafood platter, with prawns, oysters, Alaskan king crab, and fresh steamed lobster accompanied by a trio of dipping sauces). ⊠ *Four Seasons Scottsdale at Troon North, 10600 E. Crescent Moon Dr., North Scottsdale* ☎ *480/513–5086* ⌕ *Reservations essential* ▤ *AE, D, MC, V* ⊙ *No lunch.*

$$$–$$$$ ✕ **Rancho Pinot Grill.** The attention to quality paid by the husband-and-wife proprietors here—he manages, she cooks—has made this one of the town's top dining spots. The inventive menu changes daily, depending on what's fresh. If you're lucky, you might come on a day when the kitchen has made *posole*, a mouthwatering broth with hominy, salt pork, and cabbage. Entrées might include quail with soba noodles, rosemary-infused chicken with Italian sausage, and grilled sea bass atop basmati rice. ⊠ *6208 N. Scottsdale Rd., Central Scottsdale* ☎ *480/367–8030* ⌕ *Reservations essential* ▤ *AE, D, MC, V* ⊙ *Closed Sun. and Mon. and mid-Aug.–mid-Sept. No lunch.*

$$–$$$$ ✕ **Cowboy Ciao.** Looking for a culinary kick? This kitchen weds Southwestern fare and Italian flair, and it's no shotgun wedding, either. Main dishes, such as the Chianti-marinated filet mignon, fennel-seasoned meat loaf, and wild mushrooms in an ancho chile–cream sauce heaped over polenta, are creative without going off the deep end. The chocolate lottery—complete with an actual lottery ticket—is a dessert hoot. You can also order one of several affordable flights of wine, which will give you a different glass with each course. ⊠ *7133 E. Stetson Dr., Central Scottsdale* ☎ *480/946–3111* ▤ *AE, D, MC, V* ⊙ *No lunch Sun. and Mon.*

$$–$$$$ ✕ **Michael's at the Citadel.** One of this town's best-looking places has a two-story sandstone waterfall, warm fireplaces, and lush desert landscaping. The contemporary American fare is simply elegant: roast salmon mignon on vegetable ribbons; grilled lamb with a goat-cheese potato tart; grilled prawns on chive-and-mushroom risotto. Sunday brunch showcases offerings like rolled Swedish pancakes with cinnamon apples and mascarpone. If you're celebrating a special occasion, Michael's is the

spot. ⊠ *8700 E. Pinnacle Peak Rd., North Scottsdale* ☎ *480/515–2575* ▤ *AE, DC, MC, V* ☉ *No lunch weekends.*

$$–$$$$ ✕ **Roaring Fork.** Elk-antler chandeliers, earth-tone fabrics and leathers, barbed-wire accessories, and a buffalo skull above the bar add up to a comfortable, rustic restaurant named after the river that winds past Aspen in Colorado. Chef Robert McGrath's creations include mustard-crusted trout, a pork porterhouse steak, and such side dishes as smoked-tomato grits and green-chile macaroni. For dessert, "Lucky 7" is a chocolate tart filled with chocolate silk and smothered in (you guessed it) chocolate ice cream and milk-chocolate sauce. The reasonably priced saloon menu is served in the bar from 7 to 10 PM. ⊠ *Finova Building, 4800 N. Scottsdale Rd., Central Scottsdale* ☎ *480/947–0795* ▤ *AE, D, DC, MC, V* ☉ *No lunch.*

$$–$$$ ✕ **Razz's Restaurant and Bar.** There's no telling what part of the globe chef-proprietor Erasmo "Razz" Kamnitzer will use for culinary inspiration. However, you can count on his creations to give dormant taste buds a wake-up call: black-bean paella is a twist on a Spanish theme; South American bouillabaisse is a fragrant fish stew, stocked with veggies; and *bah mie goreng* teams noodles with fish, meat, and vegetables, perked up with dried cranberries and almonds. Count on it—Razz'll dazzle. ⊠ *10315 N. Scottsdale Rd., North Scottsdale* ☎ *480/905–1308* ▤ *AE, D, MC, V* ☉ *Closed Sun. and Mon. No lunch.*

$$ ✕ **L'Ecole.** You'll have no regrets putting yourself in the talented hands of the student chefs at the Valley's premier cooking academy. A complete dinner costs as little as $25 and lunch around $13, a real bargain. The three-course prix-fixe dinner menu selections change frequently, as the restaurant is taken over by a different class each week. You can expect inventive appetizers like ginger-soy–marinated gravlax, entrées such as fillet Rossini (with foie gras, truffles, and a demi-glace sauce), and such desserts as crème brûlée. Because the students also pull server duty, you can count on being pampered, too. ⊠ *Scottsdale Culinary Institute, 8100 E. Camelback Rd., Central Scottsdale* ☎ *480/423–2530* ⌂ *Reservations essential* ▤ *D, MC, V* ☉ *Closed weekends.*

$ ✕ **L'Academie Café.** It's hard to find a better bargain in Scottsdale than this student-run restaurant at the Scottsdale Culinary Institute. The bistro-style café's à la carte menu focuses on the cuisine of the Mediterranean, particularly the Italian and French rivieras. The student chefs create selections of fresh fish and veal, panini, salads, and desserts. Although menus rotate regularly, diners clamor to try such offerings as Italian sausage, Portobello, and mozzarella pizza; seafood lasagna filled with plump pieces of fresh fish, shrimp, and clams; and decadent desserts like a chocolate flourless torte with raspberry coulis. ⊠ *Scottsdale Culinary Institute, 4301 N. Scottsdale Rd., Central Scottsdale* ☎ *480/941–0229* ▤ *D, MC, V* ☉ *Closed weekends.*

French

★ $$$$ ✕ **Mary Elaine's.** Formal and elegant, this is the Valley's finest high-end dining experience. The austerity of Mary Elaine's (in the Phoenician Hotel) is a perfect backdrop for dramatic city-light views of Scottsdale from every table. French-inspired offerings may include fricassee of lobster, foie gras drizzled with maple syrup and 100-year-old balsamic vinegar, and a pan-roasted wild turbot with black truffle–lobster sauce. Desserts like the warm chocolate-soufflé tart are breathtaking. An extensive wine cellar, impeccable service, and a pleasant jazz vocalist make this an exceptional dining experience. ⊠ *The Phoenician, 6000 E. Camelback Rd., Camelback Corridor* ☎ *480/423–2530* ⊕ *www.phoenician. com* ⟟ *Reservations essential* ⟟ *Jacket required* ⊟ *AE, D, MC, V* ⊘ *Closed Sun. No lunch.*

Italian

★ **$$–$$$** ✕ **Maria's When in Naples.** In a town teeming with Italian restaurants, this is a standout. The antipasto spread laid out just inside the entrance tastes as good as it looks. Maria, herself, makes all of the homemade pasta. Check out the *salsiccia Pugliese* (fettuccine topped with homemade sausage, leeks, porcini mushrooms, and white-wine sauce) or the *orecchiette Barese* (ear-shape pasta tossed with cauliflower, pancetta, sundried tomatoes, olive oil, and cheese). ⊠ *7000 E. Shea Blvd., North Scottsdale* ☎ *480/991–6887* ⊟ *AE, D, DC, MC, V* ⊘ *No lunch weekends.*

Japanese

$–$$$ ✕ **Sushi on Shea.** You may be in the middle of the desert, but the sushi here will make you think you're at the ocean's edge. Yellowtail, toro, shrimp, scallops, freshwater eel, and even monkfish liver pâté are among the long list of delights. *Nabemono* (hot pot or meals-in-a-bowl) are prepared at your table. The best dish? Maybe it's the *una-ju* (broiled freshwater eel with a sublime smoky scent), served over sweet rice. The fact that some people believe eel is an aphrodisiac only adds to its charm. ⊠ *7000 E. Shea Blvd., North Scottsdale* ☎ *480/483–7799* ⊟ *AE, D, DC, MC, V* ⊕ *www.sushionshea.com* ⊘ *No lunch.*

Latin

$$–$$$ ✕ **Havana Patio Cafe.** Tapas are marvelous here, particularly the shrimp pancakes, potato croquettes, and Cuban tamales. There's an intoxicating choice of entrées including paella heaped with a whole Maine lobster. And there's even something for vegetarians: *cho cho,* a fresh chayote squash stuffed with loads of veggies and topped with a Jamaican curry sauce. ⊠ *6245 E. Bell Rd., North Scottsdale* ☎ *480/991–1496* ⊟ *AE, D, DC, MC, V.*

Mexican

★ **$$$** ✕ **La Hacienda.** La Hacienda is widely considered to be among the finest Mexican restaurants in North America. To ensure authentic cuisine, chef Reed Groban took tasting tours through Mexican villages and towns. You'll find no burritos or tacos here, just appetizers like the ancho chile stuffed with dried fruit, nuts, and chicken, and such entrées as *camarones salteados* (braised, sautéed shrimp) with a poblano-rice casserole and tamarind sauce, and *cochinillo asado,* La Hacienda's signature dish—spit-roasted suckling pig marinated in tamarind and bitter orange, wheeled up to the table and carved to order. The restaurant occupies a re-created turn-of-the-20th-century ranch house on the grounds of the Fairmont Scottsdale Princess Resort. ⊠ *Fairmont Scottsdale Princess Resort, 7575 E. Princess Dr., North Scottsdale* ☎ *480/585–4848* ⊟ *AE, D, DC, MC, V* ⊘ *Closed Wed. No lunch.*

¢–$$ ✕ **Carlsbad Tavern.** This casual and busy New Mexico–style eatery serves big portions of such tasty dishes as a half-pound burger grilled over pecan wood, green-chile mashed potatoes, chipotle barbecue baby-back ribs, and a spicy chorizo meat loaf on focaccia with brown gravy. They'll custom-mix your margarita with fresh lime and lemon juice and blend it with your choice of some 35 tequilas. There's a late-night menu for the after 10 PM crowd. ⊠ *3313 N. Hayden Rd., Central Scottsdale* ☎ *480/970–8164* ▤ *AE, D, MC, V.*

★ ¢–$$ ✕ **Los Sombreros Mexican Cantina.** Los Sombreros has moved to a converted brick home with lovely patio seating in Scottsdale, and the new location is as enticing as the freshly-prepared food. Chef-owner Jeffrey Smedstad creates dishes not found in typical Mexican restaurants. Start with the smoked salmon tostada, a crisp corn tortilla spread with cream cheese and chipotle chile, then topped with smoked salmon. Entrées include lamb *adobo,* a shank braised in a piquant sauce of ancho chiles, garlic, and cinnamon. Ice creams are house-made, and there's a *tamal de chocolate* made with Mexican chocolate, sugar, and ground almonds. Los Sombreros also serves the best flan you'll find this side of Mexico City. ⊠ *2534 N. Scottsdale Rd., South Scottsdale* ☎ *480/994–1799* ▤ *AE, D, DC, MC, V* ⊘ *Closed Mon. No lunch.*

Pan-Asian

$$$ ✕ **Restaurant Hapa.** Hapa, meaning "half" in Hawaiian, is a salute to the Asian-American ancestry of chef-owner James McDevitt. The Pan-Asian contemporary fare served in the minimalist dining room has received national recognition and with good reason. McDevitt is masterful at fusing exotic flavors and textures and wrapping them into such offerings as skillet-roasted mussels in a Thai-style coconut broth scented with lemongrass, mint, basil, and ginger, or into the superb house specialty—beef tenderloin brushed with hot mustard and caramelized sugar. ⊠ *6204 N. Scottsdale Rd., Central Scottsdale* ☎ *480/998–8220* ▤ *AE, MC, V* ⊘ *Closed Sun. No lunch.*

FodorśChoice ★

Pizza

¢–$ ✕ **Nello's.** Leave it to two guys from Chicago to come up with some of the best pizza in the Valley. The motto is "In Crust We Trust," and Nello's excels in both thin-crust and deep-dish pies. Try the traditional varieties heaped with homemade sausage and mushrooms, or go vegetarian with the spinach pie, which is piled with fresh spinach, mozzarella, and feta. There's even a seafood pizza prepared with white sauce and Alaskan king crab. Pasta entrées are also good, and the huge, family-style salads are inventive and fresh. A rather plain and noisy atmosphere is all forgiven when you've been greeted by the friendly waitstaff and sunken your teeth into the award-winning pizza. ⊠ *8658 E. Shea Blvd., North Scottsdale* ☎ *480/922–5335* ▤ *AE, MC, V* ⊘ *Closed Mon.*

Seafood

$$–$$$$ ✕ **Salt Cellar.** It's rare to find a restaurant in a cellar, especially in the desert. Originally an ASU hamburger joint with concrete walls and floors, the space has been transformed with crisp linen tablecloths and nautical decor. The kitchen dishes out straightforward, fresh seafood. For starters try Chesapeake Bay crab cakes, oysters Rockefeller, or tur-

tle soup. Then move on to well-prepared entrées such as Idaho trout, Yakimono Hawaiian ahi, or charcoal-broiled king salmon. If you're really hungry, splurge on a gigantic 5-pound Maine lobster. ⊠ *550 N. Hayden Rd., South Scottsdale* ☎ *480/947–1963* ▤ *AE, D, DC, MC, V* ⊗ *Closed Mon. No lunch.*

Southwestern

$$–$$$ ✕ **Old Town Tortilla Factory.** Aside from the tasty Sonoran cuisine and the best homemade tortillas in Scottsdale, the draw here is the location in a historic adobe home in the heart of Old Town Scottsdale. Hundred-year-old pecan trees shade the large flagstone patio, which is the spot for alfresco dining or for sipping a margarita made with one of the premium tequilas. Signature dishes include ancho raspberry–encrusted pork chops and Shawnee sea bass—pan-seared and served with a rock shrimp and cheese quesadilla, topped with shoestring sweet potatoes. Save room for dessert: the banana crisp wrapped in a sweet tortilla with blackberry compote is out of this world. ⊠ *6910 E. Main St., Downtown Scottsdale* ☎ *480/945–4567* ▤ *AE, D, DC, MC, V* ⊗ *No lunch.*

Spanish

$$$$ ✕ **Marquesa.** Polished marble, antiques, and floor-to-ceiling oil paintings
Fodor'sChoice adorn this Spanish colonial–style dining room in the Fairmont Scottsdale
★ Princess Resort. Herbs and flavors indigenous to northeast Spain season such appetizers as *anec d' Napoléon,* phyllo dough pouches stuffed with duck, foie gras, and mushrooms. Main courses include expertly prepared seafood, meats, and poultry; however, the real triumph is the paella, bursting with lobster, chicken, mussels, shrimp, escargots, pork, and mussels. Marquesa also serves a wonderful market-style Sunday brunch that can be enjoyed alfresco on the garden patio. ⊠ *Fairmont Scottsdale Princess Resort, 7575 E. Princess Dr., North Scottsdale* ☎ *480/585–4848* ⩘ *Reservations essential* ▤ *AE, D, DC, MC, V* ⊗ *No lunch.*

Steak

$$$ ✕ **Don & Charlie's.** A favorite with major-leaguers in town for spring training, this venerable chophouse specializes in prime-grade steak and baseball memorabilia—the walls are covered with pictures, autographs, and uniforms. The New York sirloin, prime rib, and double-thick lamb chops are a hit; sides include au gratin potatoes and creamed spinach. Serious carnivores will not strike out here. ⊠ *7501 E. Camelback Rd., Camelback Corridor* ☎ *480/990–0900* ▤ *AE, D, DC, MC, V* ⊗ *No lunch.*

$$–$$$$ ✕ **Morton's of Chicago.** The Windy City chain is famous for exceptional service, immense steaks, and entertaining tableside presentations, but most of all for consistency. If you've been hankerin' for a great aged prime steak, you won't go wrong here. The monstrous 24-ounce porterhouse or 14-ounce double-cut fillet can satisfy the hungriest cowpoke. The seafood is excellent, too, but plays second fiddle to the beef. ⊠ *15233 N. Kierland Blvd., North Scottsdale* ☎ *480/951–4440* ⩘ *Reservations essential* ▤ *AE, D, DC, MC, V* ⊗ *No lunch.*

Thai

$–$$ ✕ **Malee's on Main.** This fashionable, casual eatery in the heart of Scottsdale's Main Street Arts District serves sophisticated, Thai-inspired fare.

The *ahoi phannee* is a medley of seafood in a bamboo-leaf bowl moistened with red curry sauce, coconut, lime leaf, and Thai basil. The Thai barbecued chicken is grilled to a sizzle and coated with rum. Everything is made to order here, so you specify the spiciness—from mild to flaming. But even the "mild" dishes have a bite. ⊠ *7131 E. Main St., Downtown Scottsdale* ☎ *480/947–6042* ⊕ *www.maleesonmain.com* ⊟ *AE, DC, MC, V* ⊘ *No lunch Sun.*

East Valley: Tempe, Mesa, Chandler

American

$–$$$ ✕ **Landmark.** In a 1908 building that was originally a Mormon church, this family-run restaurant serves the kind of all-American home cooking that Norman Rockwell would've loved. The dining room, decorated with lace curtains, chandeliers, and white linens, looks like it could be a backdrop for one of his paintings. The food is straightforward and comfy—roast turkey, chicken potpie, fried chicken, and baked fish. However, the real draw is the salad *room,* probably the largest salad bar you'll ever see, featuring nearly 100 items that include soups, breads, salad fixings, and hot dishes. Don't forget to save room for apple pie with a slice of cheddar on top. ⊠ *809 W. Main St., Mesa* ☎ *480/962–4652* ⊟ *AE, D, MC, V* ⊘ *No lunch Sun.*

¢–$ ✕ **Four Peaks Brewing Company.** The redbrick, historic Bordens Creamery is the location for this college-town hangout. Ten different brews—such as 8th Street Ale and Kilt Lifter Scottish Amber—are on tap. Pub grub, pizza, and burgers fill the menu. If you like beer, burgers, and noise, this is the next best thing to being at the game on a Sunday during football season. ⊠ *1340 E. 8th St., Tempe* ☎ *480/303–9967* ⊟ *AE, D, DC, MC, V.*

Chinese

$–$$ ✕ **C-Fu Gourmet.** This is serious Chinese food, the kind you'd expect to find on Mott Street in New York City's Chinatown or Grant Avenue in San Francisco. C-Fu's specialty is fish, and you can see several species in big holding tanks. Shrimp are fished out of the tank, steamed, and bathed in a potent garlic sauce. Clams in black-bean sauce and tilapia in a ginger-scallion sauce also hit all the right buttons. If you don't find what you're looking for on the menu, tell them what you want and they'll make it. There's a daily dim sum brunch, too. ⊠ *2051 W. Warner Rd., Chandler* ☎ *480/899–3888* ⊟ *AE, D, MC, V.*

Contemporary

$$–$$$ ✕ **House of Tricks.** There's nothing up the sleeves of Robert and Robin Trick, who work magic on their eclectic menu emphasizing the freshest available seafood. The appetizer list is known for its offbeat creations, such as cheese and avocado blintzes and stuffed grape leaves in chipotle plum sauce. Main dishes are just as clever. The roasted eggplant–and–goat cheese lasagna and grilled rack of pork with jalapeño-orange marmalade, scallops, saffron, and Pernod get high marks. An old elm tree towers over the outdoor bar and patio at this intimate restaurant converted from a 1920s home. ⊠ *114 E. 7th St., Tempe* ☎ *480/ 968–1114* ⊟ *AE, D, MC, V* ⊘ *Closed Sun.*

French

★ **$$–$$$** ✕ **Citrus Cafe.** Elegant yet casual, this small restaurant does everything right to create an inviting atmosphere, from the romantic candlelit dining room to a daily menu featuring what's freshest from the market (it's written out on a board). For starters, try the baked Brie with almonds and apples or the superb leek-and-potato soup. The main dishes are pure French comfort food: veal kidneys, sweetbreads, leg of lamb, roast pork, and occasionally even rabbit. ✉ *2330 N. Alma School Rd., Chandler* ☎ *480/899–0502* ▤ *AE, D, DC, MC, V* ☾ *Closed Mon. No lunch.*

Mexican

⟲ **¢–$** ✕ **Rosa's Mexican Grill.** This festive, family-friendly restaurant summons up images of a Baja beach taqueria. The tacos are Rosa's true glory: beef, pork, and chicken are marinated in fruit juices and herbs for 12 hours, slowly oven-baked for another 10, then shredded and charbroiled. The fish taco, pepped up with cabbage, radishes, and lime, is also in a class by itself. Spoon on one of Rosa's five fresh homemade salsas. But beware the fiery habanero version—it can strip the enamel right off your teeth. ✉ *328 E. University Dr., Mesa* ☎ *480/964–5451* ▤ *No credit cards* ☾ *Closed Sun. and Mon.*

Middle Eastern

¢–$ ✕ **Tasty Kabob.** The Middle Eastern food here is heavily seasoned, but never spicy hot. Perfumed basmati rice is often teamed with several grilled kabobs—skewers of ground beef, lamb, chicken, or beef tenderloin. The stews, called *khoresht* and *polo,* give you a taste of authentic Persian fare. If *baghali polo*—dill-infused rice tossed with lima beans and lamb shank—is on the menu, don't hesitate to order it. ✉ *1250 E. Apache Blvd., Tempe* ☎ *480/966–0260* ▤ *AE, D, MC, V* ☾ *Closed Mon.*

Vietnamese

¢–$$ ✕ **Cyclo.** It's always exciting to find an outstanding one-of-a-kind restaurant in a town filled with corporate-chain establishments. Cyclo is just that. Friendly and gracious owner Justina Dwong is as much a draw as the well-prepared Vietnamese food. Try the *bánh xéo,* a crispy, tumeric-yellow crepe filled with juicy bites of pork and shrimp, or crispy *cha gío,* a spicy lemongrass chicken. A French-inspired, jasmine-scented crème brûlée provides a perfect ending to the meal. ✉ *1919 W. Chandler Blvd., Chandler* ☎ *480/963–4490* ▤ *AE, D, MC, V* ☾ *Closed Sun.*

West Valley: West Phoenix, Glendale, Litchfield Park

Chinese

★ **$$** ✕ **Silver Dragon.** This is one of the best Chinese restaurants in town—as long as you order properly. Insist on sitting in the big room to the left as you walk in the door, and ask for the Chinese menu (it has brief English descriptions). Your boldness will be rewarded with some of the best Hong Kong–style Chinese fare between the two coasts. Crispy Hong Kong–Style Chicken is a plump whole bird steamed, flash-fried, and cut into bite-size pieces. Hot-pot dishes, noodles, fish, and vegetarian dishes—the Buddhist-style rolls are outstanding—make it hard to eat

Chinese food anyplace else in the Valley. ⊠ *8946 N. 19th Ave., West Phoenix* ☎ *602/674–0151* ⊟ *AE, D, MC, V* ☻ *No lunch Sat.*

German

$–$$ ✕ **Haus Murphy's.** On weekends, kick back with the accordionist at this charming storefront restaurant in downtown Glendale. Schnitzel is a specialty, especially the spicy paprika version, teamed with crispy chunks of fried potatoes and green beans. Sauerbraten, paired with tart red cabbage and two huge potato dumplings, is not for the faint of appetite. Wash everything down with a German beer—there are eight on tap—and save room for the homemade apple strudel and hazelnut torte. ⊠ *5819 W. Glendale Ave., Glendale* ☎ *623/939–2480* ⊟ *AE, D, MC, V.*

Mexican

¢–$ ✕ **Lily's Cafe.** Friendly mom-and-pop proprietors, a jukebox with south-of-the-border hits, and low-priced, fresh Mexican fare have kept patrons coming here for almost 50 years. Beef is the featured ingredient. The chimichanga is stuffed with tender beef and covered with cheese, guacamole, and sour cream. Fragrant tamales, spunky red-chile beef, and chiles rellenos right out of the fryer also shine. ⊠ *6706 N. 58th Dr., Glendale* ☎ *623/937–7757* ⌕ *Reservations not accepted* ⊟ *No credit cards* ☻ *Closed Mon., Tues., and Aug.*

¢–$ ✕ **Pepe's Taco Villa.** The neighborhood's not fancy, and neither is this restaurant. But in a town filled with gringo-ized, south-of-the-border fare, this is the real deal. Tacos *rancheros*—spicy, shredded pork pungently lathered with adobo paste—are a dream. So are the green-corn tamales, *machacado* (air-dried beef), and chiles rellenos. But don't leave here without trying the sensational mole, a rich, exotic sauce fashioned from chiles and chocolate. ⊠ *2108 W. Camelback Rd., West Phoenix* ☎ *602/242–0379* ⊟ *No credit cards* ☻ *Closed Tues.*

Southwestern

$$–$$$$ ✕ **Arizona Kitchen.** With the help of a historian of Native American foods, the chef here has put together a bold Southwestern menu. Appetizers such as blue corn *piki* rolls, stuffed with capon and goat cheese, and the wild boar Anasazi bean chile give you an indication of what's to come. Entrées include grilled sirloin of buffalo and venison medallions in a blackberry-zinfandel cocoa sauce. For dessert, try the chile-spiked ice cream in the striking turquoise "bowl" of hardened sugar. It's worth the 20-minute drive from downtown Phoenix to the Wigwam Resort. ⊠ *Wigwam Resort, 300 E. Wigwam Blvd., Litchfield Park* ☎ *623/935–3811* ⊕ *www.wigwamresort.com* ⊟ *AE, D, DC, MC, V* ☻ *Closed Mon.*

Vietnamese

$–$$ ✕ **Pho Bang.** What makes this little hole-in-the-wall restaurant so appealing—aside from price—is the simplicity and freshness of the food: rice, noodles, vegetables, beef, seafood, pork, and chicken. The house specialty is *tom va bo nuong vi* (#35 on the menu): the server brings three plates, one with transparently thin slices of marinated beef and raw shrimp; another with piles of mint, lettuce, cilantro, pickled leeks, cucumber, and carrot; and the last with rice paper. You fire up the portable grill and cook the beef and shrimp. When they're done, combine with the veggies, fold into rice paper, and start dunking. ⊠ *1702 W. Camelback Rd., West Phoenix* ☎ *602/433–9440* ⌘ *Reservations not accepted* ▭ *MC, V.*

WHERE TO STAY

The Valley of the Sun has long been the domain of resorts. Historic resorts, including the Arizona Biltmore, Camelback Inn, and Royal Palms—all in Phoenix and Paradise Valley—are still among the Valley's most popular getaways. Most others are in the neighboring, tourist-friendly city of Scottsdale.

Competition among the newest megaresorts is fierce. The properties vie for family and leisure business with immaculately manicured golf courses and incredible water features. The Valley of the Sun is carpeted with green and, surprisingly, filled with water. Rivers, large waterfalls, lakes, slides, pools, and even canals replete with gondolas put the humble hotel pool to shame. Superlatives like biggest, tallest, longest, twistiest, and wettest are bandied back and forth—at resorts, not theme parks. The resorts come in all shapes and sizes. Some of the properties consist of a large main hotel, but others are spread out in casitas (little houses) surrounding the golf courses.

Most downtown Phoenix properties are business and family hotels, closer to the heart of the city—and to the average vacationer's budget. Many properties cater to corporate travelers during the week but lower their rates on weekends to entice leisure travelers. Ask about weekend specials when making reservations. For a true Western experience, guest-ranch territory is 60 mi northwest, in the town of Wickenburg.

Many people flee snow and ice to bask in the warmth of the Valley. As a result, winter is the high season, peaking in January through March. Summer season—mid-May through the end of September—is giveaway time, when a night at one of the fanciest resorts often goes for half of the winter price.

With more than 55,000 hotel rooms in the metro area, you can take your pick of anything from a luxurious resort to a guest ranch to an extended-stay hotel.

WHAT IT COSTS				
$$$$	**$$$**	**$$**	**$**	**¢**
FOR 2 PEOPLE over $250	$175–$250	$120–$175	$70–$120	under $70

Prices are for two people in a standard double room in high season.

Downtown Phoenix

$$$$ ▦ **Wyndham Phoenix.** When Wyndham took over this former Crowne Plaza in 2003, the chain immediately invested $6 million into renovations. It sits in the center of bustling Copper Square within 1 mi of Heritage and Science Parks, America West Arena, Bank One Ballpark, and the Arizona Center. Rooms have high-speed Internet, large desks, and ergonomic desk chairs. Although this hotel is geared primarily toward business travelers, children under 18 stay free with parents. Rascal's Comedy Club books stand-up comedy shows on weekends. ⊠ *50 E. Adams St., Downtown Phoenix, 85004* ☎ *602/333–0000* ⊕ *www.wyndham. com* ⇆ *445 room, 87 suites* ⚭ *Restaurant, room service, in-room data ports, some refrigerators, cable TV with movies, pool, gym, hair salon, sauna, bar, comedy club, shop, laundry service, Internet, business services, airport shuttle, car rental, parking (fee), no-smoking rooms* ⊟ *AE, D, MC, V.*

$$–$$$$ ▦ **Hyatt Regency Phoenix.** A quintessential Hyatt, this convention-oriented hotel efficiently handles the arrival and departure of hundreds of business travelers each day. The seven-story atrium has huge sculptures, colorful tapestries, potted plants, and comfortable seating areas. Rooms are spacious, but be aware that the atrium roof blocks east views on floors 8 through 10. There's a revolving restaurant with panoramic views of the Phoenix area. ⊠ *122 N. 2nd St., Downtown Phoenix, 85004* ☎ *602/252–1234* 🗈 *602/254–9472* ⊕ *www.hyatt.com* ⇆ *667 rooms, 45 suites* ⚭ *4 restaurants, in-room data ports, cable TV with movies, pool, wading pool, gym, outdoor hot tub, 2 bars, concierge, business services, meeting rooms, car rental, parking (fee), no-smoking rooms* ⊟ *AE, D, DC, MC, V.*

$–$$ ▦ **Hotel San Carlos.** Built in 1928 in an Italian Renaissance design, the seven-story San Carlos is the only historic hotel still operating in downtown Phoenix. Among other distinctions, the San Carlos was the Southwest's first air-conditioned hotel, and suites bear the names of such movie-star guests as Marilyn Monroe and Spencer Tracy. Big-band music, wall tapestries, Austrian crystal chandeliers, shiny copper elevators, and an accommodating staff transport you to a more genteel era. The rooms are snug by modern standards but have attractive period furnishings and coffeemakers. ⊠ *202 N. Central Ave., Downtown Phoenix, 85004* ☎ *602/253–4121 or 800/678–8946* 🗈 *602/253–6668* ⊕ *www. hotelsancarlos.com* ⇆ *133 rooms* ⚭ *In-room data ports, cable TV with movies, pool, dry cleaning, laundry service, meeting rooms, parking (fee), no-smoking rooms* ⊟ *AE, D, DC, MC, V.*

Central Phoenix

$$$–$$$$ ▦ **Hilton Suites.** This practical hotel is a model of excellent design within tight limits. It sits off Central Avenue, 2 mi north of downtown amid the Central Corridor cluster of office towers. The marble-floor, pillared lobby opens into an 11-story atrium containing palm trees, natural boulder fountains, glass elevators, and a lantern-lit café. Each suite has an exercise bike and a large walk-through bathroom between the living room and bedroom. A complimentary beverage reception in the evening and full breakfast make this hotel an outstanding value. ⊠ *10 E. Thomas Rd., Central Phoenix, 85012* ☎ *602/222–1111* 🗈 *602/ 265–4841* ⊕ *www.hilton.com* ⇆ *226 suites* ⚭ *Restaurant, room service, in-room data ports, kitchenettes, cable TV with movies and video games, in-room VCRs, indoor pool, exercise equipment, gym, hot tub, sauna, bar, shop, laundry facilities, laundry service, concierge, business*

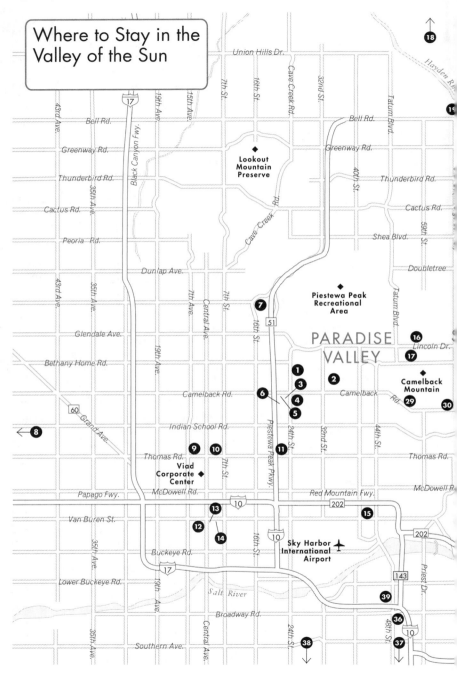

Where to Stay in the Valley of the Sun

101

22

↑

0   4 miles

0   6 km

Scottsdale Rd.

Pima Rd.

21

Rhodes Aqueduct

20

19

Scottsdale
Municipal
Airport

✈

Frank Lloyd Wright Blvd.

64th St. (Invergordon Rd.)

Scottsdale Rd.

Hayden Rd.

104th St.

23

Shea Blvd.

24

96th St.

Ranch Rd.

25

26

27

SCOTTSDALE

Indian Bend Rd.

McDonald Dr.

28

32

31

33

Indian School Rd.

87

Alma School Rd.

96th St.

Beeline Hwy.

Mesa Dr.

McKellips Rd.

Salt River

Country Club Rd.

Brown Rd.

MESA

34

University Dr.

Scottsdale Rd.

Hayden Rd.

Rd.

Apache Blvd.

35

Main St.

Broadway Rd.

Cooper Rd.

Gilbert Rd.

Mill Ave.

Rural Rd.

TEMPE

101

Dobson Rd.

87

Superstition Fwy.

60

Phoenix & Paradise Valley ▼

Doubletree Phoenix
Gateway Center Suites **15**

Embassy Suites
Phoenix Airport West **11**

Hampton Inn Airport **39**

Hermosa Inn **2**

Hilton Suites **10**

Hotel San Carlos **12**

Hyatt Regency Phoenix **14**

JW Marriott's Camelback Inn ... **16**

JW Marriott Desert Ridge **18**

Pointe Hilton at Squaw Peak ... **7**

Pointe South
Mountain Resort **37**

Sanctuary on
Camelback Mountain **17**

Sheraton Wild Horse Pass ... **38**

Sunshine Hotel & Suites **9**

Wyndham Phoenix **13**

Camelback Corridor ▼

Arizona Biltmore **1**

Courtyard Phoenix
Camelback **5**

Homewood Suites **6**

Phoenix Inn Suites Phoenix ... **3**

Ritz-Carlton **4**

Royal Palms **29**

Scottsdale ▼

Comfort Inn **24**

Country Inn & Suites **23**

Fairmont Scottsdale Princess ... **21**

Four Seasons Scottsdale
at Troon North **22**

Gainey Suites Hotel **26**

Hampton Inn & Suites **20**

Hotel Waterfront Ivy **28**

Hyatt Regency Scottsdale at
Gainey Ranch **25**

James Hotel Scottsdale **33**

Motel 6 Scottsdale **32**

The Phoenician **30**

Radisson Resort and Spa **26**

Ramada Ltd. Scottsdale **31**

Westin Kierland **19**

Tempe & Chandler ▼

Tempe Mission Palms Hotel ... **34**

Twin Palms Hotel **35**

Wyndham Buttes Resort **36**

Litchfield Park ▼

Wigwam Resort **8**

services, free parking, some pets allowed, no-smoking rooms ⊟ *AE, D, DC, MC, V* ⦿| *BP.*

$$–$$$ ⊡ **Embassy Suites Phoenix Airport West.** Just minutes from downtown, this four-story all-suites hotel has lush palms and olive trees surrounding bubbling fountains and a sunken pool in its enclosed atrium. Complimentary breakfast (cooked to order) and an evening social hour are offered in the spacious atrium lounge. Suites have hair dryers, irons and ironing boards, and kitchenettes. ⊠ *2333 E. Thomas Rd., Central Phoenix, 85016* ☎ *602/957–1910* 🖷 *602/955–2861* ⦿ *www.embassy- suites.com* ⌕ *183 suites ⟁ Restaurant, kitchenettes, cable TV, pool, gym, hot tub, lounge, laundry service, airport shuttle, free parking, no-smok- ing rooms* ⊟ *AE, D, DC, MC, V* ⦿| *BP.*

$ ⊡ **Sunshine Hotel & Suites.** The 1½-acre Getaway Lagoon at the Sunshine Hotel Suites is ringed by exotic palms and bamboo. Rooms and public areas are simply furnished; the VIP floor offers cabana suites and a private rooftop pool with views of downtown's ever-changing skyline. Be prepared for occasional lapses in service, but at these prices, you are getting your money's worth. ⊠ *3600 N. 2nd Ave., Central Phoenix, 85013* ☎ *602/248–0222* 🖷 *602/265–6331* ⦿ *www.getawayresort.com* ⌕ *257 rooms, 23 suites ⟁ Restaurant, cable TV with movies and video games, putting green, 4 pools, gym, hot tub, basketball, shuffleboard, volleyball, bar, video-game room, playground, laundry facilities, laundry service, busi- ness services, free parking, no-smoking rooms* ⊟ *AE, D, DC, MC, V.*

Phoenix: Camelback Corridor

$$$$ ⊡ **Arizona Biltmore.** Designed by Frank Lloyd Wright's colleague Albert
Fodor'sChoice Chase McArthur, the Biltmore has been Phoenix's premier resort since
★ it opened in 1929. The lobby, with its stained-glass skylights, wrought-iron pilasters, and cozy sitting alcoves, fills with piano music each evening. Spacious guest rooms (the smallest is 400 square feet), appointed with Southwestern-print fabrics and Mission-style furniture, have a sitting area and desk. Accommodating, guest-focused staff are unobtrusive. The Biltmore sits on 39 impeccably manicured acres of cool fountains, open walkways, and colorful flower beds. ⊠ *2400 E. Missouri Ave., Camelback Corridor, 85016* ☎ *602/955–6600 or 800/950– 0086* 🖷 *602/381–7600* ⦿ *www.arizonabiltmore.com* ⌕ *720 rooms, 50 villas ⟁ 4 restaurants, in-room safes, minibars, cable TV with movies, golf privileges, miniature golf, putting green, 7 tennis courts, 8 pools, gym, hair salon, 3 outdoor hot tubs, sauna, spa, bicycles, badminton, croquet, horseshoes, lobby lounge, children's programs (ages 6–12), laun- dry service, concierge, business services, car rental, free parking, no-smok- ing rooms* ⊟ *AE, D, DC, MC, V.*

★ $$$$ ⊡ **Ritz-Carlton.** The sand-colored neo-Federal facade facing Biltmore Fash- ion Park hides a graceful luxury hotel well known for impeccable ser- vice. Large public rooms are decorated with 18th- and 19th-century European paintings and a handsome china collection. Feather and foam pillows and marble baths distinguish the guest rooms. Maid service is twice-daily. Both mountain and city vistas can be best appreciated from the rooftop terrace, where the heated pool is found. ⊠ *2401 E. Camel- back Rd., Camelback Corridor, Phoenix 85016* ☎ *602/468–0700 or 800/*

241–3333 🖷 *602/468–0793* ⊕ *www.ritzcarlton.com* ⟅ *281 rooms, 14 suites* Ꮡ *Restaurant, room service, in-room safes, refrigerators, cable TV, pool, gym, 2 saunas, bicycles, 3 bars, shop, laundry service, concierge floor, Internet, business services, meeting rooms, parking (fee), no-smoking rooms* ☱ *AE, D, DC, MC, V.*

★ **$$$$** 🖅 **Royal Palms Resort & Spa.** Once the home of Cunard Steamship executive Delos T. Cooke, this Mediterranean-style resort has a stately row of the namesake palms at its entrance, courtyards with antique fountains, and individually designed rooms. The deluxe casitas are each done in a different style—trompe l'oeil, romantic retreat, Spanish colonial—by members of the American Society of Interior Designers. The restaurant, T. Cook's, is renowned in the Valley, and the bi-level, open-air Alzadora Spa has every imaginable amenity, including an outdoor rain shower. ⊠ *5200 E. Camelback Rd., Camelback Corridor, 85018* 🕾 *602/840–3610 or 800/672–6011* 🖷 *602/840–6927* ⊕ *www. royalpalmshotel.com* ⟅ *34 rooms, 35 suites, 45 casitas* ᏑᏑ *Restaurant, room service, in-room safes, refrigerators, cable TV, golf privileges, tennis court, pool, gym, spa, bicycles, croquet, hiking, bar, laundry service, business services, meeting rooms, parking (fee), no-smoking rooms* ☱ *AE, D, DC, MC, V.*

$$$ 🖅 **Phoenix Inn Suites Phoenix.** The Phoenix representative of this Arizona chain is a remarkable bargain, considering it has amenities not generally seen in properties of the same price category—including leather love seats in each room. Local calls and high-speed Internet access are free, and several rooms have corner jetted tubs. The three-story hotel is a block off a popular stretch of Camelback Road. ⊠ *2310 E. Highland Ave., Camelback Corridor, 85016* 🕾 *602/956–5221 or 800/956–5221* 🖷 *602/ 468–7220* ⊕ *www.phoenixinn.com* ⟅ *120 suites* ᏑᏑ *In-room data ports, some in-room hot tubs, microwaves, refrigerators, cable TV with movies, pool, gym, hair salon, hot tub, shop, laundry facilities, no-smoking rooms* ☱ *AE, D, DC, MC, V* ⍥ *CP.*

$–$$$ 🖅 **Homewood Suites Phoenix-Biltmore.** This all-suites chain is a major value, especially considering its location in the heart of the upscale Biltmore District. Suites have a spacious living and working area with a sleeper-sofa and one or two separate bedrooms; each has a full kitchen. From Monday to Thursday evening there's a "manager's reception," a minifeast featuring anything from a taco bar to baked potatoes with all the trimmings. Guests also get free passes to a nearby fitness club and transportation within a 5-mi radius of the hotel. ⊠ *2001 E. Highland Ave., Camelback Corridor, 85016* 🕾 *602/508–0937* 🖷 *602/508–0854* ⊕ *www. homewood-suites.com* ⟅ *124 rooms* ᏑᏑ *In-room data ports, kitchens, cable TV with movies, pool, gym, laundry facilities, laundry service, no-smoking rooms* ☱ *AE, D, DC, MC, V* ⍥ *BP.*

$$ 🖅 **Courtyard Phoenix Camelback.** Public areas in this four-story hotel are mostly glass and tile, filled with plenty of greenery. Rooms are equipped with complimentary coffee as well as irons and ironing boards. A lap pool and Jacuzzi await in the landscaped courtyard. You won't go hungry staying here—there's a small café on premises that serves breakfast, lunch, and dinner or, if you prefer, there are more than 50 restaurants within a 1½-mi radius. ⊠ *2101 E. Camelback Rd., Camelback Corri-*

dor, 85016 ☎ *602/955–5200 or 800/321–2211* 🖨 *602/955–1101* ⊕ *www.marriott.com* ⇨ *155 rooms, 12 suites* ⚹ *Restaurant, in-room data ports, some microwaves, some refrigerators, cable TV with movies, pool, gym, hot tub, bar, laundry facilities, laundry service, meeting rooms, free parking* ☰ *AE, D, DC, MC, V.*

North Phoenix

☾ **\$\$\$\$** 🖾 **JW Marriott Desert Ridge Resort & Spa.** The Valley's newest resort and Arizona's largest is in the burgeoning northeastern corridor. The immense entryway has floor-to-ceiling windows that allow the sandstone lobby, the Sonoran Desert, and the resort's amazing water features to meld together in a single prospect. Four acres of water fun include the "lazy river," where you can flop on an inner tube and float the day away, and there are two golf courses. Rooms have balconies or patios. Roy Yamaguchi's newest Phoenix restaurant is just one of nine eateries vying for attention on the property. ✉ *5350 E. Marriott Dr., 85054* ☎ *480/293– 5000 or 888/236–2427* 🖨 *480/905–0032* ⊕ *www.marriott.com* ⇨ *870 rooms, 80 suites* ⚹ *9 restaurants, coffee shop, room service, in-room data ports, in-room safes, minibars, some refrigerators, cable TV with movies, 2 18-hole golf courses, 8 tennis courts, 5 pools, hair salon, spa, 2 lounges, shops, baby-sitting, children's programs (ages 5–12), Internet, business services, meeting rooms, free parking, no-smoking rooms* ☰ *AE, D, DC, MC, V.*

☾ **\$\$\$–\$\$\$\$** 🖾 **Pointe Hilton at Squaw Peak.** The real highlight of the Squaw Peak, the more family-oriented of the two Pointe Hiltons in Phoenix, is a 9-acre recreation area known as the Hole-in-the-Wall River Ranch. It has swimming pools fed by man-made waterfalls, a 130-foot water slide, and a 1,000-foot "river" that winds past a miniature golf course, tennis courts, outdoor decks, and artificial buttes with stunning mountain vistas. Accommodations in the pink-stucco buildings vary in size from standard two-room suites to a grand three-bedroom house; all have two or more TVs and balconies. The resort is adjacent to the Phoenix Mountain Preserve, making it an ideal base for hiking and biking trips. ✉ *7677 N. 16th St., North-Central Phoenix, 85020* ☎ *602/997–2626 or 800/ 876–4683* 🖨 *602/997–2391* ⊕ *www.pointehilton.com* ⇨ *431 suites, 130 casitas, 1 house* ⚹ *3 restaurants, some kitchens, minibars, cable TV, golf privileges, miniature golf, 3 tennis courts, 7 pools, gym, spa, mountain bikes, hiking, Ping-Pong, 2 lounges, shops, children's programs (ages 6–12), meeting rooms, parking (fee), no-smoking rooms* ☰ *AE, D, DC, MC, V.*

Near Sky Harbor Airport

\$\$\$ 🖾 **Doubletree Phoenix Gateway Center Suites.** In the Gateway Center, just 1½ mi north of the airport, this honeycomb of six-story towers is the best of a dozen choices for anyone who just wants to get off the plane and into a comfortable, central hotel. Vacationers, beware: bedroom furnishings definitely cater to the corporate crowd who are traveling light— two-drawer credenzas serve as bureaus, and dinky wardrobes function as closets. ✉ *320 N. 44th St., Airport, 85008* ☎ *602/225–0500* 🖨 *602/*

225–0957 ⊕ *www.doubletree.com* ⟳ *242 suites ⚴ Restaurant, room service, in-room data ports, microwaves, refrigerators, cable TV with movies, pool, gym, sauna, bar, laundry facilities, laundry service, Internet, meeting rooms, free parking, airport shuttle, no-smoking rooms* ▭ *AE, D, DC, MC, V* ⦿ *BP.*

$–$$ ⊞ **Hampton Inn Phoenix-Airport Tempe.** More affordable than many of the other airport options, this four-story hotel is 5 mi from downtown. Rooms are moderate in size and appointed with handsome armoires and bright-colored prints for drapes and bedspreads. Free continental breakfast is available in the lobby, where a good-size TV is tuned to the local wake-up news show. Take advantage of free local calls and the hotel airport shuttle, running from 5 AM to midnight. ⊠ *4234 S. 48th St., Tempe, 85040* ☎ *602/438–8688 or 800/426–7866* 🖷 *602/431–8339* ⊕ *www. hamptoninn.com* ⟳ *130 rooms, 4 suites ⚴ Restaurant, refrigerators, cable TV with movies, in-room VCRs, pool, gym, hot tub, bar, laundry facilities, laundry service, meeting rooms, airport shuttle, free parking, no-smoking rooms* ▭ *AE, D, DC, MC, V* ⦿ *CP.*

South Phoenix

☾ $$$–$$$$ ⊞ **Pointe South Mountain Resort.** This all-suites resort next to South Mountain Park was spiffed up in 2003, adding a redesigned golf course and the largest water park in Arizona. At the Oasis, you can tube down a river, splash in the wave pool, or zoom down the nation's tallest water slide. When you've had your fill of the wet and wild, there's a four-story sports center, golf, tennis, horseback riding, and mountain biking. Each suite has two TVs and a sofa bed. For an extra $15 a night per suite, you can have up to four kids in the room. ⊠ *7777 S. Pointe Pkwy., South Phoenix, 85044* ☎ *602/438–9000 or 877/800–4888* 🖷 *602/431–6535* ⊕ *www.pointesouthmtn.com* ⟳ *640 suites ⚴ 6 restaurants, room service, in-room data ports, minibars, 18-hole golf course, 10 tennis courts, pro shop, 6 pools, health club, hair salon, sauna, mountain bikes, hiking, horseback riding, racquetball, volleyball, laundry facilities, meeting rooms, free parking* ▭ *AE, D, DC, MC, V.*

$$$–$$$$ ⊞ **Sheraton Wild Horse Pass Resort & Spa.** The grounds of the Gila River Indian community, 11 mi south of Sky Harbor airport, shelter this resort from the hustle and bustle of the city. The culture and heritage of the Pima and Maricopa tribes are reflected in every aspect of the property. Guest rooms are detailed with Native art and textiles, and Kai (Pima for "seed") Restaurant combines Southwestern- and Native-culinary traditions. A 2½ mi replica of the the Gila River meanders throughout the property; you can take a boat ride to the Whirlwind Golf Clubhouse or to nearby Wild Horse Pass Casino. The Koli Equestrian Center organizes horseback rides, hayrides, and even cattle drives and rodeos. Keep your eyes open, and you might just catch a glimpse of the wild horses for which the resort is named. ⊠ *5594 W. Wild Horse Pass Blvd., Chandler 85070* ☎ *602/225–0100 or 800/325–3535* 🖷 *602/225–0300* ⊕ *www.wildhorsepassresort.com* ⟳ *474 rooms, 26 suites ⚴ 4 restaurants, in-room data ports, in-room safes, minibars, cable TV with movies, 2 18-hole golf courses, 2 tennis courts, 4 pools, gym, hair salon, spa, boating, hiking, horseback riding, 2 lounges, casino, children's* *programs (ages 5–12), laundry service, Internet, business services, meeting rooms, free parking, no smoking rooms* ☰ *AE, D, DC, MC, V.*

Paradise Valley

★ **$$$$** ⊞ **JW Marriott's Camelback Inn Resort, Golf Club & Spa.** This historic resort is a swank spot for comfort and relaxation in the gorgeous valley between Camelback and Mummy mountains. Built on 125 acres in the mid-1930s, the latilla beam buildings ooze Southwestern charm; the grounds are adorned with stunning cacti and desert flowers. Rooms are notably spacious, and seven suites even have private swimming pools. A gallery exhibits Barry Goldwater's photographs, which display a real talent with a camera. Visit one of 32 treatment rooms in the expanded spa for a para-joba body wrap or an adobe-mud purification treatment. ✉ *5402 E. Lincoln Dr., Paradise Valley 85253* ☎ *480/948–1700 or 800/242–2635* 🖷 *480/951–8469* ⊕ *www.camelbackinn.com* ⇋ *453 rooms, 27 suites* △ *6 restaurants, coffee shop, in-room fax, some kitchenettes, cable TV with movies, 2 18-hole golf courses, 6 tennis courts, 3 pools, hot tub, sauna, spa, hiking, lounge, shops, children's programs (ages 5–12), Internet, business services, meeting rooms, free parking, no-smoking rooms* ☰ *AE, D, DC, MC, V.*

★ **$$$$** ⊞ **Sanctuary on Camelback Mountain.** This luxurious boutique hotel is the only resort perched on the north slope of Camelback Mountain. Secluded, contemporary casitas are painted in desert hues; beds are covered with luxury linens and custom duvets. Bathrooms are travertine marble with elegant sinks, custom cabinetry, and roomy tubs. An infinity-edge pool, Zen meditation garden, and Asian-inspired Sanctuary Spa make this property a haven for relaxation and retreat. The hotel's restaurant, elements, is the hotspot for a martini at sunset. ✉ *5700 E. McDonald Dr., Paradise Valley 85253* ☎ *480/948–2100 or 800/245–2051* 🖷 *480/607–3386* ⊕ *www.sanctuaryoncamelback.com* ⇋ *98 casitas* △ *Restaurant, room service, in-room data ports, some kitchenettes, minibars, cable TV, 6 tennis courts, 4 pools, gym, massage, spa, bar, shop, business services, meeting rooms, free parking, no-smoking rooms* ☰ *AE, D, DC, MC, V.*

$$$–$$$$ ⊞ **Hermosa Inn.** The ranch-style lodge at the heart of this small resort
Fodor'sChoice was the home and studio of cowboy artist Lon Megargee in the 1930s;
★ today the adobe structure houses Lon's at the Hermosa, justly popular for its new American cuisine. Villas as big as private homes and individually decorated casitas hold an enviable collection of art. The Hermosa, on 6 acres of lushly landscaped desert, is a blessedly peaceful alternative to some of the larger resorts. ✉ *5532 N. Palo Cristi Rd., Paradise Valley 85253* ☎ *602/955–8614 or 800/241–1210* 🖷 *602/955–8299* ⊕ *www.hermosainn.com* ⇋ *4 villas, 3 haciendas, 22 casitas, 17 ranchos* △ *Restaurant, in-room data ports, some kitchenettes, minibars, cable TV, 3 tennis courts, pool, 2 hot tubs, massage, bar, free parking; no smoking* ☰ *AE, D, DC, MC, V* ❍ *CP.*

Scottsdale

★ ☺ **$$$$** ⊞ **Fairmont Scottsdale Princess.** Home of the TPC Stadium golf course, this resort covers 450 breathtakingly landscaped acres of desert. Willow Stream Spa, hailed as one of the top spots in the country, has a dramatic rooftop pool. Kids love the fishing pond and water slides. Rooms are Southwestern in style, with walk-around tile showers and immense closets. Service is what you'd expect at a resort of this caliber, both excellent and unobtrusive. Even pets get the royal treatment with the "Paws On Board" service: a specially designated pet room comes with treats and turn-down service. ☒ 7575 E. Princess Dr., North Scottsdale, 85255 ☎ 480/585–4848 or 800/344–4758 🖷 480/585–0091 ⊕ www. fairmont.com ☞ 650 rooms, 21 suites, 125 casitas, 75 villas ♻ 5 restaurants, some in-room data ports, in-room safe, minibars, cable TV with movies and video games, 2 18-hole golf courses, 7 tennis courts, pro shop, 5 pools, health club, spa, racquetball, squash, 3 bars, 4 shops, children's programs (ages 6–12), business services, free parking, some pets allowed, no-smoking rooms ▤ AE, D, DC, MC, V.

$$$$ ▦ **Four Seasons Scottsdale at Troon North.** This is a logical choice for serious golfers, as it's adjacent to two Troon North premier courses, where guests receive preferential tee times and free shuttle service. The resort is tucked in the shadows of Pinnacle Peak, near the Pinnacle Peak hiking trail. Large, casita-style rooms have separate sitting and sleeping areas as well as out-of-doors garden showers, fireplaces, and balconies or patios. Suites come with telescopes and star charts. A smart destination on Sunday morning is Acacia, the hotel's main restaurant, for one of the best brunches in town. ☒ 10600 E. Crescent Moon Dr., North Scottsdale, 85255 ☎ 480/515–5700 or 888/207–9696 🖷 480/515–5599 ⊕ www.fourseasons.com ☞ 210 rooms, 22 suites ♻ 3 restaurants, in-room data ports, in-room safes, minibars, cable TV, golf privileges, 4 tennis courts, 2 pools, gym, hair salon, sauna, spa, steam room, bicycles, hiking, 2 lounges, shops, children's programs (ages 5–12), laundry service, business services, meeting rooms, parking (fee), no-smoking rooms ▤ AE, D, DC, MC, V.

☺ $$$$ ▦ **Hyatt Regency Scottsdale at Gainey Ranch.** When you stay here, it's easy to imagine that you're relaxing at an oceanside resort instead of the desert. Shaded by towering palms, with manicured gardens and walking paths, you'll find water everywhere—a large pool area has waterfalls, a lagoon, and if you want, you can take a ride in a *sandolo* (small gondola). The dramatic, two-story lobby, filled with stunning Native American art, opens to outdoor conversation areas where cozy fires burn in huge stone fireplaces on cool desert nights. Large rooms with all the amenities have balconies or patios. Three golf courses will suit any duffer's fancy. ☒ 7500 E. Doubletree Ranch Rd., North Scottsdale, 85258 ☎ 480/991–3388 or 800/233–1234 🖷 480/483–5550 ⊕ www.hyatt.com ☞ 493 rooms, 7 casitas ♻ 4 restaurants, in-room data ports, cable TV with movies, 3 18-hole golf courses, 8 tennis courts, 10 pools, health club, hair salon, sauna, spa, bicycles, croquet, bars, children's programs (ages 6–12), concierge floor, business services, free parking, no-smoking rooms ▤ AE, D, DC, MC, V.

★ $$$$ ▦ **The Phoenician.** In a town where luxurious, expensive resorts are the rule, the Phoenician still stands apart, primarily in the realm of service. The gilded, marbled lobby with towering fountains is the backdrop for the $8 million collection of authentic Dutch masterworks. Large rooms, decorated with rattan furniture, have private patios and oversize marble bathrooms. There is a secluded tennis garden and 27 holes of premier golf. The Center for Well Being Spa has a meditation atrium and pool lined with mother of pearl tiles. Mary Elaine's is one of the finest (and most expensive) restaurants in the state. ⊠ *6000 E. Camelback Rd., Camelback Corridor, 85251* ☎ *480/941–8200 or 800/888–8234* ⊕ *www.thephoenician.com* ⟿ *581 rooms, 57 suites, 119 casitas ⚭ 4 restaurants, room service, in-room data ports, in-room safes, minibars, cable TV, 18-hole golf course, 9-hole golf course, 12 tennis courts, pro shop, 9 pools, health club, hair salon, sauna, steam room, archery, badminton, basketball, billiards, croquet, Ping-Pong, volleyball, children's programs (ages 5–12), business services, meeting rooms, parking (fee), no-smoking rooms* ⊟ *AE, D, DC, MC, V.*

$$$$ ▦ **Westin Kierland Resort & Spa.** Original artwork by Arizona artists is displayed throughout the Westin Kierland (a self-guided art walking tour brochure available). Spacious rooms in relaxing earth tones have the Westin's signature Heavenly Beds, and all have balconies or patios with views of the mountains or of the resort's water park and tubing river. Kierland Commons, within walking distance of the resort, is a planned village of upscale specialty boutiques and restaurants. ⊠ *6902 E. Greenway Pkwy., North Scottsdale, 85254* ☎ *480/624–1000* 🖶 *480/624–1001* ⊕ *www.westin.com* ⟿ *735 rooms, 63 suites, 32 casitas ⚭ 8 restaurants, in-room data ports, minibars, cable TV with movies and video games, 3 9-hole golf courses, 2 tennis courts, pro shop, 2 pools, gym, hot tub, sauna, spa, hiking, lounge, game room, children's program (ages 4–12), business services, meeting rooms, free parking, no-smoking rooms* ⊟ *AE, D, DC, MC, V.*

$$$–$$$$ ▦ **Radisson Resort and Spa.** One of the biggest and most affordable tennis resorts in Scottsdale, this hotel is the perfect match for active types who desire the facilities of a low-key, but upscale, hotel along with excellent tennis facilities. Massive fountains dominate the lobby, and the rooms have patios or balconies as well as sitting areas. Stay connected with high-speed Internet access and complimentary newspapers delivered to your door. ⊠ *7171 N. Scottsdale Rd., Central Scottsdale, 85253* ☎ *480/991–3800 or 800/333–3333* 🖶 *480/948–9843* ⊕ *www.radissonscottsdale.com* ⟿ *318 rooms, 34 suites ⚭ Restaurant, patisserie, room service, in-room data ports, minibars, cable TV with movies, golf privileges, 21 tennis courts, 3 pools, health club, hair salon, sauna, spa, steam room, volleyball, 2 bars, shop, children's programs (ages 3–11), Internet, parking (fee)* ⊟ *AE, D, DC, MC, V.*

$$–$$$$ ▦ **James Hotel Scottsdale.** On Scottsdale's Civic Center Mall, stylish James (formerly the Old Town Hotel & Conference Center) is up-to-the-minute. All rooms have pillow-top mattresses and expensive linens, as well as the latest high-tech toys, including wireless-Internet access and 42-inch plasma TVs with DVD players; there's even curbside check-in. The hotel's northern Italian restaurant, Fiamma, is a desert rendition of chef Michael White's Manhattan hotspot, and J Bar is quite the scene. James is a short stroll from the arts district and swanky 5th Avenue. ⊠ *7353 E. Indian School Rd., Downtown Scottsdale, 85251* ☎ *480/994–9203 or 866/505–2637* 🖶 *480/308–1200* ⊕ *www.*

jameshotels.com ⟿ *177 rooms, 17 suites* ⟡ *Restaurant, room service, minibars, cable TV, in-room VCRs, 2 pools, gym, outdoor hot tub, spa, bar, laundry service, Internet, business services, convention center, free parking, some pets allowed, no-smoking rooms* ⊟ *AE, D, DC, MC, V.*

☾ **$$–$$$** ▦ **Hotel Waterfront Ivy.** Near downtown shopping and attractions, the Ivy is a boutique extended-stay hotel geared to business travelers that also serves families well with its reasonably priced suites and recreational facilities. The studio guest rooms are a bit snug, but they do have minifridges and microwaves; one- and two-bedroom suites have full kitchens with dishwashers and unexpected amenities like coffee grinders and fresh coffee beans. Freebies include a full breakfast buffet; a nightly social hour with beer, wine, and munchies; fresh-baked cookies at night; and shuttle service from 8 AM to 8 PM to within 5 mi of the hotel. The pools are a bit small, but kids will enjoy them as well as the out-of-doors play area and in-room TV video games. ⊠ *7445 E. Chaparral Rd., Central Scottsdale, 85250* ☎ *480/994–5282 or 877/284–3489* ▤ *480/994–5625* ⊕ *www.hotelwaterfrontivy.com* ⟿ *25 studios, 80 suites* ⟡ *In-room data ports, in-room safes, some kitchens, some microwaves, some refrigerators, cable TV with movies and video games, 2 tennis courts, 5 pools, gym, hot tub, bicycles, playground, laundry facilities, meeting rooms* ⊟ *AE, D, DC, MC, V* ⦙◎⦙ *BP.*

$$ ▦ **Gainey Suites Hotel.** In the posh Gainey Ranch area, this independently-owned boutique hotel is a rare find in both amenities and price. Floorplans vary from studio suites for two to two-bedroom suites that sleep eight. All include such extra touches as plush pillow top mattresses and original art work on the walls. Cozy conversation areas in the lobby and an evening hors d'ouevres reception create an warm atmosphere. The hotel is directly adjacent to the Gainey Village development, which encompasses boutique shopping and upscale dining, as well as a spa. Golfers are not forgotten; the hotel can book advanced tee times at over 50 courses in the area. ⊠ *7300 East Gainey Suites Dr., North Scottsdale 85258* ☎ *480/922–6969 or 800/970–4666* ▤ *480/922–1689* ⊕ *www.gaineysuiteshotel.com* ⟿ *162 suites* ⟡ *In-room data ports, kitchens, microwaves, refrigerators, cable TV with movies and video games, golf privileges, pool, outdoor hot tub, laundry facilities, no-smoking rooms* ⊟ *AE, D, V, MC* ⦙◎⦙ *CP.*

☾ **$$** ▦ **Hampton Inn & Suites.** The Hampton Inn is within easy walking distance of restaurants and shops; plus there is complimentary shuttle service within 5 mi of the hotel. This is a newer property, and the rooms are outfitted with coffeemakers, irons, and ironing boards. Each room also has either a balcony or a patio, and there's a children's wading pool. It's a good choice for families traveling with kids or for those attending the PGA's FBR Open. ⊠ *16620 N. Scottsdale Rd., North Scottsdale, 85254* ☎ *480/348–9280* ▤ *480/348–9281* ⊕ *www.hamptoninn.com* ⟿ *126 rooms, 4 suites* ⟡ *BBQs, in-room data ports, microwaves, refrigerators, cable TV with movies, 2 pools, gym, hot tub, laundry facilities, shop, Internet, business services, free parking, no-smoking rooms* ⊟ *AE, D, DC, MC, V* ⦙◎⦙ *CP.*

☾ **$–$$** ▦ **Country Inn & Suites.** The reasonable price and prime location within one block of shops and restaurants make this national-chain outpost a great bargain. The cozy lobby has comfortable seating around a flagstone fireplace, and the guest rooms all include a bedroom and living room. Every suite has two TVs, two phones, coffeemaker, and activity table. Several specialty suites offer fireplaces and whirlpool baths. ✉ *10801 N. 89th Pl., North Scottsdale, 85260* ☎ *480/314–1200 or 800/456–4000* 📠 *480/317–7367* 🌐 *www.countryinns.com* *163 rooms* *BBQs, in-room data ports, minibars, microwaves, refrigerators, cable TV with movies and video games, 2 pools, gym, hot tub, free parking, pets allowed, no-smoking rooms* 💳 *AE, D, DC, MC, V* *CP.*

$ Fodor'sChoice ★ **Comfort Inn.** This may be one of the nicest Comfort Inns you ever lay eyes on, and it's in a quiet, upscale North Scottsdale neighborhood along the Scottsdale Road corridor. The two-story glass entryway is as welcoming as the enthusiastic staff inside. Rooms are utilitarian but clean and have irons and ironing boards and free HBO. There are several trendy restaurants and lots of shopping opportunities within easy walking distance. It's a comfortable, affordable, and family-friendly alternative in a town filled with expensive resorts. ✉ *7350 E. Gold Dust Rd., at Scottsdale Rd., North Scottsdale 85258* ☎ *480/596–6559 or 888/296–9776* 📠 *480/596–0554* 🌐 *www.comfortinn.com* *123 rooms, 3 suites* *In-room data ports, refrigerators, cable TV with movies, pool, gym, hot tub, Internet, business services, free parking, no-smoking rooms* 💳 *AE, D, DC, MC, V* *CP.*

$ **Ramada Limited Scottsdale.** There are two attractive things about this exterior-corridor, three-story motel: the location, which is within walking distance of Scottsdale's Old Town, and the price, which is hard to beat in the heart of Scottsdale. The simple but clean rooms have standard, serviceable furnishings. ✉ *6935 E. 5th Ave., Downtown Scottsdale, 85251* ☎ *480/994–9461 or 800/528–7396* 📠 *480/947–1695* 🌐 *www.ramada.com* *92 rooms* *Some microwaves, refrigerators, cable TV, pool, gym, hot tub, laundry facilities, free parking, no-smoking rooms* 💳 *AE, D, DC, MC, V* *CP.*

¢–$ **Motel 6 Scottsdale.** The best bargain in downtown Scottsdale has a small sign and is set back from the road, so it can be easy to miss. It's worth the hunt, however, because it's close to the specialty shops of 5th Avenue and Scottsdale's Civic Plaza Mall. Rooms are small and spare with few amenities, but the price is remarkable for the area. Anyway, how many Motel 6 properties have a pool surrounded by palms and rooms with a view of Camelback Mountain? ✉ *6848 E. Camelback Rd., Downtown Scottsdale, 85251* ☎ *480/946–2280 or 800/466–8356* 📠 *480/949–7583* 🌐 *www.motel6.com* *122 rooms* *In-room data ports, cable TV, pool, hot tub, free parking, some pets allowed, no-smoking rooms* 💳 *AE, D, DC, MC, V.*

East Valley: Tempe

$$–$$$ **Twin Palms Hotel.** Across the street from ASU's Gammage Auditorium and minutes from Old Town Tempe shopping, dining, and entertainment venues, this seven-story high-rise has a domed-window facade. Faux finishes creatively mask dated, textured walls in the rooms, and corner basins create more space in cramped bathrooms. Hotel guests receive free admission to facilities at the nearby ASU Recreation

Complex, with three Olympic-size pools, badminton and squash courts, and aerobics classes. ✉ *225 E. Apache Blvd., Tempe 85281* ☎ *480/ 967–9431 or 800/367–0835* 🖨 *480/303–6602* ⊕ *www.twinpalmshotel. com* ✒ *140 rooms, 1 suite △ Restaurant, room service, in-room data ports, cable TV with movies, pool, bar, laundry facilities, laundry service, concierge floor, airport shuttle, free parking, no-smoking rooms* ▭ *AE, D, DC, MC, V.*

$$–$$$ 🏨 **Wyndham Buttes Resort.** Two miles east of Sky Harbor airport, nestled in desert buttes at Interstate 10 and AZ 60, this hotel joins dramatic architecture (the lobby's back wall is the volcanic rock itself) and classic Southwest design (pine and saguaro-rib furniture, works by major regional artists) with stunning Valley views. "Radial" rooms are largest, with the widest views; inside rooms face the huge free-form pools, with waterfall, hot tubs, and poolside cantina. The elegant Top of the Rock restaurant is a definite plus. ✉ *2000 Westcourt Way, Tempe 85282* ☎ *602/ 225–9000 or 800/843–1986* 🖨 *602/438–8622* ⊕ *www.wyndham.com* ✒ *353 rooms △ 2 restaurants, in-room data ports, minibars, cable TV with movies, 4 tennis courts, 2 pools, gym, 4 hot tubs, massage, sauna, bicycles, hiking, 3 bars, shop, laundry service, concierge floor, business services, meeting rooms, some pets allowed (fee), free parking, no-smoking rooms* ▭ *AE, D, DC, MC, V.*

$–$$$ 🏨 **Tempe Mission Palms Hotel.** A handsome, casual lobby—Matisse-inspired upholstery on overstuffed chairs—and an energetic young staff set the tone at this three-story courtyard hotel. Rooms are Southwestern in style, and comfortable. Between the Arizona State University campus and Old Town Tempe, this is a particularly convenient place to stay if you're attending ASU sports and pro-football Cardinals events (the stadium is virtually next door). The hotel's Harry's Bar becomes a lively sports lounge at game time. ✉ *60 E. 5th St., Tempe 85281* ☎ *480/894– 1400 or 800/547–8705* 🖨 *480/968–7677* ⊕ *www.missionpalms.com* ✒ *303 rooms △ Restaurant, room service, 3 tennis courts, pool, gym, sauna, bar, business services, meeting rooms, airport shuttle, free parking; no smoking* ▭ *AE, D, DC, MC, V.*

West Valley: Litchfield Park

$$$$ 🏨 **Wigwam Resort.** Built in 1918 as a retreat for executives of the Goodyear Company, the Wigwam has the pleasing feel of an upscale lodge. Casita-style rooms, situated along paths overflowing with cacti, palms, and huge bougainvillea, are decorated in a Southwestern style: distressed-wood furniture, iron lamps, pastel walls, and brightly patterned spreads. Local art adorns the walls, and all rooms have patios. This isolated world of graciousness inspires a fierce loyalty in its guests, some of whom have been returning for more than 50 years. ✉ *300 Wigwam Blvd., Litchfield Park 85340* ☎ *623/935–3811 or 800/327–0396* 🖨 *623/ 935–3737* ⊕ *www.wigwamresort.com* ✒ *261 rooms, 70 suites △ 3 restaurants, cable TV, 3 18-hole golf courses, 9 tennis courts, pro shop, 2 pools, gym, hair salon, 2 hot tubs, basketball, croquet, Ping-Pong, shuffleboard, volleyball, 3 bars, children's programs (ages 6–12), business services, meeting rooms, free parking* ▭ *AE, D, DC, MC, V.*

NIGHTLIFE & THE ARTS

The Arts

For weekly listings of theater, arts, and music events, check out "The Rep Entertainment Guide" in Thursday's *Arizona Republic*; pick up a free issue of the independent weekly *New Times* from street-corner boxes; or check out *Where Phoenix/Scottsdale Magazine,* available free in most hotels. A good online source of information on events in the Valley is **Digital City** (⊕ www.digitalcity.com). The online arm of the *Arizona Republic* (⊕ www.azcentral.com) has extensive nightlife and arts listings.

TICKETS **Arizona State University Public Events Box Office** (☎ 480/965–6447 ⊕ www. herbergercollege.asu.edu) sells tickets for events performed at ASU through the Herberger College of Fine Arts. **Tickets.com** (⊕ www.tickets. com) sells tickets for ASU Public Events at Gammage Auditorium, Kerr Theatre, and the ASU Sundome. **Ticketmaster** (☎ 480/784–4444 ⊕ www. ticketmaster.com) sells tickets for nearly every event in the Valley and has outlets at all Robinsons-May department stores, Fry's, Wherehouse, and Tower Records stores.

Classical Music

Arizona Opera (✉ 4600 N. 12th St., Downtown Phoenix ☎ 602/266–7464 ⊕ www.azopera.com) stages an opera season, primarily classical, in both Tucson and Phoenix. The Phoenix season runs from October to March. Due to an extensive renovation project at Symphony Hall, the 2005 series will be held at rotating venues—Gammage Auditorium, Orpheum Theatre, and Herberger Theater. They expect to return to Symphony Hall in 2006.

Phoenix Symphony Orchestra (Box Office ✉ Arizona Center, 455 N. 3rd St., Suite 390, Downtown Phoenix ☎ 602/495–1999 ⊕ www. phoenixsymphony.org) is the resident company at Symphony Hall. Its season, which runs September through May, includes orchestral works from classical and contemporary literature, a chamber series, composer festivals, and outdoor Pops concerts. Due to renovation of Symphony Hall, Phoenix Symphony Orchestra performances in 2005 will be held at different venues.

Dance

Ballet Arizona (✉ 3645 E. Indian School Rd., Central Phoenix ☎ 602/381–1096 ⊕ www.balletaz.org), the state's professional ballet company, presents a full season of classical and contemporary works (including pieces commissioned for the company) in Tucson and Phoenix, where it performs at the Orpheum Theater. The ballet's season runs from October through May. The ballet box office is open weekdays 9 to 4:30.

Film

Farrelli's Cinema Supper Club (✉ 14202 N. Scottsdale Rd., North Scottsdale ☎ 480/905–7200 ⊕ www.farrellis.com) offers dinner and a movie. Watch new releases on a big screen while dining on contemporary American cuisine.

Valley Art Theatre (✉ 509 S. Mill Ave., Tempe ☎ 480/829–6668) shows major foreign releases and domestic art films if you're looking for something besides the latest blockbuster.

Theater

Actors Theatre of Phoenix (✍ Box 1924, Phoenix 85001 ☎ 602/253–6701 ⊕ www.atphx.org) is the resident theater troupe at the Herberger Theater Center. The theater presents a full season of drama, comedy, and musical productions; it runs from September through May.

Arizona Theatre Company (✉ 808 N. 1st St. ☎ 602/252–8497 ⊕ www. aztheatreco.org) is the only resident company in the country with a two-city (Tucson and Phoenix) operation. Productions, held from September through June, range from classic dramas to musicals and new works by emerging playwrights.

Black Theater Troupe (✉ 333 E. Portland St., Downtown Phoenix ☎ 602/258–8128) performs at its own house, the Helen K. Mason Center, a half-block from the city's Performing Arts Building on Deck Park. It presents original and contemporary dramas and musical revues, as well as adventurous adaptations, between September and May.

☺ **Childsplay** (✍ Box 517, Tempe 85280 ☎ 480/350–8101 ⊕ www.azeats. com/childsplay) is the state's theater company for young audiences and families, which runs during the school year. Rotating through many a venue—Herberger Theater Center, Scottsdale Center for the Arts, and Tempe Performing Arts Center—these players deliver colorful, high-energy performances.

Great Arizona Puppet Theatre (✉ 302 W. Latham St., Downtown Phoenix ☎ 602/262–2050 ⊕ www.azpuppets.org), which performs in a historic building featuring lots of theater and exhibit space, mounts a year-long cycle of inventive puppet productions that change frequently; it also offers puppetry classes.

Phoenix Theatre (✉ 100 E. McDowell Rd., Downtown Phoenix ☎ 602/254–2151 ⊕ www.phxtheatre.org), across the courtyard from the Phoenix Art Museum, stages a musical and dramatic performances as well as productions for children by the Cookie Company.

DINNER THEATER **Broadway Palm Dinner Theatre** (✉ 5247 E. Brown Rd., Mesa ☎ 480/325–6700 or 888/504–7256 ⊕ www.broadwaypalmwest.com) offers a buffet dinner followed by a live, full-length Broadway-style musical in its 500-seat theater.

WILD WEST At **Rawhide Western Town & Steakhouse** (✉ 23023 N. Scottsdale Rd., North
SHOWS Scottsdale ☎ 480/502–1880 ⊕ www.rawhide.com), the false fronts on
☺ the dusty Main Street contain a train depot, saloons, and gift shops. Reenacted Old West shoot-outs and cheesy souvenirs make this a venue for down-home, tacky fun. City slickers can take a ride on a stagecoach or gentle burro, and there are barnyard animals at the Petting Ranch for small children. Hayrides travel a short distance into the desert for nightly Sundown Cookouts under the stars. There are often special events going on here as well as an occasional rodeo.

☺ **Rockin' R Ranch** (✉ 6136 E. Baseline Rd., Mesa ☎ 480/832–1539 ⊕ www.rockinr.net) includes a petting zoo, a reenactment of a wild shoot-out, and—the main attraction—a nightly cookout with a Western stage show. Pan for gold or take a wagon ride until the "vittles" are served, followed by music and entertainment.

Nightlife

From brewpubs, sports bars, and coffeehouses to dance clubs, mega-concerts, and country venues, the Valley of the Sun offers nightlife of all types. Nightclubs, comedy clubs, and upscale lounges abound in downtown Phoenix; along Camelback Road in north-central Phoenix; and in Scottsdale and Tempe, as well as other suburbs.

Among music and dancing styles, country-and-western has the longest tradition here. Jazz venues, rock clubs, and hotel lounges are also numerous and varied. Phoenix is getting hipper and more cosmopolitan as it gets older: cigar lovers and martini sippers will find plenty of places to indulge their tastes. There are also more than 30 gay and lesbian bars, centered primarily on 7th Avenue, 7th Street, and the stretch of Camelback Road between the two.

You can find listings and reviews in the *New Times* free weekly newspaper, distributed Wednesday, and "The Rep Entertainment Guide" of the *Arizona Republic. PHX Downtown,* a free monthly available in downtown establishments, has an extensive calendar for the neighborhood's events from art exhibits and poetry readings to professional sporting events. The local gay scene is covered in *Echo Magazine,* which you can pick up all over town.

Bars & Lounges

America's Original Sports Bar (⊠ Arizona Center, 455 N. 3rd St., Downtown Phoenix ☎ 602/252–2112) offers more than 40,000 square feet of boisterous fun, with more than 60 TVs (seven giant screens among them). Locals, conventioneers, and vacationers show up for the big games.

Buddha Bar (⊠ 7419 E. Indian Plaza, Central Scottsdale ☎ 480/970–1945) is a twenty- to thirtysomething hangout with a large center bar, a tasting-dipping menu, and a DJ-controlled dance wing.

Fox Sports Bar (⊠ 16203 N. Scottsdale Rd., North Scottsdale ☎ 480/368–0369) is a sports bar where you can watch live Fox Sports broadcasts while you're drinking and dining. It's the first of its kind.

Jilly's American Grill (⊠ 7301 E. Butherus Dr., North Scottsdale ☎ 480/368–8663) is the new "in" place to watch sports on 45 monitors or at a private TV booth. The weeknight TV clientele turns into a nightclub scene on weekends with music and dancing for a thirty- to fortysomething crowd.

Majerle's Sports Grill (⊠ 24 N. 2nd St., Downtown, Phoenix ☎ 602/253–9004), operated by former Suns basketball player Dan Majerle, is within striking distance of the major sports facilities and offers a comprehensive menu as well as a bar for pre- and post-game celebrations.

Postino Winebar (⊠ 3939 E. Campbell Ave., Central Phoenix ☎ 602/852–3939) occupies a former post office in the Arcadia neighborhood. Over 40 wines are poured by the glass, with prices ranging from $7–$12. Order a few grazing items off the appetizer menu and settle in, or carry out a bottle of wine, hunk of cheese, and loaf of bread for a twilight picnic.

Seamus McCaffrey's Irish Pub (✉ 18 W. Monroe St., Downtown P
☎ 602/253–6081) is a fun and friendly place to enjoy a joke, a song, or one of the dozen European brews on draft. A small kitchen turns out traditional Irish fare.

Top of the Rock Bar (✉ 2000 W. Westcourt Way, Tempe ☎ 602/431–2370), the lounge in Top of the Rock restaurant at the Buttes, attracts an older, professional crowd to drink in cocktails and spectacular views.

Blues & Jazz

The **Blue Note** (✉ 8040 E. McDowell Rd., Central Scottsdale ☎ 480/945–9573) is always packed with locals for live shows nightly.

Char's Has the Blues (✉ 4631 N. 7th Ave., Central Phoenix ☎ 602/230–0205) is the Valley's top blues club, with nightly bands.

J. Chew & Co. (✉ 7320 Scottsdale Mall, Downtown Scottsdale ☎ 480/946–2733) is the spot for listening to live jazz and sipping a drink. Patio seating centers on a cozy wood-burning fireplace.

A League of Our Own (✉ 40 E. Camelback Rd., Camelback Corridor ☎ 602/265–2354), a large club filled with oversized booths and vintage furniture, has cool jazz and blues Tuesday through Saturday 4 PM to 1 AM.

Leland's House of Fine Food & New Orleans Jazz (✉ 37433 Cave Creek Rd., Cave Creek ☎ 480/488–4094) features New Orleans and Chicago-style jazz Thursday through Saturday, and there's a Sunday jazz brunch.

★ **Remington's Lounge** (✉ Scottsdale Plaza Resort, 7200 N. Scottsdale Rd., North Scottsdale ☎ 480/948–5000) has a popular piano player, Danny Long, who delivers jazz standards as well as ballads to a very appreciative following from Tuesday to Saturday night.

Rhythm Room (✉ 1019 E. Indian School Rd., Central Phoenix ☎ 602/265–4842) hosts local and touring blues artists. On Saturday night, there's barbecue in the parking lot.

Sugar Daddy's Blues (✉ 3102 N. Scottsdale Rd., North Scottsdale ☎ 480/970–6556) serves rhythm, blues, and food nightly until 1 AM.

Casinos

Casino Arizona at Indian Bend (✉ 9700 E. Indian Bend Rd., North Scottsdale ☎ 480/850–8642) draws Scottsdale locals for live blackjack, poker, keno, over 200 slot machines and musical entertainment nightly.

Casino Arizona at Salt River (✉ Loop 101 and McKellips Rd., South Scottsdale ☎ 480/850–7777, 480/850–7790 for free transportation) is the largest casino in the area, with five restaurants, four lounges, a sports bar, a 250-seat theater featuring live performances, a 50-table card room, a keno parlor, and a bingo hall. The off-track betting room features wide-screen TVs.

Fort McDowell Casino (✉ AZ 87 at Fort McDowell Rd., Fountain Hills ☎ 602/843–3678 or 800/843–3678) is popular with the Scottsdale resort crowd. In addition to the cards, slot machines, and keno games, off-track greyhound wagering takes place in a classy mahogany room with 18 giant video screens. Take advantage of the casino's free Valley-wide shuttle.

Gila River Casino (✉ 5550 W. Wildhorse Pass, Chandler ☎ 480/796–7777 or 800/946–4452) near Wildhorse Pass Resort & Spa includes 500 slots, live poker, blackjack, keno, and complimentary drinks.

Coffeehouses

Willow House (✉ 149 W. McDowell Rd., Downtown Phoenix ☎ 602/
252–0272) is a uniquely fun and funky spot in a city not overflowing
with great coffeehouses. Thursday-night poetry readings are a big draw.
The espresso flows until midnight on weeknights, 1 AM on weekends.

Comedy

The **Comedy Spot** (✉ 7117 E. 3rd Ave., Downtown Scottsdale ☎ 480/
945–4422 ⊕ www.thecomedyspot.net) is Scottsdale's only comedy
venue featuring local and national stand-up talent. They also offer
classes to wanna-be comedians on Sunday. Cover is $5 to $10.
The **Jester'Z Live Improv Comedy Show** (✉ 7117 E. McDowell Rd., Central Scottsdale ☎ 480/423–0120) has clean, family-friendly comedy
shows, performed by Jester'Z Improvisational Troupe on Thursday and
Friday night. There is a cover charge of $5 to $10.
Rascal's (✉ 100 N. 1st St., Wyndham Hotel, Downtown Phoenix ☎ 602/
254–0999) is part of a national chain that features headlining comics.
Cover is $9 to $20 Thursday through Saturday and $7 on Sunday for
open-mike night.
The **Tempe Improv** (✉ 930 E. University Dr., Tempe ☎ 480/921–9877),
part of a national chain, showcases better-known headliners from Thursday to Sunday; shows cost between $10 and $20.

Country & Western

★ **Greasewood Flats** (✉ 27500 N. Alma School Pkwy., North Scottsdale
☎ 480/585–7277) isn't fancy; in fact, it's downright ramshackle, but
the burgers are delicious and the crowds friendly. There's a dance floor
with live music from Thursday through Sunday. In winter, wear jeans
and a jacket here, since everything is outside; to keep warm, folks con-
gregate around fires burning in halved 42-gallon oil drums.
Handlebar-J (✉ 7116 E. Becker La., Central Scottsdale ☎ 480/948–
0110) is a lively restaurant and bar with a Western line-dancing, 10-
gallon-hat–wearing crowd.
Marquee Theatre (✉ 730 N. Mill Ave., Tempe ☎ 480/829–0607) hosts
mainly headlining country and Western entertainers.
Mr. Lucky's (✉ 3660 N.W. Grand Ave., West Phoenix ☎ 602/246–0686)
is the granddaddy of Phoenix Western clubs, where you can dance the
two-step all night (or learn how, if you haven't before).

Dance Clubs

Axis and Radius (✉ 7340 E. Indian Plaza Rd., Central Scottsdale ☎ 480/
970–1112) is the dressed-to-kill locale where you can party at side-by-
side clubs connected by a glass catwalk while watching a laser light show.
Bash on Ash (✉ 230 W. 5th St., Tempe ☎ 480/966–8200) plays alternative and indie rock for a college crowd.
Cajun House (✉ 7117 E. 3rd Ave., Downtown Scottsdale ☎ 480/945–
5150), one of the hottest spots in the Valley, is a Louisiana-themed venue
decorated as a two-story block of Bourbon Street. Locals sip Hurricanes
while listening to touring acts play rock, jazz, and Cajun music. On weekends there's a line.
Sanctuary (✉ 7340 E. Shoeman La., North Scottsdale ☎ 480/970–
5000) is an ultra-swanky dance club where lasers flash to the DJ's tunes

and the bartender lights your martini with a blow torch. There's a cigar bar, too.

Scorch (✉ Desert Ridge Marketplace, 21001 N. Tatum Blvd., North Phoenix ☎ 480/513–7211) is a subterranean dance club and bar, LA-style. Dancers behind a translucent screen entertain the crowd with their shadowy forms. Plush booths, lava lights, and a small dance floor complete the scene. The $5 to $10 cover is suspended on Tuesday and Sunday.

Gay & Lesbian Bars

Ain't Nobody's Bizness (✉ 3031 E. Indian School Rd., Central Phoenix ☎ 602/224–9977) is the most popular lesbian bar in town; you'll also find a few gay men at this male-friendly establishment, well known as one of the most fun in town.

Amsterdam (✉ 718 N. Central Ave., Downtown Phoenix ☎ 602/258–6122) attracts a young crowd that wants to see and be seen; it's where Phoenix's beautiful (gay) people hang out.

B. S. West (✉ 7125 E. 5th Ave., Downtown Scottsdale ☎ 480/945–9028) is tucked behind a shopping center on Scottsdale's main shopping drag and draws a stylish, well-heeled crowd.

Charlie's (✉ 727 W. Camelback Rd., West Phoenix ☎ 602/265–0224), a longtime favorite of local gay men, has a country-western look (cowboy hats are the accessory of choice) and friendly staff.

Microbreweries

Bandersnatch Brew Pub (✉ 125 E. 5th St., Tempe ☎ 480/966–4438) is a popular pre- and post-game hangout for Arizona State University Sun Devils' fans. It brews several *cervezas* daily.

Rock Bottom Brewery (✉ 8668 E. Shea Blvd., North Scottsdale ☎ 480/998–7777) has casual dining and beer brewed on the premises.

The **Unlikely Cowboy** (✉ 20751 N. Pima Rd., North Scottsdale) serves brewed-on-the-premises German-style beers as well as good food in an upscale atmosphere.

Rock

Long Wong's on Mill (✉ 701 S. Mill Ave., Tempe ☎ 480/966–3147) may not be the most elegant joint you'll ever see, but huge crowds of students pack the graffiti-covered room to catch the sounds of local musicians playing raw rock and roll.

Mason Jar (✉ 2303 E. Indian School Rd., Central Phoenix ☎ 602/956–6271) has nightly shows, mostly hard rock.

SPORTS & THE OUTDOORS

Central Arizona's dry desert heat imposes particular restraints on outdoor endeavors—even in winter, hikers and cyclists should wear lightweight opaque clothing, a hat or visor, and high-UV-rated sunglasses and should carry a quart of water for each hour of activity. The intensity of the sun makes strong sunscreen (SPF 15 or higher) a must, and don't forget to apply it to your hands and feet. From May 1 to October 1, you shouldn't jog or hike from one hour after sunrise until a half hour before sunset. During those times, the air is so hot and dry that your body will lose moisture at a dangerous, potentially lethal rate. Don't

CloseUp

BASEBALL'S THREE SEASONS

FOR DYED-IN-THE-WOOL BASEBALL **FANS,** there's no better place than the Valley of the Sun. Baseball has become nearly a year-round activity in the Phoenix area, beginning with Spring Training in late February and continuing through the Arizona Fall League championships in mid-November.

Professional baseball sunk its roots in the warm Sonoran Desert more than a half-century ago, in 1947, when Bill Veeck brought his Cleveland Indians to Tucson and Horace Stoneham brought the New York Giants to Phoenix for spring training. Before 1947, only a few exhibition games had been played in Arizona. Most spring training games took place in the Florida Grapefruit League, as they had since 1914. Some teams trained in California in the 1930s, and a few teams played in such places as San Antonio, Savannah, Puerto Rico, and even Havana, Cuba. But Veeck's move was the catalyst. In 1951, baseball fans in Arizona watched Joe DiMaggio and rookie Mickey Mantle train and play at the Phoenix Municipal Stadium, when the New York Yankees came over from Florida for a year, brought by owner—and Phoenix resident—Del Webb.

Spring
Today, the Cactus League consists of 12 major league teams (9 in the Valley and 3 in Tucson). Ticket prices are reasonable, around $7 to $8 for bleacher seats to $15 for reserved seats. Many of the stadiums have lawn-seating areas in the outfield, where you can spread a blanket and bring a picnic. Cactus League stadiums are more intimate than big-league parks, and often players come right up to the stands to say hello to fans and to sign autographs. Special events such as fireworks nights, bat and T-shirt giveaway nights, and visits from sports mascots add

to the festive feeling during spring training. A Cactus League game allows a family to enjoy nine innings of baseball, a hotdog, and some peanuts without absorbing the national debt.

Tickets for some teams go on sale as early as December. Brochures listing game schedules and ticket information are available by calling the Arizona teams' venues or checking the Cactus League's Web site.

Summer
During the regular major-league season, the hometown Arizona Diamondbacks play on natural grass at Bank One Ballpark (BOB), in the heart of Phoenix's Copper Square (the team does spring training in Tucson). The stadium is a technological wonder; if the weather's a little too warm outside, they close the roof, turn on the gigantic air-conditioners, and keep you as cool as a cucumber while you enjoy the game. You can tour the stadium, except on afternoon-game days and holidays.

Fall
At the conclusion of the regular season, the Arizona Fall League runs until the week before Thanksgiving. Each major league team sends six of their most talented young prospects to compete with other young promising players—180 players in all. There are six teams in the league, broken down into two divisions. It's a great way to see future Hall of Famer's in their early years. Tickets for Fall League games are $5 for adults, $4 for kids and seniors, or you can get season tickets.

— Bob and Gloria Willis

head out to desert areas at night to jog or hike in summer; that's when rattlesnakes and scorpions are on the prowl.

Tickets for most sporting events can be purchased from **Ticketmaster** (☎ 480/784–4444 ⊕ www.ticketmaster.com).

Auto Racing

Bob Bondurant School of High Performance Driving (✉ I–10 and Maricopa Rd., Chandler ☎ 480/961–0143 ⊕ www.bondurant.com) is the world's largest driver-training facility with programs at all levels, from Teen Defensive Driving to Advanced Road Racing. The school has 200 race-prepared vehicles and a 1.6-mi road course.

Phoenix International Raceway (✉ 11901 W. Baseline Rd., Avondale ☎ 602/252–2227 ⊕ www.phoenixintlraceway.com), the Valley's NASCAR track—south of Litchfield Park—hosts the Skoal Bandit Copper World Classic, Phoenix 200 Indy Car race, and Phoenix 500 NASCAR race.

Baseball

Take one step outside during March and you'll realize why many of the major-league baseball teams choose Phoenix for spring training. It can't get much better. The 12 teams of the **Cactus League** (⊕ www.cactus-league. com) start playing in late February and reside in the Valley through March. You can information on teams on the Web site of **Major League Baseball** (⊕ www.mlb.com), where you can also buy tickets to games. Additionally, the Arizona Diamondbacks major-league team is based in Phoenix and holds spring training games at Tucson's Electric Park.

LOCAL TEAMS The **Arizona Diamondbacks** (✉ Bank One Ballpark, 401 E. Jefferson St., between S. 4th and S. 7th Sts., Downtown Phoenix ☎ 602/462–6000 team offices, 602/514–8400 tickets ⊕ www.azdiamondbacks.com), the 2001 World Series Champions, play at the 48,500-seat Bank One Ballpark, which has a retractable roof, a natural-grass playing surface, and a slew of restaurants, luxury boxes, and party suites. Their Cactus League spring training takes place in Tucson's Electric Park. (✉ 2500 E. Ajo Way, Tucson ☎ 520/434–1111).

SPRING **Anaheim Angels** (✉ Tempe Diablo Stadium, Tempe ☎ 480/784–4444
TRAINING TEAMS ⊕ www.angelsbaseball.com).

Chicago Cubs (✉ HoHoKam Stadium, Mesa ☎ 480/964–4467 or 800/ 905–3315 ⊕ www.cubspringtraining.com).

Kansas City Royals (✉ Surprise Stadium, Surprise ☎ 623/594–5600 ⊕ www.kcroyals.com).

Milwaukee Brewers (✉ Maryvale Baseball Park, West Phoenix ☎ 602/ 895–1200 or 800/933–7890 ⊕ www.milwaukeebrewers.com).

Oakland A's (✉ Phoenix Municipal Stadium, Downtown Phoenix ☎ 602/ 392–0217 or 800/352–0212 ⊕ www.oaklandathletics.com or www. springtrainingtours.com).

San Diego Padres (✉ Peoria Sports Complex, Peoria ☎ 800/409–1511 ⊕ www.padres.com).

San Francisco Giants (✉ Scottsdale Stadium, Downtown Scottsdale ☎ 480/990–7972 ⊕ www.sfgiants.com).

Seattle Mariners (✉ Peoria Sports Complex, Peoria ☎ 800/409–1511 ⊕ www.seattlemariners.com).

Texas Rangers (⊠ Surprise Stadium, Surprise ☎ 623/594–5600 ⊕ www. texasrangers.com).

Basketball

Phoenix Mercury (⊠ America West Arena, 201 E. Jefferson St., at 2nd St., Downtown Phoenix ☎ 602/379–7867 team offices, 602/379–2000 America West Arena Ticket Office ⊕ www.wnba.com/mercury) draw among the top crowds in the Women's NBA (WNBA).

Phoenix Suns (⊠ America West Arena, 201 E. Jefferson St., at 2nd St., Downtown Phoenix ☎ 602/379–7867 team offices, 602/379–2000 America West Arena Ticket Office ⊕ www.suns.com) often fill all 19,000 spectator seats in the America West Arena on game nights, and they remain the Valley's marquee pro team.

Bicycling

The desert climate can be tough on cyclists. Be sure to have a helmet and a mirror when riding in the streets: there are few adequate bike lanes in the Valley.

Scottsdale's Indian Bend Wash (along Hayden Road, from Shea Boulevard south to Indian School Road) has paths suitable for bikes winding among its golf courses and ponds. **Pinnacle Peak,** about 25 mi northeast of downtown Phoenix, is a popular place to take bikes for the ride north to Carefree and Cave Creek, or east and south over the mountain pass and down to the Verde River, toward Fountain Hills. Mountain bikers will want to check out the **Trail 100,** which runs throughout the Phoenix Mountain preserve (enter at Dreamy Draw park, just east of the intersection of Northern Avenue and 16th Street). **South Mountain Park** is the prime site for mountain bikers, with its 40-plus mi of trails—some of them with challenging ascents and all of them quiet and scenic. **Phoenix Parks and Recreation** (☎ 602/262–6861 ⊕ www. ci.phoenix.az.us/parks) has detailed maps of Valley bike paths.

ABC/Desert Biking Adventures (☎ 602/320–4602 or 888/249–2453 ⊕ www.desertbikingadventures.com) provides transportation from Scottsdale hotels and offers two-, three-, and four-hour mountain-biking excursions through the McDowell Mountains and the Sonoran Desert. **Wheels N' Gear** (⊠ 7607 E. McDowell Rd., Central Scottsdale ☎ 480/945–2881) rents bikes by the day or the week.

Four-Wheeling

Taking a jeep or a wide-track Humvee through the backcountry has become a popular way to experience the desert terrain's saguaro-covered mountains and curious rock formations.

Arizona Desert Mountain Jeep Tours (⊠ 6303 E. Cochise, North Scottsdale ☎ 480/860–1777 ⊕ www.azdesertmountain.com) ventures down to the Verde River on its own trail and offers wilderness cookouts.

Arrowhead Desert Jeep Tours (⊠ 841 E. Paradise La., North Phoenix ☎ 602/942–3361 or 800/514–9063 ⊕ www.azdeserttours.com) offers gold-panning on a private claim, cookouts, cattle drives, river crossings, and Native American–dance demonstrations.

Wild West Jeep Tours (⊠ 7127 E. Becker La., Scottsdale ☎ 480/922–0144 ⊕ www.wildwestjeeptours.com) has special permits that allow it to conduct four-wheeler excursions in the Tonto National Forest and to visit thousand-year-old Indian ruins listed on the National Register of Historic Places.

Football

The **Arizona Cardinals** (✉ Sun Devil Stadium, Stadium Dr., Tempe ☎ 602/379–0102 ⊕ www.azcardinals.com), the area's professional football team, currently plays at ASU's outdoor Sun Devil Stadium in Tempe but will be moving to a new stadium (now under construction) in Glendale for the 2006 NFL season.

Golf

Arizona has more golf courses per capita than any other state west of the Mississippi River, making it one of the most popular golf destinations in the United States. It's also one of Arizona's major industries, as greens fees can run from $35 at a public course to more than $500 at some of Arizona's premier golfing spots. New courses seem to pop up monthly: there are more than 200 in the Valley (some lighted at night), and the PGA's Southwest section has its headquarters here. Call well ahead for tee times during the cooler months. During the summer, fees drop dramatically and it's not uncommon to schedule a round before dawn. Check course Web sites for discounts before making your reservations. Also, package deals abound at resorts as well as through booking agencies like **Arizona Golf Adventures** (☎ 877/841–6570 ⊕ www.azteetimes.com), who will plan and schedule a nonstop golf holiday for you. For a copy of the *Arizona Golf Guide,* contact the **Arizona Golf Association** (✉ 7226 N. 16th St., Phoenix 85020 ☎ 602/944–3035 or 800/458–8484 ⊕ www.azgolf.org).

Arizona Biltmore Country Club (✉ Arizona Biltmore Resort & Spa, 24th St. and Missouri Ave., Camelback Corridor ☎ 602/955–9655 ⊕ www.arizonabiltmore.com), the granddaddy of Valley golf courses, has two 18-hole PGA championship courses, lessons, and clinics.

Fodor'sChoice ★ **ASU Karsten Golf Course** (✉ 1125 E. Rio Salado Pkwy., Tempe ☎ 480/921–8070 ⊕ www.asukarsten.com) is the Arizona State University 18-hole golf course where NCAA champions train.

Encanto Park (✉ 2775 N. 15th Ave., West Phoenix ☎ 602/253–3963 ⊕ www.phoenix.gov) has an attractive, affordable public course with 9- and 18-hole courses.

Fodor'sChoice ★ **Gold Canyon Golf Club** (✉ 6100 S. King's Ranch Rd., Gold Canyon ☎ 480/982–9449 ⊕ www.gcgr.com), near Apache Junction in the East Valley, offers fantastic views of the Superstition Mountains and challenging golf. Don't miss this 36-hole course.

★ **Grayhawk Country Club** (✉ 8620 E. Thompson Peak Pkwy., North Scottsdale ☎ 480/502–1800 ⊕ www.grayhawk.com), a 36-hole course, is always in excellent condition and has beautiful mountain views.

Hillcrest Golf Club (✉ 20002 Star Ridge Dr., Sun City West ☎ 623/584–1500) is the best course in the Sun Cities development, with 18-holes on 179 acres of well-designed turf.

Ocotillo Golf Resort (✉ 3751 S. Clubhouse Dr., Chandler ☎ 480/917–6660 ⊕ www.ocotillogolf.com) is designed around 95 acres of man-made lakes; there's water in play on nearly all 27 holes.

Papago Golf Course (✉ 5595 E. Moreland St., North-Central Phoenix ☎ 602/275–8428) is a low-priced 18-holes and Phoenix's best municipal course.

★ The **Phoenician Golf Club** (✉ The Phoenician, 6000 E. Camelback Rd., Camelback Corridor ☎ 480/423–2449 ⊕ www.thephoenician.com) has a 27-hole course that plays up against the mountains.

Raven Golf Club at South Mountain (✉ 3636 E. Baseline Rd., South Phoenix ☎ 602/243–3636 ⊕ www.ravengolf.com) has thousands of drought-resistant Aleppo pines and Lombardy poplars, making it a cool, shady 18-hole haven for summertime golfers.

★ **Tournament Players Club of Scottsdale** (✉ Fairmont Scottsdale Princess Resort, 17020 N. Hayden Rd., North Scottsdale ☎ 480/585–3600 ⊕ www. fairmont.com), a 36-hole course by Tom Weiskopf and Jay Morrish, is the site of the PGA FBR Open each January.

Fodor'sChoice **Troon North** (✉ 10320 E. Dynamite Blvd., North Scottsdale ☎ 480/585–
★ 5300 ⊕ www.troonnorthgolf.com) is a challenge for the length alone (7,008 yards). The million-dollar views add to the experience at this perfectly maintained 36-hole course.

Wigwam Golf and Country Club (✉ Wigwam Resort, 300 Wigwam Blvd., Litchfield Park ☎ 623/935–3811 ⊕ www.wigwamresort.com) is the home of the famous Gold Course, as well as two other 18-hole courses.

Hiking

One of the best ways to see the beauty of the Valley of the Sun is from above. Hikers of all calibers seek a better vantage point in the mountains surrounding the flat Valley. No matter the season, be sure to bring sunscreen, plenty of water, and a camera to capture a dazzling sunset. The city's **Phoenix Mountain Preserve System** (⌂ Phoenix Mountain Preservation Council, Box 26121, Phoenix 85068 ☎ 602/262–6861 ⊕ www. phoenixmountains.org) administers the mountainous regions that surround the city and has its own park rangers who can help plan your hikes. It also publishes a book, *Day Hikes and Trail Rides in and around Phoenix*.

★ At **Camelback Mountain and Echo Canyon Recreation Area** (✉ Tatum Blvd. and McDonald Dr., Paradise Valley ☎ 602/256–3220 Phoenix Parks & Recreation Dept.), there are intermediate to difficult hikes up the Valley's most outstanding landmark.

☺ The **Papago Peaks** (✉ Van Buren St. and Galvin Pkwy., Central Scottsdale ☎ 602/256–3220 Phoenix Parks & Recreation Dept. Eastern and Central District) were sacred sites for the Tohono O'odham. The softsandstone peaks contain accessible caves, some petroglyphs, and splendid views of much of the Valley. This is a good spot for family hikes.

Pinnacle Peak Trail (✉ 26802 N. 102nd Way [1 mi south of Dynamite and Alma School Rds.], North Scottsdale ☎ 480/312–0990), closed for over six years because of luxury-home development around its base, has finally reopened, much to the joy of area hikers. The well-maintained trail offers a moderately challenging 3½-mi round-trip hike or horseback experience. Interpretive programs and trail signs along the way describe the geology, flora, fauna, and cultural history of the area.

★ **South Mountain Park** (✉ 10919 S. Central Ave., South Phoenix ☎ 602/261–8457) is the jewel of the city's Mountain Park Preserves. Its mountains and arroyos contain more than 40 mi of marked and maintained trails—all open to hikers, horseback riders, and mountain bikers. It also has three auto-accessible lookout points, with 65-mi sight lines. Rangers can help you plan hikes to view some of the 200 petroglyph sites.

Hockey

The **Phoenix Coyotes** (☎ 602/379–7825 team offices ⊕ www. phoenixcoyotes.com) are the local NHL team; hockey great Wayne Gretzky is managing partner. The Coyotes skate in the $180 million **Glendale Arena** (✉ 9400 W. Maryland Ave., Glendale ☎ 623/772–3200 ⊕ www.glendalearenaaz.com).

Horseback Riding

More than two dozen stables and equestrian tour outfitters in the Valley attest to the saddle's enduring importance in Arizona—even in this auto-dominated metropolis. Stables offer rides for an hour, a whole day, and even some overnight adventures.

All Western Stables (✉ 10220 S. Central Ave., South Phoenix ☎ 602/276–5862), one of several stables at the entrance to South Mountain Park, offers rentals, guided rides, hayrides, and cookouts.

Cowboy College (✉ 30208 N. 152nd St., North Scottsdale ☎ 480/471–3151 or 888/330–8070 ⊕ www.cowboycollege.com) has wranglers who will teach you everything you need to know about ridin', ropin', and ranchin'.

MacDonald's Ranch (✉ 26540 N. Scottsdale Rd., North Scottsdale ☎ 480/585–0239 ⊕ www.macdonaldsranch.com) offers one- and two-hour trail rides and guided breakfast, lunch, and dinner rides through desert foothills above Scottsdale.

★ **OK Corral & Stable** (✉ 2665 E. Whiteley St., Apache Junction ☎ 480/982–4040 ⊕ www.okcorrals.com) offers one-, two-, and four-hour horseback trail rides and steak cookouts as well as one- to five-day horse-packing trips. Ron Feldman, an authority on the history and secrets of the Lost Dutchman Mine, is the guide for historical pack trips through the Superstition Mountains.

Hot-Air Ballooning

A sunrise or sunset hot-air–balloon ascent is a remarkable desert sightseeing experience. The average fee—there are more than three dozen Valley companies to choose from—is $135 per person, and hotel pickup is usually included. Since flight paths and landing sites vary with wind speeds and directions, a roving land crew follows each balloon in flight. Time in the air is generally between 1 and 1½ hours, but allow 3 hours for the total excursion. Be prepared for changing temperatures as the sun rises or sets, but it's not actually any colder up in the balloon.

Adventures Out West (☎ 602/996–6100 or 800/755–0935 ⊕ www. adventuresoutwest.com) will send you home with a free video of your flight taped from the balloon.

Hot Air Expeditions (☎ 480/502–6999 or 800/831–7610 ⊕ www. hotairexpeditions.com) is the best ballooning in Phoenix. Flights are long, the staff is charming, and the snacks are out of this world.

Unicorn Balloon Company (☎ 480/991–3666 or 800/468–2478 ⊕ www. unicornballoon.com), operating since 1978, is run by the state's ballooning examiner for the FAA and is headquartered at Scottsdale Airport.

Sailplaning/Soaring

Arizona Soaring Inc. (✉ Maricopa ☎ 480/821–2903 or 800/861–2318 ⊕ www.azsoaring.com), at the Estrella Sailport in Maricopa, 35 mi south of Phoenix, off Interstate 10, gives sailplane rides in a basic trainer or high-performance plane. The adventuresome can opt for a wild 15-minute acrobatic flight.

Tennis

With all of the blue sky and sunshine in the Valley, it's a perfect place to play tennis or to watch the pros. The Fairmont Scottsdale Princess hosts several national championships, including the annual Franklin Templeton Men's Classic and the State Farm Women's Tennis Championship. All major resorts, such as the Radisson, Phoenician, Wigwam, Fairmont Princess, and JW Marriott Desert Ridge (and many smaller properties), have tennis courts. Tennis plays second fiddle to golf here; however, many of the larger resorts offer package deals for tennis as well. If you are not staying at a resort, there are more than 60 public facilities in the area.

Kiwanis Park Recreation Center (✉ 6111 S. All America Way, Tempe ☎ 480/350–5201 Ext. 5) has 15 lighted premier-surface courts (all for same-day or one-day-advance reserve). Before 5 PM, courts rent for $4.50; after 5 PM, the rate is $6, and $2 drop-in programs are offered for single players weekdays, 10:30–noon.

Phoenix Tennis Center (✉ 6330 N. 21st Ave., West Phoenix ☎ 602/249–3712), a city facility with 22 lighted hard courts, charges $11 per hour per court for doubles.

Scottsdale Ranch Park (✉ 10400 E. Via Linda, North Scottsdale ☎ 480/312–7774) is a city facility with 12 lighted courts, ranging from $3 to $6 per hour. Lessons are available here too.

Village Camelback Racquet & Health Club (✉ 4444 E. Camelback Rd., Camelback Corridor ☎ 602/840–6412 ⊕ www.dmbclubs.com) is a private tennis facility, health club, and spa featuring lighted courts, ball-machine clinics, and lessons. Out-of-towners can enjoy club amenities for $17 a day.

Tubing

The Valley may not be known for its wealth of water, but locals manage to make the most of whatever they can. A popular summer stop is the northeast side of the Salt River, where sun worshippers can rent an inner tube and float down the river for an afternoon. Tubing season runs from May to September. Several Valley outfitters rent tubes. **Salt River Recreation** (✉ Usery Pass and Power Rds., Mesa ☎ 480/984–3305 ⊕ www.saltrivertubing.com), offering shuttle-bus service to and from your starting point, rents tubes for $12 (cash only) for the day.

SHOPPING

Since its resorts began multiplying in the 1930s and 1940s, Phoenix has acquired a healthy share of high-fashion clothiers and leisure-wear boutiques. But long before that, Western clothes dominated fashion here—jeans and boots, cotton shirts and dresses, 10-gallon hats, and bola ties (the state's official neckwear). In many places around town, they still do.

On the scene as well were the arts of the Southwest's true natives—Navajo weavers, sand painters, and silversmiths; Hopi weavers and katsina-doll carvers; Pima and Tohono O'odham (Papago) basket makers and potters; and many more. Inspired by the region's rich cultural traditions, contemporary artists have flourished here, making Phoenix—and in particular Scottsdale, a city with more art galleries than gas stations—one of the Southwest's largest art centers (alongside Santa Fe, New Mexico).

Today's shoppers find the best of the old and the new—all presented with Southwestern style. Upscale stores, one-of-a-kind shops, and outlet malls sell the latest fashions, cowboy collectibles, handwoven rugs, traditional Mexican folk art, and contemporary turquoise jewelry.

Most of the Valley's power shopping is concentrated in central Phoenix, downtown Scottsdale, and the Kierland area in North Scottsdale. But auctions and antiques shops cluster in odd places—and as treasure hunters know, you've always got to keep your eyes open.

Shopping Centers

Arizona Mills (✉ 5000 Arizona Mills Circle, I–10 and Superstition Fwy., Tempe ☎ 480/491–9700), the leader in the local discount-shopping competition, is a mammoth center featuring almost 200 outlet stores, including Off 5th–Saks 5th Avenue, Kenneth Cole, and Neiman Marcus Last Call. When you tire of bargain hunting relax in the food court, cinemas, or faux rain forest.

Biltmore Fashion Park (✉ 24th St. and Camelback Rd., Camelback Corridor ☎ 602/955–8400), across Camelback Road from the Ritz-Carlton, has posh shops and 12 restaurants in a parklike setting. Macy's and Saks 5th Avenue are the anchors for more than 60 stores and upscale shops, such as Gucci, Betsey Johnson, and Cartier.

The **Borgata** (✉ 6166 N. Scottsdale Rd., Central Scottsdale ☎ 480/998–1822), an outdoor re-creation of the Italian village of San Gimignano with courtyards, stone walls, turrets, and fountains, is a lovely setting for browsing upscale boutiques or merely sitting at an the outdoor cafés.

Cofco Chinese Cultural Center (✉ 2425 E. Camelback Rd., Central Phoenix ☎ 602/955–7229) is adorned by beautiful replicas of pagodas, statutes, and traditional Chinese gardens. It's the place to find Asian restaurants, gift shops, and the 99 *Market*, an Asian grocery store. Make sure to take a stroll through the market's fish department—you'll forget you're in the desert.

♻ **Desert Ridge Marketplace** (✉ Tatum Blvd. and Loop 101, North Phoenix ☎ 480/513–7586), an outdoor megamall, has more than 1 million square feet of shops and restaurants, but it's also a family entertainment destination. The District area of the mall has an 18-theater cineplex, bowling alley, rock-climbing wall, and Jillian's, a multivenue entertainment center with a virtual-reality game room and dance club.

Kierland Commons (⊠ Greenway Pkwy. at Scottsdale Rd., North Scottsdale ☎ 480/348–1577), next to the Westin Kierland Resort, is one of the city's newest shopping areas. "Urban village" is the catchphrase for this outdoor pedestrian mall with restaurants and upscale chain retailers, among them Crate & Barrel, J. Crew, and Tommy Bahama.

★ **Scottsdale Fashion Square** (⊠ Scottsdale and Camelback Rds., Central Scottsdale ☎ 480/941–2140) has a retractable roof and many specialty shops unique to Arizona. Nordstrom, Dillard's, Neiman Marcus, Macy's, Robinsons-May, a huge food court, sit-down restaurants, and a cineplex complete the picture.

Open-air Markets

Two of metropolitan Phoenix's best markets can be found in the tiny town of Guadalupe, which is tucked between Interstate 10, Baseline Road, and Warner Road, almost entirely surrounded by Tempe. Take Interstate 10 south to Baseline Road, go east ½ mi, and turn south on Avenida del Yaqui to find open-air vegetable stalls, roadside fruit stands, and tidy houses covered in flowering vines.

Guadalupe Farmer's Market (⊠ 9210 S. Ave. del Yaqui, Guadalupe ☎ 480/730–1945) has all the fresh ingredients you'd find in a rural Mexican market—tomatillos, varieties of chile peppers (fresh and dried), fresh-ground *masa* (cornmeal) for tortillas, spices like cumin and cilantro, and on and on. It's open from 9 to 7 every day but Wednesday.

Mercado Mexico (⊠ 8212 S. Ave. del Yaqui, Guadalupe ☎ 480/831–5925) carries ceramics, paper, tin, and lacquerware, all at unbeatable prices. Stock up from 10 to 6 daily.

Patriot's Square Marketplace (⊠ Patriot's Square Park, Washington St. and Central Ave., Downtown Phoenix ☎ 623/848–1234) sells arts and crafts, locally grown produce, baked goods, and homemade jams and salsas, livening up downtown every Wednesday 10 to 2, from October through April.

Scottsdale Downtown Farmer's Market (⊠ 6th Ave. between Scottsdale Rd. and Stetson Dr., Downtown Scottsdale) peddles fresh produce, flowers and a host of specialty items every Saturday morning from 9 to 1.

Specialty Shops

Antiques & Collectibles

The central Phoenix corridor, between 7th Street and 7th Avenue, has many antiques stores. Most shops sit north of Thomas and south of Camelback. Prices, though reasonable, are firm at most shops. A surprise to many visitors is the old-town district of suburban Glendale, with more than 80 antiques and collectible shops nestled around Historic Old Towne and Catlin Court, which are listed on the National Register of Historic Places.

Antique Centre (⊠ 2012 N. Scottsdale Rd., Central Scottsdale ☎ 480/675–9500) has a hodgepodge of collectibles and trinkets.

Antique Trove (⊠ 2020 N. Scottsdale Rd., Central Scottsdale ☎ 480/947–6074), next door to Antique Centre, has similar "you never know what you might find" merchandise.

Central Antiques (⊠ Uptown Plaza, Central Ave. and Camelback Rd., Camelback Corridor ☏ 602/241–1174) is one of the best places in the Valley to find fine china and silver and high-end antiques.

Glendale Old Towne & Catlin Court (⊠ 59th and Glendale Aves., Glendale) antiques district has more than 80 shops and restaurants in colorful, century-old bungalows. Stop in at antiques-filled Aunt Pittypat's Kitchen for breakfast or lunch or have a cup of tea at the Spicery, which is in an 1895 Victorian home.

Arts & Crafts

The best option, if you're interested in touring Scottsdale's galleries, is
★ the **Art Walk** (⊠ Main St., Downtown Scottsdale ☏ 480/990–3939), held from 7 PM to 9 PM each Thursday year-round (except Thanksgiving). Main Street and Marshall Way, the two major gallery strips, take on a party atmosphere during the evening hours when tourists and locals are browsing.

Art One (⊠ 4120 N. Marshall Way, Central Scottsdale ☏ 480/946–5076) carries works by local art students.

Cosanti Originals (⊠ 6433 Doubletree Ranch Rd., North Scottsdale ☏ 480/948–6145) is the studio where architect Paolo Soleri's famous bronze and ceramic wind chimes are made and sold. You can watch the craftspeople at work, then pick out your own—prices are surprisingly reasonable.

Drumbeat Indian Arts (⊠ 4143 N. 16th St., Central Phoenix ☏ 602/266–4823) is a small, interesting shop specializing in Native American music, movies, books, drums, and craft supplies. If you're lucky, you might find a Native American selling homemade fry bread and Navajo tacos in the parking lot on weekends.

★ The **Heard Museum Shop** (⊠ 22 E. Monte Vista Rd., Downtown Phoenix ☏ 602/266–4823) is hands-down the best place in town for Southwestern Native American and other crafts, both traditional and modern. Prices tend to be high, but quality is assured, with many one-of-a-kind items among the collection of rugs, katsina dolls, pottery, and other crafts; there's also a wide selection of lower-priced gifts.

Suzanne Brown Galleries (⊠ 7156 Main St., Downtown Scottsdale ☏ 480/945–8475) has a fabulous collection of innovative glasswork, painting, and other fine arts.

Trailside Gallery (⊠ 7330 Scottsdale Mall, Downtown Scottsdale ☏ 480/945–7751) has been showcasing works by members of the Cowboy Artists of America for more than 40 years and specializes in traditional American paintings and sculptures.

Xanadu Gallery (⊠ Shops at Gainey Village, 8977 N. Scottsdale Rd., North Scottsdale ☏ 480/368–9929) specializes in paintings and sculptures of desert scenes, children, and flower gardens.

Books

Barnes and Noble (⊠ Metrocenter, I–17 and Peoria Ave., West Phoenix ☏ 602/678–0088 ⊠ 4847 E. Ray Rd., South Phoenix ☏ 480/940–7136

✉ 10500 N. 90th St., North Scottsdale ☎ 480/391–0048 ✉ Kierland Commons, 7030 E. Greenway Pkwy., North Scottsdale ☎480/948–8551) has the most stores in Arizona of any chain.

Bookstar (✉ 2073 E. Camelback Rd., Camelback Corridor ☎ 602/957–2001 ✉ 12863 N. Tatum Blvd., North-Central Phoenix ☎ 602/953–8066) is a good place to find deep discounts on popular books.

B. Dalton (✉ Metrocenter, I–17 and Peoria Ave., West Phoenix ☎ 602/997–5847 ✉ Paradise Valley Mall, Cactus Rd. and Tatum Blvd., Paradise Valley ☎ 602/996–7430) has two stores in the Valley.

Borders Books and Music (✉ 2402 E. Camelback Rd., Camelback Corridor ☎ 602/957–6660 ✉ 4555 E. Cactus Rd., North-Central Phoenix ☎ 602/953–9699) is a popular chain with a good music selection.

Brentano's Bookstore (✉ Scottsdale Fashion Square South, 7014-590 E. Camelback Rd., Camelback Corridor ☎ 480/423–8717) is a small bookstore with an assortment of stationery and cards.

Changing Hands Bookstore (✉ 6428 S. McClintock Dr., Tempe ☎ 480/730–0205) has three stories of new and used books and an inviting atmosphere that will tempt you to linger.

Gifts Anonymous (✉ 4524 N. 7th St., Central Phoenix ☎ 602/277–5256) carries books and small gifts exclusively for those in 12-step programs.

Guidon (✉ 7117 E. Main St., Downtown Scottsdale ☎ 480/946–0521), a small, independent bookshop in Scottsdale's art district, specializes in out-of-print and hard-to-find Western fiction and nonfiction titles.

The **Poisoned Pen** (✉ 4014 N. Goldwater Blvd., Central Scottsdale ☎ 480/947–2974) specializes in mysteries.

Those Were the Days (✉ 516 S. Mill Ave., Tempe ☎ 480/967–4729) sells used and rare books.

Waldenbooks (✉ Metrocenter, I–17 and Peoria Ave., West Phoenix ☎ 602/997–8861 ✉ Paradise Valley Mall, Cactus Rd. and Tatum Blvd., Paradise Valley ☎ 602/953–2407 ✉ 302 E. Bell Rd., North-Central Phoenix ☎ 602/863–2424) is a large, primarily mall-based chain scattered throughout the Valley.

SIDE TRIPS NEAR PHOENIX

All the following sights are within a 1- to 1½-hour drive of Phoenix. To the north, the thriving artist communities of Carefree and Cave Creek are popular Western attractions. Arcosanti and Wickenburg are half- or full-day trips from Phoenix. Stop along the way to visit the petroglyphs of Deer Valley Rock Art Center and the reenactments of Arizona territorial life at the Pioneer Arizona Living History Museum. You also might consider Arcosanti and Wickenburg as stopovers on the way to or from Flagstaff, Prescott, or Sedona.

South of Phoenix, an hour's drive takes you back to prehistoric times and the site of Arizona's first known civilization at Casa Grande Ruins National Monument, a vivid reminder of the Hohokam who began farming this area more than 1,500 years ago. The nearby town of Florence, one of central Arizona's first cities, is filled with territorial architecture.

Deer Valley Rock Art Center

❹ *15 mi north of downtown Phoenix on Interstate 17. Exit at W. Deer Valley Road and drive 2 mi west.*

On the lower slopes of the Hedgepeth Hills, Deer Valley Rock Art Center has the largest concentration of ancient petroglyphs in the metropolitan Phoenix area. Some 1,500 of the cryptic symbols are found here, left behind by Native American cultures that lived in the Valley (or passed through) during the past 1,000 years. After watching one of the videos about the petroglyphs, pick up a pair of binoculars for $1 and an informative trail map and set out on the ¼-mi path. Telescopic tubes point to some of the most well-formed petroglyphs, but you'll soon be picking them out everywhere: mysterious, enduring, and beautiful, they range from human and animal forms to more abstract figures. Even the cars whizzing by in the distance can't spoil this trip through ancient art and culture. For more information about petroglyphs, *see* The Writing on the Wall Closeup box *in Chapter 5.* ⊠ *3711 W. Deer Valley Rd., North Phoenix* ☎ *623/582–8007* ⊕ *www.asu.edu/clas/anthropology/ dvrac* ⌂ *$5* ☉ *May–Sept., Tues.–Fri. 8–2, Sat. 9–5, Sun. noon–5; Oct.–Apr., Tues.–Sat. 9–5, Sun. noon–5.*

Pioneer Arizona Living History Museum

☾ ❺ *25 mi north of downtown Phoenix on Interstate 17 (Exit 225 [Pioneer Road]), just north of the Carefree Highway (AZ 74).*

The Pioneer Arizona Living History Museum contains 28 original and reconstructed buildings from throughout territorial Arizona. Costumed guides filter through the bank, schoolhouse, and print shop, as well as the Pioneer Opera House, where classic melodramas are performed daily. This museum is popular with the grade-school field-trip set, and it's your lucky day if you can tag along for their tour of the site—particularly when John the Blacksmith forges, smelts, and answers sixth-graders' questions that adults are too know-it-all to ask. For an extra $5 per adult, tour the grounds via a reproduction Conestoga wagon. ⊠ *3901 W. Pioneer Rd., North Phoenix, Phoenix* ☎ *623/465–1052* ⊕ *www.pioneer-arizona.com* ⌂ *$7* ☉ *Wed.–Sun. 9–5.*

Cave Creek & Carefree

❻ *15 mi. north of downtown Phoenix on Interstate 17. Exit at Carefree Highway and turn right, then go 12 mi. Turn left onto Cave Creek Road and go 3 mi to downtown Cave Creek then another 4 mi on Cave Creek Road to Carefree.*

Some 30 mi north of Phoenix, resting high in the Sonoran Desert at an elevation of 2,500 feet, the towns of Cave Creek and Carefree look back to a lifestyle far different than that of their more populous neighbors to the south.

Cave Creek got its start with the discovery of gold in the region. When the mines and claims "played out," the cattlemen arrived, and

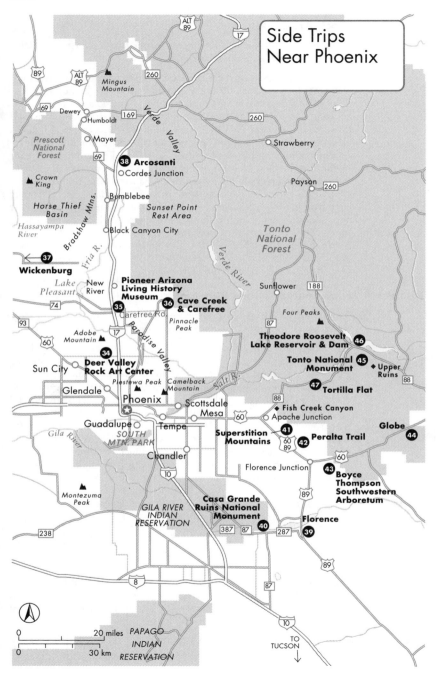

Side Trips
Near Phoenix

ALT 89

17

ALT 89

89

69

▲ *Mingus Mountain*

260

Dewey ○

Humboldt ○

169

Verde Valley

260

Prescott National Forest

○ Mayer

○ Strawberry

69

38 Arcosanti
○ Cordes Junction

Payson

260

▲ Crown King

Bumblebee

Sunset Point Rest Area

Horse Thief Basin

Bradshaw Mtns.

Tonto National Forest

Hassayampa River

○ Black Canyon City

Verde River

Fria R.

37 ←
Wickenburg

Lake Pleasant

New River

Pioneer Arizona Living History Museum

Sunflower

188

93

74

17

35 Carefree Rd.

36 Cave Creek & Carefree

Pinnacle Peak

87

Four Peaks ▲

60

▲ *Adobe Mountain*

Paradise Valley

Theodore Roosevelt Lake Reservoir & Dam **46**

34 Deer Valley Rock Art Center

Tonto National Monument **45**

♦ Upper Ruins

88

Sun City

Piestewa Peak ▲

Camelback Mountain ▲

Salt R.

47 Tortilla Flat

Glendale

Phoenix ★

Scottsdale

88

♦ *Fish Creek Canyon*

Globe

Mesa

60

○ Apache Junction

44

Guadalupe ○

Tempe

41

Gila River

SOUTH MTN. PARK

Superstition Mountains

60
89

42 Peralta Trail

60

Chandler

10

Florence Junction ○

43 Boyce Thompson Southwestern Arboretum

89

▲ *Montezuma Peak*

GILA RIVER INDIAN RESERVATION

Casa Grande Ruins National Monument

Florence

238

387

87

40

287

39

8

87

89

⊛

0 ____ 20 miles

0 ____ 30 km

PAPAGO INDIAN RESERVATION

10

TO TUCSON
↓

the sounds of horse hooves and lowing cattle replaced those of miners' picks. The area grew slowly and independently from Phoenix to the south, until a paved road connected the two in 1952. Today, the mile-long main stretch of town on Cave Creek Road is a great spot to have some hot chili and cold beer, try on Western duds, or learn the two-step in a "cowboy" bar. Or, you can amble up the hill and rent a horse for a trip into the Tonto National Forest in search of some long forgotten native petroglyphs.

Just about the time the dirt road–era ended in Cave Creek, planners were sketching out a new community, which became neighboring Carefree. The world's largest sundial, at the town's center, is surrounded by crafts shops, galleries, artists' workshops, and cafés. Today Cave Creek and Carefree sit cheek by jowl—but the one has beans, beef, biscuits, and beer, while the other discreetly orders up a notch or two.

Pick up maps and information about the area at the **Carefree-Cave Creek Chamber of Commerce.** ⊠ *748 Easy St., No. 9, Carefree 85377* ☎ *480/ 488–3381* ⊕ *www.carefree-cavecreek.com* ⊙ *Weekdays 8–4.*

Exhibits at the **Cave Creek Museum** depict pioneer living, mining, and ranching. There's a restored 1920s tuberculosis cabin and a collection of Indian artifacts from the Hohokam and Yavapai tribes. ⊠ *6140 E. Skyline Dr., Cave Creek* ☎ *480/488–2764* ⊕ *www.cavecreekmuseum. org* ⊠ *$3* ⊙ *Oct.–May, Wed.–Sun. 1–4:30.*

⚘ Pseudo-Western **Frontier Town** (⊠ 6245 E. Cave Creek Rd., Cave Creek) has wooden sidewalks, ramshackle buildings, and souvenir shops. You can grab a sandwich and a bottle of locally-brewed Cave Creek Chile Beer (with a real chile pepper in each bottle) at **Crazy Ed's Satisfied Frog** (⊠ 6245 E. Cave Creek Rd., Cave Creek ☎ 480/488–3317).

The **Heard Museum North,** a small satellite of the big Heard in downtown Phoenix, has one gallery with its own small, permanent collection of Native American art; it also hosts two rotating exhibits during the year, which may be made up of items from the parent Heard's permanent collection or exhibits on loan from other museums. The gift shop is well stocked with expensive, high-quality items. ⊠ *el Pedregal Shopping Mall, 34505 N. Scottsdale Rd., at Carefree Hwy., Carefree* ☎ *480/ 488–9817* ⊕ *www.heard.org* ⊠ *$3* ⊙ *Mon.–Sat. 10–5:30, Sun. noon–5.*

Sports & the Outdoors

GOLF   The **Boulders Resort Golf Club** (⊠ The Boulders, 34831 N. Tom Darlington Dr., Carefree ☎ 480/488–9028 ⊕ www.wyndham.com) has two 18-hole, par-72 courses.

HORSEBACK RIDING   **Spur Cross Stable** (⊠ 44029 Spur Cross Rd., Cave Creek ☎ 480/488– 9117 or 800/758–9530 ⊕ www.horsebackarizona.com) has well-cared-for horses that will take you on one- to seven-hour rides to the high Sonoran Desert of the Spur Cross Preserve and the Tonto National Forest. Longer rides include visits to petroglyph sites and a saddlebag lunch.

Where to Stay & Eat

$$-$$$ ✕ **Tonto Bar & Grill at Rancho Manana.** Old West ambience oozes from every corner of the Tonto Bar & Grill, from the hand-carved beams of the ceiling to the latilla (stick)-covered patios with views of the pristine Sonoran Desert. Try the cowboy Cobb salad or the Tonto burger piled with fried onions and Tillamook cheddar for lunch; lamb chops with leek fondue or grilled grouper with orange-tomato salsa are good choices at dinner. ⊠ *5736 E. Rancho Manana Blvd., Cave Creek* ☎ *480/488–0698* ⊟ *AE, D, DC, MC, V.*

$-$$$ ✕ **Horny Toad Restaurant.** The Horny Toad is a rustic spot for barbecued pork ribs and steak, but the real star here is the crispy fried chicken. There's a chapel out back in case you feel like "making it legal." ⊠ *6738 E. Cave Creek Rd., Cave Creek* ☎ *480/488–9542* ⊟ *AE, D, DC, MC, V.*

$$$$ 🏨 **The Boulders Resort and Golden Door Spa.** One of the country's top re-
Fodor'sChoice sorts hides amid hill-sized, 12-million-year-old granite boulders and the
★ lush Sonoran Desert. Casitas snuggled against the rocks have exposed log-beam ceilings and curved, pueblo-style half-walls and shelves. Each has a patio with a view, a wood-burning fireplace, and a spacious bathroom with deep soaking tub. El Pedregal Market Place, an upscale mall, adjoins the resort, and there are two golf courses. The Golden Door spa is one of the best in the state. ⊠ *34631 N. Tom Darlington Dr., Carefree 85377* ☎ *480/488–9009 or 800/553–1717* ⊟ *480/488–4118* ⊕ *www.wyndham.com* ⇆ *160 casitas, 46 patio homes* ⟺ *5 restaurants, room service, in-room data ports, in-room safes, some kitchens, minibars, cable TV, 2 18-hole golf courses, 6 tennis courts, 2 pools, gym, hair salon, spa, hiking, horseback riding, concierge, Internet, business services, meeting rooms, car rental, free parking* ⊟ *AE, D, DC, MC, V.*

$-$$ 🏨 **Cave Creek Tumbleweed Hotel.** Innkeepers Gary and Jeri Rust have kept the 1950s flavor of Cave Creek's only hotel intact. There's a fireplace in the lobby and a quiet pool outside. Red and tan rooms have Southwestern and cowboy accents. The hotel is a short walk from restaurants and shops in town. ⊠ *6333 E. Cave Creek Rd., Cave Creek 85327* ☎ *480/488–3668* ⊕ *www.tumbleweedhotel.com* ⇆ *32 rooms, 8 casitas* ⟺ *Picnic area, BBQs, some kitchenettes, cable TV, pool, hot tub, shop, Internet, some pets allowed (fee), non-smoking rooms* ⊟ *AE, MC, V.*

Nightlife

Watch real cowboys and cowgirls doing the two-step to live music at **Buffalo Chip Saloon** (⊠ 6811 E. Cave Creek Rd., Cave Creek ☎ 480/488–9118). Chow down on Mesquite grilled chicken and Buffalo Chips (hot, homemade potato chips). Reservations are suggested for the all-you-can-eat Friday night fish fry that draws crowds. **Harold's Cave Creek Corral** (⊠ 6895 E. Cave Creek Rd., Cave Creek ☎ 480/488–1906) is just across the dirt parking lot from the Buffalo Chip Saloon. Harold's has two full bars, a restaurant (serving some of the best ribs in the Valley), a huge dance floor with live bands on weekends, a game room, and 15 TVs. If you're a Steeler's fan, this is the place to be on Sunday during football season.

Shopping

Cave Creek and Carefree are home to a thriving arts community with hundreds of artists and dozens of galleries. Galleries open their doors for exhibitions, demonstrations, and artist receptions on **Cave Creek/Carefree: Art Night.** Most participating galleries are scattered along Cave Creek Road. Look for lighted ART NIGHT signs outside the shops. You can also pick up a list of participating galleries at the Gallery Association offices, at local restaurants, or on the Web. ✉ *Cave Creek/Carefree Gallery Association, 38252 N. Jacqueline Dr., Cave Creek* ☎ *480/488–2334* ⊕ *www. cavecreekcarefreegalleries.com* ☯ *Nov.–May, Fri. 6 PM–9 PM.*

El Pedregal Festival Marketplace (✉ Scottsdale Rd. and Carefree Hwy., Carefree ☎ 480/488–1072) is a two-tiered shopping plaza at the foot of a 250-foot boulder formation. In spring and summer there are open-air Thursday-night concerts in the courtyard amphitheater. In addition to its posh boutiques and specialty stores, el Pedregal contains the Heard Museum North, a satellite of the downtown Heard with its own gift shop. The **Spanish Village** (✉ Ho and Hum Rds., Carefree ☎ 480/488–0350), an outdoor shopping area, comes complete with bell tower, fountains, courtyards, and winding alleyways. While away an afternoon browsing 30 shops and contemplating dinner at one of several casual restaurants.

Wickenburg

❸❼ *70 mi from Phoenix. Follow Interstate 17 north for about 25 mins to the Carefree Highway (AZ 74) junction. About 30 mi west on AZ 74, take U.S. 89/93 north and go another 10 mi to Wickenburg.*

This town, land of guest ranches and tall tales, is named for Henry Wickenburg, whose nearby Vulture Mine was the richest gold strike in the Arizona Territory. By the late 1800s, Wickenburg was a booming mining town on the banks of the Hassayampa River with a seemingly endless supply of gold, copper, and silver. Resident miners developed a reputation for waxing overenthusiastic about the area's potential wealth, helping to coin the term "Hassayamper" for tellers-of-tales throughout the Old West. Legend has it that a drink from the Hassayampa River will cause one to fib forevermore—a tough claim to test, since for most of the river's 100-mi course it flows underground. Nowadays, Wickenburg's Old West history attracts visitors to its sleepy downtown and Western museum. There is a group of good antiques shops, most of which are found on Tegner and Frontier streets. On the northeast corner of Wickenburg Way and Tegner Street, check out the **Jail Tree,** to which prisoners were chained, the desert heat sometimes finishing them off before their sentences were served. Maps for self-guided walking tours of the town's historic buildings are available at the **Wickenburg Chamber of Commerce** (✉ 216 N. Frontier St. ☎ 928/684–5479 ⊕ www. wickenburgchamber.com), in the city's old Santa Fe Depot.

The **Desert Caballeros Western Museum** has a collection of paintings and sculpture by Remington, Bierstadt, Joe Beeler (founder of the Cowboy Artists of America), and others. The re-creation of a turn-of-the-20th-century Main Street includes a general store. ✉ *21 N. Frontier St.* ☎ *928/684–7075 or 928/684–2272* ⊕ *www.westernmuseum.org* 💲 *$6* ☯ *Mon.–Sat. 10–5, Sun. noon–4.*

The self-guided trails of **Hassayampa River Preserve** wind through lush cottonwood-willow forests, mesquite trees, and around a 4-acre, spring-fed pond and marsh habitat. Waterfowl, herons, and Arizona's rarest raptors shelter here. ⊠ *3 mi southeast of Wickenburg on U.S. 60* ☎ *928/684-2772* 🖼 *$5* ⊘ *Mid-Sept.–mid-May, Wed.–Sun. 8–5; mid-May–mid-Sept., Fri.–Sun. 8–5.*

The **Vulture Mine** was once the largest producing gold mine in Arizona, though its vein has long since run out. A small town originally grew up around the mine, but the only thing left today are a few storage buildings and a home where caretakers live. The self-guided tour through this "ghost town" wanders past mining memorabilia (still in place on the grounds); old buildings including bunkhouses, the jail, and a blacksmith shop; the mine shaft itself; and the infamous hanging tree where some of the town's more notorious residents were hanged. The raw ore was crushed in the Hassayampa River about 10 mi away, and the town of Wickenburg sprung up there to provide services to miners working at the Vulture operation. Head west from Wickenburg on U.S. 60 for about 6 mi; then turn left onto Vulture Mine Road and travel 12 mi to the mine at the end of the pavement. ⊠ *Vulture Mine Rd., Vulture Mine* ☎ *520/859-2743* 🖼 *$7* ⊘ *Fall and winter, Thurs.–Mon. 8–4; spring and summer, Fri.–Sun. 8–4.*

Where to Stay & Eat

¢–$$ ✕ **Anita's Cocina.** Reliable Tex-Mex fare is served at Anita's. Fresh, steaming tamales are especially tasty, for either lunch or dinner. Try a fruit burrito for dessert. ⊠ *57 N. Valentine St.* ☎ *928/684-5777* 🖃 *MC, V.*

$$$$ 🏨 **Kay El Bar Ranch.** Personable, low-key, and remote—this is what guest ranches used to be. John and Nancy Loftis accept only 24 guests at a time at their ranch, which is tucked into a hollow by the Hassayampa River. Some of the biggest mesquite trees in Arizona shade the lodge, a family cottage with private patio (built in 1914), two separate casitas, and charming adobe cookhouse, where family-style meals are served. Each compact room in the lodge—designed for sleeping rather than hanging out—has a small, modern bathroom. In the evening everyone gathers in the living room for cocktails and homemade hors d'oeuvres by the stone fireplace. ⊠ *37500 S. Rincon Rd.* ⬦ *Box 2480, 85358* ☎ *928/684-7593* ⊕ *www.kayelbar.com* ➥ *8 rooms, 1 house, 2 casitas* ⚹ *Dining room, golf privileges, pool, hot tub, horseback riding, Ping-Pong, volleyball, library; no room phones, no room TVs* 🖃 *MC, V* ⊘ *Closed May–mid-Oct.* ⦿ *FAP.*

$$$$ 🏨 **Rancho de los Caballeros.** This 20,000-acre property combines the guest-ranch experience with first-class amenities. Meals are served in the lodge's bright, festive dining room, and everyone is asked to dress for each night's sit-down dinner. Rooms are spacious, done in low-key Southwestern style. Some contain two queen-size beds and can be creatively configured—through a system of adjoining doors—to annex separate living rooms or sleeping quarters for children. The Los Caballeros Golf Club course is considered one of the country's top resort courses. ⊠ *1551 S. Vulture Mine Rd., 85390* ☎ *928/684-5484* 🖷 *928/684-2267* ⊕ *www.guestranches.com/caballeros* ➥ *79 rooms* ⚹ *Dining room,*

driving range, 18-hole golf course, 4 tennis courts, pool, massage, bicycles, horseback riding, lounge, children's programs (ages 5–12) ⊟ *No credit cards* ⊙ *Closed mid-May–Oct.*

Nightlife

The **Rancher Bar** (⊠ 910 W. Wickenburg Way ☎ 928/684–5957) is a modern-day saloon where real live wranglers and cowboys meet up to shoot some pool after a hard day's work. A live country-music combo plays weekend nights, when the two-stepping locals really file in.

Arcosanti

38 *65 mi north of Phoenix on Interstate 17, near the exit for Cordes Junction (AZ 69).*

Two miles down a partly paved road northeast from the gas stations and cafés, the evolving complex and community of Arcosanti was masterminded by Italian architect Paolo Soleri to be a self-sustaining habitat in which architecture and ecology function in symbiosis. Arcosanti is a bit tired-looking these days and hasn't quite achieved Soleri's original vision. However, it's still worth a stop to take a tour, have a bite at the café, and purchase one of the hand-cast bronze wind-bells made at the site. The town is off Interstate 17 at Cordes Junction, near the town of Mayer. ☎ 928/632–7135 ⊕ *www.arcosanti.org* ⊠ *Tour $8* ⊙ *Daily 9–5; tours hrly 10–4.*

en route | If you're continuing from Arcosanti to Prescott, consider stopping in at **Young's Farm** (⊠ AZ 69 at AZ 169, Dewey ☎ 928/632–7272). Family run since 1947, Young's sells fresh turkeys for the holidays, has hayrides and a pumpkin festival in October, a petting zoo, and a restaurant serving hearty lunches and dinners. The store has become a beloved purveyor of fresh vegetables, potpies and pumpkins, sweet corn and cider, honey and fresh bread.

Florence

39 *Take U.S. 60 east (Superstition Freeway) to Florence Junction (U.S. 60 and AZ 79) and head south 16 mi on AZ 79 to Florence.*

A Victorian courthouse and more than 150 other sites listed on the National Register of Historic Places distinguish this Old West town southeast of Phoenix. It was once a tough place where saloons outnumbered churches by 28 to 1 and even women robbed stagecoaches. You may recognize Florence as the location where *Murphy's Romance* was filmed. The **Pinal County Visitor's Center** (⊠ 330 W. Butte St. ☎ 520/868–4331 ⊕ www.co.pinal.az.us/visitorcenter) answers questions and provides brochures September through May, weekdays 8 to 3, and June–August, weekdays 9 to 2.

The **Pinal County Historical Society** (⊠ 715 S. Main St. ☎ 520/868–4382), a free museum open Tuesday through Saturday 11 to 4 and Sunday noon to 4, displays furnishings from 1900s houses and Native American crafts and tools. There is also a rather unsettling collection of nooses from actual executions. Open Thursday through Monday 8 to 5, **McFarland State Historic Park** (⊠ Main and Ruggles Sts. ☎ 520/868–5216 ⊕ www.pr.state.az.us) houses memorabilia of former governor and U.S. senator Ernest W. McFarland in the circa-1878 Pinal County Courthouse.

Where to Eat

¢–$$ ✕ **Old Pueblo Restaurant.** Of the down-home Mexican and American fare served in this simple restaurant, the steak fajita burros, chimichangas, and *carne asada* (grilled beefsteak) are favorites. ⊠ *505 S. Main St.* ☎ *520/868–4784* ▭ *AE, D, DC, MC, V* ⊘ *Closed Sat.*

Casa Grande Ruins National Monument

⓯ *9 mi west of Florence on AZ 287 or, from Interstate 10, 16 mi east on AZ 387 and AZ 87. Note: follow the signs to the ruins, not to the town of Casa Grande. When leaving the ruins, take AZ 87 north 35 mi back to U.S. 60.*

The ruins of Casa Grande were unknown to European explorers until Father Kino, a Jesuit missionary, first recorded their existence in 1694. The ruins were named a national monument in 1918. Allow an hour to explore the site, longer if park rangers are giving a talk or leading a tour.

Start at the visitor center, where a small museum displays artifacts and information on the Hohokam, who lived here and farmed irrigated fields of corn, beans, squash, cotton, tobacco, and other crops until they vanished mysteriously in about AD 1450. Begin your self-guided tour with an inspection of the 35-foot-tall (that's four stories) Casa Grande (Big House), the tallest Hohokam building known, built in the early 14th century. Today it sits underneath a modern roof erected on posts to protect it from sun and wind. Neighboring structures are much smaller, and only a bit of the 7-foot wall around the compound is still in evidence. The original purpose of Casa Grande still eludes archaeologists; some think it was an ancient astronomical observatory or a center of government, religion, trade, or education. On your way out, cross the parking lot by the covered picnic grounds and climb the platform for a view of a ball court and two platform mounds, said to date from the 1100s. Although only a few prehistoric sites can be viewed, more than 60 are included in the monument area. ⊠ *AZ 87, Coolidge* ☎ *520/723–3172* ⊕ *www.nps.gov/cagr* ▱ *$3* ⊘ *Daily 8–5.*

THE APACHE TRAIL

Fodor'sChoice   President Theodore Roosevelt called this 150-mi drive "the most awe-in-
★   spiring and most sublimely beautiful panorama nature ever created." A stretch of winding highway, the AZ 88 portion of the Apache Trail closely follows the route forged through wilderness in 1906 to move construction supplies to build Roosevelt Dam, which lies at the northernmost part of the loop. Take a day to drive the trail, which makes large loop east of Phoenix, drink in the vistas, and stop to explore along the way.

THE LOST DUTCHMAN MINE

NOT MUCH IS KNOWN ABOUT JACOB "THE DUTCHMAN" WALTZ, *except that he was born around 1808 in Germany (he was "Deutsch," not "Dutch") and emigrated to the United States, where he spent several years at mining camps in the Southeast, in the West, and finally in Arizona. There is certainly enough documentation that he indeed did have access to a large quantity of gold, though he never registered a claim for the mine that was attributed to him.*

In 1868, Waltz appeared in the newly developing community of Pumpkinville, soon to become Phoenix. He kept to himself on his 160-acre homestead on the banks of the Salt River. From time to time, he would disappear for a few weeks and return with enough high-quality ore to keep him in a wonderful fashion. Soon word was out that "Crazy Jake" had a vast gold mine in the Superstition Mountains, east of the city near the Apache Trail.

Stories also were circulating at that time about a wealthy gold mine discovered by the Peralta family of Mexico. The local Apaches raided the mine, which was near their sacred Thunder Mountain. The Peraltas and more than 100 peons working for them at the mine were killed, their mules were slaughtered and eaten, and the bags of gold emptied upon the ground. Rumors soon spread that Waltz had saved the life of a young Apache and was shown the Peralta's mine as a reward.

As the legend of the Dutchman's mine grew, numerous opportunists attempted to follow Waltz into the Superstition Mountains. A crack marksman, Waltz quickly discouraged several who tried to track him. At least two others mysteriously disappeared and were never heard from again. The flow of gold continued for several years.

In 1891 the Salt River flooded, badly damaging Waltz's home. When the floodwaters receded, neighbors found Waltz there in a weakened condition. He was taken to the nearby home and boarding house of Julia Thomas, who nursed the Dutchman for months. Finally, when his death was imminent, he reportedly gave Julia the directions to his mine. He died early in the morning of October 25, 1891.

Julia and another German boarder searched for the mine fruitlessly. In her later years, she sold maps to the treasure, based upon her recollections of Waltz's description. Dozens upon dozens of maps have appeared over the years. Thousands have searched for the lost mine; many losing their lives in the process. More than a century later, gold seekers are still trying to connect the pieces of the puzzle.

There's no doubt that the Dutchman had a source of extremely rich gold ore. Was it in the Superstition Mountains, or the nearby Goldfields, or even in the Four Peaks region? New evidence has surfaced in the case. Not too many years ago a pile of rich ore was found atop pieces of a rotting leather bag of Spanish or Mexican origin. The source of the Dutchman's gold remains hidden somewhere in the parched desert surrounding Phoenix. Perhaps the best-researched books on the subject are T.E. Glover's The Lost Dutchman Mine of Jacob Waltz *and the companion book,* The Holmes Manuscript. *Ron Feldman of OK Corral (www.okcorrals.com) in Apache Junction has become an expert on the subject during his 30-plus years in the region. He leads adventurers on pack trips into the mysterious mountains to relive the lore and legends.*

— Bob and Gloria Willis

From the town of Apache Junction, you can choose to drive the trail in either direction; there are advantages to both. If you begin the loop going clockwise—heading eastward on AZ 88—your drive may be more relaxing; you'll be on the farthest side of this narrow dirt road some refer to as the "white-knuckle route," with its switchbacks and drop-offs straight down into spectacular Fish Creek Canyon. But if you follow the route counterclockwise—continuing on U.S. 60 past the town of Apache Junction—you'll be able to appreciate each attraction better.

The tour below follows the route counterclockwise. Although the drive itself can be completed in one day, it's advisable to consider spending a night in Globe and continuing the loop back to Phoenix the following day.

Superstition Mountains

❹① *From Phoenix, take Interstate 10 and then U.S. 60 (the Superstition Freeway) east through the suburbs of Tempe, Mesa, and Apache Junction.*

As the Phoenix metro area gives way to cactus- and creosote-dotted desert, the massive escarpment of the Superstition Mountains heaves into view and slides by to the north. The Superstitions are supposedly where the legendary Lost Dutchman Mine is, the location—not to mention the existence—of which has been hotly debated since pioneer days. (⇨ Legend of the Lost Dutchmine Mine Closeup). The best place to learn about the "Dutchman" Jacob Waltz and the Lost Dutchman Mine is at **Superstition Mountain Museum** (⊠ 4087 N. Apache Trail [AZ 88], Apache Junction 85217 ☏ 480/983–4888 ⊕ www. superstitionmountainmuseum.org ☒ $4 ⊙ daily 9–4). The museum exhibits include a collection of mining tools, historical maps, and artifacts relating to the "gold" age of the Superstition Mountains. Western history buffs take note: the gift shop has a large collection of books on the region.

Goldfield became an instant city of about 4,000 residents after a gold strike in 1892. The town dried up five years later when the gold mine flooded. Today, **Goldfield Ghost Town** (⊠ 4650 N. Mammoth Mine Rd., 4 mi northeast of Apache Junction on AZ 88, Goldfield ☏ 480/983–0333 ⊕ www.goldfieldghosttown.com) is really a tourist trap, but it is nonetheless an interesting place to grab a cool drink, pan for gold, or go for a mine tour. The ghost town's shops are open daily 10 to 5, the saloon daily 10 to 8.

Peralta Trail

❹② *About 11½ mi southeast of Apache Junction, off U.S. 60, take the Peralta Trail Road (just past King's Ranch Road), an 8-mi, rough gravel road that leads to the start of the Peralta Trail.*

The 4-mi round-trip Peralta Trail winds 1,400 feet up a small valley for a spectacular view of **Weaver's Needle**, a monolithic rock formation that is one of Arizona's more famous sights. Allow a few hours for this rugged and challenging hike, bring plenty of water and a snack or lunch, and don't hike it in the middle of the day in summer.

Boyce Thompson Southwestern Arboretum

★ ⓸ *12 mi east of Florence Junction (U.S. 60 and AZ 79).*

At the foot of Picketpost Mountain, the Boyce Thompson Southwestern Arboretum is one of the treasures of the Sonoran Desert. From the visitor center, well-marked, self-guided trails traverse 35 acres, winding through all of the desert's varied habitats—from gravelly open desert to lush creekside glades. Native flora coexists alongside imported exotic specimens such as Canary Islands date palms and Australian eucalyptus. The Smith Interpretive Center, a National Historic Site, has two greenhouses and displays on geology, plant propagation, and native basketry. Benches with built-in misting machines are a relief on hot days, and natural exhibits illustrate such subjects as herbs used in traditional Sonoran healing. Bring a sack lunch and enjoy the arboretum's lovely picnic grounds. ✉ *37615 U.S. 60, Superior* ☎ *520/689–2811* ⊕ *www. ag.arizona.edu/bta* ✍ *$6* ⊘ *Daily 8–5.*

en route A few miles farther past the arboretum, **Superior** is the first of several modest mining towns and the launching point for a dramatic winding ascent through the Mescals to a 4,195-foot pass that affords panoramic views of this copper-rich range and its huge, dormant, open-pit mines. Collectors will want to watch for antiques shops through these hills, but be forewarned that quality varies considerably. A gradual descent will take you into **Miami** and **Claypool,** once-thriving boomtowns that have carried on quietly since major-corporation mining ground to a halt in the 1970s. Working-class buildings are dwarfed by the mountainous piles of copper tailings to the north. At a stoplight in Claypool, AZ 88 splits off northward to the Apache Trail, but continue on U.S. 60 another 3 mi to make the stop in the city of Globe.

Globe

⓸ *U.S. 60, 51 mi east of Apache Junction, 25 mi east of Superior, and 3 mi east of Claypool's AZ 88 turnoff.*

In the southern reaches of Tonto National Forest, Globe is the most cosmopolitan of the area's mining towns. Initially, it was gold and silver that brought miners here—the city allegedly got its name from a large, circular boulder of silver, with lines like continents, found by prospectors—although the region is now known for North America's richest copper deposits. If you're driving the Apache Trail loop, be sure to stop in Globe to fill up the tank, as it is the last chance to gas up until looping all the way back to U.S. 60 at Apache Junction. But Globe is worth more than a quick pit stop; its charm is its lack of prestige—and, in some cases, modernity. At the **Globe Chamber of Commerce** (✉ 1¼ mi north of downtown on U.S. 60 ☎ 928/425–4495 or 800/ 804–5623 ⊕ www.globemiamichamber.com), open weekdays 9–5, you can pick up brochures detailing the self-guided Historic Downtown Walking Tour.

A good place to begin a visit to Globe is the **Gila County Historical Museum** (✉ 1330 N. Broad St. ☎ 928/425–7385) to see the collection of memorabilia from the area's mining days. The museum, which is free, is open weekdays 9 to 5. The restored late-19th-century Gila County Courthouse houses the **Cobre Valley Center for the Arts** (✉ 101 N. Broad St. ☎ 928/425–0884), showcasing works by local artists. Also visit the ladies and their looms in the basement Weaver's Studio, open Thursday through Saturday 10 to 3.

For a step 800 years back in time, tour the 2 acres of excavated Salado Indian ruins on the southeastern side of town at the **Besh-Ba-Gowah Archaeological Park.** After a trip through the small museum and a video introduction, enter the area full of remnants of more than 200 rooms occupied here by the Salado during the 13th and 14th centuries. Public areas include the central plaza (also the principal burial ground; archaeologists have uncovered more than 150 burials), roasting pits, and open patios. Besh-Ba-Gowah is a name given by the Apaches, who, arriving in the 17th century, found the pueblo abandoned and moved in. Loosely translated, the name means "metal camp," as remains left on the site point to it as part of an extensive commerce and trading network. ✉ *150 N. Pine St.* ☎ *928/425–0320* ⊕ *www.jqjacobs.net/ southwest/besh_ba_gowah.html* ⊜ *$3* ☉ *Daily 9–5.*

Where to Stay & Eat

¢–$ ✕ **Chalo's.** This casual roadside spot offers top-notch Mexican food. Try an order of the savory stuffed sopaipillas, which are filled with pork and beef, beans, and red or green chiles. ✉ *902 E. Ash St.* ☎ *928/425–0515* ⊟ *MC, V.*

¢–$ 🏨 **Noftsger Hill Inn.** Built in 1907, this bed-and-breakfast was originally the North Globe Schoolhouse; now classrooms serve as guest rooms, filled with mining-era antiques and affording fantastic views of the Pinal Mountains and historic Old Dominion Mine. All rooms have private baths; one has air-conditioning, and the rest have evaporative coolers, which work well at this cooler elevation. Innkeepers Rosalie and Dom Ayala promise you'll enjoy walking off "miner-size" breakfasts with a hike through the scenic Copper Hills behind the old school. ✉ *425 North St., 85501* ☎ *928/425–2260 or 877/780–2479* ⊕ *www. noftsgerhillinn.com* ⋙ *6 rooms* ♺ *VCRs in some rooms; no a/c in some rooms, no TV in some rooms, no smoking* ⊟ *MC, V* ❙❁❙ *BP.*

¢ 🏨 **El Rey Motel.** Hosts Rebecca and Ricardo Bernal lovingly operate this quintessential roadside motel, where wagon wheels and potted plants dot the grounds. This vintage motor court offers small, immaculate rooms; covered parking spaces; and a shared central picnic and barbecue area. ✉ *1201 E. Ash St., 85501* ☎ *928/425–4427* 🖷 *928/402–9147* ⋙ *23 rooms* ♺ *Picnic area, BBQ, cable TV* ⊟ *AE, D, MC, V.*

Nightlife

Run by the San Carlos Apache tribe, **Apache Gold** (✉ U.S. 70, 5 mi east of Globe ☎ 928/425–7800 or 800/272–2433) has more than 500 slots, keno, and video and live poker. Call about the free shuttle from most of Globe's hotels and motels.

Shopping

Broad Street, Globe's main drag, is lined with a number of antiques and gift shops. On Ash, between Hill and South East streets, **Copper City Rock Shop** (✉ 566 Ash St. ☎ 928/425–7885) specializes in mineral products, many from Arizona. **Past Times** (✉ 1068 Adonis Ave. ☎ 928/473–3791) carries antiques. **Simply Sarah** (✉ 294 N. Broad St. ☎ 928/425–2248), with its ornately carved stone arch, has upscale ladies' clothing in predominantly natural fibers and high-quality accessories. **True Blue Jewelry** (✉ 200 N. Willow St., Globe ☎ 928/425–8361) carries high-quality jewelry made with turquoise supplied by Globe's Sleeping Beauty Mine. Ask to watch the five-minute video about turquoise mining and preparing it for use. Try **Turquoise Ladies** (✉ 996 N. Broad St. ☎ 928/425–6288) for owner June Stratton's collection of uniquely Globe souvenirs and stories.

en route — At the stoplight 3 mi south of Globe on U.S. 60, AZ 88 splits off to the northwest. About 25 mi later on AZ 88, heading toward the Tonto National Monument, you'll see towering quartzite cliffs about 2 mi in the distance—look up and to the left for glimpses of the 40-room **Upper Ruins**, 14th-century condos left behind by the Salado people. They can't be seen from within the national monument, so make sure you've got binoculars.

Tonto National Monument

45 *30 mi northwest of U.S. 60 on AZ 88.*

This well-preserved complex of 13th-century Salado cliff dwellings is worth a stop. There is a self-guided walking tour of the Lower Cliff Dwellings, but if you have time, take a ranger-led tour of the 40-room Upper Cliff Dwellings, offered on selected mornings from November to April. Tour reservations are required and should be made as far as a month in advance. To reach Tonto National Monument, go northwest on AZ 88, 30 mi beyond the intersection of U.S. 60 and AZ 88. ✉ *AZ 88, Roosevelt* 🖃 *HC 02, Box 4602, 85545* ☎ *928/467–2241* ⊕ *www.nps.gov/tont* 🖾 *$3* ☉ *Daily 8–5; Nov.–Apr., tours Thurs. and weekends at 9:30 AM; May–Oct., tours Tues., Thurs., and weekends at 9:30 AM.*

Theodore Roosevelt Lake Reservoir & Dam

46 *5 mi northwest of Tonto National Monument on AZ 88.*

Flanked by the desolate Mazatzal and Sierra Anchas mountain ranges, this aquatic recreational area is a favorite with bass anglers, water-skiers, and boaters. Not only is this the largest masonry dam on the planet, but the massive bridge is the longest two-lane, single-span, steel-arch bridge in the nation.

en route — Past the reservoir, AZ 88 turns west and becomes a meandering dirt road, eventually winding its way back to Apache Junction via the magnificent, bronze-hued volcanic cliff walls of **Fish Creek Canyon,** with views of the sparkling lakes, towering saguaros, and, in the springtime, vast fields of wildflowers.

Tortilla Flat

47 *AZ 88, 38 mi southwest of Roosevelt Dam; 18 mi northeast of Apache Junction.*

Close to the end of the Apache Trail, this old-time restaurant and country store are what is left of an authentic stagecoach stop. This is a fun place to stop for a well-earned rest and refreshment—miner- and cowboy-style grub, of course—before heading back the last 18 mi to civilization. Enjoy a hearty bowl of killer chili and some prickly-pear-cactus ice cream while sitting at the counter on a saddle barstool.

VALLEY OF THE SUN A TO Z

To research prices, get advice from other travelers, and book travel arrangements, visit www.fodors.com

AIR TRAVEL

Phoenix Sky Harbor International Airport (PHX) is served by most major airlines, including Aeromexico, Air Canada, Alaska Airlines, Aloha Airlines, America West Airlines, American Airlines, ATA, Arizona Express, British Airways, Continental, Delta, Frontier, Great Lakes, Hawaiian Airlines, Lufthansa, Midwest Express, Northwest, Southwest, Sun Country, United, and US Airways. It's a major hub for both America West and Southwest.

AIRPORT

Most air travelers visiting Arizona fly into Phoenix Sky Harbor International Airport. Just 3 mi east of downtown Phoenix, it is surrounded by freeways linking it to almost every part of the metro area.

🛫 Sky Harbor International Airport (PHX) ☎ 602/273–3300 ⊕ www.phxskyharbor.com.

AIRPORT TRANSFERS It's easy to get from Sky Harbor to downtown Phoenix (3 mi west) and Tempe (3 mi east). The airport is also only about 30 minutes by freeway from Glendale (to the west) and Mesa (to the east). Scottsdale (to the northeast) can be reached by AZ 101; depending on your destination, expect the trip to take anywhere from 25 minutes to downtown Scottsdale to an hour to North Scottsdale.

Valley Metro buses can get you directly from Terminal 2, 3, or 4 to the bus terminal downtown (at 1st and Washington streets) or to Tempe (Mill and University avenues). With free transfers, the bus can take you from the airport to most other Valley cities (Glendale, Sun City, Scottsdale, etc.), but the trip is likely to be slow unless you take an express line.

The Red Line runs westbound to Phoenix every half hour from about 6 AM until after 9 PM weekdays. Saturday, take Bus 13 and transfer at Central Avenue to Bus 0 north. The Red Line runs eastbound to Tempe every half hour from 3:30 AM to 7; 25 minutes later, it goes to downtown Mesa (Center and Main streets). Fares range from $.60 to $1.75.

The blue vans of SuperShuttle cruise Sky Harbor, each taking up to seven passengers to their individual destinations, with no luggage fee or airport surcharge. Wheelchair vans are also available. Drivers accept credit cards and expect tips. Fares are $6 to downtown Phoenix, around $16 to most places in Scottsdale, and $18 to $35 to places in far north Scottsdale or Carefree.

Only a few taxi firms are licensed to pick up at Sky Harbor's commercial terminals. All cabs add a $1 surcharge for airport pickups, do not charge for luggage, and are available 24 hours a day. A trip to downtown Phoenix can range from $8 to $12. The fare to downtown Scottsdale averages about $18. If you're headed to the East Valley, expect to shell out more than $20. Checker/Yellow Cab and Courier Cab are the Valley's main taxi services and charge about $3 for the first mile and $1.50 per mile thereafter (not including tips).

A few limousine firms cruise Sky Harbor, and many more provide airport pickups by reservation. Scottsdale Limousine requires reservations but offers a toll-free number; rates start at $65 (plus tip).
🚖 **Checker/Yellow Cab** ☎ 602/252-5252. **Courier Cab** ☎ 602/232-2222. **Scottsdale Limousine** ☎ 480/946-8446 or 800/747-8234. **SuperShuttle** ☎ 602/244-9000 or 800/258-3826 ⊕ www.supershuttle.com. **Valley Metro buses** ☎ 602/253-5000.

BUS TRAVEL
Greyhound Lines has statewide and national routes from its main terminal near Sky Harbor airport.
🚌 **Greyhound Lines** ✉ 2115 E. Buckeye Rd., Phoenix ☎ 602/389-4200 or 800/229-9424 ⊕ www.greyhound.com.

BUS TRAVEL WITHIN THE VALLEY
Valley Metro routes service most of the Valley suburbs, but these routes are not really suitable for vacationers and offer limited service evenings and weekends. Fares are $1.25 for regular service, $1.75 for express, with free transfers. The city of Phoenix also runs a free Downtown Area Shuttle (DASH), with purple minibuses circling the area between the Arizona Center and the state capitol at 15-minute intervals from 6:30 AM to 11 PM weekdays and from 11 AM to 11 PM weekends; this system also serves major thoroughfares in several suburbs—Glendale, Scottsdale, Tempe, Mesa, and Chandler. The city of Tempe operates the Free Local Area Shuttle (FLASH), which serves the downtown Tempe and Arizona State University area from 7 AM until 8 PM. Check the Valley Metro Web site for all public transit options (including DASH and FLASH) in the Valley.
🚌 **Valley Metro** ☎ 602/262-7433 ⊕ www.valleymetro.org.

CAR RENTALS
To get around Phoenix, *you will need to rent a car*. Only the major downtown areas (Phoenix, Scottsdale, Tempe) are pedestrian-friendly. There is no mass transit beyond a commuter -bus system. At the airport most rental companies offer shuttle services to their lots. Don't expect to nab a car without a reservation, however, especially in the high season, from January to April. Most companies keep nearly all of their stock on the roads.
🚗 **Alamo** ☎ 602/244-0897. **Avis** ☎ 602/273-3222. **Budget** ☎ 602/267-1717. **Dollar** ☎ 602/224-2349. **Enterprise** ☎ 602/225-0588. **Hertz** ☎ 602/267-8822. **National** ☎ 602/275-4771. **Thrifty** ☎ 602/244-0311.

CAR TRAVEL

If you're coming to Phoenix from the west, you'll probably come in on Interstate 10. The trip from the Los Angeles basin, via Palm Springs, takes six to seven hours, depending on where you start. From San Diego, Interstate 8 slices across the low desert to Yuma and on toward the Valley on what the Spanish called El Camino del Diablo (the Devil's Highway); at Gila Bend, take AZ 85 up to Interstate 10. The trip takes a total of six to seven hours. From the east, Interstate 10 takes you from El Paso, across southern New Mexico, and through Chiricahua Apache country into Tucson, then north to Phoenix (a total of about 6 to 7 hours).

From the northwest, Interstate 40 crosses over from California and runs along old Route 66 to Flagstaff. East of Kingman, however, U.S. 93 branches off diagonally to the southeast, becoming U.S. 60 at Wickenburg and continuing into Phoenix.

The northeastern route, Interstate 40 from Albuquerque, crosses Hopi and Navajo historic lands to Flagstaff, where Interstate 17 takes you south to Phoenix—an eight-hour journey. For a scenic shortcut, take AZ 377 south at Holbrook to Heber and the pines of the Mogollon Rim; then take AZ 260 down the 2,000-foot drop to Payson and AZ 87 through the forests of saguaro cactus into Phoenix.

Around downtown Phoenix, AZ 202 (Papago Freeway), AZ 143 (Hohokam Freeway), and Interstate 10 (Maricopa Freeway) make an elongated east–west loop, encompassing the state capitol area to the west and Tempe to the east. At mid-loop, AZ 51 (Piestewa—formerly Squaw—Peak Parkway) runs north into Paradise Valley. From AZ 202 east, the AZ 101 runs north to Scottsdale and makes a loop west to Sun City. And from the loop's east end, Interstate 10 runs south to Tucson, 100 mi away (although it's still referred to as Interstate 10 east, as it is eventually headed that way); U.S. 60 (Superstition Freeway) branches east to Tempe and Mesa.

Roads in Phoenix and its suburbs are laid out on a single, 800-square-mi grid. Even the freeways run predominantly north–south and east–west. (Grand Avenue, running about 20 mi from northwest downtown to Sun City, is the *only* diagonal.)

Central Avenue is the main north–south grid axis: all roads parallel to and west of Central are numbered *avenues*; all roads parallel to and east of Central are numbered *streets*. The numbering begins at Central and increases in each direction.

RULES OF THE ROAD Camera devices are mounted on several streetlights to catch speeders and red-light runners, and their locations are constantly changing. You may think you've gotten away with a few miles over the limit and return home only to find a ticket waiting for you.

Many accidents in the Valley are created as a result of confusion in the left-turn lanes. Each individual jurisdiction varies. In some jurisdictions, the left-turn arrow precedes the green light and in other jurisdictions it follows the green light. As well, the yellow lights tend to be shorter than most drivers are accustomed to. Therefore, be prepared for sudden stops and watch intersections for yellow-light runners. Weekdays 6 AM to 9 AM and 4 PM to 6 PM, the center or left-turn lanes on the major surface arteries of 7th Street and 7th Avenue become one-way traffic-flow lanes between McDowell Road and Dunlap Avenue. These specially marked lanes are dedicated mornings to north–south traffic (into downtown) and afternoons to south–north traffic (out of downtown).

Arizona requires seat belts on front-seat passengers and children 16 and under.

EMERGENCIES

🔢 Emergencies **Ambulance, Fire, and Police Emergencies** ☎ 911.
🔢 Hospitals **Maricopa County Medical Center** ✉ 2601 E. Roosevelt St., Central Phoenix ☎ 602/344–5011. **Scottsdale Memorial Hospital** ✉ 7400 E. Osborn Rd., Central Scottsdale ☎ 480/481–4000 or 480/860–3000. **Doctor Referral** ☎ 602/252–2844.
🔢 Pharmacies **Osco Drug** ✉ 3320 N. 7th Ave., Central Phoenix ☎ 602/266–5501 ✉ 35th and Glendale Aves., West Phoenix ☎ 602/841–7861 ✉ Scottsdale and Shea Rds., North Scottsdale ☎ 480/998–3500 ✉ 1836 W. Baseline Rd., Mesa ☎ 480/831–0212. **Walgreens** ✉ 4114 N. 24th St., Central Phoenix ☎ 602/381–0275 ✉ 3605 E. Thomas Rd., Central Phoenix ☎ 602/267–0648 ✉ 1120 S. 16th St., South Phoenix ☎ 602/252–8758 ✉ 4006 E. Bell Rd., North-Central Phoenix ☎ 602/971–1096 ✉ 8449 E. Mac-Donald Dr., Paradise Valley ☎ 480/483–0628 ✉ 3420 N. Scottsdale Rd., Central Scottsdale ☎ 480/941–0525.

SIGHTSEEING TOURS

Reservations for tours are a must all year, with seats often filling up quickly in the busy season, October through April. All tours provide pickup services at area resorts, but some offer lower prices if you drive to the tour's point of origin.

FLOAT TRIPS Cimarron Adventures and River Co. arranges half-day float trips down the Salt and Verde rivers. Trips cost about $35 per person.
🔢 **Cimarron Adventures and River Co.** ✉ 7901 E. Pierce St., Scottsdale ☎ 480/994–1199 ⊕ www.thetent.com/arcadia/az/azcr_cimarron.htm.

ORIENTATION Gray Line Tours gives seasonal, three-hour narrated tours including down-
TOURS town Phoenix, the Arizona Biltmore hotel, Camelback Mountain, mansions in Paradise Valley, Arizona State University, Papago Park, and Scottsdale's Old Town; the price is about $40.

Open Road Tours offers excursions to Sedona and the Grand Canyon, Phoenix city tours, and Native American–culture trips to the Salt River Pima–Maricopa Indian Reservation.

For $38, Vaughan's Southwest Custom Tours gives a 4½-hour city tour for 11 or fewer passengers in custom vans, stopping at the Pueblo Grande Museum, the Arizona Biltmore, and the state capitol. Vaughan's will also take you east of Phoenix on the Apache Trail. The tour is offered on Tuesday, Friday, and Saturday; the cost is $75.
🔢 **Gray Line Tours** 🗄 Box 21126, Phoenix 85036 ☎ 602/495–9100 or 800/732–0327 ⊕ www.graylinearizona.com. **Open Road Tours** ✉ 522 E. Dunlap Ave., No. 2, Phoenix 85020 ☎ 602/997–6474 or 800/766–7117 ⊕ www.openroadtours.com. **Vaughan's Southwest Custom Tours** 🗄 Box 31250, Phoenix 85046 ☎ 602/971–1381 or 800/513–1381 ⊕ www.southwesttours.com.

TAXIS

Taxi fares are unregulated in Phoenix, except at the airport. The 800-square-mi metro area is so large that one-way fares in excess of $50 are not uncommon; you might want to ask what the damages will be before you get in, since it will often be cheaper to rent a car, even if you are renting for only a day. Except within a compact area, such as central Phoenix, travel by taxi is not recommended.

TRAIN TRAVEL

Amtrak provides train service in Arizona with bus transfers to Phoenix. Eastbound train passengers will stop in Flagstaff, where Amtrak buses depart daily for Phoenix each morning. Westbound train travelers will likely make the transfer in Tucson, where Amtrak-run buses have limited service to Phoenix on Sunday, Tuesday, and Thursday nights. What used to be Phoenix's downtown train terminal is now the Amtrak Thruway Bus Stop.

🚆 **Amtrak** ⊠ 4th Ave. and Harrison St. 🕾 602/253-0121 or 800/872-7245 ⊕ www.amtrak.com.

VISITOR INFORMATION

The Arizona Office of Tourism is open weekdays 8 to 5. The Native American Tourism Center aids in arranging tourist visits to reservation lands; it can't afford to send information packets, but you can call or stop in weekdays 8 to 5. You can find more information at the Greater Phoenix Convention and Visitors Bureau and at the Phoenix Chamber of Commerce. The Scottsdale Convention and Visitors Bureau is open weekdays 8:30 to 6:30, Saturday 10 to 5, and Sunday 11 to 5.

🚆 Before You Leave **Arizona Office of Tourism** ⊠ 1110 W. Washington, Suite 155, Phoenix 85007 🕾 602/364-3730 or 888/520-3444 ⊕ www.arizonaguide.com. **Native American Tourism Center** 🕾 480/945-0771 🖷 480/945-0264.

🚆 In Phoenix & Central Arizona **Greater Phoenix Convention and Visitors Bureau** ⊠ Arizona Center, 2nd and Adams Sts., Downtown, Phoenix 🕾 602/254-6500 ⊕ www.phoenixcvb.com. **Scottsdale Convention and Visitors Bureau** ⊠ 4343 N. Scottsdale Rd., at Drinkwater Blvd., Downtown, Scottsdale 🕾 480/421-1004 or 800/782-1117 ⊕ www.scottsdalecvb.com.

NORTH-CENTRAL ARIZONA

WONDER AS YOU WANDER
the ancient cliff dwellings at
Montezuma Castle ⇨*p.97*

STROLL PAST VICTORIAN HOMES
in Prescott, capital of the Arizona Territory ⇨*p.102*

TAKE THE SCENIC ROUTE
in Oak Creek Canyon ⇨*p.113*

POSE FOR A PICTURE-PERFECT SWING
at Sedona Golf Resort's 10th hole ⇨*p.114*

ESCAPE TO A STUNNING HACIENDA
with red-rock views at El Portal ⇨*p.118*

INDULGE IN RETAIL THERAPY
at Sedona's galleries and New Age shops ⇨*p.122*

GRAB HIKING BOOTS OR A HYBRID
and hit the trails near Flagstaff ⇨*p.129*

Updated by
Matt Baatz

RED-ROCK BUTTES ABLAZE in the slanting light of late afternoon, the San Francisco peaks tipped with white from a fresh snowfall, pine forests clad in dark green needles—north-central Arizona is rich in natural attractions. The landscape of north-central Arizona is a series of vast plateaus punctuated by steep ridges and canyons. To the north of Flagstaff, a string of tall volcanic mountains, the San Francisco Peaks, rises above 12,000 feet, tapering to the 9,000-foot Mount Elden and a scattering of diminutive cinder cones. To the south, a seemingly endless stand of ponderosa pines covers this part of the Colorado Plateau before the terrain plunges dramatically into Oak Creek Canyon. The canyon then opens up to reveal red buttes and mesas in the high-desert areas surrounding Sedona. The desert gradually descends to the Verde Valley, crossing the Verde River before reaching the 7,000-foot Black Range, over which lies the Prescott Valley.

Flagstaff, the hub of this part of Arizona, was historically a way station en route to southern California. First the railroads, then Route 66 carried westbound traffic right through the center of town. The ranks of modern-day transients are filled with vacationers on their way north to the Grand Canyon, students at Northern Arizona University, and Phoenix weekenders fleeing the heat of the valley. But many of those who were just "passing through" have stayed and built a community, revitalizing downtown with cafés, an activity-filled square, eclectic shops, and festivals. Flagstaff has earned its reputation as a progressive mountain town. The town's large network of bike paths and parks abuts hundreds of miles of trails and forest roads, an irresistible lure for outdoors enthusiasts. There is a long backlog of future projects, proposing new trails and bike paths for years to come. Not surprisingly, the typical resident of Flagstaff is outdoorsy, young, and has a large, friendly dog in tow.

Down AZ 89A a bit, in Sedona, the average age and income rises considerably. This was once a hidden hamlet used by Western filmmakers true to Zane Grey's vision. New Age enthusiasts flocked to the region throughout the 1980s believing that it was the center of spiritual powers. Well-off retirees followed soon after, populating clusters of maze-like cul-de-sacs all along the two highways through Sedona. Sophisticated restaurants, upscale shops, luxe accommodations, and New Age entrepreneurs cater to both of these populations, as well as to the tourist trade, which brings close to five million visitors a year to the area. It can be difficult, though not impossible, to find a moment of serenity, even in wilderness areas. A hike into apparently remote territory is often disturbed by a tour plane buzzing above or a gonzo mountain biker who brakes for no one. Despite these quibbles, the beauty here is unsurpassed. For this reason, Sedona and much of north-central Arizona attracts more than its share of artists and galleries.

Pioneers and miners are now part of north-central Arizona's past, but the wild and woolly days of the Old West are not forgotten. The preserved fort at Camp Verde recalls frontier life, and the decrepit facades of the funky former mining town of Jerome have an infectious charm. Jerome's hillside streets are blessed with a sublime panorama from the red-rock buttes to the snowcapped peaks of the San Francisco range.

A short stay can give you a little taste of this rich part of the state, but at least five days are necessary for the full flavor. Linger longer if you want to savor the region's history and landscape or enjoy some outdoor activities. The following itineraries assume you'll start out in Phoenix, as most folks do, and head north.

If you have 3 days
Spend the first two nights in 🏨 **Sedona** ⑫ ⌐ –㉒. Take a jeep tour or a hike in **Red Rock State Park** ㉒, and then explore the town's shops and sights. On the next day, visit the ghost town of **Jerome** ⑥. On your third day, drive through scenic **Oak Creek Canyon** ㉑ to 🏨 **Flagstaff** ㉓–㉜, where you can visit the **Riordan State Historic Park** ㉖ or the **Museum of Northern Arizona** ㉙ in the afternoon and the **Lowell Observatory** ㉕ at night.

If you have 5 days
Expand your time in 🏨 **Sedona** ⑫ ⌐ –㉒ by exploring **Oak Creek Canyon** ㉑ and **Red Rock State Park** ㉒ on the first day and shopping or exploring the town on the second. Enjoy a good part of the third day in **Jerome** ⑥; then continue on to 🏨 **Prescott** ⑦–⑪, where you can spend the night in one of the many Victorian-era lodgings. Next day, poke around the town's antiques shops and **Sharlot Hall Museum** ⑨ and in the late afternoon drive up to 🏨 **Flagstaff** ㉓–㉜. Then make excursions to the adjacent **Sunset Crater Volcano National Monument** ㉟ and **Wupatki** ㊱ national monuments, where Native American artifacts may be explored in an inactive volcanic field.

If you have 7 days
Take your time driving up from Phoenix to Sedona, spending the morning of the first day at **Fort Verde State Historic Park** ① ⌐ and **Montezuma Castle National Monument** ②. In the afternoon, ride the **Verde Canyon Railroad** and spend the night in 🏨 **Jerome** ⑥. Continue on to 🏨 **Prescott** ⑦–⑪ for a day or two before heading over to 🏨 **Flagstaff** ㉓–㉜, where you can ski in the winter or view the entire San Francisco Peaks region from the Agassiz ski lift in summer. Conclude your trip in 🏨 **Sedona** ⑫–㉒ for a very satisfying circle of the area.

The many Victorian houses in temperate Prescott attest to the attempt to bring "civilization" to Arizona's territorial capital.

North-central Arizona is also rich in artifacts from its earliest inhabitants: several national and state parks—among them Walnut Canyon, Wupatki, Montezuma Castle, and Tuzigoot national monuments—hold well-preserved evidence of the architectural accomplishments of Native American Sinagua and other ancestral Puebloans who made their homes in the Verde Valley and the region near the San Francisco Peaks.

Exploring North-Central Arizona

Avoid the interstates as much as possible; the back ways are sometimes the most direct and usually provide the best vantage points from which to view the stunning contrasts of the landscape. It's wise, especially if you are an outdoors enthusiast, to start in the relatively lowland areas of Prescott and the Verde Valley, climbing gradually into Sedona and Flagstaff. It can take several days to grow accustomed to high elevation in Flagstaff. If you can, plan to be in Sedona midweek, when the perennial weekend crowds aren't around to crowd the streets.

About the Restaurants

Sedona and Flagstaff have the largest number of good, multiethnic restaurants in the region, but even little Cottonwood has become more food conscious in the last couple of years. Prescott and Jerome have their share of good cafés, but beyond the main streets of these towns, restaurants tend toward standard American and Mexican road food, some of which is homey and delicious.

About the Hotels

Flagstaff has many comfortable motels (most of the familiar U.S. chains are represented) and pleasant bed-and-breakfasts, but no real luxury. There's a nearly continuous string of motels lining Route 66 once you're within the city limits, and if you aren't too particular about accommodations and rumbling trains, you can usually book a room on the fly even during the busy summer season. Otherwise, it's good to make reservations, if only a day or two ahead of your arrival. Stunning settings and outstanding amenities abound in Sedona, but there are few bargains. Book rooms well ahead of time in the busy spring and fall seasons; you might find some relative bargains in winter and summer, when tourism in the area isn't quite as brisk. Sedona has springlike temperatures even in January, when it's sure to be snowing in Flagstaff, but summer temperatures well above 100°F are common. Many of Prescott's hotels have fabled pasts. Little Jerome a few reliable B&Bs, but it's smart to call ahead if you think you might want to spend the night here.

	WHAT IT COSTS				
	$$$$	**$$$**	**$$**	**$**	**¢**
RESTAURANTS	over $30	$20–$30	$12–$20	$8–$12	under $8
HOTELS	over $250	$175–$250	$120–$175	$70–$120	under $70

Restaurant prices are per person for a main course at dinner. Hotel prices are for two people in a standard double room in high season, excluding taxes and service charges.

Timing

Autumn, when the wet season ends, the stifling desert temperatures moderate, and the mountain aspens reach their full golden splendor, is a great time to visit. Hotel rooms in Prescott and Flagstaff are less expensive in winter, but mountain temperatures dip below zero, and snowstorms often occur weekly, especially near Flagstaff. Prescott and Flagstaff hold most of their festivals and cultural events in summer. Sedona's biggest event, the Jazz on the Rocks Festival, takes place in September.

2

Camping The Prescott and Coconino national forests cover a large part of north-central Arizona. Campgrounds close to Sedona often fill up in summer, especially those along Oak Creek in Oak Creek Canyon; if you want to camp near the red rocks, two good places to try are Manzanita and Banjo Bill. In Coconino National Forest near Flagstaff, the campgrounds near Mormon Lake and Lake Mary—including Pinegrove, Lakeview, Forked Pine, Double Springs, and Dairy Springs—are popular to the point of overcrowding in summer. Sites near Prescott and Jerome in the Prescott National Forest are generally less visited; Potato Patch and Granite Basin are both scenic, and sleeping out on top of Mingus Mountain is unforgettable.

Hiking Ancient seas, colliding land masses, spewing volcanoes, and other geological forces have cast and recast northern Arizona into a sprawling sculpture of incredible contrasts. Hikes along the canyon rims often look out among red rock monoliths, and treks to the barren crests of the San Francisco Peaks overlook verdant pine forests stretching to the edge of the Grand Canyon to the north and the Mogollon Rim to the south. You can hike through thickly wooded areas in the Verde Valley and the Prescott National Forest in the state's highest alpine region (and even ascend a volcano), and among the rock formations around Sedona. National Forest Service offices in Camp Verde, Prescott, Sedona, and Flagstaff direct trekkers to the best trails.

Native American Culture The achievements of the Sinagua people, who lived in north-central Arizona from the 8th through the 15th centuries, reached their height in the 12th and 13th centuries, when various related groups occupied most of the San Francisco Volcanic Field and a large portion of the upper and middle Verde Valley. The Sinagua sites around modern-day Camp Verde, Clarkdale, and Flagstaff provide a window onto this remarkable culture. Some of the best examples of surviving Sinagua architecture can be found at Wupatki National Monument, northeast of Flagstaff.

THE VERDE VALLEY, JEROME & PRESCOTT

About 90 mi north of Phoenix, as you round a curve approaching Exit 285 of Interstate 17, the valley of the Verde River suddenly unfolds in a panorama of grayish-white cliffs, tinted red in the distance and dotted with desert scrub, cottonwood, and pine. For hundreds of years many Native American communities, especially those of the southern Sinagua people, lined the Verde River. Rumors of great mineral deposits brought Europeans to the Verde Valley as early as 1583, when Hopi Indians guided Antonio de Espejo here, but it wasn't until the second half of the 19th century that this wealth was commercially exploited. The discovery of silver and gold in the Black Hills, which border the valley on the southwest, gave rise to such boomtowns as Jerome—and to military installations such

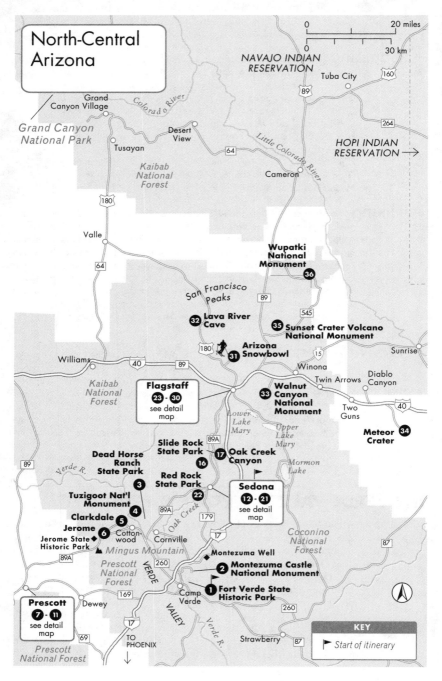

North-Central
Arizona

0 _____ 20 miles
0 _____ 30 km

NAVAJO INDIAN
RESERVATION

Tuba City

89   160

264

HOPI INDIAN
RESERVATION →

Grand
Canyon Village

Colorado River

Grand Canyon
National Park

Desert
View

Tusayan

64

Little Colorado River

Cameron

Kaibab
National
Forest

180

Valle

64

San Francisco
Peaks

Wupatki
National
Monument
36

89

545

32 Lava River
Cave

35 Sunset Crater Volcano
National Monument

180   31 Arizona
Snowbowl

15

Sunrise

Williams

40   89

Kaibab
National
Forest

Flagstaff
23 - 30
see detail
map

Winona

Twin Arrows

Diablo
Canyon

33 Walnut
Canyon
National
Monument

Two
Guns

40

Meteor
Crater   34

Lower
Lake
Mary

Upper
Lake
Mary

89A

Slide Rock
State Park
16

17 Oak Creek
Canyon

Mormon
Lake

Dead Horse
Ranch
State Park
3

Red Rock
State Park
22

Sedona
12 - 21
see detail
map

Verde R.

Tuzigoot Nat'l
Monument
4

89A

Oak Creek

179

Coconino
National
Forest

87

89

Clarkdale 5
Jerome 6
Jerome State ◆
Historic Park
89A

Cotton-
wood

Cornville

17

Mingus Mountain

Montezuma Well ◆

2 Montezuma Castle
National Monument

Prescott
National
Forest

VERDE

260

1 Fort Verde State
Historic Park

Prescott
7 - 11
see detail
map

Dewey

169

Camp
Verde

260

69

17

Verde R.

Strawberry

87

TO
PHOENIX
↓

Prescott
National Forest

VALLEY

KEY

▶ Start of itinerary

as Fort Verde, set up to protect the white settlers and wealth seekers from the Native American tribes they displaced. Mineral wealth was also the impetus behind the establishment of Prescott, across the Mingus Mountains from Verde Valley, as a territorial capital by President Lincoln and other Unionists who wanted to keep the riches out of Confederate hands.

Numbers in the text correspond to numbers in the margin and on the North-Central Arizona, Prescott, Sedona, and Flagstaff maps.

Camp Verde

94 mi north of Phoenix on Interstate 17.

▶ ❶ The military post for which **Fort Verde State Historic Park** is named was built between 1871 and 1873 as the third of three fortifications in this part of the Arizona Territory. To protect the Verde Valley's farmers and miners from Tonto Apache and Yavapai raids, the fort's administrators oversaw the movement of nearly 1,500 Native Americans to the San Carlos and Fort Apache reservations. A museum details the history of the area's military installations, and three furnished officers' quarters show the day-to-day living conditions of the top brass. Signs from any of Interstate 17's three Camp Verde exits will direct you to the 10-acre park. ⊠ *125 Hollomon St.* ☎ *928/567–3275* ⊕ *www.pr.state.az.us* ⊠ *$3* ⊙ *Daily 8–5.*

❷ The five-story 20-room cliff dwelling at **Montezuma Castle National**
 Monument was named by explorers who believed it had been erected by
★ the Aztecs. Southern Sinagua Native Americans actually built the structure, one of the best-preserved prehistoric ruins in North America—and one of the most accessible. An easy paved trail (⅓ mi round-trip) leads to the dwelling and to adjacent Castle A, a badly deteriorated 6-story living space with about 45 rooms. No one is permitted to enter the ruins, but the viewing area is very close by. From Camp Verde, take Main Street to Montezuma Castle Road.

Somewhat less accessible than Montezuma's Castle—but equally striking—is the **Montezuma Well** (☎ 928/567–4521) unit of the national monument. Although there are some Sinagua and Hohokam ruins here, the limestone sinkhole with a limpid blue-green pool lying in the middle of the desert is the park's main attraction. This cavity—55 feet deep and 365 feet across—is all that's left of an ancient subterranean cavern; the water remains at a constant 76°F year-round. It's a short hike up here, but the peace, quiet, and the views of the Verde Valley reward the effort. To reach Montezuma Well from Montezuma Castle, return to Interstate 17 and go north to Exit 293; signs direct you to the well, which is 4 mi east of the freeway. The drive includes a short section of dirt road. ⊠ *Montezuma Castle Rd., 7 mi northeast of Camp Verde* ☎ *928/567–3322 Montezuma Castle, 928/567–3322 Ext. 15 bookstore* ⊕ *www.nps. gov/moca* ⊠ *$3 per person* ⊙ *Labor Day–Memorial Day, daily 8–5; Memorial Day–Labor Day, daily 8–7.*

Sports & the Outdoors

The **Verde Ranger District** office of the **Prescott National Forest** (⊠ 300 E. AZ 260, Camp Verde ☎ 928/567–4121 ⊕ www.fs.fed.us/r3/prescott)

is a good resource for places to hike—as well as to fish and boat—along the Verde River.

The **Black Canyon Trail** (⊹ AZ 260, 4 mi south of Cottonwood, west on FR 359 4½ mi) is a bit of a slog, rising over 2,200 feet in 6 mi, but the reward is grand views from the gray cliffs of Verde Valley to the red buttes of Sedona to the blue range of the San Francisco Peaks.

Dead Horse Ranch State Park

❸ *20 mi northwest of Montezuma Castle National Monument; 1 mi north of Cottonwood, off Main St.*

In the late 1940s, when Calvin "Cap" Ireys asked his family to help him choose among the ranches he was thinking about buying in the Verde Valley, his son immediately picked "the one with the dead horse on it." Ireys sold the land to the state in 1973 at one-third of its value, with the stipulation that the park into which it was to be converted retain the ranch's colorful name.

The 423-acre spread, which combines high-desert and wetlands habitats, is a pleasant place to wile away the day. You can fish in the Verde River or the well-stocked Park Lagoon, or hike on some 6 mi of trails that begin in a shaded picnic area and wind along the banks of the river; adjoining forest service pathways are available for those who enjoy longer treks. Birders can check off more than 100 species from the Arizona Audubon Society lists provided by the rangers. Bald eagles perch along the Verde River in winter, and the common black hawks—a misnomer for these threatened avians—nest here in summer. ⊠ *675 Dead Horse Ranch Rd., Cottonwood* ☎ *928/634–5283* ⊕ *www.pr.state.az.us* ⊠ *Day use $5 per car; camping without electricity $12, with electricity $19* ☉ *Daily 8–5.*

Sports & the Outdoors

FISHING   The best time to fish the upper Verde River is from November through March, when selected pools are stocked with six species of fish, including catfish, bass, and trout. The trout fishing is especially good. Catches average about 10 inches. Access the river from either Dead Horse State Park or Tuzigoot National Monument. If you're lucky, you'll be fishing alongside bald eagles that nest here during the winter. In March, springtime runoff may make the river muddy. Be aware of the three endangered native species—the spikedace, razorback sucker, and Colorado pike minnow—and throw them back.

Despite all the good fishing, there are no tackle shops in the sparsely populated Verde Valley. The closest shop, **On the Creek Sedona Outfitters** (⊠ 274 Apple Ave., #C, Sedona ☎ 928/203–9973), is almost 20 mi up AZ 89A in Sedona.

Where to Eat

$$ ✕ **Kramer's at the Manzanita Restaurant & Lounge.** You wouldn't expect
Fodor'sChoice   to find sophisticated cooking in Cornville, 6 mi east of Cottonwood,
★   but here a European-born chef (who came to the Verde Valley via Los Angeles) prepares Continental fare, using organic produce and locally

raised meat whenever possible. Roast duckling à l'orange and rack of lamb are beautifully presented; try the mushroom soup if it's available. The hours are not as cosmopolitan as the food: dinner ends at 8 PM. ⊠ *11425 E. Cornville Rd., Cornville* ☎ *928/634–8851* ▤ *MC, V* ⊙ *Closed Mon. and Tues.*

¢–$$ ✕ **Page Springs Restaurant.** Come to these two rustic, wood-paneled rooms in Cornville, on the loop to the town of Page Springs—off AZ 89A—for down-home Western chow: great chili, burgers, and steaks. You'll get an Oak Creek view for a lot less than you'd pay closer to Sedona. ⊠ *1975 N. Page Springs Rd., Cornville* ☎ *928/634–9954* ▤ *No credit cards.*

¢ ✕ **Gabriela's Mexican Food.** Off the main Camp Verde drag, this tiny eatery serves traditional Mexican food. Try the *carne asada* (marinated, grilled beef) tacos and the chicken *burros* (what burritos are often called in this part of Arizona). ⊠ *522 W. Finnie Flats Rd., Camp Verde* ☎ *928/567–4484* ▤ *No credit cards* ⊙ *Closed Sun.*

Tuzigoot National Monument

❹ *3 mi north of Cottonwood.*

Not as well preserved as Montezuma Castle but more impressive in scope, Tuzigoot is another complex of ruins of the Sinagua people, who lived on this land overlooking the Verde Valley from about AD 1000 to 1400. Items used for food preparation, as well as jewelry, weapons, and farming tools excavated from the site, are displayed in the visitor center. Within the ruins, you can step into a reconstructed room. ⊠ *Broadway Rd., between Cottonwood's Old Town and Clarkdale, Clarkdale* ☎ *928/634–5564* ⊕ *www.nps.gov/tuzi* ▤ *$3* ⊙ *Labor Day–Memorial Day, daily 8–5; Memorial Day–Labor Day, daily 8–7.*

Clarkdale

❺ *19 mi northwest of Camp Verde, via AZ 260 and AZ 89A; 23 mi southwest of Sedona on AZ 89A; 2 mi southwest of Tuzigoot National Monument.*

There's little to see in Clarkdale, but the town once provided the smelter for copper mines in nearby Jerome. Its current incarnation is said to have arisen from a colony of prostitutes and hard-core gamblers who were tossed out of a rowdy mining camp in one of its periodic purges of "sinners."

★ Train buffs come to catch the 22-mi **Verde Canyon Railroad** (⊠ Arizona Central Railroad, 300 N. Broadway, Clarkdale ☎ 800/320–0718 ⊕ www.verdecanyonrr.com), whose knowledgeable announcers regale riders with the area's colorful history and point out natural attractions along the way—in winter, you're likely to see bald eagles. This trip, which takes about four hours, is especially popular in fall-foliage season and in the spring, when the desert wildflowers bloom; make reservations well in advance. Round-trip rides cost $39.95. For $59.95 you can ride the much more comfortable living-room like first-class cars, where hot hors d'oeuvres, coffee, and a cocktail are included in the price.

Jerome

★ ❻　*3½ mi southwest of Clarkdale, 20 mi northwest of Camp Verde, 33 mi northeast of Prescott, 25 mi southwest of Sedona on AZ 89A.*

Jerome was once known as the Billion Dollar Copper Camp, but after the last mines closed in 1953, the booming population of 15,000 dwindled to 50 determined souls, earning Jerome the "ghost town" designation it still holds, although its population has risen back to almost 500. It's hard to imagine that this town—which doesn't have a single convenience store—once was the location of Arizona's largest JCPenney department store and one of the state's first Safeway supermarkets. Jerome saw its first revival during the mid-1960s, when hippies arrived and turned it into an art colony of sorts, and it's since become a tourist attraction. In addition to its shops and historic sites, Jerome is worth visiting for its scenery: it's built into the side of Cleopatra Hill, and from here you can see Sedona's red rocks, Flagstaff's San Francisco Peaks, and even eastern Arizona's Mogollon Rim country.

Jerome is about a mile above sea level, but structures within town sit at elevations that vary by as much as 1,500 feet, depending on whether they're on Cleopatra Hill or at its foot. Blasting at the United Verde (later Phelps Dodge) mine regularly shook buildings off their foundations—the town's jail slid across a road and down a hillside, where it sits today. That's not all that was unsteady about Jerome. In 1903 a reporter from a New York newspaper called Jerome "the wickedest town in America," due to its abundance of drinking and gambling establishments; town records from 1880 list 24 saloons. Whether by divine retribution or drunken accidents, the town burned down several times.

Jerome has around 50 retail establishments (that's more than one for every 10 residents). You can get a map of the town's shops and its attractions at the visitor-information trailer on AZ 89A. Except for the state-run historic park, attractions and businesses don't always stay open as long as their stated hours when things are slow.

Of the three mining museums in town, the most inclusive is part of **Jerome State Historic Park.** Just outside town, signs on AZ 89A will direct you to the turnoff for the park, reached by a short, precipitous road. The museum occupies the 1917 mansion of Jerome's mining king, Dr. James "Rawhide Jimmy" Douglas Jr., who purchased Little Daisy Mine in 1912. You can see some of the tools and heavy equipment used to grind ore, but accounts of the town's wilder elements—such as the House of Joy brothel—are not so prominently displayed. ⊠ *State Park Rd.* ☎ *928/ 634–5381* ⊕ *www.pr.state.az.us* 🎟 *$4* ⊙ *Daily 8–5.*

The **Mine Museum** in downtown Jerome is staffed by the Jerome Historical Society. The museum's collection of mining stock certificates alone is worth the (small) price of admission—the amount of money that changed hands in this town 100 years ago boggles the mind. ⊠ *200 Main St.* ☎ *928/634–5477* 🎟 *$2* ⊙ *Daily 9–4:30.*

Where to Stay & Eat

$–$$ ✕ **Haunted Hamburger/Jerome Palace.** After the climb up the stairs from Main Street to this former boardinghouse, you'll be ready for the hearty burgers, chili, cheese steaks, and ribs that dominate the menu. Lighter fare, including such meatless selections as the guacamole quesadilla, is also available. An outdoor deck that overlooks Verde Valley helps to compensate for the often indifferent service. ⊠ *410 Clark St.* ☎ *928/634–0554* ▤ *MC, V.*

¢ ✕ **English Kitchen.** One of the oldest continually operating restaurants in the country, this space has housed some kind of restaurant since 1899, when Chinese immigrant Charley Hong arrived in Jerome and set up shop. Nearly 100 years later, in 1986, Tim and Jayne Toth bought the restaurant, and they serve salads, burgers, and sandwiches at lunch, as well as the usual breakfast fare, to residents who might prefer to keep this place a secret. ⊠ *416 Main St.* ☎ *928/634–2132* ▤ *MC, V* ⊙ *Closed Mon. No dinner.*

¢ ✕ **Red Rooster Café.** The old Safeway is now a café with tin ceilings and country accents, yet the delicious meat-loaf sandwich is nontraditional, served on whole wheat bread with Dijon mustard *sans* mashed potatoes. A compact but eclectic lunch menu includes green-chile quiche and a turkey wrap topped with bacon, avocado, and chipotle mayonnaise. On the weekends, live music rounds out the homey atmosphere. ⊠ *363 Main St.* ☎ *928/634–7087* ▤ *MC, V* ⊙ *Closed Tues. No dinner.*

$–$$ ⊞ **Ghost City Inn.** The outdoor verandah at this 1898 B&B affords sweeping views of the Verde Valley and Sedona. Most rooms are decorated in Victorian style, but one has contemporary Western touches and another has a rustic appeal. Afternoon tea with cookies is an unexpected luxury for this formerly rough-and-ready town. ⊠ *541 N. Main St., 86331* ☎☏ *928/634–4678 or 888/634–4678* ⊕ *www.ghostcityinn.com* ⇌ *6 rooms, 2 with bath* ⌕ *Some in-room VCRs, outdoor hot tub; no kids under 14, no smoking* ▤ *AE, D, MC, V* ⦿ *BP.*

$–$$ ⊞ **Jerome Grand Hotel.** This full-service hotel is housed in a former hospital built by the United Verde Mine Company in 1927. It's on Cleopatra Hill, so many rooms have splendid views. ⊠ *200 Hill St., 86331* ☎ *928/634–8200 or 888/817–6788* ☏ *928/639–0299* ⊕ *www.jeromegrandhotel.net* ⇌ *22 rooms, 1 suite* ⌕ *Restaurant, in-room VCRs, lounge* ▤ *AE, D, MC, V.*

★ **$–$$** ⊞ **Surgeon's House.** Abundant plants, knickknacks, bright colors, and plenty of sunlight make this Mediterranean-style home, which once belonged to Jerome's sawbones, a most welcoming place to stay. The friendly ministrations of innkeeper Andrea Prince enhance the experience. Her multicourse breakfasts might include potato–sour cream soup, overstuffed burritos, or a marinated fruit compote. There are two suites and two rooms, including a former chauffeur's quarters, which has a skylight and private patio. All have private bathrooms. Knockout vistas can be seen from almost everywhere in the house. A plus: pets are welcome. ⊠ *101 Hill St., 86331* ☎ *928/639–1452 or 800/639–1452* ⊕ *www.surgeonshouse.com* ⇌ *2 rooms, 2 suites* ⌕ *Some kitchenettes, some pets allowed (fee); no room TVs* ▤ *MC, V* ⦿ *BP.*

CAMPING For information about camping near Jerome at Mingus Mountain, Playground, or Potato Patch—all open May through October—contact the Prescott National Forest's **Verde Ranger District** (✉ 300 E. AZ 260, Camp Verde ☎ 928/567–4121 ⊕ www.fs.fed.us/r3/prescott).

Nightlife

Paul & Jerry's Saloon (✉ Main St. ☎ 928/634–2603) attracts a rowdy crowd to its two pool tables and old wooden bar. On weekends there's live music and a lively scene at the **Spirit Room** (✉ Main St. and AZ 89A ☎ 928/634–8809); the mural over the bar harks back to the days when it was a dining spot for the prostitutes of the red-light district.

Shopping

Jerome has its share of art galleries (some perched precariously on Cleopatra Hill), along with boutiques, but they're funkier than those in Sedona. Main Street and, just around the bend, Hull Avenue are Jerome's two primary shopping streets. Your eyes may begin to glaze over after browsing through one boutique after another, most offering tasteful Southwestern paraphernalia.

Aurum (✉ 369 Main St. ☎ 928/634–3330) focuses on contemporary art jewelry in silver and gold; about 30 artists are represented. **Designs on You** (✉ 233 Main St. ☎ 928/634–7879) carries attractively styled women's clothing. **Jerome Artists Cooperative Gallery** (✉ 502 Main St. ☎ 928/639–4276) specializes in jewelry, sculpture, painting, and pottery by local artists. The **Jewel** (✉ 420 Hull Ave. ☎ 928/639–0259) specializes in Australian opals. **Nellie Bly** (✉ 136 Main St. ☎ 928/634–0255) stocks perfume bottles and outstanding kaleidoscopes. Among the work of 300 artists at the **Raku Gallery** (✉ 250 Hull Ave. ☎ 928/634–2876) you'll find wrought-iron furniture, free-blown glass, and fountains. **Sky Fire** (✉ 140 Main St. ☎ 928/634–8081), the most sophisticated shop in Jerome, has two floors of items to adorn your person and your house, from Southwestern-pattern dishes to handcrafted Mission-style hutches.

en route The drive down a mountainous section of AZ 89A from Jerome to Prescott is gorgeous (if somewhat harrowing in bad weather), filled with twists and turns through **Prescott National Forest.** If you're coming from Phoenix, the route that crosses the Mogollon Rim, overlooking the Verde Valley, is scenic but less precipitous.

Prescott

33 mi southwest of Jerome on AZ 89A to U.S. 89, 100 mi northwest of Phoenix via Interstate 17 to AZ 69.

In a forested bowl 5,300 feet above sea level, Prescott is a prime summer refuge for Phoenix-area dwellers. It was proclaimed the first capital of the Arizona Territory in 1864 and settled by Yankees to ensure that gold-rich northern Arizona would remain a Union resource. (Tucson and southern Arizona were strongly pro-Confederacy.) Although early territorial settlers thought that ruins in the area were of Aztec origin, today it is believed that ancestors of the Yavapai, whose reservation is today on the outskirts of town, were the area's original inhabitants. You can see the results of this notion—inspired by *The History and Conquest of Mexico,* a popular book by historian William Hickling Prescott, for whom the town was named—in such street names as Montezuma, Cortez, and Alarcon.

Despite a devastating downtown fire in 1900, Prescott remains the Southwest's richest town of late-19th-century New England–style architecture (some have called it the "West's most Eastern town"). With two institutions of higher education, Yavapai College and Prescott College, Prescott could be called a college town, but it doesn't really feel like one, perhaps because so many retirees also reside here, drawn by the temperate climate and low cost of living.

The city's main drag is Gurley Street, named after John Addison Gurley, who was slated to be the first governor but died days before he was to move to the Arizona Territory. Those interested in architecture should be sure to get a map of the town's Victorian neighborhoods. Most are within walking distance of the chamber office. Many Queen Annes have been beautifully restored, and a number of them are now B&Bs. Antiques and collectibles shops line both sides of Cortez Street to the north of the courthouse.

a good tour

Start walking around **Courthouse Plaza** ⑦ and down **Whiskey Row** ⑧ on Montezuma Street, browsing through the curio shops, or grabbing a drink in an Old West saloon as you do. Once you reach the Hotel St. Michael on the corner, make a left onto Gurley Street and tour the **Sharlot Hall Museum** ⑨, a block to the west. It's 10 blocks east on Gurley then one block north on Arizona Street to the **Smoki Museum** ⑩. You may want to drive over, or you could stroll through the south side of town. Cortez Street near Gurley is the antiques district; there are many shops to browse. Backtrack to Gurley Street and continue east for four more blocks. Make a detour to the right on Mount Vernon Avenue to see some of the most beautiful Victorian homes in Prescott. Unless you visit around Christmastime, the private homes are not open for touring. It's four more blocks on Gurney to Arizona Street and the Smoki. Six miles northeast of here Gurley Street turns into U.S. 89. The **Phippen Museum of Western Art** ⑪ is directly to the east.

TIMING Tourism in Prescott can be bustling but rarely overwhelming. Any day will do to tour the Victorian homes and antique shops, but if you enjoy museums, avoid going on Sunday. The museum hours are stunted on this day, and you won't want to be rushed through the extensive grounds of the Sharlot Hall Museum. Devoting a full day to tour Prescott is plenty, with time left over, perhaps, to watch the sunset from Thumb Butte.

What to See

⑦ **Courthouse Plaza.** The 1916 Yavapai County Courthouse stands in the heart of Prescott, guarded by an equestrian bronze of turn-of-the-20th-century journalist and lawmaker Bucky O'Neill, who died while charging San Juan Hill in Cuba with Teddy Roosevelt during the Spanish-American War. At the south end of the plaza, across from the courthouse's main entrance, the chamber of commerce is a good place

Courthouse
Plaza **7**

Phippen
Museum of
Western Art . . **11**

Sharlot Hall
Museum **9**

Smoki
Museum **10**

Whiskey
Row **8**

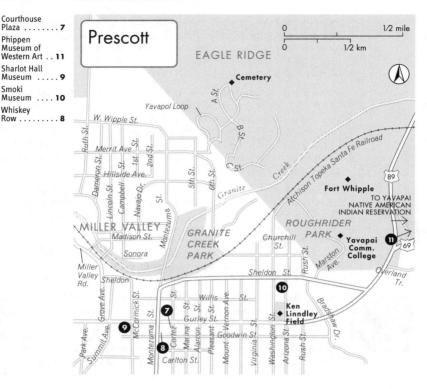

to get your bearings. ✉ *Bounded by Gurley and Goodwin Sts. to the north and south and by Cortez and Montezuma Sts. to the west and east, Downtown.*

⓫ **Phippen Museum of Western Art.** The paintings and bronze sculptures of George Phippen, along with works by other artists of the West, form the permanent collection of this museum, about 5 mi north of downtown. Phippen met with a group of prominent cowboy artists in 1965 to form the Cowboy Artists of America, a group dedicated to preserving the Old West as they saw it. Phippen became the president of the Cowboy Artists, but he died the next year. A memorial foundation set up in his name opened the doors of this museum in 1984. ✉ *4701 U.S. 89 N, Hwy. 89* ☎ *928/778–1385* ⊕ *www.phippenartmuseum.org* ✆ *$5* ☉ *Mon.–Sat. 10–4, Sun. 1–4.*

🅒 ⓿ **Sharlot Hall Museum.** Local history is documented at this remarkable mu-
Fodor'sChoice seum. Along with the original ponderosa-pine log cabin, which housed
★ the territorial governor, and the museum, named for historian and poet Sharlot Hall, the parklike setting contains three fully restored period homes and a transportation museum. Territorial times are the focus, but natural history and artifacts of the area's prehistoric peoples are also on display. ✉ *415 W. Gurley St., 2 blocks west of Courthouse Plaza,*

Downtown ☎ *928/445–3122* ⊕ *www.sharlot.org* ✉ *$5 donation requested per family* ☉ *May.–Sept., Mon.–Sat. 10–5, Sun. 1–5; Oct.–Apr., Mon.–Sat. 10–4.*

❿ **Smoki Museum.** The 1935 stone-and-log building, which resembles an Indian pueblo, is almost as interesting as the Native American artifacts inside. Priceless baskets and katsinas, as well as pottery, rugs, and beadwork, make up this fine collection, which represents Native American culture from the pre-Columbian period to the present. ⊠ *147 N. Arizona St., Downtown* ☎ *928/445–1230* ⊕ *www.smokimuseum.org* ✉ *$4* ☉ *Apr.–Dec., Mon.–Sat. 10–4, Sun. 1–4; Jan.–Mar., Fri., Sat., and Mon. 10–4, Sun. 1–4.*

❽ **Whiskey Row.** Twenty saloons and houses of pleasure once lined this stretch of Montezuma Street. Social activity is more subdued these days, and the historic bars provide an escape from the street's many boutiques. ⊠ *Montezuma St. along west side of Courthouse Plaza, Downtown.*

> **need a break?**
>
> **Caffe St. Michael** is a great place to mull over a coffee or to grab a bowl of black-bean chili and watch the people on Whiskey Row. The café and bar has been restored to its original 1901 style. The service at the counter is brisk and will leave you plenty of time for antiquing or museum browsing for the remainder of the day. ⊠ *205 W. Gurley St. Downtown* ☎ *928/776–7318.*

Sports & the Outdoors

HIKING & CAMPING More than a million acres of national-forest land surround Prescott. Thumb Butte is a popular hiking spot, but there are lots of other trekking and overnighting options. Contact the **Bradshaw Ranger District** (⊠ 2230 E. AZ 69, Hwy. 69 ☎ 928/445–7253 ⊕ www.fs.fed.us/r3/prescott) for information about hiking trails and campgrounds in the Prescott National Forest south of town down to Horse Thief Basin. Campgrounds near Prescott are generally not crowded.

The **Thumb Butte Loop Trail** (⊹ Thumb Butte Rd., 3 mi west of Prescott following Gurley St.), a 2 mi trek, takes you 600 feet up near the crest of its namesake. The vistas are large, but you won't be alone on this popular trail.

HORSEBACK RIDING **Granite Mountain Stables** (⊠ 2400 W. Shane Dr., 7 mi northeast of Prescott, Hwy. 89 ☎ 928/771–9551) has daily guided rides as well as group specials, such as hay-wagon outings.

Where to Stay & Eat

$$–$$$ ✕ **Murphy's.** Mesquite-grilled meats and beer brewed exclusively for the restaurant are the specialties here. The baby-back ribs, fresh steamed clams, and fresh fried catfish are your best bets. The bar has a good selection of microbrews as well. ⊠ *201 N. Cortez St., Downtown* ☎ *928/ 445–4044* ⊟ *AE, D, MC, V.*

$–$$$ ✕ **Agostino's Italian Cucina.** On Prescott's main square, Agostino's specializes in the standard fare of the Italian-American kitchen. Chicken Parmigiana, spaghetti with meatballs, and calamari marinara are all solid choices. Pasta can be overcooked, so order it al dente if you prefer it that way. ☒ *107 S. Cortez St., Downtown* ☏ *928/778–6818* ▭ *AE, D, MC, V.*

$$ ✕ **The Palace.** Legend has it that the patrons who saved the Palace's ornately carved 1880s Brunswick bar from a Whiskey Row fire in 1900 continued drinking at it while the rest of the row burned across the street. Whatever the case, the bar remains the centerpiece of the beautifully restored turn-of-the-20th-century structure, with a high, pressed-tin ceiling. Steaks and chops are the stars here, but the grilled fish and hearty corn chowder are fine, too. ☒ *120 S. Montezuma St., Downtown* ☏ *928/541–1996* ▭ *AE, MC, V.*

$–$$ ✕ **Prescott Brewing Company.** Good beer, good food, good service, and good prices—for a casual meal, it's hard to beat this cheerful, multilevel restaurant. In addition to the chili, fish-and-chips, and British-style bangers (sausage) and mash, vegetarian enchiladas made with tofu, and a pasta salad with sundried tomatoes, avocado, broccoli, and two types of cheese are on the menu. Fresh-baked beer bread comes with many of the entrées. ☒ *130 W. Gurley St., Downtown* ☏ *928/771–2795* ▭ *AE, D, DC, MC, V.*

$–$$ ✕ **Zuma's Woodfire Café.** One of the more sophisticated restaurants in town, Zuma's offers pizzas made in a wood-burning oven, with such toppings as goat cheese, grilled onions, and fresh basil. The large menu also includes salads, pastas, and grilled meats and fish. ☒ *124 N. Montezuma St., Downtown* ☏ *928/541–1400* ▭ *AE, D, MC, V.*

¢–$ ✕ **El Charro Restaurant.** This is the best Mexican food in town, mostly heavy Sonoran food, and most of it homemade. The restaurant has been open since 1959, and the enchiladas, fajitas, and basic soft tacos are perennial customer favorites. The salsa has been tamed over the years, but ask for hot sauce and your wish will be granted. ☒ *120 N. Montezuma St., Downtown* ☏ *928/445–7130* ▭ *AE, MC, V.*

¢ ✕ **Kendall's Famous Burgers and Ice Cream.** A great diner in the middle of downtown, Kendall's serves hamburgers cooked to order with your choice of 14 condiments. Be sure to try the homemade french fries. ☒ *113 S. Cortez St., Downtown* ☏ *928/778–3658* ▭ *No credit cards.*

¢ ✕ **Plaza Café.** A bustling lunch place, the Plaza, as the locals call it, serves some of the most healthful meals in town. Light pasta dishes, homemade soups, veggie burgers, and rice bowls are just a few of the selections on the lengthy menu. Service is homey and brisk. ☒ *106 W. Gurley St., Downtown* ☏ *928/445–3234* ▭ *AE, MC, V.*

★ $$–$$$ ▦ **Hassayampa Inn.** Built in 1927 for early automobile travelers, the Hassayampa Inn oozes character: The ceiling in the lobby is hand-painted, and some rooms still have the original furnishings. A free full breakfast of your choice at the restaurant gilds the lily of reasonable rates. The Peacock Room, the hotel's pretty—if overly formal—dining room, has tapestried booths, dim lighting, and better than average Continental food. ☒ *122 E. Gurley St., Downtown, 86301* ☏ *928/778–9434 or 800/322–1927* ☐ *928/445–8590* ⊕ *www.hassayampainn.com* ⇱ *58 rooms, 10 suites* ⌂ *Restaurant, cable TV, bar* ▭ *AE, D, DC, MC, V* ⦿ *BP.*

$$–$$$ ▦ **Prescott Resort Conference Center and Casino.** On a hill on the outskirts of town, this upscale property has views of the mountain ranges surrounding Prescott or the Valley. Many guests hardly notice, so riveted

RODEO LESSON

COWBOYS VIED *for the unofficial titles of best roper and rider at the end of the big cattle drives of the late 19th century. As their day jobs were curtailed in scope by the spread of railroads and the fencing-in of the West, they made the contests more formalized. The sport of rodeo was born.*

The five standard events in contemporary rodeo are calf roping, bull riding, steer wrestling, saddle bronc-riding, and bareback bronc-riding. ("Bronc" is short for bronco, an unbroken range horse with a tendency to buck, or throw, a rider.) Two other events are recognized in championship competitions: single-steer roping and team roping. The barrel race, a saddle-horse race around a series of barrels, is a popular contest for women.

Participants pay entry fees, and the prize money won is their only compensation. More than half of all rodeos are

independent of state and county fairs, livestock shows, or other attractions, and many are held in arenas devoted to the purpose. The equipment, however, is simple and may be improvised.

In 1929 the Rodeo Association of America was formed to regulate the sport. The contestants themselves took a hand in 1936 after a strike in Boston Garden and organized the Cowboy Turtles Association—"turtles" because they had been slow to act. This group was renamed the Rodeo Cowboys Association (RCA) in 1945 and the Professional Rodeo Cowboys Association (PRCA) in 1975. Its rules became accepted by most rodeos.

Prescott's annual rodeo started in 1888 and is claimed to be the world's oldest. The rodeo is part of the popular Frontier Days during the week surrounding the 4th of July.

are they by the poker machines and slots in Arizona's only hotel casino. There are plenty of recreational facilities to occupy those able to resist the one-armed bandits. ✉ *1500 AZ 69, Hwy. 69, 86301* ☎ *928/776–1666 or 800/967–4637* 🖨 *928/776–8544* ⊕ *www.prescottresort.com* ➥ *161 rooms* ⚐ *Restaurant, coffee shop, refrigerators, cable TV, 4 tennis courts, pool, gym, hot tub, sauna, racquetball, piano bar, casino, no-smoking rooms* ▤ *AE, D, DC, MC, V.*

$–$$ 🏨 **Marks House Victorian Bed and Breakfast.** Victoria still reigns at this B&B, once owned by the mayor of territorial Prescott. It now belongs to Beth Maitland, a star of the daytime soap *The Young and the Restless,* and is ably managed by her parents. Rooms are impeccably furnished with period antiques: the suite in the circular turret, overlooking Thumb Butte, is particularly impressive. Breakfast is served in the formal dining room. ✉ *203 E. Union St., Downtown, 86303* ☎ *928/778–4632 or 800/370–6275* ✉ *markshouse@cableone.net* ➥ *2 rooms, 2 suites* ⚐ *Dining room; no room TVs* ▤ *D, MC, V* ⏻ *BP.*

$ 🏨 **Hotel Vendome.** This World War I–era hostelry has seen miners, health seekers, and such celebrities as cowboy star Tom Mix walk through its doors. Old-fashioned touches, including the original claw-foot tubs, remain. Like many other historic hotels, the Vendome has its obligatory resident ghost (her room costs slightly more). Only a block from Courthouse Plaza, this is a good choice for those who want to combine sightseeing, modern comforts, and good value. ⊠ *230 Cortez St., Downtown, 86303* ☎ *928/776–0900 or 888/468–3583* 🖨 *928/771–0395* ⊕ *www. vendomehotel.com* ⟿ *16 rooms, 4 suites* ⚬ *Fans, cable TV, bar; no smoking* ☰ *AE, D, DC, MC, V* ⦿| *CP.*

¢–$ ▦ **Hotel St. Michael.** Don't expect serenity on the busiest corner of Courthouse Plaza, but for low rates and historic charm it's hard to beat this hotel in operation since 1900. Rooms have 1920s–40s-era antiques; some face the plaza and others look out on Thumb Butte. The first-floor Café St. Michael serves great coffee and croissants. ⊠*205 W. Gurley St., Downtown, 86303* ☎ *928/776–1999 or 800/678–3757* 🖨 *928/776–7318* ⟿ *71 rooms* ⚬ *Coffee shop, cable TV, shop* ☰ *AE, D, MC, V.*

Nightlife & the Arts

Prescott's popular **Bluegrass Festival on the Square** takes place in June. The town, which had its first organized cowboy competition in 1888, lays claim to having the world's oldest rodeo: the annual **Frontier Days** roundup, held on the Fourth of July weekend at the Yavapai County Fairgrounds. In August, the **Cowboy Poets Gathering** brings together campfire bards from around the country.

The **Prescott Fine Arts Association** (⊠208 N. Marina St., Downtown ☎928/ 445–3286) sponsors musicals and dramas, a series of plays for children, and a concert series. The association's gallery also presents rotating exhibits by local, regional, and national artists. The **Prescott Jazz Society** (⊠ 129½ N. Cortez St., Downtown ☎ 928/445–0000) has an intimate storefront lounge. The **Yavapai Symphony Association** (⊠ 107 N. Cortez St., Suite 105B, Downtown ☎ 928/776–4255) hosts performances by the Phoenix and Flagstaff symphonies; call ahead for schedules and venues.

Montezuma Street's Whiskey Row, just off the central Courthouse Plaza, is nowhere near as wild as it was in its historic heyday, but most bars have live music—and a lively collegiate crowd—on the weekends. The **Cadillac Bar and Grill** (⊠216 W. Gurley St., Downtown ☎928/777–0018) offers live blues, jazz, rock, and pop Friday and Saturday at 9 PM. It also has "Fat Tuesday" happy-hour entertainment beginning at 5 PM. For a more refined experience, head over to the art nouveau–piano bar at the **Hassayampa Inn** (⊠ 122 E. Gurley St., Downtown ☎ 928/778–9434); there's always someone tickling the ivories on the weekend. The Brunswick bar at **Lyzzard's Lounge** (⊠ 120 N. Cortez St., Downtown ☎ 928/778–2244) was shipped from overseas from England via the Colorado River.

Shopping

Shops selling antiques and collectibles line Cortez Street, just north of Courthouse Plaza. There is fun stuff—especially Western kitsch—as well as some good buys on valuable pieces. Many of the stores gather together groups of retailers. Courthouse Plaza, especially along Montezuma Street, is lined with specialty and gift shops. Many match those in Sedona for quality and price. Be sure to check out **Arts Prescott** (⊠ 134 S. Montezuma St., Downtown ☎ 928/776–7717), a cooperative gallery of talented local craftspeople and artists. **Bashford Courts** (⊠ 130 Gurley St., Downtown ☎ 928/445–9798) has three floors of artsy stores. At 14,000 square feet, the **Merchandise Mart Antique Mall** (⊠ 205 N. Cortez St., Downtown ☎ 928/776–1728) is the largest of the town's collections of collectors. To get your fill of Old West kitsch, stop at **Prescott Museum & Trading Company** (⊠ 142 S. Montezuma St., Downtown ☎ 928/776–8498), which also displays vintage boots, saddles, and taxidermy. **Sun West Gallery** (⊠ 152 S. Montezuma St., Downtown ☎ 928/778–1204) has artwork, furnishings, and Zapotec rugs.

SEDONA & OAK CREEK CANYON

119 mi north of Phoenix, Interstate 17 to AZ 179 to AZ 89A; 60 mi northeast of Prescott, U.S. 89 to AZ 89A; 27 mi south of Flagstaff on AZ 89A.

It's easy to see what draws so many people to Sedona. Red-rock buttes—Cathedral Rock, Bear Mountain, Courthouse Rock, and Bell Rock, among others—reach up into an almost always clear blue sky, both colors intensified by dark-green pine forests. Surrealist Max Ernst, writer Zane Grey, and many filmmakers drew inspiration from these vistas (more than 80 Westerns were shot in the area in the 1940s and '50s alone).

These days, Sedona lures enterprising restaurateurs and gallery owners from the East and West coasts. New Age followers, who believe that the area contains some of the Earth's more important vortices (energy centers), also come in great numbers in the belief that the area's "vibe" confers a sense of balance and well-being and enhances creativity. Several entrepreneurs have set up crystal shops and New Age bookshops that cater to the curious and true devotees.

Expansion since the early 1980s has been rapid, and lack of planning has taken its toll in unattractive developments and increased traffic, especially on weekends and during busy summer months, when Phoenix residents flee north to cooler elevations. Still, the future looks promising. The town has been chosen to take part in the federally sponsored Main Street program, which means, among other things, that a number of Red Rock Territorial–style buildings in the Uptown section will be preserved and that a separate parking district will be built. A proposed bridge over Oak Creek should help alleviate some of the traffic, but it will also impinge on the natural glory of Red Rock Crossing, one of the town's most-photographed vistas.

The town itself is young and there are few historic sites. The main downtown activity is shopping, mostly for Southwestern-style paintings, clothing, rugs, jewelry, and Native American artifacts. Just beyond the shops and restaurants, however, canyons, creeks, Indian ruins, and the red rocks beckon. The area is thrilling and easy to hike. Another option is to take one of the ubiquitous jeep tours. During warmer months visit air-conditioned shops at midday and do hiking and jeep tours in the early morning or late afternoon, when the light is softer and the heat less oppressive.

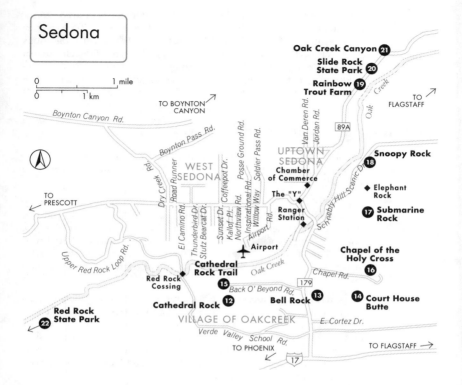

Any whimsical turn off the main drag of Sedona, save an errant one into a subdivision, is almost certain to lead to somewhere worthwhile. The following excursions will divert you for a hastily-spent hour to a full day. Those with their own wheels might want to take the drive out to **Boynton Canyon,** sacred to the Yavapai Apache, who believe it was their ancient birthplace. It's where you'll find the Enchantment Resort, where all are welcome to hike the canyon and stop in for lunch or a late-afternoon drink. Weather permitting, the rather bumpy **Schnebly Hill Scenic Drive** is another inspiring option too rocky for anything but all-terrain vehicles. The vistas of Sedona from **Airport Mesa** at sunset can't be beat. The **Upper Red Rock Loop** will likely consume a roll or two of film. Many of the most picturesque spots in Sedona are considered energy centers; vortex maps of the area are available at most of Sedona's New Age stores.

Exploring Sedona

a good drive

Start this tour early when the favorable angle of the sun's rays sets the crimson buttes ablaze. Begin your drive on AZ 179 at the outlet mall on the south side of the Village of Oak Creek. To the west, on the right, is Verde Valley School Road, which meanders northwest for 5 mi. The last several miles is a smooth dirt road leading to Red Rock Crossing and excellent views of **Cathedral Rock** ⑫. Backtrack to AZ 179 and turn

VORTEX TOUR

WHAT IS A VORTEX? *The word "vortex" comes from the Latin* vertere, *which means "to turn or whirl." In Sedona, a vortex is a funnel created by the motion of spiraling energy. Sedona has long been believed to be a center for spiritual power because of the vortices of subtle energy in the area. This energy isn't described as electricity or magnetism, though it is said to leave a slight residual magnetism in the places where it is strongest.*

New Agers believe there are four major vortices in Sedona: Airport, Red Rock Crossing/Cathedral Rock, Boynton Canyon, and Bell Rock. Each manifests a different kind of energy, and this energy interacts with the individual in its presence. People come from all over the world to experience these various energy forms, hoping for guidance in spiritual matters, health, and relationships.

Juniper trees, which are all over the Sedona area, are said to respond to vortex energy in such a way that reveals where this energy is strongest. The stronger the energy, the more axial twist the junipers bear in their branches.

Airport Vortex is said to strengthen one's "masculine" side, aiding in self-confidence and focus. Red Rock Crossing/Cathedral Rock Vortex nurtures one's "feminine" aspects, such as patience and kindness. You'll be directed to Boynton Canyon Vortex if you're seeking balance between the masculine and feminine. And finally, Bell Rock Vortex, the most powerful of all, strengthens all three aspects: masculine, feminine, and balance.

These energy centers are easily accessed, and vortex maps are available at crystal shops all over Sedona.

left, continuing north several blocks to **Bell Rock ⓭**, which has a clearly signed trailhead on the right. **Court House Butte ⓮** is the large monolith behind it. Drive north on AZ 179 3 mi and turn left onto Back o' Beyond Road to reach **Cathedral Rock Trail ⓯**. Head back to AZ 179, make a left and another ½ mi farther on the right is the turnoff for the **Chapel of the Holy Cross ⓰** on Chapel Road. In 1 mi you must park and walk the last stretch up a steep, but brief, spiraling road to the chapel's vestibule. Step inside the small church to see inspired views of the buttes framed by the rectangular altar window.

Morgan Road is 1½ mi north on AZ 179, leading to the path and jeep trail to **Submarine Rock ⓱**. From Morgan Road, you can pull over and gaze off to the right to make out the easily recognizable **Elephant Rock.** Immediately before the highway veers sharply left across Oak Creek, continue straight, and off AZ 179, to Schnebly Hill Road to find the best views of **Snoopy Rock ⓲**. Backtrack, cross Oak Creek on AZ 179, then turn right onto AZ 89A. Continue for 3 mi to the **Rainbow Trout Farm ⓳**, a good place to take the kids fishing. It's about 4 mi farther to **Slide Rock State Park ⓴** where you can slip down a red-rock waterslide. The state park is in **Oak Creek Canyon ㉑**. Head back to and through Sedona on AZ 89A. Approximately 6 mi out of town is Red Rock Loop

Road, which will be on your left and leads to **Red Rock State Park** ㉒. The park has great panoramic views of Sedona's buttes from vistas on several easy trails, an ideal place to watch the sunset and end your day.

TIMING   Arrange your time in Sedona for midweek, if possible. The notorious crowds clog AZ 179 to near gridlock on the weekends, and finding a place to park, both in town and by the trails, is a chore. When you stop to explore a sight more closely, remember that a Red Rock Pass is required to park in the Coconino National Forest. If driving, you can tour all of the famous buttes in a day with time to linger over the vistas. Otherwise, allow several days to enjoy the full palate of outdoor activities. You can spend entire mornings hiking, mountain biking, or jeep touring, and afternoons swimming in Oak Creek.

What to See

⓭ **Bell Rock.** With its distinctive shape right out of your favorite Western film and its proximity to the main drag ensuring a steady flow of admirers, you may want to arrive early to see this very popular butte. The parking lot next to the Bell Rock Pathway often fills by mid-morning even in the middle of the week. The views from the parking lot are good, but an easy and fairly accessible path follows mostly gentle terrain for 1 mi to the base of the butte. Mountain bikers, parents with all-terrain baby strollers, and not-so-avid hikers should have little problem getting there. No official paths climb the rock itself, but many forge their own routes (at their own risk). ⊠ *AZ 179, several hundred yards north of Bell Rock Blvd., Village of Oak Creek.*

⓬ **Cathedral Rock.** It's almost impossible not to be drawn to this butte's towering, variegated spires. The approximately 1,200-foot-high Cathedral Rock looms dramatically over almost every part of town. When you emerge from the narrow gorge of Oak Creek Canyon, this is the first recognizable formation you'll spot. The butte is best seen toward dusk from a distance. Hikers may want to drive to the Airport Mesa and then hike the rugged but generally flat path that loops around the airfield. The trail is a ½ mi up Airport Road off of AZ 89A in West Sedona. The reward is a panoramic view of Cathedral Rock without the crowds. Those not hiking should drive through the Village of Oak Creek, and 5 mi west on Verde Valley School Road to its end, to a small park called Red Rock Crossing, where you can view the butte from a beautiful streamside vantage point and take a dip in Oak Creek if you wish. ⊠ *5 mi to the end of Verde Valley School Rd., west off of AZ 179, Village of Oak Creek.*

⓯ **Cathedral Rock Trail.** A vigorous but nontechnical 1½-mi scramble up the slickrock, this path leads to a nearly 360-degree view of red-rock country. Follow the cairns, the rock piles faithfully marking the trail, and look for the footholds in the rock. Carry plenty of water. Though short, the trail offers little shade and the pitch is steep. You can see the Verde Valley and Mingus Mountain in the distance. Look for the barely discernible "J" etched on the hillside marking the former ghost town of Jerome 30 mi distant. ✛ *Trailhead: About ½ mi down Back O' Beyond Rd. off of AZ 179, 3 mi south of Sedona.*

16 Chapel of the Holy Cross. You needn't be religious to be inspired by the setting and the architecture here. Built in 1956 by Marguerite Brunwige Staude, a disciple of Frank Lloyd Wright, this modern landmark, with a huge cross on the facade, rises between two red-rock peaks. Vistas of the town and the surrounding area are spectacular. There are no regular services, but anyone is welcome for quiet meditation. A small gift shop sells religious artifacts and books. A trail east of the chapel leads you—after a 20-minute walk over occasional loose-rock surfaces—to a seat surrounded by voluptuous red-limestone walls, worlds away from the bustle and commerce around the chapel. ⌂ *Chapel Rd., off AZ 179, Village of Oak Creek* ☎ *928/282–4069* ✉ *Free* ☉ *Daily 9–5.*

14 Courthouse Butte. The red sandstone seems to catch on fire toward sunset when the large monolith is free of any shadow. From the perspective of the highway, it sits in back of Bell Rock and can be viewed at the same time without any additional hiking or driving. ⌂ *AZ 179, Village of Oak Creek.*

21 Oak Creek Canyon. Whether you want to swim, hike, picnic, or enjoy
Fodor'sChoice beautiful scenery framed through a car window, head north through the
★ wooded Oak Creek Canyon. It's the most scenic route to Flagstaff and the Grand Canyon and worth a drive-through even if you're not heading north. Although the forest is primarily evergreen, the fall foliage is glorious. The road winds through a steep-walled canyon, where you crane your neck for views of the dramatic rock formations above. Oak Creek, which runs along the bottom, is lined with tent campgrounds, fishing camps, cabins, motels, and restaurants. ⌂ *AZ 89A, beginning 1 mi north of Sedona, Oak Creek Canyon.*

19 Rainbow Trout Farm. Anglers young and old always enjoy a sure catch. Rent a cane pole with a hook and bait for $1. There's no charge if your catch is under 8 inches; above that it's $2.85 to $5.85, depending on the length. The real bargain is that the staff will clean and pack your fish for 50¢ each. ⌂ *3500 N. AZ 89A, 3 mi north of Sedona, Oak Creek Canyon* ☎ *928/282–3379* ✉ *$1* ☉ *Daily 9–5.*

22 Red Rock State Park. Two miles west of Sedona via AZ 89A is the turnoff for this 286-acre state park, a less-crowded alternative to the popular Slide Rock State Park, though without the possibility for swimming. The 5 mi of interconnected-park trails are well marked and provide beautiful vistas. There are daily ranger-guided nature walks, bird-watching excursions on Wednesday and Saturday, and a guided hike to Eagle's Nest scenic overlook—the highest point in the park—every Saturday. Call ahead for times, which change with the season. ⌂ *4050 Red Rock Loop Rd., West* ☎ *928/282–6907* ⊕ *www.pr.state.az.us* ✉ *$6 per car* ☉ *Daily 8–5.*

20 Slide Rock State Park. A good place for a picnic, Slide Rock is 7 mi north of Sedona. On a hot day, you can plunge down a natural rock slide into a swimming hole (bring an extra pair of jeans to wear on the slide). The only downside to this trip is the traffic, particularly on summer weekends; you might have to wait to get in. Unfortunately, the popularity of the stream has led to the occasional midsummer closing due to e coli–bacteria infestations. ⌂ *6871 N. AZ 89A, Oak Creek Canyon* ☎ *928/282–*

3034 ⊕ *www.pr.state.az.us* 🖃 *$8 per vehicle for up to 4 persons* ☉ *Labor Day–Memorial Day, daily 8–5; Memorial Day–Labor Day, daily 8–7.*

 Snoopy Rock. When you look almost directly to the east, this butte looks like the famed Peanuts beagle laying atop red rock instead of his doghouse. You can distinguish the formation from several places around town including the mall in Uptown Sedona, but to get a clear view, venture up Schnebly Hill Road. Park by the trailhead on the left immediately before the paved road deteriorates to dirt. Marg's Draw, one of several trails originating here, is worthwhile, gently meandering 100 feet down-canyon, through the tortured desert flora to Morgan Road. Backtrack to the parking lot for close to a 3-mi hike. Always carry plenty of water, no matter how easy the hike appears. ⊠ *Schnebly Hill Rd., off of AZ 179, Central.*

⑰ **Submarine Rock.** This elongated vessel of a rock has an interesting shape, but is not as photogenic as the others. Nestled in the canyon and colored in beige tones, it doesn't catch the sunlight in the same way. Getting to Submarine Rock is perhaps more interesting than seeing the rock itself. It can be reached several ways. You can drive up FR 179F, a very technical jeep trail that should be attempted only by highly skilled off-road-vehicle drivers, or alternately you can take a popular jeep tour offered in town. For experienced mountain bikers, Broken Arrow Trail, used heavily by both cyclists and hikers, rolls across washes, red clay, and large mounds of slickrock. The 2 mi hike is moderate but best done in the early morning in summer. However, Submarine Rock is not the best retreat for serenity seekers. The rock abuts the jeep trail, which is clogged with tour jeeps revving over the rugged terrain. ⊠ *End of Morgan Rd., off of AZ 179, Central.*

Sports & the Outdoors

A Red Rock Pass is required to park in the Coconino National Forest from Oak Creek Canyon through Sedona and the Village of Oak Creek.

Golf

The **Oak Creek Country Club** (⊠ 690 Bell Rock Blvd., Village of Oak Creek
Fodor's Choice 📞 928/284–1660) is a good semiprivate course. The 18-hole **Sedona Golf
★ Resort** (⊠ 7260 AZ 179, Village of Oak Creek 📞 928/284–9355) was designed by Gary Panks to take advantage of the many changes in elevation and scenery. The 10th hole, said to be the most-photographed hole in all of Arizona, takes in a sweeping view of the Sedona Valley's red rocks.

Hiking & Backpacking

For free detailed maps, hiking advice, and information on campgrounds, contact the rangers of the **Coconino National Forest** (⊠ Sedona Ranger District, 250 Brewer Rd., West, 86339 📞 928/282–4119 ⊕ www.fs.fed. us/r3/coconino ☉ Weekdays 8–4:30). Ask here or at your hotel for directions to trailheads for Doe's Mountain (an easy ascent, with many switchbacks), Loy Canyon, Devil's Kitchen, and Long Canyon.

Among the paths in Coconino National Forest, the popular **West Fork Trail** (✛ Trailhead: AZ 89A, 9½ mi north of Sedona) traverses the Oak

Creek Canyon for a 3-mi hike. A walk through the woods in the midst of sheer red-rock walls and a dip in the stream make a great summer combination. The trailhead is about 3 mi north of Slide Rock State Park.

Any backpacking trip in the **Secret Mountain Wilderness** near Sedona guarantees stunning vistas, otherworldly rock formations, zenlike serenity, but little water. Pack in a full supply. Plan your trip for the spring or fall: summer brings 100 degree heat and sudden thunderstorms that flood canyons without warning. Most individual trails in the wilderness are too short for anything but an overnighter, but several trails can be linked up to form a memorable multiday trip. Contact the Sedona Ranger District for full details.

Horseback Riding

Among the equine tour options at **Trail Horse Adventures** (⊠ 5 J La., Lower Red Rock Loop Rd., West ☎ 928/282–7252) are a midday picnic and an Oak Creek swim and a full-moon ride with a campfire cookout.

Mountain Biking

Given the red-rock splendor, challenging terrain, miles of rideable single track, and mild weather, you might think Sedona would be a mountain biking destination on the order of Moab or Durango. Inexplicably, you won't find the lycra-clad throngs patronizing pasta bars or throwing back microbrews on the Uptown mall, but that's all the better for you. The mountain -biking culture of the area remains fervent but lowkey. A few strategically located, and excellent, bike shops can outfit you and dole out their best advice.

As a general rule, mountain bikes are allowed on all trails and jeep paths unless designated as wilderness or private property. The rolling terrain, which switches between serpentine trails of buff red clay and mounds of slickrock, has few sustained climbs. But be careful of blind drop-offs that often step down several feet in the most unexpected places. The thorny trailside flora makes carrying one or two extra inner tubes a must, and an inner tube sealant may be a good idea. If you plan to ride for several hours, pack close to a gallon of water and start rides early in the morning on hot days. Shade is rare, and with the nonpotable exception of Oak Creek, water is nonexistent.

For the casual rider, **Bell Rock Pathway** (✛ Trailhead: 5 mi south of Sedona on AZ 179) is a scenic and easy ride traveling 3 mi through some of the most breathtaking scenery in red-rock country. Several single-track trails spur off of this one making it a good starting point for many other rides in Sedona. **Submarine Rock Loop** is perhaps the most popular single-track loop in the area, and for good reason. The 10-mi trail is a heady mixture of prime terrain and scenery following slickrock and twisty trails up to Chicken Point, a sandstone terrace overlooking colorful buttes. The trail continues as a bumpy romp through washes almost all downhill. Be wary of blind drop-offs in this section. It wouldn't be overly cautious to scout any parts of the trail that look sketchy.

A few hundred yards south of Bell Rock Pathway, **Bike and Bean** (⊠ 6020 AZ179, Village of Oak Creek ☎ 928/284-0210) offers rentals, tours, and their own blend of gourmet coffee.

Where to Stay & Eat

Some Sedona restaurants close in January and February, so call before you go; make reservations in high season (April to October). Sedona is roughly divided into three neighborhoods: Uptown, which is a walkable shopping district; West Sedona, which is a 4-mi-long commercial strip; and Central Sedona, which encompasses everything south of the "Y" where AZ 179 and AZ 89A intersect.

★ **$$$-$$$$** ✕ **L'Auberge.** The most formal dining room in Sedona promises a quiet, civilized evening of indulgence. Chef Mark May's specialties include inventive twists on traditional French cuisine, such as chilled mango soup with champagne and mint, foie gras with prosciutto, striped bass with haricot verts, and rack of lamb with goat cheese gnocchi and artichokes. Save room for the chocolate soufflé at all costs. The restaurant has one of the best (and priciest) wine lists in Arizona. Don't miss the lavish Sunday brunch. ⊠ *L'Auberge de Sedona, 241 AZ 89A, Uptown* ☎ *928/ 282–4200* ▭ *AE, D, DC, MC, V.*

$$$-$$$$ ✕ **Shugrue's Hillside.** Almost everything is good here, which has made this one of the most popular restaurants in Sedona, but the salads and meats are particularly noteworthy. The Caesar salad is refreshingly traditional and the inventive ginger-walnut chicken salad is large enough to share. Rack of lamb and filet mignon are prepared and presented simply. There's a small, thoughtful, and well-priced wine list as well. Don't be confused: Shugrue's Hillside is not owned by the same folks who own Shugrue's West, a less appealing restaurant. ⊠ *671 AZ 179, Central* ☎ *928/282–5300* ▭ *AE, DC, MC, V.*

$$-$$$$ ✕ **Cowboy Club.** At this upscale restaurant, you can either hang out in the casual Cowboy Club or dine in the more formal Silver Saddle Room. High-quality cuts of beef are the specialty, but the fried chicken served with cumin-mashed potatoes is good, too. The wine list, however, is surprisingly meager. ⊠ *241 AZ 89A, Uptown* ☎ *928/282–4200* ▭ *AE, D, DC, MC, V.*

$$-$$$$ ✕ **Sasaki.** Somewhat off the tourist path, this understated restaurant serves a limited selection of impeccably fresh sushi and sashimi. There's a full Japanese menu, too. Pork *katsu* (lightly battered and fried cutlets of pork) and *ten-zura* (cold buckwheat noodles with tempura) are good cooked options. The service couldn't be friendlier. ⊠ *65 Bell Rock Rd., Village of Oak Creek* 928/284–1757 ▭ *AE, MC, V.*

$$-$$$$ ✕ **Takashi.** Those seeking some serenity and a respite from heavy meals will enjoy this Japanese restaurant, which provides aesthetic pleasure in everything from tea (with little bits of floating popcorn and brown rice) to dessert (sweet ginger or red-bean ice cream). Salads include a spicy sushi tuna with Japanese mayonnaise on a bed of cabbage and fresh vegetables. Combination dinners such as sashimi with tempura or teriyaki let you sample a little bit of everything. ⊠ *465 Jordan Rd., Uptown* ☎ *928/282–2334* ▭ *AE, DC, MC, V* ☾ *Closed Mon. No lunch Sun.*

$$$ ✕ **René at Tlaquepaque.** Ease into the plush banquettes of this lace-curtained restaurant for classic Continental dishes. Recommended starters include a delicate French-onion soup and the salade Walter—baby-spinach leaves and sautéed mushrooms in a hazelnut vinaigrette. Rack of lamb is the house specialty, and the true Dover sole is a real find, far from the white cliffs. Crêpes suzette for two, prepared table-side, is an impressive dessert. There's a well-selected wine list, too. Service is formal, as befits the room and menu, but casual attire is acceptable. ✉ *Tlaquepaque Arts & Crafts Village, Unit B–117, AZ 179, Central* ☎ *928/282–9225* ▭ *AE, MC, V.*

★ **$$–$$$** ✕ **Dahl & DiLuca.** A husband-and-wife team—Andrea DiLuca and Lisa Dahl—has created one of the most popular Italian restaurants in town with this colorful, eclectic space. Andrea runs the kitchen, and Lisa meets and greets diners as they enter. Lisa also slips into the kitchen every day to make delicious homemade soups like white bean with ham and hearty minestrone. ✉ *2321 W. AZ 89A, West* ☎ *928/282–5219* ▭ *AE, D, MC, V* ☾ *No lunch.*

★ **$$–$$$** ✕ **Heartline Café.** Fresh flowers and innovative, modern Southwestern cuisine are this attractive café's hallmarks. The oak-grilled salmon is marinated in tequila and lime, and the chicken breast has a prickly-pear sauce. Appealing vegetarian plates are also on the menu. On nice days grab a seat on the rosebush-lined terrace. Desserts include a phenomenal crème brûlée, as well as homemade truffles at the chef's whim. ✉ *1610 W. AZ 89A, West* ☎ *928/282–0785* ▭ *AE, D, MC, V* ☾ *No lunch Tues.–Thurs. and Sun.*

$$–$$$ ✕ **Pietro's.** Good northern Italian cuisine plus a friendly and attentive staff have made this lively and casual dining spot one of Sedona's most popular. Don't miss anything made with buffalo mozzarella from Naples. Homemade soups are always fabulous, and Leon is almost always on hand to help you decide on your *secondi piatti* if you can't make up your mind. ✉ *2445 W. AZ 89A, West* ☎ *928/282–2525* ▭ *AE, D, DC, MC, V* ☾ *No lunch.*

★ **$$–$$$** ✕ **Robert's.** A long-standing favorite on the banks of Oak Creek gained notoriety when Regis Philbin breezed through town and fell in love with the restaurant's peach cobbler. It's quite good, as are the grilled polenta, baby-back ribs, and prime rib. Nightly specials, such as fresh mako shark, are always intriguing, and stellar views of the buttes from the patio make for a sublime dining experience. ✉ *251 AZ 179, Central* ☎ *928/282–3671* ▭ *AE, MC, V.*

¢–$ ✕ **Mesquite Tree Barbecue.** Although it offers limited indoor seating, this Uptown hideaway behind a long row of tourist shops is worth a visit. Follow your nose to the mesquite-burning grill, where you can watch beef, chicken, and pork cook slowly and fall off the bone. The sauce has a slight kick, and the homemade french fries are fabulous. ✉ *250 Jordan Rd., No. 9, Uptown* ☎ *928/282–6533* ▭ *MC, V.*

¢–$ ✕ **Thai Spices.** This small, unadorned restaurant has a loyal following **Fodor'sChoice** of vegetarians and health-food enthusiasts, though not everything is meat- ★ less. If you call a day ahead, chef Pearl will create a special macrobiotic platter. The curries, especially red curry with tempeh, are delicious and can be prepared at the spice level of your choice. There's plenty here for carnivores, too: traditional pad thai with chicken is satisfyingly homey, and the spicy beef salad will make your hair stand on end. ✉ *2986 W. AZ 89A, West* ☎ *928/282–0599* ▭ *MC, V.*

¢ ✕ **Sedona Coffee Roasters.** Not only does this café serve the best coffee in town by a mile, but the lunch sandwiches are perfect fare before or after a red-rock hike. Daily specials might include a healthful chicken salad with sprouts, as well as the more decadent jumbo-beef Polish hot dog. You can also choose your own sandwich fixings from a list of fresh ingredients. More than 20 house-roasted coffees are sold by the pound. ⊠ *2155 W. AZ 89A, West* ☎ *928/282–0282* ▭ *No credit cards.*

★ **$$$$** ▣ **L'Auberge de Sedona.** This hillside resort consists of a central lodge building; a motel-style structure called the Orchards, reached by means of an incline railway; and—the major attraction—cabins in the woods along Oak Creek. Rooms in the Orchards are less expensive—and more standard-motel issue—while rooms in the lodge are decorated in lush Provençal style. The large cabins along the creek have wood-burning fireplaces. Phoenix couples flock to these country-French hideaways and dine in the hotel's French restaurant, one of the most romantic eateries in Arizona. ⊠ *L'Auberge La., Uptown* ⬤ *Box B, 86336* ☎ *928/282–1661 or 800/272–6777* 🖷 *928/282–2885* ⊕ *www.lauberge.com* ⬦ *69 rooms, 32 cottages* ♿ *2 restaurants, minibars, refrigerators, cable TV, pool, hot tub* ▭ *AE, D, DC, MC, V.*

★ **$$$$** ▣ **El Portal Sedona.** Opened in summer 2003 beside Tlaquepaque Arts & Crafts Village, this stunning hacienda has quickly earned a reputation as one of the most beautifully designed small hotels in the Southwest. The decor pays homage to the Arts and Crafts movement—accents include authentic Tiffany and Roycroft pieces, French doors leading to balconies or a grassy central courtyard, stained-glass windows and ceiling panels, river-rock or tile fireplaces, and huge custom-designed beds. All rooms have flat-screen TVs with DVD players and free high-speed Internet. Guests enjoy gym, spa, and pool privileges next door at Los Abrigados Resort. Wine and hors d'oeuvres are served in the afternoon, and the inn also presents prix-fixe ($45 per person) dinners on Saturday night, to the sounds of classical guitar. ⊠ *95 Portal La., Central, 86336* ☎ *928/203–9405 or 800/313–0017* 🖷 *928/203–9401* ⊕ *www.innsedona.com* ⬦ *11 rooms, 1 suite* ♿ *In-room data ports, some in-room hot tubs, refrigerators, cable TV, some pets allowed; no smoking* ▭ *AE, D, MC, V* ⦿ *BP.*

$$$–$$$$ ▣ **Amara Resort.** You might not expect to find this urbane boutique hotel in small, outdoorsy Sedona, but Amara fits right in here with its ochre-and-tan–sandstone exterior and secluded setting adjacent to gurgling Oak Creek. Sleek rooms deviate from the usual Sedona look, with mod low-slung beds and work desks with ergonomically correct seating. Other cushy extras include in-room DVD players, free high-speed Internet, and Aveda bath products. Step out onto your room's private balcony or terrace to take in expansive red-rock views. You can reach the shops and restaurants of Oak Creek up a long driveway; right on property, Amara Grille serves creative, globally inspired contemporary victuals. ⊠ *310 N. AZ 89, Oak Creek, 86336* ☎ *928/282–4828 or 866/455–6610* 🖷 *928/282–4825* ⊕ *www.amararesort.com* ⬦ *92 rooms, 8 suites* ♿ *Restaurant, in-room data ports, some in-room hot tubs, minibars, cable TV, lounge, concierge, meeting rooms, no-smoking rooms* ▭ *AE, D, DC, MC, V.*

★ **$$$–$$$$** 🏨 **Enchantment Resort.** Southwest-style rooms and suites at this resort are tucked into pueblo-style buildings in serene Boynton Canyon. Accommodations come in a variety of configurations, some with kitchens, separate living and dining areas, and multiple bedrooms, which can be joined to create large, elaborate suites. All have beehive gas fireplaces and superb views. Fresh-squeezed orange juice and a newspaper greet you each morning. The Yavapai Room serves excellent Southwestern cuisine. The resort's full-service spa, Mii Amo, offers cutting-edge treatments like hot stone massage and myo-facial release. ⊠ *525 Boynton Canyon Rd., West, 86336* 📞 *928/282–2900 or 800/826–4180* 🖷 *928/ 282–9249* ⊕ *www.enchantmentresort.com* 🛏 *107 rooms, 115 suites* ⌂ *2 restaurants, in-room safes, some kitchens, some kitchenettes, putting green, 12 tennis courts, pro shop, 4 pools, health club, spa, mountain bikes, boccie, croquet, hiking, Ping-Pong, bar, children's programs (ages 4–12)* ▭ *AE, D, MC, V.*

★ **$$$–$$$$** 🏨 **Graham Inn and Adobe Village.** Some of the attractive rooms at this inn south of Sedona have Jacuzzi tubs and balconies that look out onto the red rocks. Each of the four large, individually decorated casitas on the lot next door has a gas fireplace that opens into both the sitting area and the bathroom area, which is outfitted with a two-person Jacuzzi tub. What makes this place special, though, is the impeccable yet casual service, and the French chef makes breakfasts worth the price of admission. The owners are committed to always having at least one room under $200. ⊠ *150 Canyon Circle Dr., Village of Oak Creek, 86351* 📞 *928/284–1425 or 800/228–1425* 🖷 *928/284–0767* ⊕ *www. sedonasfinest.com* 🛏 *6 rooms, 1 suites, 4 private villas* ⌂ *Some in-room hot tubs, some kitchenettes, some refrigerators, cable TV, in-room VCRs, pool, hot tub, mountain bikes, library, Internet; no smoking* ▭ *D, MC, V* ⓘ *BP.*

★ **$$–$$$$** 🏨 **Alma de Sedona.** One of Sedona's most enchanting B&Bs, this family operation, run by Lynn McCarroll, has large rooms with spectacular views and ultracomfortable beds. When Lynn and her husband, Ron, were planning the inn, they told their architect that their top priorities were views and privacy; they've achieved both unequivocally. Understated, elegant, and inviting rooms all have private entrances and patios; bath salts and candles await in the bathrooms. ⊠ *50 Hozoni Dr., West, 86336* 📞 *928/282–2737 or 800/923–2282* 🖷 *928/203–4141* ⊕ *www. almadesedona.com* 🛏 *12 rooms* ⌂ *Some in-room hot tubs, cable TV, pool, meeting room; no smoking* ▭ *AE, MC, V* ⓘ *BP.*

$$–$$$$
Fodor'sChoice
★ 🏨 **Briar Patch Inn.** In a verdant canyon with a rushing creek, this B&B has rooms in wooden cabins (in Native American and Mexican styles), some with decks overlooking Oak Creek. On summer mornings you can sit outside and enjoy home-baked breads and fresh egg dishes while listening to live classical music. New Age and crafts workshops are sometimes held on the premises. Winter is equally beautiful; request a cabin with a fireplace and wake to see icicles hanging from the trees. ⊠ *3190 N. AZ 89A, Oakcreek Canyon, 86336* 📞 *928/282–2342* 🖷 *928/282– 2399* ⊕ *www.briarpatchinn.com* 🛏 *13 two-person cabins, 4 four-person cabins* ⌂ *Fans, some kitchenettes, massage, fishing, library, meeting room; no room TVs, no smoking* ▭ *AE, MC, V* ⓘ *BP.*

$$–$$$$ ▦ **Junipine Creekside Retreat.** These one- and two-bedroom cabins—here called creek houses—nestled in a juniper and pine forest (hence the name) are spacious and airy, with vaulted ceilings and fireplaces. They are an excellent value for groups of four or more, and some of the cabins comfortably sleep six. But Junipine's most enchanting feature is the sound of Oak Creek roaring below, lulling you to sleep by the fire. ⊠ *8351 N. AZ 89A, Oakcreek Canyon, 86336* ☎ *928/282–3375* 🖨 *928/282–7402* ⊕ *www.junipine.com* ⇘ *50 suites* ⚴ *Restaurant, kitchens, outdoor hot tub, no-smoking rooms; no TV in some rooms* ▭ *AE, D, MC, V.*

$$$ ▦ **Garland's Oak Creek Lodge.** In the heart of Oak Creek Canyon, this 1930s lodge and its 16 comfortably furnished cabins—some with fireplaces and pullout beds—are owned by Gary and Mary Garland. This mile-high, 17-acre spread has its own apple orchard, and accommodations look out over the rugged cliffs of the canyon or the creek. Excellent daily breakfast and dinner are included in the room price, along with afternoon tea. It's often booked solid a year in advance, but it's worth a call to check for vacancies. ⊠ *AZ 89A, 8 mi north of Uptown, Oakcreek Canyon* ✆ *Box 152, 86339* ☎ *928/282–3343* ⊕ *www. garlandslodge.com* ⇘ *16 cabins* ⚴ *Restaurant, tennis court, fishing, croquet, volleyball; no room phones, no room TVs, no smoking* ▭ *MC, V* ⊘ *Closed late Nov.–Mar.* ⦿| *MAP.*

$$–$$$ ▦ **Apple Orchard Inn.** Within walking distance of Uptown, nestled among pine and juniper trees, Apple Orchard Inn is an affordable choice. Each room has a different theme, and the inn can provide you with a personal guide to the area. Or you might choose to just relax in the massage room. ⊠ *656 Jordan Rd., Uptown, 86336* 🖨 *928/282–5328 or 800/663–6968* 🖨 *928/204–0044* ⊕ *www.appleorchardbb.com* ⇘ *7 rooms* ⚴ *Refrigerators, cable TV, in-room VCRs, pool; no smoking* ▭ *AE, MC, V* ⦿| *BP.*

$$–$$$ ▦ **Boots & Saddles.** Irith and Sam are the worldly and consummate hosts at this quiet inn tucked behind the main street in West Sedona. The rooms are decorated in an upscale Western motif, complete with genuine cowboy artifacts, and the Gentleman Cowboy room has unparalleled red-rock views and a telescope for stargazing. ⊠ *2900 Hopi Dr., West, 86336* 🖨 *928/282–1944 or 800/201–1944* ⊕ *www.oldwestbb. com* ⇘ *4 rooms* ⚴ *BBQ, refrigerators, in-room VCRs, hot tub, shop; no smoking* ▭ *AE, D, MC, V* ⦿| *BP.*

$$–$$$ ▦ **Lodge at Sedona.** Rooms in this rambling wood-and-stone house are Mission-style; some have fireplaces, redwood decks, or hot tubs. For solitude, walk the seven-path classic labyrinth (made of local rock) and through the gardens outside. A chef prepares a five-course breakfast each morning, which you can linger over either inside or on the outdoor terrace with a view of the red rocks in the distance. ⊠ *125 Kallof Pl., West, 86336* 🖨 *928/204–1942 or 800/619–4467* 🖨 *928/204–2128* ⊕ *www. lodgeatsedona.com* ⇘ *6 rooms, 8 suites* ⚴ *Dining room, some in-room hot tubs, some in-room VCRs, pool, gym, massage, library, concierge, meeting room; no room phones, no TV in some rooms, no smoking* ▭ *D, MC, V* ⦿| *BP.*

★ $$ ▦ **The Canyon Wren.** The best value in the Oak Creek Canyon area, this small B&B has free-standing cabins with views of the canyon walls. Milena and Mike (she's Slovenian, he's Floridian) regard guests' privacy first and foremost. It's likely that their two lovable dogs, Nasa and Stubby, will greet you on arrival. Cabins have private decks and fireplaces. Breakfast is a selection of delicious baked goods from Milena's kitchen. ✉ *6425 N. AZ 89A, Oakcreek Canyon, 86336* ☎ *928/282–6900 or 800/437–9736* 🖷 *928/282–6978* ⊕ *www.canyonwrencabins.com* ➦ *4 cabins* ⚿ *In-room hot tubs, kitchens; no room phones, no room TVs, no smoking* ▭ *AE, D, MC, V* ¶⊙¶ *CP.*

$–$$ 🏨 **Sky Ranch Lodge.** There may be no better vantage point in town from which to view Sedona's red-rock canyons than the private patios and balconies at Sky Ranch Lodge, near the top of Airport Mesa. Some rooms have stone fireplaces and some have kitchenettes; a few are a bit worn, but all are very clean. Paths on the grounds wind around fountains and, in summer, through colorful flower gardens. This is an excellent value, primarily because of the views. ✉ *Airport Rd., West, 86339* ☎ *928/282–6400* 🖷 *928/282–7682* ⊕ *www.skyranchlodge.com* ➦ *92 rooms, 2 cottages* ⚿ *Some kitchenettes, some refrigerators, cable TV, pool, hot tub, no-smoking rooms* ▭ *AE, MC, V.*

$ 🏨 **Desert Quail Inn.** Close to a lion's share of the trailheads, but out of the main flow of tourist traffic, the motel is a good base for outdoor adventures. The front desk is well stocked with maps and advice. The rooms are spacious and bright, and a few are done up in a Western motif. ✉ *6626 AZ 179, Village of Oak Creek, 86351* ☎ *800/385–0927 or 928/284–1433* 🖷 *928/284–0487* ⊕ *www.desertquailinn.com* ➦ *41 rooms* ⚿ *Some in-room hot tubs, some microwaves, refrigerators, cable TV, pool, laundry facilities* ▭ *AE, D, DC, MC, V.*

¢–$ 🏨 **Sedona Motel.** A typical motel in most other aspects, the structure is built on a terrace removed from the highway, affording it the very same expansive, red-rock views as the much more expensive resorts. Almost at the exact center of the "Y," it is within easy reach of most of Sedona's attractions. The rooms, which have coffeemakers, are new-looking and well kept. ✉ *218 AZ 179, Central, 86336* ☎ *928/282–7187* ➦ *16 rooms* ⚿ *Microwaves, refrigerators, cable TV* ▭ *D, MC, V.*

CAMPING 🏕 **Cave Springs and Pine Flat Campgrounds.** Try to arrive midweek to
¢ secure one of the popular national-forest campsites in Oak Creek Canyon. Reservations are a good idea but are limited to 29 sites. These neighboring campgrounds are the only two in the canyon to accept RVs as well as tents, but there are no hookups provided. The sites are near or next to Oak Creek, and at 5,500 feet in elevation, the summer nights are pleasantly cool. Stays are limited to one week. ⊹ *AZ 89A, 12 miles north of Sedona* ⊙ *Red Rock Ranger District, Box 300, Sedona, 86336* ☎ *877/444-6777 reservations only, 928/282-4119 information* ⊕ *www. reserveusa.com* ➦ *136 sites* ⚿ *Pit toilets, drinking water, showers, grills, picnic tables* ⊙ *Closed late Sept.–mid-Apr.*

Nightlife & the Arts

Find out about cultural events in Sedona at the **Book Loft** (✉ 175 AZ 179, just south of the "Y," Central ☎ 928/282–5173), which often hosts poetry readings, theatrical readings, book signings, and lectures. The Se-

dona **Jazz on the Rocks Festival** (☎ 928/282–1985 ⊕ www.sedonajazz.
com), held every September, always attracts a sellout crowd that fills
the town to capacity. The **Sedona Arts Center** (⊠ N. AZ 89A and Art
Barn Rd., Uptown ☎ 928/282–3809) sponsors events ranging from classical concerts to plays; there's an innovative and growing film festival
every March. The **Sedona Heritage Day Festival** (☎ 928/282–7038), a fam-
ily-oriented event in early October, includes pioneer storytellers, square-
dance exhibitions, music, and a barbecue.

Nightlife in Sedona tends to be fairly sedate. On high-season weekends,
there's usually live music at the Enchantment Resort. Shugrue's Hillside
also regularly presents local musicians. Offerings vary from jazz to rock
and pop; in all cases, call ahead. **Casa Rincon** (⊠ 2620 W. AZ 89A, West
☎ 928/282–4849) hosts an otherworldly dance party along with local
bands and open-mike nights. The closest thing to a rollicking cowboy
bar in Sedona is **Rainbow's End** (⊠ 3235 W. AZ 89A, West ☎ 928/282–
1593), a steak house with a large dance floor and country-and-western
bands on weekends.

Shopping

Shopping Areas & Malls

Most stores in what is known as the **Uptown** area, north of the "Y," running along AZ 89A to the east of its intersection with AZ 179, cater to
the tour-bus trade. There are several exceptions, though. The largest concentration of stores and galleries is in **Central** Sedona, along AZ 179,
south of the "Y." **West** Sedona, the more residential area that stretches
west of the "Y" along AZ 89A, doesn't have such concentrated areas
of shops as Uptown and Central.

It's worth a trip over to the West Sedona to visit **Artisans Galleria**
(⊠ 1420 W. AZ 89A, West ☎ 928/284–0077), which showcases the out-
put of more than 100 artists and craftspeople. A minute or two south
of the Hozho Center on AZ 179 is the **Hillside Courtyard & Marketplace**
(⊠ 671 AZ 179, Central ☎ 928/282–4500). The **Hozho Center** (⊠ 431
AZ 179, Central ☎ 928/204–2257) is a small, upscale complex in a beige
Santa Fe–style building. Inveterate bargain hunters will want to head
south on AZ 179, 2 mi past Chapel of the Holy Cross, to the Village of
Oak Creek. At the **Oak Creek Factory Outlets** (⊠ 6601 S. AZ 179, Village of Oak Creek ☎ 928/284–2150) are such stores as Corning/Revere,
Mikasa, Anne Klein, Bass, Jones New York, and Van Heusen. **Tlaquepaque Arts & Crafts Village** (⊠ AZ 179, just south of the "Y", Central
☎ 928/282–4838) gathers together more than 100 artisans, many of
them painters and sculptors. The complex of red-tile-roof buildings arranged around a series of courtyards shares its name and architectural
style with a crafts village just outside Guadalajara. It's a lovely place to
browse, but prices tend to be high; locals joke that it's pronounced "to-
lock-your-pocket."

Stores & Galleries

Clay Pigeon (⊠ Hillside Courtyard & Marketplace, 671 AZ 179, Central
☎ 928/282–2845) carries boldly designed dishes and sculptures with a

Western accent. A good bet for Southwestern art is **El Prado Gallery by the Creek** (✉ Tlaquepaque, AZ 179, No. 101, Bldg. E, Central ☎ 928/282–7390). **Esteban's** (✉ Tlaquepaque, AZ 179, No. 103, Bldg. B, Central ☎ 928/282–4686) focuses on ceramics and Native American crafts. **Garland's Navajo Rugs** (✉ 411 AZ 179, Central ☎ 928/282–4070) has a dazzling collection of new and antique carpets, as well as Native American–katsina dolls, pottery, and baskets. **Isadora** (✉ Tlaquepaque, AZ 179, No. 120, Bldg. A, Central ☎ 928/282–6232) has beautiful handwoven jackets and shawls. **James Ratliff Gallery** (✉ 431 AZ 179, Central ☎ 928/282–1404) has fun and functional pieces by not-yet-established artists. **Kuivato** (✉ Tlaquepaque, AZ 179, No. 122, Bldg. B, Central ☎ 928/282–1212) carries gorgeous glassware. **Lanning Gallery** (✉ Hozho Center, 431 AZ 179, Central ☎ 928/282–6865) sells attractive Southwestern art and jewelry. **Looking West** (✉ 242 N. AZ 89A, Uptown ☎ 928/282–4877) sells the spiffiest cowgirl-style getups in town. **Robert Shields Design** (✉ Sacajawea Plaza, 301 N. AZ 89A, Uptown ☎ 928/204–9253) carries colorful clay snakes and unusual silver jewelry. (If you still remember them, it's the same Shields who used to perform with Yarnell.) **Sedona Pottery** (✉ 411 AZ 179, Central ☎ 928/282–1192) sells unusual pieces, including flower-arranging bowls, egg separators, and life-size ceramic statues by shop owner Mary Margaret Sather.

FLAGSTAFF

146 mi northwest of Phoenix, 27 mi north of Sedona via Oak Creek Canyon.

Few travelers slow down long enough to explore Flagstaff, a town of 54,000, known locally as "Flag." Most stop only to spend the night at one of the town's many motels before making the last leg of the trip to the Grand Canyon, 80 mi north. Flag makes a good base for day trips to Native American ruins and the Navajo and Hopi reservations, as well as to the Petrified Forest National Park and the Painted Desert. But the city is a worthwhile destination in its own right. Set against a lovely backdrop of pine forests and the snowcapped San Francisco Peaks, Flagstaff retains a frontier flavor downtown.

Flagstaff has more fast-food outlets than most cities, no doubt because of the incredible demand for them: two major interstate highways meet just south of downtown; thousands of tourists drive through; thousands of students attending Northern Arizona University reside here; and many Native Americans come in from nearby reservations. During the summer, Phoenix residents head here, seeking relief from the desert heat. At any time of the year, temperatures in Flagstaff are about 20°F cooler than in Phoenix.

Phoenicians also come to Flagstaff in winter to ski at the small Arizona Snowbowl, about 15 mi northeast of town among the San Francisco Peaks. Accommodation rates are low at this time of year, making winter visits an excellent option for downhill and cross-country enthusiasts. Flagstaff has many accommodations (although no major hotels or resorts), but you should make reservations, especially during the summer.

Exploring Flagstaff

a good drive

Start your exploration of Flagstaff in the **Historic Downtown District** ㉓ ↾, the heart of which is the restored Santa Fe Depot on Route 66, still a functioning train station and also a visitor center. Drive east from here on Route 66/Santa Fe Avenue to reach the raucous **Museum Club** ㉔. Backtrack on Route 66/Santa Fe Avenue past the Depot. Continue straight on Santa Fe when Route 66 splits off sharply to the left. Santa Fe ends in a fork a few blocks later; take the right fork onto Mars Hill Road to reach the **Lowell Observatory** ㉕. Backtrack from the Observatory and turn right onto Route 66. Take the Milton Road branch off 66 to the turnoff for **Riordan State Historic Park** ㉖ and, a little farther to the south, one for the **Northern Arizona University Observatory** ㉗. Drive back up Milton Road, which merges with Route 66, then turn left on Humphreys Street, a major downtown thoroughfare; about a mile after it becomes Fort Valley Road, you'll reach Fort Valley Park and the **Pioneer Museum** ㉘. Continue north for just a few minutes on Fort Valley Road to reach the **Museum of Northern Arizona** ㉙. On the opposite side of Fort Valley Road, a few hundred yards farther down, is the turnoff for Schultz Pass Road, which leads to a number of the trailheads for the **Mount Elden Trail System** ㉚. Five miles farther along Fort Valley Road is the turnoff for **Arizona Snowbowl** ㉛. Drive another 6 mi north on Fort Valley Road, keeping a close eye out for FR 245, the easily missed turnoff on your left leading to the **Lava River Cave** ㉜.

TIMING You can see almost all of Flagstaff's attractions in a single day if you can visit the Lowell Observatory or the Northern Arizona University Observatory in the evening—which is also when the Museum Club is best experienced. Consult the schedule of tour times if you want to visit the Riordan State Historic Park. Plan on devoting at least an hour to the excellent Museum of Northern Arizona. The Historic Railroad District is a good place to have lunch. If you're a skier, you might be spending a good part of a winter's day at Arizona Snowbowl; in summer, allot a couple of hours to the sky ride and scenic trails at the top. Take your time enjoying the trails on Mount Elden, and remember to pace yourself in the higher elevations; allow a full day if you decide to hike these trails. The Lava River Cave is an easy—if dark—hike that can be comfortably completed in an hour.

What to See

㉛ **Arizona Snowbowl.** One of Flagstaff's most popular winter attractions also lures patrons in the summer, when the Agassiz ski lift, which climbs to a height of 11,500 feet in 25 minutes, doubles as a sky ride through the Coconino National Forest. From this vantage point, you can see up to 70 mi; views may even include the North Rim of the Grand Canyon. There's a lodge at the base with a restaurant and bar. To reach the ski area, take U.S. 180 north from Flagstaff; it's 7 mi from the Snowbowl exit to the skyride entrance. ✉ *Snowbowl Rd., North Flagstaff* ☎ *928/779–1951* ⊕ *www.arizonasnowbowl.com* 🎫 *Skyride $10* ☉ *Skyride Memorial Day–early Sept., daily 10–4; early Sept.–mid-Oct., Fri.–Sun. (weather permitting) 10–4.*

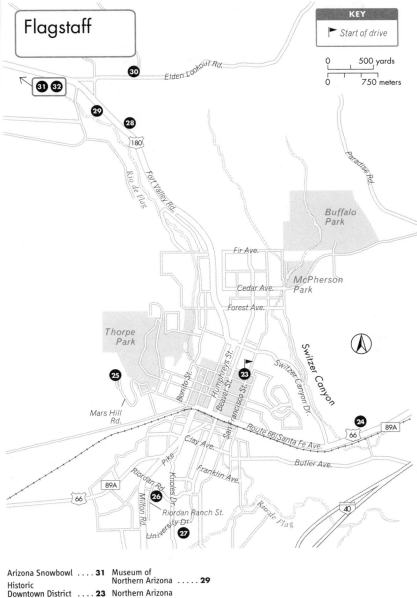

Flagstaff

KEY

▶ Start of drive

Arizona Snowbowl **31**

Historic
Downtown District **23**

Lava River Cave **32**

Lowell Observatory **25**

Mt. Elden
Trail System **30**

Museum Club **24**

Museum of
Northern Arizona **29**

Northern Arizona
University
Observatory **27**

Pioneer Museum **28**

Riordan State
Historic Park **26**

▶ **㉓ Historic Downtown District.** Storied Route 66 runs right through the heart of downtown Flagstaff. The late Victorian, Tudor Revival, and early-art-deco architecture in this district recalls the town's heyday as a logging and railroad center. A walking-tour map of the area is available at the visitor center in the Tudor Revival–style **Santa Fe Depot** (⊠ 1 E. Rte. 66, Downtown), an excellent place to begin sightseeing.

Highlights include the 1927 **Hotel Monte Vista** (⊠ 100 N. San Francisco St., Downtown), built after a community drive raised $200,000 in 60 days. The construction was promoted as a way to bolster the burgeoning tourism in the region, and the hotel was held publicly until the early 1960s. The 1888 **Babbitt Brothers Building** (⊠ 12 E. Aspen Ave., Downtown) was constructed as a building-supply store and then turned into a department store by David Babbitt, the mastermind of the Babbitt empire. The Babbitts are one of Flagstaff's wealthiest founding families. Bruce Babbitt, the most recent member of the family to wield power and influence, was the governor of Arizona from 1978 through 1987 and secretary of the Interior under President Clinton (1993–2001). Most of the area's first businesses were saloons catering to railroad construction workers, which was the case with the 1888 **Vail Building** (⊠ 5 N. San Francisco St., Downtown), a brick art deco–influenced structure covered with stucco in 1939. It now houses Crystal Magic, a New Age shop. ✛ *Downtown Historic District, Rte. 66 north to Birch Ave., and Beaver St. east to Agassiz St.*

need a break? The town's most interesting shops are concentrated downtown, and there are a couple of brewpubs and some spots where you can grab a quick bite. Students, skiers, new and aging hippies, and just about everyone else who likes good coffee jam into **Macy's** (⊠ 14 S. Beaver St., Downtown ☎ 928/774–2243) for the best cup in town. The **Black Bean** (⊠ 12 E. Rte. 66, Downtown ☎ 928/779–9905) is the place for do-it-yourself burritos, as healthful or as guacamole-smothered as you like.

㉜ Lava River Cave. Subterranean lava flow formed this mile-long cave roughly 700,000 years ago. Once you descend into its boulder-strewn maw, the cave is spacious, shaped like a railroad tunnel with 40-foot ceilings. But claustrophobes take heed: about halfway through the cave tapers to a 4-foot-high squeeze that can be a bit unnerving. Pack an extra flashlight and warm clothing. A yearlong 40°F chill pervades the cave. To reach the turnoff for the cave, go approximately 14 mi north of Flagstaff on U.S. 180, and then turn west onto FR 245. Turn left at the intersection of FR 171 and look for the sign to the cave. Although the cave is on National Forest Service property, the only thing here is an interpretive sign, so it's definitely something you tackle at your own risk. ⊠ *FR 171B.*

㉕ Lowell Observatory. In 1894, Boston businessman, author, and scientist Percival Lowell founded this observatory from which he studied the planet Mars. His theories of the existence of a ninth planet sowed the seeds for the discovery of Pluto at Lowell in 1930 by Clyde Tombaugh. V. M. Slipher's observations here between 1912 and 1920 led to the theory of the expanding universe. The 6,500-square-foot Steele Visitor Center hosts exhibits and lectures and has a gift shop; a "Tools of the Astronomer" display explains what professional stargazers do. Several interactive exhibits—among them the Pluto Walk, a scaled-down version of the solar system—will interest children. On some evenings the public is invited to peer through the 24-inch Clark telescope or through a more up-to-date 16-inch reflecting telescope. Four viewings a week are offered from June through August; call ahead for a schedule. The observatory dome is open and unheated, so dress for the outdoors. To reach the observatory, which is less than 2 mi from downtown, drive west on Route 66, which resumes its former name, Santa Fe Avenue, before it merges into Mars Hill Road. ⊠ *1400 W. Mars Hill Rd., West Flagstaff* ☎ *928/774–2096* ⊕ *www.lowell.edu* ⊡ *$5* ⊙ *Visitor center and night viewing hrs change seasonally; call ahead.*

㉚ Mount Elden Trail System. Most trails in the 35-mi-long Mount Elden Trail System lead to prodigious views from the dormant volcanic field, across the vast ponderosa pine forest, all the way to Sedona. The most challenging trail in the Mount Elden system, which happens to be the route with the most rewarding views, is along the steep switchbacks of the **Elden Lookout Trail** (⊠ off U.S. 89, 3 mi east of downtown Flagstaff). If you traverse the full 3 mi to the top, keep your focus on the landscape rather than the tangle of antennae and satellite dishes that greet you at the top. The 4-mi-long **Sunset Trail** (⊠ off U.S. 180, 3 mi north of downtown Flagstaff, then 6 mi east on FR 420 [Schultz Pass Rd.]) proceeds with a gradual pitch through the pine forest, finally emerging onto a narrow ridge nicknamed the Catwalk. By all means take pictures of the stunning valley views, but make sure your feet are well placed. This trail is closed in winter.

㉔ Museum Club. For real Route 66 color, don't miss this local institution fondly known as the Zoo because the building housed an extensive taxidermy collection in the 1930s. Luckily, most of the stuffed animals—including such bizarre specimens as a one-eyed sheep—are gone, but some owls still perch above the dance floor of what is now a popular country-and-western club. Even if you don't like crowds or country music, it's worth coming to see this gigantic log cabin constructed around five trees; the entryway consists of a huge wishbone-shaped pine. ⊠ *3404 E. Rte. 66, Downtown* ☎ *928/526–9434* ⊕ *www.museumclub.com* ⊡ *Free* ⊙ *Sun.–Thurs. noon–1 AM, Fri. and Sat. noon–3 AM.*

★ ℭ ㉙ Museum of Northern Arizona. Visiting here is worthwhile, if only to see the striking native-stone building in a cool, tree-shaded site. But the institution, founded in 1928, is also respected worldwide for its research and its collections centering on the natural and cultural history of the Colorado Plateau; only 1% of its vast holdings on the archaeology, ethnology, geology, biology, and fine arts of the region is on display at any given time. Among the permanent exhibitions are an extensive collection of Navajo rugs and an authentic Hopi kiva (men's ceremonial chamber).

A gallery devoted to area geology is usually a hit with children: it includes a life-size model dilophosaurus, a carnivorous dinosaur that once roamed northern Arizona. Outdoors, a life-zone exhibit shows the changing vegetation from the bottom of the Grand Canyon to the highest peak in Flagstaff. A nature trail, open only in summer, heads down across a small stream into a canyon and up into an aspen grove. In summer the museum hosts exhibits and the works of Native American artists, whose wares are also sold in the museum gift shop. The museum's education department sponsors excellent tours of the area and as far away as New Mexico and Utah. ☒ *3101 N. Fort Valley Rd., University* ☎ *928/774–5213* ⊕ *www.musnaz.org* ☞ *$5* ☉ *Daily 9–5.*

㉗ Northern Arizona University Observatory. The observatory, with its 24-inch telescope, was built in 1952 by Dr. Arthur Adel, a scientist at Lowell Observatory until he joined the college faculty as a professor of mathematics. His work on infrared astronomy pioneered research into molecules that absorb light passing through the Earth's atmosphere. Today's studies of Earth's shrinking ozone layer rely on some of Dr. Adel's early work. Visitors to the observatory—which houses one of the largest telescopes that the public is allowed to move and manipulate—are usually hosted by friendly students and faculty members of the university's Department of Physics and Astronomy. ☒ *Bldg. 47, Northern Arizona Campus Observatory, Dept. of Physics and Astronomy, S. San Francisco St., just north of Walkup Skydome, University* ☎ *928/523–8121 weekdays, 928/523–7170 Fri. night* ⊕ *www.phy.nau.edu/~naaa* ☞ *Free* ☉ *Viewings Fri. 7:30–10 PM, weather permitting.*

㉘ Pioneer Museum. The Arizona Historical Society operates this museum in a volcanic-rock building constructed in 1908. The structure was Coconino County's first hospital for the poor, and the current displays include one of the depressingly small nurses' rooms, an old iron lung, and a reconstructed doctor's office. Most of the exhibits, however, touch on more cheerful aspects of Flagstaff history—for example, road signs and children's toys. The museum holds a folk-crafts festival on the 4th of July, complete with blacksmiths, weavers, spinners, quilters, and candle makers at work. Their crafts, and those of other local artisans, are sold in the museum's gift shop, a tiny space filled with teddy bears, dolls, hand-dipped candles, and the like. The museum is part of the Fort Valley Park complex, in a wooded residential section at the northwest end of town. ☒ *2340 N. Fort Valley Rd., North Flagstaff* ☎ *928/774–6272* ☞ *$1 suggested donation per individual, $3 per family* ☉ *Mon.–Sat. 9–5.*

㉖ Riordan State Historic Park. This must-see artifact of Flagstaff's logging heyday is near Northern Arizona University. Its centerpiece is a mansion built in 1904 for Michael and Timothy Riordan, lumber-baron brothers who married two sisters. The 13,300-square-foot, 40-room log-and-stone structure—designed by Charles Whittlesley, who was also responsible for the El Tovar Hotel at the Grand Canyon—contains furniture by Gustav Stickley, father of the American Arts and Crafts–design movement. Fascinating details abound: one room holds "Paul Bunyan's shoes," a 2-foot-long pair of boots made by Timothy in his workshop. Everything on display is original to the house, half of which was occupied by members of the family until 1986. The mansion may be explored on a guided tour only. ☒ *1300 Riordan Ranch St., Uni-*

FodorśChoice
★

versity ☎ *928/779–4395* ⊕ *www.pr.state.az.us* 🎫 *$6* ☉ *May–Oct.,
daily 8:30–5, with tours on the hr 9–4; Nov.–Apr., daily 10:30–5, with
tours on the hr 11–4.*

Sports & the Outdoors

Camping

Contact the **Coconino National Forest** (✉ Peaks Ranger Station, 5075 N.
U.S. 89, North Flagstaff ☎ 928/526–0866 ⊕ www.fs.fed.us/r3/coconino)
for information on campgrounds in the area.

Hiking & Rock Climbing

You can explore Arizona's alpine tundra in the San Francisco Peaks, where
more than 80 species of plants grow on the upper elevations. The habitat is fragile, so hikers are asked to stay on established trails (and there
are lots of them). The altitude here will make even the hardiest hikers
breathe a little harder, so individuals with cardiac or respiratory problems should be cautious about overexertion. Flatlanders should give themselves a day or two to adjust to the altitude.

The rangers of the **Coconino National Forest** (✉ 2323 Greenlaw La.,
North Flagstaff ☎ 928/527–3600 ✉ Peaks Ranger Station, 5075 N.
U.S. 89, North Flagstaff ☎ 928/527–3630 ⊕ www.fs.fed.us/r3/coconino)
maintain many of the region's trails and can provide you with details
on hiking in the area; the forest's main office is open weekdays 7:30 to
4:30, and the ranger station has excellent hiking and recreation guides.

Flagstaff is in the Peaks District of the Coconino National Forest, and
there are many trails to explore. The **Humphreys Peak Trail** (⊕ Trailhead: Snowbowl Rd., 7 mi north of U.S. 180) is 9-mi round-trip, with
a vertical climb of 3,843 feet to the summit of Arizona's highest mountain (12,643 feet). Those who don't want a long hike can do just the
first mile of the adjacent, 5-mi-long **Kachina Trail** (⊕ Trailhead: Snowbowl Rd., 7 mi north of U.S. 180); completely flat, this route is surrounded
by huge stands of aspen and offers fantastic vistas. It's particularly
worthwhile in fall, when changing leaves paint the landscape shades of
yellow, russet, and amber. Others, such as the rewarding 2-mi **Fatmans
Loop** (⊕ Trailhead: AZ 89, across from Flagstaff Mall) on Mount
Elden, can be accessed in town. The 600-foot climb opens up great vistas of Flagstaff and the craggy face of Mount Elden.

Flagstaff Mountain Guides (☎ 928/635–0145) organizes peak rock-climbing trips around town or as far away as Sedona. If you'd prefer to hone
your skills first, **Vertical Relief Rock Gym** (✉ 205 S. San Francisco St., Downtown ☎ 928/556–9909) provides the tallest indoor climbing walls in
the Southwest.

Horseback Riding

The wranglers at **Hitchin' Post Stables** (✉ 4848 Lake Mary Rd., South
Flagstaff ☎ 928/774–1719) lead rides into Walnut Canyon and operate horseback or horse-drawn wagon rides with sunset barbecues. In
winter, they'll take you through Coconino National Forest on a sleigh—
bells and all.

Mountain Biking

With more than 30 mi of challenging trails a short ride from town, it was inevitable that one of Flagstaff's best-kept secrets would leak out. The mountain biking on Mount Elden is on par with that of more celebrated trails in Colorado and Utah.

The **Coconino National Forest** (⇨ Hiking & Rock Climbing) holds some of the best trails in the region. A good place to start is the **Lower Oldham Trail** (✛ Trailhead: Cedar St.), which originates on the north end of Buffalo Park in Flagstaff; there's a large meadow with picnic areas and an exercise path. The terrain rolls, climbing about 800 feet in 3-mi, and the trail is technical in spots but easy enough to test your tolerance of the elevation.

The very popular **Schultz Creek Trail** (✛ Trailhead: Schultz Padd Rd., near the intersection with U.S. 180) is very fun and suitable for strong beginners, though seasoned experts will be thrilled as well. Most opt to start at the top of the 600-foot-high hill and swoop down the smooth, twisting path through groves of wildflowers and stands of ponderosa pines and aspens and end at the trailhead four giddy miles later.

You can rent mountain bikes at **Absolute Bikes** (⊠ 18 N. San Francisco St., Downtown ☎ 928/779–5969). From mid-June through mid-October, the **Flagstaff Nordic Center** (⊠ U.S. 180, 16 mi north of Flagstaff, North Flagstaff ☎ 928/779–1951), which is operated by the Arizona Snowbowl, opens its cross-country trails to mountain bikers, gratis if you bring your own wheels; rentals are also available. **Mountain Sports** (⊠ 1800 S. Milton Rd., University ☎ 928/779–5156 or 800/286–5156) offers competitive rates for bike rentals. A map of the **Urban Trails System** (⊠ 1 E. Rte. 66, Downtown ☎ 928/774–9541 or 800/842–7293), available at the Flagstaff Visitor Center, details biking options in the area.

Skiing & Snowboarding

The ski season usually starts in mid-December and ends in mid-April. The **Arizona Snowbowl** (⊠ Snowbowl Rd., North Flagstaff ☎ 928/779–1951, 928/779–4577 snow report ⊕ www.arizonasnowbowl.com), 7 mi north of Flagstaff off U.S. 180, has 30 downhill runs (37% beginner, 42% intermediate, and 21% advanced), four chairlifts, and a vertical drop of 2,300 feet. Those who have skied Colorado's Rockies might find Snowbowl disappointing—there are a couple of good bump runs, but it's better for beginners or those with moderate skill. Still, it's a fun place to spend the day. Snowboarders share trails with downhill skiers. The Hart Prairie Lodge has an equipment-rental shop and a SKIwee center for ages 4 to 8. All-day adult lift tickets are $42. Half-day discounts are available, and group-lesson packages (including two hours of instruction, an all-day lift ticket, and equipment rental) are a good buy at $64. A children's program (which includes lunch, progress card, and full supervision 9–3:30) runs $65. Many Flagstaff motels offer ski packages, including transportation to Snowbowl.

The **Flagstaff Nordic Center** (⊠ U.S. 180, 16 mi north of Flagstaff, North Flagstaff ☎ 928/779–1951, 928/779–4577 snow report ⊕ www.arizonasnowbowl.com), owned and operated by Arizona Snowbowl, is 9 mi north of Snowbowl Road. There are 25 mi of well-groomed cross-country trails here. Instruction packages and rental combinations are available.

Where to Stay & Eat

By city ordinance, all restaurants in Flagstaff forbid smoking.

$$-$$$ ✕ **Black Bart's Steakhouse Saloon & Old West Theater.** The Wild West atmosphere at this rollicking, brightly lit barn of a restaurant is a rather cornball creation. However, the barbecued chicken is tender and flavorful, and the biscuits stick to your ribs. Just don't expect to see any vegetables on your plate unless they're deep-fried. Northern Arizona University music students entertain while they wait on tables, so don't be surprised if your server suddenly jumps onstage to belt out a couple of show tunes. ⊠ *2760 E. Butler Ave., Downtown* ☎ *928/779–3142* ⌘ *Reservations not accepted* ⊟ *AE, MC, V* ⊘ *No lunch.*

★ **$$-$$$** ✕ **Cottage Place.** An unexpectedly elegant spot in a town known for fast food and drive-through service, this cozy restaurant in a 50-year-old cottage has intimate dining rooms and an extensive wine list. The menu strays only slightly from Continental to include some classic American dishes, such as charbroiled lamb chops. Try the artichoke chicken breast or chateaubriand for two carved table-side. Dinner includes soup and salad, but save room for Chocolate Decadence and other desserts. ⊠ *126 W. Cottage Ave., Downtown* ☎ *928/774–8431* ⊟ *AE, MC, V* ⊘ *Closed Mon. No lunch.*

$$-$$$ ✕ **Sakura Restaurant.** The excellent fish at this Japanese restaurant in the Radisson is flown in every other day from the West Coast. If sushi doesn't entice you, dine at a large grill table where the well-seasoned, large portions of steak or seafood with vegetables are flipped in front of you. ⊠ *Radisson Woodlands Plaza Hotel, 1175 Rte. 66, East Flagstaff* ☎ *928/773–9118* ⊟ *AE, D, DC, MC, V* ⊘ *No lunch Sun.*

$$ ✕ **Pasto.** This downtown Italian restaurant—two intimate dining rooms in adjacent historic buildings—is popular with a young crowd for good food at reasonable prices. Such southern Italian standards as lasagna and spaghetti with meatballs appear on the menu along with more innovative fare, such as artichoke orzo and salmon Caesar salad. A courtyard in the back, tucked away among higher buildings, has a romantic urban feel. ⊠ *19 E. Aspen St., Downtown* ☎ *928/779–1937* ⊟ *MC, V* ⊘ *No lunch Sept.–May.*

$-$$ ✕ **Buster's Restaurant.** At lunchtime, families and students from nearby Northern Arizona University settle into the comfortable booths and enjoy fresh seafood, homemade soups, salads, giant burgers, and mesquite-grilled steaks. Try the *lahvosh* appetizer—a giant cracker heaped with toppings ranging from smoked salmon to mushrooms—or the Caesar salad with grilled Cajun chicken. At night, single professionals and skiers crowd the bar and work through its impressive beer selection. ⊠ *1800 S. Milton Rd., Downtown* ☎ *928/774–5155* ⊟ *AE, D, DC, MC, V.*

$ ✕ **Beaver Street Brewery.** Popular among the wood-fired pizzas here is the Enchanted Forest, with Brie, Portobello mushrooms, roasted red peppers, spinach, and artichoke pesto. Whichever pie you order, expect serious amounts of garlic. Sandwiches, such as the Southwestern chicken with three types of cheese, come with a hefty portion of tasty fries. You won't regret ordering one of the down-home desserts, such as the super-gooey chocolate bread pudding. Among the excellent microbrews usually on tap, the raspberry ale is a local favorite. An outdoor beer garden opens up in summer. ⊠ *11 S. Beaver St., Downtown* ☎ *928/779–0079* ⊟ *AE, D, DC, MC, V.*

¢–$ ✕ **Café Espress.** The menu is largely vegetarian at this natural-foods restaurant. Stir-fried vegetables, pasta dishes, Mediterranean salads, tempeh burgers, pita pizzas, fish or chicken specials, and wonderful baked goods made on the premises all come at prices that will make you feel good, too. This is an artsy and hip place (the work of local artists hangs on the walls) but friendly, and it's open for breakfast every day at 7. ⊠ *16 N. San Francisco St., Downtown* ☎ *928/774–0541* ⊟ *MC, V.*

¢–$ ✕ **Salsa Brava.** This cheerful Mexican restaurant, with light-wood booths and colorful designs, eschews heavy Sonoran-style fare in favor of the grilled dishes found in Guadalajara. The fish tacos are particularly good, and this place has the only salsa bar in town. On weekends, come for a huevos rancheros breakfast. ⊠ *1800 S. Milton Rd., Downtown* ☎ *928/774–1083* ⊟ *AE, MC, V.*

¢ ✕ **La Bellavia.** At this favorite bohemian breakfast nook, the trout and eggs platter is the standard—two eggs served with Idaho trout flavored with a hint of lemon, and rounded off by a buttermilk pancake. Other options include Swedish oat pancakes, seven-grain French toast, and nine varieties of eggs Benedict. A palette of creative sandwiches and familiar salads makes this a worthwhile lunch stop as well. The café doubles as a gallery for local artists whose artwork hangs on the walls beneath an azure-painted ceiling scattered with, perhaps, the few clouds you'll see that day. ⊠ *18 S. Beaver St., Downtown* ☎ *928/774–8301* ⊟ *No credit cards* ☉ *No dinner.*

¢ ✕ **Bun Huggers.** The best burger in town is flipped over a mesquite-fired grill. Also try the tasty, if decadent, deep-fried zucchini served with shredded cheddar cheese and ranch dressing. There is a small salad bar here, but it seems like an afterthought, existing only to heal guilty consciences. ⊠ *901 S. Milton Rd., Downtown* ☎ *928/779–3743* ⊟ *AE, D, MC, V.*

★ $$–$$$ 🖼 **Inn at 410.** An inviting alternative to the chain motels in Flagstaff, this B&B has a convenient but quiet downtown location. All the accommodations in the beautifully restored 1907 residence are suites with private baths. Some have private entrances and fireplaces; all have coffeemakers. Monet's Garden is a lovely Jacuzzi suite with fireplace. Pancakes with blue cornmeal and piñon nuts, and curried cornbread pudding with pumpkin sauce highlight a tantalizing breakfast menu. ⊠ *410 N. Leroux St., Downtown, 86001* ☎ *928/774–0088 or 800/774–2008* 🖨 *928/774–6354* ⊕ *www.inn410.com* ➦ *9 suites* ᇋ *Some in-room hot tubs, refrigerators, room TVs, in-room VCRs; no kids in some rooms, no smoking* ⊟ *MC, V* ❏ *BP.*

$$ 🖼 **Jeanette's.** If you prefer the clean lines of 1920s design to Victorian froufrou, consider staying at this stylish B&B. Rooms in this residence on the city's east side are all beautifully appointed with art deco pieces; one room has a private porch, another a fireplace. Details such as fine

china at breakfast enhance the time-travel experience, as does owner Jeanette's devotion to antique clothing, which she often dons. ✉ *3380 E. Lockett Rd., East Flagstaff, 86004* ☎ *928/527–1912 or 800/752–1912* ⊕ *www.jeanettesbb.com* ➪ *4 rooms* ♿ *No room TVs, no smoking* ⊟ *D, MC, V* ♨ *BP.*

★ **$$** ☷ **Little America of Flagstaff.** The biggest hotel in town is a deservedly popular place. It's far from the roar of the trains, the grounds are surrounded by evergreen forests, and it's one of the few places in Flagstaff with room service. Plush rooms have chandeliers, comfortable sitting areas with French provincial–style furniture, phones in bathrooms, and large stereo TVs. Other pluses are courtesy van service to the airport and the Amtrak station and a gift shop with great Southwestern stuff. ✉ *2515 E. Butler Ave., Downtown, 86004* ☎ *928/779–2741 or 800/352–4386* ☷ *928/779–7983* ⊕ *www.flagstaff.littleamerica.com* ➪ *248 rooms* ♿ *Restaurant, coffee shop, room service, kitchenettes, refrigerators, cable TV with movies and video games, pool, gym, hair salon, croquet, hiking, horseshoes, bar, shop, playground, laundry facilities, laundry service, meeting rooms, airport shuttle* ⊟ *AE, D, DC, MC, V.*

$–$$ ☷ **Birch Tree Inn.** This historic home in a tree-filled neighborhood near downtown is nicely appointed with antiques. The place feels relaxed, in part because the hosts (two friendly couples who trade off inn-keeping stints) enjoy chatting with their guests. The billiard table adjoining the living room gets people talking to each other, too. Start your day well fueled for sightseeing: the morning meal might consist of a cheese, sausage, and potato casserole accompanied by fresh fruit and banana bread made on the premises. ✉ *824 W. Birch Ave., Downtown, 86001* ☎ *928/774–1042 or 800/645–5805* ⊕ *www.birchtreeinn.com* ➪ *5 rooms, 3 with bath* ♿ *Outdoor hot tub; no room TVs, no kids under 12, no smoking* ⊟ *AE, MC, V* ♨ *BP.*

$–$$ ☷ **Sled Dog Inn.** This inn is on just 4 acres, but its grounds seem vastly larger, since the land borders the immense Coconino National Forest. A big draw here is, as the name implies, the owners' Siberian huskies, which are lovingly cared for. Sometimes during the winter you can even accompany the owners on a dog-sled run, but they no longer offer regular rides to guests. Rooms are contemporary rustic. ✉ *10155 Mountainaire Rd., South Flagstaff, 86001* ☎ *928/525–6212 or 800/754–0064* ⊕ *www.sleddoginn.com* ➪ *8 rooms, 2 suites* ♿ *Hot tub, sauna; no room TVs, no kids under 6, no smoking* ⊟ *AE, MC, V* ♨ *CP.*

¢–$$ ☷ **Hotel Monte Vista.** Over the years many Hollywood stars, including Bob Hope and Spencer Tracy, have stayed at this downtown hotel. Funky room designs are inspired by the famous guests: golden cherubs descend from an azure ceiling in the Air Supply Room, and framed antique postcards of Western novel book-covers hang on the walls of the Zane Grey Room. The 1926 building has a restored Southwestern-deco lobby with curved archways. ✉ *100 N. San Francisco St., Downtown, 86001* ☎ *928/779–6971 or 800/545–3068* ☷ *928/779–2904* ⊕ *www.hotelmontevista.com* ➪ *48 rooms* ♿ *Restaurant, cable TV, bar, laundry service* ⊟ *AE, D, MC, V.*

¢ ☷ **Hotel Weatherford.** With a columned veranda that wraps around the block, this hotel, built in 1897, is a dramatic presence at the hub of town.

Imbued with a creaky charm, the rooms are spartan and a bit worn around the edges but comfortable nonetheless. Forgo TV and a telephone for a taste of the Old West. The Exchange Pub downstairs has a bustling nightlife scene. ⊠ *23 N. Leroux St., Downtown, 86001* ☎ *928/779–1919* 🖷 *928/773–8951* ⊕ *www.weatherfordhotel.com* 🛏 *8 rooms, 5 with bath* 🍴 *Restaurant, 2 bars; no a/c, no room phones, no room TVs* 🖃 *AE, D, DC, MC, V.*

Nightlife & the Arts

THE ARTS   Northern Arizona University's **College of Creative and Performing Arts** (⊠ Ardrey Auditorium, Knoles and Riordan Rds., University ☎ 928/523–5661) is a top-quality performance venue. The **Flagstaff Symphony Orchestra** (☎ 928/774–5107) offers year-round musical events. **Theatrikos Theater Company** (⊠ 11 W. Cherry Ave., Downtown ☎ 928/774–1662) is a highly regarded troupe, featuring an eclectic lineup of plays.

A Celebration of Native American Art (⊠ 3101 N. Fort Valley Rd., University ☎ 928/774–5211), featuring exhibits of work by Zuni, Hopi, and Navajo artists, is held at the Museum of Northern Arizona from late May through September. During the month of August, the **Flagstaff Festival of the Arts** (☎ 928/774–7750 or 800/266–7740) fills the air with the sounds of classical music and pops performances, many by world-renowned artists. **Flagstaff SummerFest** (⊠ Fort Tuthill Coconino County Park, S. AZ 89A, South Flagstaff ☎ 928/774–5130), held the first weekend in August, includes an arts-and-crafts fair. Flagstaff's observatories help make September's **Festival of Science** (☎ 800/842–7293) a stellar attraction.

NIGHTLIFE   Flagstaff's large college contingent has plenty of places to gather after dark, most of them in the historic downtown district and most of them charging little or no cover. It's easy to walk from one rowdy spot to the next. For current information on what's going on in town, pick up the free *Flagstaff Live*. There's also no shortage of cultural entertainment in Flagstaff, not to mention summer festivals.

The ground floor of the **Hotel Weatherford** (⊠ 23 N. Leroux St., Downtown ☎ 928/779–1919) has a double bill, with both Charly's, which hosts late-night jazz and blues bands, and the Exchange Pub, which tends to attract folksy ensembles. Dark, smoky, and decked with a neon sign, **Joe's Place** (⊠ 200 E. Rte. 66, Downtown ☎ 928/774–6281) is a Route 66 classic and a favorite place for locals to shoot pool. The **Mogollon Brewing Company** (⊠ 15 N. Agassiz St., Downtown ☎ 928/773–8950) rolls out live music and hardy stout. The **Monte Vista Lounge** (⊠ 100 N. San Francisco St., Downtown ☎ 928/774–2403) packs them in with nightly live blues, jazz, classic rock, punk, and an open mike on Wednesday.

Shopping

Flagstaff's prime shopping area is downtown. Even if you're not looking for anything in particular, it's fun to stroll along San Francisco Street and Route 66. The **Flagstaff Mall** (⊠ 4650 N. U.S. 89, East Flagstaff ☎ 928/526–4827) is just east of town off Interstate 40 at Exit

201. This mall has the greatest number of department and specialty stores in the area, including Dillard's, Sears, and JCPenney. There's also a food court and a two-screen cinema.

For fine arts and crafts—everything from ceramics and stained glass to weaving and painting—visit the **Artists Gallery** (⊠ 17 N. San Francisco St., Downtown ☎ 928/773–0958), a local artists' cooperative. You can pick up sporting goods at **Babbitt's Backcountry Outfitters** (⊠ 12 E. Aspen Ave., Downtown ☎ 928/774–4775). The **Black Hound Gallerie** (⊠ 120 N. Leroux St., Downtown ☎ 928/774–2323) specializes in posters, prints, and funky kitsch of all kinds. **Candles by Night** (⊠ 113 W. Phoenix Ave., Downtown ☎ 928/774–1461) displays whimsical handcrafted candles. The 20-odd vendors at **Carriage House Antique and Gift Mall** (⊠ 413 N. San Francisco St., Downtown ☎ 928/774–1337) sell vintage clothing and jewelry, furniture, fine china, and other collectibles. The **Museum of Northern Arizona Gift Shop** (⊠ 3101 N. Fort Valley Rd., University ☎ 928/774–5213) carries high-quality jewelry and crafts. **Winter Sun Trading Company** (⊠ 107 N. San Francisco St., Downtown ☎ 928/774–2884) sells medicinal herbs, jewelry, and crafts. **Zani** (⊠ 111-C S. San Francisco St., Downtown ☎ 928/774–9409) stocks hip home furnishings and greeting cards in addition to futons.

SIDE TRIPS NEAR FLAGSTAFF

Travelers who head straight through town, bound for the Grand Canyon, often neglect the area north and east of Flagstaff. But a detour has its rewards. If you don't have enough time to do everything, take a quick drive to Walnut Canyon—only about 15 minutes out of town.

East of Flagstaff

★ ❸ **Walnut Canyon National Monument** consists of a group of cliff dwellings constructed by the Sinagua people, who lived and farmed in and around the canyon starting around AD 700. The more than 300 dwellings here were built between 1080 and 1250 and abandoned, like those at so many other settlements in Arizona and New Mexico, around 1300. The Sinagua traded far and wide with other Native Americans, including people at Wupatki. Even macaw feathers, which would have come from tribes in what is now Mexico, have been excavated in the canyon. The area wasn't explored by Europeans until 1883, when early Flagstaff settlers shamelessly looted the site for pots and "treasure." Woodrow Wilson declared the site a national monument in 1915, which began a 30-year process of stabilizing the ruins.

Part of the fascination of Walnut Canyon is the opportunity to enter the dwellings themselves, stepping back in time to an ancient way of life. Some of the Sinagua homes are in near-perfect condition, in spite of all the looting, because of the dry, hot climate and the protection of overhanging cliffs. You can reach them by descending 185 feet on the 1-mi stepped **Island Trail,** which starts at the visitor center. As you follow the trail, look across the canyon for other dwellings not accessible on the path.

Island Trail takes about an hour to complete at a normal pace. Those with health concerns should opt for the easier ½-mi **Rim Trail,** which has overlooks from which dwellings, as well as an excavated, reconstructed pit house, can be viewed. Attractive picnic areas dot the grounds and line the roads leading to the park. Guides conduct tours on Wednesday, Saturday, and Sunday from late May through early September. You are permitted to enter about two dozen ruins. ⊠ *Walnut Canyon Rd., 3 mi south of Interstate 40, Exit 204, Winona* ☎ *928/526–3367* ⊕ *www. nps.gov/waca* ☑ *$3* ⊙ *Sept.–May, daily 9–5; June–Aug., daily 9–6.*

🕐 ㉞ **Meteor Crater,** a natural phenomenon, set in a privately owned park 43 mi east of Flagstaff, is impressive if for no other reason than its sheer size. A hole in the ground 600 feet deep, nearly 1 mi across, and more than 3 mi in circumference, Meteor Crater is large enough to accommodate the Washington Monument or 20 football fields. It was created when a meteorite came hurtling through space at a speed of 43,000 mph and crashed here 49,000 years ago. The area looks so much like the surface of the moon that NASA made it one of the official training sites for the Project Apollo astronauts. You can't descend into the crater because of the efforts of its owners to maintain its condition—scientists consider this to be the best-preserved crater on Earth—and guided rim tours, given every hour on the hour from 9 to 3, give you some useful background information. There's a small snack bar, and rock hounds will enjoy the Rock Shop's raw specimens from the area and jewelry made from native stones. Take Interstate 40 east of Flagstaff to Exit 233, then 6 mi south on Meteor Crater Road. ⊠ *Meteor Crater Rd., 43 mi east of Flagstaff* ☎ *800/289–5898* ⊕ *www.meteorcrater.com* ☑ *$12* ⊙ *Memorial Day–Labor Day, daily 7–7; Labor Day–Memorial Day, daily 8–5.*

San Francisco Volcanic Field

The San Francisco Volcanic Field north of Flagstaff encompasses 2,000 square mi of fascinating geological phenomena—ancient volcanoes, cinder cones, and valleys carved by water and ice, and the San Francisco Peaks themselves, some of which soar to almost 13,000 feet—as well as some of the most extensive Native American ruins in the Southwest: don't miss Sunset Crater and Wupatki. These national monuments can be explored in relative solitude during much of the year. The area is short on services, so fill up on gas and consider taking along a picnic. A good source for hiking and camping information in the San Francisco Volcanic Field area are the rangers of **Coconino National Forest** (⊠ Peaks Ranger Station, 5075 N. U.S. 89, North Flagstaff ☎ 928/526–0866 ⊕ www.fs.fed.us/r3/coconino). If you camp, do not pitch your tent in a low-lying area, where dangerous flash floods can literally wipe you out.

★ ㉟ **Sunset Crater Volcano National Monument** lies 14 mi northeast of Flagstaff off U.S. 89. Sunset Crater, a cinder cone that rises 1,000 feet, was an active volcano 900 years ago. The final eruption contained iron and sulfur, which gives the rim of the crater its glow and thus its name. You can walk around the base, but you can't descend into the huge, fragile cone. The **Lava Flow Trail,** a half-hour, mile-long, self-guided walk, provides a good view of the evidence of the volcano's fiery power: lava formations and holes in the rock where volcanic gases vented to the surface. Three smaller cones to the southeast were formed at the same time and along the same fissure.

If you're interested in hiking a volcano, head to **Lenox Crater,** about 1 mi east of the visitor center, and climb the 280 feet to the top of the cinder cone. Wear closed, sturdy shoes; the cinder is soft and crumbly. From **O'Leary Peak,** 5 mi from the visitor center on Forest Route 545A, great views can be had of the San Francisco Peaks, the Painted Desert, and beyond. The road is unpaved and rutted, however, so it's advisable to take only high-clearance vehicles, especially in winter. In addition, there's a gate, about halfway along the route, that is usually closed. This will mean a steep 2½-mi hike to the top on foot. To get to the area from Flagstaff, take Santa Fe Avenue east to U.S. 89, and head north for 12 mi; turn right onto the road marked Sunset Crater and go another 2 mi to the visitor center. ⊠ *Sunset Crater–Wupatki Loop Rd., 14 mi northeast of Flagstaff* ☎ *928/556–7042* ⊕ *www.nps.gov/sucr* ⊡ *$3, including Wupatki National Monument and Doney Mountain* ☉ *Daily 8–5; hrs may be extended in summer.*

Families from the Sinagua and other ancestral Puebloans are believed to have lived together in harmony on the site that is now **Wupatki National Monument,** farming and trading with one another and with those who passed through their "city." The eruption of Sunset Crater may have caused migration to this area a century after the event, as freshly laid volcanic cinders held in moisture needed for crops—and may have disrupted the settlement more than once around AD 1064. Although there is evidence of earlier habitation, most of the settlers moved here around 1100 and left the pueblo by about 1250. The 2,700 identified sites contain archaeological evidence of a Native American settlement.

36
Fodor'sChoice
★

The site for which the national monument was named, the Wupatki (meaning "tall house" in Hopi), was originally three stories high, built above an unexplored system of underground fissures. The structure had almost 100 rooms and an open ball court—evidence in itself of Southwestern trade with Mesoamerican tribes for whom ball games were a central ritual. Next to the ball court is a blowhole, a geologic phenomenon in which air is forced upward by underground pressure; scientists speculate that early inhabitants may have attached some spiritual significance to the region's many blowholes.

Other ruins to visit are Wukoki, Lomaki, and the Citadel, a pueblo on a knoll above a limestone sink. Although the largest remnants of Native American settlements at Wupatki National Monument are open to the public, other sites are off-limits to casual visitors. Rules regarding entering closed sites are strictly enforced. If you are interested in an in-depth tour, consider taking a ranger-led overnight hike to the **Crack-in-Rock Ruin.** The 14-mi (round-trip) trek covers areas marked by ancient petroglyphs and dotted with well-preserved ruins. The trips are conducted in April and October; call by February or August if you'd like to take part in the lottery for one of the 100 available places on these $25 hikes.

Between the Wupatki and Citadel ruins, the **Doney Mountain** affords 360-degree views of the Painted Desert and the San Francisco Volcanic Field. It's a perfect spot for a sunset picnic. In summer, rangers give lectures. ⊠ *Sunset Crater–Wupatki Loop Rd., 19 mi north of Sunset Crater visitor center* ☎ *928/556–7040* ⊕ *www.nps.gov/wupa* ⌨ *$3, including Wupatki National Monument and Doney Mountain* ☉ *Daily 8–5; hrs may be extended in summer.*

NORTH-CENTRAL ARIZONA A TO Z

To research prices, get advice from other travelers, and book travel arrangements, visit www.fodors.com.

AIR TRAVEL

America West flies frequently from Phoenix into Prescott Municipal Airport and to Flagstaff Pulliam Airport. Sedona Airport is a base for several air tours and has no regularly scheduled flights.

🛈 **America West** ☎ 800/235-9292 ⊕ www.americawest.com.

AIRPORTS

Prescott Municipal Airport is 8 mi north of town on U.S. 89. Flagstaff Pulliam Airport is 3 mi south of town off Interstate 17 at Exit 337. Sedona Airport is in West Sedona.

🛈 **Flagstaff Pulliam Airport** ☎ 928/556-1234. **Prescott Municipal Airport** ☎ 928/445-7860. **Sedona Airport** ☎ 928/282-1046.

FLAGSTAFF AIRPORT TRANSFERS A taxi ride from the airport to the downtown area should cost about $8 to $10. Cabs are not regulated; some, but not all, have meters. It's wise to agree on a rate with a driver before you leave for your destination.

🛈 **A Friendly Cab** ☎ 928/774-4444. **Sun Taxi** ☎ 928/774-7400.

BUS TRAVEL

Greyhound Lines has daily connections from throughout the West to Flagstaff, but none to Sedona. Buses also run between Prescott and Phoenix Sky Harbor International Airport.

The Sedona/Phoenix Shuttle Service makes eight trips daily between those cities; the fare is $40 one-way, $65 round-trip. You can also get on or off at Camp Verde or Cottonwood. The bus leaves from three terminals of Sky Harbor International Airport in Phoenix. Reservations are required.

🛈 **Greyhound Lines** ⊠ 399 S. Malpais La., Flagstaff ☎ 928/774-4573 or 800/231-2222 ⊠ 820 E. Sheldon Ave., Prescott ☎ 928/445-5470 ⊕ www.greyhound.com. **Sedona/ Phoenix Shuttle Service** ☎ 928/282-2066, 800/448-7988 in Arizona ⊕ www.sedona-phoenix-shuttle.com.

CAR RENTALS

It makes sense to rent a car in this region. Trails and monuments stretch miles past city limits and many area towns cannot be reached by the major bus companies. Major rental agencies have offices in Flagstaff, Prescott, and Sedona. If you want to explore the red rocks of Sedona, you can even rent a four-wheel drive.

🚗 Flagstaff **Avis** ✉ Flagstaff Pulliam Airport, Flagstaff ☎ 928/774-8421. **Budget** ✉ Flagstaff Pulliam Airport, Flagstaff ☎ 928/779-0306. **Enterprise** ✉ 800 W. Rte. 66, Flagstaff ☎ 928/774-9407. **Hertz** ✉ Flagstaff Pulliam Airport, Flagstaff ☎ 928/774-4452. **National** ✉ Holiday Inn, 2320 E. Lucky La., Flagstaff ☎ 928/779-1975. **Sears** ✉ 100 N. Humphreys St., Flagstaff ☎ 928/774-1879 or 800/527-0770.

🚗 Prescott **Budget** ✉ 1031 Commerce Dr. ☎ 928/778-3806. **Enterprise** ✉ 202 S. Montezuma St. ☎ 928/778-6506. **Hertz** ✉ Prescott Municipal Airport ☎ 928/776-1399.

🚗 Sedona **Budget** ✉ Sedona Airport, Sedona ☎ 928/282-4602. **Canyon Jeep Rentals** ✉ Oak Creek Terrace Resort, 4548 AZ 89A, Sedona ☎ 928/282-6061 or 800/224-2229. **Sedona Jeep Rentals** ✉ Sedona Airport, Sedona ☎ 928/282-2227 or 800/879-5337.

CAR TRAVEL

Flagstaff lies at the intersection of Interstate 40 (east–west) and Interstate 17 (running south from Flagstaff), 134 mi north of Phoenix via Interstate 17. The most direct route to Prescott from Phoenix is to take Interstate 17 north for 60 mi to Cordes Junction and then drive northwest on AZ 69 for 36 mi into town. Interstate 17, a four-lane divided highway, has several steep inclines and descents (complete with a number of runaway-truck ramps). However, it's generally an easy and scenic thoroughfare. If you want to take the more leisurely route through Verde Valley to Prescott, continue north on Interstate 17 another 25 mi past Cordes Junction until you see the turnoff for AZ 260, which will take you to Cottonwood in 12 mi. Here you can pick up AZ 89A, which leads southwest to Prescott (41 mi) or northeast to Sedona (19 mi).

Sedona stretches along AZ 89A, its main thoroughfare, which runs roughly east–west through town. AZ 89A is bisected by AZ 179. The more commercial section of AZ 89A east of AZ 179 is known as Uptown; locals tend to frequent the shops on the other side, called West Sedona. To the south of AZ 89A, AZ 179 is lined with upscale retailers for a couple of miles. To reach Sedona more directly from Phoenix, take Interstate 17 north for 113 mi until you come to AZ 179; it's another 15 mi on that road into town. The trip should take about 2½ hours. The 27-mi drive from Sedona to Flagstaff on AZ 89A, which winds its way through Oak Creek Canyon, is breathtaking.

Weekend traffic near Sedona, especially during the high season, can approach gridlock on the narrow highways. Leave for your destination at first light, and you'll bypass most day-trippers and late risers as well as avoiding the midday heat.

PARKING A Red Rock Pass is required to park anywhere in the Coconino National Forest from Oak Creek Canyon through Sedona. Passes cost $5 for the day, $15 for the week, or $20 for an entire year and can be purchased at four visitor centers surrounding and within Sedona. Passes are also available from vending machines at the most popular trailheads including Boynton Canyon, Bell Rock, and Huckaby. Locals widely resent the pass, feeling that free access to National Forests is a right with no exceptions. The Forest Service counters that it is doesn't receive enough federal funds to maintain the land surrounding Sedona, trampled by five million visitors each year, and that a parking fee is the best way to raise the revenue.

🚗 **Red Rock Pass** ☎ 928/282-4119 information only ⊕ www.redrockcountry.org.

EMERGENCIES

🚑 **Ambulance & Fire** Ambulance and Fire Emergencies ☎ 911.

🏥 Hospital in Flagstaff **Flagstaff Medical Center** ✉ 1200 N. Beaver St., Flagstaff ☎ 928/779-3366.

🏥 Hospital in Prescott **Yavapai Regional Medical Center** ✉ 1003 Willow Creek Rd., Prescott ☎ 928/445-2700.

🏥 Hospital in Sedona The **Sedona Medical Center** ✉ 3700 W. AZ 89A, Sedona ☎ 928/204-4900.

💊 Pharmacies in Flagstaff **Flagstaff Medical Center Pharmacy** ✉ 1200 N. Beaver St., Flagstaff ☎ 928/779-3366. **Fry's Food and Drug** ✉ 201 N. Switzer Canyon Dr., at Rte. 66, Flagstaff ☎ 928/774-3389. **Walgreens** ✉ 1500 E. Cedar Ave., Flagstaff ☎ 928/773-1011.

💊 Pharmacy in Prescott **Goodwin Street Pharmacy** ✉ 406 W. Goodwin St., Prescott ☎ 928/776-9939.

💊 Pharmacies in Sedona **Rite Aid** ✉ 2350 W. AZ 89A, Sedona ☎ 928/282-9734. **Walgreens** ✉ 1995 W. AZ 89A, Sedona ☎ 928/282-2528.

👮 **Police** Police Emergencies ☎ 911.

TAXIS

In Sedona, try Bob's Sedona Taxi. A–1 Quick Cab & Tours in Flagstaff provides local and long-distance service.

🚕 **A-1 Quick Cab & Tours** ☎ 928/214-8294. **Bob's Sedona Taxi** ☎ 928/282-1234.

TOURS

IN FLAGSTAFF The Ventures program, run by the education department of the Museum of Northern Arizona, offers tours of the area led by local scientists, artists, and historians. Trips might include rafting excursions down the San Juan River, treks into the Grand Canyon or Colorado Plateau backcountry, or bus tours into the Navajo reservation to visit with Native American artists. Prices start at about $100 for cultural tours and go up to $1,500 for outdoor adventures, with most tours in the $900 to $1,100 range.

🏛 **Museum of Northern Arizona** ☎ 928/774-5213 ⊕ www.musnaz.org.

IN PRESCOTT On Monday and Friday at 10 AM from late May through early September, volunteer guides offer free orientation tours of Prescott that leave from the Chamber of Commerce. The rest of the year, tours can be booked directly with Melissa Roughner, who'll be wearing period clothing from Arizona's territorial days when she guides you around town.

🏛 **Melissa Roughner** ☎ 928/445-4567. **Prescott Chamber of Commerce** ✉ 117 W. Goodwin St., 86303 ☎ 928/445-2000 or 800/266-7534 ⊕ www.prescott.org.

IN SEDONA Sedona Trolley offers two types of daily orientation tours, both departing from the main bus stop in Uptown and lasting less than an hour. One goes along AZ 179 to the Chapel of the Holy Cross, with stops at Tlaquepaque and some galleries; the other passes through West Sedona to Boynton Canyon (Enchantment Resort). Rates are $7 for one or $11 for both.

Several jeep-tour operators headquartered along Sedona's main Uptown drag conduct excursions, some focusing on geology, some on astronomy, some on vortices, some on all three. You can even find a combination jeep tour and horseback ride. The ubiquitous Pink Jeep Tours are a popular choice. Sedona Adventures offers both full- and half-day options. Sedona Red Rock Jeep Tours is also a reliable operator. Prices start at about $22 per person for one hour and go up to $65 per person for four hours. Although all the excursions are safe, many are not for those who dislike heights or bumps.

Prices for hot-air-balloon tours generally start at $135 per person for a one- to two-hour tour. The only two companies with permits to fly over Sedona are Northern Light Balloon Expeditions, open since 1974 and the longest operating in northern Arizona, and Red Rock Balloon Adventures.

Sedona Art Tours guides visitors through the town's art galleries. Sedona Photo Tours will take you to all the prime spots and help you take your best (photographic) shot. Rates are $35 per person for a basic two-hour tour.

Northern Light Balloon Expeditions ☎ 928/282-2274 or 800/230-6222 ⊕ www. sedona.net/fun/balloon. **Pink Jeep Tours** ✉ 204 N. AZ 89A, Sedona ☎ 928/282-5000 or 800/873-3662 ⊕ www.pinkjeep.com. **Red Rock Balloon Adventures** ☎ 928/284-0040 or 800/258-3754 ⊕ www.redrockballoons.com. **Sedona Adventures** ✉ 276 N. AZ 89A, Suite A, Sedona ☎ 928/282-3500 or 800/888-9494 ⊕ www.sedonaadventures.com. **Sedona Art Tours** ☎ 928/282-0788. **Sedona Photo Tours** ✉ 252 N. AZ 89A, Sedona ☎ 928/282-4320 or 800/973-3662. **Sedona Red Rock Jeep Tours** ✉ 270 N. AZ 89A, Sedona ☎ 928/282-6826 or 800/848-7728 ⊕ www.redrockjeep. com. **Sedona Trolley** ☎ 928/282-6826 or 928/282-5400 ⊕ www.sedonatrolley.com.

TRAIN TRAVEL

Amtrak comes into the downtown Flagstaff station twice daily. There is no rail service into Prescott or Sedona.

Amtrak ✉ 1 E. Rte. 66 ☎ 928/774-8679.

VISITOR INFORMATION

Camp Verde Chamber of Commerce ✉ 435 S. Main St., 86322 ☎ 928/567-9294 ⊕ www.campverde.org. **Clarkdale Chamber of Commerce** ⬠ Box 161, 86324 ☎ 928/634-3382 ⊕ www.clarkdalechamber.com. **Cottonwood/Verde Valley Chamber of Commerce** ✉ 1010 S. Main St., Cottonwood 86326 ☎ 928/634-7593 ⊕ http://cottonwood. verdevalley.com. **Flagstaff Visitors Center** ✉ 1 E. Rte. 66, 86001 ☎ 928/774-9541 or 800/842-7293 ⊕ www.flagstaffarizona.org. **Jerome Chamber of Commerce** ⬠ Box K, 86331 ☎ 928/634-2900. **Prescott Chamber of Commerce** ✉ 117 W. Goodwin St., 86303 ☎ 928/445-2000 or 800/266-7534 ⊕ www.prescott.org. **Sedona-Oak Creek Canyon Chamber of Commerce** ✉ 331 Forest Rd., at N. AZ 89A, Sedona 86339 ☎ 928/282-7722 or 800/288-7336 ⊕ www.sedonachamber.com.

THE GRAND CANYON

INCLUDING HAVASU CANYON & GRAND CANYON WEST

3

BOARD A VINTAGE STEAM TRAIN
bound for the South Rim ⇨*p.147*

HIKE PAST 10 CLASSIC OVERLOOKS
on the Rim Trail to Hermit's Rest ⇨*p.159*

LEARN TO TRUST A MULE
on the Bright Angel Trail ⇨*p.159*

BEAT THE HEAT
by a blue-green waterfall ⇨*p.171*

DETOUR TO CAMERON TRADING POST
for Navajo and Hopi crafts ⇨*p.174*

TAKE THE STATE'S BIGGEST THRILL RIDE
on the Colorado River rapids ⇨*p.176*

COMMUNE WITH THE CANYON
at Point Sublime on the North Rim ⇨*p.181*

Updated by
Carrie Miner

THE GRAND CANYON IS FAR MORE than an experience. It's an emotion. Ask anyone who's visited, hiked, worked, or lived here. Many think it deserves a greater superlative than just "Grand." Although it's easy to list the statistics of the canyon—both geological and historical—that all becomes immaterial as you lose your breath when standing at the edge for the first sunrise or the thousandth sunset.

As you gaze out from the rim, you're viewing 2 billion years of geologic history, exposed for all to see in the canyon's rock walls. There is more Paleozoic and Pre-Cambrian Earth history on view here than anywhere else on the planet. As the river has carved its course through the canyon's walls, it has exposed fossil records that date from the very earliest living organisms.

Far below the rim, the Colorado River continues its timeless carving process. Prior to the completion of the Glen Canyon Dam in the 1960s, it's been estimated that an average of 400,000 tons of silt was carried away every day. That equates to 80,000 5-ton dump-truck loads—one per second, nonstop. During the last million years—give or take a few—some experts believe the Colorado may have actually flowed north instead of south.

If you were to travel from one end of the Grand Canyon to the other, you would journey just under 280 mi from Lees Ferry near the junction of the Paria and Colorado rivers in northern Arizona to the western border shared by Arizona and Nevada. At its deepest point, the canyon is nearly 6,000 feet. From the North Rim to the South Rim, the distance across varies from 18 mi to less than ½ mi. However, to travel between rims by car requires a journey of 200 mi. Hiking steep and arduous trails from rim to rim is a strenuous trek of at least 21 mi. The earliest trails into the canyon were animal trails that were used and modified by the native people and later upgraded by miners. A rim-to-rim hike for the very fit is well worth the effort, though. You'll travel through four of the seven life zones—that is, regions sharing the same climate and plant and animal life—found in North America. To otherwise witness this, you'd need to travel south to north from the Mexican desert to the Canadian woods.

There is ample evidence of early habitation from ruins that are between 8,000 and 10,000 years old in some of the highest, most inaccessible areas of the canyon. The Paleo-Indians were nomadic peoples known as Elephant Hunters, whose existence depended upon hunting large prehistoric elephants, mastodons, and mammoths. Then, about 1,500 years ago, the Puebloan people more popularly known as the Anasazi (a name that means both "ancient ones" and "enemy ancestors") arrived on the scene. More than 2,000 of their sites have been found, including Tusayan Pueblo, some 3 mi west of Desert View in the South Rim. The last of the Native Americans to occupy the region were the Navajo, who came into the area some 600 years ago.

The first Europeans to view the canyon were Spanish Conquistadors, who were more interested in finding the fabled Cibola, the Seven Cities of Gold. Don Garcia Lopez de Cardenas's band spent four days vainly searching for a path to the bottom of the canyon. They were not able to reach the Colorado River to obtain the water they so desperately needed and left uninspired and disappointed.

The first recorded Americans to visit the region were an army survey party seeking an alternate southern supply route to Utah. They, too, left in despair and recorded that the canyon was of dubious value. Then, in 1869, John Wesley Powell undertook a famous voyage down the Colorado that created the first everlasting interest in the Grand Canyon. In 1908 the area was declared a national monument, and in 1919 Congress passed legislation making it a national park.

Today, nearly a century later, more than five million people each year stand in awe at the canyon and leave with a sense of fulfillment and realization that they have witnessed nature at her finest. "Leave it as it is," President Teddy Roosevelt proclaimed. "You can not improve on it. Keep it for your children, your children's children, and for all who come after you as the one great sight which every American should see."

Exploring the Grand Canyon

Although the average length of stay for the South Rim is about a half-day, you'll need to spend several days here to appreciate this very special place. A word of caution is in order though—*plan ahead*. Each year, fewer than 30,000 can be accommodated on rafting trips, and the famous mule rides into the canyon require at least a six-month advance reservation.

Because the North Rim is less crowded than its southern counterpart, a trip here allows you to explore the Grand Canyon in a more pleasant and leisurely way. Although there are lodgings available, your best bet is to pack your camping gear and hiking boots and take several days to explore the lush Kaibab Forest and the highest, most dramatic rim views.

About the Restaurants

Throughout the Grand Canyon region, restaurants that offer fast-food, standard American fare, and Native American specialties at reasonable prices prevail. One exception to this rule is El Tovar, the oldest existing hotel in the canyon and a pleasant surprise for anyone expecting traditional National Park Service dining. Though dress is casual, you might want to don your best jeans for a meal in its dining room.

About the Hotels

Reservations at Grand Canyon National Park are a must, especially during the busy summer season when rooms on both rims book up fast. You might find a last-minute cancellation, but you shouldn't count on it. If you can't find accommodations on the South Rim or in Tusayan (the development of hotels and restaurants 7 mi south of Grand Canyon Village), you may find available lodging 60 mi south in Williams or 80 mi southeast in Flagstaff. Although lodging in Tusayan and at the South Rim will keep you close to the action, the frenetic activity and crowded facilities are off-putting to some people. If you don't mind the hour-long jaunt to and from Williams, the cozy mountain town can give you a respite from the multitudes at the South Rim and also a break on prices for food

If you have 2 or 3 days

Begin your adventure in ⊞ **Williams** ❶ ⊩, west of Flagstaff on Interstate 40, which runs roughly parallel to the old Route 66. Board the Grand Canyon Railway, which will carry you to the South Rim of the canyon. You'll want several hours to explore the South Rim area and Canyon Village. Taxis and shuttle buses can transport you into Tusayan to view the Grand Canyon IMAX film. There's authentic Native American entertainment each weeknight at the Grand Hotel in ⊞ **Tusayan** ❷. You can spend the night here or in one of the lodges in ⊞ **Grand Canyon Village.** The next morning, take a tour of the **Village Rim** ❸–❿; then take the afternoon train back to Williams. If you decide to spend the evening in Tusayan, you'll have time the next morning for a hike or an exciting airplane or helicopter tour.

If you are more adventurous and a hardy hiker, you might consider going to ⊞ **Havasu Canyon** ㉗. Hike 8 mi down into the canyon to the small village of Supai and the Havasupai Lodge. It's a healthy drive to the trailhead, and you'll need a Havasupai tribal permit to hike here; however, it's an unforgettable hike. Reservations are required for staying at the lodge and are highly recommended for the backpacker's campground. You'll need plenty of time and water for your rigorous climb back to the rim. You might even consider returning to the top by mule.

If you have 4 or 5 days

To capture the full "canyon" experience, absorb it from above and from within. This trip will require reservations many months in advance. After spending your first night in one of the lodges at ⊞ **Grand Canyon Village,** take the mule-pack journey from the **Bright Angel Trailhead** ❿, which stops on an especially scenic plateau and includes a trailside lunch. Arrive at ⊞ **Phantom Ranch** for dinner and a welcome night's rest. Next morning, return by mule to the South Rim. Another day or two at the canyon's rim, staying in ⊞ **Tusayan** ❷ or at the ⊞ **Cameron Trading Post** ㉘, will round out your experience.

---

and lodging. Even though the North Rim is dramatically less crowded than the South Rim, the number of rooms is severely limited. With short notice, the best time to find a room on the South Rim is in winter (the North Rim is closed from mid-October through mid-May). The snow only increases the canyon's sublime beauty, which makes up for the chance of encountering icy roads and chilly winds.

WHAT IT COSTS					
	$$$$	$$$	$$	$	¢
RESTAURANTS	over $30	$20–$30	$12–$20	$8–$12	under $8
HOTELS	over $250	$175–$250	$120–$175	$70–$120	under $70

Restaurant prices are per person for a main course at dinner. Hotel prices are for two people in a standard double room in high season, excluding taxes and service charges.

Timing

There's not a bad time to visit the canyon, though summer and spring-break season are the busiest times. Spring heralds colorful blankets of wildflowers. In summer, afternoon thunderstorms paint the canyon walls, darkening the colorful strata. Autumn color on the canyon oaks and snow-capped stone create images of change and peace in the fall and winter months. March is the month with the best chance for snow at the South Rim. Since the North Rim gets considerable snowfall, the highways and facilities are closed from mid-October until mid-May. The South Rim, open year-round, is an exposed high-desert region, where the weather changes on a whim. Thanksgiving, Christmas, and New Year's can also get quite busy.

The Grand Canyon covers 1,900 square mi on the Colorado Plateau; elevations range from 1,200 to 9,100 feet, which means that climatic conditions in the region vary immensely. Rainfall, for example, reaches more than 25 inches annually at the North Rim, while the South Rim collects but 16 inches in a typical year. The North Rim accumulates considerably more snow—about 130 inches per year—compared to less than half of that at the South Rim. Temperatures vary widely, too. In summer, the canyon floor may easily reach 115°F, at the South Rim temperatures rarely exceed 90°F, and it's seldom more than 80°F at the North Rim.

Numbers in the text correspond to numbers in the margin and on the Grand Canyon South Rim and Grand Canyon North Rim maps.

APPROACHING THE SOUTH RIM: WILLIAMS & TUSAYAN

As a result of the tremendous popularity of the Grand Canyon as a destination in itself, few visitors to this remote part of Arizona realize that there are other places to rest their heads than at the lodgings within the park boundaries. However, it can be much more relaxing to retreat to either Tusayan or Williams than it is to fight the crowds at the Canyon for lodging and dining facilities. Once purchased, the park pass is valid for seven days, and it allows you to to bypass the regular traffic lines approaching the Grand Canyon on return visits. Tusayan offers less selection and style than the historic town of Williams, which sits on the shoulders of the Mother Road—Historic Route 66.

Williams

▶ ❶ *30 mi west of Flagstaff on Interstate 40 and AZ 64. 55 mi south of Grand Canyon Village.*

At the turn of the 20th century, Williams was a rough-and-tumble town replete with saloons and bordellos. Today, it reflects a much milder side of the Wild West, with 2,900 residents and some 1,400 motel rooms. Wander along main street, named—like the town—after mountain man Bill Williams and indulge in Route 66 nostalgia. There are antiques shops, cozy eateries, and the ever-present souvenir and T-shirt stores.

3

Bicycling

Rangers say the best bet for mountain bikers is the Rainbow Rim Trail, which goes along the North Rim of the canyon through a ponderosa-pine forest and up and down through side canyons, aspen groves, and pristine meadows. Mountain bikers heading to the North Rim will enjoy testing the many dirt access roads found in this remote area—including the 17-mi trek to Point Sublime. It's a rarity to spot other people any time of the year on these primitive roads. On the other hand, bikers wanting to see the South Rim of the Grand Canyon on two wheels might be disappointed by the experience, because of narrow shoulders on park roads and the heavy auto traffic. Bicycles are prohibited on park trails with the exception of the Greenway System, which is currently under development on the South Rim, so the opportunities for off-road biking are also limited here. Mountain bikers visiting the South Rim may be better off meandering through the ponderosa pine forest on the Tusayan Bike Trail.

Hiking

Hikers can choose from a plethora of canyon trails including everything from an easy rim hike to a strenuous trek into the depths of this massive gorge. Even though an immense network of trails winds through the Grand Canyon, the popular corridor trails are recommended for the first overnight trip in the canyon for hikers new to the region. Although permits are not required for day hikes, you must have a backcountry permit for longer trips. Some of the more popular paths and trails are listed in this chapter, and more detailed information and maps can be obtained from the Backcountry Information Center.

Rafting

Those who have taken a white-water raft trip down the Colorado River often list it as one of their most memorable lifetime experiences. Trips begin at Lees Ferry, a few miles below the Glen Canyon Dam near Page. There are tranquil half- and full-day float trips from the Glen Canyon Dam to Lees Ferry as well as raft trips that run from three days to three weeks. Many of these voyages end at Phantom Ranch at the bottom of the Grand Canyon at river mile 87. You'll encounter some good white water along the way, including Lava Falls, which is considered by many to be the wildest navigable rapids on the continent.

The town sits at 6,700 feet in the world's largest stand of ponderosa pines. Often considered just a jumping-off point for the Grand Canyon (it's only an hour away from the South Rim by car and a little more than two hours by train), Williams is temperate in summer, offers skiing in the winter, and is within minutes of seven mountain lakes.

In 1989 service on the **Grand Canyon Railway** was reinaugurated along a route first established in 1901. The 65-mi trek from Williams Depot to the South Rim (2¼ hours each way) takes the vintage train through prairie, ranch, and national park land to the log-cabin train station in Grand Canyon Village. The ride includes refreshments, commentary, and corny but fun onboard entertainment by Wild West characters from

CloseUp
TIPS FOR AVOIDING CANYON CROWDS

It's hard to commune with nature while you're searching for a parking place, dodging video cams, and stepping away from strollers. However, this scenario is only likely to occur during the very peak months of mid-May through mid-October. One option is to bypass Grand Canyon National Park altogether and head to the West Rim of the canyon, tribal land of the Hualapai and Havasupai. If only the park itself will do, the following tips will help you to keep your distance and your cool.

In peak season, avoid the noon inbound rush at the South Rim by getting an early start. For the most part, challenges will be finding lodging within the park and reserving a saddle for the mule trek down the canyon trails. Make your reservations well in advance, especially in the summer. If you want to escape the crowds that gather at the South Rim in summer, here are a few alternative suggestions.

Take Another Route
Avoid road rage by choosing a different route to the South Rim, avoiding the traditional highways AZ 64 and U.S. 180 from Flagstaff. Take U.S. 89 north from Flagstaff instead, passing near the Sunset Crater and Wupatki national monuments. When you reach the Cameron Trading Post at the junction with AZ 64, take a break (you can even stay here). This is a good place to shop for Native American artifacts, souvenirs and the usual postcards, dream-catchers, recordings, and T-shirts. There's also high-quality Navajo rugs, jewelry, and other authentic handicrafts. You can sample Navajo tacos before heading out. U.S. 64 to the west takes you directly into the park at the East Entrance; the scenery along the Little Colorado River Gorge en route is eye-popping. It's 25 mi from the Grand Canyon East Entrance to the visitor center at Canyon View Information Plaza.

Bypass the South Rim Altogether
Although the North Rim is just 10 mi across from the South Rim, the trip to get there by car is a five-hour drive of about 215 mi. At first it might not sound like the trip would be worth it, but your paybacks are huge. Along the way you will travel through some of the prettiest parts of the state and you'll be granted even more stunning views than you would find on the more easily accessible South Rim. Those who make the North Rim trip usually insist it offers the most beautiful scenic views and the best hiking. To get to the North Rim from Flagstaff, take U.S. 89 north past Cameron, turning left onto U.S. 89A at Bitter Springs. En route you'll pass the area known as Vermilion Cliffs. At Jacob Lake, take AZ 67 directly to the Grand Canyon North Rim. The road to the North Rim closes in mid-October because of heavy snow, but in summer months and early fall, it's a wonderful way to beat the crowds at the South Rim.

Take the Grand Canyon Railway
There is no need to deal with all of the other drivers racing to the South Rim. Forget the hassle of the twisting rim roads, jaywalking pedestrians, and jammed parking lots. Instead, sit back and relax in the comfy train cars of the Grand Canyon Railway. Live music and storytelling enliven the trip as you journey past the unfolding landscape. The train departs from the depot every morning at 9:30 sharp and makes the 65-mi journey in 2¼ hours. You can do the round-trip in a single day; however, you may choose to stay overnight at the South Rim and return to Williams the following afternoon.

the Cataract Creek Gang. Passengers ride in restored 1923 cars. Club Class, with its fully stocked mahogany bar and complimentary morning pastries and coffee, costs an additional $21. A First-Class ($58 upgrade), Deluxe Observation Dome, or Luxury Parlor Car ($79–$89 upgrade) ticket gets you Continental breakfast and complimentary afternoon champagne and snacks. Both Coach and Club Classes provide the basics, with padded benches to sit on and ceiling fans to keep you cool; the other three classes provide much more comfortable seating and air-conditioning.

Even if you don't take the train, it's worth visiting the **Williams Depot,** where the trains depart. It was built in 1908 to replace the terminal where the Williams Visitor Center now resides. Attractions at the depot include a passenger car and the locomotive of a turn-of-the-20th-century steam train, a gift shop where you can find bizarre souvenirs such as a tie that plays "I've Been Working on the Railroad," and Max and Thelma's, a full-service restaurant. A small **Railroad Museum** is next to the depot in the original dining room of the former Harvey House hotel. The museum holds a collection of old railroad and Harvey-girl photographs and is a good place to learn about the history of the Grand Canyon Railway, which once carried American presidents, Franklin D. Roosevelt among them, on their whistle-stop campaigns through the West. ⊠ *Williams Depot, 233 N. Grand Canyon Blvd. at Fray Marcos Blvd.* ☎ *800/843–8724 railway reservations and information* ⊕ *www.thetrain. com* ⊠ *$58–$147 round-trip, not including 9.525% tax and $8 national park entrance fee* ☉ *Departs daily from Williams at 10* AM, *from the South Rim at 3:30* PM.

The **Williams Visitor Center,** also housing the Williams-Grand Canyon Chamber of Commerce and National Forest Service office, is the former passenger-train depot, which was built in 1901. Its brick walls still show graffiti scrawled by early railroad workers and hobos. A small bookstore offers a selection of regional materials and an interactive exhibit on the history of the town and Route 66. ⊠ *200 W. Railroad Ave., at Grand Canyon Blvd.* ☎ *928/635–1418 or 800/863–0546* ⊕ *www. williamschamber.com* ☉ *Spring, fall and winter, daily 8–5; summer, daily 8–6:30.*

Children enjoy the **Grand Canyon Deer Farm,** a petting zoo with pygmy goats and deer, including fawns born every June, July, and August. Buffalo, pot-bellied pigs, pronghorn antelope, reindeer and exotic birds are also in residence. ⊠ *6752 E. Deer Farm Rd., 8 mi east of Williams off I-40, Exit 171* ☎ *928/635–4073 or 800/926–3337* ⊕ *www.deerfarm. com* ⊠ *$6.75* ☉ *Mar.–May, Sept., and Oct., daily 9–6; June–Aug., daily 8–7; Nov.–Feb., daily 10–5 (weather permitting).*

Sports & the Outdoors

FISHING Fish for trout, crappie, catfish, and smallmouth bass at a number of lakes surrounding Williams. Anglers age 14 and older are required to obtain a fishing license from the **Arizona Game and Fish Department** (⊕ 3500 S. Lake Mary Rd., Flagstaff 86001 ☎ 928/774–5045 or 866/462–0433 ⊕ www.gf.state.az.us) in order to fish on public land. You can also order fishing licenses online.

SKIING The **Williams Ski Area** (✉ off I–40 ⏰ Box 953, 86046 ☎ 928/635–
♺ 9330 ⊕ www.williamsskiarea.com) is usually open from mid-December through much of March, weather permitting. There are four groomed
runs (including one for beginners), areas suitable for cross-country skiing, and a hill set aside for tubing. The lodge rents skis, snowboards,
and inner tubes. From Williams, take South 4th Street for 2 mi, and then
turn right at the sign and go another 1½ mi.

Where to Stay & Eat

¢–$$$ ✗ **Cruisers Café 66.** Talk about nostalgia. Imagine your favorite 1950s-
Fodor'sChoice style, high school hangout—with cocktail service. Good burgers, steaks,
★ ribs, seafood, salads, and, of course, malts are on the menu. The large
mural, stuffed buffalo, and historic cars out front make this a Route 66
favorite. Kids especially enjoy the relaxed atmosphere and the jukebox
tunes. ✉ *233 W. Rte. 66* ☎ *928/635–2445* ▭ *AE, DC, MC, V.*

★ $–$$ ✗ **Pancho McGillicuddy's.** Established in 1893 as the Cabinet Saloon, this
restaurant is on the National Register of Historic Places. Gone are the spit-
toons and pipes—the smoke-free dining area now has Mexican-inspired
decor and such specialties as "armadillo eggs," the local name for deep-
fried jalapeños stuffed with cheese. Some other favorites are the fish tacos
and the pollo verde—chicken breasts smothered in a sauce of cheese, sour
cream, and green chiles. The bar—on the smoking side of the restaurant—
has two TVs tuned to sporting events and pours more than 30 tequilas.
✉ *141 Railroad Ave.* ☎ *928/635–4150* ▭ *AE, D, MC, V.*

$–$$ ✗ **Rod's Steak House.** You can't miss this steak house with the plastic
Angus cow out front. Obviously the emphasis here is on meat—sizzling
mesquite-broiled steaks, prime rib, and the like. The local favorite is Rod's
special charred steak, a hefty sirloin dipped in sugar and grilled over
mesquite. Other specialties at this landmark steak house include chicken,
ribs and seafood. ✉ *301 E. Rte. 66* ☎ *928/635–2671* ▭ *D, MC, V.*

¢–$ ✗ **Pine Country Restaurant.** This cozy and spotless restaurant is across
from the Grand Canyon Railway Depot. Owner Dee Seehorn serves
homemade pies and ample, hearty meals such as country-fried steak and
hamburgers. The crafts that make up most of the decor are all for sale
and are handmade by local artists. Don't leave without trying some of the
fabulous fudge, in flavors ranging from maple nut to vanilla chocolate
caramel. Open daily at 5:30 AM, the restaurant serves breakfast, lunch,
and dinner; for an extra 15% charge, they will deliver to any hotel in town.
✉ *107 N. Grand Canyon Blvd.* ☎ *928/635–9718* ▭ *AE, D, MC, V.*

¢ ✗ **Grand Canyon Coffee Café.** You'll find good espresso drinks here,
along with wonderful sandwiches on homemade focaccia. The mountain man sandwich is piled-high roast beef with cheddar cheese and onions
on Italian bread. Try an egg-cream soda with Ghirardelli chocolate if
you're feeling nostalgic. Harley-Davidson artifacts fill the space, and some
of them are for sale. ✉ *125 W. Rte. 66* ☎ *928/635–1255* ▭ *AE, MC,
V* ⊙ *Closed Jan.–Mar.*

¢ ✗ **Twisters.** Get your kicks on Route 66 at this old-fashioned soda fountain and gift shop. Dine on hamburgers and hot dogs, or skip the road
food altogether and get a famous Twisters sundae, a Route 66 Beer Float,
or a cherry phosphate—all to the sounds of hip-shaking 1950s tunes.
The adjoining gift shop is a blast from the past with Route 66 merchandise,

classic Coca Cola memorabilia, and fanciful items celebrating the careers of such characters as Betty Boop, James Dean, Elvis, and Marilyn Monroe. ⊠ *417 E. Rte. 66* ☎ *928/635–0266* ⊕ *www.route66place.com* ⊟ *AE, D, MC, V.*

★ **$$–$$$** 🏨 **Sheridan House Inn.** A more civilized alternative to crowded Grand Canyon National Park or Tusayan lodgings, this B&B is nestled among 2 acres of pine trees just a few blocks from Route 66. Outside there are decks looking out to the tall ponderosa pines and a flagstone patio with a hot tub. Hearty breakfasts (such as eggs Benedict or buttermilk pancakes) will ready you for the hour-long drive to the canyon. K. C. and Mary Seidner are gracious hosts who happily help guests plan their itineraries. Every afternoon the Seidners lay out a spread of hors d'oeuvres and open the bar for a relaxing social hour. ⊠ *460 E. Sheridan Ave., 86046* ☎ *928/635–9441 or 888/635–9345* ⇒ *6 rooms, 2 suites* ♻ *Dining room, cable TV, in-room VCRs, gym, hiking, hot tub; no a/c* ⊟ *AE, D, MC, V* ⊙ *BP.*

★ **$$** 🏨 **Fray Marcos Hotel.** This hotel was designed to resemble the train depot's original Fray Marcos lodge. Neoclassical Greek columns flank the grand entrance leading into a lobby with maplewood balustrades, an enormous flagstone fireplace, and oil paintings of the Grand Canyon by local artist Kenneth McKenna. Original bronzes by Frederic Remington, from the private collection of hotel owners Max and Thelma Biegert, also adorn the lobby. The Southwestern-style accommodations have large bathrooms. At this writing, the hotel was adding a new wing, which will include another 102 rooms, 10 two-room suites, and a meeting room. Adjacent to the lobby is Spenser's, a pub with an ornate 19th-century hand-carved bar. ⊠ *235 N. Grand Canyon Blvd., 86046* ☎ *928/635– 4010 or 800/843–8724* ⊕ *www.thetrain.com* ⇒ *196 rooms* ♻ *Cable TV, indoor pool, gym, hot tub, bar, no-smoking rooms* ⊟ *AE, D, MC, V.*

$–$$ 🏨 **Mountainside Inn Gateway to the Grand Canyon.** At the east entrance to town, this basic motel has comfortable rooms, a good American restaurant called Miss Kitty's Steakhouse, and country-and-western bands in summer. ⊠ *642 E. Rte. 66, 86046* ☎ *928/635–4431 or 800/462–9381* 🖷 *928/635–2292* ⇒ *95 rooms, 1 suite* ♻ *Restaurant, cable TV, pool, hot tub* ⊟ *AE, D, DC, MC, V.*

☺ **$** 🏨 **Quality Inn Mountain Ranch & Resort.** Seven miles east of town, off Exit 171, the warm lights and friendly staff of this motel beckon. Rooms are basic and predictable; however, included with the room rate is a full breakfast in the coffee shop, which has views of the San Francisco Peaks. In season, evening hay rides—complete with singing cowboys, staged gunfights, and a cookout—are offered. There is also horseback riding available at **Mountain Ranch Stables** (928/635–0706). One hour is $22, two hours is $44, and half-day rides are $85. ⊠ *6701 E. Mountain Ranch Rd., 86046* ☎ *928/635–2693 or 866/687–2624* 🖷 *928/635–4188* ⊕ *www.mountainranchresort.com* ⇒ *73 rooms* ♻ *Restaurant, coffee shop, microwaves, refrigerators, cable TV, in-room VCRs, putting green, 2 tennis courts, pool, hot tub, horseback riding, horseshoes, volleyball, bar, some pets allowed (fee), no-smoking rooms* ⊟ *AE, D, MC, V* ☉ *Closed Nov.–Apr.* ⊙ *BP.*

$ 🏨 **Red Garter.** A restored saloon and bordello dating from 1897 now houses a small B&B. The Victorian Romanesque brick building is filled with antiques. Guest rooms are on the second floor; ask for the Best Gal's room, with its own sitting room overlooking the train tracks. Despite the inn's location, all four rooms (two are interior, with skylights but no windows) are very quiet, as the only train traffic is the Grand Canyon Railway, with one daily arrival and departure. Even if you don't stay here, the fresh scones, rolls, croissants, and pastries served in the first-floor coffee shop are worth a stop. ✉ *137 W. Railroad Ave., 86046* ☎ *928/635–1484 or 800/328–1484* ⊕ *www.redgarter.com* ➳ *4 rooms* ☌ *Coffee shop; no kids under 8, no smoking* ☰ *D, MC, V* �‖ *CP* ☉ *Closed Dec.–mid-Feb.*

♺ ¢–$ 🏠 **Canyon Motel.** Elk and deer roam this forested 10-acre property on the outskirts of Williams. The best room in the house is the 1931 Santa Fe red caboose (Suite 2). The family-friendly caboose has two sides separated by a bathroom, giving parents a little privacy. The original wooden floor and tool equipment add to the authenticity. The other caboose looks much like a standard hotel room inside as do the flagstone cottage rooms and rail-car suites. Owners Shirley and Kevin Young have been slowly remodeling the rooms. Be sure to check out the guest book in the office, where you'll find good-luck charms in the form of currency from countries such as Brazil, Haiti, India, Kenya, and Uruguay. The motel also has a few dry camping and RV sites available ($10). ✉ *1900 E. Rodeo Rd., 86046* ☎ *928/635–9371 or 800/482–3955* 🖷 *928/635–4138* ➳ *18 rooms, 5 suites* ☌ *BBQs, microwaves, refrigerators, cable TV, in-room VCRs, indoor pool, hiking, horseshoes, playground, some pets allowed (fee); no room phones* ☰ *D, MC, V* �‖ *CP.*

CAMPING   Both developed and undeveloped campsites are available on a first-come, first-served basis in the **Kaibab National Forest** (☎ 928/635–4061 or 800/863–0546 ⊕ www.fs.fed.us/r3/kai), which surrounds the Williams area and goes up to the Grand Canyon itself. Campgrounds in the region include Cataract Lake, Kaibab Lake, Dogtown Lake, and White Horse Lake.

Shopping

Whether you're looking for Grand Canyon souvenirs, Western kitsch, or the best in Native American art and jewelry, you'll likely find what you are looking for in the shops on Historic Route 66. **The Pueblo Indian Gallery** (✉ 202 W. Rte. 66 ☎ 928/635–4966 ⊕ www.puebloindiangallery.com) offers authentic Native American jewelry as well as Indian arts, including sculpture, painting, pottery, and rugs. For the most comprehensive collection of Route 66 memorabilia on offer, pull over to the **Route 66 Roadstore** (✉ 320 W. Rte. 66 ☎ 928/635–0700 ⊕ www.route66roadstore.com). **The Rustic Raspberry** (✉ 309 W. Rte. 66 ☎ 928/635–3024 ⊕ www.rusticraspberry.com) sells creative country crafts in its cheery store. **Thunder Eagle** (✉ 221 W. Rte. 66 ☎ 928/625–9260) has the most extensive collection in town of Navajo and Hopi jewelry.

Tusayan

❷ *48 mi north of Williams on AZ 64/U.S. 180. 7 mi south of Grand Canyon Village*

The village of Tusayan, the gateway to the South Entrance of the national park, is 7 mi from Grand Canyon Village on the South Rim. Here you'll find basic amenities, including restaurants and motels, several stores, and an airport that serves as a starting point for airplane and helicopter tours of the canyon; there's also an IMAX theater.

At the **Grand Canyon IMAX Theater** you can watch river runners battle rapids, experience the Grand Canyon from the air, and discover the canyon's natural history in a 34-minute film, *Grand Canyon—The Hidden Secrets*, on an 82-foot-wide screen that stands six stories high. At the theater, you'll also find an **Arizona Tourist Information Center**, where you can schedule and purchase air tours and daily Colorado River trips. ⊠ *AZ 64/U.S. 180* ☎ *928/638–2203 or 928/638–2468* ⊕ *www. grandcanyonimaxtheater.com* ⊡ *$10* ☉ *Mar.–Oct., daily 8:30–8:30; Nov.–Feb., daily 9:30–6:30; shows every hr on the ½ hr.*

Sports & the Outdoors

BICYCLING Pedal through the depths of the Kaibab National Forest on the **Tusayan Bike Trail** (⊠ Tusayan Ranger District, Tusayan ☎ 928/638–2443). By following linked loop trails at an elevation of 6,750 feet, you can bike as few as 3 mi or as many as 32 mi round-trip along old logging roads. The lightly used dirt roads meander through ponderosa pine forest. Along the way, keep an eye out for elk, mule deer, hawks, eagles, pronghorn antelope, turkeys, coyote, and porcupines. Open for biking from March through October, the trail is accessed on the west side of AZ 64 between Tusayan and the Moqui Lodge.

HORSEBACK You can rent gentle horses at the **Apache Stables** (⊠ AZ 64/U.S. 180
RIDING ☎ 928/638–2891 ⊕ www.apachestables.com), at the former Moqui Lodge, which is now closed, for $30.50 an hour or $55.50 for a two-hour guided tour of the Kaibab National Forest. A four-hour ride though Long Jim Canyon ($95.50) will take you through rugged canyon country to the viewpoint on the rim. The stables open in March, and rides are offered, weather permitting, through the end of November.

Where to Stay & Eat

$$–$$$ ✕ **Canyon Star.** Relax Western-style in the rustic dining room at the Grand Hotel for breakfast, lunch, or dinner. Some favorite menu items include wild mushroom enchiladas, barbecue buffalo brisket, grilled elk tenderloin, and panfried mountain trout. Live entertainment in the evenings includes dance performances, live music, and storytelling by the Diné Nation Performers–a group of Navajo entertainers. ⊠ *AZ 64/U.S. 180* ☎ *928/638–3333* ⚭ *Reservations suggested* ⊟ *AE, DC, MC, V.*

$$–$$$ ✕ **The Coronado Room.** When pizza and burgers just won't do, the restaurant at the Best Western Grand Canyon Squire Inn is the best upscale choice in Tusayan. The menu is primarily Continental with some Southwestern touches, encompassing everything from escargots to elk steak. Even though the Coronado Room takes pride in its fine-dining atmosphere, dress is casual and comfortable, as is most everything about the Grand Canyon. Reservations are usually a good idea, particularly in the busy season. ⊠ *AZ 64/U.S. 180* ☎ *928/638–2681* ⊟ *AE, D, DC, MC, V* ☉ *No lunch.*

¢–$$ ✕ **Café Tusayan.** Homemade pies and local microbrews from Sedona, Flagstaff, and Tucson brighten up the menu in this clean but ordinary dining room. Standard American fare—salads, burgers, pastas, and prime rib—fills out the selection at this basic restaurant. ⊠ *AZ 64/U.S. 180* ☎ *928/638–2151* ▭ *MC, V.*

★ **$$–$$$** ▣ **The Grand Hotel.** At the south end of Tusayan, this popular hotel has bright, clean rooms decorated in Southwestern colors. The warm lobby area has a stone-and-timber design and cozy seating areas. The restaurant offers good steaks, Mexican fare, and barbecue. At the bar, you can sit on a saddle that was once used for the canyon mule trips. Don't miss the well-stocked, reasonably priced gift shop, and keep in mind that most of the photos displayed in the lobby are for sale. ⊠ *AZ 64/U.S. 180* ☐ *Box 3319, Grand Canyon 86023* ☎ *928/638–3333* ☐ *928/638–3131* ⊕ *www.visitgrandcanyon.com* ⇝ *120 rooms* ⚭ *Restaurant, in-room data ports, cable TV, indoor pool, gym, hot tub, bar, meeting rooms, some pets allowed (fee); no-smoking rooms* ▭ *AE, DC, MC, V.*

♺ **$$–$$$** ▣ **Holiday Inn Express Hotel and Suites.** The main building of this hotel at the south end of Tusayan contains most of the rooms, which are modern but plain. You'll get a better deal at the Arizona Rooms, an adjacent all-suites annex, which has Western-theme suites with separate sitting rooms, coffeemakers, and VCRs—amenities you won't find next door. Kids Suites cater to families with bunk beds and PlayStation games. ⊠ *AZ 64/U.S. 180* ☐ *Box 3251, Grand Canyon 86023* ☎ *928/638–3000 or 888/538–5353* ☐ *928/638–0123* ⊕ *www.grandcanyon. hiexpress.com* ⇝ *165 rooms, 30 suites* ⚭ *Some microwaves, some refrigerators, in-room data ports, cable TV, some in-room VCRs, indoor pool, hot tub, business services* ▭ *AE, MC, V.*

★ ♺ **$–$$$** ▣ **Best Western Grand Canyon Squire Inn.** About 2 mi south of the park's South Entrance, this motel lacks the historic charm of the older lodges at the canyon rim, but it has more amenities, including a small cowboy museum in the lobby, a bowling alley, and an upscale gift shop. The rooms are spacious and furnished in Southwestern style. Those in the rear have a view of the woods. The Coronado Dining Room has an adventurous menu and good service. ⊠ *AZ 64/U.S. 180* ☐ *Box 130, Grand Canyon 86023* ☎ *928/638–2681 or 800/622–6966* ☐ *928/638–2782* ⊕ *www.grandcanyonsquire.com* ⇝ *250 rooms, 4 suites* ⚭ *Restaurant, coffee shop, cable TV, 2 tennis courts, pool, gym, hair salon, sauna, hot tub, billiards, bowling, bar, video game room, laundry facilities, concierge, meeting rooms, travel services, no-smoking rooms* ▭ *AE, D, DC, MC, V.*

$–$$ ▣ **Rodeway Inn Red Feather Lodge.** Some of the rooms here are worn around the edges, but this motel is still a good value, largely because of the pool, whirlpool, and game room for children. A restaurant serves standard American food. ⊠ *AZ 64/U.S. 180* ☐ *Box 1460, Grand Canyon 86023* ☎ *928/638–2414 or 800/538–2345* ☐ *928/638–9216* ⊕ *www.redfeatherlodge.com* ⇝ *230 rooms* ⚭ *Restaurant, cable TV with movies and video games, pool, gym, hot tub, video game room, business services, some pets allowed (fee)* ▭ *AE, D, DC, MC, V* ⊺◯ *CP.*

CAMPING ⚠ **Grand Canyon Camper Village and RV Park.** More a city than a village, this popular RV park and campground has 200 utility hookups
¢ and 50 tent sites. Hookups for two people run $22 for electric, $24 for water and electric, and $26 for full. There is an additional fee of $2 for

each additional person over the age of 12. Tent sites are $18. Reservations are a good idea during the busy spring and summer seasons. ⊠ *Off AZ 64/U.S. 180, Grand Canyon* ⌁ *Box 490, 86023* ☏ *928/ 638–2887* ↯ *200 full hookups, 50 tent sites* ⟺ *Flush toilets, full hookups, dump station, drinking water, showers, fire grates, picnic tables, general store, play area* ☉ *Open Mar.–Nov.*

¢ ⌂ **Ten X Campground.** Two miles south of Tusayan, this campground offers 70 sites with water and pit toilets but no electrical hookups or showers. Unlike in campgrounds in the Grand Canyon National Park itself, campfires are allowed. Learn about the surrounding ponderosa pine forest on a self-guided nature trail or check out one of the evening, ranger-led weekend programs. No reservations are accepted, except for groups of six or more. ⊠ *Kaibab National Forest, 9 mi south of Grand Canyon National Park east of AZ 64/U.S. 180* ⌁ *Tusayan Ranger District, Box 3088, Grand Canyon 86023* ☏ *928/638–2443* ⊕ *www. fs.fed.us/r3/kai* ↯ *70 tent sites* ⟺ *Pit toilets, drinking water, fire pits, grills, picnic tables* ⟺ *Reservations not accepted* ☉ *Open mid-Apr.–Sept.*

GRAND CANYON NATIONAL PARK: THE SOUTH RIM

Out of the roughly 5 million people who visit the Grand Canyon each year, 4 million throng into the South Rim's collection of lodges, restaurants, and breathtaking viewpoints. Visiting during the peak summer weekends and holidays requires patience and a tolerance for crowds. Even while they are jostling for a spot at the most popular viewpoints, most visitors are enthralled by the sheer scope of the deepest, most stunning canyon on the planet. But the canyon offers a much more intimate experience in the off-season, including winter, when snow mantles the landscape and contrasts vividly with the reds, oranges, yellows, blues, and purples of the canyon.

Most people don't give the canyon enough time, flitting quickly from viewpoint to viewpoint near the main lodge in a fit of drive-by sightseeing. Many drive to the main visitors center, then take the 25-mi Desert View Drive, which follows the rim and offers frequent viewpoints. But even during the peak times you can find some solitude from the pressing crowds. A bus shuttles passengers to the less-visited and less-crowded viewpoints to the west of the main lodge. You can also walk down several different trails from various viewpoints, although the steep climb and the high elevation can pose problems for people who aren't in shape or have heart or respiratory problems.

Another option is to start from the main lodge and stroll along the mostly paved Rim Trail for miles. Crowds drop off sharply as soon as you start walking, even during the busy seasons. Try to arrange your schedule to take in at least one sunrise or sunset at the canyon. The flat light of midday flattens even the Grand Canyon, but the early and the late light makes the lurid sandstone cliffs glow and fills the canyon's depths with shadow. The drama of the canyon is only enhanced with a glimpse of one of the endangered California condors, which were reintroduced to their historical canyon habitat in 1996. The condors often visit the South Rim, although watchful biologists try to shoo them away to prevent them from getting used to human beings.

HOURS   The South Rim is open year-round.

The entrance gates are open 24 hours but are generally staffed from about 7 AM to 7 PM. If you arrive when there's no one at the gate, you may enter legally without paying.

ADMISSION FEES   A fee of $20 per vehicle (regardless of the number of passengers) is collected at the East Entrance near Cameron and also at the South Entrance near Tusayan; pedestrians and cyclists pay $10 per person. In all cases, this fee is for one week's access.

Grand Canyon Village

Most of the services at the South Rim are concentrated in Grand Canyon Village, where you'll find accommodations and dining as well as many attractions. Grand Canyon Village and the Village Rim can be explored on foot via a paved footpath that runs along the rim, about 1 mi round-trip. You can leave your car at the El Tovar parking lot, but more often than not, this lot is full, so try parking along the railroad tracks below the historic hotel.

❾ Bright Angel Lodge was built in 1935 from Oregon pine logs and native stone; rustic cabins are set off from the main building. The rocks used to make the "geologic" fireplace are arranged in the order in which they are layered in the Grand Canyon, and the history room displays memorabilia from the South Rim's early years.

★ ❿ Bright Angel Trailhead is the starting point for one of America's most famous hiking trails. It began as a path used by bighorn sheep, later used by the Havasupai, and was improved and widened in the late 1800s for prospectors. It's now a well-maintained path for foot and mule traffic. Before you start your trek to the bottom, keep in mind that the trail descends 5,510 feet to the Colorado River. Be certain to have an adequate supply of water, food, and sunscreen before you begin. Rangers discourage hikers from attempting to make it to Phantom Ranch on the river and back up to the South Rim as a day hike. Permits are required for overnight hikes. Directly south of the trailhead are rails once used by the Santa Fe trains and the barn that houses the famous mules.

★ ❹ Canyon View Information Plaza, near Mather Point, cannot be reached by private vehicle. It's just a short walk from Mather Point, or you can take one of the free shuttle buses from anywhere in the village area. Here, park rangers can answer questions and assist in planning your excursions. This orientation center has the usual—rest rooms, bookstore, exhibits, and a schedule for ranger-led hikes and lectures. ⊠ *East side of Grand Canyon Village, about 2 mi east of El Tovar Hotel* ☎ *928/638-7888* ⊡ *Free after $20 per vehicle park admission* ⊙ *Late May–early Sept., daily 8–6; early Sept.–late May, daily 8–5.*

★ ❻ El Tovar Hotel has been the man-made focal point of a visit to the South Rim since it opened in 1905, when it was recognized as the most ele-

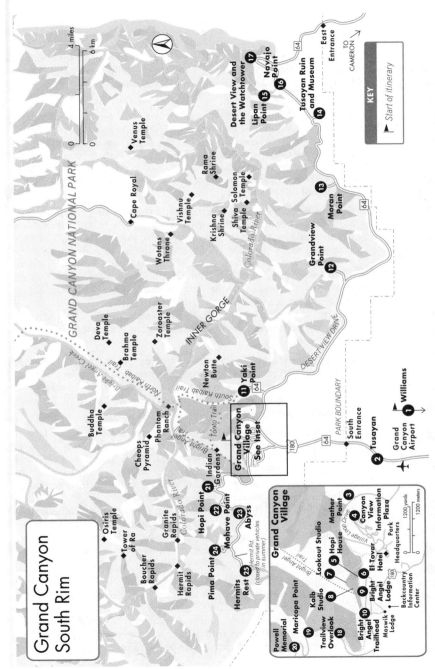

Grand Canyon South Rim

GRAND CANYON NATIONAL PARK

GRAND CANYON NATIONAL PARK

INNER GORGE

Colorado River

North Kaibab Trail

Bright Angel Creek Trail

South Kaibab Trail

Tonto Trail

Bright Angel Trail

DESERT VIEW DRIVE

PARK BOUNDARY

KEY

▲ Start of itinerary

0 — 4 miles
0 — 6 km

Osiris Temple
Tower of Ra
Boucher Rapids
Hermit Rapids
Granite Rapids
Buddha Temple
Cheops Pyramid
Phantom Ranch
Indian Gardens
Newton Butte
Deva Temple
Brahma Temple
Zoroaster Temple
Wotans Throne
Krishna Shrine
Shiva Temple
Solomon Temple
Rama Shrine
Vishnu Temple
Cape Royal
Venus Temple
Desert View and the Watchtower

11 Yaki Point
12 Grandview Point
13 Moran Point
14 Tusayan Ruin and Museum
15 Lipan Point
16 Navajo Point
17 Desert View and the Watchtower
21 Hopi Point
22
23 Abyss
24 Pima Point
25 Hermits Rest

Mohave Point
Hermit Rd. (closed to private vehicles in summer)

1 Williams
2 Tusayan
Grand Canyon Airport
South Entrance
East Entrance
TO CAMERON
PARK BOUNDARY

Grand Canyon Village
See Inset

64
180

Grand Canyon Village

3 Mather Point
4 Canyon View Information Plaza
5 Hopi House
6 El Tovar Hotel
7 Lookout Studio
8 Kolb Studio
9 Bright Angel Lodge
10 Bright Angel Trailhead
18 Trailview Overlook
19 Maricopa Point
20 Powell Memorial

Village Loop Drive
Bright Angel Trail
Park Headquarters
Maswik Lodge
Backcountry Information Center

0 — 1200 yards
0 — 1200 meters

gant hotel west of the Mississippi. Built of Oregon pine logs at a cost of $250,000, it was designed as a cross between a Swiss chalet and a Norwegian villa. Originally, the hotel had a coal-fired generator for electricity, a greenhouse to supply fresh vegetables, a henhouse for eggs, and a dairy herd for milk. When the weather gets chilly, you'll be glad to sit for a spell in front of the rustic lobby's stone fireplace for some good people-watching.

⑤ Hopi House, a multistory structure of rock and mortar, was modeled after buildings found in the Hopi village of Oraibi, Arizona, the oldest continuously inhabited community in the United States. An attempt by the Fred Harvey Company to encourage Southwest Native American crafts at the turn of the 20th century, Hopi House was one of the first gift shops to open in the Grand Canyon, where it catered to the desires of early westbound rail passengers.

⑧ Kolb Studio, built in 1904, was the Grand Canyon's original photo studio. The Kolb brothers, Ellsworth and Emery, bought a photo studio in Flagstaff and moved the equipment to the canyon. The brothers photographed those departing on the mule trip into the canyon. As there was no water available at the rim, the Kolbs would then travel 4½ mi to the Indian Garden (visible from the studio window), where they set up a lab with the available water to process the film and prints, returning to the rim in time to sell the finished images to the mule riders. Emery operated the studio until his death in 1976 at age 95. The gallery displays photography, paintings, and crafts exhibits year-round. There's also a bookstore.

★ ⑦ Lookout Studio was built in 1914 to compete with the Kolbs' photographic studio. Architect Mary Jane Colter designed it to blend into the surrounding landscape. A paved trail at the rim leads here from El Tovar Hotel. The upstairs loft provides an excellent overlook into the gorge below and a good photo spot.

③ Mather Point, about 4 mi north of the South Entrance, gives you the first glimpse of the canyon from one of the most impressive and accessible vista points on the rim—you can see nearly one quarter of the Grand Canyon. This overlook, named for the National Park Service's first director, Stephen Mather, yields extraordinary views of the Inner Gorge and the numerous buttes that rise out of the eroded chasm: Wotan's Throne, Brahma Temple, Zoroaster Temple, and many others. This overlook can be very busy—to the point of overcrowding—during peak periods. The Grand Canyon Lodge, on the North Rim, is almost directly north from Mather Point and only 10 mi away—yet you have to drive nearly 210 mi to get from one spot to the other.

Sports & the Outdoors

HIKING It's important to remember that there are large elevation changes and, in summer, extreme temperature ranges in the Grand Canyon. **Carry plenty of water** and energy foods including salty and high-carbohydrate snacks. Each year there are scores of unnecessary rescues simply because hikers underestimate the enormous size of the canyon, hike beyond their ability, or do not take with them sufficient quantities of food and water. Overnight hikes into the canyon require a backcountry permit (*see* Hiking Permits *in* the A to Z section at the end of this chapter).

The well-maintained **Bright Angel Trail** is one of the most scenic hiking paths from the South Rim to the bottom of the canyon (9 mi). Rest houses are equipped with water at the 1½- and 3-mi points from May through September and at Indian Gardens year-round. Water is also available at Campground, 9¼ mi below the trailhead. Plateau Point, about 1½ mi below Indian Garden, is as far as you should attempt to go on a day hike. Bright Angel Trail is the easiest of all the footpaths into the canyon, but because the climb out from the bottom is an ascent of 5,510 feet, the trip should be attempted only by those in good physical condition and should be avoided in midsummer due to extreme heat. The top of the trail, a tight set of switchbacks called Jacob's Ladder, can be icy in winter. Note that you will be sharing the trail with mule trains, which have the right-of-way and sometimes leave unpleasant surprises in your path.

If you've been driving too long and want some exercise along with great views of the canyon, it's an easy mile-long hike from the **Information Plaza to El Tovar Hotel.** There's a quiet wooded area for about ½ mi, and then the path runs along the rim for another ¾ mi.

The most popular walking path at the South Rim is 9-mi (one-way) **Rim Trail,** which runs along the edge of the canyon from Mather Point to Hermits Rest. This walk, which is paved to Maricopa Point, allows visits to several of the South Rim's historic landmarks. The Rim Trail is an ideal day hike as it only varies a few hundred feet in elevation from Mather Point (7,120 feet) to the trailhead at Hermits Rest (6,640 feet). The trail can also be accessed from the major viewpoints along Hermit Road, which you can reach by the shuttle bus during the busy summer months.

MULE TOURS Mule trips, which are run by **Xanterra Parks & Resorts** (⌖ 14001 E. Illiff, Suite 600, Aurora, CO 80014 ☎ 303/297–2757 or 888/297–2757 🖷 303/297–3175 ⊕ www.grandcanyonlodges.com), go down the precipitous trails to the Inner Gorge of the Grand Canyon and are nearly as well known as the canyon itself. But it's hard to get reservations unless you make them months in advance, especially in summer; write to the Reservations Department or make reservations online. Reservations are usually accepted up to 23 months in advance. These trips have been conducted since the early 1900s, and no one has ever been killed by a mule falling off a cliff. Nevertheless, the treks are not for the faint of heart or people in questionable health. Riders must be at least 4 foot 7 inches tall, weigh less than 200 pounds, and understand English. Pregnant women are not allowed to ride, and children under 15 must be accompanied by an adult. The all-day ride to Plateau Point costs $129.12 (lunch included). An overnight with a stay at Phantom Ranch at the bottom of the canyon is $360.54 ($641.57 for two) for one night. Two nights at Phantom Ranch, an option available from November through March, cost $493.76 ($832.56 for two, $1,555.57 for four). Meals are included.

SKIING Although you can't schuss down into the Grand Canyon, you can cross-country ski in the woods near the rim when there's enough snow. The best season for cross-country skiing is from mid-December though early March. Groomed trails, suitable for beginners and intermediate skiers, begin ³⁄₁₀-mi north of the Grandview Lookout and travel through the Kaibab National Forest. Contact the **Tusayan Ranger District** (🕾 Box 3088, Grand Canyon 86023 ☎ 928/638–2443) for details. The **Canyon Marketplace** (✉ Grand Canyon Village ☎ 928/638–2234 or 928/638–2262) rents equipment and can guide you to the best trails.

Where to Stay & Eat

If you want to get your first choice (especially the Lodge or El Tovar), it's a very good idea to make reservations as far in advance as possible, but there is often some option available even nearing the last minute.

$$–$$$ ✕ **Arizona Room.** This casual Southwestern-style steak house serves chicken, steak, and seafood on a first-come, first-served basis. Standard fare includes such steak-house favorites as prime rib, New York–strip steak, and baby back ribs. The quality is no more than what you might expect at a mid-range steak house. Prices reflect the restaurant's choice location; canyon views from the dining room are the best of any restaurant at the South Rim. The restaurant opens for dinner at 4:30; come early if you want to avoid the crowds. ✉ *Bright Angel Lodge, West Rim Dr., Grand Canyon Village* ☎ *928/638–2631* ⌖ *Reservations not accepted* ▤ *AE, D, DC, MC, V* ⊘ *Closed Jan.–mid-Feb.*

$–$$$ ✕ **El Tovar Dining Room.** Modeled after a European hunting lodge, this
Fodor's Choice   rustic 19th-century dining room built of hand-hewn logs is worth a visit
★   in itself. Breakfast, lunch, and dinner are served beneath the beamed ceiling. The cuisine is modern Southwestern, and the menu includes such dishes as sautéed rainbow trout served with a wild rice salad topped with an apple pumpkin seed salsa and a grilled New York strip steak framed with buttermilk-cornmeal onion rings and pepper jack au gratin potatoes. ✉ *El Tovar Hotel, West Rim Dr., Grand Canyon Village* ☎ *928/ 638–2631* ⌖ *Reservations essential* ▤ *AE, D, DC, MC, V.*

¢   ✕ **Yavapai Lodge Cafeteria.** Families favor the home-style food at Yavapai Lodge, which offers dining on a budget. Fast-food favorites here include the pastries, burgers, and pizza. Open for breakfast, lunch, and dinner, the cafeteria also serves pasta, chicken potpie, fried catfish, and fried chicken. ✉ *Grand Canyon Village* ☎ *928/638–2631* ⌖ *Reservations not accepted* ▤ *AE, D, DC, MC, V* ⊘ *Closed mid-Dec.–Feb.*

$$–$$$$ 🏨 **El Tovar Hotel.** A registered National Historic Landmark, El Tovar was built in 1905 of Oregon pine logs and native stone. The hotel's proximity to all of the canyon's facilities, its European hunting-lodge atmosphere, and its renowned dining room make it the best place to stay on the South Rim. It's usually booked well in advance (up to nine months ahead), though it's easier to get a room here during winter months. Only three suites have canyon views—the Fred Harvey, Mary Jane Colter, and El Tovar suites— and these are usually booked two years in advance, but you can enjoy the view anytime from the cocktail-lounge back porch. ✉ *West Rim Dr., Grand Canyon Village* 🕾 *Box 699, Grand Canyon 86023* ☎ *303/297– 2757 reservations only, 928/638–2631 direct to hotel (no reservations)*

🖹 *303/297–3175 reservations only, 928/638–2855 direct to hotel (no reservations)* ⊕ *www.grandcanyonlodges.com* 🗗 *70 rooms, 8 suites* ⚇ *Restaurant, room service, some in-room hot tubs, some refrigerators, cable TV, bar; no smoking* ☰ *AE, D, DC, MC, V.*

✪ **$–$$** 🏨 **Bright Angel Lodge.** Famed architect Mary Jane Colter designed this
Fodor'sChoice 1935 log-and-stone structure, which sits within a few yards of the
★ canyon rim and blends superbly with the natural environment. It offers as much atmosphere as El Tovar for about half the price. Accommodations are in motel-style rooms or cabins. Most rooms in the main lodge share baths; cabins, some with fireplaces and/or canyon views (No. 6158 has both), are scattered among the pines. Expect historic charm and bargain prices but not luxury. The restaurant serves family-style meals all day; the Arizona Room serves dinner only. An ice-cream parlor, a well-stocked gift shop, and a small history museum with exhibits on Fred Harvey and Mary Jane Colter add to the experience. ⊠ *West Rim Dr., Grand Canyon Village* ⌖ *Box 699, Grand Canyon 86023* 📞 *303/ 297–2757 reservations only, 928/638–2631 direct to hotel (no reservations)* 🖹 *303/297–3175 reservations only, 928/638–2876 direct to hotel (no reservations)* ⊕ *www.grandcanyonlodges.com* 🗗 *30 rooms, 6 with shared bath; 42 cabins* ⚇ *Restaurant, coffee shop, bar, shop; no a/c, no TV in some rooms* ☰ *AE, D, DC, MC, V.*

$ 🏨 **Kachina Lodge.** Half of the rooms at this contemporary motel-style lodge have a partial canyon view ($10 extra). The rooms with two queen beds are your best bet for families and for people with physical disabilities. Check in at El Tovar Hotel to the east. At the time of this writing the Kachina Lodge was closed for complete upgrading and remodeling. ⊠ *West Rim Dr., Grand Canyon Village* ⌖ *Box 699, Grand Canyon 86023* 📞 *303/297–2757 reservations only, 928/638–2631 direct to hotel (no reservations)* 🖹 *303/297–3175 reservations only* ⊕ *www. grandcanyonlodges.com* 🗗 *50 rooms* ⚇ *In-room data ports, refrigerators, cable TV, no-smoking rooms* ☰ *AE, D, DC, MC, V.*

$ 🏨 **Maswik Lodge.** At the southwest end of Grand Canyon Village, the lodge, named for a Hopi Kachina who is said to guard the canyon, is ¼ mi from the rim. Accommodations, nestled in the ponderosa pine forest, range from rustic cabins to more modern rooms. The rustic log cabins are the cheapest option but are available only in summer. Make sure to bring layered clothing if you stay here, because the log cabins have neither heat nor air-conditioning; regular rooms have heat but no air-conditioning. Maswik cafeteria offers typical national-park fare; there's a lounge here, too, where you can shoot pool, throw darts, or watch the big-screen TV. Kids under 16 stay free. ⊠ *Grand Canyon Village* ⌖ *Box 699, Grand Canyon 86023* 📞 *303/297–2757 reservations only, 928/638–2631 direct to hotel (no reservations)* 🖹 *303/297–3175 reservations only* ⊕ *www.grandcanyonlodges.com* 🗗 *250 rooms, 28 cabins* ⚇ *Cafeteria, sports bar, shop, no-smoking rooms; no a/c* ☰ *AE, D, DC, MC, V.*

$ 🏨 **Thunderbird Lodge.** This motel-style lodge is next to Bright Angel Lodge in Grand Canyon Village. For $10 more, you can get a room with a partial view of the canyon. All rooms have two queen beds. Check in at Bright Angel Lodge, the next hotel to the west. At this writing the Thunderbird Lodge was closed for complete upgrading and remodeling. ⊠ *West Rim Dr., Grand Canyon Village* ☐ *Box 699, Grand Canyon 86023* ☎ *303/297–2757 reservations only, 928/638–2631 direct to hotel (no reservations)* ⎙ *303/297–3175 reservations only* ⊕ *www. grandcanyonlodges.com* ⇥ *55 rooms* ☼ *In-room data ports, refrigerators, no-smoking rooms* ☰ *AE, D, DC, MC, V.*

$ ▦ **Yavapai Lodge.** The largest motel-style lodge in the park is tucked in a piñon and juniper pygmy forest at the eastern end of Grand Canyon Village, near the RV park. The basic rooms are conveniently near the park's general store, the visitor center (½ mi), and the rim (¼ mi). The cafeteria, open for breakfast, lunch, and dinner, serves standard park service food. ⊠ *Grand Canyon Village* ☐ *Box 699, Grand Canyon 86023* ☎ *303/297–2757 reservations only, 928/638–2631 direct to hotel (no reservations)* ⎙ *303/297–3175 reservations only* ⊕ *www. grandcanyonlodges.com* ⇥ *358 rooms* ☼ *Cafeteria, fans, shop, no-smoking rooms; no a/c in some rooms* ☰ *AE, D, DC, MC, V* ☉ *Closed Jan. and Feb.*

¢–$ ▦ **Phantom Ranch.** Phantom Ranch, in a grove of cottonwood trees on the canyon floor, is accessible only to hikers, mule trekkers, or rafters. The wood-and-stone buildings were originally a hunting camp built in 1922. For hikers, there are 40 dormitory beds and 14 beds in cabins, all with shared baths. Seven additional cabins are reserved for mule riders, who buy their trips as a package. The restaurant at Phantom Ranch, probably the most remote eating establishment in the United States, serves family-style meals, with breakfast, dinner, and box lunches available. Food and lodging reservations should be made 9 to 11 months ahead. ⊠ *On canyon floor at intersection of the Bright Angel and Kaibab trails* ☎ *303/297–2757 reservations only (no direct phone)* ⎙ *303/ 297–3175 reservations only* ⊕ *www.grandcanyonlodges.com* ⇥ *4 dormitories and 2 cabins for hikers, 7 cabins with outside showers for mule riders* ☼ *Dining room; no a/c, no room phones, no room TVs* ☰ *AE, D, DC, MC, V.*

CAMPING ⛺ **Campground.** This free campground is near Phantom Ranch on the ¢ South and North Kaibab trails, at the bottom of the canyon. There are toilet facilities and running water but no showers. A backcountry permit, which serves as your reservation, is required to stay here. ⊠ *Intersection of South and North Kaibab trails, Grand Canyon* ☐ *Backcountry Office, Box 129, Grand Canyon 86023* ☎ *928/638– 7875* ⎙ *928/638–2125* ⇥ *32 tent sites* ☼ *Flush toilets, drinking water, picnic tables* ⌀ *Reservations essential* ☉ *Open year-round.*

¢ ⛺ **Indian Garden.** About halfway down the canyon is this free campground, located en route to Phantom Ranch on the Bright Angel Trail. Running water and toilet facilities are available, but there are no showers. A backcountry permit, which serves as a reservation, is required. ⊠ *Bright Angel Trail, Grand Canyon* ☐ *Backcountry Office, Box 129, Grand Canyon 86023* ☎ *928/638–7875* ⎙ *928/638–2125* ⇥ *15 tent sites* ☼ *Pit toilets, drinking water, picnic tables* ⌀ *Reservations essential* ☉ *Open year-round.*

¢ ⛺ **Mather Campground.** Mather has both RV and tent sites but no hookups. No reservations are accepted from December to March, but during the rest of the year they are a good idea, especially during the busy spring and summer seasons. Reservations can be made up to five months in advance. ⊠ *Off Village Loop Dr., Grand Canyon Village* ⌾ *National Park Reservation Service, Box 1600, Cumberland, MD 21501* ☎ *800/365–2267* ⊕ *reservations.nps.gov/index.cfm* ⟿ *97 RV sites, 190 tent sites* ⚭ *Flush toilets, drinking water, guest laundry, showers, fire grates, picnic tables* ☉ *Open year-round* ⚭ *Reservations suggested Apr.–Nov.*

¢ ⚲ **Trailer Village.** This campground in Grand Canyon Village has RV sites with full hookups and bathroom facilities, though they are ½ mi from the campground. The fee is good for two people; there is an extra fee of $2 for each additional person over the age of 16. No reservations are accepted from December to March, but they are a good idea the rest of the year, especially during the busy spring and summer seasons. The dump station is closed in the winter. ⊠ *Off Village Loop Dr., Grand Canyon Village* ☎ *303/297–2757 or 888/297–2757 reservations only, 928/638–2631 direct to village (no reservations)* ⌸ *303/297–3175 reservations only* ⊕ *www.xanterra.com* ⟿ *78 RV sites* ⚭ *Flush toilets, full hookups, dump station, drinking water, guest laundry, showers, fire grates* ☉ *Open year-round.*

Nightlife & the Arts

If you are looking for exciting nightlife of any variety, you're in the wrong place. Nightlife in these parts consists of watching a full moon above the soaring buttes of the Grand Canyon, crawling into your bedroll beside some lonely canyon trail, or attending a free evening program on area lore. The following Grand Canyon properties have cocktail lounges: **Bright Angel Lodge** (occasional live entertainment), **El Tovar Hotel** (casual relaxation), and **Maswik Lodge** (sports bar).

★ The **Grand Canyon Chamber Music Festival** (☎ 928/638–9215 or 800/997–8285) is held each September at the Shrine of Ages amphitheater and stages nearly a dozen concerts. In the early 1980s, music aficionados Robert Bonfiglio and Clare Hoffman hiked through the Grand Canyon and decided the stunning spectacle should be accompanied by the strains of a symphony. One of the park rangers agreed, and the wandering musicians performed an impromptu concert. Encouraged by the experience, Bonfiglio and Hoffman started up the Grand Canyon Music Festival in 1984. Concerts are held Friday and Saturday evenings and several other nights during the course of the three-week event.

Shopping

Nearly every lodging facility and retail store at the South Rim stocks Native American arts and crafts and Grand Canyon books and souvenirs. Prices are comparable to other souvenir outlets, though you may find some better deals in Williams. However, a portion of the proceeds from items purchased at Hopi House, Desert Watchtower, and the visitor center go to the Grand Canyon Association. **El Tovar Hotel Gift Shop** (⊠ West Rim Dr., Grand Canyon Village ☎ 928/638–2631) carries Native American jewelry, rather expensive casual wear, and souvenir gifts. **Hopi**

★ **House** (⊠ West Rim Dr., east of El Tovar Hotel, Grand Canyon Village ☎ 928/638–2631) has the widest selection of Native American handicrafts in the vicinity. **Verkamp's** (⊠ West Rim Dr., across from El Tovar Hotel, Grand Canyon Village ☎ 928/638–2242 ⊕ www.verkamps. com) is the best place on the South Rim to buy inexpensive souvenirs of your Grand Canyon adventure.

Desert View Drive

The breathtaking Desert View Drive proceeds east for about 25 mi along the South Rim from Grand Canyon Village to Desert View. Before beginning the drive, consider stopping to see the exhibits and attend the free lectures offered by park naturalists at Yavapai Observation Station. There are four marked picnic areas along the route and rest rooms at Tusayan Museum and Desert View. This is the road you come into the park on if you enter at the East Entrance.

⟳ ❶ **Desert View and the Watchtower** make for a climactic final stop if you are driving Desert View Drive from Grand Canyon Village. They are also a dramatic beginning if you enter the park through the East Entrance. From the top of the 70-foot stone-and-mortar Watchtower even the muted hues of the distant Painted Desert to the east and the 3,000-feet-high Vermilion Cliffs rising from a high plateau near the Utah border are visible. In the chasm below, angling to the north toward Marble Canyon, you can see an imposing stretch of the Colorado River. The Watchtower houses a glass-enclosed observatory with powerful telescopes. Desert View originally served as a trading post; now the building is a small museum and information center. ⊠ *Desert View Dr., Grand Canyon* ☎ *928/638–2736, 928/638–2360 trading post* ☒ *Watchtower 25¢* ☉ *Daily 8–7 or 8–8 in summer, daily 9–5 in winter.*

❷ **Grandview Point** (⊠ Desert View Dr., Grand Canyon), at an altitude of 7,496 feet, has large stands of ponderosa pine, piñon pine, oak, and juniper. The view from here is one of the finest in the canyon. To the northeast is a group of dominant buttes, including Krishna Shrine, Vishnu Temple, Rama Shrine, and Shiva Temple. A short stretch of the Colorado River is also visible. Directly below the point and accessible by the rugged Grandview Trail is Horseshoe Mesa, where you can see ruins of the Last Chance Copper Mine. Grandview Point was also the site of the Grandview Hotel, constructed in the late 1890s but closed in 1908; logs salvaged from the hotel were used for the Kiva Room of the Desert View and the Watchtower.

❺ **Lipan Point** (⊠ Desert View Dr., Grand Canyon), 1 mi northeast of Tusayan Ruin, is the canyon's widest point. From here you can get an astonishing visual profile of the gorge's geologic history, with a view of every eroded layer of the canyon. You can also see Unkar Delta, where a wide creek joins the Colorado to form powerful rapids and a broad beach. Ancestral Puebloan farmers worked the Unkar Delta for hundreds of years, growing corn, beans, squash, and melons.

❸ **Moran Point** (⊠ Desert View Dr., Grand Canyon), about 5 mi east of Grandview Point, was named for American landscape artist Thomas Moran, who painted Grand Canyon scenes from many points on the rim but was especially fond of the play of light and shadows from this location. He first visited the canyon with John Wesley Powell in 1873, and his vivid canvases helped persuade Congress to create a national park at the Grand Canyon. "Thomas Moran's name, more than any other, with the possible exception of Major Powell's, is to be associated with the Grand Canyon," wrote the noted canyon photographer Ellsworth Kolb. It's fitting that Moran Point is a favorite spot for photographers and painters.

16 **Navajo Point** (⊠ Desert View Dr., Grand Canyon) is just over 1 mi east of Lipan Point at 7,461 feet. It is the probable site of the first Spanish descent into the canyon, in 1540. Just west of Navajo Point—the highest natural elevation on the South Rim, at 7,498 feet—is the head of the unmaintained Tanner Trail, a rugged route once favored by prospectors, rustlers (it's also called Horsethief Trail), and bootleggers.

14 **Tusayan Ruin and Museum** is three miles east of Moran Point on the south side of the highway. This archaeological site contains evidence of early habitation in the Grand Canyon, and the accompanying museum provides plenty of information about ancestral Pueblo people who once lived here. *Tusayan* comes from a Hopi phrase meaning "country of isolated buttes," which certainly describes the scenery. The partially intact rock dwellings here were occupied for roughly 20 years around AD 1200 by 30 or so Native American hunters, farmers, and gatherers. They eventually moved on like so many others, perhaps pressured by drought and depletion of natural resources. The museum displays artifacts, models of the dwellings, and exhibits on modern tribes of the region. Free 30-minute guided tours—as many as five during the summer, fewer in winter—are given daily. ⊠ *Desert View Dr., 3 mi east of Moran Point, Grand Canyon* ☎ *928/638–2305* 🔲 *Free* ☉ *Daily 9–5.*

11 **Yaki Point** (⊠ Desert View Dr., Grand Canyon), east of Grand Canyon Village on AZ 64, has an exceptional view of Wotan's Throne, a majestic flat-top butte named by François Matthes, a U.S. Geological Survey scientist who developed the first topographical map of the Grand Canyon. Due north is Buddha Temple, capped by limestone. Newton Butte, with its flat top of red sandstone, lies to the east. At Yaki Point the popular South Kaibab Trail starts the descent to the Inner Gorge, crosses the Colorado over a steel suspension bridge, and wends its way to rustic Phantom Ranch, the only lodging facility at the bottom of the Grand Canyon. If you plan to go more than a mile, carry water with you. If you encounter a mule train, the animals have the right-of-way. Move to the inside of the trail and wait as they pass. Yaki Point is accessible only by the park shuttle bus most of the year. Sometimes, during winter months when visitation is low, the road is open to private vehicles.

Sports & the Outdoors

HIKING Accessible from the parking area at Grandview Point, the trailhead for **Grandview Trail** is at 7,400 feet. The path heads down into the canyon for 4⁸⁄₁₀ mi to the junction at East Horseshoe Mesa Trail. Classified as a wilderness trail, the route is aggressive and not as heavily traveled as some of the more well-known trails, such as Bright Angel and Hermit. There is no water available along the trail and it follows a steep descent

CloseUp

FREEBIES AT THE CANYON

WHILE YOU'RE HERE, make sure you take advantage of the many freebies offered at Grand Canyon National Park. The most useful of these services is the system of free shuttle buses at the South Rim that will ease the road-weary with three routes winding through the park—Hermits Rest Route, Village Route, and Kaibab Trail Route. Of the bus routes, the Hermits Rest Route runs only from March through November; the other two run year-round, and the Kaibab Trail Route provides the only access to Yaki Point. Hikers coming or going from the Kaibab Trailhead can catch the Hikers Express, which departs three times each morning from the Bright Angel Lodge, makes a quick stop at the Backcountry Office, and then heads out to the South Kaibab Trailhead.

Ranger-led programs are always free and are offered year-round, though more programs are scheduled during the busy spring and summer seasons. These might include such activities as stargazing and topics as geology and the cultural history of prehistoric peoples. Some programs are held during the day and others in the evening. Some of the more in-depth programs include a fossil walk and a condor talk. Also make sure to check with the visitor center for seasonal programs including wildflower walks and fire ecology.

Kids ages 4 to 14 can get involved as well with the park's Junior Ranger program, with activities including a ranger-led rim hike and hands-on experiments detailing how the Grand Canyon was formed.

However, rangers will tell you that the best free activity in the canyon is watching the magnificent splashes of color on the canyon walls during sunrise and sunset.

to 4,800 feet at Horseshoe Mesa, where Hopi Indians once collected mineral paints.

The **New Hance Trail** was blazed in the late 1800s by the famous canyon guide and storyteller John Hance. The strenuous hike begins at 7,000 feet and descends 8 mi to the Colorado River at 2,600 feet. The trailhead is 1 mi south of Moran Point. This primitive wilderness trail can occasionally be blocked with small rock slides or washouts, making for a more interesting and difficult hike than the regularly maintained trails within the park. Make sure to take plenty of water and don't attempt to hike down to the river and back in one day. As Hance once remarked to a tourist, "You can't imagine how hot it is [in the canyon]. Why I'll give my word, I've been down there when it was so hot it melted the wings off the flies."

The **South Kaibab Trail**, starting near Yaki Point on Desert View Drive near Grand Canyon Village, connects at the bottom of the canyon (after the Kaibab Bridge across the Colorado River) with the **North Kaibab Trail.** Plan on two to three days if you want to hike the gorge from rim to rim (it's easier to descend from the North Rim, as it is more than 1,000 feet higher than the South Rim). The South Kaibab Trail is steep, descending from the trailhead at 7,260 feet to 2,480 feet at the Colorado River. Although there is no water and no campgrounds and very little shade, there are portable toilets at Cedar Ridge (6,320 feet) 1½ mi from the trailhead. Toilets and an emergency phone are also located at the Tipoff, 4½ mi down the trail (3 mi past Cedar Ridge). The trail corkscrews down through some spectacular geology, closely following the 300-million-year-old Supai and Redwall formations. Look for (but don't remove) fossils in the limestone when you take your frequent water breaks. If you're going back up to the South Rim, ascend **Bright Angel Trail.** Accommodations along the way include the backcountry campgrounds at Indian Garden and Phantom Ranch (reservations are required far in advance for the latter). Don't forget–hikers traveling down the canyon are required to yield to mules and to hikers going uphill. Overnight hikes into the canyon require a backcountry permit (*see* Hiking Permits *in* the A to Z section at the end of this chapter).

Where to Stay

CAMPING   �' **Desert View Campground.** Popular for the spectacular views of the canyon at nearby Watchtower, this campground gets booked up fast in summer. Fifty RV (without hookups) and tent sites are available on a first-come, first-served basis. ⚿ *Flush toilets, drinking water, grills, picnic tables* ⛺ *50 campsites* ✉ *Desert View Dr., 23 mi east of Grand Canyon Village off AZ 64* 📮 *Box 129, Grand Canyon 86023* ☎ *928/638–7875* 🖷 *928/638–2125* ⚓ *Reservations not accepted* 🕐 *Mid-May–mid-Oct.*

Shopping

Desert View Trading Post (✉ Desert View Dr., near the Watchtower at Desert View, Grand Canyon ☎ 928/638–2360) sells a mix of traditional Southwestern souvenirs and authentic Native American arts and crafts.

Hermit Road

The Santa Fe Company built Hermit Road, formerly known as West Rim Drive, in 1912 as a scenic tour route. There are 10 scenic overlooks along this 8-mi stretch, each worth a visit. Hermit Road is filled with hairpin turns; be certain to adhere to posted speed limits. Hermit Road is usually closed to private auto traffic from March through November because of congestion; during this period, a free shuttle bus can carry you to all the overlooks. To ride the bus round-trip without getting off at any of the viewpoints takes 75 minutes, as the return trip only stops at Mohave and Hopi points. Make sure to take plenty of water with you for the ride—the only water along the way is at Hermits Rest.

㉓ The Abyss (✉ Hermit Rd., Grand Canyon), at an elevation of 6,720 feet, is one of the most awesome stops on Hermit Road, revealing a sheer drop of 3,000 feet to the Tonto Platform. From the Abyss you'll also see several isolated sandstone columns, the largest of which is called the Monument.

★ ㉕ **Hermits Rest** (✉ Hermit Rd., Grand Canyon), the westernmost viewpoint, and the Hermit Trail that descends from it were named for the "hermit" Louis Boucher, a 19th-century French-Canadian prospector who had a number of mining claims and a roughly built home down in the canyon. Canyon views from here include Hermit Rapids and the towering cliffs of the Supai and Redwall formations. The stone building at Hermits Rest sells curios and refreshments and—more important—has the only rest rooms on Hermit Road.

㉑ Hopi Point (✉ Hermit Rd., Grand Canyon) is at an elevation of 7,071 feet, and a large section of the Colorado River is visible from here; although it appears as a thin line, the river is nearly 350 feet wide below this overlook. Across the canyon to the north is Shiva Temple, which remained an isolated section of the Kaibab Plateau until 1937. In that year, Harold Anthony of the American Museum of Natural History led an expedition to the rock formation in the belief that it supported life that had been cut off from the rest of the canyon. Imagine the expedition members' surprise when they found an empty Kodak film box on top of the temple. Directly below Hopi Point lies Dana Butte, named for a prominent 19th-century geologist. In 1919 an entrepreneur proposed connecting Hopi Point, Dana Butte, and the Tower of Set across the river with an aerial tramway, a technically feasible plan that, fortunately, has not been realized.

⑲ Maricopa Point (✉ Hermit Rd., Grand Canyon) merits a stop for its arresting scenery and a view of the Colorado River below. On your left as you face the canyon are the Orphan Mine and (below) a mine shaft and cable lines leading up to the rim. The Orphan Mine was operated briefly as a copper mine around the beginning of the 20th century. In the 1950s, it was reopened as a uranium mine and closed again in the late '60s. It was one of the few profitable mines in the region.

㉒ Mohave Point (✉ Hermit Rd., Grand Canyon) also has striking views of the Colorado River and of 5,401-foot Cheops Pyramid, the grayish rock formation behind Dana Butte. Granite and Salt Creek rapids can also be seen from this spot.

㉔ Pima Point (✉ Hermit Rd., Grand Canyon) provides a bird's-eye view of the Tonto Platform and the Tonto Trail, which wends its way through the canyon for more than 70 mi. Also to the west, two dark cone-shaped mountains—Mount Trumbull and Mount Logan—are visible on clear days. They rise in stark contrast to the surrounding flat-top mesas and buttes. From here you can see the scars from Hermit Camp, which can be seen up close if you hike the Hermit Trail.

★ ⑳ The Powell Memorial (✉ Hermit Rd., Grand Canyon), a large, granite monument, stands as a tribute to the first man to ride the wild rapids of the Colorado River through the canyon in 1869. John Wesley Powell measured, charted, and named many of the canyons and creeks along the river. It was here that the dedication ceremony for Grand Canyon National Park took place on April 3, 1920.

⑱ Trailview Overlook (✉ Hermit Rd., Grand Canyon) provides a dramatic view of the Bright Angel and Plateau Point trails as they zigzag down the canyon. Across the canyon, in the deep gorge to the north, flows

Bright Angel Creek, one of the permanent tributary streams of the Colorado River in the region. Toward the south is an unobstructed view of the distant San Francisco Peaks, Arizona's highest mountains (the tallest is 12,633 feet), as well as of Bill Williams Mountain (on the horizon) and Red Butte (about 15 mi south of the canyon rim).

Sports & the Outdoors

HIKING The steep, 9-mi **Hermit Trail** beginning just west of Hermits Rest (8 mi west of Grand Canyon Village) is recommended for experienced long-distance hikers only. The trail descends from the trailhead at 6,640 feet to the Colorado River at 2,400 feet. Day hikers should not go past Santa Maria Springs at 4,880 feet. For much of the year, no water is available along the way; ask a park ranger about the availability of water at Santa Maria Springs and Hermit Creek before you set out. But all water from these sources should be treated before drinking. The route leads down to the Colorado River and has inspiring views of Hermit Gorge and the Redwall and Supai formations. Six miles from the trailhead you'll come across the scattered ruins of Hermit Camp, which the Santa Fe Railroad ran as a tourist camp from 1911 until 1930. Hiking here requires a backcountry permit (*see* Hiking Permits *in* the A to Z section at the end of this chapter).

GRAND CANYON: THE WEST RIM

West of Grand Canyon National Park, the tribal lands of the Hualapai and the Havasupai lie on the West Rim of the Canyon.

The Hualapai tribe has been attempting to foster tourism to the little known West Rim, where a road travels through their reservation lands down to the Colorado River. The only place upriver that offers the same opportunity is Lees Ferry. This is a launch point for the region's river runners and, because few others know about the road, traffic is a rarity.

Some 12,000 people a year hike, ride, or fly deep into the Grand Canyon to visit the more well-known Havasupai, the "people of the blue green waters." Dubbed the "Shangri-la of the Grand Canyon," the remote, inaccessible Indian reservation includes some of the world's most beautiful and famous waterfalls, together with streams and pools tinted a mystical blue green by dissolved travertine.

The Hualapai Tribe & Grand Canyon West

🗓 *78 mi west of Williams via Interstate 40 and AZ 66.*

The region occupied by the Hualapai tribe was explored by the Franciscan Father Garcés in 1775 and later by Lieutenant Ives in 1857. There is no record of where the creek and peak originally earned their gleaming designations—but, interestingly enough, a diamond swindle was attempted in the region, years after Ives passed through. However, the scheme was quickly debunked by a geologist who claimed that the geology isn't conducive to creating the precious gems.

The Hualapai Tribe is expanding its tourism offerings on the West Rim, but you definitely won't be shoulder to shoulder with other visitors. Hualapai guides also add a Native American perspective to a canyon trip that you won't find on North and South Rim tours. **Diamond Creek Road,** directly north of the Hualapai Lodge in Peach Springs, is the access point for adventures in this developing section of the Grand Canyon. The winding, 22-mi Diamond Creek Road leads past Diamond Peak to the Colorado River just above Diamond Creek Rapid. The road is at river mile 226, which is 138 mi downstream from Phantom Ranch (as the crow flies the distance is about half of that). Diamond Creek Road can be braved by high clearance passenger vehicles, but your best bet is four-wheel-drive capabilities, especially in the summer season when storms are commonplace.

The Hualapai Tribe requires visitors to obtain permits to enter the West Rim. A sightseeing permit is $6 per person (ages 7 and above); a hiking permit, which includes road travel fees, is $8 per person. Another option while you are here is to visit the Hualapai Mountain Park for hiking and camping. For more information on the park, *see* Kingman *in* Chapter 8. ⊠ *Hualapai Tourist Information, Peach Springs 86434* ☎ *928/769–2230 or 888/255–9550* ⊕ *www.grandcanyonresort.com* ⌨ *$6–$8* ⊙ *Daily.*

Sports & the Outdoors

RAFTING One-day river trips are offered by the Hualapai tribe through the **Hualapai River Runners** (⊠ 887 Rte. 66, Peach Springs 86434 ☎ 928/769–2230 or 888/255–9550 ⊕ www.grandcanyonresort.com) from March through October. The trips, which cost $265 with a $100 advance deposit, leave from the Hualapai Lodge at 8 AM and return between 6:30 and 8:30 PM. Lunch, snacks, and beverages are provided. Children must be eight or older to take the trip, which runs several rapids with the most difficult rated as Class V or VI, depending on the river flow.

Where to Stay & Eat

¢–$ ✕⌂ **Hualapai Lodge.** This lodge and its small café provide basic rooms and hearty food. The comfortable lobby has a large fireplace that is welcoming on chilly nights. The rooms are clean, but basic. The Diamond Creek Café offers standard American fare, including hamburgers and sandwiches along with a few specialties, such as Hualapai tacos, which are worth a stop on their own. ⊠ *900 Rte. 66, Peach Springs 86434* ☎ *928/769–2230 or 888/255–9550* ⊕ *www.grandcanyonresort.com* ↪ *62 rooms* ⌂ *Restaurant, cable TV, laundry facilities, no-smoking rooms* ⊟ *AE, D, MC, V.*

CAMPING The Hualapai permit camping on their tribal lands. An overnight camping permit is $10 per person per night and can be purchased at the **Hualapai Lodge** (⊠ 900 Rte. 66, Peach Springs 86434 ☎ 928/769–2230 or 888/255–9550). The camping on the beach area on the Colorado River is accessed by Diamond Creek Road. The camping area is primitive and offers only a picnic table and pit toilets. No fires are allowed; however, grills may be used.

The Havasupai Tribe & Havasu Canyon

㉗ *141 mi from Williams (to head of the Hualapai Trail), west on Interstate 40 and AZ 66, north on Indian Highway 18. Note: Last gas is at the junction of AZ 66 and Indian Highway 18.*

Havasu Canyon, south of the middle part of the national park and away from the crowds, is the home of the Havasupai, a tribe that has lived in this isolated area for centuries. Their name means "people of the blue green waters," and you'll know why when you see the canyon's waterfalls, as high as 200 feet, cascading over red cliffs into travertine pools surrounded by thick foliage and sheltering trees.

The striking falls, plunging into the deep turquoise pools, seem like something from Hawaii or Shangri La, rather than a desert canyon. The travertine in the water coats the walls and lines the pools with bizarre, drip-castle rock formations. Centuries of accumulated travertine formations in some of the most popular pools were washed out in massive flooding decades ago, destroying some of the otherworldly scenes pictured in older photos. But the travertine, the color of the water, and the abundance of spring-fed waterfalls still make the place magical. The Havasupai have woven a rich myth around the deep canyons, rushing water, long falls, and pools of their canyon. They also excel in basketry and beadwork.

The 500 tribal members now live in the village of Supai, accessible only down the 8-mi-long **Hualapai Trail,** which drops 3,000 feet. The quiet and private Havasupai mostly remain apart from the modest flow of tourists, which nevertheless plays a vital role in the tribal economy.

To reach Havasu's waterfalls, you must hike downstream from the village of Supai. The first fall, 1½ mi from Supai, is the 75-foot-high **Navajo Falls,** named after a 19th-century Havasupai chief who was abducted as a child and raised by the Navajo, until he eventually discovered his origin and returned to his tribe as an adult. Navajo Falls rushes over red-wall limestone and collects in a beautiful blue-green pool perfect for swimming. Not much farther downstream, the striking **Havasu Falls** dashes over a ledge into another pool of refreshing 70°F water. The last of the enchanting waterfalls is **Mooney Falls,** 2 mi down from Navajo Falls. Mooney Falls, named after a prospector who fell to his death here in 1880, plummets 196 feet down a sheer travertine cliff. The hike down to the pool below is a steep descent down slippery rocks with only the assistance of chains suspended along a series of iron stakes.

The Havasupai restrict the number of visitors to the canyon; you must have reservations. They ask that hikers call ahead before taking the trek into the canyon. Hualapai Trail leaves from Hualapai Hilltop, 63 mi north on Indian Route 18 from Route 66. From an elevation of 5,200 feet, the trail travels down a moderate grade to Supai village at 3,200 feet. Be sure to bring plenty of water and avoid hiking during the middle of the day, when canyon temperatures can reach into the 100s. If you'd rather ride, you can rent a horse for the trip down for $150 round-trip, or $75 one-way. Riders must be able to mount and dismount by themselves. You must also be at least 4 feet, 7 inches and weigh less than 250 pounds. Reservations must be made at least six weeks in advance with Havasupai Tourist Enterprise, which requires a 50% deposit. You'll need to spend the night if you're hiking or riding.

Another option is to take a helicopter ride into the canyon with **Air West Helicopters** (☎ 623/516–2790). Flights leave from Hualapai Hilltop and cost $85 per person each way. Air West Helicopters does not accept reservations. Visitors are taken into the canyon on a first-come, first-served basis.

There is a $20 entrance fee for visiting the Havasupai tribal lands. You are expected to respect the land and its people. The tribe does not allow alcohol, drugs, pets, or weapons. ⊠ *Havasupai Tourist Enterprise, Supai 86435* ☎ *928/448–2141 general information, 928/448–2111 lodging reservations* ⊕ *www.havasupaitribe.com* 🍴 *$20* ☉ *Daily.*

Where to Stay & Eat

¢–$ ✕🛏 **Havasupai Lodge.** These are fairly spartan accommodations, but you won't notice it too much when you see all of the natural beauty surrounding you. The lodge and restaurant are at the bottom of Havasu Canyon and are operated by the Havasupai tribe. The restaurant serves three meals a day, mostly sandwiches and fast-food-type fare, and a daily special; dinner main-course prices are about $8 to $10. ⊠ *Supai 86435* ☎ *928/448–2111 or 928/448–2201* ⇥ *24 rooms* ⚬ *Restaurant; no room phones, no room TVs, no smoking* ▤ *MC, V.*

CAMPING   For information about camping in Havasu Canyon, call the **Havasupai Tourist Enterprise** (☎ 928/448–2141) You can stay in the primitive campgrounds for $10 per person per night, which is in addition to your $20 entry fee.

APPROACHING THE NORTH RIM: LEES FERRY & JACOB LAKE

John Wesley Powell, the one-armed Civil War veteran who first explored the depths of the Grand Canyon on the Colorado River, wrote: "Mountains of music swell in the river, hills of music billow in the creek . . . while other melodies are heard in the gorges of the lateral canyons. The Grand Canyon is a land of song."

This land of song has one vital crossing point—Lees Ferry. There isn't another crossing point until you reach river mile 226 at Diamond Creek on the West Rim. Lees Ferry, the junction of several canyons just 15 mi below Glen Canyon dam, has for thousands of years offered one of the best places to cross the deep gash of the Grand Canyon. Today, the town; the Lonely Dell Ranch Historic District; a small, sad cemetery; and a scattering of historic buildings offer a glimpse of frontier life. But most people journey to Lees Ferry to get onto the river. Commercial raft trips take off from the boat ramps, and fly-fishing guides regularly shuttle people upstream to the base of Glen Canyon dam.

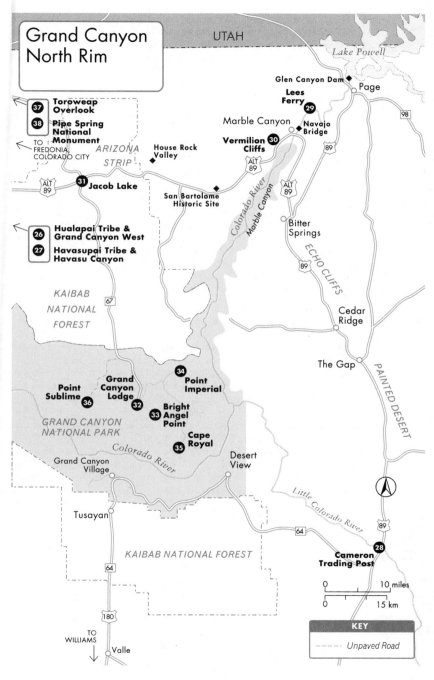

Grand Canyon North Rim

UTAH

ARIZONA STRIP

37 Toroweap Overlook

38 Pipe Spring National Monument

TO FREDONIA, COLORADO CITY

ALT 89

31 Jacob Lake

26 Hualapai Tribe & Grand Canyon West

27 Havasupai Tribe & Havasu Canyon

Lake Powell

Glen Canyon Dam

Page

Lees Ferry **29**

Marble Canyon

Navajo Bridge

Vermilion Cliffs **30**

House Rock Valley

ALT 89

San Bartolome Historic Site

98

89

ALT 89

Colorado River

Marble Canyon

Bitter Springs

89

ECHO CLIFFS

KAIBAB NATIONAL FOREST

67

Cedar Ridge

The Gap

PAINTED DESERT

34 Point Imperial

Point Sublime **36**

Grand Canyon Lodge **32**

33 Bright Angel Point

GRAND CANYON NATIONAL PARK

Colorado River

35 Cape Royal

Grand Canyon Village

Desert View

Tusayan

64

Little Colorado River

KAIBAB NATIONAL FOREST

64

180

TO WILLIAMS

Valle

Cameron Trading Post **28**

89

0   10 miles
0   15 km

KEY
- - - - - Unpaved Road

The tiny town of Jacob Lake, nestled high in pine country at an elevation of 7,925 feet, was named after the Mormon explorer Jacob Hamblin, who was also known as the "Buckskin Missionary." Jacob Lake is mostly just an en route point for visitors heading to the North Rim, but the lush mountain countryside is worth a day or two of exploration in its own right.

Cameron Trading Post

28 *53 mi north of Flagstaff on U.S. 89, 57 mi east of Grand Canyon Village on AZ 64.*

If you are heading to the Eastern Entrance on the South Rim or to the North Rim via U.S. 89 from Flagstaff and points south, **Cameron Trading Post** on the Navajo Indian Reservation is a worthwhile stop along the way. Most of the jewelry, rugs, baskets, and pottery sold here are made by Navajo and Hopi artisans, but some are created by New Mexico's Zuni and Pueblo Indians. Come armed with knowledge of Native American artisanship if you're looking at high-ticket items, some of which are sold at a separate gallery. Also at the post are a restaurant, cafeteria, grocery store, butcher shop, and post office. An outlet of the **Navajo Arts and Crafts Enterprises** (⊠ AZ 64/U.S. 89 ☎ 928/679–2244) stocks authentic Navajo products.

Where to Stay & Eat

$-$$ ✕🍴 **Cameron Trading Post.** Fifty-four miles north of Flagstaff, this historic trading post dates back to 1916. Southwestern-style rooms have carved-oak furniture, tile baths, and balconies overlooking the Colorado River. Native-stone landscaping—including fossilized dinosaur tracks—and a small, well-kept garden with lilacs, roses, and crab-apple trees are pleasant. Make your reservations far in advance for high season. The dining room (¢–$) serves a delicious homemade green chili and fry bread that is worth the stop alone. ⊠ *U.S. 89* ⌂ *Box 339, Cameron 86020* ☎ *928/679–2231 or 800/338–7385 Ext. 414* 🖷 *928/679–2350* ⊕ *www.camerontradingpost.com* ⇝ *62 rooms, 4 suites* ♨ *Restaurant, cafeteria, grocery, cable TV* ⊟ *AE, DC, MC, V.*

Fodor's Choice
★

¢ ⚠ **Cameron RV Park.** This park, open year-round, is adjacent to the Cameron Trading Post. There are 60 spaces with hookups for $15 a day. However, there are no public rest rooms or showers. No reservations accepted. ⊠ *U.S. 89* ⌂ *Box 339, Cameron 86020* ☎ *928/679–2231 or 800/338–7385* 🖷 *928/679–2350* ⊕ *www.camerontradingpost.com* ⇝ *60 RV sites* ♨ *Full hookups, dump station, drinking water, food service, general store* ☉ *Open year-round.*

en route | The route north from Cameron Trading Post on U.S. 89 offers a stunning view of the **Painted Desert** to the right. The desert, which covers thousands of square miles and stretches to the south and east, is a vision of subtle, almost harsh beauty, with windswept plains and mesas, isolated buttes, and barren valleys in pastel patterns. The sparse vegetation is mostly desert scrub, which provides sustenance for only the hardiest wildlife. Most of the undulating hills belong to the 200-million-year-old Chinle formation, the depository of countless fossil records.

About 30 mi north of Cameron Trading Post, the Painted Desert country gives way to sandstone cliffs that run for miles off to the right. Brilliantly hued and ranging in color from light pink to deep orange, the **Echo Cliffs** rise to more than 1,000 feet in many places. They are essentially devoid of vegetation, but in a few places high up, thick patches of tall cottonwood and poplar trees, nurtured by springs and water seepage from the rock escarpment, manage to thrive.

At Bitter Springs, 60 mi north of Cameron, U.S. 89A branches off from U.S. 89, running north and providing views of **Marble Canyon,** the geographical beginning of the Grand Canyon. Like the Grand Canyon, Marble Canyon was formed by the Colorado River. Traversing a gorge nearly 500 feet deep is **Navajo Bridge,** a narrow steel span built in 1929 and listed on the National Register of Historic Places. Formerly used for car traffic, it now functions only as a pedestrian overpass. The visitor center is informational and handy.

Lees Ferry Area

76 mi north of Cameron Trading Post, U.S. 89 to U.S. 89A.

★ **29** A turnoff at Marble Canyon Lodge, about 1 mi past Navajo Bridge in the small town of Marble Canyon, leads to historic **Lees Ferry,** 3 mi away. On a sharp bend in the Colorado River where Echo Cliffs and Vermilion Cliffs intersect, Lees Ferry is considered "mile zero" of the river—the point from which all distances on the rivers system in the Grand Canyon are measured.

This spot, one of the last areas in the mainland United States to be completely charted, was first visited by non–Native Americans in 1776, when Spanish priests Fray Francisco Atanasio Domínguez and Fray Silvestre Velez de Escalante tried, but failed, to cross the Colorado. In March of 1864, Mormon frontiersmen and missionary Jacob Hamblin made the first crossing by raft. Efforts by the Mormons to establish colonies in the area generated high ferry traffic in the 1870s through the 1890s. It became part of the Honeymoon Trail, a gateway to Utah for young couples who wanted their civil marriages in Arizona sanctified at the Latter-Day Saints temple in St. George. The ferry also became a crossing and a supply point for miners and other pioneers who shaped the American West. Its most infamous ferryman was John Doyle Lee, who tended the crossing for years before he was arrested and finally executed in connection with the Mountain Meadows massacre in Utah. The ferry was operational until 1928, when a bridge was finally built to span the river.

Lees Ferry retains a number of vestiges of the mining era, but it's now primarily known as the spot where most of the Grand Canyon river rafts put into the water. In addition, huge trout lurk in the river near here, so there are several places to pick up angling gear and a guide.

★ **30** West from the town of Marble Canyon, rising to the right of the highway, are the sheer, spectacular **Vermilion Cliffs,** in many places more than 3,000 feet high. Keep a sharp eye out for condors; these giant endangered birds were reintroduced into the area in the winter of 1996–97. Reports suggest that the birds, once in captivity, are surviving well in the wilderness.

Sports & the Outdoors

FISHING The Colorado River in the Lees Ferry area is known for good-size German brown and rainbow trout. This stretch of ice-cold, crystal clear water provides arguably the best trout fishing in the Southwest. Many rafters and fishermen stay the night in a campground near the river or in nearby Marble Canyon before hitting the river at dawn. Marble Canyon Lodge sells Arizona fishing licenses. **Lees Ferry Anglers** (⊠ Milepost 547, N. U.S. 89A, Marble Canyon ☎ 928/355–2261, 800/ 962–9755 outside Arizona ⊕ www.leesferry.com) operates guided fishing trips, starting from $280 per day; it practices year-round catch and release.

RAFTING **Arizona Raft Adventures** (⊠ 4050 E. Huntington Rd., Flagstaff, 86004 ☎ 928/526–8200 or 800/786–7238 ⊟ 928/526–8246 ⊕ www.azraft. com) organizes 6- to 14-day combination paddle-and-motor trips, all paddle and all motor trips for all skill levels. Trips, which average from $1,510 to $3,040, depart from May through October. With a reputation for high quality and a roster of 3- to 13-day trips, **Canyoneers** (⌂ Box 2997, Flagstaff, 86003 ☎ 928/526–0924 or 800/525–0924 ⊟ 928/527–9398 ⊕ www.canyoneers.com) is popular with those who want to include some hiking as well. The five-day "Best of the Grand" includes a hike down to Phantom Ranch. The April through September trips cost between $695 and $2,700.

Owned and operated by a mother-and-daughters team, **Diamond River Adventures** (⌂ Box 1300, Page, 86040 ☎ 928/645–8866 or 800/343–3121 ⊟ 928/645–9536 ⊕ www.diamondriver.com) offers both oar-powered and motorized river trips from 4 to 14 days from May through September. Prices range from $800 to $2,500. Expert and long-established **Grand Canyon Expeditions** (⊠ Box O, Kanab, UT 84741 ☎ 435/ 644–2691 or 800/544–2691 ⊟ 435/644–2699 ⊕ www.gcex.com) has guided the likes of the Smithsonian Institution along the Colorado River. You can count on them to take you down the river safely and in style: They limit the number of people on each boat to 14, and evening meals might include filet mignon, pork chops, or shrimp. The April through October trips cost $2,095 to $2,995 for 8 to 14 days.

Where to Stay & Eat

★ ¢–$$$ ✕⊞ **Marble Canyon Lodge.** This Arizona Strip lodge opened in 1929 on the same day the Navajo Bridge was dedicated. Three types of accommodations are available: rooms in the original building; standard motel rooms in the newer building; and two-bedroom apartments. You can sit on the porch swing of the native-rock lodge and look out on Vermilion Cliffs and the desert or play the 1920s piano. Zane Grey and Gary Cooper are among the well-known past guests. The restaurant ($–$$) serves steaks, seafood, pasta, and sandwiches. ⊠ ¼ *mi west of Navajo Bridge on U.S. 89A* ⌂ *Box 6001, Marble Canyon 86036* ☎ *928/355– 2225 or 800/726–1789* ⊟ *928/355–2227* ⊅ *52 units* ⌂ *Restaurant,* *room TVs, lounge, shop, laundry facilities, meeting room, airstrip, some pets allowed* ⊟ *AE, D, MC, V.*

¢–$ ✕▦ **Lees Ferry Lodge.** Geared toward the Lees Ferry trout-fishing trade, this lodge will outfit you, guide you, and freeze your catch. At the end of the day you can sit out on one of the garden patios of this rustic 1929 building, constructed of native stone and rough-hewn beams. Rooms are charming, if a bit quirky in their plumbing. The hotel's Vermilion Cliffs Bar and Grill ($–$$) is a popular gathering spot for river raft guides, and it serves good American fare—especially the steaks and ribs—in an authentic Western setting. The bar serves only wine and beer, but the extensive beer collection includes more than 100 beers brewed everywhere, from California to Czechoslovakia. ⊠ *4 mi west of Navajo Bridge on U.S. 89A* ⌂ *HC 67, Box 1, Marble Canyon 86036* ☎ *928/ 355–2231 or 800/451–2231* ⊕ *www.leesferrylodge.com* ⟵ *10 rooms, 2 5-person trailers* ⟐ *Restaurant, beer garden; no room phones, no TV in some rooms* ⊟ *AE, MC, V.*

¢–$ ▦ **Cliff Dwellers Lodge.** Built in 1949, this dining and lodging complex sits at the foot of Vermilion Cliffs. Rooms in the modern motel building are attractive and clean. **Lees Ferry Anglers** (☎ 928/355–2261 or 800/962–9755 ⊕ www.leesferry.com) is headquartered at this lodge, adding to the convenience of a fly-fishing trip on the Colorado River. ⊠ *U.S. 89A, 9 mi west of Navajo Bridge* ⌂ *HC 67, Box 30, Marble Canyon 86036* ☎ *928/355–2228 or 800/433–2543* ⊞ *928/355–2229* ⟵ *22 rooms* ⟐ *Restaurant, cable TV, fishing, bar, shops, some pets allowed (fee)* ⊟ *AE, D, MC, V.*

en route As you continue the journey to the North Rim, the immense blue-green bulk of the Kaibab Plateau stretches out before you. About 18 mi past Navajo Bridge, a sign directs you to the **San Bartolome Historic Site,** an overlook with plaques that tell the story of the Domínguez-Escalante expedition of 1776. At **House Rock Valley,** a large road sign announces the House Rock Buffalo Ranch, operated by the Arizona Game and Fish Department. A 23-mi dirt road leads to the home of one of the largest herds of American bison in the Southwest. You may drive out to the ranch, but be aware that you may not see any buffalo—the expanse of their range is so great that they frequently cannot be spotted from a car.

As it nears its junction with AZ 67, U.S. 89A starts climbing to the top of the **Kaibab Plateau,** heavily forested, filled with animals and birds, and more than 9,000 feet at its highest point. The rapid change from barren desert to lush forest is dramatic.

Jacob Lake

③① *25 mi west of town of Marble Canyon on U.S. 89A, at AZ 67.*

Jacob Lake junction is a good base camp for exploring the beautiful Kaibab Plateau, often described as an "island in the sky." The Kaibab squirrel— a tassel-eared squirrel found nowhere else in the world—is one of the many species of wildlife encountered here. The U.S. Forest Service's

Kaibab Plateau Visitor's Center (⊠ U.S. 89A/AZ 67 ☎ 928/643–7298) is open May–mid-October and offers several interpretive displays, books, and educational gifts. Gas and groceries are also available in the area.

Where to Stay & Eat

$–$$ ✕⌨ **Jacob Lake Inn.** The bustling lodge center at Jacob Lake Inn is a popular stop for those heading to the North Rim; it has a grocery store, a coffee shop, a restaurant (¢–$), and a large gift shop. Even if you don't plan to stay here, make sure to stop for one of their famous malts or milk shakes. The modest 5-acre complex in Kaibab National Forest has basic cabins and standard motel rooms that overlook the highways. ⊠ *AZ 67/U.S. 89A, 86022* ☎ *928/643–7232* ⊕ *www.jacoblake.com* ⤳ *14 rooms, 22 cabins* ⚭ *Restaurant, café, grocery; no a/c, no room phones, no room TVs* ⊟ *AE, D, MC, V.*

CAMPING   ⚠ **Demotte Campground.** Surrounded by tall pines, this U.S. Forest Ser-
¢   vice campground is 25 mi south of Jacob Lake. It has 23 single-unit (RV or tent) sites but no hookups, for $14 per day. The campground can only accommodate RVs that are 30 feet and under. There are interpretive campfire programs in summer. ⊠ *Off AZ 67* ⌂ *North Kaibab Ranger District, Box 248, Fredonia 86022* ☎ *928/643–7395* ⤳ *23 campsites* ⚭ *Flush toilets, fire pits, grill, picnic tables* ⚭ *Reservations not accepted* ☉ *Open mid-May–mid-Oct.*

¢   ⚠ **Jacob Lake Campground.** Fifty-three family and group RV and tent sites (no hookups) are available for $14 per vehicle per day at this U.S. Forest Service campground on a first-come, first-served basis. On summer evenings, rangers present interpretive programs. No reservations are accepted (except for groups of 10 or more). ⊠ *U.S. 89A/AZ 67* ⌂ *North Kaibab Ranger District, Box 248, Fredonia 86022* ☎ *928/ 643–7395* ⤳ *53 campsites* ⚭ *Flush toilets, fire pits, grills, picnic tables* ⚭ *Reservations not accepted* ☉ *Open May–Oct.*

¢   ⚠ **Kaibab Camper Village.** Fire pits and more than 70 picnic tables are spread out in this wooded spot, which is near a gas station, store, and restaurant. Reservations are accepted by the Canyoneers outfitter and are recommended, particularly during the height of the busy summer season. There are 50 tent sites ($12 for two people) and 80 RV and trailer sites ($22 for a pull-through with full hookup, $12 without hookup). ⊠ *AZ 67, ¼ mi south of U.S. 89A* ⌂ *Box 3331, Flagstaff 86003* ☎ *928/643–7804 in season, 800/525–0924, 800/525–0924 outside AZ in winter* 🖷 *928/527–9398* ⊕ *www.canyoneers.com* ⤳ *80 full hookups, 50 tent sites* ⚭ *Portable toilets, full hookup, drinking water, showers, fire pits, picnic tables* ☉ *Open mid-May–mid-Oct.*

en route   AZ 67 runs south from U.S. 89A to the North Rim; the route passes through one of the thickest stands of ponderosa pine in the United States. You'll frequently see mule deer and Kaibab squirrels, which live only on this plateau. You can recognize the squirrels by their all-white tails and the long tufts of white hair on their ears. The mule deer are recognizable by their large antlers. Keep an eye out for mountain lions, elk, and black bear . . . they're here, but seeing them is rare. You're more likely to see wild turkeys.

GRAND CANYON NATIONAL PARK: THE NORTH RIM

The North Rim, within the 14,000-square-mi Arizona Strip, draws only about 10% of the Grand Canyon's visitors but is, many believe, even more gorgeous than the South Rim. Sitting at an elevation 1,000 feet higher than the South Rim, the northern edge offers a more stretched out view of the buttes and ridges scattered though the wide expanse cut by the Colorado River millions of years ago. Because of its remote location, the North Rim provides a much more intimate and unhurried experience than the heavily trafficked South Rim. The atmosphere is much more relaxed here, leaving you time to wander through the old-growth ponderosa-pine forest. However, the North Rim is closed during the long, hard winter. The 8,000-foot elevation, which keeps things cool in the summer, is arduous in the winter.

Author Edward Abbey once wrote: "I find that in contemplating the natural world my pleasure is greater if there are not too many others contemplating it with me, at the same time." The North Rim will give you that opportunity.

HOURS   The North Rim is open mid-May through mid-October, depending on the weather. AZ 67 from Jacob Lake is often closed due to snowfall from mid-October to mid-May, and during these times all facilities at the North Rim are closed.

The entrance gates are open 24 hours but are generally staffed from about 7 AM to 7 PM. If you arrive when there's no one at the gate, you may enter legally without paying.

ADMISSION FEES   A fee of $20 per vehicle (regardless of the number of passengers) is collected as you enter the North Entrance. Those on foot, bicycle, or motorcycle pay $10 per person. In all cases, this fee is for one week's access to the entire park.

The North Rim

Fodor's Choice   *44 mi south of Jacob Lake on AZ 67.*
★

Unlike the tourist-driven South Rim, the north side only offers one historic lodge and restaurant and a single campground. The easily accessible Bright Angel Point offers a wonderful view of the canyon and is the starting point for several rim trails. You can drive to three different, developed viewpoints. Point Imperial and Cape Royal await at the end of a winding, scenic drive—with several stops along the way, the trip can easily consume half a day. The highest point on the North Rim at 8,800 feet, Point Imperial overlooks the Painted Desert to the east and dramatic views of the Grand Canyon. Cape Royal, a popular sunset destination, showcases the jagged landscape within the canyon. At this viewpoint, you'll also get a glimpse of the Colorado River, which is framed by a natural stone arch whimsically called the Angels Window. The third developed viewpoint, Point Sublime, requires four-wheel drive and half a day of effort, but in return offers some of the best views in the canyon.

CloseUp
GRAND CANYON NATURE PRIMER

ALMOST TWO BILLION YEARS WORTH of the Earth's history is written between the colored layers of sedimentary rock that are stacked from the river bottom to the top of the plateau. The South Rim's Coconino Plateau is fairly flat, at an elevation of about 7,000 feet, and covered with stands of piñon and ponderosa pine, juniper, and Gambel's oak. On the Kaibab Plateau on the North Rim, Douglas fir, spruce, quaking aspen, and more ponderosa-pine trees prevail. In spring, you're likely to see asters, sunflowers, and lupine in bloom at both rims.

Eighty-eight mammal species inhabit the park, as well as 300 species of birds, 24 kinds of lizard, and 24 kinds of snake. The rare Kaibab squirrel is found only on the North Rim, and the pink Grand Canyon rattlesnake lives at lower elevations within the canyon. Hawks and ravens are visible year-round, usually coasting on the wind above the canyon. The endangered California condor has been reintroduced to the canyon. Park rangers give daily talks on the magnificent birds, whose wingspan measures nine feet. In spring, summer, and fall, mule deer are abundant at the South Rim, even aggressive. Don't be tempted to feed them; it's illegal, and it will disrupt their natural habits and increase your risk of being bitten.

Both sunrise and sunset in the park are spectacular when skies are clear. In any season, some of the best spots to enjoy or photograph them are along Hermit Road west of Grand Canyon Village and Yaki and Lipan points between the Village and Desert View, and Cape Royal on the North Rim.

★ ③③ The trail to **Bright Angel Point** (⊠ North Rim Dr., Grand Canyon), one of the most awe-inspiring overlooks on either rim, starts on the grounds of the Grand Canyon Lodge and runs along the crest of a point of rocks that juts into the canyon for several hundred yards. The walk is only 1 mi round-trip, but it's an exciting trek accented by sheer drops just a few feet away on each side of the trail. In a few spots where the route is extremely narrow, metal railings ensure visitors' safety. The temptation to clamber out to precarious perches to have your picture taken could get you killed. Every year several people die from falls at the Grand Canyon.

★ ③⑤ **Cape Royal** (⊠ AZ 67, Grand Canyon) is about 23 mi southeast of Grand Canyon Lodge. A short walk on a paved road from the parking lot leads to this southernmost viewpoint on the North Rim. In addition to a large slice of the Grand Canyon, Angels Window, a giant, erosion-formed hole, can be seen through the projecting ridge of Cape Royal. At Angels Window Overlook, ⅓ mi north of here, **Cliff Springs Trail** starts its 1-mi route (round-trip) through a forested ravine. The trail, narrow and precarious in spots, passes ancient dwellings, winds beneath a limestone overhang, and terminates at Cliff Springs, where the forest opens on another impressive view of the canyon walls.

🌙 ㉜ **Grand Canyon Lodge** (✉ AZ 67, Grand Canyon) is literally at the end of the road. Built in 1928 by the Union Pacific Railroad, the massive stone structure is listed on the National Register of Historic Places. Its huge sunroom has hardwood floors, high-beam ceilings, and a marvelous view of the canyon through plate-glass windows. Don't forget to pay your respects to Brighty, the faithful burro of children's-book fame, honored by a bronze sculpture near the lounge's west entrance. On warm days visitors sit in the sun and drink in the surrounding beauty at an equally spacious outdoor viewing deck, where National Park Service employees deliver free lectures on geology and history. Lunch, dinner, or a snack in the lodge's rock-and-log dining room is an integral part of the North Rim experience; the food is good and reasonably priced. If you don't want a full meal, just buy a soda at Pizza Place or a drink at the saloon and sit out on the west veranda to watch the sun set over the canyon.

🌙 The **Transept Trail** (✉ AZ 67, Grand Canyon) begins near the corner of the Grand Canyon Lodge's east patio. This 3-mi (round-trip) trail stays near the rim for part of the distance before it plunges into the forest, ending at the North Rim Campground and General Store, 1½ mi from the lodge.

㉞ Eleven miles northeast of Grand Canyon Lodge is one of the North Rim's most popular lookouts, **Point Imperial** (✉ AZ 67, Grand Canyon), the highest vista point (elevation 8,803 feet) at either rim, offering magnificent views of both the canyon and the distant country: the Vermilion Cliffs to the north, the 10,000-foot Navajo Mountain to the northeast in Utah, the Painted Desert to the east, and the Little Colorado River canyon to the southeast.

㉟ Talk about solitude. There's plenty of it at **Point Sublime** (✉ North Rim Dr., Grand Canyon), where you can camp within a few feet of the canyon's edge. Sunrises and sunsets are spectacular and worth a roll or two of film every day. The winding road, through gorgeous high country, to Point Sublime is only 17 mi, but it will take you at least an hour, more if you want to absorb the scenery en route. The road is intended only for vehicles with high-road clearance (pickups and four-wheel-drive vehicles). It is also necessary to be properly equipped for wilderness road travel. Check with a park ranger or at the information desk at Grand Canyon Lodge before taking this journey. You may camp here only with a permit from the Backcountry Office at the park-ranger station.

FodorsChoice ★

Sports & the Outdoors

BICYCLING The **Rainbow Rim Trail** is an 18-mi, one-way trail that begins at Parissawampitts. It travels past four other fantastic viewpoints—Fence, Locust, North Timp, and Timp—winding through a ponderosa pine forest and up and down through side canyons, aspen groves, and pristine meadows. The trail's elevation of 7,550 feet doesn't vary more than a 200 feet along the way. The Rainbow Rim Trail is in the **Kaibab National Forest** (☎ 928/635–4061 or 800/863–0546 ⊕ www.fs.fed.us/r3/kai).

HIKING **Cliff Springs Trail** is an easy 1-mi North Rim walk near Cape Royal. The trailhead begins across from Angels Window Overlook and descends through a forested ravine. Narrow and precarious in spots, the trail passes ancient dwellings, winds beneath a limestone overhang, and terminates at the boulder-protected Cliff Springs.

Ken Patrick Trail begins at a trailhead on the east side of the North Kaibab trailhead parking lot. It travels 10 mi from the trailhead at 8,250 feet to Point Imperial at 8,803 feet. There is no water on this primitive trail, which crosses drainages and occasionally detours around fallen trees. But the trip is worth it—with the views at the highest point on either rim at the end of the road.

The trailhead to **North Kaibab Trail** is about 2 mi north of the Grand Canyon Lodge. Only open from May through October, the trail begins at 8,250 feet and travels down to the Colorado River at 2,400 feet. This is a long, steep hike that drops 5,850 feet over a distance of 14½ mi and is recommended for experienced hikers only. The National Park Service recommends that day hikers not go any farther than Roaring Springs (5,020 feet) before turning to hike back up out of the canyon. Cottonwood Campground (4,080 feet) has drinking water in summer, rest rooms, shade trees, and a ranger. Like Bright Angel and South Kaibab trails, this one also leads to Phantom Ranch.

ⓒ **Transept Trail** is a popular 1½-mi trail that starts near Grand Canyon Lodge, ducks through dense forests, and emerges on the rim to a dramatic view of a large stream through Bright Angel Canyon. The trail, which begins at 8,255 feet, has little elevation change. The well-marked route leads to a side canyon called Transept Canyon, which geologist Clarence Dutton named in 1882—announcing that it was "far grander than Yosemite."

Round-trip, **Widforss Trail** is 9⁹⁄₁₀ mi with an elevation change of 200 feet, unusually great for a rim hike. The Widforss trailhead, at 8,100 feet, is across from the North Kaibab Trail parking lot. The trail passes through shady forests of pine, spruce, fir, and aspen on its way to Widforss Point, at 7,900 feet. You are likely to see wildflowers in summer, and this is the best trail on the North Rim for viewing fall foliage. It is named in honor of Gunnar M. Widforss, an artist renowned for his paintings of National Park landscapes.

MULE RIDES   **Canyon Trail Rides** (☎ 435/679–8665 ⊕ www.canyonrides.com) conⓒ ducts short mule rides suitable for children on the easier trails along the North Rim. A one-hour ride, available to those seven and older, runs about $30. Half-day trips on the rim or into the canyon (minimum age 8) cost $55; full-day trips (minimum age 12), which include lunch and water, go for $105. These excursions are very popular, so try to make reservations in advance. Rides are available daily from May 15 to October 15.

Where to Stay & Eat

$ ✕⊡ **Grand Canyon Lodge.** This historic property, constructed mainly in Fodor'sChoice the 1920s and '30s, is the premier lodging facility in the North Rim area. ★ The main building has limestone walls and timbered ceilings. Lodging options include small, rustic cabins; larger cabins (some with a canyon view and some with two bedrooms); and newer, traditional motel rooms. You might find marinated pork kebabs or linguine with cilantro on the dining room's dinner menu ($$). Dining room reservations are essential and should be made as far in advance as possible. ✉ *AZ 67, Grand Canyon National Park, North Rim 86052* ☎ *303/297–2757 reservations only, 928/638–2611 direct to hotel (no reservations)* 🖷 *303/297–3175 reservations only* 🌐 *www.grandcanyonnorthrim.com* 🛏 *44 rooms, 157 cabins* ♨ *Cafeteria, dining room, bar, shop, laundry facilities; no a/c, no room TVs, no smoking* 🚭 *AE, D, MC, V* ☯ *Closed mid-Oct.–mid-May.*

$–$$ 🏨 **Kaibab Lodge.** In the woods 5 mi north of the North Rim entrance, this 1920s property comprises rustic cabins with simple furnishings. The lodge has a cozy fireplace that's welcome in the early evening, as the chill can be felt shortly after the sun sets—even in summer. ✉ *AZ 67, Grand Canyon* 🖈 *HC 64, Box 30, Fredonia 86022* ☎ *928/638–2389 or 928/526–0924 in winter* 🛏 *36 rooms* ♨ *Restaurant, some pets allowed; no a/c, no room TVs* 🚭 *D, MC, V* ☯ *Closed mid-Oct.–mid-May.*

CAMPING 🏕 **North Rim Campground.** The only designated campground at the
¢ North Rim of Grand Canyon National Park, 3 mi north of the rim, has 83 RV and tent sites (no hookups) for $15 per day. ✉ *AZ 67, Grand Canyon* 🖈 *National Park Reservation Service, Box 1600, Cumberland, MD 21501* ☎ *800/365–2267* 🌐 *reservations.nps.gov/index.cfm* 🛏 *83 campsites* ♨ *Flush toilets, dump station, drinking water, guest laundry, showers, fire grates, picnic tables, general store* 🗺 *Reservations essential* ☯ *Open mid-May–mid-Oct.*

Elsewhere in the Arizona Strip

The Arizona Strip—the part of the state directly north of Grand Canyon National Park—is sometimes called the American Tibet because of its isolation; it has only two small towns, Fredonia and Colorado City. The combined population of these two towns is less than 7,000, and fewer than 700 permanent residents—including 150 members of the Kaibab-Paiute tribe—live in the rest of the strip. Services in this part of the state are extremely limited; top off your tank when you find a gas station, and keep an ample supply of drinking water in your car. Once you get away from the paved highways in this region, roadways tend to be rough and may be impassable when wet.

③⑧ **Pipe Spring National Monument,** ninety miles from the North Rim and
Fodor'sChoice 14 mi from Fredonia, has one of the few reliable sources of water in the
★ Arizona Strip. The park contains a restored rock fort and ranch, with exhibits of Southwestern frontier life. In summer there are living-history demonstrations of ranching operations or weaving. The fort was intended to fend off Native American attacks (which never came because a peace treaty was signed before the fort was finished). It ended up functioning mainly as headquarters for a dairy and ranching operation and in 1871 became the first telegraph station in the Arizona Territory. About ½ mi north of the monument is a campground and picnic area. While you're here check out the expanded museum and visitor center, which is now operated jointly by the National Park Service and the Kaibab-Paiute tribe. ✉ *401 N. Pipe Spring Rd.* 🖈 *HC 65, Box 5 Fredonia 86022* ☎ *928/643–7105* 🌐 *www.nps.gov/pisp* 🎟 *$4* ☯ *Historic structures daily 8:30–4:30, visitor center and museum daily 8–5.*

Six miles back toward Fredonia from Pipe Spring on AZ 389, a dirt road leads 50 mi south through starkly beautiful, uninhabited country to **Toroweap Overlook,** a lonely and awesome viewpoint over one of the narrowest stretches of the Grand Canyon (less than 1 mi across). The overlook also contains the deepest sheer cliff (more than 3,000 feet straight down) in the Grand Canyon. From this vantage point, you can see upstream to sedimentary ledges, cliffs, and talus slopes. Looking downstream, you can see miles of the lava flow that forms steep deltas, some of which look like black waterfalls frozen on the cliff. Be sure you have plenty of gas, drinking water, good tires, and a reliable car; a high-clearance vehicle (one that sits high up off the ground, like a pickup truck) is best for this trip. It's a rough drive, especially over the last 3 mi over slickrock. Allow up to three hours to drive from the highway to the overlook. Don't try to go in wet weather, when the dirt road is likely to be washed out. There's a ranger station near the rim as well as a primitive campground, which has 11 first-come, first-served tent sites, picnic tables, grates and compost toilets. If you plan to return the same day, you should make motel reservations in advance at an Arizona Strip motel.

THE GRAND CANYON A TO Z

To research prices, get advice from other travelers, and book travel arrangements, visit ⊕ *www.fodors.com*

ACCESSIBILITY

Rim Trail and all the viewpoints along the South Rim are accessible to wheelchairs. Private vehicles with accessibility permits are allowed access to Hermit Road and the access road to Yaki Point year-round. The North Rim viewpoints are steeper than those on the South Rim but are wheelchair-accessible. TDD phones are available as well. For detailed information, see the *Grand Canyon Accessibility Guide,* free from Canyon View Information Plaza, Yavapai Information Station, Tusayan Museum, Desert View Information Center, and all entrance stations. There are free wheelchairs for use inside the park; inquire at one of the information centers. Temporary handicapped-parking permits are available at Canyon View Information Plaza, Yavapai Observation Center, and all entrance stations.

For handicapped shuttle services within the park, make your request a day in advance. Wheelchair-accessible tours are offered by prior arrangement through Grand Canyon National Park Lodges.
🚩 Grand Canyon National Park Lodges ☎ 928/638-2631. **Handicapped shuttle reservations** ☎ 928/638-2631.

AIR TRAVEL

Several carriers fly to the Grand Canyon Airport from Las Vegas, including Air Vegas, Scenic Airlines, and Vision Air, which offer service from North Las Vegas Airport to the Grand Canyon.
🚩 **Air Vegas** ☎ 800/255-7474 ⊕ www.airvegas.com. **Scenic Airlines** ☎ 800/634-6801 ⊕ www.scenic.com. **Vision Air** ☎ 702/261-3850.

AIRPORTS

North Las Vegas Airport in Las Vegas is the primary air hub for flights to Grand Canyon Airport. You can also make connections into the Grand Canyon from Sky Harbor International Airport in Phoenix.

🚹 **Grand Canyon National Parks Airport** ☏ 928/638-2446. **North Las Vegas Airport** ☏ 702/261-3806. **Phoenix Sky Harbor International Airport (PHX)** ☏ 602/273-3300.

TRANSFERS The Tusayan/Canyon Airport Shuttle operates between Grand Canyon Airport and the nearby towns of Tusayan and Grand Canyon Village; it makes hourly runs daily between 8:15 AM and 5:15 PM, with additional trips in the summer months.

Fred Harvey Transportation Company offers 24-hour taxi service at Grand Canyon Airport, Grand Canyon Village, and the nearby village of Tusayan. Taxis also make trips to other destinations in and around Grand Canyon National Park.

🚹 **Fred Harvey Transportation Company** ☏ 928/638-2822. **Tusayan/Canyon Airport Shuttle** ☏ 928/638-0821.

BIKE TRAVEL

Bicycles are not permitted on any of the Grand Canyon's designated trails, but there are miles of scenic paved and unpaved roads in the national park, which are accessible to bikers. The Greenway Trail and Hermit Road are open to bike traffic year-round. The park roads have narrow shoulders and are heavily trafficked, so if you ride on them use extreme caution. There are no rentals or tours available at either North or South Rim.

BUS TRAVEL

There is no public bus transportation to the Grand Canyon. Greyhound Lines provides bus service Williams, Flagstaff, and Kingman. Schedules change frequently; call or check the Web site for information.

🚹 **Greyhound Lines** ☏ 800/231-2222 ⊕ www.greyhound.com.

BUS TRAVEL WITHIN THE GRAND CANYON

Within the park, there are three shuttle routes. Hermits Rest Route operates from March through November between Grand Canyon Village and Hermits Rest. You can catch this shuttle every 15 to 30 minutes at one hour before sunrise until one hour after sunset, depending on the season. Check for exact shuttle times. The Village Route operates year-round in the village area and offers shuttles from one hour before sunrise until after dark. This shuttle service is the easiest access to the Canyon View Information Center. The Kaibab Trail Route travels from Canyon View Information Center to Yaki Point, including a stop at the South Kaibab Trailhead.

From mid-May to late October, the Trans Canyon Shuttle leaves Bright Angel Lodge at 1:30 PM and arrives at the North Rim's Grand Canyon Lodge about 6 PM. The return trip leaves the North Rim each morning at 7 AM, arriving at the South Rim at about noon. One-way fare is $65, round-trip $110. A 50% deposit is required two weeks in advance.

🚹 **Trans Canyon Shuttle** ☏ 928/638-2820.

CAMPING SUPPLIES

The Canyon Marketplace has three locations in the South Rim area: at Grand Canyon Village, in the nearby village of Tusayan, and at Desert View near the park's east entrance. The main store, in Grand Canyon Village, is a department store that has a deli and sells a full line of camping, hiking, and backpacking supplies, in addition to groceries. The store also rents hiking supplies including backpacks, tents, and walking sticks.

The North Rim General Store, inside the park at the North Rim Campground, carries groceries, some clothing, and travelers' supplies.

🚶 **The Canyon Marketplace** ⊠ Grand Canyon Village ☎ 928/638-2262 ⊠ Tusayan ☎ 928/638-2854 ⊠ Desert View ☎ 928/638-2393. **North Rim General Store** ⊠ North Rim Campground, Grand Canyon North Rim ☎ 928/638-2611.

CAR TRAVEL

Most of Arizona's scenic highlights are many miles apart, and a car is essential for touring the state. However, you won't really need one if you're planning to visit only the Grand Canyon's most popular area, the South Rim. Some people choose to fly to the Grand Canyon and then hike, catch a shuttle or taxi, or sign on for bus tours or mule rides in Grand Canyon Village.

If you are driving to Arizona from the east, or coming up from the southern part of the state, the best access to the Grand Canyon is from Flagstaff. You can take U.S. 180 northwest (81 mi) to Grand Canyon Village on the South Rim. Or, for a scenic route with stopping points along the canyon rim, drive north on U.S. 89 from Flagstaff, turn left at the junction of AZ 64 (52 mi north of Flagstaff), and proceed north and west for an additional 57 mi until you reach Grand Canyon Village on the South Rim.

To visit the North Rim of the canyon, proceed north from Flagstaff on U.S. 89 to Bitter Springs. Then take U.S. 89A to the junction of AZ 67. Travel south on AZ 67 for approximately 40 mi to the North Rim, which is 210 mi from Flagstaff.

If you are crossing Arizona on Interstate 40 from the west, your most direct route to the South Rim is on AZ 64 (U.S. 180), which runs north from Williams for 58 mi to Grand Canyon Village.

GASOLINE The only gas station inside the national park is at Desert View, and this station operates only from March 31 to September 30 dependent on snowfall. Gas is available year-round near the South Entrance at Moqui Lodge (though the lodge itself is now closed), in Tusayan, and at Cameron, to the east.

At the South Rim, in Grand Canyon Village, the Public Garage is a fully equipped AAA garage that provides auto repair daily 8 to noon and 1 to 5 as well as 24-hour emergency service. This is a garage for repairs only and does not sell gasoline.

At the North Rim, the Chevron service station, which repairs autos, is located inside the park on the access road leading to the North Rim Campground. No diesel fuel is available at the North Rim.

🚶 **Chevron** ☎ 928/638-2611. **Public Garage** ☎ 928/638-2225.

ROAD
CONDITIONS
When driving off major highways in low-lying areas, watch for rain clouds. Flash floods from sudden summer rains can be deadly.

The South Rim stays open to auto traffic year-round, although access to Hermits Rest is limited to shuttle buses in summer because of congestion. Roads leading to the South Rim near Grand Canyon Village and the parking areas along the rim are badly congested in summer as well. However, if you visit from October through April, you should experience only light to moderate traffic and have no problem with parking.

Reaching elevations of 8,000 feet, the more remote North Rim has no services available from late October through mid-May. AZ 67 south of Jacob Lake is closed by the first heavy snowfall in November or December and remains closed until early to mid-May.

To check on Arizona road conditions, call the Arizona Department of Transportation's recorded hot line.
🗂 **Arizona Department of Transportation** ☎ 888/411-7623 ⊕ www.dot.state.az.us.

EMERGENCIES
There are no pharmacies at the North or South Rim. Prescriptions can be delivered daily to the South Rim Clinic from Flagstaff.
🗂 Ambulance, Fire & Police **Emergency services** ☎ 911, 9-911 from in-park lodgings.
🗂 Hospitals **Grand Canyon Walk-in Clinic** ⊠ Grand Canyon Village ☎ 928/638-2551. **North Rim Clinic** ⊠ Grand Canyon Lodge, Cabin 1, Grand Canyon North Rim ☎ 928/638-2611 Ext. 222.

FEES
It costs $20 per motorized vehicle to enter the park. Individuals arriving by bicycle or foot pay $10. In all cases, this fee is for one week's access. Backcountry permits are $10 plus $5 per person per night.

HEALTH
The Grand Canyon is unforgiving, and it claims several lives each year. Most of those deaths are avoidable.

The trek down into the canyon appears deceptively easy; the route back up is much longer than most other mountain day hikes and is very fatiguing. Before hiking into the canyon, assess the proposed hiking conditions versus your physical condition. During summer months, temperatures inside the canyon can climb to 105°F. Carry water on hikes to the Inner Canyon—at least 1 to 1½ gallons per day. To avoid dehydration, drink frequently, about every 10 minutes, especially during summer months. Likewise, take food—preferably salty energy snacks such as trail mix and pretzels, along with bananas, fig bars, and other fructose-rich foods. Do not drink alcohol or caffeine, which accelerate dehydration; for the same reason, avoid processed sugar. Wear hiking boots that have been broken in and proven on previous hikes. Also wear sunscreen and a hat. Carry a first-aid kit. In case of a medical emergency, stay with the distressed person and ask the next hiker to go for help. Do not attempt to make the round-trip to the Colorado River in one day. More than 250 hikers are rescued from the depths of the canyon each year, and most of those are attempting to hike from the rim to the canyon and back in a day.

Be careful when you or your children are near the edge of the canyon or walking along any of the trails that descend into it. Guardrails exist only on portions of the rims. Before engaging in any strenuous exercise, be aware that the canyon rims are more than 7,000 feet in altitude. Being at this height can cause some people—even those in good shape—to become dizzy, faint, or nauseated.

HOURS
The South Rim is open year-round. The North Rim is open mid-May through mid-October. AZ 67 from Jacob Lake is often closed due to snowfall from mid-October to mid-May, and during these times all facilities at the North Rim are closed.

The entrance gates are open 24 hours but are generally staffed from about 7 AM to 7 PM. If you arrive when there's no one at the gate, you may enter legally without paying.

LOST & FOUND
Report lost or stolen items or turn in found items at Canyon View Information Plaza or Yavapai Observation Station at 928/638–7798 from Tuesday to Friday, 8 AM to 5 PM. For items lost or found at a dining or lodging establishment, call 928/638–2631.

MAIL & SHIPPING
There's a U.S. Post Office in the Market Plaza shopping center near Yavapai Lodge. It's open weekdays 9 to 4:30 and Saturday 11 to 3.

MONEY MATTERS
There is a 24-hour teller machine at the Bank One South Rim office in Market Plaza near the General Store and at the Maswik Lodge. There are also ATM machines at several hotels and stores in Tusayan. No banking facilities are located within Grand Canyon National Park at the North Rim. **fi Bank One** ☎ 928/638-2437.

OUTDOOR ACTIVITIES & SPORTS
HIKING PERMITS Overnight hikes in the Grand Canyon require a permit that can be obtained by written or faxed requests to the Backcountry Information Center. Permits cost $10, plus $5 per person, per night. The free Backcountry Trip Planner should answer all of your hiking questions. Permits are limited; however, reservations can be made up to four months in advance. If you arrive at the canyon without a permit, go to the Backcountry Office at either rim—at the South Rim near Maswik Lodge, at the North Rim at the Ranger Station. Space may be available due to a last-minute cancellation—but don't count on it. **fi Backcountry Office** ⬧ Box 129, Grand Canyon 86023 ☎ 928/638-7875 🖷 928/ 638-2125.

PETS
Pets are allowed in Grand Canyon National Park; however, they must be on a leash at all times. Pets are not allowed below the rim or on the

park buses, with the exception of service animals. There is a kennel, near the Maswik Lodge, which houses cats and dogs. It is open daily from 7:30 AM to 5 PM. Reservations are highly recommended.

🖪 **Grand Canyon Kennel** ☎ 928/638-0534.

TOURS

AIR TOURS Flights by plane and helicopter over the canyon are offered by a number of companies, departing for the Grand Canyon Airport at the south end of Tusayan. Prices and lengths of tours vary, but you can expect to pay about $75 per adult for short plane trips and approximately $100 for a brief helicopter tour.

🖪 **Air Grand Canyon** ⊠ Grand Canyon Airport, Tusayan ☎ 928/638-2686 ⊕ www.airgrandcanyon.com. **AirStar Helicopters/Airlines** ⊠ Grand Canyon Airport, Tusayan ☎ 928/638-2622 or 800/962-3869 ⊕ www.airstar.com. **Grand Canyon Airlines** ⊠ Grand Canyon Airport, Tusayan ☎ 928/638-2463 or 866/235-9422 ⊕ www.grandcanyonairlines.com. **Grand Canyon Helicopters** ⊠ Grand Canyon Airport, Tusayan ☎ 928/638-2764 or 800/541-4537 ⊕ www.grandcanyonhelicoptersaz.com. **Papillon Helicopters** ⊠ Grand Canyon Airport, Tusayan ☎ 928/638-2419 or 800/528-2418 ⊕ www.papillon.com.

BUS TOURS The Fred Harvey Transportation Company in Grand Canyon Village operates daily motor-coach sightseeing trips along the South Rim. Prices range from $13 for shorter trips to $34 for the longer ones. Children under 16 ride free with an adult.

🖪 **Fred Harvey Transportation Company** ⊠ Grand Canyon Village ☎ 928/638-2631.

HIKING TOURS The Grand Canyon Field Institute leads a full program of educational guided hikes around the canyon year-round. Topics include everything from archaeology and backcountry medicine to photography and natural history. Reservations are essential for the tours, which range from $85 to $1,200. For a personalized tour of the Grand Canyon and surrounding sacred sites, contact Marvelous Marv, the Indiana Jones of Williams, whose knowledge of the area is as extensive as his repertoire of local legends.

🖪 The **Grand Canyon Field Institute** ⊡ Box 399, Grand Canyon 86023 ☎ 928/638-2485 or 866/471-4435 ⊕ www.grandcanyon.org/fieldinstitute. **Marvelous Marv** ⊡ Box 544, Williams 86046 ☎ 928/635-4948 ⊕ www.marvelousmarv.com.

JEEP TOURS If you'd like to get off the pavement and see parts of the park that are accessible only by dirt road, a jeep tour can be just the ticket. Rides can be rough; if you have had back injuries, check with your doctor before taking a jeep tour. From March through October, Grand Canyon Outback Jeep Tours leads daily, 1½- to 4½-hour, off-road tours within the park, as well as in Kaibab National Forest. Expect to pay from $35 to $83, and reservations are essential.

🖪 **Grand Canyon Outback Jeep Tours** ⊡ Box 1772, Grand Canyon 86023 ☎ 928/638-5337 or 800/320-5337 🖷 928/638-5337 ⊕ www.grandcanyonjeeptours.com.

RAFTING TOURS Nearly two dozen companies currently offer excursions, reservations for raft trips (excluding smooth-water, one-day cruises) often need to be made more than six months in advance. A complete list of concessionaires offering trips on the Colorado River is available on the Grand Canyon National Park Web site. National Park Service white-water concessionaires include Arizona River Runners, Canyoneers, Diamond River Adventures, Grand Canyon Expeditions, and Tour West. For a smooth-water, one-day trip check out Wilderness River Adventures. Prices for river-raft trips vary greatly, depending on type and length. Half-day trips on smooth water run as low as $54 per person. Trips that negotiate the entire length of the canyon and take as long as 12 days can cost more than $2,000.

🏇 **Arizona River Runners** ☎ 602/867-4866 or 800/477-7238 ⊕ www.raftarizona.com. **Canyoneers, Inc.** ☎ 928/526-0924, 800/525-0924 outside Arizona ⊕ www.canyoneers. com. **Diamond River Adventures, Inc.** ☎ 928/645-8866 or 800/343-3121 ⊕ www. diamondriver.com. **Grand Canyon Expeditions** ☎ 435/644-2691 or 800/544-2691 ⊕ www.gcex.com. **Tour West, Inc.** ☎ 801/225-0755 or 800/453-9107 ⊕ www.twriver. com. **Wilderness River Adventures** ☎ 928/645-3279 or 800/992-8022 ⊕ www. riveradventures.com.

SPECIAL INTEREST TOURS The National Park Service sponsors all sorts of free Ranger Programs at both the South and the North rims. These orientation activities include daily guided hikes and talks. The focus may be on any aspect of the canyon—from geology, flora, and fauna to history and early inhabitants. Programs change seasonally. For schedules, go to Canyon View Information Plaza on the South Rim or the Grand Canyon Lodge on the North Rim.

Several of the free programs are designed especially for children. Children ages 9 to 11 use field guides, binoculars, magnifying glasses, and other exploration tools on the one-hour Junior Ranger Discovery Pack Program. Park rangers also coordinate Way Cool for Kids, free, hour-long introductions to the park for children ages 7 to 11. Kids and rangers walk around the Village Rim area and talk about local plants and animals, history, or archaeology. These two programs are only offered in the summer; check for a schedule of times at the Canyon View Information Plaza.

🏇 **Ranger Programs** ✉ Box 129, Grand Canyon 86023 ☎ 928/638-7888 ⊕ www.nps. gov/grca

VISITOR INFORMATION

Every person arriving at the South or North Rim is given a detailed map of the area. Centers at both rims also publish a free newspaper, the *Guide,* which contains a detailed area map; it is available at the visitor center, entrance stations, and many of the lodging facilities and stores. The park also distributes *Accessibility Guide,* a free newsletter that details the facilities accessible to travelers with disabilities. Grand Canyon National Park is the contact for general information. Write ahead for a complimentary *Trip Planner,* updated regularly by the National Park Service.

Several Web sites are useful for trip-planning information, including the National Park Service's Web site, which has information on fees and permits. Try thecanyon.com, a commercial site where you'll find information on lodging, dining, and general park information. You can use the Xanterra Parks & Resorts Grand Canyon Web site to make reservations for park lodging, mule rides, bus tours, and some smooth-water rafting trips. The park service allows camping reservations to be made online as well, through the campground reservation vendor.

In summer, transportation-services desks are maintained at Lodge, Maswik Lodge, and Yavapai Lodge in Grand Canyon Village; in winter, the one at Yavapai is closed. The desks provide information and handle bookings, sightseeing tours, taxi and bus services, mule and horseback rides, and accommodations at Phantom Ranch (at the bottom of the Grand Canyon). The concierge at El Tovar can also arrange most tours, with the exception of mule rides and lodging at Phantom Ranch.

Grand Canyon Lodge has lodging and general information about the North Rim year-round, but you cannot make reservations for the lodge directly through the hotel. For information on local services during the season in which the North Rim is open, generally mid-May to late October, depending on the weather, you can phone the lodge directly.

The Williams and Forest Service Visitor Center, run jointly by the U.S. Forest Service and the Williams Chamber of Commerce, offers information on the Kaibab National Forest and the entire Grand Canyon region.

🔝 Grand Canyon Contacts **Grand Canyon Lodge** ☎ 928/638-2611 direct to hotel or 303/297-2757 during the winter off-season. **Grand Canyon National Park** ✉ Box 129, Grand Canyon 86023 ☎ 928/638-7888 recorded message 🖷 928/638-7797 ⊕ www. nps.gov/grca. **Grand Canyon National Park Lodges** ✉ Xanterra Parks and Resorts, 14001 E. Iliff Ave., Suite 600, Aurora, CO 80014 ☎ 303/297-2757 🖷 303/297-3175 ⊕ www.grandcanyonlodges.com. **North and South Rim Camping** ✉ National Park Reservation Service, Box 1600, Cumberland, MD 21501 ☎ 800/365-2267 ⊕ http://reservations.nps.gov/index.cfm. **The Canyon.com** ⊕ www.thecanyon.com. **Williams and Forest Service Visitor Center** ✉ 200 W. Railroad Ave., at Grand Canyon Blvd., Williams 86046 ☎ 928/635-4061.

THE NORTHEAST

4

STAND IN THE SHADOW
of the sheer walls of Canyon de Chelly ⇨*p.201*

WITNESS A KATSINA DANCE
on a remote Hopi Mesa ⇨*p.197*

PAY TRIBUTE
to the Navajo code-talkers of World War II ⇨*p.214*

RIDE OFF INTO A HOLLYWOOD SUNSET
in Monument Valley ⇨*p.215*

BE A RUBBERNECKER
in the Goosenecks Region of Utah ⇨*p.216*

EXPLORE ANCIENT PUEBLOS
in the cliffs of Tgesi Canyon ⇨*p.218*

GET THE BIG PICTURE
in Antelope Canyon ⇨*p.223*

MAKE YOURSELF AT HOME
on a houseboat on Lake Powell ⇨*p.227*

Updated by
Bob & Gloria
Willis

NORTHEAST ARIZONA IS a vast and magnificent land of lofty buttes, towering cliffs, and turquoise skies so clear that horizons appear endless. Most of the land in the area belongs to the Navajo and Hopi peoples, who cling to ancient traditions based on spiritual values, kinship, and an affinity for nature. In many respects life on the Hopi Mesas has changed little during the last two centuries, and visiting this land can feel like traveling to a foreign country. In such towns as Tuba City and Window Rock it's not uncommon to hear the gliding vowels and soft consonants of the Navajo language, a tongue as different from Hopi as English is from Chinese. As you drive in the vicinity, tune your AM radio to 660 KTNN, the Voice of the Navajo Nation. You'll quickly understand why the U.S. Marine Navajo "code talkers" communicating in their native tongue were able to devise a code within their language that was never broken by the Japanese.

The Navajo Nation encompasses more than 27,000 square mi, an area that would rank it larger than 10 of the 50 states. In its approximate center sits the 4,000-square-mi Hopi Reservation, a series of adobe villages built on high mesas overlooking cultivated land. On Arizona's northern and eastern borders, where the Navajo Nation continues into Utah and New Mexico, the Navajo National Monument and Canyon de Chelly contain haunting cliff dwellings of ancient people who lived in the area 1,500 years ago. Glen Canyon Dam, which abuts the far northwestern corner of the reservation on U.S. 89, holds back more than 200 mi of emerald waters known as Lake Powell.

Most of northeast Arizona is desert country, but it is far from boring: eerie and spectacular rock formations as colorful as desert sunsets highlight immense mesas, canyons, and cliffs; towering stands of ponderosa pine cover the Chuska Mountains to the north and east of Canyon de Chelly. Navajo Mountain to the north and west in Utah soars more than 10,000 feet, and the San Francisco Peaks climb to similar heights to the south and west by Flagstaff. According to the Navajo creation myth, these are two of the four mountainous boundaries of the sacred land where the Navajo first emerged from the Earth's interior.

Exploring the Northeast

The Navajo Nation, which encircles the Hopi Reservation, occupies most of northeastern Arizona. Canyon de Chelly is in the eastern part of the reservation. The Navajo National Monument and Monument Valley are in north-central "Navajoland" (a term used by the Navajo in promotional material). In the northwestern corner of the Arizona portion of the reservation are Lake Powell and Glen Canyon Dam. Note: Northeastern Arizona is a sparsely inhabited area with few roads and services. Rarely do establishments have numbered street addresses; even the post office operates on the basis of landmarks. Don't count on using your cell phone in many portions of the region, though talks are under way with the Navajo Nation to install cell-phone towers in some areas.

Numbers in the text correspond to numbers in the margin and on the Northeast Arizona map.

About the Restaurants

Northeastern Arizona is a vast area with small hamlets and towns scattered miles apart, and there are very few stores or restaurants along the highway. Most of the restaurants serve basic Native American and Southwestern cuisine and are very casual, with "formal dining" virtually nonexistent. Navajo and Hopi food consists mainly of mutton stew, Hopi *piki* (paper-thin, blue-corn bread), and Navajo fry bread. Navajo tacos are fry bread piled with refried beans, ground beef, lettuce, tomato, scallions, cheese, avocado, sour cream, and salsa. When spread with butter, honey, and confectioner's sugar, Navajo fry bread becomes a delicious dessert. In the smaller reservation communities, only fast-food may be available.

About the Hotels

One of the most important things to know when traveling in northeastern Arizona is which of the scattered communities have motels. Bed-and-breakfasts have begun to proliferate in Page. Contact the Page/Lake Powell Chamber of Commerce or the Navajo Nation Visitors Center for a list of area B&Bs, campgrounds, and RV facilities. Accommodations are also available in Native American hogans, eight-side domed houses made of mud, logs, or even contemporary building materials. During summer months, it is especially wise to make reservations. Most motels throughout this region are national chains and are clean, comfortable, and well maintained. Unless otherwise indicated, all rooms have air-conditioning, private baths, telephones, and TVs.

WHAT IT COSTS				
$$$$	**$$$**	**$$**	**$**	**¢**
RESTAURANTS over $30	$20–$30	$12–$20	$8–$12	under $8
HOTELS over $250	$175–$250	$120–$175	$70–$120	under $70

Restaurant prices are per person for a main course at dinner. Hotel prices are for two people in a standard double room in high season, excluding taxes and service charges.

Timing

Summer is a busy time around Lake Powell, and reservations for accommodations are suggested. Travelers seeking a quieter vacation should plan to visit between early November and late March, when the crowds—and the prices—ebb. The first weekend of September after Labor Day is a good time to be at Window Rock, when the Navajo Nation Annual Tribal Fair takes place. It's the world's largest Native American fair and includes a rodeo, traditional Navajo music and dances, food booths, and an intertribal powwow. August and September bring the Hopi Harvest Festival, a celebration featuring Harvest and Butterfly social dances.

NAVAJO NATION EAST

Land has always been central to the history of the Navajo people: it's embedded in their very name. The Tewa were the first to call them *Navahu*—which means "large area of cultivated land." But according to the Navajo creation myth, they were given the name *ni'hookaa diyan*

If you have
2 days

If you are just driving through the area on your way west, you might start off in ► 🖾 **Window Rock** ❶. From there, it's an easy drive to some of the most interesting sights in northeastern Arizona. On your first day, visit **Canyon de Chelly** ❷. On the second, set out for the **Hopi Mesas** ❺–❼, stopping along the way at **Hubbell Trading Post National Historic Site** ❸ and, perhaps, **Keams Canyon Trading Post** ❹ for a mid-morning snack.

If you have
5 days

If you plan to spend a bit more time exploring the region after a trip to the Grand Canyon, head north on U.S. 89 on your first day to ► 🖾 **Tuba City** ❽. Along the way, you might wish to stop by ► **Cameron Trading Post** ❾. Explore the area, and relax for the night. On the second day, head east at Moenkopi on AZ 264 for the **Hopi Mesas** ❺–❼. (And fill your tank before you leave since Tuba City is the last stop for gas before the mesas.) Have lunch at the **Hopi Cultural Center,** then return to Tuba City and head northeast on U.S. 160 toward 🖾 **Kayenta** ❿, where you can spend your second night. Get up early the next day to visit the **Navajo National Monument** ⓮ and hike to Beta-Takin or Keet Seel pueblo (if you have made reservations in advance). Spend your third night at the lodge at 🖾 **Goulding's Trading Post** ⓭ in Monument Valley. The next day, visit **Monument Valley Navajo Tribal Park** ⓫, and then take U.S. 160 north to where it connects with U.S. 191 near the town of Mexican Water. Head south for Chinle, a good base for touring 🖾 **Canyon de Chelly** ❷.

diné—"holy earth people"—by their creators. Today, among tribal members, they call themselves the Diné. The eastern portion of the Arizona Navajo Nation (in Navajo, *diné bikéyah*) is a dry but often surprisingly green land, especially in the vicinity of the aptly named Beautiful Valley, south of Canyon de Chelly along U.S. 191. A landscape of rolling hills, wide arroyos, and small canyons, the area is dotted with traditional Navajo hogans, sheepfolds, cattle tanks, and wood racks. The region's easternmost portion is marked by tall mountains and towering sandstone cliffs cut by primitive roads that are generally accessible only by horse or four-wheel-drive vehicles.

Window Rock

► ❶ *192 mi from Flagstaff, east on Interstate 40 and north on Indian Highway 12; 26 mi from Gallup, New Mexico, north on U.S. 191 and west on NM and AZ 264.*

Named for the immense arch-shaped "window" in a massive sandstone ridge above the city, Window Rock is the capital of the Navajo Nation and the center of its Tribal Government. With a population of fewer than 5,000, this community serves as the business and social center for Navajo families throughout the reservation. Window Rock is a good place to stop for food, supplies, and gas. The **Navajo Nation Council Chambers** is a handsome structure that resembles a large ceremonial hogan.

The murals on the walls depict scenes in the history of the tribe, and the bell beside the entrance was a gift to the tribe by the Santa Fe Railroad to commemorate the thousands of Navajos who worked to build the railroad. Visitors can observe sessions of the council, where 88 delegates representing 110 reservation chapters meet on the third Monday of January, April, July, and October. Turn east off Indian Highway 12, about ½ mi north of AZ 264, to reach the Council Chambers. **Window Rock Navajo Tribal Park,** near the Council Chambers, is a memorial park honoring Navajo veterans, including the famous World War II code talkers. ⊠ *AZ 264* ☎ *928/871–6417.*

The **Navajo Nation Museum,** on the grounds of the former Tse Bonito Park off AZ 264, is devoted to the art, culture, and history of the Navajo people and has an excellent selection of books on the Navajo Nation. The museum hosts exhibitions of native artists each season; call for a listing of shows. Housed in the same building as the Navajo Nation Museum is the **Navajo Nation Visitor Center,** a great resource for all sorts of information on reservation activities. Within walking distance of the Navajo Nation Museum, the **Navajo Arts and Crafts Enterprises** displays local artwork, including pottery, jewelry, and blankets. ⊠ *AZ 264, next to Navajo Nation Inn* ☎ *928/871–6673 museum, 928/871–7371 visitor center* ☎ *Free* ☉ *Weekdays 1–5.*

Many all-Indian rodeos are held near the center of downtown at the **Navajo Tribal Fairgrounds.** The community hosts the annual Fourth of July celebration, with a major rodeo, ceremonial dances, and a parade. The Navajo Nation Tribal Fair, much like a traditional state fair, is held in early September. It offers standard county-fair rides, midway booths, contests, powwow competitions, and an all-Indian rodeo. ⊠ *AZ 264* ☎ *928/871–6282 Navajo Nation Fair Office.*

Where to Stay

¢ 🏨 **Navajo Land Day's Inn.** This motel in St. Michaels, 4 mi west of Window Rock, offers standard rooms appointed with Southwestern-style decor. A Denny's restaurant is also on the property. ⊠ *392 W. AZ 264, St. Michaels 86511* ☎ *928/871–5690 or 800/329–7466* ☎ *928/871–5699* ⊕ *www.daysinn.com* 🛏 *65 rooms, 8 suites* ᐃ *Restaurant, cable TV, indoor pool, gym, hot tub, sauna, meeting rooms, some pets allowed (fee), no-smoking rooms* ⊟ *AE, D, MC, V.*

¢ 🏨 **Navajo Nation Inn.** Rooms in this two-story beam-and-stucco motel are decorated with a Navajo-style palette of tan, orange, and yellow that complements the basic pine furniture. The upstairs Haskeneini Restaurant serves Navajo cuisine in addition to regular American fare (you can build your own Navajo tacos), and the gift shop sells authentic Navajo jewelry. ⊠ *48 W. AZ 264, at Indian Hwy. 12, 86515* ☎ *928/871–4108 or 800/662–6189* ☎ *928/871–5466* ⊕ *www.navajonationinn.com* 🛏 *56 rooms* ᐃ *Restaurant, cable TV, shop, Internet, meeting rooms, some pets allowed, no-smoking rooms* ⊟ *AE, D, MC, V* ⧓ *CP.*

Shopping

An outlet of the **Navajo Arts and Crafts Enterprises** (⊠ AZ 264 at Indian Hwy. 12, next to Navajo Nation Inn ☎ 928/871–4090) stocks au-

4

Fishing

Lake Powell, known for its bass fishing, also holds other varieties including bluegill and pike, and the Colorado River below Glen Canyon Dam is known for its large trout. Keep in mind that Lake Powell stretches into Utah; a fishing license is required for each state. The eastern region of the Navajo Reservation has scattered lakes, most of them remote and small, but two of the more popular and accessible lakes are near Canyon de Chelly: Wheatfields Lake, on Indian Highway 12 about 11 mi south of the community of Tsaile, and Many Farms Lake, near the community of Many Farms, on U.S. 191. Permits are required for fishing on the reservation.

Hiking

Some of the best hikes in this region are in Canyon de Chelly, up the streambed between the soaring orange-and-white sandstone cliffs, with the remains of the ancient ancestral Puebloan communities frequently in view. Mummy Cave is especially worth a look, its three-story watchtower nearly perfectly preserved. The more weathered Antelope House and White House stand against the sweeping canyon cliffs as impressive reminders of a bygone era. The Navajo National Monument offers impressive hikes to two ruins: Beta-Takin, a settlement dating back to AD 1250, and Keet Seel, which dates back as far as AD 950. Both are in alcoves at the base of gigantic overhanging cliffs. Remember, you cannot hike on private property or tribal land without permission; it's important to be respectful of this law.

Hopi Ceremonies

The Hopi are well known for colorful ceremonial dances, many of which are supplications for rain, fertile crops, and harmony with nature. Most of these ceremonies take place in village plazas and kivas (underground ceremonial chambers) and last two days or longer; outsiders are sometimes permitted to watch segments of some ceremonies but are never allowed into kivas unless invited. Seasonal katsina dances performed at agricultural ceremonies may be restricted, so it's best to inquire upon arrival. Each clan has its own sacred rituals, starting times, and dates, which are determined by tribal elders. Outsiders should be respectful, dress appropriately (no baseball caps), and adhere to the proper etiquette while observing dances.

Shopping

Most visitors to the area are tempted by the beautiful pottery, turquoise and sterling-silver jewelry, handwoven baskets, Navajo wool rugs, and other examples of Native American crafts. Many trading posts also carry the work of some New Mexico tribes, including exquisite inlaid Zuni jewelry and the world-acclaimed pottery of the Pueblo people. A vast majority of the products sold on the Hopi and Navajo Reservations are authentic, but the possibility of imitations does exist. Trading posts are very reliable, as are most roadside stands, which can offer some outstanding values, but be wary of solo vendors hanging around parking lots. If you're planning on shopping on the Hopi Reservation or elsewhere outside the Navajo trading posts, it's a good idea to carry cash or traveler's checks. Phone lines in the region are sometimes unreliable, which can make credit-card use impossible.

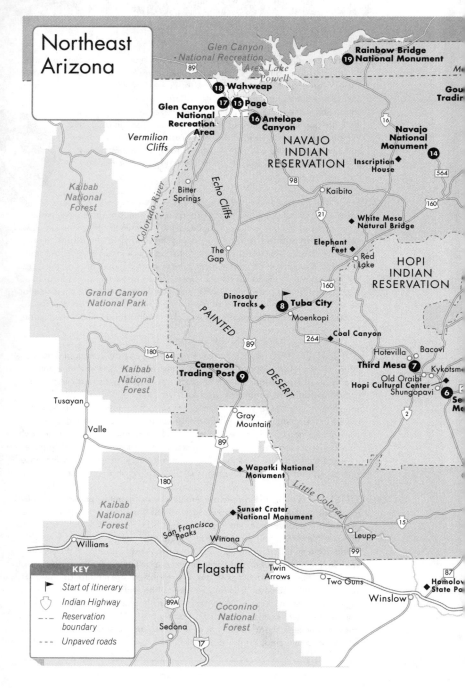

Northeast Arizona

Glen Canyon National Recreation Area Lake Powell

89

18 Wahweap

17 15 Page

Glen Canyon National Recreation Area

16 Antelope Canyon

19 Rainbow Bridge National Monument

Gou Tradir

Navajo National Monument 14

564

NAVAJO INDIAN RESERVATION

Inscription House

Vermilion Cliffs

Kaibab National Forest

Colorado River

Bitter Springs

Echo Cliffs

98

Kaibito

160

21

White Mesa Natural Bridge

The Gap

Elephant Feet

Red Lake

HOPI INDIAN RESERVATION

Grand Canyon National Park

Dinosaur Tracks

8 Tuba City

160

Moenkopi

Coal Canyon

180 64

PAINTED

89

264

Hotevilla

Bacovi

Third Mesa 7

Kykotsm

DESERT

Old Oraibi

Hopi Cultural Center

Shungopavi

6

Cameron Trading Post 9

Tusayan

Kaibab National Forest

Valle

Gray Mountain

89

Se Me

2

Wapatki National Monument

180

Little Colorad

Sunset Crater National Monument

15

Kaibab National Forest

Williams

San Francisco Peaks

Winona

Leupp

99

89A

Twin Arrows

Two Guns

87

Homolo State Pa

Sedona

17

Coconino National Forest

Flagstaff

Winslow

KEY

- ⚑ Start of itinerary
- ⬡ Indian Highway
- --- Reservation boundary
- --- Unpaved roads

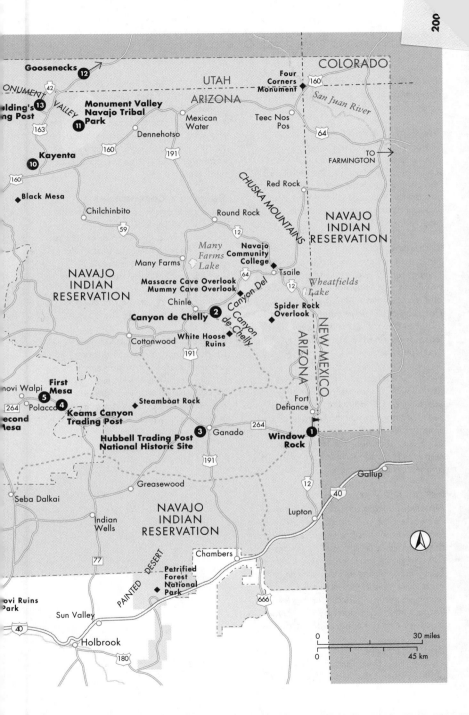

RESERVATION RULES

Visitors to the Navajo Nation and Hopi Reservation should observe several rules when visiting either reservation.

Alcohol & Drugs
The possession and consumption of alcoholic beverages or illicit drugs is illegal on both Hopi and Navajo land. You cannot purchase alcohol legally while you are on the reservations, and you should not bring any alcohol onto the reservations with you.

Camping
No open fires are allowed in reservation campgrounds; you must use grills or fireplaces. You may not gather firewood on the reservation—bring your own. Camping areas have quiet hours from 11 PM to 6 AM. Pets must be kept on a leash or confined. Pick up after yourself and don't litter.

Hopi Shrines
Don't touch shrines. Hopi spirituality is intertwined with daily life, and objects that seem ordinary to you might have deeper significance. If you come upon a collection of objects at or near the Hopi Mesas, respect the person who left the offerings and do not disturb them.

Permits & Permissions
No off-trail hiking or rock climbing is allowed unless you are accompanied by a local guide. A tribal permit is required for fishing in lakes or streams. Violations of fish and game laws are punishable by heavy fines, imprisonment, or both. Off-road travel is not allowed unless accompanied by a local tour guide. Respect private property by not wandering across or through residential areas.

Photography
Always ask permission before taking photographs of the locals. You may have to pay to take the picture, and even if no money is requested, consider offering a dollar or two to the person whose photograph you have taken. The Navajo are very open about photographs; the Hopi do not allow photographs at all, including videos, tape recordings, notes, and even sketches.

Religious Ceremonies
Should you see a ceremony in progress while traveling, look for posted signs indicating who is welcome. If there are no signs, check with local shops or the village community to see if the ceremony is open to the public. Unless you are specifically invited, stay out of kivas (ceremonial rooms) and stay on the periphery of dances or processions.

Respect for the Land
Do not wander across or through residential areas or disturb property. Do not disturb or remove animals, plants, rocks, petrified wood, or artifacts. They are protected by Tribal Antiquity and federal laws, which are strictly enforced.

thentic tribal artworks purchased from craftspeople across the reservation. Local artisans are occasionally at work here. Major credit cards are accepted.

Canyon de Chelly

2 *25 mi west of Window Rock on AZ 264, then north on U.S. 191.*

Fodor's Choice
★

Home to ancestral Puebloans for more than 1,000 years, the nearly 84,000-acre Canyon de Chelly (pronounced d'*shay*) is one of the most spectacular natural wonders in the Southwest. On a smaller scale, it rivals the Grand Canyon for beauty. Its main gorges—the 26-mi-long Canyon de Chelly ("canyon in the rock") and the adjoining 35-mi Canyon del Muerto ("canyon of the dead")—have sheer, heavily eroded sandstone walls that rise to 1,100 feet. Ancient pictographs and petroglyphs decorate some of the cliffs, and within the canyon complex there are more than 7,000 archaeological sites. Gigantic stone walls rise hundreds of feet above streams, hogans, tilled fields, peach orchards, and sheep-grazing lands.

The first inhabitants of the canyons arrived more than 2,000 years ago. In AD 750, these Basket Makers disappeared and were replaced by Pueblo tribes who constructed stone cliff dwellings. The departure of the Pueblo people around AD 1300 is widely believed to have resulted from changing climatic conditions, soil erosion, dwindling local resources, disease, and internal conflict. Present-day Hopis see these people as their ancestors. Beginning around AD 780, Hopi farmers settled here, followed by the Navajo around 1300. The Navajo migrated from far northern Canada; no one is sure when they arrived in the Southwest. Despite evidence to the contrary, most Navajos hold that their people have always lived here and that the Diné passed through three previous underworlds before emerging into this, the fourth or Glittering World.

Prehistoric ruins can be found near the base of cliffs and perched on high, sheltering ledges. The dwellings and cultivated fields of the present-day Navajo lie in the flatlands between the cliffs, and those who inhabit the canyon today farm much the way their ancestors did. Most residents leave the canyon in winter but return in early spring to farm and tend their sheep.

The **visitor center** has exhibits on the history of the cliff dwellers and provides information on scheduled hikes, tours, and National Park Service programs offered throughout the summer months.

Both Canyon de Chelly and Canyon del Muerto have a paved rim drive with turnoffs and parking areas. Each drive takes about two hours. Overlooks along the rim drives provide incredible views of the canyon; be sure to stay on trails and away from the canyon edge, and to control children and pets at all times.

The **South Rim Drive** (36 mi round-trip with seven overlooks) of Canyon de Chelly starts at the visitor center and ends at **Spider Rock Overlook**, where cliffs plunge 1,000 feet to the canyon floor. The view here is of two pinnacles, Speaking Rock and Spider Rock; the latter rises about

800 feet from the canyon floor and is considered a sacred place. Other highlights on the South Rim Drive are Junction Overlook, where Canyon del Muerto joins Canyon de Chelly; White House Overlook, from which a trail leads to the **White House Ruin,** with dwelling remains of nearly 60 rooms and several kivas; and Sliding House Overlook, where you can see ruins on a narrow, sloped ledge across the canyon. The carved and sometimes narrow trail down the canyon side to White House Ruin is the only access to Canyon de Chelly without a guide. If you have a fear of heights, this may not be a hike you want to make.

The **North Rim Drive** (34 mi round-trip with four overlooks) of Canyon del Muerto also begins at the visitor center and continues northeast on Indian Highway 64 toward the town of Tsaile. Major stops include Antelope House Overlook, the site of a large ruin named for the animals painted on an adjacent cliff; the Mummy Cave Overlook, where two mummies were found inside a remarkably unspoiled pueblo dwelling, the monument's largest; and Massacre Cave Overlook, the last stop, which marks the spot where an estimated 115 Navajo were killed by the Spanish in 1805. (The rock walls of the cave are still pockmarked from the Spaniards' ricocheting bullets.) ⊠ *Indian Hwy. 7, 3 mi east of U.S. 191, Chinle* 🕾 *928/674–5500 visitor center* ⊕ *www.nps.gov/cach* 🖾 *Free* ⊙ *Daily 8–5.*

In Tsaile, Navajo medicine men worked in conjunction with architects to design the town's six-story **Diné College.** Because all important Navajo activities traditionally take place in a circle (a hogan is essentially circular), the campus was laid out in the round, with all of the buildings inside its perimeter. Diné College's **Hatathli Museum** is actually two museums in one: one concentrates on Navajo culture, and the other contains intertribal exhibits from across the United States. ⊠ *Indian Hwy. 12, south of Indian Hwy. 64, Tsaile* 🕾 *928/724–3311 college, 928/724– 6653 museum* 🖾 *By donation* ⊙ *Museum weekdays 8:30–4.*

To the north of Tsaile are the impressive **Chuska Mountains,** covered with sprawling stands of ponderosa pine. There are no established hiking trails in the Chuska Mountains, but up-to-date hiking information and backcountry-use permits (rarely granted if a Navajo guide does not accompany the trip) can be obtained through the Navajo Nation. ⊠ *Navajo Nation Parks and Recreation Department, Bldg. 36A, E. AZ 264, Window Rock* 🕾 *Box 2520, 86515* 🕾 *928/871–6647* ⊕ *www. navajonationparks.org.*

Sports & the Outdoors

HIKING From late May through early September, free three-hour ranger-led hikes depart from the visitor center at 9 AM. Also in summer, two four-hour hikes (about $10 per person) leave from the visitor center in the morning and afternoon. Some trails are strenuous and steep; others are easy or moderate. Regardless, those with health concerns or a fear of heights should proceed with caution. Call ahead if you are interested in a hike: they're canceled occasionally due to local customs or events.

Only one hike within Canyon de Chelly National Monument—the **White House Ruin Trail** on the South Rim Drive—can be done without an authorized guide. The trail starts near White House Overlook and runs along sheer walls that drop about 550 feet. If you have concerns about height, be aware that the path gets narrow and somewhat slippery along the way. The hike is 2½ mi round-trip, and hikers should carry their own drinking water.

Private, guided hikes to the interior of the canyons cost about $20 per hour with a three-hour minimum for groups of up to four people. (Don't venture into the canyon without a guide, or you'll face a stiff fine.) For overnights, you'll need a guide as well as permission to stay on private land. If you have a four-wheel-drive vehicle and want to drive yourself, guides will accompany you for a charge of about $20 an hour with a three-hour minimum for up to three vehicles. All Navajo guides are members of the **Tsegi Guide Association** (⊠ Canyon de Chelly Visitor Center, Indian Hwy. 7, Chinle ☎ 928/674–5500 ⊕ www.nps.gov/cach). You can hire a guide on the spot at the visitor center, or you can call ahead and make a reservation.

HORSEBACK RIDING

Justin's Horse Rental (⊠ Indian Hwy. 7, near the South Rim Drive entrance ⌂ Box 881, Chinle 86503 ☎ 928/674–5678) conducts horseback rides into the canyon for $10 per hour for each horse plus $15 per hour for a guide. Two-day, one-night guided tours run about $190 per person and include dinner and lunch. Owner Justin Tso will gladly arrange longer or shorter rides through either canyon. **Totsonii Ranch** (⊠ South Rim Dr. ⌂ Box 434, Chinle 86503 ☎ 928/755–6209), 13 mi from visitor center to the end of the paved road, offers four-hour round-trip horseback rides 1,000 feet down Bat Trail to Spider Rock. Rates are $10 per hour for each horse plus $15 per hour for a guide. Contact Lee Bigwater for more information.

JEEP TOURS

Canyon de Chelly Tours (☎ 928/674–3772) offers private jeep tours into Canyon de Chelly and arranges group tours and overnight camping in the canyon as well as late day and evening tours. Entertainment such as storytellers, music, and Navajo legends can be arranged with advance reservation. Treks with **Thunderbird Lodge Canyon Tours** (⊠ Thunderbird Lodge Gift Shop, Indian Hwy. 7, Chinle ☎ 928/674–5841 or 800/679–2473), in six-wheel-drive vehicles, are available from late spring to early fall. Half-day tours are $39.95 and start at 9 AM and 2 PM daily; all-day tours cost $64.95 and include lunch.

Where to Stay & Eat

Chinle is the closest town to Canyon de Chelly. There are several comfortable and good lodgings with restaurants as well as a supermarket and a campground. Be aware that you'll probably be approached by panhandlers in the grocery store parking lot, as well as hungry, forlorn, homeless dogs. In late August each year, Chinle is host to the Central Navajo Fair, a public celebration complete with a rodeo, carnival, and traditional dances.

★ $–$$ ✕▦ **Thunderbird Lodge.** In an ideal location within the national monument's borders, this pleasant establishment has stone-and-adobe units that match the architecture of the site's original 1896 trading post. Rooms have rough-hewn beam ceilings, rustic wooden furniture, and

Navajo-style decor. The cafeteria (¢–$) is in the original trading post and serves reasonably priced soups, salads, sandwiches, and entrées, including charbroiled steaks. The lodge also offers truck tours of Canyon de Chelly and Canyon del Muerto. ⊠ *Indian Hwy. 7* ⌂ *Box 548, Chinle 86503* ☎ *928/674–5841 or 800/679–2473* ⊕ *www.tbirdlodge. com* ↙ *74 rooms* ♨ *Cafeteria, cable TV, shop, travel services* ▤ *AE, D, DC, V.*

$ ✕▥ **Best Western Canyon de Chelly Inn.** This two-story motel about 3 mi from Canyon de Chelly has cheerful rooms with modern oak furnishings and Native American–print bedspreads and drapes. All rooms have coffeemakers. The on-site Junction restaurant (¢–$$) opens for breakfast at 6:30 AM; traditional Navajo, Mexican, and American fare is served until 9 PM. ⊠ *100 Main St.* ⌂ *Box 295, Chinle 86503* ☎ *928/674–5875 or 800/327–0354* 🖷 *928/674–3715* ⊕ *www.canyondechelly.com* ↙ *102 rooms* ♨ *Restaurant, cable TV, pool, some pets allowed, no-smoking rooms* ▤ *AE, D, DC, MC, V.*

$ ✕▥ **Holiday Inn Canyon de Chelly.** Once Garcia's Trading Post, this motel near Canyon de Chelly is less generic than you might expect: the exterior is territorial fort in style. Rooms, on the other hand, are predictably pastel and contemporary. The lobby restaurant (¢–$$), low-key by most standards, is the most upscale eatery in the area, serving well-prepared specialties such as mutton stew with fry bread and honey. The hotel restaurant offers a box picnic ($5.95) for its guests and has a gift shop stocked with local Native American arts and crafts. ⊠ *Indian Hwy. 7* ⌂ *Box 1889, Chinle 86503* ☎ *928/674–5000* 🖷 *928/674–8264* ⊕ *www.sixcontinentshotels.com* ↙ *108 rooms* ♨ *Restaurant, cable TV, pool, shop, no-smoking rooms* ▤ *AE, D, DC, MC, V.*

¢ ▥ **Many Farms Inn.** Many Farms High School runs this facility, which is staffed by Navajo students of hotel management. It's not fancy, but rooms are pleasant and contain two single beds, which means single or double occupancy only. Bathrooms are shared, and you'll have to go to the first floor to use pay phones or watch TV. ⊠ *U.S. 191 and Indian Hwy. 59* ⌂ *Box 307, Many Farms 86538* ☎ *928/781–6362* 🖷 *928/781–6355* ↙ *30 rooms with shared bath* ♨ *Refrigerators; no room phones, no room TVs* ▤ *No credit cards* ⊙ *Closed weekends Aug.–May.*

CAMPING ⛺ **Cottonwood Campground.** This sometimes cramped and noisy camp-
¢ ground has 52 RV sites (maximum length 35 feet; no hookups) and 95 tent sites that are available free, on a first-come, first-served basis. Cottonwood trees shade the sites. Although it's open year-round, there are limited facilities from November to March. No reservations. ⊠ *Indian Hwy. 7, near Canyon de Chelly visitor center, Chinle 86503* ☎ *928/674–5501* ⊕ *www.nps.gov/cach* ↙ *52 RV sites, 95 tent sites* ♨ *Flush toilets, drinking water, grills, picnic tables* ⊙ *Open year-round.*

¢ ⛺ **Spider Rock Campground.** Cordial Navajo owner Howard Smith makes everyone feel comfortable at this informal campground nestled in low piñons within a few hundred yards of the canyon. Howard occasionally offers "sweat lodges." The hand-hewn hogans have interior fire pits and are ideal for winter camping. The camp is just a short drive from the famous Spider Rock site and overlook. There's a 3-mi self-guided hike to the rim overlooking ancestral Puebloan ruins in Wild Cherry Canyon, and Howard will also customize guided hikes into the Canyon on such routes as Grandmother's Trail, which has ancestral Puebloan footholds and handholds worn into the sandstone. Howard sells firewood and limited food and camping items. ⊠ *Indian Hwy. 7, 10 mi east of Canyon de Chelly Visitor Center* ☎ *Box 2509, Chinle 86503* ☏ *928/674–8261 or 877/910–2267* ⊕ *www.home.earthlink.net/~spiderrock* ⊠ *Tent sites $10, partial hookups $15, hogans $25* ⊸ *30 camp sites, 2 hogans* ⚬ *Pit toilets, partial hookups (electricity), dump station, drinking water, showers, fire pits, picnic tables* ⊙ *Open year-round.*

Hubbell Trading Post National Historic Site

❸ *40 mi south of Canyon de Chelly, off AZ 264; 32 mi west of Window Rock.*

John Lorenzo Hubbell, a merchant and friend of the Navajo, established this trading post in 1878. Hubbell taught, translated letters, settled family quarrels, and explained government policy to the Navajo, and during an 1886 smallpox epidemic, he turned his home into a hospital and ministered to the sick and dying. Hubbell died in 1930 and is buried near the trading post.

The National Park Service Visitor Center exhibits illustrate the post's history, and you can take a self-guided tour of the grounds and visit the Hubbell Trading Post, which contains a fine display of Native American artistry. The visitor center has a fairly comprehensive bookstore specializing in Navajo history, art, and culture; local weavers often demonstrate their craft on site.

The **Hubbell Trading Post Store** is famous for "Ganado red" Navajo rugs, which are sold at the store here. The quality is outstanding and prices are high but fair—rugs can cost anywhere from $100 to around $30,000. Considering the time that goes into weaving each one, the prices are quite reasonable. It is hard to resist these beautiful designs and colors, and it's a pleasure just to browse around this rustic spot, where Navajo artists frequently show their work. Documents of authenticity are provided for all works. Note: When photographing weavers, ask permission first. They expect a few dollars in return. ⊠ *AZ 264, 1 mi west of town, Ganado* ☎ *928/755–3475 park office, 928/755–3254 store* ⊕ *www.nps.gov/hutr* ⊠ *Free* ⊙ *Daily 8–5.*

⬭ en route | About 20 mi west of Hubbell Trading Post on AZ 264 is **Steamboat Rock,** an immense, jutting peninsula of stone that resembles an early steamboat, complete with a geologically formed waterline. At Steamboat Rock you are only 5 mi from the eastern boundary of the Hopi Reservation.

THE HOPI MESAS

The Hopi occupy 10 villages in regions referred to as First Mesa, Second Mesa, and Third Mesa. Although these areas have similar languages and traditions, each has its own individual features. Generations of Hopitu, "the peaceful people," much like their Puebloan ancestors, have lived in these settlements of stone-and-adobe houses, which blend in with the earth so well that they appear to be natural formations. Television aerials, satellite dishes, and automobiles notwithstanding, these Hopi villages still impart the air of another time.

Descendants of the ancient Hisatsinom, the Hopi number about 10,000 people today. Their culture can be traced back 2,000 years, making them one of the oldest known tribes in North America. They successfully developed "dry farming" and grow a variety of vegetables and corn—called maize—as their basic food. The Hopi, who are often called the "corn people," incorporate nature's cycles into most of their religious rituals. In the celebrated Snake Dance ceremony, dancers carry venomous snakes in their mouths in order to appease the gods and to bring rain. Aside from farming the land, the Hopi create fine pottery and basketwork and excel in wood carving of katsina dolls—the spirits of the invisible life forces of the Hopi. The dolls are carved not as toys but as tools to instruct children about the hundreds of katsina spirits. Today the finer carvings are collector's items.

Although you do not need permission before entering the Hopi Reservation, you must obtain a permit to visit certain areas. Since all Hopi villages are separate and autonomous, each has its own governing policies, which are sometimes posted at the entrance to the village. Many villages don't allow cars, and some close to the public when they are participating in religious ceremonies. Lodging is available on Second Mesa and recommended if you wish to see the Hopi Mesas at a leisurely pace.

Keams Canyon Trading Post

❹ *48 mi west of Hubbell Trading Post on AZ 264.*

The trading post established by Thomas Keam in 1875 to do business with local tribes is now the area's main tourist attraction, offering a primitive campground, restaurant, service station, and shopping center. An administrative center for the Bureau of Indian Affairs, Keams Canyon also has a number of government buildings. A road, accessible by passenger car, winds northeast 3 mi into the 8-mi wooded canyon. At **Inscription Rock**, about 2 mi down the road, frontiersman Kit Carson engraved his name in stone. There are several picnic spots in the canyon.

Where to Eat

¢ ✕ **Keams Canyon Restaurant.** A typical roadside diner with Formica tabletops, Keams offers both American and Native American dishes, including Navajo tacos heaped with ground beef, chili, beans, lettuce, and grated cheese. Daily specials, offered at $1 to $2 off the regular price, may include anything from barbecued ribs to lamb chops to crab legs. ⊠ *Keams Canyon Shopping Center, AZ 264, Keams Canyon* ☎ *928/738–2296* ▭ *D, MC, V* ☾ *No dinner weekends.*

Shopping

Keams Canyon Arts and Crafts and McGee's Art Gallery (⊠ AZ 264, Keams Canyon ☎ 928/738–2295), upstairs from the Keams Canyon

RESERVATION REALITIES

BOTH THE NAVAJO AND HOPI *base their culture on the land around them, but they are two distinct peoples, as different from each other as the French are from the Germans. The similarities and contrasts between them are reflected in the harsh realities of life on the reservation.*

The Navajo refer to themselves as the Diné (pronounced din-eh)—"the people"—and live on 17 million acres in Arizona, New Mexico, Utah, and Colorado. Although it is not officially part of the reservation, many Navajo consider southwestern Colorado part of their sacred land. The Hopi trace their roots back to the original settlers of the area, whom they call the Hisatsinom, or "people of long ago." But these ancestral Puebloans are also popularly known as Anasazi, a Navajo word meaning both "ancient ones" and "ancient enemies." Hopi culture is far more formal and structured than that of the Navajo, and their religion has remained much stronger and purer. But for both tribes, unemployment is very high on the reservation, and poverty is a constant presence.

Most Navajo and Hopi disapprove of the practice, but some panhandlers nevertheless cluster at shopping centers and view sites, hoping to glean a few tourist dollars. Visitors should respond to panhandlers with a polite but firm "no." The phrases "she bay-so at-den" or "dough-da" (roughly translated, "no money") generally work. If you wish to help, make a donation to one of the legitimate organizations that raise funds at reservation grocery stores.

The sight of stray dogs, both starving and dead, is another unpleasant fact of life on the reservation. Among the Navajo in particular, dogs have never been held in high esteem, and in Navajo mythology dogs represent chaos and mischief. On both reservations, federal funding for animal control has been cut, and people struggling to make ends meet have few resources to devote to animal care. Visitors are encouraged not to feed the dogs, as this just exacerbates the problem.

Hopi mythology holds that a white-skinned people will save the tribe from its difficult life. Long ago, however, in the face of brutal treatment by whites, most Hopi became convinced that their salvation would originate elsewhere. (Some Hopi now look to the Dalai Lama of Tibetan Buddhism for redemption.) Although not easy to witness, the disappointment of the Hopi and the despair of the Navajo are easy to understand after a visit to the reservation.

To learn more about the Navajo, visit ⊕ www.navajocentral.org, www. navajoland.com, or www.navajo.org. To learn more about the Hopi, visit ⊕ www. hopi.nsn.us.

— Ed Tomchin

Restaurant, sells first-rate, high-quality Hopi crafts such as handcrafted jewelry, pottery, beautiful carvings, basketry, and artwork.

First Mesa

★ **5** *11 mi west of Keams Canyon, on AZ 264.*

First Mesa villages arerenowned for their polychrome pottery and katsina-doll carvings. The first village that you approach is Polacca; the older and more impressive villages of Hano, Sichomovi, and Walpi are at the top of the mesa. From Polacca, a paved road (off AZ 264) angles up to a parking lot near the village of Sichomovi, and to the Punsi Hall Visitor Center. You must get permission at Punsi Hall to take the guided walking tour of Hano, Sichomovi, and Walpi. Admission is by tour only, so be sure to call ahead to find out when they're offered.

All the older Hopi villages have structures built of rock and adobe mortar in a simple architectural style. **Hano** actually belongs to the Tewa, a New Mexico Pueblo tribe. In 1696, the Tewa Indians sought refuge with the Hopi on First Mesa after an unsuccessful rebellion against the Spanish in the Rio Grande Valley. Today, the Tewa live in close proximity to the Hopi but still maintain their own language and ceremonies. **Sichomovi** is built so close to Hano that only the residents can tell where one ends and the other begins. Constructed in the mid-1600s, this village is believed to have been built to ease overcrowding at Walpi, the highest point on the mesa. **Walpi,** built on solid rock and surrounded by steep cliffs, frequently hosts ceremonial dances. It is the most pristine of the Hopi villages, with cliff-edge houses and vast scenic vistas. Inhabited for more than 1,000 years (dating back to 900 AD). Walpi's cliff-edge houses—the mesa measures only 15 feet across at its narrowest point—seem to grow out of the nearby terrain. Today, only about 10 residents occupy this settlement, which has neither electricity nor running water. Walpi's surroundings make it a less than ideal destination for acrophobes. ⊠ *Punsi Hall Visitor Center, First Mesa* ☎ *928/737–2262* ⊕ *www.hopi.nsn.us* ⊠ *Guided tours $8* ☉ *Tours Nov.–mid-Mar., daily 9:30–4:30; mid-Mar.–Oct., daily 8:30–4:30, except when ceremonies are being held.*

Second Mesa

6 *10 mi southwest of First Mesa, on AZ 264.*

The Mesas are the Hopi universe, and Second Mesa is the "Center of the Universe." **Shungopavi,** the largest and oldest village on Second Mesa, which was founded by the Bear Clan, is reached by a paved road angling south off AZ 264, between the junction of AZ 87 and the Hopi Cultural Center. The villagers here make silver overlay jewelry and coil plaques. Coil plaques are woven from galleta grass and yucca and are adorned with designs of katsinas, animals, and corn. The art of making the plaques has been passed from mother to daughter for generations, and fine coil plaques have become highly sought after collector's items. The famous Hopi snake dances (closed to the public) are held here in August during even-numbered years. Two smaller villages are off a paved road that runs north from AZ 264, about ⅓ mi east of the Hopi Cultural Center. **Mishongnovi,** the easternmost settlement, was built in the late 1600s. For permission to visit **Sipaulovi** (☎ 928/737–2570), which was originally located at the base of the mesa before being moved to its present site in 1680, call the Sipaulovi Village Community Center.

At the **Hopi Cultural Center,** you can stop for the night, learn about the people and their reservation, and eat authentic Hopi cuisine. The museum here is dedicated to preserving the Hopi traditions and to presenting those traditions to non-Hopi visitors. A gift shop sells works by local Hopi artisans at reasonable prices, and a modest picnic area on the west side of the building is a pleasant spot for lunch with a view of the San Francisco Peaks. ⊠ *AZ 264, Second Mesa* ☎ *928/734–6650* ⊕ *www. psv.com/hopi.html* 🖾 *Museum $3* ⊙ *Mid-Mar.–Oct., weekdays 8–5 and weekends 9–3; Nov.–mid-Mar., weekdays 8–5.*

Where to Stay & Eat

¢ ✕🖾 **Hopi Cultural Center Restaurant and Motel.** This Hopi-run establishment is the only place to eat or sleep in the immediate area, but because of its remote location it almost always has vacant rooms. The motel offers clean, quiet, moderately priced rooms with coffeemakers. The restaurant (¢–$) serves traditional Hopi dishes, including Indian tacos, Hopi blue-corn pancakes, fry bread (delicious with honey or salsa), and *nok qui vi* (a tasty stew made with tender bits of lamb, hominy, and mild green chiles). ⊠ *5 mi west of AZ 87 on AZ 264, Second Mesa 86403* ☎ *928/734–2401* ⊕ *www.psv.com/hopi.html* ↰ *33 rooms* ♨ *Cable TV; no smoking* ☐ *DC, MC, V.*

Shopping

The **Hopi Arts and Crafts/Silvercrafts Cooperative Guild** (⊠ AZ 264, Second Mesa ☎ 928/734–2463), west of the Hopi Cultural Center, hosts craftspeople selling their wares; you might even see silversmiths at work here. Shops at the **Hopi Cultural Center** (⊠ AZ 264, Second Mesa ☎ 928/734–2401) carry the works of local artists and artisans. At **Hopi Fine Arts** (⊠ AZ 264 at AZ 87, Second Mesa ☎ 928/737–2222), proprietor Alph Secakuku is a native of the Hopi Pueblo of Supawlavi on the Second Mesa and an authority on all arts and crafts of the Hopi people. He represents about 75 active artisans in this user-friendly gallery. **Tsakurshovi** (⊠ AZ 264, Second Mesa ☎ 928/734–2478), 1½ mi east of the Hopi Cultural Center, is a small shop where Hopi come to buy bundles of sweet grass and sage, deer hooves with which to make rattles, and ceremonial belts adorned with seashells. The proprietor's wife, Janice Day, is a renowned Hopi basket maker. The shop has one of the largest collections of Hopi baskets in the Southwest.

Third Mesa

❼ *10 mi northwest of Second Mesa, on AZ 264.*

Third Mesa villages are known for their agricultural accomplishments, textile weaving, wicker baskets, and plaques. You'll find crafts shops and art galleries, as well as occasional roadside vendors, along AZ 264. The Hopi Tribal Headquarters and Office of Public Relations in

Kykotsmovi should be visited first for necessary permissions to visit the villages of Third Mesa.

Kykotsmovi, at the eastern base of Third Mesa, is literally translated as "ruins on the hills" for the many ruin sites on the valley floor and in the surrounding hills. Present-day Kykotsmovi was established by Hopi people from Oraibi—a few miles west—who either converted to Christianity or who wished to attend school and be educated. Kykotsmovi is the seat of the Hopi Tribal Government.

Old Oraibi, a few miles west and on top of Third Mesa, is believed to be the oldest continuously inhabited community in the United States, dating from around AD 1150. It was also the site of a rare, bloodless conflict between two groups of the Hopi people; in 1906, a dispute, settled uniquely by a "push of war" (a pushing contest), sent the losers off to establish the town of Hotevilla. Oraibi is a dusty spot, and, as an act of courtesy, tourists are asked to park their cars outside and approach the village on foot.

Hotevilla and **Bacavi** are about 4 mi west of Oraibi, and their inhabitants are descended from the former residents of that village. The men of Hotevilla continue to plant crops and beautiful gardens along the mesa slopes. ⊠ *Cultural Preservation Office, AZ 264* ⌖ *Box 123 Kykotsmovi 86039* ☎ *928/734–3000 or 928/734–2441* ⊕ *www.hopi.nsn.us* ⊗ *Weekdays 8–5.*

en route

Beyond Hotevilla, AZ 264 descends from Third Mesa, exits the Hopi Reservation, and crosses into Navajo territory, past **Coal Canyon,** where Native Americans have long mined coal from the dark seam just below the rim. The colorful mudstone, dark lines of coal, and bleached white rock have an eerie appearance, especially by the light of the moon. Twenty miles west of Coal Canyon, at the junction of AZ 264 and U.S. 160, is the town of Moenkopi, the last Hopi outpost. Established as a farming community, it was settled by the descendants of former Oraibi residents.

NAVAJO NATION WEST

The Hopi Reservation is like a donut hole surrounded by the Navajo Nation. If you approach the Grand Canyon from U.S. 89, via Flagstaff, north of the Wupatki National Monument, you'll find two significant sites in the western portions of the Navajo Reservation, the Cameron Trading Post and Tuba City. Situated 45 mi west of the Hopi town of Hotevilla, Tuba City is a good stop over if you're traveling east to the Hopi Mesas or northeast to Page.

At Cameron, the turnoff point for the Grand Canyon South Rim, the Cameron Trading Post was built in 1916 and commemorates Ralph Cameron, a pre-statehood territorial-legislative delegate. The sheer walls of the Little Colorado River Canyon about 10 mi west of U.S. 89 along AZ 64 are quite impressive and also worth a stop.

Tuba City

▶ ⑧ *50 mi northwest of Third Mesa on AZ 264.*

Tuba City, with about 12,000 permanent residents, is the administrative center for the western portion of the Navajo Nation. In addition to a motel, hostel, and a few restaurants, this small town has a hospital, a bank, a trading post, and a movie theater. In late October, Tuba City hosts the Western Navajo Fair, a celebration combining traditional Navajo song and dance with a parade, pageant, and countless arts-and-crafts exhibits. The octagonal **Tuba City Trading Post** (⊠ Main St. ☎ 928/283–5441), founded in the early 1870s, sells groceries and authentic, reasonably priced Navajo rugs, pottery, baskets, and jewelry.

About 5½ mi west of Tuba City, between mileposts 316 and 317 on U.S. 160, is a small sign for the **Dinosaur Tracks.** More than 200 million years ago, dilophosaurus—a carnivorous bipedal reptile more than 10 feet tall— left tracks in soft mud that subsequently turned to sandstone. There's no charge for a look. Ask the locals about guiding you to the nearby petroglyphs and freshwater springs. Four miles west of the dinosaur tracks on U.S. 160 is the junction with U.S. 89. This is one of the most colorful regions of the **Painted Desert,** with amphitheaters of maroon, orange, and red rocks facing west; it's especially glorious at sunset.

Where to Stay & Eat

¢–$ ✕ **Kate's Cafe.** A favorite of locals, this all-American café serves breakfast—try the vegetarian omelet—lunch, and dinner. Choose from hearty burgers, Kate's club sandwich, grilled chicken, or salads at lunchtime; dinner selections include five daily pasta specials and a charbroiled New York–strip steak. There may be a wait, but for local color and fine food at reasonable prices, this is the place. ⊠ *Main St. (AZ 264)* ☎ *928/283–6773* ▭ *No credit cards.*

¢–$ ✕ **Tuba City Truck Stop Cafe.** Home cooking and fast service are the specialties at this small, convenient restaurant. The popular Navajo vegetarian taco, available for lunch and dinner, is a mix of beans, lettuce, sliced tomato, shredded cheese, and green chiles served open face on fry bread. Meatier options include mutton stew served with fry bread and hominy. It's open at 6 AM for breakfast and closes at 10 PM every day. ⊠ *Main St. (AZ 264) at U.S. 160* ☎ *928/283–4975* ▭ *MC, V.*

$ 🏨 **Quality Inn Navajo Nation.** This hotel has a trading post and shops for essentials, gifts, and souvenirs. The standard rooms are spacious and well maintained, fine for an overnight stop before or after a visit to the Hopi Mesas. The on-site Hogan Restaurant serves basic fare. ⊠ *Main St. at Moenave Rd.* ✉ *Box 247, 86045* ☎ *928/283–4545 or 800/644–8383* 📠 *928/283–4144* ⊕ *www.choicehotels.com* 🛏 *78 rooms, 2 suites* ☍ *Restaurant, some in-room data ports, cable TV, shop, laundry facilities, some pets allowed, no-smoking rooms* ▭ *AE, D, DC, MC, V.*

¢ 🏨 **Grey Hills Inn.** Hotel management students at Grey Hills High School run this unusual lodging, a former dormitory with large, clean rooms and comfortable beds. Paintings and other eclectic touches add character to the otherwise plain rooms. Bathrooms and showers are down the hall, and it's hard to find the inn's entrance in the large high-school complex at night, but the rates are reasonable. A share of the inn's profits helps support the students' class. ⊠ *Grey Hills High School, U.S. 160, ½ mi north of AZ 264* ⬧ *Box 160, 86045* ☎ *928/283–6271 Ext. 142, 928/283–4450 weekends and after school hrs* ↩ *32 rooms with shared bath* ☰ *MC, V.*

CAMPING   ⚠ **Quality Inn Tuba City Campground.** Adjacent to the Quality Inn, this
¢   park has some shade trees and is geared toward RVs. Several tent sites situated along the perimeter of the campground are little more than concrete slabs. However, it is safe and close to restaurants. Reservations are accepted through the hotel's 800 number and check-in is at the hotel's front desk. ⊠ *Main St. (AZ 264)* ⬧ *Box 247, 86045* ☎ *928/283–4545 or 800/644–8383* ⎙ *928/283–4144* ↩ *25 RV sites, 6 tent sites* ♨ *Flush toilets, full hookups, dump station, drinking water, guest laundry, showers, grills, picnic tables* ☰ *AE, D, DC, MC, V* ☼ *Open year-round.*

Shopping

The **Native American swap meet** (⊠ Main St.), behind the community center and next to the baseball field, held every Friday from 8 AM on, has great deals on jewelry, jewelry-making supplies, semiprecious stones, rugs, pottery, and other arts and crafts; there are also food concessions and booths selling herbs. The **Toh Nanees Dizi Shopping Center** (⊠ U.S. 160), ½ mi northeast of town, has a pizza parlor, supermarket, and the Silver Screen Twin Theaters. **Van's Trading Company** (⊠ U.S. 160 ☎ 928/283–5343), on the western outskirts of town, has a "dead-pawn" auction at 3 PM on the 15th of each month. Dead pawn means that the time limit for the original owner to repurchase a pawned item has expired. You can generally find some older pieces of Navajo turquoise and silver jewelry.

Cameron Trading Post

❾ *25 mi southwest of Tuba City on U.S. 89*

Cameron Trading Post and Motel, established in 1916, is one of the few remaining authentic trading posts in the Southwest. A convenient stop if you're driving from the Hopi Mesas to the Grand Canyon, it has reasonably priced dining, lodging, camping, and shopping (⇨ *see* the listing in Chapter 3 for more detailed information). Fine authentic Navajo products are sold at an outlet of the **Navajo Arts and Crafts Enterprises** (⊠ U.S. 89 at AZ 64, Cameron ☎ 928/679–2244). ⊠ *U.S. 89, Cameron* ☎ *928/679–2231.*

 en route   As you proceed toward Kayenta, 22 mi northeast of Tuba City on U.S. 160, you'll come to the tiny community of Red Lake. Off to the left of the highway is a geologic phenomenon known as **Elephant Feet.** These massive eroded-sandstone buttes offer a great family photo opportunity, posing beneath these enormous columns. Northwest of here at the end of a graded dirt road in Navajo backcountry is **White Mesa Natural Bridge,** a massive arch of white sandstone that extends from the edge of White Mesa. The long **Black**

Mesa plateau runs for about 15 mi along U.S. 160. Above the prominent escarpments of this land formation, mining operations—a major source of revenue for the Navajo Nation—delve into the more than 20 billion tons of coal deposited there.

NAVAJO NATION NORTH & MONUMENT VALLEY

The magnificent Monument Valley stretches to the northeast of Kayenta into Utah. At a base altitude of about 5,500 feet, the sprawling, arid expanse was once populated by ancestral Puebloan people (more popularly known by the Navajo word *Anasazi,* which means both "ancient ones" and "enemy ancestors") and in the last few centuries has been home to generations of Navajo farmers. The soaring red buttes, eroded mesas, deep canyons, and naturally sculpted rock formations of Monument Valley are easy to enjoy on a leisurely drive. Scenes from many movies—among them *National Lampoon's Vacation, How the West Was Won, Forrest Gump, Stagecoach, 2001: A Space Odyssey,* and *Wind Talkers*—have been filmed here. Monument Valley is also the world's most popular backdrop for TV and magazine advertisements. At U.S. 163 and the Monument Valley entrance is a street of disheveled buildings called Vendor Village. Here you can purchase trinkets and souvenirs without paying sales tax. Bartering is perfectly acceptable and expected.

Kayenta

🔟 *80 mi northeast of Tuba City, on U.S. 160, 25 mi south of Monument Valley*

Kayenta, a small town with a few grocery stores, a handful of chain motels, and a hospital, is a good base for exploring nearby Monument Valley Navajo Tribal Park and the Navajo National Monument. The Burger King in town has an excellent Navajo Code Talker exhibit with lots of memorabilia relative to this heroic World War II marine group.

Take a self-guided walking tour through the small outdoor cultural park, the **Navajo Cultural Center of Kayenta,** and see the way of life, beliefs, and traditions that have shaped North America's largest Native American tribe. ⊠ *U.S. 160 between Hampton Inn and Burger King* ☎ *928/697–3170* 🎫 *Free* ⊙ *Daily 7 AM–sunset.*

Where to Stay & Eat

¢–$ ✕ **Amigo Cafe.** The tables here are packed with locals who frequent this small, clean establishment where everything on the menu is made from scratch. The delicious fry bread is the real drawing card. If you've never had a Navajo taco or Navajo hamburger, this is a good place to be initiated. ⊠ *U.S. 163* ☎ *928/697–8448* 🗐 *MC, V* ⊙ *Closed Sun.*

¢–$ ✕ **Golden Sands.** The decor and the service at this local café next to the Best Western Wetherill Inn are equally unrefined, but you can fuel up on hamburgers, Navajo tacos, and other regional specialties. It's also a good place to learn about the area from residents who stop in for coffee. ⊠ *U.S. 163* ☎ *928/697–3684* 🗐 *No credit cards* ⊙ *Closed Mon.*

CloseUp

TRAVELING IN NAVAJOLAND

CONTRARY TO FIRST IMPRESSIONS IN PHOENIX, Arizona is not all desert, shopping, and golf. Traveling north from the valley's sprawl toward northeastern Arizona and the Utah border, you climb to higher altitudes where giant saguaro cacti give way to pines. Piñons and juniper hug the earth as if to give a better view of the views ahead. This is the land of the Navajo.

The Navajo Reservation encompasses nearly 27,000 square mi, about the size of West Virginia. Navajos call themselves the "Diné"—"The People"—and have been living here for more than 400 years. Rugged mountains, lakes, forests, deserts, and spectacular canyons combine to create a landscape of wonder and awe. There are few towns; rather clusters of houses, trailers, and hogans dot the landscape. Small herds of cattle, sheep, and goats move freely along and across the roads.

The Navajos use few words and possess a subtle sense of humor that can pass you by quickly if you're not a good listener. From childhood they are taught not to talk too much, be loud, or show off. Eye contact is considered impolite. If you are conversing with Navajos, some may look down or away even though they are paying attention to you. Likewise, touching is seen differently; handshaking may be the only physical contact that you see. When shaking hands, a light touch is preferred to a firm grip which is considered overbearing.

Although most Navajos speak English with varying degrees of mastery, listen closely to the language of the Diné. From the Athabascan family, the language is difficult for outsiders to learn because of subtle accentuation. The famous Marine Corps Navajo "Code Talkers" of World War II saved thousand of lives in the South Pacific by creating a code within their native Navajo language thereby mystifying the Japanese. Their unbreakable messages got safely through by radio to American troops quickly and accurately. These Native Americans are true patriots who today speak humbly of their accomplishments. Many of those still living reside in the area around Tuba City.

Navajo art centers around jewelry (often silver and turquoise) and weaving. Historians think that Navajos first learned weaving skills from the Pueblo Indians, but the Navajo believe their knowledge of weaving comes from the mythical Navajo deity Spider Woman. The prices of handwoven rugs may seem high, even in Navajoland. However, keep in mind that weaving a rug is a slow, painstaking process that begins with shearing the wool. The wool is then spun by hand as often as as 15 to 20 times. The threads can be left in their natural state or dyed with vegetable dyes as those from prickly pear cactus, Navajo tea, juniper and wild plum roots. A medium-sized rug may take five to six months to weave and the finished product is one of stunning craftsmanship.

Traveling the Navajo Nation offers a special opportunity to meet and converse with the Diné. They have a wonderful culture and heritage to share. You will not regret the time you spend getting to know them.

Bob & Gloria Willis

$–$$ ✕▦ **Hampton Inn of Kayenta.** Warm and inviting, this lodgepole-style motel is a good spot to get a night's rest. The simple rooms and lobby are tastefully decorated with Southwest textures, and the on-site restaurant (¢–$) is staffed by Native Americans wearing traditional Navajo garb. Stick with the Native American cuisine; a good choice is the Sheepherder's Taco. There's a free Continental-breakfast bar, patio with a beehive fireplace, and fantastic gift shop with a large selection of top-quality Native American art and unique gifts. ✉ *U.S. 160* ✆ *Box 1217, 86033* ☎ *928/697–3170* 🖷 *928/697–3189* ⊕ *www.hamptoninn.com* ⇨ *73 rooms* ⚐ *Restaurant, cable TV, pool, shop, no-smoking rooms* ☱ *AE, D, DC, MC, V* ¶❍ *CP.*

$–$$ ✕▦ **Holiday Inn Monument Valley.** This contemporary motel has everything you would expect from a Holiday Inn. The on-site Wagonwheel Restaurant ($–$$) offers both standard and Native American fare, and the gift shop offers traditional local arts and crafts. ✉ *U.S. 160 at U.S. 163* ✆ *Box 307, 86033* ☎ *928/697–3221 or 800/465–4329* 🖷 *928/ 697–3349* ⊕ *www.holiday-inn.com* ⇨ *160 rooms* ⚐ *Restaurant, cable TV, pool, shop, no-smoking rooms* ☱ *AE, D, DC, MC, V.*

Monument Valley Navajo Tribal Park

☾ ⓫ *24 mi northeast of Kayenta, off U.S. 163.*

Fodor'sChoice
★

For generations, the Navajo have grown crops and herded sheep in Monument Valley, considered to be one of the most scenic and mesmerizing destinations in the Navajo Nation. Director John Ford made this amazing land of buttes, towering rock formations, and mesas popular by filming *Stagecoach* here in 1938. Within Monument Valley lies the 30,000-acre Monument Valley Navajo Tribal Park where eons of wind and rain have carved the mammoth red-sandstone monoliths into memorable formations. The monoliths, which jut hundreds of feet above the desert floor, stand on the horizon like sentinels, frozen in time and unencumbered by electric wires, telephone poles, or fences . . . a scene virtually unchanged for centuries. These are the very same nostalgic images so familiar to movie buffs who recall the early Western films of John Wayne. A 17-mi self-guided driving tour on a dirt road (there's only one road, so you can't get lost) passes the memorable **Mittens** and **Totem Pole** formations, among others. Drive slowly, and be sure to walk (15 minutes round-trip) from North Window around the end of Cly Butte for the views. The park has a 99-site campground, which closes from early October through April. Call ahead for road conditions in winter. Bring plenty of extra film and batteries to capture this surreal landscape that constantly changes with the rising and setting sun.

The **Monument Valley Visitor Center** holds a small crafts shop and exhibits devoted to ancient and modern Native American history. Most of the independent guided tours here use enclosed vans and charge about $20 for 2½ hours; you can generally find Navajo Native American guides in the center or through the booths in the parking lot. They will escort you to places that you are not allowed to visit on your own. ✉ *Visitor Center, off U.S. 163, 24 mi north of Kayenta, Monument Valley* ✆ *Box 2520, Window Rock 86515* ☎ *435/727–3353 park visitor* center, 928/871–6647 Navajo Parks & Recreation Dept. ⊕ www. navajonationparks.org 🔲 $3 ☉ Visitor center May–Sept., daily 7–7; Oct.–Apr., daily 8–5.

Sports & the Outdoors

HIKING & JEEP TOURS   Jeep tours of the valley from hour-long to overnight can be arranged through Roland Cody Dixon at **Roland's Navajoland Tours** (🖃 Box 1542, Kayenta 86033 ☎ 928/697–3524); he offers cultural tours with crafts demonstrations, camping, and photography. **Simpson's Trailhandler Tours** (🖃 Box 360–377, Monument Valley, UT 85436 ☎ 435/727–3362 ⊕ www.trailhandlertours.com) offers four-wheel-drive jeep tours as well as photography and hiking tours. **Totem Pole Tours** (🖃 Box 360306, Monument Valley, UT 85436 ☎ 435/727–3313 or 800/345–8687 ⊕ www.moab-utah.com/totempole) offers jeep tours, some that include entertainment and outdoor barbecues.

HORSEBACK RIDING   Have you ever wanted to ride off into the sunset into the land of sandstone spires and sweeping red rock? **Homeland Horseback Tours** (🖂 Monument Valley Tribal Park Visitor Center, off U.S. 163, 24 mi north of Kayenta ☎ 435/727–3227 ⊕ http://cas-biz.com/homelandtours), at the Monument Valley visitor center, offers 1½-hour, half-day, full-day, and overnight tours into Monument Valley.

Where to Stay

CAMPING   🏕 **Mitten View Campground.** This RV and tent campground is within the
¢   Navajo Tribal Park, next to the park headquarters at an elevation of 5,500 feet. The sites here are crowded together, but most offer spectacular views of Monument Valley. Rest rooms and showers are open in summer only. Only group sites can be reserved. 🖂 Monument Valley Navajo Tribal Park, near visitor center, off U.S. 163, 25 mi north of Kayenta, 86003 ☎ 435/727–3287 🔲 $10 summer, $5 winter, $20 group site ⌨ 99 sites ⚲ Flush toilets, dump station, drinking water, showers, picnic tables ➡ No credit cards ☉ Open May–Oct.; some sites year-round.

| off the beaten path |

FOUR CORNERS MONUMENT – An inlaid concrete slab marks the only point in the United States where four states meet: Arizona, New Mexico, Colorado, and Utah. Most visitors—in summer, nearly 2,000 a day—stay only long enough to snap a photo; you'll see many a twisted tourist trying to get an arm or a leg in each state. The monument, a 75-mi drive from Kayenta, is administered by the Navajo Nation Parks & Recreation Department. 🖂 7 mi northwest of the U.S. 160 and U.S. 64 junction, Teec Nos Pos 🖃 Box 9000, Window Rock 86515 ☎ 928/871–6647 Navajo Parks & Recreation Dept ⊕ www.navajonationparks.org 🔲 Free.

Goosenecks Region, Utah

⑫   33 mi north of Monument Valley Navajo Tribal Park, on UT 316.

Fodor'sChoice   Monument Valley's scenic route, U.S. 163, continues from Arizona into
★   Utah, where the land is crossed, east to west, by a stretch of the San Juan River known as the Goosenecks—so named for the myriad twists

and curves it takes at the bottom of a wildly carved canyon. This barren, erosion-blasted gorge has a stark beauty. This spot is a well-known take-out point for white-water runners on the San Juan, a river that vacationing sleuths will recognize as the setting of many of Tony Hillerman's Jim Chee mystery novels. The scenic overlook for the Goosenecks is reached by turning west from U.S. 163 onto UT 261, 4 mi north of the small community of **Mexican Hat** (named for the sombrero-like rock formation on the hills to your right as you drive north), then proceeding on UT 261 for 1 mi to a directional sign at the road's junction with UT 316. Turn left onto UT 316 and proceed 4 mi to the vista-point parking lot.

Where to Stay & Eat

★ ¢ ✕⌖ **San Juan Inn & Trading Post.** The inn's Southwestern-style, rustic rooms overlooking the river at Mexican Hat are clean and well maintained. Diners can watch the river flow by at the Old Bridge Bar & Grill ($–$$), which serves great grilled steak and juicy hamburgers. Fresh trout and inexpensive Navajo dishes add variety to the menu. ⌖ *U.S. 163* ⌖ *Box 310276, Mexican Hat, UT 84531* ⌖ *435/683–2220 or 800/447–2022* ⌖ *435/683–2210* ⌖ *www.sanjuaninn.net* ⌖ *36 rooms* ⌖ *Restaurant, cable TV, gym, laundry facilities, no-smoking rooms* ⌖ *AE, D, DC, MC, V.*

Goulding's Trading Post

⓭ *1 mi west of Monument Valley Navajo Tribal Park, off U.S. 163 on Indian Hwy. 42.*

Established in 1924 by Harry Goulding and his wife "Mike," this trading post provided a place where Navajos could exchange livestock and handmade goods for necessities. However, Goulding's is probably best known for being used as a headquarters by director John Ford when he filmed the Western classic *Stagecoach*. Numerous Westerns shot in the area have brought the site a measure of international fame. Today the compound has a lodge, restaurant, museum, gift shop, grocery story, and campground. The Goulding Museum displays Native American artifacts and Goulding family memorabilia as well as an excellent multimedia show about Monument Valley.

Where to Stay & Eat

$$ ✕⌖ **Goulding's Lodge.** With spectacular views of Monument Valley from each room's private balcony, this motel often serves as headquarters for film crews. The lodge has handsome stucco buildings, and all the rooms have balconies, coffeemakers, and hair dryers. The on-premises Stagecoach restaurant, serving American fare, is decorated with Western movie memorabilia. Goulding's also conducts custom guided tours of Monument Valley and provides Navajo guides into the backcountry. The lodge is 2 mi off U.S. 163, at the Monument Valley Tribal Park turnoff. ⌖ *Off U.S. 163, 24 mi north of Kayenta* ⌖ *Box 360001, Monument Valley, UT 84536* ⌖ *435/727–3231* ⌖ *www.gouldings.com* ⌖ *62 rooms* ⌖ *Restaurant, grocery, cable TV, in-room VCRs, pool, shop, laundry facilities, travel services* ⌖ *AE, D, DC, MC, V.*

CAMPING   △ **Goulding's Good Sam Campground.** Views of Monument Valley are the
¢   draw at this clean, modern campground. Check in at Goulding's grocery
store (in Goulding's Trading Post). Campers have access—at no additional charge—to the 17-mi-loop drive around Monument Valley. Shuttle vans provide free transportation to Gouldings' restaurant and museum.
⊠ *Off U.S. 163, 24 mi north of Kayenta* ⌕ *Box 360001, Monument
Valley, UT 84536* ☎ *435/727–3231* ➥ *66 RV sites, 50 tent sites* ⌂ *Flush
toilets, full hookups, guest laundry, showers, grills, general store, play
area, swimming (indoor pool)* ▤ *$26 full hookups, $16 tent sites* ▤ *AE,
D, DC, MC, V* ⊗ *Open year-round; limited service Nov.–Mar. 15.*

Navajo National Monument

⑭   *53 mi southwest of Goulding's Trading Post. From Kayenta, take U.S.
160 southwest to AZ 564, and follow signs 9 mi north to monument.*

Fodor'sChoice   At the Navajo National Monument, two unoccupied 13th-century cliff
★   pueblos, Betatakin and Keet Seel, stand under the overhang of orange
and ocher cliffs of Tgesi Canyon. The largest ancient dwellings in Arizona, these stone-and-mortar complexes were built by ancestral Puebloans,
obviously for permanent occupancy, but abandoned after less than half
a century.

The well-preserved, 135-room **Betatakin** (Navajo for "ledge house") seems
to hang in midair before a sheer sandstone wall. When discovered in
1907 by a passing American rancher, the apartments were full of baskets, pottery, and preserved grains and ears of corn—as if the occupants
had been chased away in the middle of a meal. For an impressive view
of Betatakin, walk to the rim overlook about ½ mi from the visitor center. Ranger-led tours (a 5-mi, four-hour, strenuous round-trip hike including a 700-foot descent into the canyon) leave once a day from late
May to early September at 8 AM. No reservations are accepted; groups
of no more than 25 form on a first-come, first-served basis.

Keet Seel (Navajo for "broken pottery") is also in good condition in a
serene location, with 160 rooms and five kivas. Explorations of Keet
Seel, which lies at an elevation of 7,000 feet and is 8½ mi from the visitor center by foot, are restricted: only 20 people are allowed to visit
per day, and only between late May and early September, when a ranger
is present at the site. A permit—which also allows campers to stay
overnight near the ruins—is required. Trips to Keet Seel are very popular, so reservations are taken up to two months in advance. Anyone
who suffers from vertigo might want to avoid this trip: the trail leads
down a 1,100-foot near-vertical rock face.

The **visitor center** houses a small museum, exhibits of prehistoric pottery, and a good crafts shop. Free campground and picnic areas are nearby,
and rangers sometimes present campfire programs in summer. No food,
gasoline, or hotel lodging is available at the monument. AZ 564 turns
north off U.S. 160 at the Black Mesa gas station and convenience store
and leads to the visitor center. ⊠ *AZ 564, Black Mesa* ⌕ *HC 71, Box
3, Tonalea 86044* ☎ *928/672–2700* 🖷 *928/672–2703* ⊕ *www.nps.
gov/nava* ▤ *Free* ⊗ *Daily 8–5; tours late May–early Sept.*

Sports & the Outdoors

HIKING Now that horseback tours have been suspended in the area, hiking is the best way for adventurous souls to see Keet Seel at the Navajo National Monument. It's a pretty strenuous hike to the ruins, but if you're fit and leave early enough, it's well worth it to visit some of the best-preserved ruins in the Southwest. It's free, but the trail is open only from late May through early September, and you need to call ahead to make a reservation, usually at least two months in advance. ⌂ *Navajo National Monument, HC 71, Box 3, Tonalea 86044* ☎ *928/672–2366* ⚑ *Free* ☉ *Daily 8–5; tours late May–early Sept.*

Where to Stay & Eat

¢ ✕☒ **Anasazi Inn–Tsegi Canyon.** On U.S. 160, 10 mi east of Black Mesa and 9 mi west of Kayenta, this is the closest lodging to Navajo National Monument. The one-story property offers basic, clean accommodations with exterior entrances and commanding views of Tsegi Canyon. There's also a well-stocked gift shop and a restaurant that serves sandwiches, burgers, and basic Navajo fare. ⌂ *Off U.S. 160, 9 mi west of Kayenta* ⌂ *Box 1543, Kayenta, AZ 86033* ☎ *928/697–3793* 🖷 *928/697–8249* ⊕ *www.anasaziinn.com* ⌂ *57 rooms* ⌂ *Restaurant, cable TV, shop, picnic tables* ▭ *AE, D, MC, V.*

CAMPING ⛺ **Navajo National Monument Campground.** Beautiful and serene with ¢ no fee, this campground has no hookups, and open fires are not allowed (you must use camp stoves). Because of its remote locale, the campground, ¼ mi west of the visitor center, usually has available sites. Winter snows can block the road. ⌂ *AZ 564, Black Mesa* ☎ *928/672–2366* ⌂ *30 sites* ⌂ *Flush toilets, drinking water* ⌂ *Reservations not accepted* ☉ *Open year-round, weather permitting.*

GLEN CANYON DAM & LAKE POWELL

Lake Powell, 185 mi long with 2,000 mi of shoreline—longer than America's Pacific coast—is the heart of the huge 1,255,400-acre Glen Canyon National Recreation Area. Created by the barrier of Glen Canyon Dam—a 710-foot wall of concrete in the Colorado River—Lake Powell took 17 years to fill. The second-largest man-made lake in the nation, Lake Powell extends through terrain so rugged it was the last major area of the United States to be mapped. It's ringed by red cliffs that twist off into 96 major canyons and countless inlets (most accessible only by boat) with huge, red-sandstone buttes randomly jutting from the sapphire waters. You could spend 30 years exploring the lake and still not experience everything there is to see. The Sierra Club has started a movement to drain the lake in order to restore water-filled Glen Canyon, which some believe was more spectacular than the Grand Canyon, but the lake is likely to be around for years to come, regardless of the final outcome of this plan.

South of Lake Powell the landscape gives way to **Echo Cliffs,** orange-sandstone formations rising 1,000 feet and more above the highway in places. At **Bitter Springs,** the road ascends the cliffs and provides a spectacular view of the 9,000-square-mi Arizona Strip to the west and the 3,000-foot Vermilion Cliffs to the northwest.

Page

⑮ *96 mi west of the Navajo National Monument, 136 mi north of Flagstaff on U.S. 89.*

Built in 1957 as a Glen Canyon Dam construction camp, Page is now a tourist spot and a popular base for day trips to Lake Powell; it has also become a major point of entry to the Navajo Nation. The nearby Vermilion Cliffs are where the California condor, an endangered species, has been successfully reintroduced into the wild. The town's human population of 10,000 makes it the largest community in far-northern Arizona, and most of the motels, restaurants, and shopping centers are concentrated along **Lake Powell Boulevard,** the name given to U.S. 89 as it loops through the business district. Each year, more than 3 million people come to play at Lake Powell.

At the corner of North Navajo Drive and Lake Powell Boulevard is the **John Wesley Powell Memorial Museum,** whose namesake led the first known expeditions down the Green River and the rapids-choked Colorado through the Grand Canyon between 1869 and 1872. Powell mapped and kept detailed records of his trips, naming the Grand Canyon and many other geographic points of interest in northern Arizona. Artifacts from his expeditions are displayed in the museum, which has a good selection of regional books and maps. The museum also doubles as the town's visitor information center. A travel desk dispenses information and allows you to book boating tours, raft trips, scenic flights, accommodations in Page, or Antelope Canyon tours. When you sign up for tours here, concessionaires give a donation to the nonprofit museum with no extra charge to you. ⊠ *6 N. Lake Powell Blvd.* ☎ *928/ 645–9496* ⊕ *www.powellmuseum.org* ✉ *$2* ☉ *Weekdays 8:30–5:30; Memorial Day–Labor Day also open Sat. (call for hrs).*

☾ The **Navajo Village Heritage Center** imparts an understanding of life on the reservation. You can take a guided tour of a traditional Navajo hogan and bread oven. For $49.95 ($34.95 children), the village hosts a three-hour "Evening with the Navajo–Grand Tour," which includes two hours of cultural entertainment and a Navajo taco dinner around a campfire. ⊠ *531 Haul Rd.* ☎ *928/660–0304* ⊕ *www.navajo-village.com* ✉ *$10* ☉ *Apr.–Oct., daily 9–3.*

Sports & the Outdoors
For water sports on Lake Powell, *see* Wahweap *below.*

FLOAT TRIPS **Wilderness River Adventures** (☎ 928/645–3296 or 800/992–8022 ⊕ www. riveradventures.com) offers waterborne tours, including a 4½-hour guided rafting excursion down a calm portion of the Colorado River on comfortable, safe J boats ($52). The scenery—multicolor-sandstone cliffs adorned with Native American petroglyphs—is spectacular. The point of departure in Page is the Wilderness Outfitters Store at 50 South

Lake Powell Boulevard, but transportation is furnished both to the launch site and back from Lees Ferry, where the trip ends.

GOLF **Lake Powell National Golf Course** (⊠400 Clubhouse Dr., off U.S. 89 ☏928/ 645–2023 ⊕ www.lakepowellgolf.com) has wide fairways, tiered greens with some of the steepest holes in the Southwest, and a generous lack of hazards. A round at this 18-hole, par-72 course costs $45 (including cart); from the fairways you can enjoy gorgeous vistas of Glen Canyon Dam and Lake Powell. There's a 9-hole, par-36 municipal course here as well.

HIKING The **Glen Canyon Hike** (⊠ Off U.S. 89), a short walk from the parking lot down a flight of uneven rock steps, takes you to a viewpoint on the canyon rim high above the Colorado River and provides fantastic views of the Colorado as it flows through Glen Canyon. To reach the parking lot, turn west on Scenic View Drive, 1½ mi south of Carl Hayden Visitor Center.

The **Horse Shoe Bend Trail** (⊠ Off U.S. 89) has some steep up and down paths and a bit of deep sand to maneuver; however, the views are well worth the hike. The trail leads up to a bird's-eye view of Glen Canyon and the Colorado River downstream from Glen Canyon Dam. There are some sheer drop-offs here, so watch children. To reach the trail, drive 4 mi south of Page on U.S. 89 and turn west onto a blacktop road ²/₁₀ mi south of mile marker 545. It's a ¾-mi hike from the parking area to the top of the canyon.

Where to Stay & Eat

$–$$$ ✗ **Dam Bar and Grille.** Although the Grille's decor more resembles a construction site than a restaurant, the food is good, well prepared, and imaginative for the all-purpose palate. It's general American with good steaks and a few touches that take you south of the border. ⊠ *644 N. Navajo Dr.* ☏ *928/645–2161* ⊕ *www.damplaza.com* ⊟ *AE, MC, V.*

$–$$ ✗ **Zapata's.** Specials include green chile and home-style enchiladas, not to mention very good margaritas. Everything is made from "scratch" using family recipes. The basic, clean restaurant is decorated with Mexican blankets, *ristras* (strings of dried red-chiles), and pottery. ⊠ *614 N. Navajo Dr.* ☏ *928/645–9006* ⊟ *AE, D, MC, V.*

$–$$ 🏨 **Days Inn & Suites.** One of the newer hotels in the area has views of Lake Powell, the Vermilion Cliffs, and Glen Canyon Dam. Standard rooms are spacious, and 22 suites have wet bars, microwaves, refrigerators, and data ports. All are decorated in a pleasant Southwestern motif. ⊠ *961 N. U.S. 89, 86040* ☏ *928/645–2800* 🖨 *928/645–2604* ⊕ *www.daysinn. com* 📇 *82 rooms* ♢ *Some in-room data ports, some microwaves, some refrigerators, cable TV, pool, shop, laundry facilities, no-smoking rooms* ⊟ *AE, D, DC, MC, V* ❍❘ *CP.*

¢–$$ 🏨 **Courtyard by Marriott.** An attractive motel on the grounds of Lake Powell National Golf Course, the Courtyard has comfortable rooms decorated in a Southwestern motif, health and fitness facilities, and on-premises dining in Peppers, an eatery specializing in American fare. ⊠ *600 Clubhouse Dr.* ⊡ *Box 4150, 86040* ☏ *928/645–5000* ⊕ *www.courtyard. com* 📇 *153 rooms* ♢ *Restaurant, in-room data ports, cable TV, pool,*

gym, sauna, bar, shop, laundry facilities, laundry service, business services, meeting rooms, no-smoking rooms 🖃 AE, D, DC, MC, V.

★ ¢–$$ 🖼 **Uncle Bill's Place.** Interesting books to skim, witty and well-traveled
hosts, and a lovely garden complete with a grill make this the homiest
motel in town. A humorous list of house rules ensures harmonious liv-
ing in the one- to three-bedroom, suitelike apartments, in which guests
often share a bathroom, living room, and full kitchen (you can rent a
room or an entire apartment). Uncle Bill gives a good briefing on area
attractions and eateries and will lend you a discount card for the su-
permarket. ✉ 117 8th Ave., 86040 ☎ 928/645–1224 🖨 928/645–
3937 ⊕ www.canyon-country.com/unclebill ↘ 12 rooms in 5 apartments
⌂ Picnic area, BBQs, kitchens, cable TV, library, travel services; no kids
under 8, no smoking 🖃 AE, DC, MC, V.

$ 🖼 **Best Western at Lake Powell.** The newer of the two Best Westerns in
town is a modern, three-story motel on a high bluff overlooking Glen
Canyon Dam with dazzling views of the Vermilion Cliffs. The large rooms
are functional, and the beds are comfortable. ✉ 208 N. Lake Powell
Blvd., 86040 ☎ 928/645–5988 or 888/794–2888 ⊕ www.bestwestern.
com/atlakepowell ↘ 132 rooms ⌂ Some microwaves, some refrigera-
tors, cable TV, pool, gym, hot tub, laundry facilities, meeting rooms,
no-smoking rooms 🖃 AE, D, DC, MC, V � CP.

$ 🖼 **Canyon Colors B&B.** Run by New England transplants Bev and Rich
Jones, this desert-country B&B offers travelers a personal touch. The
Sunflower and Paisley rooms, which can accommodate up to five and
four, respectively, have queen beds, futons, and wood-burning stoves.
The cozier Canyon Room accommodates only two. The B&B also has
an extensive video library, including many videos of Lake Powell and
the Navajo Nation. Reservations, necessary in summer, can be made up
to a year in advance. ✉ 225 S. Navajo Dr. ⌖ Box 3657, 86040 ☎ 800/
536–2530 or 928/645–5979 🖨 928/645–5979 ⊕ www.canyoncolors.
com ↘ 3 rooms ⌂ BBQ, refrigerators, cable TV, in-room VCRs, pool;
no smoking 🖃 AE, D, DC, MC, V � BP.

$ 🖼 **Quality Inn at Lake Powell.** This modern hotel offers rooms with views
of the Vermilion Cliffs adjacent to Page's 18-hole, par-72 golf course.
All accommodations are decorated in a territorial motif. The inn also
has a picnic area. ✉ 287 N. Lake Powell Blvd., off U.S. 89 ⌖ Box 1867
86040 ☎ 928/645–8851 🖨 928/645–2523 ⊕ www.qualityinn.com
↘ 129 rooms ⌂ Refrigerators, microwaves, cable TV, pool, meeting
rooms, no-smoking rooms 🖃 AE, D, DC, MC, V � CP.

CAMPING 🏕 **Page–Lake Powell Campground.** Lake Powell is a popular destination
¢ and very busy in summer months. It's wise to make reservations well
ahead if you're planning to stay at this in-town campground. The An-
telope Point launch ramp on Lake Powell is 7 mi away. You can make
reservations online as well as by phone. ✉ 849 S. Coppermine Rd.,
86040 ☎ 928/645–3374 ⊕ http://campground.page-lakepowell.com
↘ 85 RV sites, 20 tent sites ⌂ Flush toilets, full hookups with cable,
partial hookups (electric and water), dump station, guest laundry,
showers, picnic tables, general store, swimming (indoor pool) 🍴 $28
full hookup (with cable), $24 partial hookup, $17 tent site 🖃 MC, V
☺ Open year-round.

Nightlife

The **Bowl** (⊠ 24 N. Lake Powell Blvd. ☎ 928/645–2682) is a 10-lane bowling alley with an outdoor patio, billiards, and coffee shop. **Gunsmoke Saloon & Eatery** (⊠ 644 N. Navajo Dr. ☎ 928/645–1888) is a spot where you can dance to live music, play billiards and video games, and munch on chicken wings until 1 AM. **Ken's Old West Restaurant & Lounge** (⊠ 718 Vista Ave. ☎ 928/645–5160) has country-and-western music and dancing; you can also get a pretty good steak, prime rib, seafood, or barbecued-chicken dinner. **Mesa Theater** (⊠ 42 S. Lake Powell Blvd. ☎ 928/645–9565) is Page's movie house.

Shopping

There are numerous gift shops and clothing stores in the downtown area along Lake Powell Boulevard. There's lots of junk on offer, but you can also find authentic Native American arts and crafts at Blair's and Wahweap Lodge. **Big Lake Trading Post** (⊠ 1501 AZ 98 ☎ 928/645–2404) has a gas station, convenience store, car wash, and coin laundry. **Blair's Dinnebito Trading Post** (⊠ 626 Navajo Dr. ☎ 928/645–3008 ⊕ www. blairstradingpost.com) has been around for more than half a century. Authentic Native American arts and crafts are only a small part of what this store sells. Need tack equipment, rodeo ropes, rugs, saddlery, pottery? It's all here and reasonably priced. Take time to wander upstairs and visit the Elijah Blair collection and memorabilia rooms. The busy gift shop at **Wahweap Lodge** (⊠ 100 Lake Shore Dr., Wahweap ☎ 928/ 645–2433 ⊕ www.blairstradingpost.com) carries a large selection of authentic Native American rugs, pottery, jewelry, and baskets as well as the essential tourist T-shirts and postcards.

Antelope Canyon

⓰ *4 mi east of Page on the Navajo Reservation, on AZ 98.*

★ You've probably seen dozens of photographs of Antelope Canyon, a narrow, red-sandstone slot canyon with convoluted corkscrew formations, dramatically illuminated by a ray of light streaming down from above. And you're likely to see assorted shutterbugs waiting patiently for just the right shot of these colorful, photogenic rocks, which are actually petrified-sand dunes of a prehistoric ocean that once filled this portion of North America. The best photographs are taken at high noon, when light filters through "the slot" in the canyon surface to create a breathtaking display of form and color. Take a tripod and use a slow shutter speed. This is one place that you'll definitely need to protect your camera equipment against blowing dust. Access to the canyon is limited to those on licensed tours. ⊠ *AZ 98, Page* ▱ *Box 2520, Window Rock 86515* ☎ *928/871–6647 Navajo Parks & Recreation Dept* ⊕ *www. navajonationparks.org* ▱ *$6 (included in tour cost).*

Antelope Canyon Tours

Access to Antelope Canyon is restricted by the Navajo Tribe to licensed tour operators. The tribe charges a $6 per-person fee—which is included in the price of tours offered by the licensed concessionaires in Page. The easiest way to book a tour of Antelope Canyon is in town at the John Wesley Powell Memorial Museum Visitor's Center. You pay nothing extra for the museum's service; however, if you'd like to go directly to the tour operators, you can do that, too. Most companies offer 1½-hour sightseeing tours for about $30 or longer photography tours for $48. The best time to see the canyon is between 8 AM and 2 PM.

Antelope Canyon Adventures (✉ 108 S. Lake Powell Blvd., Page ☎ 928/ 645–5501 ⊕ www.jeeptour.com) offers 1½-hour sightseeing tours. **John Wesley Powell Museum Visitor Center** (✉ 6 N. Lake Powell Blvd., Page ☎ 928/645–9496 ⊕ www.powellmuseum.org) arranges 1½-hour tours and 5-hour photography tours. Photo tours leave from various locations in Page at 8 and 9:30 AM and return about 2 PM. The shorter sightseeing tours leave frequently between 8 AM and 4 PM. **Overland Canyon Tours** (✉ 18 N. Lake Powell Blvd., Page ☎ 928/608–4072 ⊕ www. overlandcanyon.com) is the only Native American–operated tour company in Page. Tours include a narrative explaining the canyon's history and geology. **Roger Ekis' Antelope Canyon Tours** (✉ 22 S. Lake Powell Blvd., Page ☎ 928/645–9102 ⊕ www.antelopecanyon.com) offers several tours daily from 8 AM to 3 PM for sightseers and photographers. The photo tour gives serious and amateur photographers the opportunity to wait for the "right light" to photograph the canyon and get some basic information on equipment setup. Tickets can be purchased at the John Wesley Powell Museum Visitor Center.

Glen Canyon National Recreation Area

⑰ *2 mi west of Page on U.S. 89.*

Once you leave the Page business district heading northwest, the Glen Canyon Dam and Lake Powell behind it immediately become visible. This concrete-arch dam—all 5 million cubic feet of it—was completed in September 1963, its power plant an engineering feat that rivaled Hoover Dam. The dam's crest is 1,560 feet across and rises 710 feet from bedrock and 583 feet above the waters of the Colorado River. When Lake Powell is full, it is 560 feet deep at the dam. The plant generates some 1.3 million kilowatts of electricity when each generator's 40-ton shaft is generating nearly 200,000 horsepower. Power from the dam serves a five-state grid consisting of Colorado, Arizona, Utah, California, and New Mexico and provides energy for some 1.5 million users.

With only 8 inches of annual rainfall, the Lake Powell area enjoys blue skies nearly year-round. Summer temperatures range from the 60s to the 90s (occasionally rising to 100°F). Fall and spring are usually balmy, with daytime temperatures often in the 70s and 80s, but chilly weather can set in. Nights are cool even in the summer, and in winter the risk of a cold spell increases, but all-weather houseboats and tour boats make for year-round cruising.

Boaters and campers should note that regulations require the use of portable toilets on the lake and lakeshore. Park authorities vigorously enforce this rule to prevent water pollution.

Just off the highway at the north end of the bridge is the **Carl Hayden Visitor Center,** where you can learn about the controversial creation of

Glen Canyon Dam and Lake Powell and enjoy panoramic views of both. To enter the visitor center, you must go through a metal detector. Absolutely no bags are allowed inside. ⌗ *U.S. 89, 2 mi west of town, Page* ☎ *928/608–6404* ⊕ *www.nps.gov/glca* ⌗ *$10 per vehicle, $10 per week boating fee* ☉ *Visitor Center Memorial Day–Labor Day, daily 8–6; Labor Day–Memorial Day, daily 8–5.*

Wahweap

⑱ *5 mi north of Glen Canyon Dam on U.S. 89.*

Most waterborne-recreational activity on the Arizona side of the lake is centered on this vacation village, where everything needed for a lakeside holiday is available: tour boats, fishing, boat rentals, dinner cruises, and much more. Stop at Wahweap Lodge for an excellent view of the lake area. You can take a boat tour of Lake Powell from the Wahweap Marina.

★ **⑲** The best way to appreciate the stunning scenery of Lake Powell is by boat. If you don't have access to your own, a boat tour to **Rainbow Bridge National Monument** is a great way see the enormity of the lake and its incredible, rugged beauty. This 290-foot red-sandstone arch is the world's largest natural bridge and can be reached only by boat or viewed by air. To the Navajos, this is a sacred area with deep religious and spiritual significance, so outsiders are asked not to hike underneath the arch itself.

Sports & the Outdoors

BOATING Lake Powell has been called "the most scenic lake on earth." The 186 mi of clear sapphire waters are edged with vast canyons of red and orange rock. Ninety-six major side canyons intricately twist and turn into the main channel of Lake Powell, into what was once the main artery of the Colorado River through Glen Canyon. In some places the lake is 500 feet deep, and by June the lake's waters begin to warm and stay that way well into October.

At **Aramark's Lake Powell Resorts & Marinas** (✉ Box 56909, Phoenix 85079 ☎ 800/528–6154 central reservations, 928/645–1004 direct to hotel ⎙ 602/331–5258 ⊕ www.visitlakepowell.com) houseboat rentals range widely in size, amenities, and price, depending upon season. For more information on houseboats, *see* Houseboating *in* Where to Stay & Eat, *below.* You may want to rent a powerboat or personal water craft along with a houseboat for exploring the many narrow canyons and waterways on the lake. An 18-foot powerboat for eight passengers runs from approximately $139 to $232 per day. **State Line Marina** (✉ U.S. 89, State Line, UT ☎ 928/645–1111), 1½ mi north of Wahweap Lodge, is part of Aramark's Lake Powell Resorts & Marina concession and site of the boat-rental office. It's here that you pick up rental houseboats, powerboats, kayaks, Jet Skis, and personal water craft. There's also a public launch ramp in the event you're towing your own boat. **Wahweap Marina** (✉ 100 Lake Shore Dr., Wahweap ☎ 928/645–2433) is the largest of the four full-service Lake Powell marinas run by Aramark's Lake Powell Resorts & Marinas. There are 850 slips and the most facilities, including a decent diner, public launch ramp, fishing dock, and a marina store where you can buy fishing licenses and other necessities. It's the only full-service marina on the Arizona side of the lake (the other three marinas—Hite, Bullfrog, and Halls Crossing—are in Utah).

BOAT TOURS Excursions on double-decker scenic cruisers piloted by experienced guides leave from the dock of Lake Powell's **Wahweap Lodge** (⊠ 100 Lake Shore Dr., Wahweap ☎ 928/645–2433 or 800/528–6154). The most popular tour is the half-day trip to Rainbow Bridge National Monument for $80 (lemonade, water, and coffee are included, and you can bring your own snacks or lunch). The full-day cruise visits several side canyons as well as Rainbow Bridge and costs about $109; this one includes a box lunch, lemonade, water, and coffee. A 2½-hour sunset dinner cruise costs about $63 and also departs from Wahweap Lodge: a prime-rib dinner—vegetarian lasagna dinners are available if ordered in advance—is served on the fully enclosed decks of the 95-foot *Canyon King* paddle wheeler, a reproduction of a 19th-century bay boat. The dinner cruise is a 2½-hour tour with the captain's choice of routes.

FISHING Anglers delight in the world-class bass fishing on Lake Powell. You'll hear over and over how the big fish are "biting in the canyons," so you'll need a small vessel if you plan on fishing for the big one. Landing a 20-pound striper isn't unusual (the locals' secret is to use anchovies for bait). Fishing licenses for both Arizona and Utah are available at the **Marina Store at Wahweap Marina** (⊠ 100 Lake Shore Dr., Wahweap ☎ 928/645–1136). **Stix Market** (⊠ 5 S. Lake Powell Blvd., Page ☎ 928/645–2891) can recommend local fishing guides.

HIKING Bring plenty of water and electrolyte-rich beverages such as Gatorade when hiking, and drink often. It is important to remember when hiking at Lake Powell to watch the sky for storms. It may not be raining where you are; however, flooding can occur in downstream canyons—particularly slot canyons—from a storm miles away.

Only seasoned hikers in good physical condition will want to try either of the two trails leading to **Rainbow Bridge**; both are about 26 to 28 mi round-trip through very challenging and rugged terrain. This site is considered sacred by the Navajo, and it's requested that visitors show respect by not walking under the bridge. Take Indian Highway 16 north toward the Utah state border. At the fork in the road, take either direction for about 5 mi to the trailhead leading to Rainbow Bridge. Excursion boats pull in at the dock at the arch, but no supplies are sold there.

Navajo Nation Parks and Recreation Department (⊠ Bldg. 36A, E. AZ 264 ☎ Box 2520, Window Rock 86515 ☎ 928/871–6647 ⊕ www.navajonationparks.org) provides backcountry permits (a slight fee is charged), which must be obtained before hiking to Rainbow Bridge. Write to the office, and allow about a month to process the paperwork.

Where to Stay & Eat

$$ ✕⊡ **Lake Powell Resort.** This sprawling one-story lodge (formerly the Wahweap Lodge), run by Aramark, sits on a promontory above Lake Powell and serves as the center for recreational activities in the area. The

FodorsChoice
★

brightly colored Southwestern-style suites in the newest building are particularly attractive. The semicircular Rainbow Room restaurant ($–$$) offers an extensive Southwestern, American, and Continental menu and breakfast buffet, all with panoramic views of Lake Powell. In season, there are also decent pizzas from Itza Pizza. ⊠ *100 Lake Shore Dr., 7 mi north of Page off of U.S. 89, Wahweap* ⊡ *Box 1597, Page 86040* ☎ *928/645–2433 or 800/528–6154* ⊕ *www.aramarkparks.com* ⤺ *350 rooms* ⟁ *Restaurant, pizzeria, refrigerators, cable TV, 2 pools, boating, waterskiing, fishing, bar, travel services, some pets allowed* ⊟ *AE, D, DC, MC, V.*

CAMPING Beautiful campsites are abundant on Lake Powell, from large beaches to secluded coves, with the most desirable areas accessible only by boat. You are allowed to camp anywhere along the shores of the lake unless it's restricted by the National Park Service; however, camping within ¼ mi of the shoreline requires a portable toilet or bathroom facilities on your boat. Campfires are allowed on the shoreline, but since there's little firewood available around the lake, you'll need to bring your own.

¢ ⟁ **Wahweap Campground.** This campground in the Wahweap Marina complex, which is run by the National Park Service Concessionaire, has views of the lake and serves both RVers and tent campers. There are showers and coin-laundry services at the nearby grocery store. ⊠ *U.S. 89, 5 mi north of Page near shore of Lake Powell, Wahweap 86040* ☎ *928/645–1059* ⤺ *112 tent sites, 94 full hookups* ⟁ *Flush toilets, full hookups, dump station, drinking water, fire pits, grills, picnic tables* ⊞ *$15 tent site, $28 full hookup* ⊟ *AE, D, DC, MC, V* ☉ *Open year-round.*

¢ ⟁ **Wahweap Trailer Village.** This Aramark-managed park for RVs has 120 full-service hookups, showers, and a coin laundry. It's open year-round, and reservations are accepted. ⊠ *U.S. 89, 5 mi north of Page near shore of Lake Powell, Wahweap 86040* ☎ *928/645–1004 or 800/ 528–6154* ⤺ *120 RV sites* ⟁ *Flush toilets, full hookups, dump station, drinking water, guest laundry, showers, picnic tables* ⊟ *AE, D, DC, MC, V* ☉ *Open year-round.*

HOUSEBOATING Without a doubt, the most popular and fun way to vacation on Lake Powell is to rent a houseboat. Houseboats, ranging in size from 36 to 59 feet and sleeping 6 to 12 people, come complete with marine radios, fully equipped kitchens, and bathrooms with hot showers; you need only bring sheets and towels. The larger, deluxe boats are a good choice in hot summer months since they have air-conditioning. **Aramark's Lake Powell Resorts & Marinas** (⊡ Box 56909, Phoenix 85079 ☎ 800/528–6154 ⊕ www.lakepowell.com ⊟ AE, D, DC, MC, V) is the only concessionaire that rents boats on Lake Powell. There's a vast array of vacation packages available. One houseboat that sleeps eight (four double beds) can run about $900 for three nights. Larger, 59-foot Admiral Class–luxury houseboats may cost as much as $3,200 for three nights. You receive hands-on instruction before you leave the marina.

THE NORTHEAST A TO Z

To research prices, get advice from other travelers, and book travel arrangements, visit www.fodors.com.

AIR TRAVEL

No major airlines fly directly to northeastern Arizona. To get closer to this part of the state, you can fly into Sky Harbor International Airport in Phoenix and take a small plane operated by Denver-based Great Lakes Aviation to Page Municipal Airport.

🚩 Carriers **Great Lakes Aviation** ☎ 800/554-5111 ⊕ www.greatlakesav.com.

AIRPORT

🚩 **Page Municipal Airport** ☎ 928/645-4337 ⊕ www.cityofpage.org.

BUS TRAVEL

The Navajo Transit System has extensive, fixed routes throughout the Navajo Reservation as well as charter service; write or phone for schedules and bus station locations. The buses are modern, in good condition, and generally on time, but they do not make frequent runs, and when they do run they can be slow. Fares range from 50¢ for local rides to a high of $13.05 (Window Rock to Tuba City). This can be an up-close-and-personal way to travel the Navajo Nation and meet the people who live here as they go about their daily business.

🚩 **Navajo Transit System** ✎ Drawer 1330, Window Rock 86515 ☎ 928/729-4002.

CAR TRAVEL

The only practical way to tour the Navajo and Hopi nations is by car. If you are arriving from southern California or southern Arizona, Flagstaff is the best jumping-off point into northeastern Arizona. If you are traveling from Utah or Nevada, you might choose to come in from Utah on U.S. 89, starting your tour at Page. For those driving south from Colorado, logical entry points are Farmington and Shiprock, New Mexico, via U.S. 64 (what looks like a more direct route to Canyon de Chelly through Red Rock ends up crossing an unimproved road). Gallup, New Mexico, to the east, is also a convenient starting point for exploring the area.

Because a tour of Navajo-Hopi country involves driving long distances among widely scattered communities, a detailed, up-to-date road map is absolutely essential. A wrong turn could send you many miles out of your way. Gas stations carry adequate state maps, but two other maps are particularly recommended: the AAA (Automobile Association of America) guide to Navajo-Hopi country and the excellent map of the northeastern region prepared by the Navajo Nation Tourism Office.

Road service, auto repairs, and other automotive services are few and far between, so service your vehicle before venturing into the Navajo and Hopi reservations, and carry emergency equipment and supplies. If you need assistance, ask a local for the nearest auto-repair service. Diamond Towing offers a 24-hour emergency road service.

🚩 **Diamond Towing** ✉ Kayenta ☎ 928/697-8437.

ROAD CONDITIONS Most of the 27,000 square mi of the Navajo Reservation and other areas of northeastern Arizona are off the beaten track. Many travelers in northeastern Arizona generally stay on the well-maintained paved thoroughfares, which are patrolled by police officers. If you don't have the equipment for wilderness travel—including a four-wheel-drive vehicle and provisions—and do not have backcountry experience, stay off the dirt roads unless they are signed and graded and the skies are clear. Seek weather information if you see ominous rain clouds in summer or signs of snow in winter. Never drive into dips or low-lying road areas during a heavy rainstorm; they could be flooded or could flood suddenly. If you heed these simple precautions, car travel through the region will be as safe as anywhere else. While driving around the Navajo Nation, tune in to 660 AM (KTNN) for local news and weather.

EMERGENCIES

Dial 911 for emergencies on reservation lands.

⚡ Ambulance & Fire **Kayenta Ambulance** ☎ 928/697-4074. **Page Ambulance** ☎ 928/645-2461.

⚡ Hospitals **Monument Valley Health Center** ⊠ 4 Rock Door Canyon, Monument Valley, UT 84536 ☎ 801/727-3241. **Page Hospital** ⊠ 501 N. Navajo Ave., Page ☎ 928/645-2424. **Sage Memorial Hospital** ⊠ Ganado ☎ 928/755-3411. **U.S. Public Health Service Indian Hospital** ⊠ Chinle ☎ 928/674-7001 ⊠ Fort Defiance ☎ 928/729-5741 ⊠ Keams Canyon ☎ 928/738-2211 ⊠ Tuba City ☎ 928/283-2501.

⚡ Pharmacies **Safeway Pharmacy** ⊠ Page Plaza, Page ☎ 928/645-5714 or 928/645-5068. **Wal-Mart Pharmacy** ⊠ Gateway Plaza, Page ☎ 928/645-2917.

⚡ Police **Canyon de Chelly Police** ☎ 928/674-2111 or 928/674-2112. **Hopi tribal police: Hopi Mesas** ☎ 928/738-2233 or 928/738-2234. **Navajo tribal police** ⊠ Chinle ☎ 928/674-2111 or 928/674-2112 ⊠ Tuba City ☎ 928/283-3111 or 928/283-3112 ⊠ Window Rock ☎ 928/871-6111 or 928/871-6112 ⊠ Kayenta ☎ 928/697-5600 ⊠ **Page Police** ☎ 928/645-2463.

MEDIA

RADIO KTNN radio (660 AM), the Voice of the Navajo Nation, serves the Hopi and Navajo Reservations from studios in Window Rock. Some programming is in Navajo, but there are news and weather reports in English; its "sister" station is KWRK, at 106.1 on the FM dial. Another radio station you might tune to for news and weather is KOB (770 AM, 107.3 FM, or 97.9 FM). For the boater's emergency band, dial Channel 16 on the marine band.

MONEY MATTERS

Wells Fargo has branch offices with ATMs in Window Rock, Kayenta, and Tuba City on the Navajo Reservation. Near the reservation, Flagstaff, Page, Winslow, Chinle, and Holbrook have banks and ATMs.

TIME

Unlike the rest of Arizona (including the Hopi Reservation), the Navajo Reservation observes daylight saving time. Thus for half the year—April to October—it's an hour later on the Navajo Reservation than everywhere else in the state.

TOURS

AIR TOURS   Gallup Flying Service offers photo and scenic aerial tours of Navajoland from Gallup, New Mexico.

🛫 **Gallup Flying Service** ⊠ West Hwy. 66, Gallup, NM ☎ 505/863-6606.

CANYON X TOURS   On private property, the isolated slot canyon known as Canyon X slot
can be toured only by Navajo guide Harley Klemm and his company,
Overland Canyon Tour, which also operates popular tours to Antelope
Canyon. Tours depart from Page at approximately 8 AM and return at
3 PM, by advance reservation only. The six-hour tour for serious shutterbugs ($135 per person) offers treks to three different, off-the-beaten-
track canyons and is guided by a professional slot-canyon photographer.
The four-hour guided hiking tour ($85 per person) is limited to groups
of 16. Because the area is rugged, children are not allowed, and participants should have good physical mobility to climb crevasses and some
rough terrain.

🛫 **Overland Canyon Tours** ⊠ 18 Lake Powell Blvd., Page ☎ 928/608-4072 ⊕ www.
overlandcanyon.com.

TRAIN TRAVEL

No passenger trains enter the interior of the Navajo or Hopi Reservation or stop at any of the other towns along its perimeter. Amtrak
serves Flagstaff.

VISITOR INFORMATION

🛫 **Glen Canyon Recreation Area** ⓓ National Park Service, Box 1507, Page 86040-1507
☎ 928/608-6200 or 928/608-6404 ⊕ www.nps.gov/glca. **Hopi Tribe Office of Public
Relations** ⓓ Box 123, Kykotsmovi 86039 ☎ 928/734-2441 ⊕ www.hopi.nsn.us. **Navajo
Nation Tourism Office** ⓓ Box 663, Window Rock 86515 ☎ 928/871-7371 ⊕ www.
navajoland.com. **Page/Lake Powell Chamber of Commerce** ⊠ 644 N. Navajo Dr., at Dam
Plaza, Page ⓓ Box 727, 86040 ☎ 928/645-2741 ⊕ www.pagelakepowellchamber.org.

EASTERN ARIZONA

5

CLIMB FROM DESERT HEAT
to cool mountain forests via the
Salt River Canyon ⇨*p.236*

HIT THE SLOPES
at Sunrise Park in the White Mountains ⇨*p.243*

DOZE BY THE FIRE
at the Red Setter Inn in alpine Greer ⇨*p.245*

GO FISH
in the "queen of all trout lakes" ⇨*p.250*

TEST YOUR REFLEXES
on the Coronado Trail switchbacks ⇨*p.252*

TAKE A WALK ON THE WILD SIDE
in the Blue Range Primitive Area ⇨*p.254*

SEE THE SUNSET IN A LUNAR LANDSCAPE
in the badlands of the Painted Desert ⇨*p.260*

Updated by
Janet Webb
Farnsworth

IN A STATE OF DRAMATIC NATURAL WONDERS, eastern Arizona is often overlooked—truly a tragedy, as it is one of Arizona's great outdoor playgrounds. In the White Mountains, northeast of Phoenix, you can hike amid the largest stand of ponderosa pine in the world, fish for trout in babbling brooks, swim in clear reservoirs fed by unsullied mountain streams, and, at night, camp under millions of twinkling stars. The region's winter sports are just as varied: you can ski downhill or cross country, snowboard, snowshoe, and snowmobile on hundreds of miles of designated trails. And although some regions were burned in the devastating Rodeo-Chediski wildfire of 2002, visitor services were disrupted only temporarily, though the effects are still evident. At this writing, removal of the burned trees is underway, and new grass is growing in the burn areas.

The White Mountains are unspoiled high country at its best. Certain areas have been designated as primitive wilderness, removed from the touch of people. In these vast tracts, the air is rent with piercing cries of hawks and eagles, and majestic herds of elk graze in verdant, wildflower-laden meadows. Past volcanic activity has left the land strewn with cinder cones, and the whole region is bounded by the Mogollon Rim (pronounced *muh*-gee-on)—a 200-mi geologic upthrust that splits the state—made famous as the "Tonto Rim" in Zane Grey's books. Much of the plant life is unique to this region; this is one of the few places in the country where such desert plants as juniper and manzanita grow intermixed with mountain pines and aspen.

The human aspects of the landscape are equally appealing. Historic Western towns are friendly outposts of down-home hospitality, and the region's many prehistoric ruins are reminders of the rich native cultures that once flourished here. Native Americans are still a vital presence in the region. The Fort Apache Reservation, home to the White Mountain Apache Tribe, is north of the Salt River, and the San Carlos Apache Tribal Reservation is south of the river. Visitors are welcome to explore most reservation lands. All that's required is a permit—easily obtained from tribal offices.

However, there's more to eastern Arizona than the White Mountains. To the north, along historic Route 66, are the Painted Desert and Petrified Forest National Park and Homolovi Ruins State Park—extraordinary attractions in their own right. The austere mesas of the Painted Desert are world famous for their multihued sedimentary layers. Nature has also worked its wonders on the great fallen logs of the Petrified Forest National Park. In Triassic times, the park was a great, steamy swampland; some 225 million years ago, seismic activity forced the swamp's decaying plant matter (and a number of deceased dinosaurs) deep underground, where it eventually turned to stone. Fifty miles west of these unusual geologic remains, Homolovi Ruins State Park marks the site of four major ancestral Hopi pueblos, two of which contain more than 1,000 rooms. Between these artifacts of times past and the recreational bounty of the White Mountains wilderness, eastern Arizona offers a cultural and outdoor experience that defines the pleasures of Arizona.

The itineraries below assume that you're traveling between March and October. Winter travelers may have to rearrange their trips to accommodate seasonal road closures and chain requirements.

If you have Drive up to 🏨 **Pinetop-Lakeside ❸** ⊢, 🏨 **Greer ❺**, or 🏨 **Springerville-**
3 days **Eagar ❼** and take advantage of a day or two of hiking, fishing, or biking. In winter, snow enthusiasts commonly make the pilgrimage to **Sunrise Park Resort ❹** for just a day or two.

If your main priority is visiting the **Petrified Forest National Park ⓭** ⊢ and the **Painted Desert,** spend the first night in 🏨 **Snowflake-Taylor ❿**. On day two tour the park; spend the night in nearby 🏨 **Holbrook ⓬**, or make the scenic 75-mi drive southeast into 🏨 **Springerville-Eagar ❼**. Another option is to retrace your route back on AZ 77 and head east for accommodations in 🏨 **Show Low ❷**. Spend your third day driving back to Phoenix. You can return via U.S. 60 or opt for the daylong trip down the **Coronado Trail,** one of the state's most scenic byways.

If you have After exploring the **Painted Desert** and **Petrified Forest National Park ⓭** ⊢,
5 days head south to the White Mountains and spend the night in either 🏨 **Springerville-Eagar ❼** or 🏨 **Pinetop-Lakeside ❸**, depending on whether you take AZ 77 or U.S. 180. Indulge in a day of local sightseeing in either pair of twin towns, and then spend the following day working your way across east–west AZ 260 through the Apache Sitgreaves National Forest and parts of the White Mountain Apache Reservation, stopping for the night in tiny 🏨 **Greer ❺**. On the last day, retrace your route back to Phoenix via U.S. 60 or, if departing from Springerville-Eagar, via the **Coronado Trail.** If you're looking for solitude and remote beauty, skip poking along AZ 260's towns and head straight from the Petrified Forest down U.S. 180 to **Hannagan Meadow ❾**, returning on the remainder of the Coronado Trail for day five.

Exploring Eastern Arizona

Eastern Arizona runs the gamut of high-desert wonders. In the northern part of the region is the Petrified Forest National Park, covering 93,000 acres and including a portion of the Painted Desert; a straight shot west on Interstate 40 leads to important ancestral Hopi pueblos at Homolovi Ruins State Park. South of here, on the western edge of the region, is Salt River Canyon, known to many as the mini–Grand Canyon, where the San Carlos and Fort Apache Reservations abut. Much of the White Mountains is National Forest land. The mountain town of Pinetop-Lakeside is on the northern edge of the Sitgreaves National Forest; Greer is in the middle of the forest. Springerville-Eagar is just north of the Apache National Forest boundary. All three towns are connected by AZ 260. At Springerville-Eagar, you can connect to U.S. 191, also known as the Coronado Trail Scenic Byway. Towering over this southern part of the White Mountains is Mount Baldy, an 11,590-foot extinct volcano considered sacred by the Apache. Of note—and definitely worth exploring—is the Mogollon Rim, a limestone escarpment that extends 200 mi from southwest of Flagstaff to the White Mountains in eastern Arizona. In the winter months, stick to major thoroughfares, as many Forest Service roads are closed, and be sure to call for a road and weather report before setting off during this time.

About the Restaurants

In the White Mountains, you might settle in for a relaxing evening at a candlelit restaurant in the pines. "Formal dining" is almost unheard of in the mountains, and a laid-back atmosphere is preferred by residents and visitors alike. If cowboy-size steaks and Old West atmosphere are what you seek, choose a more rustic setting at one of the area's many Western-style cafés. In and around the Navajo and Hopi reservations, be sure to sample Indian tacos, an authentic treat made with scrumptious fry bread, beans, and chiles.

About the Hotels

The communities of Pinetop-Lakeside, Greer, Show Low, and Springerville-Eagar offer lodging choices including modern resorts, rustic cabins, and small bed-and-breakfasts. Note that air-conditioning is not a standard amenity in the high country, where the nights are cool enough for a blanket even in summer. Closer to the Navajo and Hopi reservations, many establishments are run by Native Americans, tribal enterprises intent on offering first-class service and hospitality.

WHAT IT COSTS				
$$$$	**$$$**	**$$**	**$**	**¢**
RESTAURANTS over $30	$20–$30	$12–$20	$8–$12	under $8
HOTELS over $250	$175–$250	$120–$175	$70–$120	under $70

Restaurant prices are per person for a main course at dinner. Hotel prices are for two people in a standard double room in high season, excluding taxes and service charges.

Numbers in the text correspond to numbers in the margin and on the Eastern Arizona map.

Timing

If you're a skier, winter is definitely the time to tour the White Mountains. The White Mountain Winter Games at Sunrise Park Resort bring real-life mushing to the region in January.

Spring is unpredictable, with snow sometimes lasting to early May. Generally, Sunrise Ski Resort closes by mid-March, and forest roads are open in May. In mid-May, the tiny hamlet of Greer comes alive to celebrate Greer Days with a parade, crafts, dances, and a fishing derby. Crowds begin converging on the White Mountains starting in late June, when school is out and Valley of the Sun temperatures start to become uncomfortably warm.

5

Hiking & Bicycling

Hikers and mountain bikers of all abilities enjoy the White Mountains' interconnecting loop trails, which are open to those on foot or on two nonmotorized wheels. Be sure to stop at ranger stations for maps and tips on trails and overnight hikes. When planning your hike, allow one hour for each 2 mi of trail covered, plus an additional hour for every 1,000 feet gained in altitude. Farther north, day hikes through the Painted Desert Wilderness are a great way to explore the park's backcountry. Mountain bikers will thrill over the White Mountain Trail System's 225 mi of interconnecting multiuse trails. Many bike routes follow narrow Forest Service roads, which carry heavy traffic during the logging season from April to November. Be especially cautious when biking on reservation roads, as bicyclists are generally unexpected. Always carry ample water and be aware that poison ivy grows in White Mountain wilderness areas.

Fishing

Anglers flock to the more than 65 lakes, streams, and reservoirs in the White Mountains, where they hook German browns, rainbow, and brook trout, as well as the occasional arctic grayling or native Apache trout, the official state fish, which is unique to Arizona. Early spring is prime trout-fishing season, but even in the winter, devoted anglers can be found ice-fishing on Nelson Reservoir or Hawley Lake. High-country warm-water fishing consists mostly of largemouth bass, bluegill, catfish, and walleye, hailed as the tastiest catch in the region. During winter months only artificial lures and flies are permitted. An Arizona fishing license is required at these sites; on tribal land, an additional White Mountain Apache fishing license is required.

Native American Ruins

North of Springerville-Eagar, Casa Malpais Archaeological Park is a prehistoric pueblo site with construction characteristics of both the ancient Puebloan peoples to the north and the Mogollon peoples to the south. Today, both the Hopi and Zuni peoples hotly claim individual affiliations with the sacred ruins of Casa Malpais, thought to have been a prominent religious center with an impressive astronomical calendar and the largest kiva (sunken ceremonial chamber) ever discovered in the United States. Nearby Lyman Lake State Park has petroglyph trails with some of the region's more accessible rock art. West of Holbrook, Homolovi Ruins State Park is home to a large complex of Hopi ancestral pueblos. Petroglyphs and pueblos dating back more than 600 years can be found at stops along the 28-mi park road in the Petrified Forest National Park.

Skiing & Snowmobiling

Famous regionally for winter skiing, the 11,000-foot White Mountains offer hilly, wooded landscapes that invite downhill and cross-country skiing adventurers. Greer is an ideal hub for cross-country skiers: The nearby Pole Knoll Trail System and surrounding Forest Service roads make for 33 mi of cross-country trails. No matter where you stay in the White Mountains, the drive to Sunrise Park Resort—the state's largest ski resort—with 65 trails on 3 mountains—is never more than an hour away, and there are equipment-rental facilities throughout the region. Snowmobilers enjoy the area's dense forest and expansive meadows; the more adventurous enjoy the long-distance routes connecting Sunrise Ski Area to Williams Valley (near Alpine) or Hannagan Meadow.

Autumn is a splendid time for a drive down the Coronado Trail, with hairpin turns winding through the yellows and golds of aspen and oak. The Pinetop-Lakeside Fall Festival is held the last weekend of September, with a parade and crafts booths. The White Mountain Apache Tribal Fair is celebrated Labor Day weekend with a parade and professional Native American rodeo.

THE WHITE MOUNTAINS

With elevations climbing to more than 11,000 feet, the White Mountains of east-central Arizona are a winter wonderland and a summer haven from the desert heat. In the 1870s John Gregory Bourke labeled the region "a strange upheaval, a freak of nature, a mountain canted up on one side; one rides along the edge and looks down two or three thousand feet into . . . a weird scene of grandeur and rugged beauty." It is still grand and rugged, carved by deep river canyons and tall cliffs covered with ponderosa pine. It is also much less remote than it was in Bourke's time, with a full-scale real-estate boom now under way.

Winter travelers through the White Mountains should be aware that weather conditions can change without notice in these higher elevations. Call for weather information before heading out to White Mountains highways.

Salt River Canyon

❶ *40 mi north of Globe on U.S. 60.*

Fodor'sChoice

★

Exposing a time lapse of 500 million years, the multicolored spires, buttes, mesas, and walls of the **Salt River Canyon** have inspired its nickname, the mini–Grand Canyon. Approaching the Salt River Canyon from Phoenix, U.S. 60 climbs through rolling hills, and the terrain changes from high desert with cactus and mesquite trees to forests of ponderosa pine. After entering the San Carlos Indian Reservation, the highway drops 2,000 feet—from the Natanes Plateau into the canyon's vast gorge—and makes a series of hairpin turns down to cross the Salt River. Stop at the viewing and interpretive display area before crossing the bridge to stretch your legs. Wander along the banks below and enjoy the rock-strewn rapids. On hot Arizona days you can slip your shoes off and dip your feet into the chilly water for a cool respite. The river and canyon are open to hiking, camping, fishing, and white-water rafting, but you will need a permit as this is tribal land. For information and recreational permits, contact either the **San Carlos Apache Tribe** (☎ 928/475–2343) or the **White Mountain Apache Tribe** (☎ 928/338–4385).

The Salt River forms the boundary between the two large Apache reservations of eastern Arizona. The **San Carlos Apache Indian Reservation** (☎ 928/475–2361 for tribal offices), established in 1871 for various Apache tribes, covers 1.8 million acres southeast of Salt River Canyon. One third of the reservation is covered with forest, and the rest is desert. The San Carlos Apaches number about 12,500 and are noted for their beadwork and basketry. Peridot, a beautiful green stone, is mined near the town of Peridot and made into jewelry. The Apache Gold Casino and cattle ranching provide most of the tribal income.

The 1.6-million-acre **Fort Apache Indian Reservation** (☎ 928/338–1230 for tribal tourism) is the ancestral home of the White Mountain Apache Tribe. The elevation of the tribal lands ranges from 3,000 feet at the bottom of Salt River to 11,000 feet in the White Mountains. Most of the over 12,000 tribal members live in nine towns, with the largest, Whiteriver (population 2,500), serving as tribal headquarters. Tribal enterprises include Sunrise Ski Resort, Hon Dah Casino, cattle ranching, and lumber.

en route

The road out of the Salt River Canyon climbs along the canyon's northern cliffs, providing views of this truly spectacular chasm, unfairly overlooked in a state full of world-famous gorges. The highway continues some 50 mi northward to the **Mogollon Rim**—a huge geologic ledge that bisects much of Arizona—and its cool upland pine woods.

Show Low

❷ *60 mi north of the Salt River Canyon on U.S. 60.*

Why, yes, Show Low *is* an odd name for a town. Local legend has it that two partners, Clark and Cooley, homesteaded the surrounding 100,000 acres in 1870 but found themselves wanting to dissolve the partnership some years later after an argument. The two decided to play cards, after which the winner would buy out the loser. On the last hand of the night, Cooley was a point behind when Clark allegedly offered "show low and you win." Cooley cut the deck and came up with the deuce of clubs, thereby winning the game and the land. Part of the partners' then-ranch is now the town of Show Low, and the main drag through town is called Deuce of Clubs.

Show Low has little of the charm of its neighboring White Mountains communities, but it is the main commercial center for the High Country. Additionally, the city is a crossing point for east–west traffic along the Mogollon Rim and traffic headed for Holbrook and points north. If you're heading up to the Painted Desert and Petrified Forest from Phoenix, you might want to spend the night here.

Sports & the Outdoors

FISHING   **Show Low Lake** (⊠ Show Low Lake Rd. ☎ 928/537–4126), south of town and 1 mi off AZ 260, holds the state record for the largest walleye catch and is well stocked with largemouth bass, bluegill, and catfish. Facilities include a bait shop, marina with boat rentals, and campsites with bathrooms and showers. **Fool Hollow Lake Recreational Area** (⊠ 2 mi north

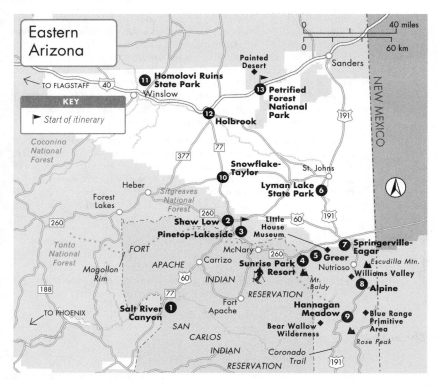

of U.S. 60 off AZ 260 ☎ 928/537–3680), is open year-round for camping, fishing, and boating. Set amid a picturesque, piney 800 acres, the lake is stocked with rainbow trout, walleye, and bass, and the surrounding area provides wonderful opportunities for wildlife viewing. **Troutback Flyfishing** (🖃 Box 864, Show Low 85902 ☎ 928/532–3473 or 800/903–4092 ⊕ www.troutback.com) has access to some of the most scenic lakes and private waters in the region. From April through October, this fishing guide company specializes in fly-fishing instruction, guided walk-wades, and float tube and boating trips.

GOLF **Show Low Golf Club** (🖃 860 N. 36th Dr., at AZ 260 ☎ 928/537–4564) is a par-70 course with a back 9 in the pines and a front 9 in a more open meadow setting. Need to practice driving or putting? You can do it here. It's closed in winter. **Silver Creek Golf Club** (🖃 2051 Silver Lake Blvd. ☎ 928/537–2744 ⊕ www.silvercreekgolfclub.com), 5 mi east of town on U.S. 60, then 7½ mi north on Bourdon Ranch Road, is an 18-hole championship golf course. Voted by the PGA as one of the top 10 golf courses in Arizona, it's also one of the more affordable. Given its lower elevation, this course is usually a few degrees warmer than Show Low and stays open year-round. Greens fees change seasonally; call for details.

Fodor's Choice
★

Where to Stay & Eat

¢–$$ ✕ **Licano's Mexican Food and Steakhouse.** You'll find everything here from nachos to prime rib and lobster tail. It's open seven days a week. The spacious but cozy lounge, with a weekday happy hour 4:30–6:30, stays open to 9:30 nightly. ✉ *573 W. Deuce of Clubs* ☎ *928/537–8220* ▭ *AE, D, DC, MC, V.*

¢–$ ✕ **High in the Pines Deli.** Locals flock to this quaint deli and coffeehouse a block east of Deuce of Clubs for tasty specialty sandwiches—the roasted pork-tenderloin sandwich is out of this world. European-style charcuterie boards include fine selections of pâtés, meats, and cheeses served with a fresh baguette. On a cold day, try their delicious Show Low hot chocolate. Box lunches are available for those planning to hit the road or spend the day exploring the local surroundings. ✉ *1191 E. Hall* ☎ *928/537–1453* ▭ *AE, D, MC, V* ⊘ *Closed Sun. No dinner.*

$–$$$ ▥ **Best Western Paint Pony Lodge.** Spacious rooms here have wood accents and large picture windows overlooking Arizona's pine-studded high country. Suites and some rooms include fireplaces, and use of an off-property gym is free for hotel guests. ✉ *581 W. Deuce of Clubs, 85901* ☎ *928/537–5773* ⊕ *www.bestwestern.com* ⇆ *46 rooms, 4 suites* ⚴ *In-room data ports, some microwaves, refrigerators, cable TV, bar, no-smoking rooms* ▭ *AE, D, DC, MC, V* ▥◎ *CP.*

★ ¢ ▥ **KC Motel.** Victorian decor, including four-poster beds, makes this a not-so-typical motel. Large rooms exude the homey feel of a B&B. All rooms have cable TV and refrigerators. ✉ *60 W. Deuce of Clubs, 85901* ☎ *928/537–4433 or 800/531–7152* ⇆ *37 rooms* ⚴ *Refrigerators, cable TV, hot tub* ▭ *AE, D, DC, MC, V* ▥◎ *CP.*

Pinetop-Lakeside

▶ ❸ *15 mi southeast of Show Low on AZ 260.*

At 7,200 feet, the community of Pinetop-Lakeside borders on the world's largest stand of ponderosa pine. Two towns, Pinetop and Lakeside, were incorporated in 1984 to form this municipality—although they still retain separate post offices. The modest year-round population is 4,500, but in summer months it can jump as high as 40,000, so the secret about this mountain resort town is now officially out. Once popular only with the retirement and summer-home set, the city now lures thousands of "flatlanders" up from the Valley of the Sun with its gorgeous scenery, excellent multiuse trails, premier golf courses, and temperatures rarely exceeding 85°F. The main drag is known as both AZ 260 and White Mountain Boulevard.

Sports & the Outdoors

BICYCLING & Ranked No. 3 in the country's "Top Ten Trail Towns" by the Ameri-
HIKING can Hiking Society, Pinetop-Lakeside is the primary trailhead for the White Mountains Trails System, roughly 180 mi of interconnecting multiuse loop trails spanning the White Mountains. All these trails are open to mountain bikers, horseback riders, and hikers.

Half a mile off AZ 260 on Woodland Road, **Big Springs Environmental Study Area** is a ½-mi loop trail that wanders by riparian meadows, two streams, and a spring-fed pond. A series of educational signs is devoted to the surrounding flora and fauna. The trailhead for **Country Club Trail** is at the junction of Forest Service Roads 182 and 185; these 3½ mi of moderate-difficulty mountain-biking and hiking trails can be spiced up by following the spur-trail to the top of Pat Mullen Mountain and back. The well-traveled and very easy **Mogollon Rim Interpretive Trail** follows a small part of the 19th-century **Crook Trail** along the Mogollon Rim; the ¼-mi path, with a trailhead just west of the Pinetop-Lakeside city limits, is well marked with placards describing local wildlife and geography. The 8-mi **Panorama Trail,** rated moderate, affords astonishing views from the top of extinct double volcanoes known as the Twin Knolls and passes though a portion of designated wildlife habitat area; the trailhead is 6 mi east on Porter Mountain Road, off AZ 260.

You can get individual trail brochures or other information from the **Apache-Sitgreaves National Forest** (⊠ Lakeside Ranger Station, 2022 W. White Mountain Blvd., Lakeside 85929 ☎ 928/368–5111 ⊕ www.fs.fed. us/r3/asnf), including a $2 booklet on the White Mountains Trail System.

FISHING   East of Pinetop-Lakeside and 9 mi south of AZ 260, 260-acre **Hawley Lake** (⊠ AZ 473, Hawley Lake) sits on Apache territory and yields mostly rainbow trout; rental boats are available in the marina. Tribal permits are required for all recreational activities: contact **Tribal Game and Fish** (☎ 928/338–4385) for details. **Bob's Bang Room Sporting Goods & Pawn Shop** (⊠ 3973 AZ 260, Lakeside ☎ 928/368–5040 or 877/368–5040 ⊕ www.bobsbangroom.com) deals in hunting, archery, and pawned fishing equipment.

GOLF   **Pinetop Lakes Golf & Country Club** (⊠ 4643 Buck Springs Rd., Pinetop ☎ 928/369–4184 ⊕ www.pinetoplakesgolf.com) has fewer trees than other area courses, but it offers several water hazards by way of compensation. The shorter course is wonderful for public play. The club has a driving range, putting greens, and tennis courts, not to mention a restaurant and lounge. It's open April to October. Greens fees range from $26 to $36 for 18 holes.

HORSEBACK   **Porter Mountain Stables** (⊠ 4048 Porter Mountain Rd., Lakeside ☎ 928/ RIDING   368–5306) offers one-hour to all-day horseback trips in the summer.

SKIING &   **Snowriders** (⊠ 857 E. White Mountain Blvd., Pinetop ☎ 928/367–3373 SNOWBOARDING   ⊕ www.azsnowriders.com) sells and rents skis and snowboards and offers special seasonal rental packages for children 12 and under. It's open December through March 15, weather permitting.

The **Skier's Edge** (⊠ 560 W. White Mountain Blvd., Pinetop ☎ 928/367–6200 or 800/231–3831 ⊕ www.skiersedgepinetop.com) has cross-country and downhill skis as well as snowboards and boots. At the same location, Paradise Creek Anglers sells fly-fishing and hiking supplies.

Where to Stay & Eat

$$–$$$ ✕ **Christmas Tree.** Year-round festive lights and displays of colorful ornaments inside this restaurant highlight a theme that's been at work here since 1977. Chicken and dumplings are the house specialty, but beef Stroganoff and honey duck served with fried apples are also highly rec-

ommended. Steaks, chops, lamb, and seafood are also available, as well as a children's menu. Save room for a piece of the Christmas Tree's famous fresh-baked fruit cobbler or Texas sheet cake à la mode. Reservations are a good idea. ⊠ *455 N. Woodland Rd., near AZ 260, Lakeside* ☎ *928/367–3107* ▭ *D, MC, V* ⊙ *Closed third week in Oct.–Thanksgiving. No lunch.*

$–$$$ ✕ **Phineas T's.** Word has it that the stuffed jumbo prawns, rack of lamb, and Creole cioppino here have no equal in the White Mountains. The wine list is high-end, and the bar sells premium liquors and beers. The separate cigar and no-smoking bars are perfect for catching live music every Tuesday night. ⊠ *1450 E. White Mountain Blvd., Pinetop* ☎ *928/ 367–7400* ▭ *AE, D, DC, MC, V.*

★ $–$$ ✕ **Annie's Gift Shop and Tea Room.** Across the highway from the Lakeside Fire Department, this genteel sandwich shop has specialty sandwiches, quiches, salads, and other delectables that make it the local "in" spot for lunch. ⊠ *2849 White Mountain Blvd., Lakeside* ☎ *928/368–5737* ▭ *AE, D, MC, V* ⊙ *Closed July–Dec.*

¢ ✕ **Artsparks and MorMor Coffee House.** The coffee here is widely regarded as the best in town. Try the fresh baked pastries and muffins to make your coffee break complete. An attached pottery store, where customers paint their own pottery, make this a lively gathering place. Saturday night musical entertainment adds to the fun. ⊠ *1450 E. White Mountain Blvd., Pinetop* ☎ *928/367–5456* ▭ *MC, V* ⊙ *Closed Mon. and Tues. Oct.–Apr.*

¢ ✕ **Khadija's Bakery & Bistro.** You won't find a more perfect spot for breakfast in Pinetop-Lakeside. Khadija's (pronounced ha-*dee*-sha's) offers scrumptious, expertly prepared eggs, bacon, hash browns, and buttermilk pancakes. If you're en route to the slopes or hiking trails, order Breakfast on the Run—a gourmet answer to the Egg McMuffin. After 11 AM, sample daily-made soups and sandwiches. Make sure to save room for pastries. ⊠ *4945 White Mountain Blvd., Lakeside* ☎ *928/537– 7776* ▭ *D, MC, V* ⊙ *Closed Tues. No dinner.*

$–$$$ ▥ **Northwoods Resort.** Each of the 14 cottage-cabins at this mountain retreat has its own covered porch and barbecue. Inside, natural wood paneling, brick fireplaces, and wall-to-wall carpeting add to the homey feel. Full electric kitchens have full-size refrigerators, ovens, microwave ovens, and adjacent dinette sets. Proprietors here keep their promise to provide "meticulously maintained" accommodations, all the way down to a daily replenishment of firewood. The honeymoon cabin features an indoor spa, and the two-story cabins can accommodate up to 18 people. ⊠ *AZ 260, Milepost 352* ⌂ *Box 397N, Pinetop 85935* ☎ *928/367– 2966 or 800/813–2966* 🖷 *928/367–2969* ⊕ *www.northwoodsaz.com* ↪ *14 cabins* ⅌ *BBQs, kitchens, cable TV, outdoor hot tub, volleyball, playground, laundry facilities; no a/c, no smoking* ▭ *D, MC, V.*

$–$$ ▥ **Hon-Dah Resort Casino and Conference Center.** A surreal staircase tableau of stuffed high-country creatures atop a mountain of boulders welcomes you to Hon-Dah. The main draw here is the casino, with hundreds of slot machines, live poker and blackjack, and weekend entertainment. Because the hotel is connected to the casino, you might pop out to fill the ice bucket but wind up at a slot machine instead. Large rooms all have coffeemakers and wet bars. A high-roof atrium holds the pool and hot tub. The Indian Pine Restaurant serves three daily meals, and a small gift shop sells local Apache crafts. The casino is on the Fort Apache Indian Reservation and operated by the White Mountain Apache Tribe. ⊠ *777 AZ 260, Pinetop 85935* ☎ *928/369–0299 or 800/929–8744* ᕦ *928/369–7405* ⊕ *www.hon-dah.com* ↝ *126 rooms, 2 suites* ⚭ *Restaurant, refrigerators, cable TV, indoor pool, hot tub, sauna, 2 bars, casino, nightclub, shop, meeting rooms, no-smoking rooms* ⊟ *AE, D, DC, MC, V.*

$–$$ 🏠 **Pinetop Country B&B and Cottages.** This inn, on 4 acres surrounded by tall ponderosa pines, has three large guest rooms plus three lakeside cottages. A common room has a cozy fireplace, a library, and an extensive video selection; a 1950s-style game room is loaded with entertaining diversions, including a jukebox, pool table, large-screen TV, and Pac-Man game. Choose from 10 items at breakfast; homemade desserts are served in the evening. Some rooms have fireplaces and small balconies. ⊠ *2444 Jan La., Pinetop 85935* ☎ *928/367–0479 or 888/521–5044* ᕦ *928/367–0479* ⊕ *www.pinetopcountry.com* ↝ *3 rooms 3 cottages* ⚭ *Refrigerators, cable TV, bicycles, billiards, recreation room, no-smoking rooms; no a/c* ⊟ *MC, V* ⟋◉⟍ *BP.*

$–$$ 🏠 **Whispering Pines Resort.** These well-maintained cabins have fireplaces, grills, and double sofa beds. One-, two-, and three-bedroom units—some with second bathrooms—have either handsome knotty-pine or more modern wood-paneled interiors. The four log cabins, three of them studio units, have that rustic hideaway vibe. Couples may want to request one of the alpine suites, with whirlpool tubs. On 12 acres bordering the Apache National Forest, cabins are within walking distance of Woodland Lake and Walnut Creek. There's a four-night minimum stay in summer and during holidays. ⊠ *AZ 260, just beyond Milepost 352* ⌖ *Box 1043, Pinetop 85935* ☎ *928/367–4386 or 800/840–3867* ᕦ *928/367–3702* ⊕ *www.whisperingpinesaz.com* ↝ *36 cabins* ⚭ *Some in-room hot tubs, some kitchens, some kitchenettes, cable TV, hot tub, laundry facilities, some pets allowed (fee), no-smoking rooms; no a/c* ⊟ *AE, D, MC, V.*

Nightlife

Charlie Clark's Steakhouse (⊠ 1701 E. White Mountain Blvd., Pinetop ☎ 928/367–4900) has been around since 1938; the cook knows how to produce a mouthwatering prime rib and other specialties over mesquite. The lounge, with a full bar, pool tables, and a bouncing jukebox, stays open until 10 PM on the weekends, which is about as late as nightlife lasts in Pinetop. Major credit cards are accepted.

Shopping

Orchard Antiques (⊠ 1664 W. White Mountain Blvd.; Lakeside ☎ 928/368–6563), open from April to October and on all major holidays, is a reliable purveyor of high-quality furniture, glass, china, and sterling and deals in some quilts and vintage clothing. **Antique Mercantile Company** (⊠ 2106 W. White Mountain Blvd., Lakeside ☎ 928/368–9090) has century-old collectibles ranging from first-edition law encyclopedias to working Victrolas. Upscale-quality glass, china, furniture, military items, and vintage sports and camera equipment are all for sale. Open by appointment only during winter. The log-cabin **Harvest Moon Antiques** (⊠ 392 W. White Mountain Blvd., Pinetop ☎ 928/367–6973), open Memorial Day through Thanksgiving weekend, specializes in Old West relics, ranging from buckskins and Apache wares to old guns and U.S. Cavalry items. This is an excellent place to find affordable Indian jewelry and Navajo rugs; look for the tepees set up outside.

Sunrise Park Resort

❻ *17 mi southeast of McNary, 7 mi south of AZ 260 on AZ 273.*

In winter and early spring, skiers and other snow lovers flock to this ski area. There's plenty more than downhill and cross-country skiing here, including snowboarding, snowmobiling, snowshoeing, ice-fishing, and sleigh rides. The resort has 10 lifts and 65 trails on 3 mountains rising to 11,000 feet. Eighty percent of the downhill runs are for beginning or intermediate skiers, there's a "ski-wee" hill for youngsters, and many less-intense trails begin at the top so skiers of varying skill levels can enjoy riding the chairlifts together. The Sunrise Express high-speed chairlift anchors the 10 lifts and has an uphill skier capacity of 16,000 skiers per hour. One-day lift tickets are $39. Sunrise's Snowboard Park features jumps of all difficulty levels and its own sound system. Restricted to snowboarders only, the area—between the Pump House and Fairway runs—can support enthusiasts' quests to "get a great ollie, hit the kicker, and go big," while simultaneously lessening tension on the hill between boarders and skiers. Cross-country skiers enjoy 13½ mi of interconnecting trails, and snowmobilers have their own 25 mi of separate, designated trails. If you don't have your own equipment, you can rent it at the resort's ski shop. In summer, a marina is open for boat rentals on beautiful Sunrise Lake. ⊠ *AZ 273, 7 mi south of AZ 260* ☜ *Box 117, Greer 85927* ☎ *928/735–7669, 800/772–7669 hotel reservations and snow reports* ▤ *AE, D, MC, V.*

Where to Stay

$–$$$ ▦ **Sunrise Park Lodge.** Catering to those who want to be as close as possible to the slopes, this hotel runs a shuttle to the slopes every half hour, has comfortable rooms with ski racks, and offers lodging and lift-ticket packages. The VIP Suite, with its wet bar, refrigerator, microwave oven, and hot tub, comes with two lift tickets that grant the holders line-cutting privileges on the slopes. Master suites feature Queen Anne–style beds and sleeper sofas. In the summer, you can enjoy boating on Sunrise Lake, "3-D" archery, scenic chairlift rides, horseback riding, and mountain biking on designated trails. ⊠ *AZ 273, 7 mi south of AZ 260* ☜ *Box 117, Greer 85927* ☎ *928/735–7669 or 800/772–7669* ☐ *928/735–7315* ⊕ *www.sunriseskipark.com* ☜ *95 rooms, 6 suites* ☒ *2 restaurants, some in-room hot tubs, some microwaves, some refrigerators, cable TV, indoor pool, lake, outdoor hot tub, sauna, boating, marina, volleyball, ski shop, lounge, recreation room, meeting rooms, no-smoking rooms; no a/c* ▤ *AE, D, DC, MC, V.*

Greer

★ ❺   *35 mi southeast of Pinetop-Lakeside and 15 mi southwest of Eagar on AZ 260; 8 mi east of AZ 273 turnoff, via AZ 373 south.*

The charming community of Greer sits just south of AZ 260 among pine, spruce, willow, and aspen on the banks of the Little Colorado River. At an elevation of 8,500 feet, this portion of gently sloping national forest land is covered with meadows and reservoirs and is dominated by 11,590-foot Baldy Peak. Much of the surrounding area remains under the control of the Apache tribe, so visitors must take care to respect Apache law and land. AZ 373 is also Greer's "Main Street"; it winds through the village and crosses the Little Colorado River, eventually coming to a dead end. It's affectionately called the Road to Nowhere.

Listed on the National Register of Historic Places, the picturesque **Butterfly Lodge Museum** was built as a hunting lodge in 1914 by John Butler, the husband of "Aunt Molly" (of Molly Butler Lodge fame), for author James Willard Schultz and his artist son, Lone Wolf, a prolific painter of Indian and Western scenes. There's a small gift shop. In spring and summer, take time to watch the surrounding meadow come to life with beautiful butterflies, from which the lodge got its name. ⊠ *AZ 373 at CR 1126* ☎ *928/735–7514* ⊕ *www.wmonline.com/butterflylodge.htm* 🎫 *$2* ☉ *Memorial Day–Labor Day, Fri.–Sun. 10–5.*

Sports & the Outdoors

The **Circle B Market** (⊠ 38940 AZ 373 ☎ 928/735–7540) rents cross-country skis and sells sleds in winter and tackle and inner tubes the rest of the year. Fishing licenses and reservation permits are also for sale.

FISHING   The three Greer Lakes are actually the Bunch, River, and Tunnel reservoirs. Bait and fly-fishing options are scenic and plentiful, and there are several places to launch a boat. Winding through Greer, the Little Colorado River's West Fork is well stocked with brookies and rainbows and has 23 mi of fishable waters.

HIKING   The difficult but accessible **Mount Baldy Trail** begins at **Sheeps Crossing,** southwest of Greer on AZ 273. In just under 8 mi (one-way), the trail climbs the northern flank of 11,590-foot Mount Baldy, the second-highest peak in Arizona. Note that the very summit of Baldy is on the White Mountain Apache Reservation. Considered sacred land, this final ¼ mi is off-limits to non-Apaches. The boundary is clearly marked; please respect it, regardless of how much you might wish to continue on to the peak.

SKIING   Cross-country skiers find Greer an ideally situated hub for some of the mountain's best trails. About 2½ mi west of AZ 373 on AZ 260, a trailhead marks the starting point for the **Pole Knoll Trail System,** nearly 30 mi of well-marked, groomed cross-country trails interlacing through the Apache Sitgreaves National Forest and color-coded by experience level. Trail maps are available from the **Apache-Sitgreaves National Forest** (⊠ Springerville Ranger District, 165 S. Mountain Ave., Springerville 85938 ☎ 928/333–4372 ⊕ www.fs.fed.us/r3/asnf).

Where to Stay & Eat

¢–$ ✕ **Greer Mountain Resort Country Cafe.** This plant-hung diner-café is open daily from 7 AM to 3 PM year-round. Grab a seat by the fireplace and sample the homemade ranch beans, a signature grilled-cheese sandwich with green chiles and tomato, or a piece of fresh-baked cobbler. ✉ *AZ 373, 1½ mi south of AZ 260* ☎ *928/735–7560* ⊟ *MC, V* ⊘ *No dinner.*

¢–$ ✕ **Rendezvous Diner.** Previous reincarnations of this cozy, colorful eatery
Fodor'sChoice include a family home as well as Greer's main post office. Rendezvous
★ Diner has earned a reputation for serving up some of Greer's tastiest dishes, not to mention the area's best hot spiced cider. Of particular note are the pineapple teriyaki and green-chile burgers, 8-ounce sirloin steak with shrimp, and generous portions of homemade desserts. It's open year-round for breakfast, lunch, and dinner. ✉ *117 Main St.* ☎ *928/735–7483* ⊟ *MC, V* ⊘ *Closed Tues.*

¢–$ ✕🏨 **Molly Butler Lodge.** Colorful quilts and barn-wood furnishings fill the comfortable rooms at Arizona's oldest lodge. There are no phones or TVs in the rooms, but both are available in the main lodge. The menu in the Molly Butler Lodge restaurant ($–$$) is divided between entrées "upstream" (sautéed scallops, halibut, trout amandine) and "downstream" (prime rib au jus, "hot dang" chili), but it's the hand-cut, aged steaks that draw locals. Sweeping views of Greer's pristine wilderness are enjoyed amid the lodge's cozy, rustic decor, with kerosene lamps on the tables and mounted hunting trophies on the walls. There is a two-night minimum. ✉ *109 Main St., 85927* ☎ *928/735–7226* ⊕ *www.mollybutlerlodge.com* ↯ *11 rooms* ♻ *Bar, video game room, some pets allowed (fee); no a/c, no room phones, no room TVs* ⊟ *AE, D, MC, V.*

$$–$$$$ 🏨 **Red Setter Inn.** From the vaulted ceiling in the breakfast room to the
Fodor'sChoice player piano in the gathering room, this hand-hewn-log inn is rich in
★ detail. Some rooms have fireplaces and private decks; the cottage rooms share a full kitchen. A spacious deck has Adirondack chairs and permits excellent wildlife viewing—don't be surprised to see mountain lions or black bear around the stream below, stopping to have a drink or to catch unsuspecting trout. Weekend guests who set out to hike or fish during the day are sent off with sack lunches. Weekends, there is a two-night minimum stay (three nights over holidays). ✉ *8 Main St.* ☎ *Box 133, 85927* ☎ *928/735–7441 or 888/994–7337* 🖷 *928/735–7425* ⊕ *www.redsetterinn.com* ↯ *13 rooms, 3 cottages* ♻ *Some in-room hot tubs, some kitchens, some in-room VCRs, fishing, hiking, cross-country skiing, recreation room; no a/c, no room phones, no TV in some rooms, no kids under 16, no smoking* ⊟ *AE, D, MC, V* ⫙ *BP.*

$–$$$ 🏨 **White Mountain Lodge.** On the banks of the Little Colorado River, this charming lodge is the oldest building in Greer. Most of the individually decorated rooms are country-cozy. Separate housekeeping cabins have gas fireplaces, and several have whirlpool tubs. An always-accessible sideboard in the lodge's great room is stocked with homemade cookies and spiced cider, as well as teas and cocoa. If you'd like a bit of sleuthing with your stay, be sure to ask about Murder Mystery Weekends. ✉ *140 Main St.* ☎ *928/735–7568 or 888/493–7568* 🖷 *928/735–7498* ⊕ *www.wmlodge.com* ↯ *6 rooms, 6 cabins* ♻ *Some in-room hot tubs, some* *kitchens, cable TV, some in-room VCRs, outdoor hot tub, hiking; no a/c, no smoking* ⊟ *AE, D, DC, MC, V* ⅦⅪ *BP.*

$–$$ ⊞ **Greer Mountain Resort.** Budget travelers and families appreciate these cabin-style accommodations. Each unit is different, but most can sleep up to six people and contain either a fireplace or a gas- or wood-burning stove. The smallest, one-bedroom, knotty-pine units have no fireplaces, but they're reasonably priced and good for couples. You may want to enjoy breakfast or lunch at the resort's roadside restaurant, or you can whip up your own feast in the fully equipped kitchens. ⊠ *AZ 373, 1½ mi south of AZ 260* ⬢ *Box 145, Greer 85927* ☎☎ *928/735–7560* ⊕ *www.wmonline.com/greermountain* ⇨ *8 units* ⚲ *Kitchens; no a/c, room phones, no room TVs* ⊟ *MC, V.*

CAMPING ⚠ **Rolfe C. Hoyer Campgrounds.** Nestled among pristine stands of pon-
¢ derosa pine, these choice campsites in the Apache-Sitgreaves National Forest have no utility hookups but are proximate to equipment rentals, gas, groceries, and restaurants in the town of Greer. A $9 surcharge (per booking, not per night) is added by the company that handles the reservations. The abundant local wildlife is one of this site's draws, but remember to secure campsites from foraging four-legged friends. There's a $3 fee to use the dump stations or to take a shower. ⊠ *AZ 373* ☎ *928/333–4372 or 877/444–6777* ⊕ *www.reserveusa.com* ⇨ *100 sites* ⚲ *Flush toilets, dump station, drinking water, showers, fire pits, grills, picnic tables* ☉ *Open May 15–Oct. 15.*

Nightlife

Tiny Greer's nightlife can be found in the bar and lounge of the **Molly Butler Lodge** (⊠ 109 Main St. ☎ 928/735–7226), where you can listen to vintage tunes on the jukebox, sink into a cozy seat near the fireplace, play an arcade game, or challenge a "local" to a game of pool or darts.

Shopping

Calamity Janet's (⊠ 96 Main St. ☎ 928/735–7610) specializes in antiques and Western collectibles, and its mid-20th-century Navajo jewelry merits a special look. This shop also has a number of impressive paintings and wood-turning pieces by well-known regional artists, and the original James Muir sculptures are breathtaking. It's open from April through October, or by appointment only the rest of the year.

Lyman Lake State Park

❻ *18 mi north of Springerville on U.S. 180/191, 55 mi southeast of Petrified Forest National Park on U.S. 180.*

Created in 1915, when the Little Colorado River was dammed for irrigation purposes, the 3-mi-long **Lyman Lake** reservoir is popular for boating, waterskiing (a permit is required for the exclusive waterskiing course on the dam end), windsurfing, and sailing. Designated swimming beaches accommodate those who prefer to stick closer to shore.

A buoyed-off "no-wake" area at the lake's west end ensures that fishing efforts there won't be disturbed by passing speedboats and waterskiers. Contributions to the creel here include largemouth bass as well

THE WRITING ON THE WALL

THE ROCK ART OF EARLY NATIVE AMERICANS is carved or painted on basalt boulders, on canyon walls, and on the underside of overhangs throughout eastern Arizona. Designs pecked or scratched into the stone are called petroglyphs; those that are painted on the surface are pictographs. Few pictographs remain because of the deleterious effects of weathering, but the more durable petroglyphs number in the thousands. No one knows the exact meaning of these signs, and interpretations vary from use in shaman or hunting rituals to clan signs, maps, or even indications of visits by extra-terrestrials.

It's just as difficult to date a "glyph" as it is to understand it. Archaeologists try to determine a general time frame by judging the style, the date of the ruins and pottery in the vicinity, the amount of patination (formation of minerals) on the design, or the superimposition of newer images on top of older ones. Most of eastern Arizona's rock art is estimated to be at least 1,000 years old, and many of the glyphs were created even earlier.

Some glyphs depict animals like big horn sheep, deer, bear, and mountain lions; others are geometric patterns. The most unusual are the anthropomorphs, strange humanlike figures with elaborate headdresses. A concentric circle is a common design. A few of these circles served as solstice signs, indicating summer and winter solstice and other important dates. At a certain time in the year, when the angle of the sun is just right, a shaft of light shines through a crack in a nearby rock, illuminating the center of the circle. Archaeologist believe these solar calendars helped determine the time for ceremonies and planting. Many solstice signs are in remote regions, but you can visit the Petrified Forest National Park around June 20 to see a concentric circle illuminated during the summer solstice. The glyph, reached by paved trail just a few hundred yards from the parking area, is visible year-round, but a finger of light shines directly in the center during the week of the solstice. The phenomenon occurs at 9 AM, a reasonable hour for looking at the calendar.

Damaged by vandalism, many rock-art sites are not open to the public, but Hieroglyphic Point in Salt River Canyon, Five-Mile Canyon in Snowflake, Lyman Lake State Park, and Petrified Forest National Park are all good spots to view petroglyphs. Do not touch petroglyphs or pictographs. The oils from your hands can cause damage the image. Make your own "interpretation" of these designs; your guess is as good as that of the experts.

— Janet Webb Farnsworth

as the "good size" (6 to 8 pounds) channel catfish that can be pulled up from May to August. Locals recommend early spring as prime season for walleye—the tastiest catch of all; Lyman Lake also has lots of crawfish, a.k.a. "poor man's shrimp."

Between early May and late October, ranger-led pontoon-boat tours go across Lyman Lake to the **Petroglyph Trail,** where some of the state's most wondrous and accessible Native American rock art lies chiseled in basalt. Check out the pueblo site, which dates to the 14th century and has three rooms and a kiva.

Other attractions in the 1,200-acre park include a volleyball court, horseshoe pits, and water-ski slalom course. There is also a campground, along with several log cabins and yurts for rent, and a camping supply and boat rental store. In nearby St. Johns, there's lodging, restaurants, and an airfield and fuel for planes. ⊠ *U.S. 180/191, 18 mi north of Springerville/Eagar* ☐ *Box 1428, St. Johns 85936* ☎ *928/337–4441* ⊕ *www.pr.state.az.us.*

en route The junction of U.S. 180/191 and U.S. 60, just north of Springerville, is the perfect jumping-off spot for a driving tour of the **Springerville Volcanic Field.** On the southern edge of the Colorado Plateau, it covers a total area larger than the state of Rhode Island and is spread across a high-elevation plain similar to the Tibetan Plateau. Six miles north of Springerville on U.S. 180/191 are sweeping westward views of the **Twin Knolls**—double volcanoes that erupted twice here about 700,000 years ago. As you travel west on U.S. 60, Green's Peak Road and various south-winding Forest Service roads make for a leisurely, hour-long drive past **St. Peter's Dome** and a stop for impressive views from **Green's Peak,** the topographic high point of the Springerville Field. A free detailed driving-tour brochure of the Springerville Volcanic Field is available from the **Springerville-Eagar Regional Chamber of Commerce** (⊠ 318 Main St. ☐ Box 31, Springerville 85938 ☎ 928/333–2123).

Springerville-Eagar

❼ *45 mi east of Pinetop-Lakeside on AZ 260, 67 mi southeast of Petrified Forest National Park on U.S. 180.*

Sister cities Springerville and Eagar are tucked into a circular, high mountain basin christened "Valle Redondo," or Round Valley, by early Basque settlers of the late 1800s. Nestled on the back side of massive 10,912-foot Escudilla Mountain, this self-proclaimed "Gateway to the White Mountains" sits in a different climate belt from nearby Greer and Sunrise Resort; insulated by its unique geography, Springerville-Eagar has markedly less severe winter temperatures and lighter snowfall than neighboring mountain towns. Geographically, the Round Valley also served as a unique Old West haven for the lawless—a great place to conceal stolen cattle and hide out for a while. Butch Cassidy, the Clantons, and the Smith gang all spent time here. So did the late John Wayne, whose former 26-Bar Ranch lies just west of Eagar off AZ 260.

The Round Valley is the favorite of skiers in the know, who appreciate the location as they commute to the lifts at Sunrise with the sun always at their back—important when you consider the glare off those blanketed snowscapes between the resort and Pinetop-Lakeside—and the dramatically lighter traffic on this less-icy stretch of AZ 260.

The 14½-acre **Casa Malpais Archaeological Park** pueblo complex is piquing the interest of a growing number of anthropologists and astronomers. The "House of the Badlands" (a sobriquet for the rough-textured ground's effect on bare feet) has a series of narrow terraces lining eroded edges of basalt (hardened lava flow) cliff, as well as an extensive system of subterranean rooms nestled within the Earth's fissures underneath. Strategically designed gateways in the walls of the complex allow for streams of sunlight to precisely illuminate significant petroglyphs prior to the setting equinox or solstice sun. Casa Malpais' Great Kiva (any kiva over 30 feet is considered great) is square cornered instead of round, consistent with Zuni heritage. Some archaeologists believe the pueblo possibly served as a regional ceremonial center for the Mogollon people and that the population included a high percentage of scholars and holy men. Both Hopi and Zuni tribes trace their history to Casa Malpais. ⊠ *318 E. Main St., Springerville* ☎ *928/333–5375* ☒ *Guided tour $5* ⊙ *Museum Mon.–Thurs. 8–5, Fri.–Sun. 8–4; guided tours of ruins daily at 9, 11, and 2.*

The 120,000-square-foot **Ensphere** may convince you that something from a galaxy far, far away landed in Eagar (especially at night, when a wafflelike grid of lights radiates eerily from its rooftop), but in fact it is the only domed high school football stadium in the country. The dome is a gift of Tucson Power & Electric (TPE), which moved into these parts and vowed to contribute something to the community. The then-absurd proposal was placed on the ballot, alongside a host of other less-extravagant options, and passed. The shocked TPE, after demanding a recount, made good on its promise. ⊠ *590 N. Butler St., Eagar.*

This **Little House Museum** has a collection of local pioneer and ranching memorabilia, but it's the mesmerizing tones from a rare collection of automatic musical instruments that you remember—that, and the museum's colorful curator, Wink Crigler, with her lore of this region's lively past. Tours to archaeological digs and petroglyphs are available by appointment. To reach the ranch, go 10 mi southwest of Eagar on AZ 260, turn south onto South Fork Road, and go 3 mi. ⊠ *X Diamond Ranch, South Fork Rd., 10 mi southwest of Eagar* ☎ *928/333–2286* ⊕ *www.xdiamondranch.com* ☒ *$7* ⊙ *By reservation only.*

The **Renée Cushman Art Collection Museum** is open to the public only by special appointment, but a visit here is worth the extra effort. Renée Cushman's extensive collection of objets d'art—some acquired on her travels, some collected with the accumulated resources of three wealthy husbands, some willed to her by her artistic father—is administered by the Church of Latter-day Saints. Her treasure of goods includes a Rembrandt engraving, Tiepolo pen-and-inks, and an impressive collection of European antiques, some dating back to the 15th century. Call the

Springerville-Eagar Regional Chamber of Commerce (☎ 928/333–2123) to arrange your visit to the Renée Cushman Art Collection Museum.

Sports & the Outdoors

For all your mountain-sport needs, stop in at the **Sweat Shop** (✉ 74 N. Main St., Eagar ☎ 928/333–2950), which rents skis, snowboards, and mountain bikes.

FISHING **Becker Lake** (✉ U.S. 60, 2 mi northwest of Springerville, Becker Lake ☎ 928/367–4281) is a "specialty lake" for trout fishing; call for seasonal bait requirements. **Big Lake** (✉ AZ 273, 24 mi south of AZ 260, Big Lake ☎ 928/735–7313), known to many as the "queen of all trout lakes," is stocked each spring and fall with rainbow, brook, and cutthroat trout. **Nelson Reservoir** (✉ U.S. 191, Nutrioso), between Springerville-Eagar and Alpine, is well stocked with rainbow, brown, and brook trout. The **Speckled Trout** (✉ 224 E. Main St., Springerville ☎ 928/333–0852 ⊕ www.cybertrails.com/~cltrout) is probably the only fly-fishing store attached to a law office anywhere. The store offers Orvis-licensed fly-fishing guide services and sells fly-fishing equipment. Springerville-Eagar's only commercial espresso machine sparkles behind a small coffee bar here. **Sport Shack** (✉ 329 E. Main St., Springerville ☎ 928/333–2222) sells camping equipment, fishing tackle, and hunting and fishing licenses. **Troutback** (✆ Box 864, Show Low 85901 ☎ 928/532–3474 ⊕ www.troutback.com) is a fly-fishing guide service that will create half- or full-day fishing trips for novices and seasoned anglers alike throughout the White Mountains. Equipment, including boats, waders, fly rods and reels, and float tubes, is available for rent. **Western United Drug** (✉ 105 E. Main St., Springerville ☎ 928/333–4321) stays open 365 days a year and has a well-stocked sporting-goods and outdoor-equipment section.

Where to Stay & Eat

¢–$$ ✕ **Booga Reds.** The delicious home-style cooking here is worth a stop. Fish-and-chips and roast beef dinners with homemade mashed potatoes and gravy top the menu; should your palate demand something spicier, however, try one of the many Mexican dishes. Save room for an unforgettable piece of the daily fruit or cream pie. Booga Reds opens at 5:30 AM for an early breakfast but closes relatively early—at 9 PM—so make your dinner an early one, too. ✉ *521 E. Main St., Springerville* ☎ *928/333–2640* ▤ *AE, MC, V.*

$–$$$ ▦ ✕ **Diamond & MLY Ranch.** This magnificent ranch has log cabins complete with porches, fireplaces, and full kitchens. Most sleep two to six, but the Butler House sleeps eight and has an atrium and private yard. Ranch activities include horseback riding, participating in the excavation of the Little Bear and Kokopelli archaeological sites, and fly-fishing on a private section of the Little Colorado. You don't have to be a ranch guest to participate in activities. Horse boarding is also available. ✉ *South Fork Rd., 10 mi southwest of Eagar off AZ 260* ✆ *Box 791, Springerville 85938* ☎ *928/333–2286* ▤ *928/333–5009* ⊕ *www. xdiamondranch.com* ⊅ *7 cabins* ⚲ *Kitchens, cable TV, fishing, hiking, horseback riding, no-smoking rooms; no a/c* ▤ *AE, D, MC, V.*

★ $ ▣ **Paisley Corner Bed & Breakfast.** From embossed-tin ceilings and stained-glass windows in the parlor to an authentic "soda shop" re-creation replete with Wurlitzer jukebox, not a detail has been overlooked in this restored 1910 colonial revival–style home. Rooms have antique beds and armoires, old-fashioned showers, and pull-chain commodes. Lush terry robes, wine, fresh fruit, and homemade munchies are included. Breakfast is served as early as you want and is prepared on a 1910 stove rescued from the Bisbee Grand Hotel. In the summer, if you time your visit right, you may even catch a vintage fashion show in the garden. ⊠ *287 N. Main St., Springerville 85938* ☎ *928/333–4665* ⊕ *www.paisleycorner.com* ⪡ *4 rooms* ⟁ *No TV in some rooms; no smoking* ☰ *MC, V* ⦿ *BP.*

¢ ▣ **Reed's Lodge.** The rooms of this mostly single-story motel have Western accents such as knotty-pine paneling and Navajo-print bedspreads. Thoughtful touches include a recreation room with pool table, video games, and a pinball machine; movie rentals for a nominal fee; a gift shop; and complimentary bicycles for guests. Proprietor Roxanne Knight, who has a wealth of local knowledge, will arrange "shared ranch" visits for guests on an actual working cowboy-style (not dude) ranch, cattle drives, customized horseback adventures, four-wheel-drive tours, wildlife and petroglyph-viewing trips, or fossil-hunting expeditions. ⊠ *514 E. Main St., Springerville 85938* ☎ *928/333–4323 or 800/814–6451* 🖷 *928/333–5191* ⊕ *www.k5reeds.com* ⪡ *45 rooms, 5 suites* ⟁ *Some microwaves, some refrigerators, cable TV, in-room VCRs, outdoor hot tub, bicycles, recreation room, shop* ☰ *AE, D, DC, MC, V.*

Fodor'sChoice
★

¢ ▣ **Rode Inn.** Don't let the John Wayne motif scare you away—two cardboard figures of "The Duke," in full cowboy regalia, are perched on a walkway above the lobby, and his photos decorate the walls; the rooms and service here are excellent. John Wayne did in fact stay here (when it was a Ramada Inn), and the room in which he slept has been converted into a plush suite. ⊠ *242 E. Main St., Springerville 85938* ☎ *928/333–4365* ⊕ *www.rodeinn.com* ⪡ *60 rooms, 3 suites* ⟁ *Some microwaves, some refrigerators, cable TV, hot tub, laundry facilities, Internet, no-smoking rooms* ☰ *AE, D, DC, MC, V* ⦿ *CP.*

CAMPING ⚠ **Big Lake Campgrounds.** On the southeast shore of Big Lake, 30 mi
¢ southwest of the Round Valley, these campgrounds are along the shore of a popular White Mountains summer destination. The lake supplies more than 300,000 trout to fishermen each year. The civilized Rainbow site offers paved loops to its more developed units. The lake's smaller sites, Grayling, Cutthroat, and Brookchar, are less swank but are within easy walking distance of Rainbow's amenities and share the picturesque tableau of looming 11,590-foot Mount Baldy. The lake has a marina where boats and motors are available for rent. ⊠ *AZ 273, 24 mi south of AZ 260, Big Lake* ☎ *928/735–7313* ⪡ *152 sites at Rainbow* ⟁ *Flush toilets, dump station, drinking water, showers, general store, swimming (lake)* ⊗ *Open mid-May–early Sept.*

Nightlife

Out on the edge of town, where U.S. 60/180 enters Springerville, the bright yellow **Main Street Lounge** (⊠ 262 W. Main St., Springerville ☎ 928/333–5790) is a cowboy bar with pool tables, darts, and live music and dancing on the weekends. Behind Booga Red's restaurant, **Tequila Red's** (⊠ 521 E. Main St., Springerville ☎ 928/333–5036) is a popular watering hole and the best place to catch a sporting event.

Shopping

K-5 Western Gallery (⊠ Reed's Lodge, 514 E. Main St., Springerville ☎ 928/333–4323) sells wares created by White Mountains artists and local craftspeople, including those from nearby reservations (check out the rustic elk-antler furniture and items made from horseshoes). The gallery teems with Western-themed paintings, stocks books on local history and wildlife, and has a selection of cowboy poetry.

Coronado Trail

Fodor'sChoice *The 127-mi stretch of U.S. 191 from Springerville to Clifton.*
★

Surely one of the world's curviest roads, this steep, winding portion of U.S. 191 was referred to as the Devil's Highway in its prior incarnation as U.S. 666. More significantly, the route parallels the one allegedly followed more than 450 years ago by Spanish explorer Francisco Vásquez de Coronado on his search for the legendary Seven Cities of Cibola, where the streets were reputedly paved with gold and jewels.

This 127-mi stretch of highway is renowned for the transitions of its spectacular scenery over a dramatic 5,000-foot elevation change—from rolling meadows to spruce- and ponderosa pine–covered mountains, down into the Sonoran Desert's piñon pine, grassland savannas, juniper stands, and cacti. A trip down the Coronado Trail crosses through Apache Sitgreaves National Forest, as well as the White Mountain Apache and San Carlos Indian reservations.

Cautious switchback-navigating will result in stretches on which motorists barely exceed 10 mph; allow a good four hours to make the drive, more if you plan to stop and leisurely explore—which you should.

Pause at **Blue Vista,** perched on the edge of the Mogollon Rim, about 30 mi outside Alpine, to take in views of the Blue Range Mountains to the east and the succession of tiered valleys dropping some 4,000 feet back down into the Sonoran Desert. Still above the rim, this is one of your last opportunities to enjoy the blue spruce, ponderosa pine, and high-country mountain meadows.

About 17 mi south of Blue Vista, the Coronado Trail continues twisting and turning, eventually crossing under 8,786-foot **Rose Peak.** Named for the wild roses growing on its mountainside, Rose Peak is also home to a fire lookout tower—staffed during the May–July dry-lightning season—from which peaks more than 100 mi away can be seen on a clear day. This is a great picnic-lunch stop.

After Rose Peak, enjoy the remaining scenery some 70 more miles until reaching the less scenic towns of Clifton and Morenci, homes to a massive Phelps Dodge copper mine. U.S. 191 then swings back west, links up with U.S. 70, and provides a fairly straight shot through Safford and across rather uninteresting desert toward Globe. ⊠ *U.S. 191 between Springerville and Clifton.*

Alpine

⑧ *27 mi south of Springerville-Eagar on U.S. 191.*

Known as the Alps of Arizona, the tiny, scenic village of Alpine promotes its winter recreation opportunities, but outdoors enthusiasts will also find that the town, sitting on the lush plains of the San Francisco River, is an ideal base for hiking, fishing, and mountain-biking excursions during the warmer months. Mormon farmers settled this high country meadow in 1879, and some of their old homes are still occupied. Originally Alpine was a farming and ranching community, but with summer cabins tucked in the pines, campgrounds, 11 lakes, and 200 mi of trout streams within a 30-mi radius, outdoor recreation drives this mountain burg now.

Sports & the Outdoors

BICYCLING   The 8-mi **Luna Lake Trail** (✉ U.S. 180, Alpine), 5 mi east of U.S. 191, is a good two-hour cruise for beginning and intermediate cyclists. The trailhead is on the north side of the lake, just before the campground entrance.

FISHING   A divergence of the San Francisco River's headwaters, 80-acre **Luna Lake** (✉ U.S. 180, Alpine), 5 mi east of U.S. 191, is well stocked with rainbow trout. **Tackle Shop** (☎ 928/339–4338), at the junction of U.S. 180 and 191, carries trout and fly fishing supplies.

Arizona MountainFlyfishing (☎ 928/339–4829 ⊕ www.azmtflyfishing.com) guides anglers to top fishing streams and teaches novices how to fly-fish.

GOLF   **Alpine Country Club** (✉ Off U.S. 180, 3 mi east of U.S. 191 ⌂ Box 526, 85920 ☎ 928/339–4944 ⊕ www.geocities.com/alpinecountryclub), at 8,500 feet above sea level, is one of the highest golf courses in the Southwest. Even if you don't play golf, stop in for Mexican food and breathtaking scenery at the club's Aspen Room Restaurant. It's 1 mi south of Alpine on Blue River Road.

HIKING   The **Escudilla National Recreation Trail** (✉ U.S. 191, Hulsey Lake) is more idyllic than arduous; the 3-mi trail wends through the Escudilla Wilderness to the summit of towering 10,912-foot **Escudilla Mountain,** Arizona's third-tallest peak. The trail climbs 1,300 feet to a fire tower ¼ mi from the summit. From Alpine, take U.S. 191 north and follow the signs to Hulsey Lake (about 5 mi).

SKIING   **Williams Valley Winter Sports Area** (✉ FR 249, Alpine ☎ 928/339–4384), 2½ mi west of town, has 12½ mi of cross-country trails of varying difficulty maintained by the Alpine Ranger District. Toboggan Hill is a favorite place for families, with sleds, toboggans, and tubes. New shelters, picnic facilities, and toilets enhance the experience.

SNOWMOBILING   Trails begin just off Forest Service Road 249, on the west side of **Williams Valley Winter Sports Area** (✉ FR 249, Alpine ☎ 928/339–4384), and the network of snow-covered Forest Service roads extends for miles. Pick up an Apache Sitgreaves National Forest map and Winter Sports brochure from the Alpine Ranger District, and call for conditions prior to heading out, as weak links in longer routes sometimes "burn out."

Where to Stay & Eat

$ ✕▦ **Tal-Wi-Wi Lodge.** This lodge draws many repeat visitors to its lush meadows. Standard motel-style rooms are simple and clean, with either two doubles or one king-size bed, and three of the most popular rooms have wood-burning fireplace-stoves, indoor hot tubs, or both. In the evening, stroll the grounds and gaze at the Milky Way in the brilliant night sky. With satellite TV and live country music on weekends, the lodge saloon draws a loyal local following. The cozy, casual restaurant is open May–November and serves breakfast on weekends and dinner Wednesday through Saturday. Tal-Wi-Wi is popular with car and motorcycle clubs and hosts an annual car show in August. ✉ *U.S. 191* 🕿 *Box 169, Alpine 85920* ☎ *928/339–4319 or 800/476–2695* 🖷 *928/339–1962* ⊕ *www.talwiwilodge.com* ⇌ *20 rooms* ⌂ *Restaurant, some in-room hot tubs, bar, some pets allowed (fee); no a/c, no room TVs* ▭ *MC, V.*

Hannagan Meadow

★ ❾ *50 mi south of Springerville-Eagar on U.S. 191, 23 mi south of Alpine on U.S. 191.*

Surely one of the state's most remote places, Hannagan Meadow is a pastorally mesmerizing location for several splendid camping areas. Lush and isolated at a 9,500-foot-plus elevation, the meadow is home to elk, deer, and range cattle, as well as blue grouse, wild turkey, and the occasional eagle. Adjacent to the meadow, the Blue Range Primitive Area gives access to miles of untouched wilderness and some beautiful rugged terrain, and it is a designated recovery area for the endangered Mexican gray wolf. It is believed that Francisco Vásquez de Coronado and his party came through the Meadow on their famed expedition in 1540 to find the Seven Cities of Cibola.

off the beaten path

BLUE RANGE PRIMITIVE AREA – Directly east of Hannagan Meadow, this unspoiled 170,000-acre area, lovingly referred to by locals as "The Blue," is the last designated primitive area in the United States. The area's diverse terrain surrounds the Blue River and is crossed by the Mogollon Rim from east to west. No motorized or mechanized equipment is allowed—including mountain bikes; passage is restricted to foot or horseback. Many trails interlace the Blue: prehistoric paths of the ancient native peoples, cowboy trails to move livestock between pastures and water sources, access routes to lookout towers and fire trails. Avid backpackers and campers may want to spend a few days exploring the dozens of hiking trails. Even though trail access is fairly good, hikers need to remember that this is primitive, rough country and to carry adequate water supplies. Contact **Apache-Sitgreaves National Forest** (✉ Alpine Ranger District, U.S. 191 🕿 Box 469, Alpine 85920 ☎ 928/339–4384 ⊕ www.fs.fed.us/r3/asnf) for trail maps and information for the Blue Range Primitive Area.

Sports & the Outdoors

FISHING Down in the Blue Range, anglers will want to cast into KP Creek and Grant Creek, both of which rush through spectacular scenery. **Bear Wallow**

Wilderness Area (⊠ west of U.S. 191 and bordered by FR 25 and 54) has a network of cool, flowing streams stocked with native Apache trout.

HIKING Twenty-one miles of maintained trail wind through the 11,000 acres of the **Bear Wallow Wilderness Area** (⊠ west of U.S. 191 and bordered by FR 25 and 54 ☎ 928/339–4384 Alpine Ranger District office ⊕ www. fs.fed.us/r3/asnf).The **Rose Spring Trail** is a pleasant 5½-mi hike with a moderate gradient and magnificent views from the Mogollon Rim's edge; the trailhead is at the end of Forest Service Road 54. **Reno Trail** and **Gobbler Trail** both drop into the main canyon from well-marked trailheads off Forest Service Road 25. Reno Trail meanders 2 mi through conifer forest and aspen stands, while Gobbler Trail is 2½ mi in length and offers views overlooking the Black River and Fort Apache Indian Reservation. This designated wilderness (and some of its trails) borders the San Carlos Indian Reservation, where an advance permit is required for entry.

SKIING The 8½ mi of groomed cross-country trails of the **Hannagan Meadow Winter Recreation Area** (⊠ U.S. 191, Hannagan Meadow ☎ 928/339–4384 Alpine Ranger District office ⊕ www.fs.fed.us/r3/asnf) are narrower than the trails of neighboring Williams Valley. The 4½-mi **Clell Lee Loop** is an easy route, partially following U.S. 191; the advanced-level, ungroomed **KP Rim Loop** traverses upper elevations of the Blue Primitive Range and provides some of the most varied (and tranquil) remote skiing in the state. There are no rental shops or outfitters nearby, so you'll have to bring your own equipment.

SNOWMOBILING The area just northeast of U.S. 191 is a snowmobile playground. Trailheads are at U.S. 191 and Forest Service Road 576. Snowmobile trail maps are available at the Alpine Ranger District office and Hannagan Meadow Lodge.

Where to Stay & Eat

★ $-$$ ✕🏠 **Hannagan Meadow Lodge.** Antiques and floral prints impart a genteel, Victorian feel to this lodge. The dining room is the pièce de résistance, with hewn-log beams and a glass wall that overlooks a pristine meadow; room rates at the lodge include breakfast. Log cabins are more rustic; some have full kitchens and fireplaces, whereas others are equipped with microwaves, stove tops, and wood-burning stoves. The solitude of the area is enhanced by the absence of phones and TVs in rooms and cabins. The general store sells sundries as well as fishing supplies and rents snowshoes, cross-country skis, and mountain bikes. From November through April there's a 20% discount Sunday to Thursday except during holidays. ⊠ *U.S. 191, 22 mi south of Alpine, Hannagan Meadow* 🖂 *HC 61, Box 335, Alpine 85920* ☎ *928/339–4370* ⊕ *www.hannaganmeadow.com* 🛏 *8 rooms, 10 cabins* ⚘ *Restaurant, some kitchens, some kitchenettes, bicycles, hiking, horseback riding, cross-country skiing, snowmobiling, some pets allowed; no a/c, no room phones, no room TVs* ⊟ *MC, V* ¶◎¶ *CP.*

CAMPING △ **Hannagan Campground.** This intimate collection of Forest Service camp-
¢ sites sits under a canopy of spruce, fir, and aspen trees and is surrounded by tall, mature forest. The area is rich in wildlife, such as elk, wild turkey,

and bear, and at night you might hear the howling of wolves. ♿ *Pit toilets, drinking water, fire pits, grills, picnic tables* ⟿ *8 campsites* ⊠ *U.S. 191, Hannagan Meadow, ¼ mi past Hannagan Meadow Lodge* ⊕ *www. fs.fed.us/r3/asnf* ⊘ *Open May–Oct.*

¢ 🔺 **KP Cienega.** These single-unit campsites in a lush meadow are a prime site for viewing the local wildlife. There are no developed facilities. ♿ *Pit toilets, drinking water, fire pits, grills, picnic tables* ⟿ *5 campsites* ⊠ *U.S. 191 and Forest Service Rd. 25, Hannagan Meadow* ⊕ *www. fs.fed.us/r3/asnf* ⊘ *Open May–Oct.*

THE PETRIFIED FOREST & THE PAINTED DESERT

Only about 1½ hours from Show Low and the lush, verdant forests of the White Mountains, Arizona's diverse and dramatic landscape changes from pine-crested mountains to the sunbaked terrain of the Petrified Forest and lunarlike landscape of the Painted Desert.

Snowflake-Taylor

🔟 *15 mi north of Show Low on AZ 77.*

Snowflake-Taylor is a good jumping-off point for exploring eastern Arizona; it's an easy day trip to the Homolovi Ruins or the Petrified Forest. The towns are also a less-crowded alternative for summer excursions in the nearby White Mountains. Most of the Phoenix weekenders head for the higher towns, so Snowflake and Taylor avoid the crush of summer visitors that results in higher prices at hotels and restaurants. Sandwiched between the White Mountains and the Colorado Plateau, the communities enjoy year-round pleasant weather with summer highs in the 90s. Yes, it does snow in Snowflake, but snow seldom lasts more than a day or so.

Snowflake and Taylor were settled by Mormons in the 1870s and named for Mormon church leaders. Snowflake's unusual name is combination of Mr. Snow, an apostle in the early Mormon church of Salt Lake City, Utah, and Mr. Flake, one of the town founders. One of only two Mormon temples in Arizona sits on Temple Hill west of Snowflake, and the towns still have a large Mormon contingent in their combined population of 7,000. Snowflake's historical district features a walking tour, antiques store, and pioneer homes.

The **Stinson Museum** once served as schoolhouse. James Stinson, the first rancher in the valley, was the original resident of the small adobe home. William J. Flake bought out Stinson's holdings and founded the town of Snowflake. Flake added on to the structure which today is a museum containing pioneer memorabilia, quilts, Indian artifacts, and a small gift shop. ⊠ *102 N. 1st St.* ☎ *928/536–4881* ⊘ *Tues.–Fri. 10–4, Sat. 9–2* 🎟 *$1.*

Sports & Outdoor Activities

GOLF The least expensive golf course in the White Mountains, the 27-hole **Snowflake Municipal Golf Course** (⊠ 90 N. Country Club Dr. ☎ 928/536–7233) is open year-round. Especially scenic with red rocks and waterfalls, the course includes a driving range, water hazard, and a restaurant. Green fees are $18, $28 with a cart.

HIKING At the junction of Silver Creek Canyon and Five-Mile Canyon, 5 mi north of Snowflake, ancient peoples left petroglyphs carved through the dark desert varnish to the light sandstone of the canyon walls. **Petroglyph Hike** (✧ Silver Creek Canyon), the trail from canyon top down to petroglyphs, is short but steep. Trail access is regulated by the city of Snowflake. To check in and get directions, contact the **Snowflake-Taylor Chamber of Commerce** (☏ 928/536–4331 or 928/536–4881).

Where to Stay & Eat

¢–$$ ✕ **Enzo's Ristorante Italiano.** Behind Heritage Antiques, in the historic district of Snowflake, the only Italian restaurant in town occupies a converted home. Sauces and bread are homemade, and everything is freshly prepared to order. Baked pastas and shrimp Alfredo are favorites. ⊠ 50 E. 1st N, Snowflake ☏ 928/243–0450 ⊟ No credit cards ☉ Closed Mon. and Tues. No lunch.

¢–$$ ✕ **Trapper's.** Opened in 1973 by "Trapper" Hatch and still family-owned, this hometown diner is decorated with Hatch's old trapping equipment and animal paintings by local artists. Chicken-fried steak and homemade barbecue sauce draw a loyal crowd. People drive out of their way just to stop for a piece of Trapper's pies, especially banana cream. Have a slice at the counter with a cup of coffee. ⊠ 9 S. Main St., Taylor ☏ 928/536–7758 ⊟ AE, MC, V ☉ Closed Sun.

¢–$ ⊞ **Osmer D. Heritage Inn.** Elegantly furnished with period antiques, this redbrick home with a white-picket fence was built in 1890 by Mormon pioneer Osmer D. Flake. Filled with pioneer style, Osmer D's is next door to Heritage Antiques and between two restaurants—making it the place to start Snowflake's historic walking tour. The Honeymoon Suite is perfect for a special occasion, and an outside patio can accommodate small weddings and parties. ⊠ 161 N. Main St., Snowflake 85937 ☏ 928/536–3322 or 866/486–5947 ⊕ www.heritage-inn.net ⮎ 9 rooms, 2 suites ⌂ Cable TV, hot tub; no smoking ⊟ AE, D, MC, V ❙❍❙ BP.

¢ ⊞ **Silver Creek Inn.** Simply furnished, clean, and near fast-food restaurants, Silver Creek sees many "regulars" who travel through the area often. There is ample parking for RVs and trailers, and it is close to Taylor's only grocery store. ⊠ 825 N. Main St., Taylor 85939 ☏ 928/536–2600 ⮎ 42 rooms ⌂ Microwaves, refrigerators, cable TV, hot tub ⊟ AE, D, DC, MC, V ❙❍❙ CP.

Homolovi Ruins State Park

⓫ *53 mi east of Flagstaff, 33 mi west of Holbrook. Exit 257 off Interstate 40.*

Fodor'sChoice ★

Homolovi is a Hopi word meaning "place of the little hills." The pueblo sites here are thought to have been occupied between AD 1200 and 1425 and include 40 ceremonial kivas and two pueblos containing more than 1,000 rooms each. The Hopi believe their immediate ancestors inhabited this place and still hold the site to be sacred. Many of rooms have been excavated and recovered for protection. Weekdays in June and July you can see archaeologists working the site. The Homolovi Visitor Center has a small museum with Hopi pottery and ancestral Puebloan artifacts; it also hosts workshops on native art, ethnobotany, and traditional foods. Mobility-impaired persons should check with the ranger station for alternate access information; rangers conduct guided tours. ⊠ *AZ 87, 5 mi northeast of Winslow* ⌕ *HCR 63, Box 5, Winslow 86047* ☎ *928/289–4106* ⊕ *www.pr.state.az.us.*

Where to Stay

Homolovi Ruins State Park is 5 mi northeast of the town of Winslow. Frequent flooding on the Little Colorado River frustrated the attempts of Mormon pioneers to settle here, but, with the coming of the railroad, the town roared into life. Later, Route 66 sustained the community until Interstate 40 passed north of town. New motels and restaurants sprouted near the interstate exits, and downtown was all but abandoned. Downtown Winslow is now revitalizing, with La Posada Hotel as its showpiece. Dining options are still scarce, however.

$–$$ 🛏 **La Posada Winslow.** One of the great railroad hotels, La Posada (which
FodorsChoice means "resting place") has the charm of an 18th-century Spanish hacienda.
★ Architect Mary Colter, famous for her work at the Grand Canyon, designed and decorated the 68,000-square-foot hotel for the Fred Harvey Company. Spanish and Native American elements, including furniture, antiques, and art, permeate her designs. Movie stars and politicians visited regularly—Charles Lindberg honeymooned here. Individually-decorated rooms are restored to 1930s style with plaster walls painted their original colors, mainly soft Southwest hues. La Posada's lush gardens are an oasis of green in the red-rock Colorado Plateau. Can't spend the night? At least take the self-guided tour ($2 donation). ⊠ *303 E 2nd St., Winslow 86047* ☎ *928/289–4366* 🖶 *928/289–3873* ⊕ *www.laposada. org* 🛏 *38 rooms* ⌂ *Restaurant, cable TV, lounge, some pets allowed (fee); no room phones, no smoking* ⊟ *AE, D, DC, MC, V.*

CAMPING ⛺ **Homolovi Ruins State Park Campground.** At an elevation of 4,900 feet,
¢ this campsite is a short walk from Homolovi I pueblo and the Little Colorado River and close to several other archaeological sites and trails leading to petroglyphs and evidence of prehistoric habitations. ⊠ *AZ 87, 5 mi northeast of Winslow* ☎ *928/289–4106* ☽ *Open year-round* ⌂ *Pit toilets, partial hookups (electric and water), dump station, drinking water, showers, fire pits, grills, picnic tables* 🛏 *53 campsites.*

Holbrook

⑫ *35 mi east of Homolovi State Park via Interstate 40.*

Downtown Holbrook is a monument to Route 66 kitsch. The famous "Mother Road" traveled through the center of Holbrook before Interstate 40 replaced it as the area's major east–west artery, and remnants of the "good ole days," when thousands of cars and big rigs rumbled through, can be found all over town.

Route 66 itself still runs through Holbrook, following Navajo Boulevard and Hopi Drive. It made a sharp corner at the intersection of these two roads, causing traffic jams. The Downtowner, a popular coffee shop on this corner, served simple meals and coffee to sleepy truck drivers. As if traffic wasn't already scrambled enough, crowds from the movie theater at what is today East Hopi Drive brought Route 66 to a standstill. Moviegoers, who thronged into the streets at the end of the show, considered it their right to block traffic; after all, many had traveled over 100 mi to see the movie.

The **Old Courthouse Museum** (☎ 800/524–2459 ⊕ www.ci.holbrook.az.us ☞ free ☉ weekdays 8–5, weekends 8–4), at the corner of Arizona Street and Navajo Boulevard, holds memorabilia from the Route 66 heyday along with Old West and railroad records. Near the railroad tracks you'll be surprised by bright green dinosaurs glaring down at you. A nearby shop makes dinosaurs and their wares are stored outside. After all, its hard to find a place to store a dinosaur.

Where to Stay & Eat

$–$$$ ✕ **Mesa Italiana Restaurant.** The chef here uses the finest herbs, spices, and other ingredients to create an authentic taste of old Italy. Fresh pastas, calzones, spaghetti with Italian mushrooms, and homemade salads are featured fare. Don't forget the spumoni for dessert. ⊠ *2318 E. Navajo Blvd.* ☎ *928/524–6696* ☰ *AE, D, MC, V* ☉ *No lunch.*

¢–$ ☷ **Best Western Arizonian Inn.** Each of the large, handsome rooms here is furnished with a suite of formal, ersatz–cherrywood furniture. A 24-hour diner is just steps across the parking lot. ⊠ *2508 E. Navajo Blvd., Holbrook 86025* ☎☎ *928/524–2611* ⊕ *www.bestwestern.com* ☞ *70 rooms, 3 suites* ⌂ *Some in-room data ports, some microwaves, some refrigerators, cable TV, pool* ☰ *AE, D, DC, MC, V* ☉ *CP.*

¢–$ ☷ **Holbrook Days Inn.** This modern Southwestern-style structure of stucco walls and Spanish-tile roofs stands amid petrified-wood landscaping. Inside, rooms are in Southwestern teal hues with whitewashed furniture. Free Continental breakfast, local phone calls, a heated indoor pool and hot tub, plus nearby restaurants, make this a pleasant, convenient choice. ⊠ *2601 Navajo Blvd., Holbrook 86025* ☎ *928/524–6949* ⊕ *www.daysinn.com* ☞ *51 rooms, 3 suites* ⌂ *Some microwaves, some refrigerators, cable TV, indoor pool, hot tub* ☰ *AE, D, DC, MC, V* ☉ *CP.*

★ ¢ ☷ **Wigwam Motel.** Classic Route 66, the Wigwam consists of 15 bright white, roadside concrete tepees where you can sleep inexpensively in a surreal environment. As you might expect, wigwams are phoneless, but— ode to Mother Progress—these have cable TV. A small lobby museum exhibits Mexican, Native American, and military relics collected by the owner's family. The 180-pound, polished petrified wood sphere is one of the largest in the Southwest. All of the classic cars parked by the teepees also belong to the owners. ⊠ *711 W. Hopi Dr., Holbrook 86025* ☎ *928/524–3048* ☞ *15 rooms* ⌂ *Cable TV; no room phones* ☰ *MC, V.*

Shopping

McGees Beyond Native Tradition (⊠ 2114 N. Navajo Blvd., Holbrook ☎ 928/524–1977 ⊕ www.hopiart.com) is the area's premier source of high-quality Native American jewelry, rugs, Hopi baskets, and katsina dolls. You may have heard the dolls referred to as kachina, but because the Hopi have no "ch" sound in their language, they are more accurately known as *katsina* dolls. The owners have long-standing, personal relationships with reservation artisans and a knowledgeable staff that adroitly assists first-time buyers and seasoned collectors alike.

Petrified Forest National Park

► ⓭ *(Northern Entrance) 54 mi east of Homolovi Ruins State Park and 27*
Fodor'sChoice *mi east of Holbrook on Interstate 40; (Southern Entrance)18 mi east*
★ *of Holbrook on U.S. 180.*

A visit to the Petrified Forest is a trip back in geological time. In 1984 the fossil remains of one of the oldest dinosaurs ever unearthed—dating from the Triassic period of the Mesozoic era 225 million years ago—were discovered here; other plant and animal fossils in the park date from the same period. Remnants of ancient human beings and their artifacts, dating back 10,000 years, have been recovered at more than 500 sites in this national park.

The park derives its name from the fact that the grounds are also covered with petrified tree trunks whose wood cells were replaced over centuries by brightly hued mineral deposits—silica, iron oxide, manganese, aluminum, copper, lithium, and carbon—which contributed to their fossilization. In many places, petrified logs scattered about the landscape resemble a fairy-tale forest turned to stone. The park's 93,000 acres include portions of the vast, pink-hue lunarlike landscape known as the **Painted Desert.** In the northern area of the park, this colorful but essentially barren series of windswept plains, hills, and mesas is considered by geologists to be part of the Chinle formation, deposited at an early stage of the Triassic period.

You can easily spend most of a day on the park's 28 mi of paved roads and walking trails. Lookouts on the north end of the park provide beautiful Painted Desert vistas. Fascinating Native American petroglyphs survive on boulders at **Newspaper Rock** and **Puerco Ruins,** which also has a partially stabilized 100-room pueblo more than 600 years old. The area around **Jasper Forest** contains stunning hunks of petrified trees scattered on the desert floor. Near the southern end of the park, **Agate House** is a pueblo structure assembled from pieces of petrified wood. The self-guided **Giant Logs Trail** starts at the Rainbow Forest Museum and Visitor Center and loops through ½ mi of huge fallen trees. One of the ancient, fallen trunks is more than 9 feet in diameter.

Because so many looters hauled away large quantities of petrified wood in the early years of the 20th century, President Theodore Roosevelt made the area a national monument in 1906. Since then, it has been illegal (not to mention bad karma) to remove even a small sliver of petrified wood from the park. Plenty of souvenir pieces are available from the park's visitor-center gift shop and surrounding trading posts. The removal of pieces from the park is a federal offense and carries with it a hefty fine and potential imprisonment. Don't miss the "Guilt Books" in each entrance's museum. These preserve letters from guilt-riddled former visitors anxiously returning their purloined souvenirs and detailing directly attributable hexes—from runs of bad luck to husbands turning into "hard-drinking strangers."

At the north entrance of the park, the **Painted Desert Visitor Center** shows a 20-minute movie entitled *Timeless Impressions,* tracing the natural history of the area. The **Rainbow Forest Museum and Visitor Center** (⊠ near the south entrance, off U.S. 180, 18 mi southeast of Holbrook) displays skeletons from the Triassic period, including that of "Gertie"—the ferocious phytosaur, a crocodile-like carnivore. The museum has numerous exhibits relating to the world of cycads (tropical plants), ferns, fish, and other early life, as well as artifacts and tools of ancient humans. Within the park's boundaries, visitors also have access to a restaurant and a service station at the north end of the park. Those interested in purchasing books or slides should know that many of the same titles are offered at the gift shops (there's one at each end of the park) and at the Painted Desert Visitor Center (at the north end of the park). Only those books purchased from the visitor center will fund the continued research and interpretive activities for the park.

Picnicking is allowed inside the park. You may hike into the nearby wilderness areas to camp overnight, but you must obtain a Wilderness Permit. Free permits are issued at both visitor centers. Petrified Forest National Park has neither dining nor lodging facilities. The closest restaurants and motels are in Holbrook, which is 27 mi west of the park's northern entrance on Interstate 40.

Visitors can begin the 28-mi drive through the park either from the northern Interstate 40 entrance or the southern entrance off U.S. 180. Those continuing on to New Mexico should enter from the park's south entrance, ending up with Interstate 40's straight shot over the border toward Albuquerque. Visitors with accommodations in Holbrook should tour the park from south end to north end, saving dramatic sunset vistas of the Painted Desert for last. As you leave the park, rangers will question you to be certain you haven't been tempted to collect a souvenir of petrified wood. *North Entrance* ⊠ *I–40, Milepost 311, 27 mi east of Holbrook, Petrified Forest* ☎ *928/524–6228* ⊕ *www.nps.gov/ pefo* ⊡ *Box 2217, Petrified Forest 86028* ⊡ *$10 per vehicle, valid for 1 wk* ⊙ *Mid-Oct.–May, daily 8–5; June–mid-Oct., daily 7–7.*

EASTERN ARIZONA A TO Z

To research prices, get advice from other travelers, and book travel arrangements, visit www.fodors.com.

BUS TRAVEL

White Mountain Passenger Lines has service between Phoenix and Show Low; one-way fares are around $44. Greyhound Lines travels from Phoenix to Winslow, 50 mi west of Petrified Forest National Park, for around $40.

🚌 **Greyhound Lines** ⊠ 2201 N. Park Dr., Winslow ☎ 928/289–2171. **White Mountain Passenger Lines** ⊠ 1041 E. Hall St., Show Low ☎ 928/537–4539 ⊠ 319 S. 24th St., Phoenix ☎ 602/275–4245.

CAMPING

Call or write the Apache-Sitgreaves National Forest for a brochure listing all public camping facilities in the region, most of which operate from April to November. To assure a site at a fee campground, call the National Recreation Reservation Service, which charges a reservation fee of $10 per transaction. Book your campground site well in advance with the Game and Fish Division of the White Mountain Apache Tribe.

🛈 **Apache-Sitgreaves National Forest** ⊠ 2022 White Mountain Blvd., Pinetop-Lakeside 85929 ☏ 928/368–5111 ⊕ www.fs.fed.us/r3/asnf. **National Recreation Reservation Service** ☏ 877/444–6777 ⊕ www.reserveusa.com. **White Mountain Apache Tribe** ⌂ Box 700, Whiteriver 85941 ☏ 928/338–4385 ⊕ www.wmat.nsn.us.

CAR RENTALS

🛈 **Enterprise Rent-A-Car** ⊠ 980 E. Deuce of Clubs, Show Low 85901 ☏ 928/537–5144. **Hatch Motor Company** ⊠ 260 W. Deuce of Clubs, Show Low 85901 ☏ 928/537–8887.

CAR TRAVEL

A car is essential for touring eastern Arizona, especially because most of the region's top scenic attractions are between towns. Rental facilities are few and far between in these parts, so you'll do well to rent a car from your departure point, whether it's Phoenix, Flagstaff, or Albuquerque.

If you're arriving from points west via Flagstaff, Interstate 40 leads directly to Holbrook, where drivers can take AZ 77 south into Show Low or U.S. 180 southeast to Springerville-Eagar. Those departing from the metropolitan Phoenix area should take the scenic drive northeast on U.S. 60, or the only slightly faster AZ 87 north to AZ 260 east, both of which lead to Show Low. From Tucson, AZ 77 north connects with U.S. 60 at Globe and continues through Show Low up to Holbrook. From New Mexico, drivers can enter the state on Interstate 40 and take U.S. 191 south into Springerville-Eagar, or continue on to Holbrook and reach the White Mountains via AZ 77. For those who want to drive the Coronado Trail south-to-north, U.S. 70 and AZ 78 link up with U.S. 191 from Globe to the west and New Mexico to the east, respectively.

ROAD CONDITIONS In winter, motorists should travel prepared, with jumper cables, a shovel, tire chains, and—for tire traction on icy roads—a bag of cat litter. Chain requirements apply to all vehicles, including those with four-wheel drive. Bridges and overpasses freeze first and are often slicker than normal road surfaces; never assume sufficient traction simply because a road appears to be sanded. If you must travel in poor visibility conditions, drivers should turn on the headlights and always keep the highway's white reflectors to their right. For road conditions through the region, call the White Mountains Road and Weather Information Line.

🛈 **White Mountains Road and Weather Information Line** ☏ 928/537–7623.

EMERGENCIES

🛈 Ambulance & Fire **Ambulance and Fire Emergencies** ☏ 911.
🛈 Hospitals **Navapache Regional Medical Center** ⊠ 2200 E. Show Low Lake Rd., Show Low ☏ 928/537–4375 ⊕ www.nrmc.org. **White Mountain Regional Medical Center** ⊠ 118 S. Mountain Ave., Springerville ☏ 928/333–4368.
🛈 Police **Police Emergencies** ☏ 911.

TRAIN TRAVEL

Amtrak trains depart daily at 6:15 AM from Flagstaff to Winslow. There is no train service to Phoenix; those traveling from Phoenix will need to take the Amtrak shuttle—which departs Phoenix-area bus stations four times daily bound for Flagstaff—and stay overnight in Flagstaff to catch the early-morning train to Winslow. From Albuquerque, Winslow is only a three-hour ride, leaving daily at 5:28 PM.

🛈 **Amtrak** ☎ 928/774-8679 in Flagstaff.

VISITOR INFORMATION

🛈 **Alpine Chamber of Commerce** ⌂ Box 410, Alpine 85920 ☎ 928/339-4330. **Holbrook Chamber of Commerce** ✉ 100 E. Arizona St., Holbrook 86025 ☎ 928/524-6558 or 800/524-2459 ⊕ www.ci.holbrook.az.us. **Pinetop-Lakeside Chamber of Commerce** ✉ 102-C W. White Mountain Blvd., Lakeside 85929 ☎ 928/367-4290 or 800/573-4031 ⊕ www.pinetoplakesidechamber.com. **Show Low Chamber of Commerce** ✉ 951 W. Deuce of Clubs ⌂ Box 1083, Show Low 85902 ☎ 928/537-2326 or 888/746-9569 ⊕ www.showlowchamberofcommerce.com. **Snowflake/Taylor Chamber of Commerce** ✉ 110 N. Main St., Snowflake 85937 ☎ 928/536-4331 ⊕ www.snowflaketaylorchamber.com **Springerville-Eagar Regional Chamber of Commerce** ✉ 318 E. Main St., Springerville 85938 ☎ 928/333-2123 ⊕ www.az-tourist.com. **White Mountain Apache Office of Tourism** ⌂ Box 710, Fort Apache 85926 ☎ 928/338-1230 ⊕ www.wmat.nsn.us.

LAND-MANAGEMENT AGENCIES 🛈 **Apache Sitgreaves National Forest** ⌂ Forest Supervisor's Office: Box 640, Springerville 85938 ☎ 928/333-4301 ⊕ www.fs.fed.us/r3/asnf ✉ Alpine Ranger District: Box 469, Alpine 85920 ☎ 928/339-4384 ✉ Lakeside Ranger District ✉ 2022 W. White Mountain Blvd., Lakeside 85929 ☎ 928/368-5111 ✉ Springerville Ranger District: Box 760, Springerville 85938 ☎ 928/333-4372. **Arizona Game & Fish Department** ✉ 2878 E. White Mountain Blvd., Pinetop 85935 ☎ 928/367-4281 ⊕ www.gf.state.az.us. **San Carlos Apache Tribe** ⌂ Box 0, San Carlos 85550 ☎ 928/475-2361. **White Mountain Apache Fish & Game Department** ⌂ Box 220, Whiteriver 85941 ☎ 928/338-4385.

TUCSON

6

CHECK OUT THE TECHNICOLOR ADOBES
in the Barrio Historico downtown ⇨*p.267*

MONITOR THE PULSE
of this college town on 4th Avenue ⇨*p.276*

BE INSPIRED
at Mission San Xavier del Bac ⇨*p.284*

SALUTE A SAGUARO
in the Sonoran Desert ⇨*p.285*

BRAVE THE TWO-CERVEZA WAIT
at Mi Nidito for the best Mexican food ⇨*p.295*

BE SPOILED LIKE A CELEBRITY
at the original Canyon Ranch ⇨*p.301*

ROUND UP YOUR LITTLE COWPOKES
for starlit campfires at a guest ranch ⇨*p.304*

SWING, BABY, SWING!
at Randolph Park Golf Course ⇨*p.313*

Updated by
Mara Levin

THE OLD PUEBLO, AS TUCSON is affectionately known, is built upon a deep Native American, Spanish, Mexican, and Old West foundation. Arizona's second-largest city is both a bustling center of business and a relaxed university and resort town. Metropolitan Tucson has more than 850,000 residents, including thousands of snowbirds who flee colder climes to enjoy the warm sun that shines on the city more than 340 days a year. Winter temperatures hover around 65°F during the day and 38°F at night. Summers are unquestionably hot—July averages 104°F during the day and 75°F at night—but, as Tucsonans are fond of saying, "it's a dry heat" (Tucson averages only 12 inches of rain a year).

Native Americans have lived along the waterways in this valley for thousands of years. During the 1500s, Spanish explorers arrived to find Pima Indians growing crops in the area. Father Eusebio Francisco Kino, a Jesuit missionary whose influence is still strongly felt throughout the region, first visited the area in 1687 and returned a few years later to build missions.

The name Tucson came from the Native American word *stjukshon* (pronounced *stook*-shahn), meaning "spring at the foot of a black mountain." (The springs at the foot of Sentinel Peak, made of black volcanic rock, are now dry.) The name became Tucson (originally pronounced *tuk*-son) in the mouths of the Spanish explorers who built a wall around the city in 1776 to keep Native Americans from reclaiming it. At the time, this *presidio* (fortified city), called San Augustin del Tuguison, was the northernmost Spanish settlement in the area known as the Pimeria Alta, and current-day Main Avenue is a quiet reminder of the former Camino Real ("royal road") that stretched from this tiny walled fort all the way to Mexico City.

Four flags have flown over Tucson—Spanish, Mexican, Confederate, and, finally, the Stars and Stripes. Tucson's allegiance changed in 1820 when Mexico declared independence from Spain, and again in 1853 when the Gadsden purchase made it part of the United States, though Arizona didn't become a state until 1912. In the 1850s the Butterfield stage line was extended to Tucson, bringing adventurers, a few settlers, and more than a handful of outlaws. The arrival of the railroad in 1880 marked another spurt of growth, as did the opening of the University of Arizona in 1891.

Tucson's 20th-century growth occurred after World War I, when veterans with damaged lungs sought the dry air and healing power of the sun, and again during World War II with the opening of Davis-Monthan Air Force Base and the rise of local aeronautical industries. It was also around this time that air-conditioning made the desert climate hospitable year-round.

Today, many transplants come from the Midwest and nearby California because of the lower housing costs, cleaner environment, and spectacular scenery. And despite the ubiquitous strip malls (Speedway Boulevard was once dubbed the "ugliest street in America" by *Life* magazine) and tract-home developments, this college town has Mexican and Native American–cultural influences, a striking landscape, and all the amenities of a resort town. High-tech industries have moved into the area, but the economy still relies heavily on tourism and the university, although, come summer, you'd never guess. When the snowbirds and students depart, Tucson can be a pretty sleepy place.

EXPLORING TUCSON

Tucson has a tri-cultural (Hispanic, Anglo, Native American) population, and the chance to see how these cultures interact—and to sample their cuisines—is one of the pleasures of a visit. The city is particularly popular among golfers, but the area's many hiking trails will keep non-duffers busy, too. If the weather is too hot to stay outdoors comfortably, museums such as the Arizona State Museum offer a cooler alternative. An influx of both new residents and visitors has given the city some growing pains, but city planners are addressing the issues of development and pollution control.

Getting Your Bearings

The metropolitan Tucson area covers more than 500-square mi in a valley ringed by mountains—the Santa Catalinas to the north, the Santa Ritas to the south, the Rincons to the east, and the Tucson Mountains to the west. You will need a car to explore the valley. The central portion of town—which has most of the shops, restaurants, and businesses—is roughly bounded by Craycroft Road on the east, Oracle Road on the west, River Road to the north, and 22nd Street to the south. The older downtown section, east of Interstate 10 off the Broadway-Congress exit, is much smaller and easy to navigate on foot. Streets downtown don't run true to any sort of grid, however, and many are one-way, so it's best to get a good, detailed map. The city's Westside area is the vast region west of Interstate 10 and Interstate 19, which includes the western section of Saguaro National Park and the San Xavier Indian Reservation.

Remember, too, that the old cliché is reversed here: it's not the humidity—it's the heat. If you are accustomed to humid conditions, then chances are you'll be unprepared for Tucson's dry climate, so use lip balm and skin moisturizer, and drink water or other noncaffeinated fluids frequently, whether you're active or not. Also, the strong solar radiation here (Tucson is second only to Cape Town, South Africa, in skin cancer incidence) makes sunscreen a must.

Downtown

The area bordered by Franklin Street on the north, Cushing Street on the south, Church Avenue on the east, and Main Avenue on the west encompasses more than two centuries of the city's architectural history, dating from the original walled El Presidio de Tucson, a Spanish fortress built in 1776, when Arizona was still part of New Spain. A good deal of Tucson's history was destroyed in the 1960s, when large sections of the downtown's barrio were bulldozed to make way for the Tucson Convention Center, high-rises, and parking lots. However, within the areas' three small historic districts it's still possible to explore parts of the original Spanish settlement and to see a number of the posh residences that accompanied the arrival of the railroad.

If you have
1 day

With only one day and a lot of ground to cover, you would be better off experiencing a taste of both the wild and developed parts of Tucson. Head out to the **Arizona–Sonora Desert Museum** ㉛. Children may enjoy a stop at the **Old Tucson Studios** ㉚, nearby. On your way back, drive through downtown's **Barrio Historico** neighborhood and **El Presidio Historic District** for a glimpse into the city's past, but with just a day, you won't have time to do much stopping.

If you have
3 days

Follow the first day's itinerary, through Old Tucson Studios. The next morning, drive out to the **Mission San Xavier del Bac** ㉝ and have some Native American–fry bread for lunch in the plaza. You might wish to continue south to the **Titan Missile Museum** ㉟ and then continue on to **Tubac** ㊲ for some shopping. On the third day, head **Downtown** ❶–⓫ to explore Tucson's early history and, in the afternoon, visit one of the several museums at the **University of Arizona** ⓬–⓲. While near the U of A, you might also want to consider heading to 4th Avenue between 2nd and 9th streets, where boutiques and used-book stores await.

If you have
4 days

What you do on the fourth day depends on the weather: if it's hot, visit **Mt. Lemmon** ㉕ to cool off; if it's not, you might enjoy breakfast at **Tohono Chul Park** ㉔ followed by a visit to beautiful **Sabino Canyon** ㉒.

El Presidio Historic District, north of the Convention Center and the government buildings that dominate downtown, is a representative mixture of Tucson's historic architecture, a thumbnail of the city's former self. The north–south streets Court, Meyer, and Main are sprinkled with traditional adobe houses. These typical Mexican structures sit cheek by jowl with territorial-style houses, with wide attics and porches. Paseo Redondo, once called Snob Hollow, is the wide road along which wealthy merchants built their homes.

The area most closely resembling 19th-century Tucson is the **Barrio Historico,** also known as Barrio Viejo. The narrow streets of this neighborhood, including Convent Avenue, have a good sampling of thick-wall adobe houses, painted in vibrant hues such as bright pink and canary yellow. The houses are close to the street, hiding the yards and gardens within. Ongoing gentrification has made this area an attractive, yet affordable, place to live.

To the east of the Barrio Historico, across Stone Avenue, lies the **Armory Park** neighborhood, mostly constructed by and for the railroad workers who settled here after the 1880s. The brick or wood territorial-style homes here were the Victorian era's adaptation to the desert climate.

Numbers in the text correspond to numbers in the margin and on the What to See in Downtown Tucson map.

a good
tour

Drive up to **"A" Mountain (Sentinel Peak)** ❶ ☞ for a great perspective of downtown Tucson (if you're squeamish about heights, be aware that the narrow, winding road has no guard rails). Come down from on high and head east along Congress Street, stopping at Santa Cruz River Park to view the religious sculptures and mosaic murals by local artists, before crossing the **Santa Cruz River** ❷. Continue east along Congress, and turn right (heading south) on Granada, passing the new Federal Court Building. The **Sosa-Carillo-Frémont House** ❸ is on the left (park at the adjacent convention center lot if no events are in progress). Continuing south on Granada, turn left onto Cushing Street and then right onto Main, to see the shrine of **El Tiradito (The Castaway)** ❹, next to El Minuto Restaurant's parking lot. As you meander through the Barrio Historico neighborhood, you'll pass adobe houses that are being restored and painted in bright colors.

Turn right onto Simpson, left onto Samaniego, left onto 17th Street, and left onto Convent, which becomes Church. One-way streets require you to drive north on Church, east on Broadway Boulevard, and then south on Stone Avenue to see **St. Augustine Cathedral** ❺. Head east on McCormick to 6th Avenue, where your kids may want to check out the hands-on activities at the **Tucson Children's Museum** ❻, in the heart of the Armory Park Historic District. To get to the **Tucson Museum of Art and Historic Block** ❼, take 6th Avenue north to Congress Street, where you'll see the historic Hotel Congress on the right. This stretch of Congress was once Tucson's bustling center, before suburban growth supplanted it. Drive west on Congress to Church Avenue, head north to Alameda, then west to Main, where you'll enter the El Presidio neighborhood and find convenient public parking. The museum and historic complex include **La Casa Cordova** ❽, the **J. Knox Corbett House** ❾, and the **Stevens Home** ❿. After your museum tour, walk east on Alameda and then south on Church to reach the **Pima County Courthouse** ⓫, downtown's architectural jewel.

TIMING You can see most of the highlights of downtown, including the Tucson Museum of Art, in about four hours. Although it is all accessible by car, the one-way streets can be frustrating and time-consuming, so you might consider parking your car and walking between destinations if the weather is not too hot. It's a good way to take in downtown, stopping for lunch or a snack along the way. On weekends, the area is less crowded and parking is easier, but some businesses and restaurants are closed.

What to See

☞ ❶ **"A" Mountain (Sentinel Peak).** The original name of this mountain west of downtown was derived from its function as a lookout point for the Spanish. In 1915, fans of the University of Arizona football team whitewashed a large "A" on its side to celebrate a victory, and the tradition has been kept up ever since—the permanent "A" is now red, white, and blue. The Pima village and cultivated fields that once lay at the base of the peak are long gone, although John Warner's 19th-century house at the base still stands. During the day, the peak's a great place to get an overview of the town's layout; at night the city lights below form a dazzling carpet, but the teenage hangout/make-out scene may make some uncomfortable. ⊠ *Congress St. on Sentinel Peak Rd., Downtown.*

Mexican- & Native-American Culture

Mexican Americans make up about 30% of Tucson's population and play a major role in all aspects of daily life. The city's south-of-the-border soul is visible in its tile-roof architecture, mariachi festivals, and abundance of Mexican restaurants. Native Americans have a strong presence in the area as well: the Tohono O'odham—the name means "desert people who have come from the Earth"—reservation borders Tucson, and the Pascua Yaqui have their villages within the city limits. Local events, especially religious festivals around Christmas and Easter, celebrate the culture of these and other Arizona tribes. Native American crafts encompass exquisite jewelry and basketry as well as the more pedestrian (but still authentic) tourist trinkets.

6

Getting Outdoors

A warm, dry climate and a varied terrain make the Tucson area wonderfully suited for outdoor sports throughout the year. The city has miles of bike paths (shared by joggers and walkers) and plenty of wide-open spaces with memorable desert views. Those same expanses contain some of the best golf courses in the country, with options ranging from well-manicured links at posh resorts to reasonably priced, excellent municipal courses. In the winter, hikers enjoy the myriad desert trails; during the summer, they go on cooler treks in nearby mountain ranges: Saguaro (pronounced suh-*war*-oh) National Park (both east and west), Sabino Canyon, and Catalina State Park are all within 20 minutes of central Tucson by car. Both equestrians and ersatz cowboys and -girls will find scenic trails and horseback riding options to suit them at one of the many area stables. City ordinances against "light pollution"—laws designed to minimize the amount of man-made light emitted into the atmosphere—allow viewing of the usually clear desert skies, even in the city center.

---

4 **El Tiradito (The Castaway).** No one seems to know the details of the story behind this little shrine, but everyone agrees a tragic love triangle was involved. A bronze plaque indicates only that it is dedicated to a sinner who is buried here on unconsecrated ground. The many candles that line the cactus-shrouded spot attest to its continuing importance in local Catholic lore. People light candles and leave *milagros* (literally, "miracles"; little icons used in prayers for healing) for their loved ones. A modern-day miracle: the shrine's inclusion on the National Register of Historic Places helped prevent a freeway from plowing through this section of the Barrio Historico. ⊠ *Main Ave. south of Cushing St., Downtown.*

9 **J. Knox Corbett House.** Built in 1906–07, this house was occupied by members of the Corbett family until 1963. The original occupants were J. Knox Corbett, successful businessman, postmaster, and mayor of Tucson, and his wife Elizabeth Hughes Corbett, an accomplished musician and daughter of Tucson pioneer Sam Hughes. Tucson's Hi Corbett field (the spring training field for the Major League Colorado Rockies) is named for their grandnephew, Hiram. The two-story, Mission Revival–style residence has been furnished with Arts and Crafts pieces: Stickley, Roy-

"A"
Mountain
(Sentinel
Peak) **1**

El Tiradito
(The
Castaway) **4**

J. Knox
Corbett
House **9**

La Casa
Cordova **8**

Pima County
Courthouse ..**11**

Santa Cruz
River **2**

Sosa-Carillo-
Frémont
House **3**

St. Augustine
Cathedral **5**

Stevens
Home **10**

Tucson
Children's
Museum **6**

Tucson
Museum
of Art and
Historic
Block **7**

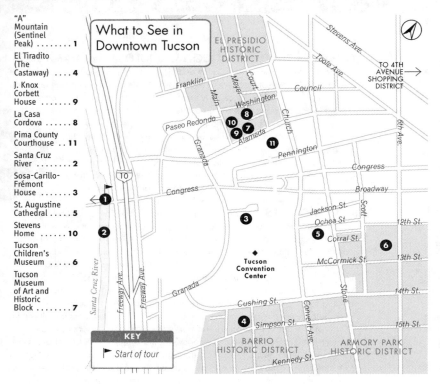

croft, Tiffany, and Morris are among the more famous manufacturers represented. ⊠ *180 N. Main Ave., Downtown* ☎ *520/624–2333* ⊕ *www.tucsonarts.com* ✉ *Included in $5 admission to Tucson Museum of Art* ⊙ *Mon.–Sat. 10–4, Sun. noon–4. Free guided tour Tues. at 11.*

⑧ La Casa Cordova. One of the oldest buildings in Tucson is also one of the best local examples of a Sonoran row house. This simple but elegant design is a Spanish style adapted to adobe construction. Adobe—brick made of mud and straw, cured in the hot sun—was used widely in early Tucson because it provides a natural insulation from the heat and cold and because it is durable in Tucson's dry climate. The oldest section of La Casa Cordova, constructed around 1848, has been restored to its original appearance and is now the Mexican Heritage Museum. Furnishings of the Native American and pioneer settlers and an exhibit on the presidio's history are inside. ⊠ *175 N. Meyer Ave., Downtown* ☎ *520/624–2333* ⊕ *www.tucsonarts.com* ✉ *Included in $5 admission to Tucson Museum of Art* ⊙ *Mon.–Sat. 10–4, Sun. noon–4.*

need a break?   On the patio of Stevens Home, a 19th-century adobe building adjacent to the Tucson Museum of Art, **Cafe A La C'Arte** (⊠ 150 N. Main Ave., Downtown ☎ 520/628–8533) serves fanciful salads, soups, and sandwiches. For a tasty frittata or panini (pressed sandwich), try **Caffé Milano** (✉ 46 W. Congress St., Downtown ☎ 520/628–1601), an Italian deli open weekdays until 3 PM.

★ ⑪ **Pima County Courthouse.** This Spanish colonial–style building with a mosaic-tile dome is among Tucson's most beautiful historic structures. It was built in 1927 on the site of the original single-story adobe court of 1869; a portion of the old presidio wall can be seen in the south wing of the courthouse's second floor. To the side of the building, the county assessor's office has a diorama depicting the area's early days (if the location seems odd, remember that the Spanish were big on taxation, too). The courthouse, still in use, is on the eastern side of El Presidio Park, a modern square once occupied by the Plaza de las Armas, the largest of El Presidio's plazas. ✉ *115 N. Church Ave., between Alameda and Pennington Sts., Downtown* ⊕ *www.jp.co.pima.az.us* 🎟 *Free* ☉ *Weekdays 8–4:30, Sat. 8–noon.*

❷ **Santa Cruz River & River Park.** The Santa Cruz is a dry wash, or arroyo, most of the year, but sudden summer thunderstorms and rainwater from upper elevations can turn it into a raging river in a matter of hours. The river has been the location of a settlement for thousands of years, and most of the archaeological finds in the valley are along its banks. When Europeans arrived, the Santa Cruz was a permanent river with wide banks suitable for irrigation. Over time its banks have been narrowed and contained and are now lined by the River Park. A favorite spot for walkers, joggers, bicyclists, and horseback riders, the park has a bike path, rest rooms, drinking fountains, and sculptures created by local artists.

❸ **Sosa-Carillo-Frémont House.** One of Tucson's oldest adobe residences, this was the only building spared when the surrounding barrio was torn down to build the Tucson Convention Center. Originally purchased by José Maria Sosa in 1860, it was owned by the Carillo family for 80 years and leased at one time to territorial governor John C. Frémont. The restored house, now a branch of the Arizona Historical Society, is furnished in 1880s fashion and has changing displays of territorial life. The house is in the Convention Center complex, between the Music Hall and the Arena. ✉ *151 S. Granada Ave., Downtown* ☎ 520/622–0956 ⊕ *www. ahs.state.az.us* 🎟 *Free; guided walking tours of the Presidio and Tucson Historic District $10* ☉ *Wed.–Sat. 10–4; walking tours Nov.–Mar., Thurs. and Sat. at 10.*

❺ **St. Augustine Cathedral.** Construction began in 1896 on one of downtown's most striking structures, in what had earlier been the Plaza de Mesilla. Although the imposing white and beige Spanish-style building was modeled after the Cathedral of Queretaro in Mexico, a number of its details reflect the desert setting: above the entryway, next to a bronze statue of St. Augustine, are carvings of local desert scenes with saguaro cacti, yucca, and prickly pears. Look closely for the horned toad. Compared with the magnificent facade, the modernized interior is a bit disappointing. For a distinctly Southwestern experience, attend the mariachi mass celebrated Sunday at 8 AM. ✉ *192 S. Stone Ave., Downtown* 🎟 *Free* ☉ *Daily 7–6.*

⑩ **Stevens Home.** It was here that wealthy politician and cattle rancher Hiram Stevens and his Mexican wife, Petra Santa Cruz, entertained many of Tucson's leaders—including Edward and Maria Fish—during the 1800s.

A drought brought the Stevens's cattle ranching to a halt in 1893, and Stevens killed himself in despair, after unsuccessfully attempting to shoot his wife (the bullet was deflected by the comb she wore in her hair). The 1865 house, just north of the Edward Nye Fish House, was restored in 1980 and now houses the Tucson Museum of Art's permanent collections of pre-Columbian, Spanish colonial, and Latin American folk art. A café on the porch and patio of this home serves lovely sandwiches, soups, and pastries to the downtown crowd weekdays 11 to 3, and it's a great place to fortify yourself against museum fatigue. ⊠ *150 N. Main Ave., Downtown* ⊕ *www.tucsonarts.com* ▣ *Included in $5 admission to Tucson Museum of Art* ⊙ *Mon.–Sat. 10–4, Sun. noon–4.*

🐾 ❻ **Tucson Children's Museum.** Youngsters are encouraged to touch and explore the science, language, and history exhibits here. They can key in on Little Tikes IBM computers or turn on the electricity in the streets of a model town. There's Dinosaur Canyon, with mechanical prehistoric creatures, and a bubble room where children can place themselves in the middle of a large vertical soap bubble. For smaller fry there's a toddler's playroom; a pretend grocery store and musical instruments add to the fun. ⊠ *200 S. 6th Ave., Downtown* ☎ *520/792–9985* ⊕ *www. tucsonchildrensmuseum.org* ▣ *$5.50* ⊙ *Tues.–Sat. 10–5, Sun. noon–5.*

★ ❼ **Tucson Museum of Art and Historic Block.** The five historic buildings on this block are listed in the National Register of Historic Places; you can enter La Casa Cordova, the Stevens Home, the J. Knox Corbett House, and the Edward Nye Fish House. The Romero House, believed to incorporate a section of the presidio wall, is not open to the public. In the center of the museum complex is the Plaza of the Pioneers, honoring Tucson's early citizens.

The museum building, the only modern structure of the complex, houses a permanent collection of modern and contemporary art and hosts traveling shows. The museum's permanent and changing exhibitions of Western art fill the Edward Nye Fish House. This 1868 adobe belonged to an early merchant, entrepreneur, and politician and to his wife, Maria Wakefield Fish, a prominent educator. The building is notable for its 15-foot beamed ceilings and saguaro cactus–rib supports. There are free docent tours of the museum, and you can pick up a self-guided tour map of the El Presidio district. Parking is in a large lot at North Main Avenue and Paseo Redondo. ⊠ *140 N. Main Ave., Downtown* ☎ *520/624–2333* ⊕ *www.tucsonarts.com* ▣ *$5, Sun. free; tours free* ⊙ *Mon.–Sat. 10–4, Sun. noon–4. Guided tours Wed., Thurs., and Sat. at 11. Closed Mon. late May–early Sept. (no guided tours during that period).*

The University of Arizona

A university might not seem to be the most likely spot for a vacation visit, but this one is unusual. The campus itself is an arboretum, and there are several museums, with exhibitions ranging from astronomy to photography, on the grounds.

The U of A (as opposed to ASU, its rival state university in Tempe), covers 353 acres and is a major economic influence with a student population of more than 34,000. The land for the university was "donated" by a couple of gamblers and a saloon owner in 1891 (their benevolence was reputed to have been inspired by a bad hand of cards), and $25,000 of territorial money was used to build Old Main (the original building) and hire six faculty members. Money ran out before Old Main's roof was placed, but a few enlightened local citizens pitched in funds to finish it. Most of the city's populace was less enthusiastic about the institution: they were disgruntled when the 13th Territorial Legislature granted the University of Arizona to Tucson and awarded rival Phoenix with what was considered to be the real prize—an insane asylum and a prison.

The university's flora is very impressive—it represents a collection of plants from arid and semiarid regions around the world. An extremely rare mutated, or "crested," saguaro grows at the northeast corner of the Old Main building. The long, grassy Mall in the heart of campus—itself once a vast cactus garden—sits atop a huge underground student activity center, and makes for a pleasant stroll or bike ride on a balmy evening.

Although the U of A prides itself on its achievements in the fields of academics (the astronomy department, medical school, and anthropology program are top-rated), undergrads seem more interested in their school's renown on the fields of athletics. The movie *Revenge of the Nerds*, filmed on campus, further contributed to the university's reputation as a "party school."

Numbers in the text correspond to numbers in the margin and on the What to See at the University of Arizona map.

a good walk

Start your tour near the northwest corner of campus, at Euclid and 2nd streets, where there is a large public parking garage. Walk a half-block east on 2nd Street to the **Arizona Historical Society's Museum** ⑫ ▶, and glimpse how far the Old Pueblo has come in 100 years. One block south on Park Avenue, just inside the main gate of the university, is the **Arizona State Museum** ⑬, the place to explore Native American culture. Heading east on University Boulevard and deeper into the campus, you'll pass by Old Main and the crested saguaro. As the road curves to the left, University Boulevard turns into the campus mall. The Student Union and University Bookstore are on your left; the sculpture in front of the complex depicts Arizona/Mexico border struggles. Cross over to the south side of the mall (watch out for Frisbees) and take a peek inside the old Gymnasium, where Wildcats fans cheered their team on before the construction of McKale Center. Continue east, passing the steps leading down to the underground activity center, and you'll come to the **Flandrau Science Center and Planetarium** ⑭, at the intersection of Cherry Avenue. Check telescope-viewing schedules, see a light show, or stock up on science-oriented gifts here.

Walk north on Cherry, then turn left onto 2nd Street, passing several fairly tame fraternity and sorority houses. Turn right on Olive Road to find the **Center for Creative Photography** ⑮, home to most of photographer Ansel Adams' negatives and a slew of other exhibits in this medium. Across from the center is the small but respectable **University of Arizona Museum of Art** ⑯. From here, it's a short walk west on Speedway Boule-

Arizona
Historical
Society's
Museum **12**

Arizona
State
Museum **13**

Center for
Creative
Photography . **15**

Flandrau
Science
Center and
Planetarium . **14**

4th Avenue .. **18**

Old Pueblo
Trolly **17**

University of
Arizona
Museum
of Art **16**

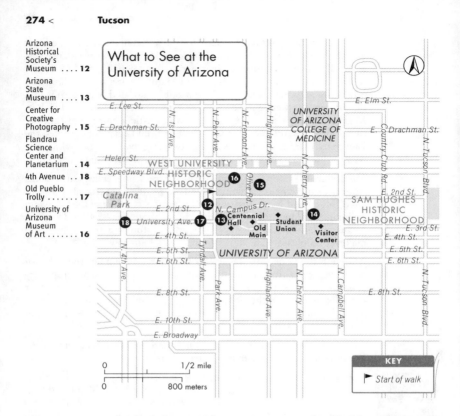

What to See at the
University of Arizona

vard to Park Avenue, where you can go south to 2nd Street and return to the Arizona Historical Society's Museum and the parking lot.

To soak up more college culture, continue down Park to University Avenue and turn right. This section of University Avenue is the hub of off-campus activity, packing a slew of restaurants, cafés, and trendy boutiques into a few blocks. At this point, you can walk—or on weekends ride aboard the **Old Pueblo Trolley** ⑰—along University to **4th Avenue** ⑱, Tucson's last bastion of bohemia, for shopping and people-watching.

TIMING   To see this huge university campus in a single day takes careful planning. Call ahead to verify hours for the university's museums, as yearly budget revisions often cause schedule changes. If you drive, leave your car in a university garage or lot; those on 2nd Street at Mountain Avenue, on Speedway Boulevard at Park Avenue, on Tyndall Avenue south of University Boulevard, and on 2nd Street at Euclid Avenue are the most convenient. Parking costs $2 for the first hour and $1 for each additional hour, with free parking on weekends and holidays. During the school semesters, you're better off visiting on the weekend when parking is both free and plentiful; there's no problem in summer when most of the students leave campus. Visit the Web site **University of Arizona** (⊕ www.arizona. edu), for parking maps and the latest visitor information.

What to See

☺ ► ⓬ **Arizona Historical Society's Museum.** Flanking the entrance to the museum are statues of two men: Father Kino, the Jesuit who established San Xavier del Bac and a string of other missions, and John Greenaway, indelibly linked to Phelps Dodge, the copper-mining company that helped Arizona earn statehood in 1912. The museum houses the headquarters of the state Historical Society, originally the Society of Arizona Pioneers, and has exhibits exploring the history of southern Arizona, the Southwest United States, and northern Mexico, starting with the Hohokam Indians and Spanish explorers. Check out the harrowing "Life on the Edge: A History of Medicine in Arizona" exhibit to gain a new appreciation of modern drugstores in present-day Tucson. Children enjoy the large exhibit on copper mining (complete with an atmospheric replica of a mine shaft and camp), the stagecoaches in the transportation area, and the pioneer clothing in the costume exhibit. The library houses an extensive collection of historic Arizona photographs and sells inexpensive reprints of most of them. If this is your first stop, park your car in the garage at the corner of 2nd and Euclid streets and then get a free parking pass in the museum. ⊠ *949 E. 2nd St., University* ☎ *520/ 628–5774* ⊕ *www.arizona.edu* ☜ *$5* ☼ *Mon.–Sat. 10–4; library weekdays 10–4, Sat. 10–1.*

⓭ **Arizona State Museum.** Inside the main gate of the university is Arizona's oldest museum, dating from territorial days (1893) and recognized as one of the world's most important resources for the study of Southwestern cultures. Exhibits in the original (south) building focus on the state's ancient history, including fossils and a fascinating sample of tree-ring dating. "Paths of Life: American Indians of the Southwest" is a permanent exhibit that explores the cultural traditions, origins, and contemporary lives of 10 native tribes of Arizona and Sonora, Mexico. ⊠ *Park Ave. at University Ave., University* ☎ *520/621–6302* ⊕ *www.statemuseum. arizona.edu* ☜ *Free* ☼ *Mon.–Sat. 10–5, Sun. noon–5.*

> [need a break?] Just outside the campus gate, University Boulevard is lined with student-oriented eateries. **Café Paraiso** (⊠ 800 E. University Blvd., University ☎ 520/624–1707) is a home-grown lunch spot serving salads and sandwiches, and it has a great patio where you can watch the passing university scene. The Chinese and Thai fast-food at **Pei Wei** (⊠ 845 E. University Blvd., University ☎ 520/884–7413) is flavorful, healthful, and affordable. Beer lovers should head over to **Gentle Ben's** (⊠ 865 E. University Blvd., University ☎ 520/624–4177), a burger-and-brew pub. The deck upstairs affords a good view of the sunset.

★ ⓯ **Center for Creative Photography.** Ansel Adams conceived the idea of a photographer's archive and donated the majority of his negatives to this museum. In addition to its superb collection of his work, the center has works by other major photographers including Paul Strand, W. Eugene Smith, Edward Weston, and Louise Dahl-Wolfe. Changing exhibits in the main gallery display selected pieces from the collection, but if you'd like to see the work of a particular photographer in the archives, call to arrange an appointment. ✉ *1030 N. Olive Rd., north of 2nd St., University* ☎ *520/621–7968* ⊕ *www.creativephotography.org* 🖾 *$5 suggested donation* ⊙ *Weekdays 9–5, weekends noon–5.*

ⓒ ⑭ **Flandrau Science Center and Planetarium.** Attractions here include a 16-inch public telescope; the impressive Star Theatre, where a multimedia show brings astronomy to life; an interactive meteor exhibit; and, in the basement, a Mineral Museum, which exhibits more than 2,000 rocks and gems, some rather rare. Bring a camera—special adapters allow you to take pictures through the telescopes. ✉ *Cherry Ave. and University Blvd., University* ☎ *520/621–4515, 520/621–7827 recorded message* ⊕ *www.flandrau.org* 🖾 *Exhibits $3; planetarium shows $5.50; observatory free* ⊙ *Exhibits Mon.–Wed. 9–5, Thurs.–Sat. 9–5 and 7 PM–9 PM, Sun. 1–5. Planetarium show times vary. Observatory Aug. 15–May 15, Wed.–Sat. 6:40 PM–10 PM; May 16–Aug. 14, Wed.–Sat. 7:30 PM–10 PM.*

⑱ **4th Avenue.** Students and counterculturists favor this ½-mi strip of 4th Avenue. Vintage-clothing stores rub shoulders with ethnic eateries from Guatemalan to Greek. After dark, 4th Avenue bars pulse with live and recorded music. ⊹ *Between University and 9th Sts.*

⑰ **Old Pueblo Trolley.** Ride historic electric trolleys through the streets of Tucson along University Boulevard and 4th Avenue past shops and restaurants. The trolley passes restored historic buildings on part of the original 1898 streetcar track. The route terminates near the Arizona Historical Society. ✉ *360 E. 8th St., University* ☎ *520/792–1802* ⊕ *www. oldpueblotrolley.org* 🖾 *Fri.–Sat. $1. 25, Sun. 25 ¢* ⊙ *Fri. 6 PM–10 PM, Sat. noon–midnight, Sun. noon–6.*

⑯ **University of Arizona Museum of Art.** This small museum houses a collection of European paintings from the Renaissance through the 17th century. One of the museum's highlights is the Kress Collection's Retablo from Ciudad Rodrigo: 26 panels of an altarpiece made in 1488 by Fernando Gallego. The museum also houses the world's second-largest collection of bronze, plaster, and ceramic sculpture by Jacques Lipschitz. ✉ *Fine Arts Complex, Bldg. 2 (southeast corner of Speedway Blvd. and Park Ave.), University* ☎ *520/621–7567* ⊕ *http://artmuseum.arizona. edu* 🖾 *Free* ⊙ *Sept.–mid-May, Tues.–Fri. 9–5, weekends noon–4; mid-May–Aug., Tues.–Fri. 10–3:30, weekends noon–4.*

---

off the beaten path

UNIVERSITY NEIGHBORHOODS – When the University of Arizona was built, it stood in the desert on the east side of town, and students either lived at home or boarded with residents. Drive slowly along University Boulevard west from the Main Gate of campus through West University Neighborhood, a wonderful mixture of stately homes built by former prominent Tucsonans and bungalows constructed for rental to students. On the other side of campus, off Campbell Avenue between Speedway and Broadway boulevards, lies Sam Hughes Neighborhood, which saw its first homes in the 1920s. Meander along 3rd Street, one of Tucson's many bike paths, to see an eclectic mix of Spanish Mission revival, bungalow, adobe, and brick homes.

Central Tucson, the Santa Catalinas & East

The U of A, built in 1891, determined the direction in ⌐____
would grow: most residential areas and major attractions are east of
the main freeway, Interstate 10. Over the years, Tucson has continued to sprawl both east and north into the the foothills of the Santa
Catalina Mountains.

*Numbers in the text correspond to numbers in the margin and on the
What to See in Greater Tucson map.*

**a good
tour**

Begin your tour in Central Tucson, where the sights worth seeing include a city park, a zoo, and botanical gardens. Then it's decision time.
To the north lie the imposing Santa Catalina Mountains, and to the far
east cacti and caverns rule. A southern detour leads to a huge reposi-
tory of old military aircraft.

Start your explorations at the **Tucson Botanical Gardens** ⑲ ⌐, at the corner of Grant Road and North Alvernon Way. Take Alvernon south from
the gardens to 22nd Street and the small **Reid Park Zoo** ⑳, a drive of
less than 10 minutes. Leave the zoo by heading east on 22nd Street to
Craycroft Road. Take a left and head north to the **Fort Lowell Park and
Museum** ㉑.

Now you're leaving Central Tucson and distances will be greater. You
can head north into the Santa Catalinas, stopping off at your choice of
Sabino Canyon ㉒, **De Grazia's Gallery in the Sun** ㉓, **Tohono Chul Park** ㉔,
or **Mt. Lemmon** ㉕. Sabino Canyon has hiking trails, a tram, and loads
of saguaros and vistas, making it a rewarding destination close to town.
Mt. Lemmon, although more time-consuming (it's a one-hour drive each
way), can be a good alternative on a warm day because of its high elevation, which produce cooler temperatures.

If caves or aviation are your fancy, you may want to head east instead,
driving to **Saguaro National Park East** ㉖ and **Colossal Cave Mountain
Park** ㉗, and then south to **Pima Air and Space Museum** ㉘.

TIMING If it's warm, visit outdoor attractions such as the Tucson Botanical Gardens, Sabino Canyon, and Saguaro National Park East in the morning.
Mt. Lemmon, with its high elevation, makes an excellent midday destination in summer. Colossal Cave stays at a constant, comfortable temperature, making it a pleasant year-round adjunct to a Saguaro National
Park East tour.

What to See

🦢 ㉗ **Colossal Cave Mountain Park.** This limestone grotto 20 mi east of Tucson
(take Broadway Boulevard or 22nd Street East to Colossal Cave Road)
is the largest dry cavern in the world. Guides discuss the fascinating crystal formations and relate the many romantic tales surrounding the cave,
including the legend that an enormous sum of money stolen in a stagecoach robbery is hidden here. Forty-five-minute cave tours begin every
30 minutes and require a ½-mi walk and 363 stairs. The park includes
a ranch area with trail rides ($20 per hour), a gemstone-sluicing area,
a small museum, nature trails, a butterfly garden, a snack bar, and a gift

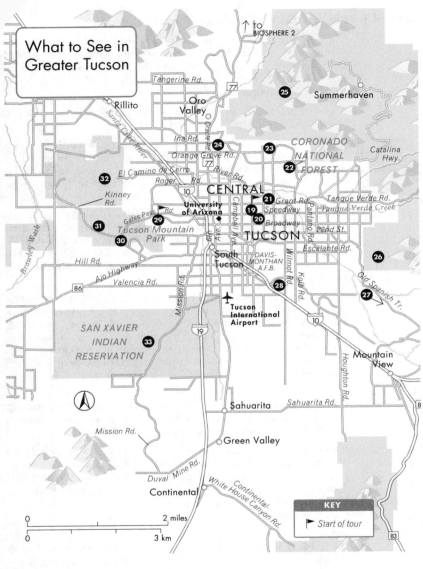

What to See in Greater Tucson

↑ TO BIOSPHERE 2

Tangerine Rd.

Rillito

Oro Valley

Summerhaven

25

CORONADO

Catalina Hwy.

Ina Rd.

24

23

NATIONAL

Orange Grove Rd.

22

FOREST

El Camino de Cerro

River Rd.

Roger Rd.

32

CENTRAL

Kinney Rd.

10

Grant Rd.

Tanque Verde Rd.

21

Tanque Verde Creek

University of Arizona

19

Speedway

Gates Pass Rd.

31

29

20

Broadway

22nd St.

30

Tucson Mountain Park

TUCSON

Escalante Rd.

Hill Rd.

South Tucson

DAVIS-MONTHAN A.F.B.

26

Ajo Highway

Valencia Rd.

86

28

27

19

Old Spanish Tr.

Tucson International Airport

10

SAN XAVIER INDIAN RESERVATION

33

Mountain View

8

Sahuarita

Sahuarita Rd.

Mission Rd.

Green Valley

Duval Mine Rd.

Continental

Continental- White House Canyon Rd.

Continental

83

| 0 | | 2 miles |
| 0 | | 3 km |

KEY

⚑ Start of tour

Arizona-Sonora Desert Museum **31**

Colossal Cave Mountain Park **27**

De Grazia's Gallery in the Sun **23**

Fort Lowell Park and Museum **21**

International Wildlife Museum **29**

Mission San Xavier del Bac **33**

Mt. Lemmon **25**

Old Tucson Studios **30**

Pima Air and Space Museum **28**

Reid Park Zoo **20**

Sabino Canyon **22**

Saguaro National Park East **26**

Saguaro National Park West **32**

Tohono Chul Park **24**

Tucson Botanical Gardens **19**

shop. ⊠ *Colossal Cave Rd. at Old Spanish Trail Rd., Eastside* ☎ ⌐ *647-7275* ⊕ *www.colossalcave.com* ☜ *Park $3 per car; cave to $7.50 per person* ⊙ *Oct.–mid-Mar., Mon.–Sat. 9–5, Sun. 9–6; mic Mar.–Sept., Mon.–Sat. 8–6, Sun. 8–7.*

❷❸ **De Grazia's Gallery in the Sun.** Arizonan artist Ted De Grazia, who depicted Southwest Native American and Mexican life in a manner some find kitschy and others adore, built this sprawling, spacious single-story museum with the assistance of Native American friends, using only natural material from the surrounding desert. You can visit De Grazia's workshop, former home, and grave. Although the original works are not for sale, the museum's gift shop has a wide selection of prints, ceramics, and books by and about the colorful artist. ⊠ *6300 N. Swan Rd., Foothills* ☎ *520/299-9191* ⊕ *www.degrazia.org* ☜ *Free* ⊙ *Daily 10–4.*

⊛ ❷❶ **Fort Lowell Park and Museum.** Fertile soil and proximity to the Rillito River once enticed the Hohokam to construct a village on this site. Centuries later, a fort was built here to protect the fledgling city of Tucson against the Apaches (1873–91). The former commanding officer's quarters display artifacts from military life in territorial days. Some of the descendants of the inhabitants of El Fuerte, a Mexican village that arose among the abandoned fort buildings in the 1890s, live in El Callejón, a narrow alley near the museum. The sprawling park has playground structures, ball fields, tennis courts, and a pond with ducks awaiting your breadcrumbs. ⊠ *2900 N. Craycroft Rd., Central* ☎ *520/885-3832* ☜ *Free* ⊙ *Wed.–Sat. 10–4.*

❷❺ **Mt. Lemmon.** In 1881, Sara Lemmon became the first woman to reach the peak of this mountain, part of the Santa Catalina range. Mt. Lemmon is the southernmost ski slope in the continental United States, but you don't have to be a skier to enjoy a visit. In spring and fall you can picnic and hike among the 150 mi of clearly marked and well-maintained trails; in summer the mountain's 9,157-foot elevation brings welcome relief from the heat.

Mt. Lemmon Highway winds and twists its way for 28 mi up the mountainside. Every 1,000-foot climb in elevation is equivalent, in terms of climate, to traveling 300 mi north. You'll move from typical Sonoran Desert plants in the foothills to vegetation similar to that found in southern Canada at the top. Rock formations along the way look as though they were carefully balanced against each other by sculptors from another planet.

At milepost 18 of your ascent, on the left-hand side of the road, is the Palisades Ranger Station of **Coronado National Forest** (☎ *520/749-8700*). Rangers have the latest information on the mountain's campgrounds, hiking trails, and picnic spots. It's open weekends 8:30 to 4:30 in winter, daily 9 to 6 in summer. Even if you don't make it to the top of the mountain, you'll find stunning views of Tucson at Windy Point, about halfway up. Look for a road on your left between the Windy Point and San Pedro lookouts; it leads to Rose Canyon Lake, a lovely little reservoir.

Just before you reach the ski area, you'll pass through the tiny alpine-style village of **Summerhaven,** which has a couple of casual restaurants, 't shops, and a few pleasant lodges. Many of Summerhaven's cabins shops were destroyed by a forest fire in summer 2003. Rebuilding is well underway, as is construction to widen the Mt. Lemmon highway, which is scheduled for completion in early 2005.

Mt. Lemmon Highway ends at **Mt. Lemmon Ski Valley.** Skiing here depends on natural conditions—there's no artificial snow, so call ahead. There are 16 runs, open daily in winter, ranging from beginner to advanced. Lift tickets cost $28 weekdays ($32 weekends and holidays) for an all-day pass and $23 weekdays ($27 weekends and holidays) for a half-day pass (starting at 1 PM). Equipment rentals and instruction are available. In off-season you can take a ride ($7.50) on the double chairlift, which whisks you to the top of the slope—some 9,100 feet above sea level. Many ride the lift and then head out hiking on one of several trails that crisscross the summit. There are some concessions at the ski lift.

There are no gas stations on Mt. Lemmon Highway, so be sure to check the road conditions in winter and to gas up before you leave town any time of year. To reach the highway, take Tanque Verde Road to Catalina Highway, which becomes Mt. Lemmon Highway as you head north. ✉ *Mt. Lemmon Hwy., Northeast* ☎ *520/576–1400 recorded snow report, 520/547–7510 winter road conditions* 🎫 *$5 per vehicle per day or $20 for an annual pass (includes Sabino Canyon)* ☉ *Daily (depending on snow during ski season).*

28 **Pima Air and Space Museum.** This huge facility ranks among the largest private collections of aircraft in the world. More than 200 airplanes are on display, including a presidential plane used by both John F. Kennedy and Lyndon B. Johnson, a full-scale replica of the Wright brothers' 1903 Wright Flyer, and a mock-up of the X-15, the world's fastest aircraft. World War II planes are particularly well-represented. Hour-long van tours of the nearby Aerospace Maintenance and Regeneration Center (AMARC) at Davis-Monthan Air Force Base provide an eerie glimpse of hundreds of mothballed aircraft lined up in long rows on a vast tract of desert; you must reserve a place in advance for this tour. ✉ *6000 E. Valencia Rd. (I–10, Exit 267), South* ☎ *520/574–0462* ⊕ *www.pimaair. org* 🎫 *$9.75, tram $4, AMARC tour $6* ☉ *Daily 9–5 (last admission at 4); AMARC tours weekdays only.*

20 **Reid Park Zoo.** This small but well-designed zoo won't tax the children's—or your—patience. There are plenty of shady places to sit, a wonderful little gift shop, and a snack bar to rev you up when your energy is flagging. The youngsters will love the zoo's adorable newborns and the South American enclosure with its rain forest and exotic birds. If you're visiting in summer, go early in the day when the animals are active. The park surrounding the zoo has multiple playground structures and a lake where you can feed ducks and rent paddleboats. ✉ *Reid Park, Randolph Way off 22nd St. between Alvernon Way and Country Club Rd., Central* ☎ *520/791–3204* ⊕ *www. tucsonzoo.org* 🎫 *$5* ☉ *Daily 9–4.*

★ ㉒ **Sabino Canyon.** Year-round, but especially in summer, locals flock to the Coronado National Forest to hike, picnic, and enjoy the waterfalls, streams, swimming holes, and shade trees that provide a respite from the heat. No cars are allowed, but a narrated tram ride (about 45 minutes round-trip) takes you up a WPA-built road to the top of the canyon; you can hop off and on at any of the nine stops. There's also a tram ride to adjacent Bear Canyon, where a much more rigorous but rewarding hike leads to the popular Seven Falls (it'll take about 1½ hours each way from the drop-off point, so carry plenty of water). If you're in Tucson near a full moon, take the special night tram and watch the desert come alive with nocturnal critters. ⊠ *Sabino Canyon Rd. at Sunrise Dr., Foothills* ☎ *520/749–2861 recorded tram information, 520/749–8700 visitor center* ⊕ *www.fs.fed.us/r3/coronado/scrd* ⊠ *$5 per vehicle per day or $20 for an annual pass (includes Mt. Lemmon), tram $6, Bear Canyon tram $3* ⊘ *Visitor center weekdays 8–4:30, weekends 8:30–4:30; call for tram schedules.*

㉖ **Saguaro National Park East.** About 16 mi from the town center is the eastern portion of the national park, which with the western district bookends Tucson. This section covers more than 67,000 acres and climbs through five climate zones, which makes for some dramatic hikes through the foothills of the Rincon Mountains. Eight-mile paved Cactus Forest Drive leads to trailheads and picnic areas. Ask for a detailed map at the visitor center for more information about the unique cacti that are concentrated here. To get here, take Speedway Boulevard or 22nd Street east. ⊠ *3693 S. Old Spanish Trail, Eastside* ☎ *520/733–5153* ⊕ *www.nps.gov/sagu* ⊠ *$6 per vehicle or $3 per person on foot or bike* ⊘ *Visitor center daily 8:30–5; park roads daily 7 AM–sunset.*

㉔ **Tohono Chul Park.** A 48-acre retreat designed to promote the conservation of arid regions, Tohono Chul—the name means "desert corner" in the language of the Tohono O'odham—uses a demonstration garden, greenhouse, and geology wall to explain this unique desert area. Enjoy the shady nooks, nature trails, small art gallery, great gift shop, and tearoom at this peaceful spot; note that only the tearoom and gift shop can be entered at no charge. ⊠ *7366 N. Paseo del Norte, Northwest* ☎ *520/742–6455* ⊕ *www.tohonochulpark.org* ⊠ *$5; free first Tues. of each month* ⊘ *Park daily 8 AM–sunset; buildings daily 9–5.*

▶ ⑲ **Tucson Botanical Gardens.** On 5 acres are a tropical greenhouse; a sensory garden, where you can touch and smell the plants and listen to the abundant bird life; historical gardens, which display the Mediterranean landscaping that the property's original owners planted in the 1930s; a garden designed to attract birds; and a cactus garden. Other special gardens showcase wildflowers, Australian plants, and Native American crops and herbs. Call ahead to find out what's blooming. All of the paths are wheelchair accessible, and there is a little gift shop near the entrance. ⊠ *2150 N. Alvernon Way, Central* ☎ *520/326–9686* ⊕ *www.tucsonbotanical.org* ⊠ *$4* ⊘ *Daily 8:30–4:30.*

CloseUp

THE DESERT'S FRAGILE GIANT

E ASY TO ANTHROPOMORPHIZE BECAUSE THEY HAVE "ARMS," saguaros are thought to be the descendants of tropical trees that lost their leaves and became dormant during drought. Carnegiea gigantea (the saguaro's scientific name) grows nowhere else on earth than the Sonoran Basin, an area that includes southern Arizona and northern Mexico.

Tourists are often amazed to find that these odd-looking plants actually bloom each May or June. Each bloom opens only for a few evening hours after sunset. The next afternoon, the creamy-white chalice closes forever. An adult saguaro produces six or seven flowers a day for about a month. They are cross-pollinated by bees, Mexican white-winged doves, and brown bats.

Because the saguaro stores massive quantities of water (enough conceivably to last two years), it is often called the "cactus camel." New saguaros are born when the seeds of the flower take root, an arduous process. Late freezes and even high heat can kill a seedling in its first days. Once a seed is established, it grows up under the protection of a "nurse" tree, such as a paloverde. Fully grown, a saguaro can weigh as much as 7 tons.

The saguaro, like many other wild plants, is protected by Arizona law. Without an Arizona Department of Agriculture permit, it is illegal to move a saguaro or sell one from private property. And the saguaro has its own means of protecting itself from would-be poachers or vandals. In the early 1980s, a hunter fired a shotgun at a large saguaro near Phoenix. It collapsed onto him, killing him instantly.

---

off the beaten path

BIOSPHERE 2 CENTER – In the little town of Oracle, some 30 minutes north of central Tucson, eight scientists walked into a self-contained, sealed ecosystem in 1992, intending to remain inside for two years. The experiment was not a complete success, but the structure itself remains an interesting phenomenon.

The miniature world within Biosphere includes tropical rain forest, savanna, desert, thorn scrub, marsh, ocean, and agricultural areas, including almost 3,000 plant and animal species. A film and a large, rotating cutaway model in the visitor center explain the project. Guided walking tours, which last about two hours and cover ¾ mi, take you inside some of the biomes, and observation areas let you peer in at the rest. A snack bar overlooks the Santa Catalina Mountains. Biosphere 2 Center is now managed by Columbia University's Earth Institute, which directs all of the current scientific, educational, and visitor-center operations. ⊠ AZ 77, Milepost 96.5, Oracle ☎ 520/838–6200 ⊕ www.bio2.edu ⊠ $19.95 ⊙ Daily 9–4.

Westside & the Sonoran Desert

If you're interested in the flora and fauna of the Sonoran Desert—as well as some of its appearances in the cinema—heed the same advice given the pioneers: go west.

a good drive

From central Tucson, take Speedway Boulevard west; when the houses begin to thin and stands of cacti begin to thicken, you'll see the **International Wildlife Museum** ㉙ ▶. Continue west on Speedway to where it joins Anklam Road and becomes Gates Pass Road; the scenic overlook on this winding road into the Tucson Mountains is a great spot for photos and catching a sunset. At the juncture of Gates Pass and Kinney roads, signs direct you south to **Old Tucson Studios** ㉚. Return to this intersection after you've had your fill of Wild West stunt shows, and continue north on Kinney Road for about 10 mi until you come to the **Arizona–Sonora Desert Museum** ㉛. It's a short drive farther north along the same road to the Red Hills Visitor Center and **Saguaro National Park West** ㉜. Note: The Gates Pass Road can be daunting to nervous drivers, and the pass itself is not navigable for large campers, RVs, or cars towing campers. As an alternative, take Interstate 10 to Interstate 19 south to Ajo Road, go west to Kinney Road, and follow the signs. Regardless of which route you choose, take Kinney Road back to Interstate 19 and continue south again. You'll soon come to the turnoff for **Mission San Xavier del Bac** ㉝.

TIMING   Although the attractions in this area are not close together, it's easy to tour all the sights in one day, as they're on a fairly direct route to one another. The best plan is to set out in the cooler early morning to Saguaro National Park, which has no shaded areas (it's also the best time to see the wildlife at its liveliest). Spend the rest of the morning at the Desert Museum, where you can have lunch at the Ironwood Terrace or the more upscale Ocotillo Café (in any case, allow at least two hours for your visit). The hottest time of the afternoon can be spent ducking in and out of attractions at Old Tucson, visiting the air-conditioned International Wildlife Museum, or enjoying the indoor sanctuary of San Xavier mission.

What to See

㉛ **Arizona–Sonora Desert Museum.** The name "museum" is misleading; this
Fodor'sChoice delightful site is a beautifully planned zoo and botanical garden featuring
★ the animals and plants of the Sonoran Desert. Hummingbirds, cactus wrens, rattlesnakes, scorpions, bighorn sheep, and prairie dogs all busy themselves in ingeniously designed habitats. An Earth Sciences Center has an artificial limestone cave and a hands-on meteor and mineral display. The coyote and javelina exhibits have "invisible" fencing that separates humans from animals, and the Riparian Corridor section affords great underwater views of otters and beavers. The gift shop carries books about Arizona and the desert, plus jewelry and crafts. ✉ *2021 N. Kinney Rd., Westside* ☎ *520/883–2702* ⊕ *www.desertmuseum.org* ⊠ *$12* ☉ *Mar.–Sept., daily 7:30–5; Oct.–Feb., daily 8:30–5.*

㉙ **International Wildlife Museum.** Dubbed by some locals the International Plush Toy Museum, this imposing structure has no real wildlife in it at all: almost 400 species of animals are stuffed and mounted in re-creations of their natural habitats. Some of the exhibits are quite naturalistic, but the "trophy room" full of mounted animal heads reminds you that hunter-conservators supplied the specimens. A "petting" menagerie allows children to touch different animal skins; they can also learn about birds and mammals from all over the world via interactive computers. ⊠ *4800 W. Gates Pass Rd., Westside* ☎ *520/629–0100* ⊕ *www. thewildlifemuseum.org* 🖻 *$7* ☉ *Weekdays 9–5, weekends 9–6.*

③③ **Mission San Xavier del Bac.** The oldest Catholic church in the United States
FodorśChoice still serving the community for which it was built, San Xavier was
★ founded in 1692 by Father Eusebio Francisco Kino, who established 22 missions in northern Mexico and southern Arizona. The current structure was constructed out of native materials by Franciscan missionaries between 1777 and 1797 and is owned by the Tohono O'odham tribe.

The beauty of the mission, with elements of Spanish, baroque, and Moorish architectural styles, is highlighted by the stark landscape against which it is set, inspiring an early-20th-century poet to dub it White Dove of the Desert. Inside, there's a wealth of painted statues, carvings, and frescoes. Paul Schwartzbaum, who helped restore Michelangelo's masterwork in Rome, supervised Tohono O'odham artisans in the restoration of the mission's artwork, completed in 1997; Schwartzbaum has called the mission the Sistine Chapel of the United States. Mass is celebrated at 8:30 AM daily in the church and three times on Sunday morning. Call ahead for information about special celebrations.

Across the parking lot from the mission, San Xavier Plaza has a number of crafts shops selling the handiwork of the Tohono O'odham tribe, including jewelry, pottery, friendship bowls, and baskets with man-in-the-maze designs. ⊠ *San Xavier Rd., 9 mi southwest of Tucson on I–19, South* ☎ *520/294–2624* ⊕ *www.sanxaviermission.org* 🖻 *Free* ☉ *Church daily 7–5, gift shop daily 8–5.*

need a
break? For wonderful Indian fry bread—large, round pieces of dough taken fresh from the hot oil and served with sweet or savory toppings like honey, powdered sugar, beans, meats, or green chiles—stop in the **Wa:k Snack Shop** (☎ no phone) at the back of San Xavier Plaza. You can also have breakfast or a lunch of Mexican food here, and if you're lucky, local dancers will be performing for one of the many tour groups that stop here.

③⓪ **Old Tucson Studios.** This film studio–cum–theme park, originally built for the 1940 motion picture *Arizona*, has been used to shoot countless movies, such as *Rio Bravo* (1959) and *The Quick and the Dead* (1994), and the TV shows *Gunsmoke, Bonanza,* and *Highway to Heaven.* Actors in Western garb perform and roam the streets talking to visitors. Youngsters enjoy the simulated gunfights, rides, stunt shows, and petting farm, while adults might appreciate the screenings of old Westerns and the little-bit-bawdy Grand Palace Hotel's Dance Hall Revue. There are plenty of places to chow down and to buy souvenirs. ⊠ *Tucson Mountain Park, 201 S. Kinney Rd., Westside* ☎ *520/883–0100* ⊕ *www.*

oldtucson.com ⊒ *$14.95* ⊙ *Thurs.–Mon. 10–6, Tues. and Wed. 10–3; no live-shows Tues. and Wed.*

③② **Saguaro National Park West.** This is the smaller (24,000 acres), more heavily visited section of the national park that flanks Tucson; the other unit
★ is east of the city. Together, the sections have the world's largest concentration of the saguaro cactus.

A native to the Sonoran Desert, the saguaro is known for its towering
height (often 50 feet) and arms that reach out in weird configurations.
The cactus is ribbed vertically with accordionlike pleats that expand to
store water gathered through its shallow roots during the infrequent desert
rain showers. In spring (usually April or May), the giant succulent's top
is covered with tiny white blooms. At any time of year, the sight of these
kings of the desert ruling over their quiet domain is awe-inspiring. The
slow-growing cacti (they can take up to 15 years to grow a foot and 75
years to grow their first arm) are protected by state and federal laws,
so enjoy but don't disturb them.

Before you venture into the desert, it's worth stopping in at the impressive Red Hills Visitor Center. A slide show (given every half hour
from 8:30 to 4:30) offers a Native American perspective of the saguaro
cactus, and a lifelike display simulates the flora and fauna of the region. A drive through the park on an unpaved loop takes ½–2 hours
depending on how many stops you make. Ask for directions to Signal Hill, where you can inspect petroglyphs (rock drawings) left by
the Hohokam Indians centuries ago. ⊠ *2700 N. Kinney Rd., 2 mi north
of Arizona–Sonora Desert Museum entrance, Westside* ☎ *520/733–
5158* ⊕ *www.nps.gov/sagu* ⊒ *Free* ⊙ *Visitor center daily 8:30–5, park
roads daily sunrise–sunset.*

WHERE TO EAT

Tucson boldly proclaims itself to be the "Mexican Food Capital of the
U.S." Most of the Mexican food in town is Sonoran style—native to
the adjoining Mexican state of Sonora—using cheese, mild peppers, corn
tortillas, pinto beans, and beef or chicken. Tucson is the birthplace of
the *chimichanga* (Spanish for "whatchamacallit"), a flour tortilla filled
with meat or cheese, rolled and deep-fried. The majority of the best Mexican restaurants are concentrated in South Tucson and Downtown.

Up in the Foothills, at resorts along Sunrise Drive, upscale, Southwestern
cuisine flourishes at such destination restaurants as Janos at the Westin
La Paloma and the Grill at Hacienda del Sol Resort. Cheaper but no less
tasty fare as varied as Chinese, Italian, and Guatemalan can be enjoyed
on the west side of U of A's campus, along University Avenue and 4th Avenue. Tucson also boasts excellent sushi restaurants, as well as good Indian, French, and Cajun food at reasonable prices, scattered around town.

Although the city's selection of restaurants is impressive, Tucson does-
n't offer much in the way of late-night dining. Most restaurants in town
are shuttered by 10 PM; some spots that keep later hours are noted below.

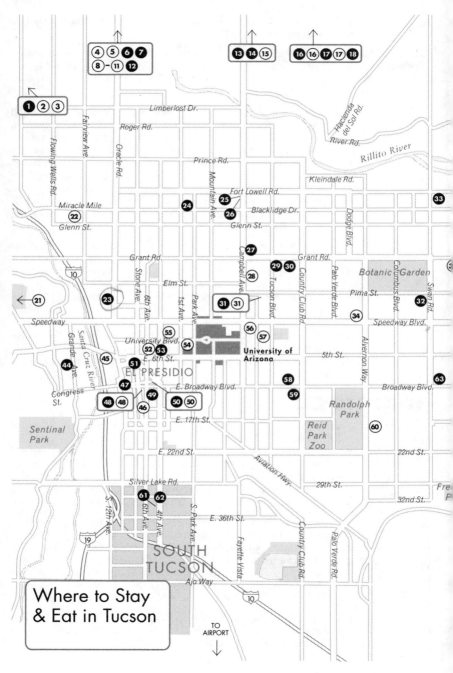

Where to Stay
& Eat in Tucson

KEY

② *Hotels*
❶ *Restaurants*

Restaurants ▼

Arizona Inn Restaurant **31**
Athens **53**
Barrio **49**
Beyond Bread **25, 43**
Bistro Zin **12**
Café Poca Cosa **48**
Café Terra Cotta **18**
Cup Café **50**
El Charro Café **51**
El Minuto Café **47**
Elle **59**
Firecracker **33**
Fuego **38**
The Gold Room **7**
Govinda **24**
The Grill at Hacienda del Sol **16**
Janos **17**
Kingfisher Bar and Grill **30**
La Fuente **23**
Le Bistro **27**
Mariscos Chihuahua **44**
Marlene's Hungry Fox **63**
Mi Nidito **62**
Micha's **61**
New Delhi Palace: Cuisine of India **65**
Nonie **29**
Olive Tree **39**
Pastiche **26**
Pinnacle Peak Steakhouse **40**
Rancher's Club **36**
Red Sky Cafe **32**
Sachiko Sushi **41**
Soleil **13**
Tohono Chul Tea Room **1**
Ventana Room **19**
Vivace **14**
Wildflower Grill **6**
Zemam **58**

Hotels ▼

Adobe Rose Inn **57**
Arizona Inn **31**
Canyon Ranch **20**
Casa Tierra **21**
Catalina Park Inn **52**
Clarion Hotel & Suites Santa Rita **48**

Doubletree Hotel at Reid Park **60**
Embassy Suites Tucson–Broadway **64**
Extended StayAmerica **35**
Four Points Sheraton Tucson University Plaza **56**
Ghost Ranch Lodge . . . **22**
Hacienda del Sol Guest Ranch Resort . . . **16**
Hilton Tucson El Conquistador **9**
Hotel Congress **50**
Inn Suites Hotel & Resort **45**
La Posada del Valle . . . **28**
La Posada Lodge and Casitas **4**
Lazy K Bar Guest Ranch **3**
Loews Ventana Canyon Resort **19**
Marriott TownePlace Suites **5**
Miraval **11**
Peppertrees B&B Inn **54**
Quail's Vista Bed and Breakfast . . . **10**
Ramada Inn Foothills **37**
The Royal Elizabeth Bed and Breakfast Inn **46**
Smuggler's Inn **42**
The SunCatcher **67**
Tanque Verde Ranch **68**
Tucson Hilton East **66**
Tucson Marriott University Park **55**
Varsity Clubs of America **34**
Westin La Paloma **17**
Westward Look Resort **8**
White Stallion Ranch **2**
Windmill Inn at St. Phillip's Plaza **15**

Costs

	$$$$	**$$$**	**$$**	**$**	**¢**
WHAT IT COSTS					
AT DINNER	over $30	$20–$30	$12–$20	$8–$12	under $8

Prices are per person for a main course. The final tab will include sales tax of 7%.

Downtown Tucson

Contemporary

$$–$$$ ✕ **Barrio.** Lively at lunchtime, this trendy grill serves the most innovative cuisine in the downtown area. Try a "little plate" of black tiger shrimp rubbed with tamarind paste, or stuffed Anaheim chile in red bell-pepper cream. Entrées are as varied as the simple but delicious fish tacos and the linguine with chicken, dried papaya, and mango in a chipotle-chardonnay cream sauce. Save room for an elegant dessert of fresh berries drenched in crème anglaise or a chilled chocolate custard topped with caramel. ⊠ *135 S. 6th Ave., Downtown* ☎ *520/629–0191* ▭ *AE, D, DC, MC, V* ⊘ *Closed Mon. No lunch weekends.*

¢–$$ ✕ **Cup Café.** This charming spot off the lobby of Hotel Congress is at the epicenter of Tucson's hippest downtown scene, but it's also a down-home, friendly place. Try Eggs in Hell (with green chile, salsa, and cayenne pepper) for breakfast or the Queer Steer Burger (a veggie burger) for lunch. The Heartbreaker appetizer (Brie melted over artichoke hearts and apple slices on a baguette) complements such entrées as chicken satay or grilled salmon. Open until 11 PM, until midnight on weekends, it becomes interestingly crowded in the evening with patrons from the Club Congress, the hotel nightclub. ⊠ *Hotel Congress, 311 E. Congress St., Downtown* ☎ *520/798–1618* ▭ *AE, D, MC, V.*

Mexican

$$ ✕ **Café Poca Cosa.** In what is arguably Tucson's most creative Mexican

Fodor'sChoice restaurant, chef-owner Susana Davila prepares recipes inspired by dif-

★ ferent regions of her native Mexico. The menu, which changes daily, might include *pollo à mole* (chicken in a spicy chocolate-based sauce) or pork *pibil* (made with a tangy Yucatán barbecue seasoning). Servings are plentiful, and each table gets a stack of warm corn tortillas and a bowl of beans to share. Order the daily Plato Poca Cosa, and the chef will select one beef, one chicken, and one vegetarian entrée for you to sample. The bold-colored walls are hung with Latin American art. ⊠ *88 E. Broadway Blvd., beside the Clarion Santa Rita, Downtown* ☎ *520/622–6400* ▭ *MC, V* ⊘ *Closed Sun.*

¢–$$ ✕ **El Charro Café.** Started by Monica Flin in 1922, El Charro still serves splendid and flavorful versions of the Mexican-American staples Flin claims to have originated, most notably chimichangas (deep-fried flour tortillas filled with seasoned beef or chicken) and cheese crisps. The *carne seca* chimichanga, made with beef that is dried on the premises—on the roof, actually—is delicious. Flin's father built the large, colorful adobe house that is El Charro today, and her great-great-nephew runs the place. ⊠ *311 N. Court Ave., Downtown* ☎ *520/622–1922* ▭ *AE, D, DC, MC, V.*

¢–$$ ✕ **Mariscos Chihuahua.** Brightly lit, cheerful, and scrupulously clean, Mariscos is popular with Tucsonans looking for a break from the usual Sonoran offerings. This Mexican place specializes in fresh—meaning un-cooked—seafood cocktails. Tostadas seviche-style loads diced fish atop a corn tortilla with plenty of salsa to spice it up. The sizable menu of well-prepared cooked seafood is highlighted by the Seven Seas soup, with all manner of fish and shellfish, and by the *camarones al mojo de ajo* (sautéed shrimp sautéed in a garlic sauce). Open 9 to 9 daily, it draws a significant crowd noon and night. ✉ *1009 N. Grande Ave., Down-town* ☎ *520/623–3563* ▭ *AE, D, DC, MC, V.*

¢–$ ✕ **El Minuto Café.** Equally popular with local families and the business crowd at lunch, this bustling restaurant is in Tucson's Barrio Historico neighborhood. Open until midnight Friday and Saturday and until 10 PM the rest of the week, it's also a good bet for those seeking a late meal downtown. For more than 50 years, El Minuto has served up *topopo* salads (a crispy tortilla shell heaped with beans, guacamole, and many other ingredients); huge burritos; and green-corn tamales (in season) made just right. The spicy *menudo* (tripe soup) is reputed to be a great hang-over remedy. ✉ *354 S. Main Ave., Downtown* ☎ *520/882–4145* ▭ *AE, D, DC, MC, V.*

University of Arizona

Continental

$$$–$$$$ ✕ **Arizona Inn Restaurant.** Executive chef Odell Baskerville presides over one of Tucson's most elegant restaurants. Dine on the patio overlook-ing the lush grounds of this inn, or enjoy the view from the dining room, which has Southwestern details from the 1930s. The culinary range is broad, from bouillabaisse to a vegetarian corn–and–butternut squash cannelloni with a carrot beurre blanc. Locals come in for weekday power-breakfast meetings, Sunday brunch, or a civilized afternoon high tea in the library. ✉ *Arizona Inn, 2200 E. Elm St., University* ☎ *520/ 325–1541* ▭ *AE, MC, V.*

Greek

$–$$ ✕ **Athens.** The tranquil dining room in this Greek spot off bustling 4th Avenue is furnished with lace curtains, wooden wainscoting, white stucco walls, and potted plants. Order a dish of creamy *taramasalata* (a Greek dip made with roe) followed by *kotopoulo stin pita* (grilled chicken breast with a yogurt-cucumber sauce on freshly baked pita). If it's Greek comfort food you're after, order the moussaka or the *pastit-sio* (a casserole made with pasta, meat, and béchamel). The house fa-vorite is braised lamb shoulder in red-wine sauce over pasta—call to reserve your order ahead of time. ✉ *500 N. 4th Ave., at 6th St., University* ☎ *520/ 624–6886* ▭ *AE, D, DC, MC, V* ☻ *Closed Sun. No lunch.*

Central Tucson

American

$$–$$$ ✕ **Kingfisher Bar and Grill.** Serving imaginative American cuisine, Kingfisher is a standout. Although the emphasis is on fresh seafood (including oys-ters and mussels), the kitchen does baby-back pork ribs and New York

steak with equal success. Try the delicately battered fish-and-chips or the clam chowder on the late-night menu, served from 10 PM to midnight. Brightly colored panels of turquoise and terra-cotta, black banquettes, and neon lighting make for a chic yet cozy space. ⊠ *2564 E. Grant Rd., Central* ☎ *520/323–7739* ⊟ *AE, D, DC, MC, V* ⊘ *No lunch weekends.*

American Casual

¢ ✗ **Beyond Bread.** Twenty-seven varieties of bread are crafted at this bakery that bustles with a morning and afternoon crowd. Highlights from the huge sandwich menu include Annie's Addiction (hummus, tomato, sprouts, red onion, and cucumber on a roll) and Brad's Beef (roast beef, provolone, onion, green chiles, and Russian dressing on white bread); soups and salads are equally scrumptious. Eat inside or on the patio (where your dog is also welcome), or order takeout and munch on daily samples while you wait. Be sure to splurge on at least one of the incredible desserts. Popular demand has extended shop hours through dinner. ⊠ *3026 N. Campbell Ave., Central* ☎ *520/322–9965* ⊠ *6260 E. Speedway Blvd., Eastside* ☎ *520/747–7477* ⊟ *AE, D, MC, V.*

¢ ✗ **Marlene's Hungry Fox.** Marlene's hungry customers have been coming here for good ol' fashioned breakfasts, served until 2 PM, since her restaurant opened in 1962. It's the home of the "double yoke," meaning when you order one egg any way you like it, you'll actually get two (and so on). You'll also get a real slice of Tucson life in this cheerful, unpretentious place decorated in a dairy theme, with cow pictures, farm photos, and an extensive spoon collection lining the walls. ⊠ *4637 E. Broadway Blvd., Central* ☎ *520/326–2835* ⊟ *AE, D, MC, V* ⊘ *No dinner.*

Cajun/Creole

¢–$$ ✗ **Nonie.** Owned by author Elmore Leonard's son, Chris, who named it for his grandmother, this restaurant has the flamboyant style of a New Orleans bistro with the good food to match. Add friendly, fast service and a hopping dose of Cajun music, and you get the idea. Try the tail gators (minced alligator tail meat, breaded and deep-fried) even if you've never eaten alligator, and you'll wish your local market carried them. It may be hard to save room for dessert, but the pecan pie and bread pudding are the standouts. ⊠ *2526 E. Grant Rd., Central* ☎ *520/319–1965* ⊟ *AE, MC, V* ⊘ *Closed Mon. No lunch weekends.*

Contemporary

$$–$$$ ✗ **Pastiche.** Colorful works by local artists line the walls at this popular spot. As is appropriate for a place named Pastiche, the menu has an eclectic mix of dishes. A favorite starter is the mushroom soufflé, made with an Asiago cream sauce and topped with fried leeks. Other highlights include the Canadian crab cakes and the thyme-crusted sea bass with smoked tomatoes and capers. The full menu is served until midnight; come in after 10 PM for half-price appetizers. ⊠ *3025 N. Campbell Ave., Central* ☎ *520/325–3333* ⊟ *AE, D, DC, MC, V* ⊘ *No lunch weekends.*

$–$$$ ✗ **Elle.** Northern Californian, French, and Italian cuisines influence Elle's menu. Choose from a long list of pasta and risotto dishes, including squash ravioli with spinach, mushrooms, and sage butter, or, if you're game, try the grilled venison in roasted-garlic sauce with rosemary polenta. Your server can provide expert assistance in selecting the perfect wine to complement your meal; of the nearly 90 vintages available (all from California, Oregon, and Washington), 45 can be ordered by the glass. The dining area is open and expansive, with contemporary furniture and slate floors. ⊠ *3048 E. Broadway Blvd., Central* ☎ *520/327– 0500* ⊟ *AE, DC, MC, V* ☉ *Closed Sun. No lunch Sat.*

$–$$ ✕ **Red Sky Cafe.** Trained in Paris at La Varenne, chef-owner Steve Schultz returned to Tucson to create his own contemporary cuisine, a fusion of French, Californian, and Southwestern flavors. The result is well-prepared, exquisitely presented meals for half the price you'd pay elsewhere. Schultz's enthusiasm pervades the Red Sky—you're made to feel like you have personally inspired every dish brought out from the kitchen. For a starter, try the foie gras with a potato pancake. All main courses include soup or salad made with fresh (and often exotic) produce from the U of A's greenhouses. ⊠ *1661 N. Swan Rd., Central* ☎ *520/326– 5454* ⊟ *AE, MC, V* ☉ *Closed Sun.*

Ethiopian

¢ ✕ **Zemam.** It can be hard at most times of the year to get a table in this small, humble eatery (except in the summer, when the lack of air-conditioning presents a challenge). The sampler plate of any three items allows you to try such dishes as *yesimir wat* (a spicy lentil-based dish) and *lega tibs* (a milder beef dish with a tomato sauce). Most of the food has a stewlike consistency; don't come if you feel the need to crunch. Everything is served on a communal platter topped with *injera,* a spongy bread, and eaten with the hands. Prices are incredibly low, considering the food quality and quantity. ⊠ *2731 E. Broadway Blvd., Central* ☎ *520/323–9928* ⌲ *Reservations not accepted* ⊟ *MC, V* ⛾ *BYOB* ☉ *Closed Mon.*

French

★ $$–$$$ ✕ **Le Bistro.** Art nouveau–etched mirrors and potted palms grace the walls of this French restaurant. The elegant yet unpretentious dining room is matched by the splendid creations of chef-owner Laurent Reux, a native of Brittany. House specialties include escargots cooked in garlic butter under a dome of puff pastry, ginger-crusted salmon in lime butter, and roasted quail flambéed with cognac. Lunch is reasonably priced, and many Tucsonans claim that the desserts here—proudly displayed as you walk in—are the best in town. ⊠ *2574 N. Campbell Ave., Central* ☎ *520/ 327–3086* ⊟ *AE, D, MC, V* ☉ *No lunch weekends, no dinner Mon.*

Mexican

¢–$$ ✕ **La Fuente.** Frank Davis owns and plays host at this family-run restaurant, long a staple of Tucson nightlife. The plain exterior belies the extravagant gardenlike interior, which bursts with color, plants, light, and the sound of live mariachi music nightly. Traditional Sonoran cuisine includes sea bass Yucatán style and enchiladas *a la bandera,* with green (guacamole), white (sour cream), and red (chile) representing the Mexican flag. The chicken mole poblano—with a spicy, dark sauce based on nuts and chocolate—is an authentic new-world dish. ⊠ *1749 N. Oracle Rd., Central* ☎ *520/623–8659* ⊟ *AE, DC, MC, V.*

Pan-Asian

$–$$ ✕ **Firecracker.** Splitting the difference between Chinese and Pacific Rim fare, this restaurant enjoys a popularity with those who like their Asian food a little on the nouvelle side. The *ahi katsu*—fresh ahi tuna wrapped in spinach and seaweed, then breaded and flash-fried—makes for a flavorful opening. Wasabi-cream chicken breast with Thai chili soy sauce is zesty and hot; the flavorful Beijing pork is roasted with sweet plum sauce. Bananas Firecracker (Foster to the rest of us) or a dense, flourless chocolate torte brings a fitting end to the meal. Choose a plush booth inside, or people-watch from patio tables shaded by umbrellas in a flower-filled courtyard of Plaza Palomino, a small outdoor shopping center. ⊠ *2990 N. Swan Rd., Central* ☎ *520/318–1118* ⊟ *AE, D, MC, V.*

Steak

$$–$$$ ✕ **Rancher's Club.** Wood-burning grills are the key to the success of this upscale Western-style restaurant. The attentive staff will help you choose the right timber—different woods impart different flavors—for your taste buds: mesquite, apple wood, and wild cherrywood are your choices. Sauces and condiments offer more traditional flavorings for the excellent and very large steaks (sharing is encouraged). Good fish and poultry dishes are also available. Local movers and shakers gather here for lunch amid side saddles, dark-wood paneling, and old photos of cowboys. ⊠ *Sheraton Tucson Hotel, 5151 E. Grant Rd., Central* ☎ *520/321–7621* ⊟ *AE, D, DC, MC, V* ☺ *Closed Sun. No lunch Sat., no dinner Mon.*

Vegetarian

¢–$ ✕ **Govinda.** One of the few places in town with a strictly meatless menu, this Hare Krishna–run restaurant has reasonably priced all-you-can-eat lunch and dinner buffets, which include vegan options. Hot and cold dishes vary daily, but ingredients are consistently fresh, and the food is tasty if not spicy. Choose from three seating areas, including an outdoor patio with a koi pond and an aviary, where you can hear the calls of the resident peacocks. No alcohol is served or permitted. ⊠ *711 E. Blacklidge Dr., Central* ☎ *520/792–0630* ⬆ *Reservations not accepted* ⊟ *MC, V* ☺ *Closed Sun. and Mon. No lunch Tues.*

Eastside

Indian

$–$$ ✕ **New Delhi Palace: Cuisine of India.** Vegetarians, carnivores, and seafood lovers will all find something to enjoy at this savory Indian restaurant, where the rich scent of curry greets you upon arrival. The congenial staff is helpful in explaining the menu, which includes lots of tandoori dishes, curries, rice, and breads. The "heat" of each dish can be adjusted to individual preference by the chef. ⊠ *6751 E. Broadway Blvd., Eastside* ☎ *520/296–8585* ⊟ *AE, MC, V.*

Japanese

$–$$ ✕ **Sachiko Sushi.** Perfectly prepared sushi, generous combinations of tempura and teriyaki, and friendly service greet you at what many locals consider the best Japanese restaurant in Tucson. Sit at the sushi bar and chat with owner-chef Tomio while you dine. Try a bowl of udon noodles, served in broth with assorted meat, seafood, or vegetables. The dish is a satisfying meal in itself. ⊠ *1101 Wilmot Rd., Eastside* ☎ *520/886–7000* ⊟ *AE, DC, MC, V* ☺ *No lunch Sun.*

Steak

¢–$$ ✕ **Pinnacle Peak Steakhouse.** Anybody caught eating newfangled foods like fish tacos or cactus jelly here would probably be hanged from the rafters—along with all the ties snipped from city slickers who overdressed. This cowboy steak house serves excellent mesquite-broiled steak (and chicken and grilled fish) with salad and pinto beans. The restaurant is part of Trail Dust Town, a re-creation of a turn-of-the-20th-century town, complete with a working antique carousel, a narrow-gauge train, and souvenir shops. Gunfights are staged in the street outside nightly at 7, 8, and 9. Expect a wait on weekends. ✉ *6541 E. Tanque Verde Rd., Eastside* ☎ *520/296–0911* ⌂ *Reservations not accepted* ▭ *AE, D, DC, MC, V* ☾ *No lunch.*

Northeast Tucson

Continental

$$$$ ✕ **Ventana Room.** This very formal restaurant is a triumph of dining elegance: muted colors, a see-through fireplace, grand views of the city lights, a classical guitarist or harpist, and waiters who attend to every detail. The contemporary Continental menu contains such entrées as a mixed grill of game (venison, quail, and buffalo) with black barley and huckleberries, and potato-wrapped striped sea bass with spinach, tomato, and sweet-basil wine sauce. There's also a spa tasting menu for those watching fat and calories. ✉ *Loews Ventana Canyon Resort, 7000 N. Resort Dr., Northeast* ☎ *520/299–2020 Ext. 5194* ⌂ *Jacket required* ▭ *AE, D, DC, MC, V* ☾ *No lunch.*

Greek

$$–$$$ ✕ **Olive Tree.** In a modern Santa Fe–style building, the Olive Tree serves fine versions of such Greek standards as moussaka, shish kebab, and stuffed grape leaves, but it has more unusual dishes on its menu as well. The Lamb Bandit is baked in foil with two types of cheese, potatoes, and vegetables. Leg of lamb is roasted in wine and served with a well-prepared orzo. Daily fresh-fish specials are broiled or sautéed in garlic, oregano, and olive oil. This is not light cuisine. If you don't have room for super-sweet baklava, a cup of strong Greek coffee makes for a satisfying finish. ✉ *7000 E. Tanque Verde Rd., Northeast* ☎ *520/298–1845* ▭ *AE, DC, MC, V* ☾ *No lunch.*

Southwestern

$$ ✕ **Fuego.** The "fire" of Alan Zeman's cooking refers not so much to hot and spicy fare but to the flambéed chorizo and tequila shrimp appetizer, which can start your meal off with tableside pyrotechnics. Fresh oysters and seafood, prickly-pear pork tenderloin, and ostrich (served according to the chef's mood that day) are all tasty selections at this comfortable bar and grill with knotty-pine floors and cozy brick fireplace. Many children will find the kids' menu here more appealing than most, with tacos and pastas as well as the usual burger and chicken-finger fare. ✉ *6958 E. Tanque Verde Rd., Northeast* ☎ *520/886–1745* ▭ *AE, MC, V* ☾ *No lunch.*

Catalina Foothills (North)

Contemporary

★ $$$–$$$$ ✕ **The Grill at Hacienda del Sol.** Tucked into the foothills and surrounded by flowering gardens, this special-occasion restaurant provides a welcome alternative to the chile-laden dishes of most Southwestern nouvelle cuisine. Steamed chicken dumplings with Havarti cheese and pecan-grilled duck with thyme are deservedly popular. Tapas (and most items on the full menu) can be enjoyed on the bar's outdoor patio, accented by live Flamenco guitar music. The lavish Sunday brunch buffet is worth a splurge. ⊠ *Hacienda del Sol Guest Ranch Resort, 5601 N. Hacienda del Sol Rd., Foothills* ☎ *520/529–3500* ⊟ *AE, DC, MC, V.*

$$–$$$ ✕ **Bistro Zin.** French cooking meets American comfort food here at the hip sister restaurant to Wildflower Grill. Indulge in their delicately flaky chicken potpie and french fries, or the succulent maple-leaf duck in drunken-cherry sauce. A hundred wines are available by the glass or "flight"—three tastes of the same type of wine from different vintners. While lunch hums with the business crowd, at night it's a place to see and be seen for singles in their 20s and 30s as well as a good number of older couples. ⊠ *1865 E. River Rd., Foothills* ☎ *520/299–7799* ⊟ *AE, D, DC, MC, V* ☼ *No lunch Sun.*

$$–$$$ ✕ **Soleil.** Watch the sun set over the Tucson Mountains from either the outdoor terrace or the panoramic picture window inside—then gaze at the twinkling city lights below as you feast on contemporary French fare like caramelized sea scallops with an Asian vegetable roll and mandarin orange sauce or filet mignon with sweet corn and shiitake mushrooms. Try a selection from the champagne bar, even if you don't usually indulge in bubbly. After dinner, stroll the fine art galleries in the imaginatively designed El Cortijo shopping complex. ⊠ *El Cortijo, 3001 E. Skyline Dr., Foothills* ☎ *520/299–3345* ⊟ *AE, D, MC, V* ☼ *Closed Mon.*

Italian

$$–$$$ ✕ **Vivace.** This nouvelle Italian bistro in the lovely St. Philip's Plaza is a consistent favorite with Tucsonans. Wild mushrooms and goat cheese in puff pastry is hard to resist as a starter. For a lighter alternative to such entrées as a rich osso buco, try the fettuccine with grilled salmon. For dessert, the chocolate molten cake, served with spumoni ice cream, is worth the 20 minutes it takes to create. Patio seating, which overlooks an expansive garden, is especially inviting on warm evenings. ⊠ *4310 N. Campbell Ave., Foothills* ☎ *520/795–7221* ⊟ *AE, D, MC, V* ☼ *No lunch Sun.*

Southwestern

$$$–$$$$ ✕ **Janos.** Chef Janos Wilder was one of the first to reinvent Southwestern cuisine, and the menu, wine list, and service place this restaurant
Fodor'sChoice among the finest in the West. The hillside location on the grounds of
★ the Westin La Paloma is a stunning backdrop for such sumptuous selections as sweet and spicy glazed quail with butternut-squash cannelloni, salmon with a scallop mousse served on mascarpone polenta, and venison loin with chile-lime paste and pecans. Have a drink or a more casual meal of Caribbean fare next door at J Bar, a lively and lower-priced venue for sampling Janos's innovative cuisine. ⊠ *Westin La*

Paloma, 3770 E. Sunrise Dr., Foothills ☎ *520/615–6100* ⊟ *AE, DC, MC, V* ⊘ *Closed Sun. No lunch.*

$$–$$$ ✕ **Café Terra Cotta.** Everything about this restaurant says Southwest—from the bright orange and purple walls, large windows and exposed beams to the contemporary art—but especially the food. Café Terra Cotta's specialties include duck two ways (grilled breast and duck *carnitas* spring roll), chiles rellenos, tortilla soup, and creative pizzas with toppings like goat cheese, artichokes, and herbed mozzarella. This is the ultimate casual yet classy place to dine in town. ⊠ *3500 E. Sunrise Dr., Foothills* ☎ *520/577–8100* ⊟ *AE, D, DC, MC, V.*

Northwest Tucson

Contemporary

★ **$$–$$$** ✕ **Wildflower Grill.** A glass wall separates the bar from the dining area, where an open kitchen, high ceilings, and plush rose-colored banquettes complete the light and airy effect. Wildflower Grill is well known for its creative American fare and stunning presentation. Everything tastes as good as it sounds on the menu, which offers compelling choices like warm Maine lobster salad; bow-tie pasta with grilled chicken, tomatoes, spinach, and pine nuts; and rack of lamb with a Dijon crust (this dish pairs well with an accompaniment from the bar's popular martini menu). Desserts are equally top-notch. ⊠ *7037 N. Oracle Rd., Northwest* ☎ *520/219–4230* ⊟ *AE, D, DC, MC, V* ⊘ *No lunch Sun.*

Southwestern

$$–$$$$ ✕ **The Gold Room.** Every seat in this casually elegant and quiet dining room at the Westward Look Resort, high in the Catalina Foothills, affords a spectacular view of the city below. The fare includes such classics as sautéed halibut and roasted rack of lamb in truffle port sauce as well as regional specialties such as mesquite-grilled buffalo sirloin. Many of the herbs and vegetables that flavor and garnish the artistically presented dishes are grown on-site. ⊠ *Westward Look Resort, 245 E. Ina Rd., Northwest* ☎ *520/297–1151* ⊟ *AE, DC, MC, V.*

¢–$ ✕ **Tohono Chul Tea Room.** The food is fine, but what stands out here is the location—inside a wildlife sanctuary and surrounded by a cactus garden. The Southwestern interior has Mexican tile, light wood, and a cobblestone patio, and the menu covers Southwestern, Mexican, and American dishes. House favorites include tortilla chicken soup with avocado, served with bread and scones baked on the premises, and grilled raspberry chipotle chicken. Open daily 8 to 5, the Tea Room is popular for Sunday brunch—which can mean long waits in high season. ⊠ *Tohono Chul Park, 7366 N. Paseo del Norte, Northwest* ☎ *520/797–1222* ⊟ *AE, MC, V* ⊘ *No dinner.*

South Tucson

Mexican

¢–$ ✕ **Mi Nidito.** A perennial favorite among locals (be prepared to wait awhile
Fodor'sChoice at dinnertime), Mi Nidito has also hosted its share of visiting celebri-
★ ties. Following President Clinton's lunch here, the rather hefty "Presidential Plate" (bean tostada, taco with barbecued meat, chile relleno,

chicken enchilada, and beef tamale with rice and beans) was added to the menu. Top that off with the mango chimichangas for dessert, and you're talkin' executive privilege. ✉ *1813 S. 4th Ave., South* ☎ *520/622–5081* ⊟ *AE, DC, MC, V* ⊗ *Closed Mon. and Tues.*

¢–$ ✕ **Micha's.** Family-owned for 24 years, this local institution is a nondescript Mexican diner serving some of the best Sonoran classics this side of the border. House specialties include *machaca* (shredded beef) enchiladas and chimichangas, and *cocido,* a hearty vegetable beef soup. Homemade chorizo spices up breakfast, which is served daily. ✉ *2908 S. 4th Ave., South* ☎ *520/623–5307* ⊟ *AE, DC, MC, V* ⊗ *No dinner Mon.*

WHERE TO STAY

In Tucson you can choose from luxurious desert resorts, basic accommodations offered by small- to medium-size hotels and motels, or area bed-and-breakfasts ranging from bedrooms in modest homes to private cottages nestled on wildlife preserves. Southwestern-style "dude" ranches—some of them former cattle ranches from the 1800s—are on the outskirts of town. Unless otherwise indicated, price categories for guest ranches include all meals and most activities.

If you like being able to walk to sights, shops, and restaurants, plan on staying in the Downtown, University, or Central Tucson neighborhoods. The posh resorts in the Foothills and Northwest areas, while farther away from town, have many activities on-site, including some of the town's top-rated restaurants, and can arrange transportation to shopping and sights. Resorts here typically charge an additional daily resort fee for "use of facilities," such as pools, tennis courts, and exercise classes and equipment. Be sure to ask what is included when you book a room.

Summer rates (late May–September) are up to 60% lower than those in the winter. Note that unless you book months in advance, you'll be hard-pressed to find a Tucson hotel room at any price the week before and during the huge gem and mineral show, which is usually held the first two weeks in February.

Costs

WHAT IT COSTS				
	$$$$	$$$	$$	$	¢
FOR 2 PEOPLE	over $250	$175–$250	$100–$175	$80–$100	under $80

Prices are for two people in a standard double room in high season.

Downtown Tucson

$$ ▦ **The Royal Elizabeth Bed and Breakfast Inn.** Fans of Victoriana will adore this B&B built in 1878 and owned for more than 100 years by the prominent Blenman family. The inn, part of the Armory Park historic district, is beautifully furnished with period antiques; the six spacious rooms are outfitted with ceiling fans. Two of the larger rooms have separate sitting areas and pull-out sofa beds. Gracious Southern hosts Robert and Jack

take turns in the kitchen, preparing eye-opener Southwestern breakfasts that might include chiles rellenos and baked eggs in tomato shells. ✉ *204 S. Scott Ave., Downtown, 85701* ☎ *520/670–9022* 🖷 *520/679–9710* ⊕ *www.royalelizabeth.com* 🛏 *6 rooms* ⚬ *Cable TV, in-room VCRs, pool, hot tub, Internet; no smoking* ▤ *AE, MC, V* �|◯| *BP.*

$ 🖼 **Clarion Hotel & Suites Santa Rita.** The modest but lush, plant-filled lobby of this historic hotel has gleaming marble floors and a sunken lounge area with comfortable overstuffed couches and chairs. The rooms are standard, but breakfast, newspapers, and local phone calls are all on the house. Ask for a room with a view of the outdoor pool and water-fall, a lovely remnant of the original hotel. It's also where you'll find the excellent Café Poca Cosa. ✉ *88 E. Broadway Blvd., Downtown, 85701* ☎ *520/622–4000 or 877/424–6423* 🖷 *520/620–0376* ⊕ *www. choicehotels.com* 🛏 *139 rooms, 22 suites* ⚬ *Restaurant, microwaves, refrigerators, cable TV with movies, pool, gym, outdoor hot tub, sauna, library, dry cleaning, laundry service, some pets allowed (fee), no-smok-ing rooms* ▤ *AE, D, DC, MC, V* ⁑◯| *CP.*

$ 🖼 **Hotel Congress.** This downtown hotel built in 1919 has been artfully
Fodor'sChoice restored to its original Western version of art deco. The gangster John
★ Dillinger was almost caught here in 1934 (his luggage, filled with guns and ammo, was suspiciously heavy; he was captured later near the uni-versity). Each room has black-and-white tile baths and the original iron bed frames, but if you want to watch TV, you'll have to share the lone set with other guests in the upstairs lounge. The convenient location down-town means it can be noisy: don't get a room over the popular Club Congress or you'll be up until the wee hours. A great place to stay for younger or more adventurous visitors, it's also a youth hostel (bring your membership card) and the center of Tucson's hippest scene. ✉ *311 E. Congress St., Downtown, 85701* ☎ *520/622–8848 or 800/722–8848* 🖷 *520/792–6366* ⊕ *www.hotcong.com* 🛏 *40 rooms* ⚬ *Restaurant, hair salon, bar, lobby lounge, nightclub, some pets allowed (fee), no-smok-ing rooms; no room TVs* ▤ *AE, D, MC, V.*

$ 🖼 **Inn Suites Hotel & Resort.** Just north of downtown and El Presidio his-toric district, this hotel is next to Interstate 10 but is nevertheless quiet. The large, peach-and-green Southwestern-theme rooms, circa 1980, face an interior courtyard with a sparkling pool and *palapas* (thatched open gazebos). Free daily extras such as a breakfast buffet, newspaper, and happy-hour cocktails, as well as a free barbecue every Wednesday night, help make this a haven in the center of the city. ✉ *475 N. Granada Ave., Downtown, 85701* ☎ *520/622–3000 or 877/446–6589* 🖷 *520/ 623–8922* ⊕ *www.innsuites.com* 🛏 *265 rooms, 35 suites* ⚬ *Restau-rant, room service, microwaves, refrigerators, cable TV with movies and video games, pool, hot tub, volleyball, bar, playground, business ser-vices, meeting rooms, some pets allowed (fee), no-smoking rooms* ▤ *AE, D, DC, MC, V* ⁑◯| *BP.*

University of Arizona

$$$ 🖼 **Arizona Inn.** Although close to the university and many sights, the
Fodor'sChoice beautifully landscaped lawns and gardens of this 1930 inn seem far away
★ from all the hustle and bustle. The spacious, individually decorated rooms

are spread out over 14 acres in pink adobe-style casitas—most have private patios and some have fireplaces. The resort also has two luxurious two-story houses, which come with their own heated pools and full hotel service. The main building houses a library, a fine restaurant, and a cocktail lounge, where a jazz pianist plays. ⊠ *2200 E. Elm St., University, 85719* ☎ *520/325–1541 or 800/933–1093* 🖶 *520/881–5830* ⊕ *www. arizonainn.com* ↩ *70 rooms, 16 suites, 3 casitas* ♲ *2 restaurants, room service, cable TV, 2 tennis courts, pool, gym, sauna, croquet, Ping-Pong, bar, library, dry cleaning, business services, meeting rooms, no-smoking rooms* ⊟ *AE, DC, MC, V.*

$$ ▦ **Catalina Park Inn.** Classical music plays softly in the living room of this beautifully restored 1927 neoclassical house behind a gate in the West University neighborhood. The original art nouveau-tile work and a butler's pantry are among many charming architectural details, and there's a collection of blue-and-white china displayed in glass cabinets. All rooms include robes, irons, and hair dryers. You may be tempted to fill your suitcase with the papaya and lime scones that are part of breakfast. ⊠ *309 E. 1st St., University, 85705* ☎ *520/792–4541 or 800/792–4885* ⊕ *www.catalinaparkinn.com* ↩ *6 rooms* ♲ *Cable TV; no kids under 10, no smoking* ⊟ *AE, D, MC, V* ⥣⦿⥣ *BP.*

$$ ▦ **Four Points Sheraton Tucson University Plaza.** Formerly the Plaza Hotel, this high-rise has a prime location, across the street from the University of Arizona, two blocks from the University Medical Center, and at the intersection of two major bus routes. A favorite of visiting faculty, prospective students, and parents, as well as the spring training home of the Chicago White Sox, it is a no-nonsense hotel with an average restaurant. Fortunately, there are many other places to eat within walking or driving distance along Speedway or Campbell. ⊠ *1900 E. Speedway Blvd., University, 85719* ☎ *520/327–7341 or 888/625–5144* 🖶 *520/327–0276* ⊕ *www.starwood.com* ↩ *150 rooms* ♲ *Restaurant, room service, in-room data ports, cable TV with movies and video games, pool, gym, bar, lounge, meeting rooms, free parking, no-smoking rooms* ⊟ *AE, D, MC, V.*

$$ ▦ **La Posada del Valle.** Noted Swiss architect Josias Joesler designed this gracious B&B in the Spanish colonial–Territorial style he popularized in the Tucson area. Breezeways and gentle arches characterize this soothing pink-adobe structure, which sits directly across from the university medical center. Guestrooms, furnished with Victorian antiques and top-of-the-line mattresses, each have private entrances off the courtyard and gardens as well as from the interior hallway. Breakfasts are copious and delicious, as are the cookies freshly baked every afternoon. ⊠ *1640 N. Campbell Ave., University, 85719* ☎ *520/795–3840 or 888/404–7113* ⊕ *www.bbonline.com/az/laposada* ↩ *6 rooms* ♲ *Some kitchenettes, cable TV; no smoking* ⊟ *AE, D, MC, V* ⥣⦿⥣ *BP.*

★ $$ ▦ **Tucson Marriott University Park.** With the University of Arizona less than a block from the front door, the Marriott is an ideal place to stay when visiting the campus. This immaculately clean hotel has a lush atrium lobby area that can be enjoyed from both the restaurant and bar. Visit the university shopping district's cafés, pubs, bookstores, and clothes stores—all within a short stroll. ⊠ *880 E. 2nd St., University, 85719* ☎ *520/*

792–4100 or 888/236–2427 🖨 520/882–4100 ⊕ *www.marriott.com*
⤴ *234 rooms, 16 suites ⟁ Restaurant, room service, in-room data ports, some refrigerators, cable TV with movies, pool, gym, outdoor hot tub, sauna, lounge, laundry service, concierge floor, Internet, business services, meeting rooms, no-smoking rooms* ☱ *AE, D, DC, MC, V.*

$–$$ 🖭 **Adobe Rose Inn.** This 1933 adobe home offers six lodgepole pine–furnished rooms, two of which have beehive fireplaces and stained-glass windows. In the historic Sam Hughes neighborhood just east of the university, the Adobe Rose is within easy walking distance of shops, restaurants, and two major bus lines. Breakfast dishes like Southwestern souflés or blueberry pancakes, always served with fruit and muffins, are enjoyed in a dining room overlooking the bougainvillea-draped pool area. ⊠ *940 N. Olsen Ave., University, 85719* 🕾 *520/318–4644 or 800/328–4122* 🖨 *520/318–4644* ⊕ *www.aroseinn.com* ⤴ *6 rooms ⟁ Dining room, cable TV, pool, outdoor hot tub, Internet; no kids under 10, no smoking* ☱ *AE, MC, V* ❙◯❙ *BP.*

$–$$ 🖭 **Peppertrees B&B Inn.** This restored 1905 Victorian just east of the U of A campus affords a degree of privacy along with B&B camaraderie. Two appealing, contemporary-style guesthouses at the rear of the tree-shaded main house have full kitchens, separate phone lines, washers and dryers, and individual patios. The antiques-filled main house (furnished with pieces from innkeeper Jill Light's family in England) has several guest rooms, as well as a separate one-bedroom apartment. Light, an award-winning pastry chef, prepares elaborate breakfasts for her visitors. ⊠ *724 E. University Blvd., University, 85719* 🕾 *520/622–7167 or 800/348–5763* ⊕ *www.peppertreesinn.com* ⤴ *3 rooms, 1 suite, 2 guest houses ⟁ Some kitchens; no smoking* ☱ *D, MC, V* ❙◯❙ *BP.*

Central Tucson

$$ 🖭 **Doubletree Hotel at Reid Park.** The municipal golf course at Randolph Park hosts the LPGA tournament every year, and most of the participants stay at the Doubletree. Reid Park (adjacent to Randolph Park) has a pleasant jogging trail and a zoo. In addition to being across the road from these two parks, this sprawling, contemporary hotel is convenient to the airport and to the center of town, and the large El Con shopping mall is nearby. ⊠ *445 S. Alvernon Way, Central, 85711* 🕾 *520/881–4200 or 800/222–8733* 🖨 *520/323–5225* ⊕ *www.doubletree. com* ⤴ *295 rooms ⟁ 2 restaurants, room service, in-room data ports, cable TV with movies, 3 tennis courts, pool, gym, hair salon, hot tub, bar, video-game room, dry cleaning, laundry service, business services, meeting rooms, no-smoking rooms* ☱ *AE, D, DC, MC, V* ❙◯❙ *BP.*

$$ 🖭 **Varsity Clubs of America.** This time-share facility also doubles as a hotel, so it may have any or all of its suites available for rental at any given time. Its handy location is also a rather busy and noisy one. One- and two-bedroom suites have whirlpool tubs and full kitchens; alternatives to cooking include the Stadium Sports Grill downstairs or any of the several restaurants within walking distance. There's a billiard room and a cozy library with a fireplace. ⊠ *3855 E. Speedway Blvd., Central, 85716* 🕾 *520/318–3777 or 888/594–2287* 🖨 *888/410–9770* ⊕ *www.ilxresorts.com* ⤴ *59 suites ⟁ Restaurant, kitchens, cable TV* *with movies and video games, pool, gym, hot tub, billiards, library, no-smoking rooms* ⊟ *AE, D, MC, V.*

$ 🏨 **Ghost Ranch Lodge.** A neon cow-skull sign lights up the entrance to the former Hotel Pack, which opened in 1941 on what was then the main road into Tucson. The single-story, Spanish tile-roof units are spread out over 8 acres that encompass an orange grove and cactus garden. Rooms are decorated with 1980s motel furnishings but retain original brick walls and sloped wood-beam ceilings. The cottages, with a separate kitchen, sitting area, and carport, are a bargain. Although this retro property has been well maintained, it's a bit west of city central, and its neighbors now include strip clubs and by-the-hour motels. ⊠ *801 W. Miracle Mile, Central, 85705* ☎ *520/791–7565 or 800/456–7565* 🖷 *520/791–3898* ⊕ *www.ghostranchlodge.com* ⤙ *72 rooms, 11 cottages* ⌂ *Restaurant, in-room data ports, some kitchenettes, cable TV, pool, hot tub, shuffleboard, bar, no-smoking rooms* ⊟ *AE, D, DC, MC, V* ⦿ *CP.*

¢ 🏨 **Extended StayAmerica.** If you're seeking convenience and value (and don't mind a certain blandness), this modern chain property will suffice. All rooms have queen-size beds and recliner chairs. Don't expect a view or coffee in the lobby, but local calls are free, and you're two blocks' walk to the Crossroads Shopping Center, where there are restaurants, a Starbucks, a grocery store, shops, and a cinema. ⊠ *5050 E. Grant Rd., Central, 85712* ☎ *520/795–9510 or 800/398–7829* 🖷 *520/795–9504* ⊕ *www.extendedstay.com* ⤙ *120 rooms* ⌂ *In-room data ports, kitchens, microwaves, refrigerators, cable TV, laundry facilities, no-smoking rooms* ⊟ *AE, D, MC, V.*

Eastside

$$$$ 🏨 **Tanque Verde Ranch.** The most upscale of Tucson's guest ranches and one of the oldest in the country, the Tanque Verde sits on 640 beautiful acres in the Rincon Mountains next to Saguaro National Park East. Rooms in one-story casitas have tasteful Western-style furnishings, fireplaces, and picture-window views of the desert. Breakfast and lunch buffets are huge, and barbecues add variety to the daily dinner menu. Horseback excursions are offered for every skill level (lessons are included in rates), and children can participate in daylong activity programs, from riding to tennis to crafts, leaving parents to their leisure. ⊠ *14301 E. Speedway Blvd., Eastside, 85748* ☎ *520/296–6275 or 800/234–3833* 🖷 *520/721–9426* ⊕ *www.tanqueverderanch.com* ⤙ *49 rooms, 23 suites, 2 casitas* ⌂ *5 tennis courts, 2 pools (1 indoor), gym, hot tub, fishing, bicycles, basketball, hiking, horseback riding, horseshoes, volleyball, children's programs (ages 4–11), no-smoking rooms* ⊟ *AE, D, MC, V* ⦿ *FAP.*

$$ 🏨 **The SunCatcher.** The four rooms in this B&B have been whimsically decorated in the style of four of the original owner's favorite hotels—the Connaught in London, the Regent in Hong Kong, the Oriental in Bangkok, and the Four Seasons in Chicago. All are charming. Focal points in the spacious living room are a large sunken seating area facing a copper-hooded fireplace and the mirrored mesquite wood bar where happy-hour snacks are served. If you're in the mood for watching a video, you can select from more than 100. All in all, it's a comfortable retreat after a day of sightseeing or hiking in nearby Saguaro National Park East.

✉ *105 N. Avda. Javelina, Eastside, 85748* ☏ *520/885–0883* ⊕ *www. thesuncatcher.com* ⤢ *4 rooms* ⟁ *Cable TV, in-room VCRs, pool, hot tub, Internet; no kids, no smoking* ⊟ *AE, D, MC, V* ⧀ *BP.*

$$ ▦ **Tucson Hilton East.** This high-rise hotel and conference center is set comfortably back off a main road on the suburban side of town. An airy atrium lobby takes full advantage of the view of the Santa Catalina Mountains; better yet, push "6" in the glass elevator for a spectacular vista. The rooms are spacious and well tended but not particularly distinctive. ✉ *7600 E. Broadway Blvd., Eastside, 85710* ☏ *520/721–5600 or 800/774–1500* ⊟ *520/721–5696* ⊕ *www.hilton.com* ⤢ *225 rooms, 8 suites* ⟁ *Restaurant, in-room data ports, cable TV, 2 pools, gym, outdoor hot tub, bar, business services, meeting rooms, no-smoking rooms* ⊟ *AE, D, DC, MC, V.*

$ ▦ **Smuggler's Inn.** At the corner of Wilmot Street and Speedway Boulevard, this comfortable suburban hotel, where you can park by your door, has easy access to Eastside activities and restaurants. A lushly landscaped central courtyard is the focus for the serviceable rooms, which have either a balcony or patio. A full, hot breakfast is included; you might also want to stock up on delectable treats from the Trader Joe's Market and Beyond Bread Bakery across the street. ✉ *6350 E. Speedway Blvd., Eastside, 85710* ☏*520/296–3292 or 800/525–8852* ⊟*520/722–3713* ⊕*www. smugglersinn.com* ⤢ *150 rooms* ⟁ *Restaurant, in-room data ports, cable TV with movies and video games, pool, outdoor hot tub, bar, laundry facilities, meeting rooms, no-smoking rooms* ⊟ *AE, D, MC, V* ⧀ *BP.*

Northeast Tucson

★ $$$$ ▦ **Canyon Ranch.** The Canyon Ranch draws an international crowd of well-to-do health seekers to its superb spa facilities on 70 acres in the desert foothills. Two activity centers include an enormous spa complex and a Health and Healing Center, where dietitians, exercise physiologists, behavioral-health professionals, and medical staff attend to body and soul. Just about every type of physical activity is possible, from Pilates to guided hiking, and the food is plentiful and healthy. Rates include all meals, activities, taxes, and gratuities. There's a four-night minimum. ✉ *8600 E. Rockcliff Rd., Northeast, 85750* ☏ *520/749–9000 or 800/742–9000* ⊟ *520/749–1646* ⊕ *www.canyonranch.com* ⤢ *240 rooms* ⟁ *Dining room, cable TV, golf privileges, 8 tennis courts, 4 pools (1 indoor), hair salon, health club, sauna, spa, steam room, basketball, racquetball, squash, library, laundry facilities, business center, airport shuttle; no kids under 12, no smoking* ⊟ *AE, D, MC, V* ⧀ *FAP.*

★ $$$–$$$$ ▦ **Loews Ventana Canyon Resort.** This is one of the most luxurious of the big resorts, with dramatic stone architecture and an 80-foot waterfall cascading down the mountains. Rooms, facing either the Catalinas or the golf course and city, are modern and elegantly furnished in muted earth tones and light woods; each bath has a miniature TV, a double-wide tub, and bubble bath. Dining options include everything from poolside snacks at Bill's Grill to fine continental cuisine at the Ventana Room. The scenic Ventana Canyon trailhead is steps away, and there's a free shuttle to nearby Sabino Canyon. ✉ *7000 N. Resort Dr., Northeast, 85750* ☏ *520/299–2020 or 800/234–5117* ⊟ *520/299–6832*

⊕ *www.loewshotels.com* ◷ *384 rooms, 14 suites* ♿ *4 restaurants, room service, in-room data ports, minibars, cable TV with movies, 2 18-hole golf courses, 8 tennis courts, pro shop, 2 pools, health club, hair salon, hot tub, sauna, spa, steam room, mountain bikes, croquet, hiking, bar, lobby lounge, shop, children's programs (ages 4–12), business services, meeting rooms, no-smoking rooms* ⊟ *AE, D, DC, MC, V.*

$$ ⛫ **Ramada Inn Foothills.** Families and business travelers stay in this Ramada on the northeastern side of town, close to many restaurants and Sabino Canyon. An attractive light stucco building with a Spanish tile roof and a fake bell tower, this property has serviceable, if generic, rooms and small suites. Complimentary beer and wine is served in the afternoon. The Southwestern restaurant next door, Fuego, provides room service. Free passes to a local health club are available; tennis facilities are nearby. ⊠ *6944 E. Tanque Verde Rd., Northeast, 85715* ☎ *520/886–9595 or 800/228–2828* 🖷 *520/721–8466* ⊕ *www.ramada.com* ◷ *50 rooms, 63 suites* ♿ *Room service, in-room data ports, cable TV, pool, sauna, laundry facilities, business services, meeting rooms, some pets allowed; no smoking* ⊟ *AE, D, DC, MC, V* ⦵⦵ *CP.*

Catalina Foothills (North)

★ **$$$$** ⛫ **Westin La Paloma.** Vying with the Hilton El Conquistador and Loews Ventana for convention business, this sprawling, pale pink resort offers views of the Santa Catalina Mountains above and the city below. It specializes in relaxation with an emphasis on fun: the golf, tennis, and spa facilities are top-notch, and the huge pool complex has an impressively long water slide, as well as a swim-up bar and grill for those who can't bear to leave the water. On-site kids' programs, including weekly "dive-in movies," make for a vacation the whole family can enjoy. Janos, one of Tucson's top restaurants, is also here. ⊠ *3800 E. Sunrise Dr., Foothills, 85718* ☎ *520/742–6000 or 888/625–5144* 🖷 *520/577–5878* ⊕ *www. starwood.com* ◷ *455 rooms, 32 suites* ♿ *4 restaurants, room service, in-room data ports, cable TV with movies and video games, 3 9-hole golf courses, 12 tennis courts, 3 pools, gym, hair salon, 3 outdoor hot tubs, spa, croquet, racquetball, volleyball, 2 bars, shops, children's programs (ages 6 months–12 years), business services, meeting rooms, no-smoking rooms* ⊟ *AE, D, DC, MC, V.*

$$–$$$ ⛫ **Hacienda del Sol Guest Ranch Resort.** This 32-acre hideaway in the Santa Catalina foothills is part guest ranch, part resort, and entirely gracious. It's a charming and lower-priced alternative to the larger resorts. Designed in classic Mexican hacienda style, this former finishing school for girls attracted stars like Clark Gable, Katharine Hepburn, and Spencer Tracy when it was converted to a guest ranch during World War II. Some of the one- and two-bedroom casitas have fireplaces and private porches, where you can watch the sun set over the Tucson Mountains. The superb Grill at Hacienda del Sol is part of the resort. ⊠ *5601 N. Hacienda del Sol Rd., Foothills, 85718* ☎ *520/299–1501 or 800/ 728–6514* 🖷 *520/299–5554* ⊕ *www.haciendadelsol.com* ◷ *22 rooms, 8 suites* ♿ *Restaurant, cable TV, pool, outdoor hot tub, horseback riding, shuffleboard, library, business services, meeting rooms; no smoking* ⊟ *AE, D, MC, V.*

$$ ⊞ **Windmill Inn at St. Philip's Plaza.** This all-suite hotel is in a chic shopping plaza filled with glitzy boutiques and good restaurants. Each 500-square-foot suite has a small sitting area, wet bar, two TVs, and three telephones (local calls are free). A few dollars extra will buy you a view of the pool and fountain rather than the parking lot. Complimentary coffee, muffins, juice, and a newspaper are delivered to your door; additional breakfast goodies are set up in the lobby. There are bicycles available for excursions along the nearby Rillito River, and free passes to a nearby gym are included in the rate. ⊠ *4250 N. Campbell Ave., Foothills, 85718* ☎ *520/577-0007 or 800/547-4747* 🖷 *520/577-0045* ⊕ *www.windmillinns.com* 🛏 *122 suites* ⚲ *Minibars, microwaves, refrigerators, cable TV, pool, hot tub, bicycles, library, laundry facilities, business services; no smoking* ☰ *AE, D, DC, MC, V* ⓧ *BP.*

Northwest Tucson

$$$$ ⊞ **Hilton Tucson El Conquistador.** A huge copper mural of cowboys and cacti and a wide view of the rugged Santa Catalina Mountains grace the lobby of the Hilton's golf and tennis resort. This friendly property draws families and conventioneers, some taking advantage of lower summer rates for the excellent sports facilities. Rooms, either in private one-bedroom casitas or the main hotel building, are decorated in desert tones of taupe, sand, and gold, and some suites have kiva-style fireplaces. ⊠ *10000 N. Oracle Rd., Northwest, 85737* ☎ *520/544-5000 or 800/325-3525* 🖷 *520/544-1224* ⊕ *www.hiltonelconquistador.com* 🛏 *328 rooms, 57 suites, 43 casitas* ⚲ *5 restaurants, in-room data ports, minibars, cable TV with movies and video games, 2 18-hole golf courses, 31 tennis courts, 3 pro shops, 4 pools, 2 gyms, spa, bicycles, basketball, horseback riding, racquetball, volleyball, piano bar, shops, business services, children's programs, meeting rooms, no-smoking rooms* ☰ *AE, D, DC, MC, V.*

$$$$ ⊞ **Lazy K Bar Guest Ranch.** In the Tucson Mountains, 16 mi northwest of town at an altitude of 2,300 feet, this family-oriented guest ranch accommodates both greenhorns and more experienced riders. Guest rooms are in eight casitas. Those in the older structures, made of Mexican stucco, have fireplaces and wood-beam ceilings; rooms in the newer, adobe-brick buildings are larger and more modern. Rides are twice-daily, but you can also enjoy guided hikes, cookouts, hayrides, and rock climbing. There are plenty of hammocks, a heated pool, and a hot tub to relax those post-equestrian muscles. There's a three-night minimum stay. ⊠ *8401 N. Scenic Dr., Northwest, 85743* ☎ *520/744-3050 or 800/321-7018* 🖷 *520/744-7628* ⊕ *www.lazykbar.com* 🛏 *19 rooms, 4 suites* ⚲ *Picnic area, pool, outdoor hot tub, hiking, horseback riding, library, meeting rooms, airport shuttle, no-smoking rooms; no room phones, no room TVs* ☰ *AE, D, MC, V* ⓧ *FAP.*

$$$$ ⊞ **Miraval.** Giving Canyon Ranch a run for its money, this New Age health spa 30 mi north of Tucson has a secluded desert setting and beautiful Southwestern rooms. The majority of its myriad spa services and wellness programs, based primarily on Eastern philosophies, help you get in touch with your inner self. Whether you prefer to be pampered with a hot stone massage, seaweed body mask, Dead Sea–salt scrub; par-

CloseUp

WHERE THE WEST IS STILL WILD

F YOU THINK THAT TUCSON HAS GONE THE WAY of sprawling suburban development like Phoenix to the north . . . well, you're partly right. Many of the wide-open spaces that once inspired the lyrics of old cowboy songs have become housing tracts, golf courses, and shopping malls. But a sliver of the rugged and free-spirited ranching life that shaped the American West is alive and well on the outskirts of town, where urban cowboys and cowgirls come to fulfill their dreams at dude ranches.

Dude ranches, also called guest ranches, are nostalgic tributes to a vanished way of life. Riding horseback under an endless blue sky with the cactus desert stretching for as far as the eyes can see, even the most cynical city slicker longs for simpler days.

Riding is the preferred activity on the ranch. Varied rides (slow, fast, mountain, and all-day) are offered daily, and some ranches allow you to help groom and feed the horses. As you ride up into Saguaro National Park or the Coronado National Forest, wranglers give sage advice on horsemanship and tell tales (some tall) of their most harrowing cattle drives. Afterwards, you can soak in the hot tub, get a massage, or laugh with new friends about the day's adventures over a pitcher of margaritas.

These lodgings are much more than resorts that offer horseback riding, however. Guests who don't saddle up can choose from birding/nature walks, mountain hikes, tennis, and swimming.

After a day of riding or hiking, or perhaps simply sitting outside enjoying a good book, all guests find a warm welcome at happy hour, dinner, and around the campfire. Lodges are outfitted with comfortable couches, crackling fireplaces, board games, and Western saloon-type bars (one even has saddles for barstools).

TVs, and the anti-social habits they encourage, are banned from guest rooms. (For those who must catch an occasional news- or sportscast, there is usually a set in the common area.) Ranch stays are popular for family vacations—parents relax while the kids make new friends who become long-distance pen-pals. The ranch experience also draws many single travelers who can easily find camaraderie in this setting.

Though accommodations are a bit more rustic than resort hotels, there are arguably more comforts: you're served three hearty meals every day, and you can mosey on into the dining room throughout the day for homemade cookies, fresh fruit, coffee, hot chocolate and "Cowboy Mix" (lemonade and iced tea). The dude ranch experience eliminates many stresses often associated with more traditional vacations. Since all meals and activities are included, you have fewer decisions about structuring your day (will it be the mountain ride or team penning?), and no anxiety about choosing a restaurant or dealing with crowds.

Three ranches are in the Tucson area. The large and luxurious *Tanque Verde Guest Ranch*, on the eastern edge of town, has two swimming pools (one indoor), a tennis pro and a fitness center. Children are separated from adults for rides and activities, which works for some dude families but not for others. The *White Stallion Ranch* is adjacent to Saguaro National Park's west unit. The owners live and work on this 3000-acre cattle ranch, the setting for High Chaparral. The *Lazy K Bar Ranch*, also in the Northwest, has extras like a rock-climbing wall, mountain biking and a separate hilltop meeting room with patio for special events.

— Mara Levin

take in the many fitness and nature activities; or just do yoga and meditate, it's all here. All gratuities and meals, including tasty buffets (with calories and fat content noted, of course), are included. ⊠ *5000 E. Via Estancia Miraval, Catalina 85739* ☎ *520/825–4000 or 800/825–4000* 📠 *520/825–5163* ⊕ *www.miravalresort.com* 📡 *106 rooms* ♻ *2 restaurants, in-room data ports, in-room safes, refrigerators, cable TV, 2 tennis courts, 3 pools, hair salon, health club, hot tub, sauna, spa, steam room, bicycles, croquet, horseback riding, bar, laundry facilities, laundry service; no smoking* ⊟ *AE, D, DC, MC, V* ⍜ *FAP.*

$$$$
Fodor's Choice
★

🏨 **White Stallion Ranch.** A 3,000-acre working cattle ranch run by the warm, hospitable True family since 1965, this place is the real deal. You can ride up to four times daily, hike in the mountains, enjoy a hayride cookout, and even compete in team cattle penning. Most rooms retain their original Western furniture, and newer deluxe rooms have whirlpool baths or fireplaces. Rates include all meals, riding, and daily entertainment such as weekend rodeos, country line dancing, telescopic stargazing, and singing cowboy songs around a campfire. ⊠ *9251 W. Twin Peaks Rd., Northwest, 85743* ☎ *520/297–0252 or 888/977–2624* 📠 *520/744–2786* ⊕ *www.wsranch.com* 📡 *24 rooms, 17 suites* ♻ *2 tennis courts, pool, hot tub, massage, basketball, billiards, horseback riding, horseshoes, Ping-Pong, shuffleboard, volleyball, bar, library, piano, recreation room, business services, meeting rooms, airport shuttle; no room phones, no room TVs* ⊟ *No credit cards* ☉ *Closed June–Aug.* ⍜ *FAP.*

$$$-$$$$

🏨 **Westward Look Resort.** Originally the 1912 homestead of William and Mary Watson, this laid-back lodging offers Southwestern character, attentive service, and all the amenities you expect at a major resort. The Watsons' original living room, with beautiful, dried ocotillo branches draped along the ceiling and antique furnishings, is now a comfortable lounge off the main lobby. The couple probably never envisioned anything like the New Age wellness center, offering hot desert-stone massages and three-mud body masks. Spacious rooms have wrought-iron beds and Mission-style furniture. Borrow a bike or take a stroll along the beautiful and well-marked nature trails. ⊠ *245 E. Ina Rd., Northwest, 85704* ☎ *520/297–1151 or 800/722–2500* 📠 *520/297–9023* ⊕ *www.westwardlook.com* 📡 *244 rooms* ♻ *2 restaurants, minibars, cable TV with movies, 8 tennis courts, 3 pools, gym, spa, mountain bikes, horseback riding, shop, concierge, business services, meeting rooms, no-smoking rooms* ⊟ *AE, D, DC, MC, V.*

$$

🏨 **Marriott TownePlace Suites.** With full kitchens in all of its studio, one-bedroom, and two-bedroom suites, this fresh newcomer is suitable for short or extended stays. In fact, the longer you stay, the lower your nightly rate. Its location is extremely handy, yet the interior hallways and the way the buildings are set back from the road make for a quiet retreat. Some suites have a view of the neighboring golf course, and a half-dozen are thoughtfully designed for wheelchair access. ⊠ *405 W. Rudasill Rd., Northwest, 85704* ☎ *520/292–9697 or 800/257–3000* 📠 *520/292–9884* ⊕ *www.towneplacesuites.com* 📡 *77 suites* ♻ *Kitchens, cable TV, pool, exercise equipment, laundry facilities, Internet, no-smoking rooms* ⊟ *AE, MC, V.*

$-$$

🏨 **La Posada Lodge and Casitas.** A 1960s motor lodge in northwest Tucson has been reborn as a charming Santa Fe–style boutique hotel.

Though most of the rooms in the three-story lodge building have Saltillo-tile floors, headboards hand-painted in Mexico, and a blend of cowboy and Mexican art, a few are whimsically decorated with royal blue–and–lime green–checkered bedspreads and curtains, along with kitschy furniture and lava lamps, as a tribute to the hotel's past life. Second- and third-floor rooms have balconies with mountain and city views, and the one-story casitas off the main grassy courtyard have sofa sleepers, kitchenettes, and private patios. The restaurant, Miguel's, is an upscale Latin-themed jewel, specializing in seafood. ⊠ *5900 N. Oracle Road, Northwest, 85704* ☎ *520/887–4800 or 800/810–2808* 🖨 *520/293–7543* ⊕ *www.laposadalodge.com* ➷ *72 rooms* ⚐ *Restaurant, room service, some kitchenettes, microwaves, refrigerators, cable TV, pool, hot tub, gym, spa, bar, Internet, meeting rooms, some pets allowed (fee); no smoking* ⊟ *AE, MC, V* ⦿*⎮ CP.*

¢–$ ⊞ **Quail's Vista Bed and Breakfast.** Innkeeper and former concierge Barbara Bauer and her husband, Richard, can direct you to all the best things to see and do in Tucson; some activities, include bird-watching or soaking in a hot tub on a redwood deck that looks out on the dramatic west face of the Santa Catalina Mountains, can be done right in the inn's backyard. Inside, peeled spruce columns support the beamed ceiling and thick, rounded walls of this rammed-earth adobe home. Fiesta dinnerware, Native American pottery, and bright Mexican blankets decorate the common area, which has cozy nooks for reading or watching the wildlife out the windows. ⊠ *826 E. Palisades Rd., Northwest, 85737* ☎ *520/297–5980* ⊕ *www.quails-vista-bb.com* ➷ *3 rooms, 1 with bath* ⚐ *Hot tub, laundry facilities, Internet; no TV in some rooms, no smoking* ⊟ *No credit cards* ⦿ *Closed June–Sept.* ⦿*⎮ CP.*

West of Tucson

$$ ⊞ **Casa Tierra.** For a real desert experience, head out to this B&B on 5
Fodor'sChoice acres near the Arizona–Sonora Desert Museum and Saguaro National
★ Park West. The last 1½ mi are on a dirt road. All rooms have private patio entrances and look out onto a lovely central courtyard with a paloverde tree, desert foliage, and a fountain. The Southwestern-style furnishings include Mexican *equipales* (chairs with pigskin seats), tiled floors, and beamed ceilings. A full vegetarian breakfast served on fine china is included in the room rate, and there is a media room for those who can't stand the quiet. There's a minimum stay of two nights. ⊠ *11155 W. Calle Pima, Westside, 85743* ☎ *520/578–3058 or 866/254–0006* 🖨 *520/578–8445* ⊕ *www.casatierratucson.com* ➷ *3 rooms, 1 suite* ⚐ *Microwaves, refrigerators, gym, hot tub, recreation room; no room TVs, no smoking* ⊟ *AE, MC, V* ⦿ *Closed mid-June–mid-Aug.* ⦿*⎮ BP.*

NIGHTLIFE & THE ARTS

The Arts

For a city of its size, Tucson is abuzz with cultural activity. It is one of only 14 cities in the United States with a symphony as well as opera, theater, and ballet companies. Wintertime, when Tucson's population swells with vacationers, is the high season, but the arts are alive and well year-round. The low cost of Tucson's cultural events comes as a pleasant surprise to those accustomed to paying East or West Coast prices: symphony tickets are as little as $5 for some performances, and touring Broadway musicals can often be seen for $22. Parking is plentiful and frequently free.

The free *Tucson Weekly* (⊕ www.tucsonweekly.com), which hits the stands on Thursday, and the Friday "Caliente" section of the *Arizona Daily Star* (⊕ www.azstarnet.com) have complete listings of what's going on in town.

Downtown Saturday Night (☎ 520/624–9977 ⊕ tucsonartsdistrict.org), an event held the first and third Saturday night of every month, keeps downtown art-district galleries, studios, and cafés hopping from 7 to 10. There's often dancing in the street—everything from calypso to square dancing—and musical performances ranging from jazz to gospel. Most of the activity takes place along Congress Street and Broadway Boulevard (from 4th Avenue to Stone Street) and along 5th and 6th avenues. You can also explore this area via such free guided tours as the Thursday Night Artwalk, or self-guided tours of art galleries and the historic districts. For more information contact the **Tucson Arts District Partnership, Inc.**

Much of the city's cultural activity takes place at or near the **Tucson Convention Center** (✉ 260 S. Church St., Downtown ☎ 520/791–4101, 520/791–4266 box office ⊕ www.ci.tucson.az.us/tcc) in the El Presidio neighborhood. Dance, music, and other kinds of performances take place at the University of Arizona's **Centennial Hall** (✉ 1020 E. University Blvd., University ☎ 520/621–3341 ⊕ uapresents.arizona.edu).

One of Tucson's hottest rock-music venues, the **Rialto Theatre** (✉ 318 E. Congress St., Downtown ☎ 520/798–3333 ⊕ www.rialtotheatre.com) was once a silent-movie theater but now reverberates with the sounds of jazz, folk, and world-music concerts, although the emphasis is on hard rock. The Rialto hosts dance and dramatic productions as well.

Each season brings visiting companies of opera, theater, and dance to Tucson, and tickets to many events can be purchased through **Ticketmaster** (✉ Robinsons-May, El Con Mall, 3435 E. Broadway Blvd., Central ☎ 520/795–3950 ✉ Robinsons-May, Tucson Mall, 4470 N. Oracle Rd., Central ☎ 520/292–0345 ⊕ www.ticketmaster.com) directly or from its outlets in the Robinsons-May stores.

Dance

Tucson shares its professional-ballet company, **Ballet Arizona** (☎ 888/322–5538 ⊕ www.balletaz.org), with Phoenix. Performances, from classical to contemporary, are held at the Music Hall in the Tucson Convention Center. Tucson's most established modern dance company, **Orts Theatre of Dance** (✉ 930 N. Stone Ave., Downtown ☎ 520/624–3799 ⊕ www.orts.org) incorporates trapeze flying into the dances. Outdoor and indoor performances are staged throughout the year.

Music

The **Arizona Opera Company** (☎ 520/293–4336 ⊕ www.azopera.com), based in Tucson, puts on five major productions each year at the Tucson Convention Center's Music Hall. From late February through late June, the **Tucson Pops Orchestra** (⊠ Lake Shore La. off 22nd St. between Alvernon Way and Country Club Rd., Central ⊕ www.theriver.com/public/tucsonpops) gives free concerts each Saturday evening at the De Meester Outdoor Performance Center in Reid Park. Arrive about an hour before the music starts (usually at 7 PM) to stake your claim on a prime viewing spot.

The **Tucson Symphony Orchestra** (⊠ 443 S. Stone Ave., Downtown ☎ 520/882–8585 box office, 520/792–9155 main office ⊕ www.tucsonsymphony.org), part of Tucson's cultural scene since 1929, holds concerts in the Music Hall in the Tucson Convention Center and at sites in the Foothills and the northwest as well.

Tucson's small but vibrant jazz scene encompasses everything from afternoon jam sessions in the park to Sunday jazz brunches at resorts in the Foothills. Call the **Tucson Jazz Society Hot Line** (☎ 520/743–3399) for information. The **Tucson Blues Society Hot Line** (☎ 520/887–2126) provides recorded updates on local blues concerts.

Poetry

Spring brings the **Tucson Poetry Festival** (☎ 520/620–2045 ⊕ www.tucsonpoetryfestival.org) and its three days of readings and related events. Such internationally acclaimed poets as Jorie Graham and Sherman Alexie have participated.

The **University of Arizona Poetry Center** (⊠ 1600 E. 1st St., University ☎ 520/626–3765 ⊕ www.coh.arizona.edu/poetry) runs a free series open to the public. Check during fall and spring semesters for information on scheduled readings.

Theater

Arizona's state theater, the **Arizona Theatre Company** (⊠ Temple of Music and Art, 330 S. Scott Ave., Downtown ☎ 520/622–2823 box office, 520/884–8210 company office ⊕ www.aztheatreco.org), performs classical pieces, contemporary drama, and musical comedy at the historic Temple of Music and Art from September through May. It's worth coming just to see the beautifully restored historic Spanish colonial/Moorish–style theater; dinner at the adjoining Temple Café makes a tasty prelude to any performance.

The University of Arizona's **Arizona Repertory Theatre** (⊠ Speedway Blvd. and Olive St., University ☎ 520/621–1162 ⊕ http://arts.music.arizona.edu/theatre) has performances during the academic year, in both the fall and spring semesters. **Borderlands Theater** (⊠ 373 S. Meyer Ave., Downtown ☎ 520/882–7406) presents new plays—often multicultural and bilingual—at venues throughout Tucson, usually from late June through April. Children of all ages love the old-fashioned and cleverly written melodramas at the **Gaslight Theatre** (⊠ 7010 E. Broadway Blvd., Eastside ☎ 520/886–9428 box office), where hissing the villain and cheering the hero are part of the audience's duty. **Invisible Theatre** (✉ 1400 N. 1st Ave., Central ☎ 520/882–9721) presents contemporary plays and musicals.

Nightlife

Bars & Clubs

In addition to the places listed below, most of the major resorts have late spots for drinks or dancing. The Westward Look Resort's Lookout Bar, with its expansive view and classic rock band on Friday and Saturday nights, is a popular spot for dancing. The bars at Westin La Paloma, Hacienda del Sol, and Loews Ventana offer live acoustic music on weekends.

BLUES & JAZZ **Boondocks** (✉ 3306 N. 1st Ave., Central ☎ 520/690–0991) is the unofficial home of the Tucson Blues Society, hosting local and touring singer-songwriters.

There's usually a lively jazz pianist at the **Arizona Inn** (✉ 2200 E. Elm St., University ☎ 520/325–1541). **Old Pueblo Grille** (✉ 60 N. Alvernon Way, Central ☎ 520/326–6000) has live jazz on Tuesday, Saturday, and Sunday nights. **Ric's Café** (✉ 5605 E. River Rd., Northeast ☎ 520/577–7272) features jazz musicians outside in the courtyard every Saturday night.

COUNTRY & WESTERN An excellent house band gets the crowd two-stepping every night except Sunday and Monday at the **Maverick** (✉ 6622 E. Tanque Verde Rd., Eastside ☎ 520/298–0430).

GAY & LESBIAN BARS **Ain't Nobody's Bizness** (✉ 2900 E. Broadway Blvd., Central ☎ 520/318–4838) is the most popular lesbian bar in town. It has a karaoke night where you may hear more than your fair share of Melissa Etheridge. **IBT's (It's 'Bout Time)** (✉ 616 N. 4th Ave., University ☎ 520/882–3053) is Tucson's most popular gay men's bar, with a patio, rock and disco DJ music, and Sunday-night drag shows. Expect long lines on weekends.

ROCK & MORE **Berky's** (✉ 5769 E. Speedway Blvd., Central ☎ 520/296–1981) has live R&B and rock and roll every night, though mostly cover songs rather than original music. The **Cactus Moon Café** (✉ 5470 E. Broadway Blvd., Central ☎ 520/748–0049), catering to a mostly yuppie crowd, offers a standard mix of Top 40, hip-hop, and modern country, often with free appetizer buffets during happy hour. The **Chicago Bar** (✉ 5954 E. Speedway Blvd., Central ☎ 520/748–8169) is a good place to catch Tucson blues legend Sam Taylor; other nightly shows include reggae and rock.

Club Congress (✉ Hotel Congress, 311 E. Congress St., Downtown ☎ 520/622–8848) is the main Friday venue for cutting-edge rock bands, with a mixed-bag crowd of jaded alternative rockers, international travelers, and college kids. Saturday brings a more outrageous crowd dancing to a big electronic beat. **El Parador** (✉ 2744 E. Broadway, Central ☎ 520/881–2808) has a live salsa band Friday and Saturday nights, with free dance lessons at 9:30 PM. The **Nimbus Brewing Company** (✉ 3850 E. 44th St., Southeast ☎ 520/745–9175) is the place for acoustic blues, folk, and bluegrass, not to mention good, cheap food and microbrewed beer.

Plush (✉ 340 E. 6th St., University ☎ 520/798–1298) hosts bands like Camp Courageous and Greyhound Soul, as well as local performers with a loyal following. Go totally retro at the **Shelter** (✉ 4155 E. Grant Rd., Central ☎ 520/326–1345), a former bomb shelter decked out in plastic 1960s kitsch, lava lamps, and JFK memorabilia, which plays Elvis videos and music by the likes of Burt Bacharach and Martin Denny.

Casinos

After a long struggle with the state of Arizona, two Native American tribes now operate casinos on their Tucson-area reservations west of the airport. The casinos are virtually the same, and quite unlike their distant and much grander cousins in Las Vegas and Atlantic City. Don't expect much glamour, ersatz or otherwise; these casinos are more like glorified video arcades, although you can lose money much faster. You'll be greeted by a wall of cigarette smoke (the reservation is exempt from the city's antismoking laws) and the wail of hundreds of slot machines and video poker, blackjack, roulette, and craps machines. The only "live" gaming is keno, bingo, blackjack, and certain types of poker. The crowd is mostly older smokers, and no one under age 21 is permitted.

The Pascua Yaqui tribe's **Casino of the Sun** (✉ 7406 S. Camino de Oeste, off W. Valencia Rd. about 5 mi west of I–19, South ☎ 520/883–1700 or 800/344–9435 ⊕ www.casinosun.com) has slot and video-gambling machines, high-stakes bingo, and live poker. Food selections include an all-you-can-eat prime rib buffet. A few miles farther west is their newer, larger facility, **Casino del Sol** (✉ 5655 W. Valencia, Southwest ☎ 520/883–1700 or 800/344–9435 ⊕ www.casinodelsol.com), with live poker and blackjack, bingo, slots, and an above-average Italian restaurant. An adjacent 4,600-seat outdoor amphitheater books entertainers like Bob Dylan and James Taylor. Free shuttle buses operate from points all over Tucson; call for a schedule. The Tohono O'odham tribe operates the dizzying **Desert Diamond Bingo and Casino** (✉ 7350 S. Old Nogales Hwy., 1 mi south of Valencia, just west of the airport, South ☎ 520/294–7777 ⊕ www.desertdiamondcasino.com), which has 500 one-arm bandits and video poker in addition to live keno, bingo, and Stud High, Texas Hold'em, Omaha, and Stud Lo poker. Players are served free nonalcoholic beverages (you'll have to pay for alcoholic ones), and can order tacos, burritos, sandwiches, and several varieties of Native American–fry bread as they play.

SPORTS & THE OUTDOORS

Ballooning

Two companies in Tucson offer hot-air-balloon flights from September to May, flown by FAA-certified pilots. Passengers toast with crystal flutes on daily champagne tours with **Balloon Rides USA** (✉ Box 31255, Tucson 85751 ☎ 520/299–7744 ⊕ www.balloonridesusa.com). Tours depart from the east side of Tucson. **Southern Arizona Balloon Excursions** (✉ Box 5265, Tucson 85703 ☎ 520/624–3599 ⊕ www.tucsoncomefly.com) offers daily sunrise flights over northwest Tucson.

Baseball

It doesn't have as many teams as Phoenix, but Tucson does have its share of baseball spring training action. Spring training brings the Arizona Diamondbacks, the Chicago White Sox, and the Colorado Rockies to the Tucson area, from the middle of February until the end of March. The Diamondbacks and White Sox play at Tucson Electric Park, south of town near the airport. The Rockies play at Hi Corbett Field, which is adjacent to Reid Park and most easily reached by driving south at the junction of East Broadway Boulevard and Randolph Way; parking is tight at Hi Corbett, so arrive early to enjoy a picnic lunch at one of the many nearby ramadas (wooden shelters that supply shade for your table). Not surprisingly, some people plan vacations around scheduled training dates; there are plenty of local fans, too. The **Pacific Coast League** (⊕ www.pclbaseball.com) includes the Tucson Sidewinders, the AAA team of the Arizona Diamondbacks, who play in Tucson Electric Park from April through July.

Arizona Diamondbacks (✉ Tucson Electric Park, 2400 E. Ajo Way, South ☎ 520/434–1000, 520/683–3900 for tickets ⊕ www.tucsonbaseball.com). **Chicago White Sox** (✉ Tucson Electric Park, 2400 E. Ajo Way, South ☎ 520/434–1000, 520/683–3900 for tickets ⊕ www.tucsonbaseball.com). **Colorado Rockies** (✉ Hi Corbett Field, 3400 E. Camino Campestre, Central ☎ 520/327–9467 ⊕ http://colorado.rockies.mlb.com). **Tucson Sidewinders** (☎ 520/325–2621, 520/434–1021 for tickets ⊕ www. tucsonsidewinders.com).

Bicycling

Tucson, ranked among America's top five bicycling cities by *Bicycling* magazine, has well-maintained bikeways, routes, lanes, and paths all over the city. Scenic loop roads in both sections of Saguaro National Park offer rewarding rides for all levels of cyclists. Most bike stores in Tucson carry the monthly newsletter of the Tucson chapter of **GABA** (Greater Arizona Bicycling Association; ✆ Box 43273, Tucson 85733 ⊕ www. bikegaba.org), which lists rated group rides. You can pick up a map of Tucson-area bike routes at the **Pima Association of Governments** (✉ 177 N. Church St., Suite 405, Downtown ☎ 520/792–1093).

Mountain bikes, comfort bikes, and road bikes can be rented by the day or week at **Fair Wheel Bikes** (✉ 1110 E. 6th St., University ☎ 520/258–0118). **Sabino Cycles** (✉ 7131 E. Tanque Verde Rd., Northeast ☎ 520/885–3666) offers a broad selection of rentals, including road bikes and mountain bikes with front or full suspension. **Tucson Bicycles** (✉ 4743 E. Sunrise Dr., Foothills ☎ 520/577–7374) rents bikes and organizes group rides of varying difficulty around town.

Bird-Watching

The naturalist and illustrator Roger Tory Peterson (1908–96) considered Tucson one of the country's top birding spots, and avid "life listers"—birders who keep a list of all the birds they've sighted and identified—soon see why. In the early morning and early evening, Sabino Canyon is alive with cactus and canyon wrens, hawks, and quail. Spring and summer, when species of migrants come in from Mexico, are great hummingbird seasons. In the nearby Santa Rita Mountains and Madera

Canyon, you can see elegant trogons nesting in early spring. The area also supports species usually found only in higher elevations.

You can get the latest word on the bird by phoning the 24-hour line at the **Tucson Audubon Society** (☎520/798–1005 ⊕www.tucsonaudubon.org); sightings of rare or interesting birds in the area are recorded regularly.

The society's **Audubon Nature Shop** (✉ 300 E. University Blvd., Suite 120, University ☎ 520/629–0510) carries field guides, bird feeders, binoculars, and natural-history books. The **Wild Bird Store** (✉ 3526 E. Grant Rd., Central ☎ 520/322–9466) is an excellent resource for bird-watching books, maps, and trail guides.

Several companies offer birding tours in the Tucson area. **Borderland Tours** (✉ 2550 W. Calle Padilla, Northwest, Tucson 85745 ☎ 520/882–7650 or 800/525–7753 ⊕ www.borderland-tours.com) leads bird-watching tours in Arizona and all over the world. **Wings** (✉ 1643 N. Alvernon Way, Suite 105, Central, Tucson 85712 ☎ 520/320–9868 ⊕ www.wingsbirds.com), a Tucson-based company, leads ornithological expeditions locally and worldwide.

Camping

The closest public campground to Tucson is at **Catalina State Park** (✉ 11570 N. Oracle Rd., Northwest ☎ 520/628–5798 ⊕ www.pr.state.az.us), about 14 mi north of town on AZ 77 in the foothills of the Santa Catalinas. The campground has 48 sites, about half with electrical hookups, accommodating both tents and RVs. Sites cost $15 with electric hookups, $10 without, and the cash- or check-only facility operates on a first-come, first-served basis. You can slumber amid saguaros at **Gilbert Ray Campground** (✉ 8451 W. McCain Loop, Westside ☎ 520/883–4200), about 15 mi west of town, just down the road from the Arizona–Sonora Desert Museum and Saguaro National Park's west unit. This campground has drinking water, flush toilets, and 130 sites with tables, grills, and electricity. Sites cost $20 with electric hookups, $10 without, and reservations can be made with a 72-hour advance payment.

Golf

For a detailed listing of the state's courses, contact the **Arizona Golf Association** (✉ 7226 N. 16th St., Phoenix 85020 ☎ 602/944–3035 or 800/458–8484 ⊕ www.azgolf.org). The **Golf Stop Inc.** (✉ 1830 S. Alvernon Way, South ☎ 520/790–0941), a shop owned and run by two LPGA pros, can fit you with custom clubs, repair your old irons, or give you lessons. For a local golf package based on your budget, interests, and experience, contact **Tee Time Arrangers** (✉ 6979 E. Broadway Blvd., Eastside ☎ 520/296–4800 or 800/742–9939). If you're planning to stay a week or more, **Tucson's Resort Golf Card** (☎ 520/886–8800), offering discounts at 13 of the area's best courses, is a good deal.

MUNICIPAL COURSES — One of Tucson's best-kept secrets is that the city's five low-priced, municipal courses are maintained to standards usually found only at the best country clubs. To reserve a tee time at one of the city's courses, call the **Tucson Parks and Recreation Department** (☎ 520/791–4653 general golf information, 520/791–4336 automated tee-time reservations ⊕www.tucsoncitygolf.com) at least a week in advance.

Fred Enke Golf Course (✉ 8251 E. Irvington, Eastside ☎ 520/791–2539) is a hilly, semi-arid 18-hole course, meaning that it has less grass and more native vegetation. It's southeast of town.

FodorsChoice **Randolph Park Golf Course–North Course** (✉ 600 S. Alvernon Way, Cen-
★ tral ☎ 520/791–4161), a long, scenic 18-hole course that has hosted the LPGA Tour for many years, is the flagship of Tucson's municipal courses. **Silverbell Golf Course** (✉ 3600 N. Silverbell Rd., Northwest ☎ 520/791–5235), with spacious fairways and ample greens, has an 18-hole layout set along the west bank of the Santa Cruz River.

PUBLIC COURSES **Rio Rico Resort & Country Club** (✉ 1069 Camino Carampi, Tubac ☎ 800/288–4746 ⊕ www.rioricoresort.com), south of Tucson, near Nogales, was designed by Robert Trent Jones Sr. This 18-hole course is one of Arizona's lesser-known gems.

San Ignacio Golf Club (✉ 4201 S. Camino del Sol, Green Valley ☎ 520/648–3468 ⊕ www.irigolfgroup.com) was designed by Arthur Hills and is a challenging 18-hole desert course.

Tubac Golf Resort (✉ 1 Otero Rd., Tubac ☎ 520/398–2021 ⊕ www.tubacgolfresort.com), an 18-hole course 45 minutes south of Tucson, will look familiar to you if you've seen the movie *Tin Cup.*

RESORTS Avid golfers check into one of Tucson's many tony resorts and head straight for the links. Those who don't mind getting up early to beat the heat will find some excellent golf packages at these places in the summer.

Hilton Tucson El Conquistador (✉ 10000 N. Oracle Rd., Northwest ☎ 520/544–5000 ⊕ www.hiltonelconquistador.com) has 45 holes of golf in the Santa Catalina foothills. The course has some panoramic views of the city.

FodorsChoice **Lodge at Ventana Canyon** (✉ 6200 N. Clubhouse La., Northeast ☎ 520/
★ 577–1400 or 800/828–5701) has two 18-hole Tom Fazio–designed courses. Their signature hole, No. 3 on the mountain course, is a favorite of golf photographers. Guests staying up the road at Loews Ventana Resort also have privileges here.

Omni Tucson National Golf Resort (✉ 2727 W. Club Dr., Northwest ☎ 520/575–7540 ⊕ www.tucsonnational.com), cohost of an annual PGA winter open, offers 27 holes and beautiful, long par 4's. The resort's orange and gold courses were designed by Robert Van Hagge and Bruce Devlin.

Starr Pass Golf Resort (✉ 3645 W. Starr Pass Blvd., Westside ☎ 520/670–0400 ⊕ www.starrpasstucson.com), with 18 magnificent holes in the Tucson Mountains, was developed as a Tournament Player's Course. Managed by Arnold Palmer, Starr Pass has become a favorite of visiting pros; playing its No. 15 signature hole has been likened to threading a moving needle.

Hiking

For hiking inside Tucson city limits, you can test your skills climbing trails up Sentinel Peak ("A" Mountain), but there are also hundreds of other trails in the immediate Tucson area. The Santa Catalina Mountains, Sabino Canyon and Saguaro National Park East and West beckon hikers with waterfalls, birds, critters, and huge saguaro cacti.

Catalina State Park (✉ 11570 N. Oracle Rd., Northwest ☎ 520/628–5798 ⊕ www.pr.state.az.us) is crisscrossed by hiking trails. One of them, the relatively easy, two-hour (5.5-mi round-trip) Romero Canyon Trail, leads to Romero Pools, a series of natural *tinajas,* or stone "jars," filled with water much of the year. The trailhead is on the park's entrance road, past the restrooms on the right side.

The Bear Canyon Trail in **Sabino Canyon** (⊠ Sabino Canyon Rd. at Sunrise Dr., Foothills ☎ 520/749–8700 ⊕ www.fs.fed.us/r3/coronado), also known as Seven Falls Trail, is a three-hour, 7.8-mi round-trip that is moderately easy and fun, crisscrossing the stream several times on the way up the canyon. Kids enjoy the boulder-hopping and all are rewarded with pools and waterfalls as well as views at the top. The trailhead can be reached from the parking area by either taking a five-minute Bear Canyon Tram ride or walking the 1.8-mi tram route.

In the west unit of **Saguaro National Park** (⊠ 2700 N. Kinney Rd., Westside ☎ 520/733–5158 ⊕ www.nps.gov/sagu) a favorite hike is the Hugh Norris Trail. Named after a Tohono O'odham police chief, this moderately difficult trail makes a gradual climb to Wasson Peak, affording wonderful views of the Tucson valley, surrounding mountain ranges, and saguaro forests below. The 9.8-mi round-trip begins on Hohokam Road, about 1 mi past the Red Hills Visitor Center.

The local chapter of the **Sierra Club** (⊠ 738 N. 5th Ave., University, Tucson ☎ 520/620–6401) welcomes out-of-towners on weekend hikes around Tucson. The **Southern Arizona Hiking Club** (☎ 520/751–4513 ⊕ www.sahcinfo.org) leads weekend hikes of varying difficulty. For hiking on your own, a good source is **Summit Hut** (⊠ 5045 E. Speedway Blvd., Central ☎ 520/325–1554), which has a collection of hiking reference materials and a friendly staff who will help you plan and outfit your trip. Packs, tents, bags, and climbing shoes can be rented here.

Horseback Riding

Pusch Ridge Stables (⊠ 13700 N. Oracle Rd., Northwest ☎ 520/825–1664), adjacent to Catalina State Park, can serve up a cowboy-style breakfast on your trail ride; gentle children's horse walks, one-hour, and overnight rides are also available. **Colossal Cave Stables** (⊠ 16600 Colossal Cave Rd., Eastside ☎ 520/647–3450) takes riders into Saguaro National Park East on one-hour or longer guided trail rides.

Rodeo

In the last week of February, Tucson hosts **Fiesta de Los Vaqueros,** the largest annual winter rodeo in the United States, a five-day extravaganza with more than 600 events and a crowd of more than 44,000 spectators a day at the **Tucson Rodeo Grounds** (⊠ 4823 S. 6th Ave., South ☎ 520/294–8896 ⊕ www.tucsonrodeo.com). The rodeo kicks off with a 2-mi parade of horseback riders (Western and fancy-dress Mexican *charro*), wagons, stagecoaches, and horse-drawn floats; it's touted as the largest nonmotorized parade in the world. Local schoolkids especially love the celebration—they get a two-day holiday from school. Daily seats at the rodeo range from $8 to $14.

Tennis

Excellent tennis facilities can be found at area resorts, among them Loews Ventana Canyon (8 courts), Hilton Tucson El Conquistador (31 courts),

Westin La Paloma (12 courts), Westward Look (8 courts), and Canyon Ranch (8 courts). **Catalina High School** (✉ 3645 E. Pima, Central), singer Linda Ronstadt's alma mater, is a favorite among local tennis enthusiasts for its well-lighted, no-charge courts, which are open to the public when school's out. **Fort Lowell Park** (✉ 2900 N. Craycroft Rd., Central ☎ 520/791–2584) has eight lighted courts and tennis instruction for all ages. **Himmel Park** (✉ 1000 N. Tucson Blvd., University ☎ 520/791–3276), 1 mi east of the university, has eight lighted tennis courts and low prices. The **Randolph Tennis Center** (✉ 50 S. Alvernon Way, Central ☎ 520/791–4896) has 24 tennis courts (and 10 racquetball courts), all of them lighted, at very reasonable rates.

SHOPPING

Much of Tucson's retail activity is focused around malls, but shops with more character and some unique wares are in the city's open plazas: St. Philip's Plaza (River Road and Campbell Avenue), Plaza Palomino (Swan and Fort Lowell roads), Casas Adobes Plaza (Oracle and Ina roads), and La Encantada (Skyline Drive and Campbell Avenue).

The 4th Avenue neighborhood near the University of Arizona—especially 4th Avenue between 2nd and 9th streets—is fertile ground for unusual items in artsy boutiques and galleries and secondhand-clothing stores. You may experience some aggressive panhandling here.

Hard-core bargain hunters usually head south to the Mexican border town of Nogales, for jewelry, liquor, home furnishings, and leather goods. For in-town deals, the outlet stores at the Foothills Mall in northwest Tucson score high marks.

Malls & Shopping Centers

Casas Adobes Plaza (✉ Oracle and Ina Rds., southwest corner, Northwest ☎ no phone ⊕ www.casasadobesplaza.com) originally served the ranchers and orange grove owners in this once remote part of town, which is now the fastest-growing area. This outdoor, Mediterranean-style shopping center has a full-service grocery with organic meats and produce, the superb Wildflower Grill, Sauce (for upscale flat-crust pizzas and salads), a bagel shop, and several boutiques and gift shops.

Foothills Mall (✉ 7401 N. La Cholla Blvd. at Ina Rd., Northwest ☎ 520/742–7191 ⊕ www.shopfoothillsmall.com) has a Barnes & Noble Superstore and a Saks Fifth Avenue outlet store; many other outlets including Samsonite, Nike, and Adidas; as well as boutiques, a 16-screen cineplex, and several restaurants.

Historic Broadway Village (✉ Country Club Rd. and Broadway Blvd., Central ☎ no phone), Tucson's first shopping center, was designed by esteemed local architect Josias Joesler and built in 1939. Although small by today's standards, this outdoor complex with a courtyard houses interesting shops such as the Clues Unlimited mystery bookstore, Zocalo for colonial Mexican furniture, Yikes! for off-the-wall toys, and Picante for Mexican clothing and crafts (get your Day of the Dead merchandise here).

La Encantada (✉ Skyline Dr. and Campbell Ave., Foothills ☎ no phone), the newest outdoor mall, has close to 50 stores (plus four restaurants) decidedly aimed at affluent consumers. Firebirds Grill, serving steaks and burgers, and North, a nouvelle Italian bistro, are the rising stars. Trendy tenants Crate & Barrel and Pottery Barn, plus a huge gourmet grocery, anchor the shopping center.

The Lost Barrio (⊠ Park Ave. and 12th St., south of Broadway, Central ☎ no phone) is a cluster of 10 shops in an old warehouse district; Southwestern and ethnic art, furniture and gifts (both antique and modern) are specialties.

Old Town Artisans Complex (⊠ 186 N. Meyer Ave., Downtown ☎ 520/623–6024), across from the Tucson Museum of Art, has a large selection of Southwestern wares, including Native American jewelry, baskets, Mexican handicrafts, pottery, and textiles.

Plaza Palomino (⊠ 2980 N. Swan Rd., at Ft. Lowell Rd., Central ☎ 520/795–1177), an outdoor mall, has many shops, galleries, and clothing boutiques, including Dark Star Leather and the Strand. On Saturday, you can sample locally grown produce, baked goods, salsas, and tamales at the farmers' market. La Placita Cafe serves tasty Mexican food.

St. Philip's Plaza (⊠ 4280 N. Campbell Ave., at River Rd., Foothills ☎ 520/886–7485) arranges its chic shops around a series of Spanish-style outdoor patios. You can shop away at more than a dozen boutiques and eye some outstanding art at Obsidian Gallery and Philabaum Contemporary Glass. When it's time to recuperate, the nearby restaurants Vivace and Ovens can provide chic sustenance.

Tucson Mall (⊠ 4500 N. Oracle Rd., at Wetmore Rd., Central ☎ 520/293–7330), an indoor mall on the west side, has Robinsons-May, Dillard's, Macy's, Mervyn's, Sears, JCPenney, and more than 200 specialty shops. For tasteful Southwestern-style T-shirts, belts, jewelry, and prickly-pear candies, try Señor Coyote, Morning Singer, or any of the other shops on Arizona Avenue, a section of the first floor that's devoted to regional items.

Specialty Shops

ART GALLERIES If you're seeking out work by regional artists, you might want to drive down to Tubac, a community 45 mi south of Tucson (⇨ Sidetrips Near Tucson). *Art Life in Southern Arizona* (⌖ Box 36777, Tucson 85740 ☎ 520/797–1271 ⊕ artlifearizona.com), published annually, lists galleries and artists statewide.

Dinnerware Contemporary Arts (⊠ 210 N. 4th Ave., Downtown ☎ 520/792–4503), a nonprofit, membership gallery, focuses on artists of Southern Arizona in various media, including painting, sculpture, digital art, and furniture.

Etherton Gallery (⊠ 135 S. 6th Ave., Downtown ☎ 520/624–7370) specializes in photography but also represents artists in other media.

Gallery Row at El Cortijo (⊠ 3001 E. Skyline Dr., Foothills ☎ 520/298–0390) is a complex of nine galleries that collectively represent regional and national artists working in all media, including Native American, Western and contemporary painting, craft, and jewelry. The highly regarded **Rosequist Galleries** (☎ 520/577–8107) is the oldest in town.

Obsidian Gallery (⊠ St. Phillip's Plaza, 4340 N. Campbell Ave., Suite 90, Central ☎ 520/577–3598) has exquisite glass, ceramic, and jewelry pieces.

Philabaum Contemporary Glass (✉ St. Phillip's Plaza, 4280 N. Campbell Ave., Suite 105, Foothills ☎ 520/299–1939) sells magnificent handblown vases, artwork, table settings, and the jewelry of Tom Philabaum and others.

BOOKS **Antigone** (✉ 411 N. 4th Ave., University ☎ 520/792–3715) specializes in books by and about women and also sells creative feminist cards and T-shirts.

Barnes & Noble (✉ 5130 E. Broadway Blvd., Eastside ☎ 520/512–1166 ✉ Foothills Mall, 7325 N. La Cholla Blvd., Northwest ☎ 520/742–6402) is capacious but comfortable, with a well-stocked children's section.

Bookman's (✉ 1930 E. Grant Rd., Central ☎ 520/325–5767 ✉ 3733 W. Ina Rd., Northwest ☎ 520/579–0303 ✉ 6230 E. Speedway Blvd., Eastside ☎ 520/748–9555) carries an eclectic selection of used and new books, music, magazines, and software in three spacious locations. The **Book Stop** (✉ 2504 N. Campbell Ave., Central ☎ 520/326–6661) is a wonderful browsing place for used and out-of-print books.

Borders Books and Music (✉ Park Place Mall, 5870 E. Broadway Blvd., Eastside ☎ 520/584–0111 ✉ 4235 N. Oracle Rd., Northwest ☎ 520/292–1331) has a vast selection of books and music, plus an above-average café.

Clues Unlimited (✉ Historic Broadway Village, 3000 E. Broadway Blvd., Central ☎ 520/326–8533) specializes in mysteries.

Crescent Tobacco and Newsstand (✉ 200 E. Congress St., Downtown ☎ 520/622–1559 ✉ 7037 E. Tanque Verde Rd., Northeast ☎ 520/296–3102) carries hundreds of daily newspapers and magazines from around the world, not to mention imported cigars and cigarettes.

Reader's Oasis (✉ 3400 E. Speedway Blvd., Central ☎ 520/319–7887), an independent bookstore, has frequent author readings and book signings. Some used books are also available.

Tucson's Map and Flag Center (✉ 3239 N. 1st Ave., Central ☎ 520/887–4234) is the place to pick up your topographical maps and specialty guides to Arizona.

Waldenbooks (✉ Tucson Mall, 4500 N. Oracle Rd., Central ☎ 520/293–6799) is handy if you need to take a break from souvenir shopping at the mall.

CACTI **B&B Cactus Farm** (✉ 11550 E. Speedway Blvd., Eastside ☎ 520/721–4687), which you'll pass en route to Saguaro National Park East, has a huge selection of cacti and other succulents and will ship anywhere in the country.

GIFTS **Del Sol** (✉ 435 N. 4th Ave., University ☎ 520/628–8765 ✉ 6536 E. Tanque Verde Rd., Eastside ☎ 520/298–3398) specializes in Mexican folk art, jewelry, and Southwest-style clothing.

Mrs. Tiggy Winkle's Toys (✉ 4811 E. Grant Rd., Central ☎ 520/326–0188) will probably remind you of the toy shops of the past—only better—with many items that are hard to find in the big-box toy stores.

United Nations Center (✉ 6242 E. Speedway Blvd., Central ☎ 520/881–7060) sells reasonably priced ethnic jewelry, apparel, and crafts from all over the world.

JEWELRY **Abbott Taylor** (✉ El Mercardo, 6372 E. Broadway Blvd., Eastside ☎ 520/745–5080) creates custom designs in diamonds and other precious stones.

Beth Friedman (✉ Joesler Village, 1865 E. River Rd., Suite 121, Foothills ☎ 520/577–6858) sells unsurpassed designs in silver and semiprecious stones. Her store also carries an eclectic selection of ladies' apparel, fine art, and home furnishings.

Patania's Originals (✉ 3000 E. Broadway Blvd., Central ☎ 520/795–0086), formerly the Thunderbird Shop, is one of the best-known jewelers in the Southwest. The Patania family has been creating unique designs in silver, gold, and platinum here and in Santa Fe for three generations. The shop is 1 mi east of the El Con mall.

Turquoise Door (✉ St. Phillip's Plaza, 4340 N. Campbell Ave., Foothills ☎ 520/299–7787) creates innovative jewelry that amounts to a modern take on classic Southwestern designs.

MEXICAN FURNISHINGS **Antigua de Mexico** (✉ 3235 W. Orange Grove Rd., Northwest ☎ 520/742–7114) sells well-made furniture and crafts that you are not likely to find elsewhere in town.

Tres Encantos (✉ 6538 E. Tanque Verde Rd., Suite 110, Eastside ☎ 520/885–4522) carries hand-carved furniture and decorative accent pieces.

NATIVE AMERICAN ARTS & CRAFTS San Xavier Plaza, across from San Xavier mission and also part of the Tohono O'odham reservation, is a good place to find vendors and stores selling the work of this and other area tribes.

Bahti Indian Arts (✉ St. Philip's Plaza, 4300 N. Campbell Ave., Foothills ☎ 520/577–0290) is owned and run by Mark Bahti, whose father, Tom, literally wrote the book on Native American art, including an early definitive work on katsinas. The store sells high-quality jewelry, pottery, rugs, art, and more.

Grey Dog Trading Company (✉ Plaza Palomino, 2970 N. Swan Rd., Central ☎ 520/881–6888) has an ample selection of jewelry, katsinas, weaving, pottery, and Zuni fetishes.

Kaibab Courtyard Shops (✉ 2837 N. Campbell Ave., Central ☎ 520/795–6905) sells traditional Native American arts, along with Mexican imports and Nambé dinnerware.

Silverbell Trading (✉ Casa Adobes Plaza, 7007 N. Oracle Rd., Northwest ☎ 520/797–6852) carries the work of local and regional artists.

WESTERN WEAR Tucsonans who wear Western gear keep it simple for the most part—jeans, a Western shirt, maybe boots. This ain't Santa Fe.

Arizona Hatters (✉ 3600 N. 1st Ave., Central ☎ 520/292–1320) can fit you for that Stetson you've always wanted.

Corral Western Wear (✉ 4525 E. Broadway Blvd., Eastside ☎ 520/322–6001) sells shirts, hats, belts, jewelry, and boots, catering to both urban and authentic cowboys and cowgirls.

Stewart Boot Manufacturing (✉ 30 W. 28th St., South Tucson ☎ 520/622–2706) has been making handmade leather boots since the 1940s.

Western Warehouse (✉ 3030 E. Speedway Blvd., Central ☎ 520/327–8005 ✉ 3719 N. Oracle Rd., Northwest ☎ 520/293–1808 ✉ 6701 E. Broadway Blvd., Eastside ☎ 520/885–4385) is the place if you want to go where native Tucsonans shop for their everyday Western duds.

SIDE TRIPS NEAR TUCSON

Interstate 19 heads south from Tucson to Tubac, carrying with it history buffs, bird-watchers, hikers, art enthusiasts, duffers, and shoppers. The road roughly follows the Camino Real (King's Road), which the conquistadors and missionaries traveled from Mexico up to what was once the northernmost portion of New Spain.

The Asarco Mineral Discovery Center

34 *15 mi south of Tucson off Interstate 19.*

Operated by the American Smelting and Refining Co. (ASARCO), this facility is designed to elucidate the importance of mining to your everyday life. Exhibits in two connected buildings include a walk-through model of an ore crusher, video stations that explain refining processes, and a film on extraction of minerals from the earth. The big draw, however, is the yawning open pit of the Mission Mine, some 2 mi long and 1¾ mi wide because a lot of earth has to be torn up to extract the 1% that is copper. It's an impressive sight, although it doesn't exactly bolster the case the center tries to make about how environmentally conscious mining has become. Tours of the Mission Mine open pit, which take about one hour, leave the center on the half hour; the last one starts at 3:30. ⊠ *1421 W. Pima Mine Rd.* ☎ *520/625–0879* ☐ *$6* ☉ *Tues.–Sat. 9–5.*

Titan Missile Museum

35 *25 mi south of Tucson, off Interstate 19.*

During the cold war, Tucson was ringed by 18 of the 54 Titan II missiles that existed in the United States. After the SALT II treaty with the Soviet Union was signed in 1979, this was the only missile-launch site left intact. Now a National Historic Landmark, the Titan Missile Museum makes for a sobering visit. Guided tours last about an hour and take you down 55 steps into the command post, where a ground crew of four lived and waited. Among the fascinating sights is the 103-foot, 165-ton, two-stage liquid-fuel rocket. Now empty, it originally held a nuclear warhead with 214 times the explosive power of the bomb that destroyed Hiroshima. Guided tours run every half hour. ⊠ *1580 W. Duval Mine Rd. (I–19, Exit 69)* ☎ *520/625–7736* ⊕ *www.pimaair.org* ☐ *$8.50* ☉ *Daily 9–5 (last tour departs at 4).*

Madera Canyon

36 *61½ mi southeast of Tucson; Exit 63 off Interstate 19, then east on White House Canyon Road for 12½ mi (it turns into Madera Canyon Road).*

This is where the Coronado National Forest meets the Santa Rita Mountains—among them Mt. Wrightson, the highest peak in southern Arizona, at 9,453 feet. With approximately 200 mi of scenic trails, the Madera Canyon recreation area is a favorite destination for hikers. Higher elevations and thick pine cover make it especially popular with Tucsonans looking to escape the summer heat. Trails vary from a steep trek up Mount

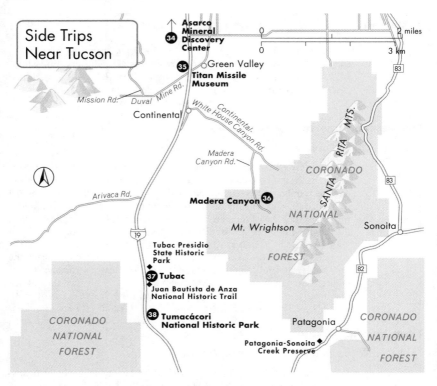

Side Trips Near Tucson

Baldy to a paved, wheelchair-accessible path. Birders flock here year-round; about 400 avian species have been spotted in the area. The small, volunteer-run visitor center is open only on weekends. Nearby, the Bog Springs Campground has 13 sites, with toilets, potable water, and grills, available on a first-come, first-served basis. The cost is $10 per vehicle per night. ⊠ *Madera Canyon Rd., Madera Canyon* ☎ *520/ 281–2296 Nogales Ranger District office* ⊕ *www.fs.fed.us/r3/coronado* ☜ *Donation requested* ⊙ *Daily.*

Tubac

★ ③⑦ *45 mi south of Tucson at Exit 40 off Interstate 19.*

Established in 1726, Tubac is the site of the first European settlement in Arizona. A year after the Pima Indian uprising in 1851, a military garrison was established here to protect early Spanish settlers, missionaries, and peaceful Native American converts of the nearby Tumacácori Mission from further attack. It was from here that Juan Bautista de Anza led 240 colonists across the desert—the expedition resulted in the founding of San Francisco in 1776. Arizona's first newspaper, the *Weekly Arizonian,* was printed here in 1859, and in 1860 Tubac was the largest town in Arizona. Today, the quiet little town is a popular art colony. More than 80 shops sell such crafts as carved wooden furniture, hand-thrown pottery, delicately painted tiles, and silk-screen fabrics (note that many shops are closed on Monday). You can also find Mexican pottery and trinkets without having to cross the border. The annual **Tubac Festival of the Arts** has been held in February for more than 30 years.

There's an archaeological display of portions of the original 1752 fort at the **Tubac Presidio State Historic Park and Museum** in the center of town. In addition to the visitor center and the adjoining museum, which has detailed the history of the early colony, the park includes Tubac's 1885 schoolhouse and a pleasant picnic area. ⊠ *Presidio Dr.* ☎ *520/398–2252* ⊕ *www.pr.state.az.us* 🔳 *$3* ⊙ *Daily 8–5.*

Where to Stay & Eat

¢ ✕ **Tubac Deli & Coffee Co.** Smack in the middle of Tubac village, this pleasant little eatery serves generous sandwiches, salads, and soups—as well as cappuccinos and pastries—every day until 4 PM. ⊠ *6 Plaza Rd.* ☎ *520/398–3330* 🚫 *No credit cards* ⊙ *No dinner.*

$$ ✕🏠 **Amado Territory Inn and Cafe.** Although this quiet, friendly B&B is directly off the highway frontage road, it feels worlds away. Part of a ranch complex that includes a plant nursery, a gem and mineral shop, an antiques store, and an artist's studio, the inn resembles a late-19th-century ranch house, but a soaring ceiling and contemporary Southwestern art make the interior distinctly modern. Rooms are furnished with handcrafted Mexican pieces, and some have a view of the garden and the Santa Rita Mountains. Breakfast is included at the inn (try the huevos rancheros); next door, the Amado Cafe serves savory Greek-style pasta, chicken, and fish specialties for lunch and dinner. ⊠ *3001 E. Frontage Rd., off Exit 48 of I–19* 🗀 *Box 81, Amado 85645* ☎ *520/398–8684 or 888/398–8684* 🖶 *520/398–8186* ⊕ *www.amado-territory-inn.com* 🛏 *9 rooms, 2 suites* 🍴 *Restaurant, putting green, meeting rooms; no room phones, no room TVs, no smoking* 🚫 *MC, V* ⍾ *BP.*

$$ 🏠 **Tubac Country Inn.** Down the lane from the shops and eateries of Tubac village, you'll find this charming two-story inn. Tastefully decorated in contemporary Southwest style, all rooms and suites have kitchenettes (stocked with coffee, tea, and cider mix). The common outdoor space is a tranquil desert flower garden with willow chairs, a Mexican fireplace, and hammocks. Each morning a breakfast basket of muffins, cheeses, fruits, and juice is brought to your door. ⊠ *13 Burruel St., Tubac 85646* ☎ *520/398–3178* 🖶 *520/398–0801* ⊕ *www.tubaccountryinn. com* 🛏 *3 rooms, 2 suites* 🍴 *Microwaves, refrigerators, cable TV; no room phones, no smoking* 🚫 *AE, D, MC, V* ⊙ *Closed July and Aug.* ⍾ *BP.*

en route   You can tread the same road as the conquistadors: the first 4½ mi of the **Juan Bautista de Anza National Historic Trail** (⊕ www.nps. gov/juba) from Tumacácori to Tubac were dedicated in 1992. You'll have to cross the Santa Cruz River (which is usually pretty low) three times to complete the hike, and the path is rather sandy, but it's a pleasant journey along the tree-shaded banks of the river.

Tumacácori National Historic Park

㊳ *3 mi south of Tubac; Exit 29 off Interstate 19.*

The site where Tumacácori National Historic Park now stands was visited by missionary Father Eusebio Francisco Kino in 1691, but the Jesuits didn't build a church here until 1751. You can still see some ruins of this simple structure, but the main attraction is the mission of San José de Tumacácori, built by the Franciscans around 1799–1803. A combination of circumstances—Apache attacks, a bad winter, and Mexico's withdrawal of funds and priests—caused the remaining inhabitants to flee in 1848. Persistent rumors of wealth left behind by both the Franciscans and the Jesuits led treasure seekers to pillage the site; it still bears those scars. The site was finally protected in 1908, when it became a national monument.

Information about the mission and the Anza trail is available at the visitor center, and guided tours are offered daily (more in winter than in summer). A small museum displays some of the mission's artifacts, and sometimes fresh tortillas are made on a wood-fire stove in the courtyard. In addition to a Christmas Eve celebration, costumed historical high masses are held at Tumacácori in spring and fall. An annual fiesta the first weekend of December has arts and crafts and food booths. ✉ *I–19, Exit 29, Tumacácori* ☎ *520/398–2341* ⊕ *www.nps.gov/tuma* ⌨ *$3* ☉ *Daily 8–5.*

Where to Stay

$$ 🏨 **Rio Rico Resort.** Too close to Tucson to be a real getaway, this ridgetop hotel and conference center languished for many years before finally coming into its own. Renovated in 2004, the three-story complex has an upscale restaurant, a Western saloon, and comfortable rooms. Most people come for the golf course, designed by Robert Trent Jones Sr.; the splendid views; and the isolation. Nogales, Mexico, is a short drive south. ✉ *1069 Camino Caralampi, off I–19 at Rio Rico Rd. (Exit 17), 85648* ☎ *520/281–1901 or 800/288–4746* 🖷 *520/281–7132* ⊕ *www.riorricoresort.com* ⇆ *166 rooms, 14 suites* ⚒ *Restaurant, refrigerators, cable TV with movies, 18-hole golf course, 4 tennis courts, pool, gym, outdoor hot tub, sauna, hiking, horseback riding, bar, laundry service, business services, meeting rooms, nosmoking rooms* ▤ *AE, D, MC, V.*

TUCSON A TO Z

To research prices, get advice from other travelers, and book travel arrangements, visit www.fodors.com.

AIR TRAVEL

Check plane fares carefully when planning your trip. Although you may not want to spend time in Phoenix, sometimes it's cheaper to fly into that city and then take a scenic 2½-hour drive down the Pinal Pioneer Parkway (U.S. 79), or a speedier (by ½-hour) trip on Interstate 10, to Tucson.

⚑ Carriers **Aerocalifornia** ☎ 800/237–6225. **Aeroméxico/Aerolitoral** ☎ 520/294–3070. **Alaska Airlines** ☎ 800/252–7522 ⊕ www.alaskaair.com. **American** ☎ 800/433–7300 ⊕ www.aa.com. **America West** ☎ 800/235–9292 ⊕ www.americawest.com. **Continental** ☎ 800/525–0280 ⊕ www.continental.com. **Delta** ☎ 800/221–1212, 0800/414–767 in the U.K. ⊕ www.delta.com. **Northwest** ☎ 800/225–2525 ⊕ www.nwa.com. **Southwest** ☎ 800/435–9792 ⊕ www.southwest.com. **United** ☎ 800/864–8331 ⊕ www.united.com.

AIRPORTS

Tucson International Airport is 8½ mi south of downtown, west of Interstate 10 off the Valencia exit.

⚑ Tucson International Airport (TUS) ☎ 520/573–8000 ⊕ www.tucsonairport.org.

TRANSFERS Many hotels provide courtesy airport shuttle service; inquire when making reservations.

It makes sense to rent a car at the airport; all the major rental-car agencies—Avis, Budget, Hertz, and National—are represented, along with Alamo, Dollar, and Thrifty. The driving time from the airport to the center of town varies, but it's usually less than half an hour; add 15 minutes during rush hours (7:30 AM–9 AM and 4:30 PM–6 PM). Parking is not a problem in most parts of town.

For $9 to $38, depending on the location, Arizona Stagecoach takes groups and individuals to all parts of Tucson and Green Valley. If you're traveling light and aren't in a hurry, you can take a city Sun Tran bus to central Tucson. Bus 11, which leaves every half hour from a stop at the left of the lower level as you come out of the terminal, goes north on Alvernon Way, and you can transfer to most of the east–west bus lines from this main north–south road; ask the bus driver which one would take you closest to the location you need. You can also transfer to several lines from Bus 6, which leaves less frequently from the same airport location and heads to the Roy Laos center at the south of town.

⚑ Arizona Stagecoach ☎ 520/889–1000. **Sun Tran** ☎ 520/792–9222.

BUS TRAVEL

Buses to Los Angeles, El Paso, Phoenix, Flagstaff, Douglas, and Nogales (Arizona) depart and arrive regularly from Tucson's Greyhound Lines terminal. For travel to Phoenix, Arizona Shuttle Service, Inc., runs express service from three locations in Tucson every hour on the hour, 4 AM to 9 PM every day; the trip takes about 2¼ hours. One-way fare is $24. Call 24 hours in advance for reservations.

⚑ Arizona Shuttle Service, Inc. ☎ 520/795–6771. **Greyhound Lines terminal** ✉ 2 S. 4th Ave., at E. Broadway Blvd., Downtown ☎ 520/792–3475 or 800/229–9424 ⊕ www.greyhound.com.

BUS TRAVEL WITHIN TUCSON

Within the city limits, public transportation, which is geared primarily to commuters, is available through Sun Tran, Tucson's bus system. On weekdays, bus service starts around 5 AM; some lines operate until 10 PM, but most go only until 7 or 8 PM, and weekend service is limited. A one-way ride costs $1; transfers are free, but be sure to request them when you pay your fare, for which exact change is required. An all-day pass costs $2. Those with valid Medicare cards can ride for 40¢. Call for information on Sun Tran bus routes.

The city-run Van Tran has specially outfitted vans for riders with disabilities. Call for information and reservations.
🚌 **Sun Tran** ☎ 520/792-9222. **Van Tran** ☎ 520/620-1234.

CAR RENTALS

You will need a car to get around Tucson and the surrounding area. If you haven't rented a car at the Tucson International Airport, or if you want to save the 10% "airport concession fee" the airport imposes on renters there, several car-rental agencies also have pick-up and drop-off locations in the central, northwest, and east areas of town. In addition, Carefree Rent-a-Car rents reliable used cars at good rates. If you think you might be interested in driving farther into Mexico than Nogales (where you can park on the U.S. side of the border), check in advance to make sure that the rental company will allow this and that you are covered on your rental-insurance policy: many rental-insurance agreements do not cover accidents or thefts that occur outside the United States.
🚌 **Alamo** ☎ 520/573-4740. **Avis** ☎ 520/294-1494. **Budget** ☎ 520/889-8800. **Carefree Rent-a-Car** ☎ 520/790-2655. **Dollar** ☎ 520/573-8486. **Enterprise** ☎ 520/792-1602. **Hertz** ☎ 520/294-7616. **National** ☎ 520/573-8050. **Thrifty** ☎ 520/790-2277.

CAR TRAVEL

From Phoenix, 111 mi northwest, Interstate 10 east is the road that will take you to Tucson. Also a major north–south traffic artery along the west side of town, Interstate 10 has well-marked exits all along the route. At Casa Grande, 70 mi north of Tucson, Interstate 8 connects with Interstate 10, bringing travelers into the area from Yuma and San Diego. From Nogales, 63 mi south on the Mexican border, take Interstate 19 into Tucson.

RULES OF THE ROAD If you drive on Broadway Boulevard or Grant Road, note that the center lanes change from left-turn lanes to through-traffic lanes during rush hour (watch the signage carefully). These are called "suicide lanes" by locals because unwitting drivers wander into them for left turns at the wrong time of day. There's a seat-belt law in the state, as well as one that requires children under the age of four to ride in a secure child-restraint seat.

Don't even think of drinking and driving; if you do, you may spend your vacation in jail. Arizona's strict laws against driving under the influence are strongly enforced.

TRAFFIC Much of the year, traffic in Tucson isn't especially heavy, but during the busiest winter months (December through March), streets in the central area of town can get congested during rush hour, between 4 and 6 PM.

EMERGENCIES

🚌 Ambulance, Fire, Police **Emergency Services** ☎ 911.
🚌 Hospitals **Columbia Northwest Medical Center** ✉ 6200 N. La Cholla Blvd., Northwest ☎ 520/742-9000. **St. Joseph's Hospital** ✉ 350 N. Wilmot Rd., Eastside ☎ 520/873-3000. **Tucson Medical Center** ✉ 5301 E. Grant Rd., Central ☎ 520/327-5461. Uni-

versity Medical Center ⊠ 1501 N. Campbell Ave., University ☎ 520/694-0111; a teaching hospital with a first-rate trauma center.

⊡ Pharmacies **Walgreens 24-Hour Pharmacy** ⊠ 4685 E. Grant Rd., Central ☎ 520/326-4341 ⊠ 7114 N. Oracle Rd., Northwest ☎ 520/297-2826.

LODGING

Several of the larger, more professionally run inns in town have formed Premier Bed & Breakfast Inns of Tucson. Write or call for a brochure.

⊡ **Premier Bed & Breakfast Inns of Tucson** ⊠ 316 E. Speedway Blvd., 85705 ☎ 520/628-1800 or 800/628-5654 🖷 520/792-1880.

SIGHTSEEING TOURS

ADVENTURE &
ECOTOURS

Sunshine Jeep Tours and Trail Dust Adventures arrange trips into the Sonoran Desert outside Tucson in open-air, four-wheel-drive vehicles. Baja's Frontier Tours and Desert Path Tours explore the natural history of Tucson and the surrounding area.

⊡ **Baja's Frontier Tours** ☎ 520/887-2340 or 888/297-2508 ⊕ www.bajasfrontiertours. com. **Desert Path Tours** ☎ 520/327-7235. **Sunshine Jeep Tours** ☎ 520/742-1943 ⊕ www.sunshinejeeptours.com. **Trail Dust Adventures** ☎ 520/747-0323 ⊕ www. traildustadventures.com.

MISSION TOURS

In the spring and fall, those interested in visiting the area's historic missions can contact Kino Mission Tours, which has professional historians and bilingual guides on staff.

⊡ **Kino Mission Tours** ☎ 520/628-1269.

ORIENTATION
TOURS

Great Western Tours takes individuals and groups to such popular sights as Old Tucson, Sabino Canyon, and the Arizona–Sonora Desert Museum; in-depth tours of the city and its neighborhoods are also available. Old Pueblo Tours, with a slightly different itinerary (including "A" Mountain and Mission San Xavier del Bac), provides a fine historical overview of the area. Many tour operators are on limited schedules (or close altogether) during the summer, but Off the Beaten Path Tours has excellent customized excursions year-round throughout the Southwest United States and Mexico.

⊡ **Great Western Tours** ☎ 520/572-1660 ⊕ www.greatwesterntours.com. **Off the Beaten Path Tours** ☎ 520/529-6090. **Old Pueblo Tours** ☎ 520/795-7448.

WALKING TOURS

The friendly, knowledgeable docents of the Arizona Historical Society conduct walking tours of El Presidio neighborhood (departing from the Sosa-Carillo-Fremont House) every Saturday at 10 from November through March; the cost is $5. Old Pueblo Walking Tours offers two-hour walking tours of the downtown historic districts led by Ken Scoville, a living encyclopedia of Tucson's history.

⊡ **Arizona Historical Society** ☎ 520/622-0956. **Old Pueblo Walking Tours** ☎ 520/323-9290.

TAXIS

Taxi rates vary widely; they are unregulated in Arizona. It's always wise to inquire about the cost of a trip before getting into a cab. You shouldn't pay much more than $18 from the airport to central Tucson. Two of the more reliable Tucson cab companies are Allstate Taxi and Yellow Cab, which also operates Fiesta Taxi, whose drivers speak both English and Spanish.

🚹 **Allstate Taxi** ☎ 520/798-1111. **Fiesta Taxi** ☎ 520/622-7777. **Yellow Cab** ☎ 520/624-6611.

TRAIN TRAVEL
Amtrak serves the city with westbound and eastbound trains six times a week.

🚹 **Amtrak** ✉ 400 E. Toole Ave., Downtown ☎ 520/623-4442 or 800/872-7245 ⊕ www.amtrak.com.

VISITOR INFORMATION
🚹 **Metropolitan Tucson Convention and Visitors Bureau** ✉ 110 S. Church Ave., Downtown, 85701 ☎ 520/624-1817 or 800/638-8350 ⊕ www.visittucson.org.

SOUTHERN ARIZONA

7

FOLLOW THE FLOCKS
to Ramsey Canyon Preserve ⇨*p.337*

SWAGGER INTO THE OK CORRAL
at twelve o'clock high ⇨*p.340*

TREK AMID VOLCANIC SPIRES
at Chiricahua National Monument ⇨*p.348*

LEARN TO LOPE
at Grapevine Canyon Ranch ⇨*p.348*

LIFT YOUR CHEEK FOR CAVE KISSES
in Kartchner Caverns State Park ⇨*p.354*

PRACTICE THE ART OF THE DEAL
in the shops of Nogales, Mexico ⇨*p.357*

Updated by
Carrie Miner

SOUTHERN ARIZONA CAN DO little to escape its cliché-ridden image as a landscape of cow skulls, tumbleweeds, dried-up riverbeds, and mother lodes—it doesn't need to. The area that evokes such American dime-novel notions as Indian wars, vast land grants, and savage shoot-'em-ups is not simply another part of the Wild West drunk on romanticized images of its former self; local farmers and ranchers here evoke the self-sufficiency and ruggedness of their pioneer ancestors and revel in the area's rowdy past. Abandoned mining towns and sleepy Western hamlets dot a lonely landscape of rugged rock formations, deep pine forests, dense mountain ranges, and scrubby grasslands.

South of Sierra Vista, just above the Mexican border, a stone marker commemorates the spot where the first Europeans set foot in what is now the United States. In 1540, 80 years before the Pilgrims landed at Plymouth Rock, Spanish conquistador Don Francisco Vásquez de Coronado led one of Spain's largest expeditions from Mexico along the fertile San Pedro River valley, where the little towns of Benson and St. David are found today. They had come north to seek the legendary Seven Cities of Cíbola, where Native American pueblos were rumored to have doors of polished turquoise and streets of solid gold.

The real wealth of the region, however, lay in its rich veins of copper and silver, not tapped until more than 300 years after the Spanish marched on in disappointment. Once word of this cache spread, these parts of the West quickly grew much wilder: fortune seekers who rushed to the region came face-to-face with the Chiricahua Apaches, led by Cochise and Geronimo, while from rugged mountain hideaways Indian warriors battled encroaching settlers and the U.S. Cavalry sent to protect them.

Although the search for mineral booty in southeastern Arizona is much more notorious, the western side of the state wasn't entirely untouched by the rage to plunder the earth. The leaching plant built by the New Cornelia Copper Company in 1917 transformed the sleepy desert community of Ajo into one of the most important mining districts in the state. Interest in going for the gold in California gave rise to the town of Yuma: the Colorado River had to be crossed to get to the West Coast, and Fort Yuma was established in part to protect the Anglo ferry business at a good fording point of the river from Indian competitors. The Yuma tribe lost that battle, but another group of Native Americans, the Tohono O'odham, fared better in this part of the state. Known for a long time as the Papago—or "bean eaters," a name given them by the Spanish—they were deeded a large portion of their ancestral homeland by the U.S. Bureau of Indian Affairs. The largest of their three reservations, stretching across an almost completely undeveloped section of southwestern Arizona, encompasses 2,774,370 acres.

Exploring Southern Arizona

The diverse geography of this region and the driving distances between sights require that you strategize when planning your tour. With Tucson as a starting point, the rolling hills and grasslands of Sonoita and

Numbers in the text correspond to numbers in the margin and on the Southeast Arizona and Southwest Arizona maps.

If you have 2 days

If you only have a short time to explore this region, you'll have to choose whether to tour the eastern or western section of southern Arizona. If you are headed east from Tucson, poke around the town of **Patagonia ②** ▶ and the Patagonia–Sonoita Creek preserve in the morning, and then continue east to **Tombstone ④** in the afternoon. After strolling the shoot-'em-up capital, head south to ▦ **Bisbee ⑤**, a good place to spend the night. Take the mine tour the next morning and devote the afternoon to exploring the shops on Main Street. Another option is to explore **Patagonia ②** and **Sonoita ①** in the morning before heading to ▦ **Nogales ⑬** for a late lunch and an afternoon of shopping in Mexico.

If you're going west, take a leisurely drive to **Kitt Peak National Observatory ⑮**. Stop at the Tohono O'odham Reservation capital, **Sells ⑯**, en route to ▦ **Ajo ⑰**, where you'll sleep. Plan to spend most of the next day hiking or driving around **Organ Pipe Cactus National Monument ⑱**, but set aside a little time to explore the pleasant mining town.

If you have 4 days

Begin your tour in Arizona wine country. First, head to **Patagonia ②** ▶, where you can visit the vineyards around ▦ **Sonoita ①** and Elgin. Stay overnight here or in ▦ **Sierra Vista ③** near Ramsey Canyon, where you're likely to be greeted by hummingbirds in the morning. Head out early for **Tombstone ④** so you can spend the morning exploring the town; in the afternoon head south to see the sights of ▦ **Bisbee ⑤** and stay overnight. Head north the next day to **Chiricahua National Monument ⑦**, hike or drive through the magnificent rock formations, and spend the night in the area. On your way back toward Tucson, stop in Dragoon at **Texas Canyon ⑩** and visit the Amerind Foundation's gallery and museum. A few miles farther west on Interstate 10 is **Benson ⑪**, where you can have lunch and then tour the huge underground world of stalactites and stalagmites in **Kartchner Caverns State Park ⑫**.

If you have 7 days

If you have a week to explore only southern Arizona, follow the four-day southeastern Arizona tour, above, and spend the night in ▦ **Benson ⑪** after your Kartchner Caverns tour. Then set out the next morning on the two-day southwestern Arizona tour, continuing on to ▦ **Yuma ⑲**, especially if desert hiking in Organ Pipe Cactus National Monument isn't to your liking.

Patagonia are little more than an hour away, as are the underground marvels in Kartchner Caverns (to the southeast) and the starry skies above Kitt Peak Observatory (to the southwest). You can explore the Old West of Tombstone, Bisbee, and the surrounding ghost towns in one day, or more leisurely in two. To see hillsides covered with Organ Pipe Cactus National Monument, however, you'll need to drive about three hours southwest to reach the national monument and then take at least a full day to hike or drive around it and the town of Ajo. A trek through the stunning Chiricahua rock formations calls for an overnight stay, since the area is a 2½-hour drive southeast of Tucson; you may wish to make an overnight stop in Texas Canyon or Willcox.

About the Restaurants

In southern Arizona, cowboy fare is more common than haute cuisine. But there are exceptions to the rule, especially in the wine-growing area of Sonoita and in Bisbee, both popular for weekend outings from Tucson. And a region that shares its border with Mexico is bound to have a fair number of good taquerias.

About the Hotels

From historic hotels, bed-and-breakfasts, and guest ranches to Nature Conservancy casitas, southern Arizona has an increasing array of properties that let you lay down your head surrounded by nature and history. Still, it's easy to find the park-your-car-outside-the-room chain-variety lodgings. Prices for the "high" season (winter and spring) tend to be a bit higher than for the "low" season (summer to early fall).

WHAT IT COSTS				
$$$$	**$$$**	**$$**	**$**	**¢**
RESTAURANTS over $30	$20–$30	$12–$20	$8–$12	under $8
HOTELS over $250	$175–$250	$120–$175	$70–$120	under $70

Restaurant prices are per person for a main course at dinner. Hotel prices are for two people in a standard double room in high season, excluding taxes and service charges.

Timing

As you might expect, the desert areas are popular in winter, and the cooler mountain areas are more heavily visited in summer months. Southern Arizona has developed seasonal travel, causing area hotels to adopt "high-season" (winter and spring) and "low-season" (summer and early fall) prices. In general, however, prices tend to be lower here than in the more touristed areas to the north.

SOUTHEAST ARIZONA

From the rugged mountain forests to the desert grasslands of Sierra Vista, the southeast corner of Arizona is one of the state's most scenic regions. Much of this area is part of Cochise County, named in 1881 in honor of the chief of the Chiricahua Apache. Cochise waged war against troops and settlers for 11 years, and he was respected by Indian and non-Indian alike for his integrity and leadership skills. Today Cochise County is dotted by small towns, many of them much smaller—and all much tamer—than they were in their heyday. Cochise County encompasses 6 and part of the 7th of the 12 mountain ranges—including the Huachucas, Mustangs, Whetstones, and Rincons—that compose the 1.7-million-acre Coronado National Forest.

7

Bird-Watching

Southern Arizona is one of the best areas for bird-watching in the United States; nearly 500 species have been spotted in the area. To the east, birders flock to the Patagonia-Sonoita Creek and Ramsey Canyon preserves, the San Pedro Riparian National Conservation Area, the ponds and dry lake beds south of Willcox, and the Portal-Cave Creek area in the Chiricahua Mountains near the New Mexico border. To the west, the Buenos Aires and Imperial national wildlife refuges are among the many places famed for their abundance of avian visitors.

Camping

Sleeping under the vast, starry desert sky reminds you that there are still huge swaths of undeveloped wilderness in the untrammeled southwest. You can find at least 100 camping areas set throughout southern Arizona. Though it can get chilly at night in the desert, the weather's usually good enough year-round to make sleeping out an appealing option. Summer is the time to camp in the state's cooler, higher-altitude campgrounds. Campgrounds in the rural areas of southern Arizona rarely come close to getting full except on holiday weekends, and even then, campers tend to stay close to major cities and towns. Keep in mind that you will find fairly primitive camping conditions (RV hookups are rare). It is advisable to bring your own fresh drinking water and be prepared to carry out what trash you bring in.

Hiking

You can trek under, over, and through dramatic rock formations in both Chiricahua National Monument and the Dragoon Mountains. Grasslands and waterways abound in Nature Conservancy preserves such as Ramsey Canyon, Arivaipa Canyon, the Patagonia-Sonoita Creek Sanctuary, and Muleshoe Ranch. Organ Pipe National Monument offers sweeping vistas of the Sonoran Desert; and hiking trails in the Huachuca, Patagonia, Rincon, and Whetstone mountain ranges afford striking ridgetop views.

Wineries

The term "Arizona wine country" may sound odd, but the soil and climate in the Santa Cruz Valley southeast of Tucson are ideal for growing grapes. Wine grapes first took root in the region 400 years ago, when the Spanish missionaries planted the first vines of "mission" grapes in what is now Arizona for the production of sacramental wine. However, it wasn't until the 1970s that the first commercial vinifera grapes were planted in the region as part of an agricultural experiment conducted by Dr. Gordon Dutt at the University of Arizona. Connoisseurs have debated the merits of the wines produced in this area since 1974, but if you want to decide for yourself, tour some of the region's wineries.

Sonoita

❶ *34 mi southeast of Tucson on Interstate 10 to AZ 83, 57 mi west of Tombstone.*

The grasslands surrounding modern-day Sonoita captured the attention of early Spanish explorers, including Father Eusebio Francisco Kino, who

mapped and claimed the area in 1701. The Tuscan-like beauty of the grasslands framed by jutting mountain ranges has been noticed more recently by Hollywood filmmakers scouting for locations. As you drive along AZ 83 and AZ 82 you might recognize the scenery from the movies filmed here, including *Oklahoma* and *Tin Cup*.

Today, this region is known for its vineyards and wineries as well as for its ranching history. Sonoita, at the junction of AZ 83 and AZ 82, offers restaurants and upscale B&Bs, but it is the nearby wineries that draw the crowds. There are several events at the wineries, including the Blessing of the Vines in the spring and the Harvest Festivals in fall. Summer is also a good time to visit the wineries, where you can sample some of Arizona's vintages and chat with a wine master or local vintner.

To explore the wineries of southern Arizona, head south on AZ 83 from Sonoita and then east on Elgin Road. Most of the growers are in and around the tiny village of Elgin, which is 9 mi southeast of Sonoita. You'll find quite a few wineries as well as several horse farms in this scenic ranching region.

Callaghan Vineyards (✉ 336 Elgin Rd., Elgin ☎ 520/455–5322 ⊕ www. callaghanvineyards.com), which is open Friday through Sunday 11 to

3, produces the best wine in Arizona. Its Buena Suerte ("good luck" in Spanish) Cuvee was named as one of the top wines in the United States by the *Wall Street Journal*. In the town of Elgin, stop in for tastings daily from 10 to 5 at **Village of Elgin Winery** (✉ The Elgin Complex, Upper Elgin Rd., Elgin ☎ 520/455–9309 🌐 www.elginwines.com), one of the largest producers of wines in the state and the home to Tombstone Red, which the winemaker claims is "great with scorpion, tarantula, and rattlesnake meat." **Sonoita Vineyards** (✉ Canelo Rd., 3 mi southwest of town, Elgin ☎ 520/455–5893 🌐 www.sonoitavineyards.com), known for its high-quality reds, offers tours and tastings daily 10 to 4. Originally planted in the early 1970s as an experiment by Dr. Gordon Dutt, former agriculture professor at the University of Arizona, this was the first commercial vineyard in Arizona.

Where to Stay & Eat

$–$$ ✕ **Steak Out Restaurant & Saloon.** A frontier-style design and a weathered-wood exterior help to create the mood at this Western restaurant and bar known for its tasty margaritas and live country music played on weekend evenings. Built and owned by the same family that operates the Sonoita Inn next door, the restaurant serves cowboy fare: mesquite-grilled steaks, ribs, chicken, and fish. ✉ *3235 AZ 82* ☎ *520/455–5205* ▭ *AE, D, DC, MC, V* ⊙ *No lunch weekdays.*

★ **¢–$** ✕ **Café Sonoita.** Like Sonoita itself, the Café Sonoita combines city sophistication with small-town charm. A local favorite, the restaurant also draws day-trippers from Tucson and tourists from afar. The dinner menu, which changes daily, incorporates locally grown produce, local wines, and beers. Be sure to save some room for the café's homemade pies, cheesecakes, and brownies. ✉ *3280 AZ 82* ☎ *520/455–5278* ▭ *MC, V* ⊙ *Closed Sun.–Tues.*

$–$$ 🏨 **Sonoita Inn.** The owner of the Sonoita also owned the Triple Crown–winning racehorse Secretariat. The walls of the inn celebrate Secretariat's career with photos, racing programs, and press clippings. Hardwood floors, colorful woven rugs, and retro-cowboy bedspreads distinguish the spacious rooms, some of which have views of the Santa Rita mountains. The inn is near the intersection of AZ 82 and AZ 83. ✉ *3243 AZ 82* 📫 *Box 99, 85637* ☎ *520/455–5935 or 800/696–1006* 📠 *520/455–5069* 🌐 *www.sonoitainn.com* ⇨ *18 rooms* ♨ *Cable TV, in-room VCRs, some pets allowed (fee)* ▭ *AE, D, MC, V* 🍽 *CP.*

$ 🏨 **Rainbow's End.** An old ranch manager's home atop a hill overlooking the Sonoita countryside is now a B&B furnished in period antiques. Four bedrooms, each with a modern bathroom, share a great room with fireplace and a big kitchen, where guests can assemble their own continental breakfast and snacks (supplied by the hosts, who live in a separate house down the hill). A few stalls at this 64-acre, working horse-breeding ranch are also available for a fee, for those who vacation with their trusty steeds. ✉ *3088 AZ 83* 📫 *Box 717, 85637* ☎ *520/455–0202* 📠 *520/455–0303* 🌐 *www.gaitedmountainhorses.com* ⇨ *4 rooms* ♨ *Dining room, library; no room TVs, no kids under 12, no smoking* ▭ *No credit cards* 🍽 *CP.*

Patagonia

② *12 mi southwest of Sonoita via AZ 82.*

Served by a spur of the Atchison, Topeka, and Santa Fe Railroad, Patagonia was a shipping center for cattle and ore. The town declined after the railroad departed in 1962, and the old depot is now the town hall. Today, art galleries and boutiques coexist with real Western saloons in this tiny, tree-lined village in the Patagonia Mountains. Most of the town's shops and eateries are closed Monday. The surrounding region is a prime birding destination with more than 275 species of birds found around Sonoita Creek.

The **Patagonia Visitors Center** (✉ 307 McKeown Ave. ☎ 520/394–0060 or 888/794–0060 ⊕ www.patagoniaaz.com) is a good first stop for an overview of the region; it's closed on Tuesday. **Mariposa Books & More** (✉ 307 McKeown Ave. ☎ 520/394–9186) shares quarters with the visitor center, and owner Ann Caston offers advice on local adventure and loves to share the region's history with visitors. The shop is closed Tuesday.

At the Nature Conservancy's **Patagonia–Sonoita Creek Preserve**, 1,400 acres of cottonwood-willow riparian habitat are protected along the Patagonia–Sonoita Creek watershed. More than 275 bird species have been sighted here, along with white-tailed deer, javelina, coati mundi, desert tortoise, and snakes. There is a self-guided nature trail; guided walks are given every Saturday at 9 AM along 2 mi of loop trails. Three concrete structures near an elevated berm of the Railroad Trail serve as reminders of the land's former life as a truck farm. To reach the preserve from Patagonia, make a right on 4th Avenue; at the stop sign, turn left onto Blue Haven Road. This paved road soon becomes dirt and leads to the preserve in about 1¼ mi. The admission fee is good for seven days. ✉ *150 Blue Haven Rd.* ☎ *520/394–2400* ⊕ *www.nature.org* 💲 *$5* ⊙ *Apr.–Sept., Wed.–Sun. 6:30–4; Oct.–Mar., Wed.–Sun. 7:30–4.*

Ⓒ Eleven miles south of town, **Patagonia Lake State Park** is the spot for water sports, picnicking, and camping. Formed by the damming of Sonoita Creek, the 265-acre reservoir lures anglers with its largemouth bass, crappie, bluegill, and catfish; it's stocked with rainbow trout in the wintertime. You can rent rowboats, paddleboats, canoes, and camping and fishing gear at the marina. Most swimmers head for Boulder Beach. The entrance fee is good for both Patagonia Lake State Park and for the Sonoita Creek State Natural Area. ✉ *400 Lake Patagonia Rd.* ☎ *520/287–6965* ⊕ *www.pr.state.az.us* 💲 *$7 per vehicle* ⊙ *Visitor center daily 9–4:30, gates closed 10 PM–4 AM.*

Arizona State Parks has designated almost 5,000 acres surrounding Patagonia Lake as **Sonoita Creek State Natural Area.** This project, funded by the Arizona State Parks Heritage Fund (lottery monies) and the State Lake Improvement Fund, offers environmental educational programs and university-level research opportunities. The riparian area is home to giant cottonwoods, willows, sycamores, and mesquites; nesting black hawks; and endangered species. Rangers offers guided birding tours (fee) every Wednesday, Saturday, and Sunday at 9 AM. The entrance fee is good for both Patagonia Lake State Park and for the Sonoita Creek State Natural Area. ⊠ *AZ 82, 5 mi south of town* ☎ *520/287–2791 or 800/285–3703* ⊕ *www.pr.state.az.us* ⊠ *$7 per vehicle.*

Where to Stay & Eat

$–$$ ✕ **Velvet Elvis Pizza Co.** There can't be too many places where you can enjoy a pizza heaped with organic veggies, a crisp salad of organic greens tossed with homemade dressing, and freshly pressed juice (try the beet, apple, and lime juice concoction), organic wine, and microbrewed and imported beer while surrounded by images of Elvis *and* the Virgin Mary. Owner Cecilia San Miguel uses a 1930s dough recipe for the restaurant's delightful crust, and you can pick up some pizza sauce in the gift shop if you want to try your hand at pizza-making at home. They also have fabulous fruit pies for dessert. ⊠ *292 Naugle Ave.* ☎ *520/394–2102* ⊕ *www.velvetelvispizza.com* ⊟ *MC, V* ⊘ *Closed Mon.–Wed.*

¢–$$ ✕ **Gathering Grounds.** This colorful little café and espresso bar serves healthful breakfasts and imaginative soups, salads, and sandwiches through the late afternoon. Whole-grain muffins and organically grown fruits and veggies make for a great repast of earthy comfort food. ⊠ *319 McKeown Ave.* ☎ *520/394–2097* ⊟ *MC, V* ⊘ *No dinner Mon.–Thurs. and Sun.*

$ ✕ **Wagon Wheel Saloon.** The Wagon Wheel's restaurant, serving ribs, steaks, and burgers, is a more recent development, but the cowboy bar, with its neon beer signs and mounted moose head, has been around since the early 1900s. This is where every Stetson-wearing ranch hand in the area comes to listen to the country jukebox and down a longneck, maybe accompanied by some jalapeño poppers (deep-fried hot peppers stuffed with cream cheese). ⊠ *400 W. Naugle Ave.* ☎ *520/394–2433* ⊟ *AE, MC, V.*

⊙ $$$$ ▦ **Circle Z Ranch.** Rimmed by giant sycamore, ash, and cottonwood trees and surrounded by the Patagonia–Sonoita Creek Preserve, this guest ranch has served as a setting in the movie *Red River* and in several episodes of *Gunsmoke*. Rooms in the adobe-style buildings have hardwood floors and area rugs, king-size or twin beds, and antique Monterrey wooden chests. Meals are prepared to suit individual tastes, which might explain why more than 60% of business here comes from repeat customers. Riders from beginners through advanced can be accommodated on adventurous, scenic trails. All meals, riding, and amenities are included. There are discounted rates for children ages 5–17; children under 5 are not allowed to ride. ⊠ *AZ 82, 4 mi southwest of town* ⊡ *Box 194, 85624* ☎ *520/394–2525 or 888/854–2525* ⊕ *www.circlez.com* ⊄ *24 rooms* ⚘ *Dining room, tennis court, pool, billiards, hiking, horseback riding, Ping-Pong, no smoking rooms; no a/c, no room phones, no room TVs* ⊟ *MC, V* ⊘ *Closed mid-May–Oct.* ❙⊙❙ *FAP.*

$ ▦ **Duquesne House Bed & Breakfast/Gallery.** The rooms of this corrugated tin–roof adobe B&B, built as a miner's boardinghouse at the turn of the 20th century, have been decorated with a wonderfully whimsical hand by artist Regina Medley. Western-period furniture collected in the Patagonia area fills the house and the four high-ceilinged suites, each with its own private entrance. Breakfast is served in your room, on the flower-filled screened porch, or in the Santa Fe–style great room. ⊠ *357*

Duquesne Ave. ⊕ *Box 772, 85624* ☏ *520/394–2732* ➪ *4 suites* ⊘ *No room TVs* ⊟ *No credit cards* ⦿ *BP.*

¢ ⊞ **Stage Stop Inn.** Old territorial appearance notwithstanding, the building isn't historic and the rooms are standard motel issue, but this is still a decent place to lay your head for the night. The public areas have character, the center-of-town location is prime, and the price is right. ✉ *303 W. McKeown Ave.* ⊕ *Box 777, 85624* ☏ *520/394–2211 or 800/923–2211* ⎙ *520/394–2212* ➪ *43 rooms* ⊘ *Restaurant, cable TV, pool, lounge* ⊟ *AE, D, DC, MC, V.*

CAMPING ⌂ **Patagonia Lake Campground.** This civilized campground in Patago-
¢ nia Lake State Park has a marina and even some boat-camping sites. Be aware that campsites do fill up quickly—plus, you can't make reservations. ⊘ *Flush toilets, partial hookups (electric and water), dump station, drinking water, showers, grills, picnic tables, public telephone, general store, swimming (lake),* ➪ *72 tent sites, 34 RV sites, 12 boat sites* ✉ *AZ 82, 4 mi southeast of town* ☏ *602/542–4174 or 800/285–3703* ⊕ *www.pr.state.az.us* ✆ *Tent site $15, RV site $22* ⌕ *Reservations not accepted* ⊟ *MC, V* ⊙ *Open year-round.*

Shopping

Patagonia is quickly turning into a shopping destination in its own right. Unlike the trendy shopping in nearby Tubac, the stores here have reasonable prices in addition to small-town charm. Some of the artist spaces are open only by appointment. Native American flute maker Odell Borg owns **High Spirits, Inc.** (✉ 714 Red Rock Ave. ☏ 520/394–2900 or 800/394–1523 ⊕ www.highspirits.com). By appointment only, you can also see the vivid clay pieces created by Martha Kelly at **Shooting Star Pottery** (✉ 370 Smelter Ave. ☏ 520/394–2752). **Kazzam Nature Center** (✉ 348 Naugle Ave. ☏ 520/394–2823 ⊕ www.kazzam.com) stocks nature books, birding supplies, and gardening items. **Global Arts Gallery** (✉ 315 McKeown Ave. ☏ 520/394–0077) showcases everything from local art and antiques to Native American jewelry and Middle Eastern rugs to exotic musical instruments. **Painted House Studio** (✉ 355 McKeown Ave. ☏ 520/394–2740) has a vibrant, creative collection of hand-painted pieces including chairs, hutches, bowls, pillows, and birdhouses. The studio is open by appointment on weekdays.

Sierra Vista

❸ *42 mi southeast of Patagonia via AZ 82 to AZ 90.*

Sierra Vista grew up as a characterless military town on the outskirts of Fort Huachuca. At 4,620 feet above sea level, Sierra Vista and the surrounding area do have the distinct benefit of a temperate climate year-round. Although there isn't much to do in town, Sierra Vista does serve as a good base from which to explore the more scenic areas that surround it. There are a few fast-food and chain restaurants for your basic dining needs, and any one of the more than 1,100 rooms in area hotels, motels, and B&Bs can shelter you for the night.

Fort Huachuca, headquarters of the army's Global Information Systems Command, is the last of the great Western forts still in operation. It dates back to 1877, when the Buffalo Soldiers (yes, Bob Marley fans—*those* Buffalo Soldiers), the first all-black regiment in the U.S. forces, came to aid settlers battling invaders from Mexico, Indian tribes reluctant to give up their homelands, and assorted American desperadoes on the lam from the law back East. Three miles from the fort's main gate are the **Fort Huachuca museums.** A late-19th-century bachelor officers' quarters houses the **Fort Huachuca Museum.** The museum and its annex across the street provide a fascinating record of military life on the frontier. Another half block south, the **U.S. Army Intelligence Museum** focuses on America intelligence operations from the Apache Scouts through Desert Storm. Code machines, code books, surveillance drones, decoding devices, and other intelligence gathering equipment are on display. Enter the main gate of Fort Huachuca on AZ 90, west of Sierra Vista. You will need your driver's license, vehicle registration, and proof of insurance to obtain a pass to get on base. ⊠ *Grierson St, off AZ 90, west of Sierra Vista., Fort Huachuca* ☎ *520/533–5736* ⊕ *huachuca-www.army. mil* ⌑ *Free* ☉ *Weekdays 9–4, weekends 1–4.*

☁ Those driving to **Coronado National Memorial,** dedicated to Francisco Vásquez de Coronado, will see many of the same stunning vistas of Arizona and Mexico the conquistador saw when he trod this route in 1540 seeking the mythical Seven Cities of Cíbola. It's a little more than 3 mi via a dirt road from the visitor center to Montezuma Pass, and another ½ mi on foot to the top of the nearly 7,000-foot Coronado Peak, where the views are best. Other trails include Joe's Canyon Trail, a steep 3-mi route (one-way) down to the visitor center, and Miller Peak Trail, 12 mi round-trip to the highest point in the Huachuca Mountains (Miller Peak is 9,466 feet). Kids ages 5 to 12 can participate in the memorial's Junior Ranger program, explore Coronado Cave, and dress up in replica Spanish armor or missionary robes. The turnoff for the monument is 16 mi south of Sierra Vista on AZ 92; the visitor center is 5 mi in. ⊠ *4101 E. Montezuma Canyon Rd., Hereford* ☎ *520/366–5515* ⊕ *www.nps.gov/coro* ⌑ *Free* ☉ *Visitor center daily 9–5.*

Ramsey Canyon Preserve, managed by the Nature Conservancy, marks the convergence of two mountain and desert systems: this spot is the northernmost limit of the Sierra Madre and the southernmost limit of the Rockies, and it's at the edge of the Chihuahuan and Sonoran deserts. The diversity of the terrain, as well as the presence of the fresh water of the San Pedro River, fosters birdlife. Rare avian species, including the elegant trogon, nest here between April and October, and 14 species of hummingbird come to the area—more varieties than anywhere else in the United States. Stop at the visitor center for maps and books on the area's natural history, flora, and fauna. To get here, take AZ 92 south from Sierra Vista for 6 mi, turn right on Ramsey Canyon Road, and then go 4 mi to the preserve entrance. ⊠ *27 Ramsey Canyon Rd., Hereford* ☎ *520/378–2785* ⊕ *www.nature.org* ⌑ *$5* ☉ *Mar.–Oct., daily 8–5, Nov.–Feb., daily 9–4.*

off the
beaten
path

SAN PEDRO RIPARIAN NATIONAL CONSERVATION AREA – The San Pedro River, partially rerouted underground by an 1887 earthquake, may not look like much for most of the year, but it sustains an impressive array of flora and fauna. In order to maintain this fragile creek-side ecosystem, a 56,000-acre area along the river (extending about 40 mi north between the Mexican border and St. David) was designated a protected riparian area in 1988. (About 70% to 80% of the state's wildlife depends on riparian habitats, which now constitute only 0.5% of Arizona's land.) More than 350 species of birds come here, as well as 82 mammal species and 45 reptiles and amphibians. Forty thousand years ago, this was the domain of woolly mammoths and mastodons: many of the huge skeletons in Washington's Smithsonian Institute and New York's Museum of Natural History came from the massive fossil pits in the area. As evidenced by a number of small, unexcavated ruins, the migratory Indian tribes who passed through centuries later also found this valley hospitable, in part because of its many useful plants. Information, guided tours, books, and gifts are available from the volunteer staff at San Pedro House, a visitor center operated by Friends of the San Pedro River. ⊠ *San Pedro House, 9800 AZ 90* ☎ *520/458–3559 Sierra Vista BLM office* ⊕ *www.az.blm.gov* ⊡ *Free* ☉ *Visitor center daily 9:30–4:30, conservation area daily sunrise–sunset.*

Where to Stay & Eat

$–$$$ ✕ **The Outside Inn.** The large, airy dining room here is decked out in green and white; meals are served with a casual flair. The Outside Inn serves salads, sandwiches, and burgers for lunch and steak, chicken, seafood, veal, and lamb for dinner. The prime rib is delicious, but it is offered only on Friday and Saturday nights. ⊠ *4907 S. AZ 92* ☎ *520/378–4645* ▱ *AE, MC, V* ☉ *Closed Sun.*

★ $$–$$$ ⌂ **Ramsey Canyon Inn Bed & Breakfast.** The Ramsey Canyon Preserve is a bird haven, and the nearby Ramsey Canyon Inn is a bird-watcher's heaven. There are three housekeeping apartments and six guest rooms, named for the hummingbirds that visit the inn's feeders and garden flowers. The furnishings are antique, and original watercolors of hummingbirds adorn the walls. Innkeeper Donna Branum serves such breakfast treats as French toast stuffed with cream cheese and nuts and topped with a cranberry sauce, as well as homemade pie in the afternoon. Children under 16 aren't allowed to stay in the inn, but they are welcome in the housekeeping suites across the creek. Reserve in advance during the busy spring season. There's a two-night minimum from March through September. ⊠ *29 Ramsey Canyon Rd., Hereford 85615* ☎ *520/378–3010* ⎙ *520/378–0487* ⊕ *www.ramseycanyoninn.com* ▱ *6 rooms, 3 suites* ♢ *Some kitchens; no a/c in some rooms, no phones in some rooms, no room TVs, no smoking* ▱ *MC, V* ⊺○⊺ *BP.*

$$–$$$ ⌂ **Windemere Hotel & Conference Center.** This large hotel complex, across from the area's sprawling shopping mall, is on AZ 92 in what used to be the eastern outskirts of Sierra Vista but is now a rapidly growing commercial corridor. Despite all this development, it's not uncommon to see roadrunners dashing about the hotel grounds. The three-story hotel has large, comfortable rooms, and most offer sweeping views of the nearby Huachuca Mountains. Rates include access to a nearby health club and evening cocktails. ⊠ *2047 S. AZ 92, 85635* ☎ *520/459–5900 or 800/825–4656* ⎙ *520/458–1347* ⊕ *www.windemerehotel.com* ▱ *149 rooms,*

3 suites ⅃ *Restaurant, in-room data ports, microwaves, refrigerators, cable TV with movies and video games, pool, hot tub, lounge, dry cleaning, laundry facilities, laundry service, business services, meeting rooms, some pets allowed, no-smoking rooms* ⊟ *AE, D, DC, MC, V* ⵔ◎ⵔ *BP.*

$$ ⛫ **Casa de San Pedro.** Bird-watchers are drawn to this contemporary hacienda-style B&B abutting the San Pedro Riparian National Conservation Area, and the hosts do everything they can to accommodate them—the computer in the high-ceilinged common room even has Robert Tory Peterson software that guests can use to identify the birds spotted through the picture windows. A number of hiking trails pass behind the house, and regular weekend birding courses and tours are offered. Each of the bright and modern rooms has its own entrance, and handcrafted wooden furnishings from northern Mexico lend local character. ✉ *8933 S. Yell La., Hereford 85615* ☎ *520/366–1300 or 888/ 257–2050* 🖷 *520/366–0701* ⊕ *www.bedandbirds.com* ⵔ⵿ *10 rooms* ⅃ *BBQs, horseshoes, library; no room phones, no room TVs, no kids under 12* ⊟ *AE, D, MC, V* ⵔ◎ⵔ *BP.*

CAMPING
¢ ⛰ **Ramsey Vista.** Though not easy to reach—you drive up the side of a mountain on an unpaved and winding road to an elevation of 7,400 feet— this National Forest Service campground is never crowded and is well worth the trip. The birding is excellent, and you are likely to see coati mundi, javelina, and deer. Go 7 mi south of Sierra Vista on AZ 92, then turn on Carr Canyon Road, and go 10 mi farther west. RVs are not allowed on this road. ⅃ *Pit toilets, fire pits, picnic tables* ⵔ⵿ *8 sites* ✉ *Carr Canyon Rd.* ☎ *520/670–4552 or 520/378–0311* ⊕ *www.fs.fed. us/r3/coronado* ⵺ *$10 per night* ⛆ *Reservations not accepted* ⊙ *Open year-round, weather permitting.*

Tombstone

❹ *28 mi northeast of Sierra Vista via AZ 90, 24 mi south of Benson via AZ 80.*

It's hard to imagine now, but Tombstone, headquarters for most of the area's gamblers and gunfighters, was once bigger than San Francisco. The legendary headquarters of Wild West rowdies, Tombstone was part of an area called Goose Flats in the late 1800s and was prone to attack by nearby Apache tribesmen. Ed Schieffelin, an intrepid prospector, wasn't discouraged by those who cautioned that "all you'll find there is your tombstone." In 1877 he struck one of the West's richest veins of silver in the tough old hills and gave the town its name as an ironic "I told you so." He called the silver mine Lucky Cuss, figuring that he fit the description himself.

The promise of riches attracted all types of folks, including outlaws. Soon gambling halls, saloons, and houses of prostitution sprang up all along Allen Street. In 1881 the Earp family and Doc Holliday battled to the death with the Clanton boys at the famous shoot-out at the OK Corral. Over the past century, scriptwriters and storytellers have done much to rewrite the exact details of the confrontation, but it's a fact that the town was the scene of several gunfights in the 1880s. On Sunday, you can witness replays of some of these on Allen Street.

Tombstone's rough-and-ready heyday was popularized by Hollywood in the 1930s and capitalized on by the local tourist industry in the decades that followed. "The town too tough to die" (it survived two major fires, an earthquake, the closing of the mines, and the moving of the county seat to Bisbee) was also a cultural center, and many of its original buildings remain intact.

Allen Street, the town's main drag, is lined with restaurants and curio shops. Many of the street's buildings still bear bullet holes from their livelier days.

Start your tour of this tiny town at **Tombstone Chamber of Commerce and Visitor Center** (✉ 4th and Allen Sts. ☎ 520/457–3929 ⊕ www.tombstone. org). There is a self-guided walking tour, but the best way to get the lay of the land is to take the 15-minute stagecoach ride ($5) around downtown. Drivers relate a condensed version of Tombstone's notorious past to the clip-clop of horse hooves.

Boot Hill Graveyard, where the victims of the OK Corral shoot-out are buried, is on the northwest corner of town, facing U.S. 80. Chinese names in one section of the "bone orchard" bear testament to the laundry and restaurant workers who came from San Francisco during the height of Tombstone's mining fever. About a third of the more than 350 graves dug here from 1879 to 1974 are unmarked. If you're put off by the commercialism of the place—you enter through a gift shop that sells novelty items in the shape of tombstones—remember that Tombstone itself is the result of crass acquisition. ✉ *U.S. 80* ☎ *520/457–9344 or 800/457–9344* 🎫 *Free* ☉ *Daily 7:30–6.*

For an introduction to the town's—and the area's—past, visit the **Tombstone Courthouse State Historic Park.** This redbrick 1882 county courthouse offers exhibits of the area's mining and ranching history; pioneer lifestyles; the 1882 judge's chambers; and the 1904 district attorney's office. ✉ *219 E. Toughnut St., at 3rd St.* ☎ *520/457–3311* ⊕ *www.pr. state.az.us* 🎫 *$4* ☉ *Daily 8–5.*

Originally a boardinghouse for the Vizina Mining Company and later a popular hotel, the **Rose Tree Inn Museum** has 1880s period rooms. Take a moment to walk under the branches of "The Shady Lady of Tombstone" in the courtyard. Covering more than 8,600-square-feet, the Lady Banksia rose tree, planted by a homesick bride in 1885, is reported to be the largest of its kind in the world. The best time to see the tree is in April when its tiny white roses bloom. Romantics wanting to take a bit of Tombstone home can purchase a healthy clipping from the tree ($10) to plant in their own yard. ✉ *116 S. 4th St., at Toughnut St.* ☎ *520/457–3326* 🎫 *$3* ☉ *Daily 9–5.*

☺ Vincent Price narrates the dramatic version of the town's past in the **Historama**—a 26-minute multimedia presentation. At the adjoining **OK Corral,** a recorded voice-over details the town's famous shoot-out, while life-size figures of the gunfight's participants stand poised to shoot. A re-enactment of the the gunfight at the OK Corral is held daily at 2 PM. Photographer C. S. Fly, whose studio was next door to the corral, didn't record this bit of history, but Geronimo and his pursuers were among the historic figures he did capture with his camera. Many of his fascinating Old West images may be viewed at the **Fly Exhibition Gallery.** ⊠ *Allen St. between 3rd and 4th Sts.* ☎ *520/457–3456* ⊕ *www.ok-corral. com* 🖃 *Historama, OK Corral, and Fly Exhibition Gallery $5.50, gunfight $2* ⊗ *Daily 9–5, Historama shows on the half hr 9:30–4:30.*

You can see the original printing presses for the town's newspaper at the **Tombstone Epitaph Museum** (⊠ 9 S. 5th St. ☎ 520/457–2211). The newspaper was founded in 1880 by John P. Clum and is still publishing today.

A Tombstone institution, known as the wildest, wickedest night spot between Basin Street and the Barbary Coast, the **Bird Cage Theater** is a former music hall where Enrico Caruso, Sarah Bernhardt, and Lillian Russell—among others—performed. It was also the site of the longest continuous poker game recorded, started when the Bird Cage opened in 1881 and lasting eight years, five months, and three days. Some of the better-known players included Diamond Jim Brady, Adolphus Busch (of brewery fame), and William Randolph Hearst's father. The cards were dealt round the clock; players had to give a 20-minute notice when they were planning to vacate their seats, because there was always a waiting list of at least 10 people ready to shell out $1,000 (the equivalent of about $30,000 today) to get in. In all, some $10 million changed hands.

When the mines closed in 1889, the Bird Cage was abandoned and locked up, but the building has remained in the hands of the same family, who threw nothing out, through five generations. Relics of the past are crammed into the Bird Cage. You can walk on the stage visited by some of the top traveling performers of the time, see the faro table once touched by the legendary gambler Doc Holliday, and pass by the black hearse that carried all of Tombstone's deceased to Boot Hill. The basement, which served as an upscale bordello and gambling hall, still has all the original furnishings and fixtures intact, and you can see the personal belongings left behind by the ladies of the night when the mines closed and they, and their clients, headed for California. ⊠ *308 E. Allen St., at 6th St.* ☎ *520/457–3421* 🖃 *$6* ⊗ *Daily 8–6.*

If you're looking to wet your whistle, stop by the **Crystal Palace** (⊠ 420 E. Allen St., at 5th St. ☎ 520/457–3611), where a beautiful mirrored mahogany bar, wrought-iron chandeliers, and tinwork ceilings date back to Tombstone's heyday. Locals come here on weekends to dance to live country-and-western music.

Where to Stay & Eat

☺ ¢–$$ ╳ **Longhorn Restaurant.** Across the street from Big Nose Kate's Saloon, named for Doc Holliday's girlfriend, the Longhorn Restaurant was originally the Bucket of Blood Saloon. Old-time saloon keepers may not have had a way with words, but they sure knew what to serve to keep the likes of the Earps, Bat Masterson, and Johnny Ringo coming back for more. Today it's noisier and definitely for the whole family, with hot dogs, burgers, steaks, ribs, tacos, and enchiladas. It may not be "cuisine," but it is filling and fun and open for three meals a day. ⊠ *501 E. Allen St.* ☎ *520/457–3405* ▤ *MC, V.*

¢–$$ ✕ **Nellie Cashman's.** You can order anything from a burger to a hearty dinner of juicy pork chops or chicken-fried steak in this homey spot, named for the original owner, a Tombstone pioneer who opened a hotel and restaurant in 1882. Old photographs and postcards decorate the walls. Nellie's is also a great place for a country breakfast complete with biscuits and gravy. ⊠ *117 5th St.* ☎ *520/457–2212* ▤ *AE, D, MC, V.*

$–$$ 🖫 **Curly Bill's Bed & Breakfast.** Though named for one of the baddest outlaws in Tombstone Territory, this B&B is quite serene. Five blocks away from all the activity on Allen Street, the adobe hacienda has views of the Dragoon Mountains from the screened sunporch and hot tub. Two rooms furnished with Victorian antiques share a bath, and two larger rooms have their own TV, VCR, and private bath. The innkeeper serves a breakfast of homemade quiche, muffins, pastries, and fresh fruit. ⊠ *210 N. 9th St., 85638* ☎ *520/457–3858* ⊕ *www.curlybillsbandb. com* ➽ *4 rooms, 2 with shared bath* ⌂ *Fans, some in-room VCRs, hot tub; no TV in some rooms, no smoking* ▤ *MC, V* ⦿| *BP.*

$ 🖫 **Best Western Look-Out Lodge.** This small, circa-1960 motel a few miles outside of town has spectacular views of the Dragoon Mountains and desert valley below. Touches such as Western-print bedspreads, Victorian-style lamps, and locally made wood-hewn clocks give the rooms character. ⊠ *AZ 80 W* ⌁ *Box 787, 85638* ☎ *520/457–2223 or 877/ 652–6772* 🖷 *520/457–3870* ⊕ *www.bestwestern.com* ➽ *40 rooms* ⌂ *Cable TV, pool, Internet, some pets (fee), no-smoking rooms* ▤ *AE, D, DC, MC, V* ⦿| *CP.*

¢   🖫 **Tombstone Boarding House Bed & Breakfast.** This friendly B&B is actually two meticulously restored 1880s adobes that sit side by side in a quiet residential neighborhood: guests sleep in one house and go next door to have a hearty country breakfast (the restaurant there is open to the public). The spotless rooms, all with private entrances, have hardwood floors and period furnishings collected from around Cochise County. Even if you don't stay here, a visit to the Lamplight Room is worth a visit. The dinner menu uses 1880s recipes from a period cookbook. Selections include Parmesan-encrusted salmon, chicken cordon bleu, and roast pork loin. ⊠ *108 N. 4th St.* ⌁ *Box 906, 85638* ☎ *520/ 457–3716 or 877/225–1319* ⊕ *www.tombstoneboardinghouse.com* ➽ *6 rooms* ⌂ *Restaurant, some pets allowed; no room phones, no room TVs, no smoking* ▤ *AE, D, MC, V* ⦿| *BP.*

¢   🖫 **Tombstone Motel.** Catercorner from the offices of the *Tombstone Epitaph*, on the town's main through street, this comfortable and well-run motel will remind you of the motor courts of years past. The major attractions of Allen Street are less than a block away. ⊠ *502 E. Fremont St.* ⌁ *Box 837, 85638* ☎ *520/457–3478 or 888/455–3478* 🖷 *520/457– 9017* ⊕ *www.tombstonemotel.com* ➽ *29 rooms* ⌂ *Some refrigerators, in-room data ports, cable TV, laundry facilities, some pets allowed (fee)* ▤ *AE, D, MC, V* ⦿| *CP.*

Shopping

Several curio shops and old-time photo emporiums await in the kitschy collection of stores lining Allen Street. To get into the spirit of the Old West, you can rent or purchase 1880s-style costumes at the **Oriental Saloon** (⊠ *500 E. Allen St., at 5th St.* ☎ *520/457–3922*), which originally opened in July of 1880 and was touted as one of the fanciest bars in town. Given the town's bloody history, it's not surprising that guns aren't permitted in most of the establishments on Allen Street. However, it is well worth the visit to the historic **G. F. Spangenberg Pioneer Gun Shop** (✉ 17 S. 4th St., at Allen St. ☎ 520/457–3227 ⊕ www.1880guns.com), established in 1880. Wyatt Earp, Virgil Earp, Doc Holliday, the Clantons, and the McLowrys all purchased weapons at this shop, which still sells 1880s-style firearms.

Bisbee

5 *24 mi south of Tombstone.*

Like Tombstone, Bisbee was a mining boomtown, but its wealth was in copper, not silver, and its success was much longer lived. The gnarled Mule Mountains aren't as impressive as some of the other mountain ranges in southern Arizona, but their rocky canyons concealed one of the richest mineral sites in the world.

Jack Dunn, a scout with Company C from Fort Huachuca chasing hostile Apaches in the area, first discovered an outcropping of rich ore here in 1877. By 1900, more than 20,000 people lived in the crowded canyons around the Bisbee mines. Phelps Dodge purchased all of the major mines by the time the Great Depression rolled around and mining continued until 1975, when the mines were closed for good. In less than 100 years of mining, the area surrounding Bisbee had yielded more than 6.1 billion dollars of mineral wealth, all of which was gleaned from a surface area of less than 3 square mi.

Once known as the Queen of the Copper Camps, Bisbee is no longer one of the biggest cities between New Orleans and San Francisco, but it clings tenaciously to the steep slopes of the Mule Mountains. It was rediscovered in the early 1980s by burned-out city dwellers and revived as a kind of Woodstock West. The permanent population is a mix of retired miners and their families, aging hippie jewelry makers, and enterprising young restaurateurs and boutique owners.

If you want to head straight into town from U.S. 80, get off at the Brewery Gulch interchange. You can park here and cross under the highway, taking Main, Commerce, or Brewery Gulch Street, all of which meet here.

About ¼ mi after AZ 80 intersects with AZ 92, you can pull off the highway into a gravel parking lot, where a short, typewritten history of the **Lavender Pit Mine** (✉ AZ 80) is attached to the hurricane fence surrounding the area (Bisbee isn't big on formal exhibits). The hole left by the copper miners is huge, with piles of lavender-hued "tailings," or waste, creating mountains around it. Arizona's largest pit mine yielded some 94 million tons of copper ore before the town's mining activity came to a halt.

For a lesson in mining history, take the **Copper Queen Mine Underground Tour.** The mine is less than ½ mi to the east of the Lavender Pit, across AZ 80 from downtown at the Brewery Gulch interchange. Tours are led by Bisbee's retired copper miners, who are wont to embellish their official spiel with tales from their mining days. They're also very capa-

A TEQUILA SNAPSHOT

AGAVE, the plant from which fine tequila is made, flourishes in southern Arizona. Many people think the agave is a cactus, but it isn't. It's a succulent, closely related to the lily or amaryllis. Only blue agave—just one of 136 species—is used to make true tequila, but other species are used to make mezcal, the more generic type of liquor. Tequila is a specific type of mezcal, just as bourbon or scotch are specific types of whiskey. Many of the cheap brands are actually mixtos, which means they aren't 100% agave; true tequila isn't cheap, and you can pay more than $50 per bottle for a premium brand.

Just across the border in Mexico, there are more than 50 tequila producers, so it's understandable that tequila is a popular drink in Arizona. In fact, more tequila is consumed in the United States than anywhere else, including Mexico. The heart of the tequila-making region is

Tequila itself, some 30 mi west of Guadalajara, in the state of Jalisco. The hills around the town are responsible for its name, "tel" meaning "hill," and "quilla," a kind of lava around the dead volcanoes in the area.

To produce tequila, the bulb of the blue agave plant is harvested (it may weigh up to 150 pounds), heated to break down the sugars, and fermented. The best brands, Herradura and El Tesoro, are fermented with wild yeasts that add distinctive flavors to the final product. The fermented tequila is then placed into pot stills, where it is double-distilled to 90 proof or higher. Bottles designated "añejo" have been aged for a minimum of a year in oak barrels and these tequilas are the most expensive.

ble, safety-minded people (any miner who survives to lead tours in his older years would have to be), so don't be concerned about the precautionary dog tags (literally—they're donated by a local veterinarian) issued to each person on the tour.

The 75-minute tours (you can't enter the mine at any other time) go into the shaft via a little open train, like those the miners rode when the mine was active. Before you climb aboard, you're outfitted in miner's garb—a yellow slicker and a hard hat with a light that runs off a battery pack strapped to your waist. You may want to wear a sweater or light coat under your slicker because the temperature in the mine is a brisk 47°F on average. You'll travel by train thousands of feet into the mine, up a grade of 30 feet (not down, as many visitors expect). Those who are a bit claustrophobic might consider taking one of the van tours of the surface mines and historic district that depart from the building at the same times as the mine tours (excluding 9 AM). ⊠ 478 N. Dart Rd. ☎ 520/432–2071 or 866/432–2071 ⊕ www.cityofbisbee.com/queenminetours.htm ⊠ Mine tour $12 ☉ Tours daily at 9, 10:30, noon, 2, and 3:30.

The **Bisbee Mining and Historical Museum** is in a redbrick structure built in 1897 to serve as the Copper Queen Consolidated Mining Offices. The rooms today are filled with exhibits, photographs, and artifacts that offer a glimpse into the everyday life of Bisbee's early mining community. This small museum was the first rural museum in the United States to become a member of the Smithsonian Institution Affiliations Program. ✉ 5 Copper Queen Plaza ☎ 520/432–7071 ⊕ www.bisbeemuseum.org 💵 $4 🕙 Daily 10–4.

The venerable **Copper Queen Hotel** (✉ 11 Howell Ave.), built a century ago, is behind the Mining and Historical Museum. It has housed the famous as well as the infamous: General John "Black Jack" Pershing, John Wayne, Theodore Roosevelt, and mining executives from all over the world made this their home away from home. The hotel also hosts three resident ghosts. Take a minute to look through the ghost journal at the front desk where guests have described their haunted encounters in words and delicate ink drawings.

Brewery Gulch, a short street running north and south, is adjacent to the Copper Queen Hotel (walk out the front door of the Copper Queen, make a left, and you'll be there in about 20 paces). In the old days, the brewery housed there allowed the dregs of the beer that was being brewed to flow down the street and into the gutter. Once largely abandoned, these structures, like many others in the area, are gradually being renovated to accommodate the demands of Bisbee's growing tourist industry.

Bisbee's **Main Street** is alive and retailing. This hilly commercial thoroughfare is lined with appealing crafts shops, boutiques, and restaurants, many of them in well-preserved turn-of-the-20th-century brick buildings.

Tom Mosier, a native of Bisbee, gives the **Lavender Jeep Tours** (✉ 45 Gila Dr. ☎ 520/432–5369) for $15 to $49. Wander Bisbee's back streets with Mosier, who regales locals and visitors alike with tales of the town and its buildings.

Where to Stay & Eat

★ $$–$$$ ✕ **Café Roka.** This is the deserved darling of the hip Bisbee crowd. The constantly changing northern Italian–style evening menu is not extensive, but you can count on whatever you order—gulf shrimp tossed with lobster ravioli, roasted quail, New Zealand rack of lamb—to be wonderful. Portions are generous, and entrées include soup or salad. Chef Rod Kass changes the menu weekly. Exposed-brick walls and soft lighting form the backdrop for original artwork, and the 1875 bar hearkens to Bisbee's glory days. ✉ 35 Main St. ☎ 520/432–5153 ⊕ www.caferoka.com ▤ AE, MC, V 🕙 Closed Sun.–Tues. No lunch.

$–$$ ✕ **The Bisbee Grill.** You might not expect diversity at a place with a reputation for having the best burger in town, but this restaurant delivers with salads, sandwiches, fajitas, pasta, salmon, steaks, and ribs. The dining room, built to resemble an old train depot, fills up fast on the weekends. Large sepia murals of Old Bisbee, exposed-brick walls, and piped jazz music create a relaxing dining experience. ✉ #2 Copper Queen Plaza ☎ 520/432–6788 ⚐ Reservations recommended ▤ AE, D, MC, V.

$–$$$ 🏨 **Canyon Rose Suites.** Steps away from the heart of downtown Bisbee, this all-suites B&B is in the 1905 Allen Block Building, formerly a furniture store and miner's rooming house. Upstairs are six spacious units,

FodorsChoice ★

all with hardwood floors, 10-foot ceilings, and fully equipped kitchens. Local art (for sale) adorns the walls. In the spa downstairs you can pamper yourself with a hot-stone massage or herbal body wrap after a day in the mines. ⊠ *27 Subway St.* ☐ *Box 1915, 85603* ☎ *520/432–5098 or 866/296–7673* ⊕ *www.canyonrose.com* ⟿ *6 suites* ♦ *Kitchens, cable TV, in-room VCRs, spa, library, laundry facilities* ⊟ *AE, D, DC, MC, V* ⟋⊙⟍ *BP.*

$–$$ ▣ **Copper Queen Hotel.** Built by the Copper Queen Mining Company (which later became the Phelps Dodge Company) when Bisbee was the biggest copper-mining town in the world, this hotel in the heart of downtown has been operating since 1902. Some of the rooms are small or oddly laid out, and the walls between them are thin, but all have a Victorian charm and were completely renovated in 2003. You might want to request room 211, where John Wayne once stayed; room 315, which is said to be inhabited by the ghost of former employee Julie Lowell; or room 406, which was once occupied by President Teddy Roosevelt. The restaurant uses china once owned by the Bisbee railroad. ⊠ *11 Howell Ave.* ☐ *Drawer CQ 85603* ☎ *520/432–2216 or 800/247–5829* 🖷 *520/432–4298* ⊕ *www.copperqueen.com* ⟿ *48 rooms* ♦ *Restaurant, coffee shop, cable TV, pool, bar* ⊟ *AE, D, DC, MC, V.*

¢–$
Fodor'sChoice
★

▣ **School House Inn Bed & Breakfast.** You may flash back to your classroom days at this B&B, a schoolhouse built in 1918 at the height of Bisbee's mining days. Perched on the side of a hill, the two-story brick building has a pleasant outdoor patio shaded by an oak tree. The inn's rooms all have a theme–history, music, library, reading, arithmetic, art, geography, and the Principal's office—reflected in the decor (though, surprisingly, there is no writing desk in the writing room). Twelve-foot ceilings contribute to an overall airy effect, but the old floors can be creaky at night. The upstairs deck provides a place to lounge or to set up the telescope for an impromptu astronomy lesson. Sip an ice-cold pop from the old-fashioned soda machine while watching the sun set over the canyon. ⊠ *818 Tombstone Canyon Rd.* ☐ *Box 32, 85603* ☎ *800/537–4333* 🖷 *520/432–2996* ⟿ *6 rooms, 3 suites* ♦ *No a/c, no room phones; no room TVs, no smoking, no kids under 14* ⊟ *AE, D, DC, MC, V* ⟋⊙⟍ *BP.*

Nightlife

Bisbee's main thoroughfare runs through Tombstone Canyon, now called Main Street, but a side canyon confluent with the main canyon earned the name Brewery Gulch. Once known for shady ladies and saloons reaching up into the canyon, Brewery Gulch retains a few shadows of its rowdy past. Established in 1902, **St. Elmo Bar** (⊠ 36 Brewery Gulch ☎ 520/432–5578) is decorated with an odd assortment of the past and present—a 1922 official map of Cochise County is next to a neon beer sign. The jukebox plays during the week, but on the weekends Buzz and the Soul Senders rock the house with rhythm and blues. **The Stock Exchange Bar** (⊠ 15 Brewery Gulch ☎ 520/432–3317), in the historic Muheim building, has the only shuffleboard in town. It also has a pool table and off-track betting. The 1914 stock board still hangs on the wall; it is the only board in Arizona ever affiliated with the New York Stock Exchange. It closed in 1964.

Shopping

Artist studios, galleries, and boutiques in historic buildings line Main Street, which runs though Tombstone Canyon. You can pick up a straw hat at **Optimo Custom Panama Hatworks** (✉ 47 Main St. ☎ 520/432–4544 ⊕ www.optimohatworks.com), which is nationally know for its custom, hand-woven Panama hats. **55 Main Street** (✉ 55 Main St. ☎ 520/432–4694) displays and sells contemporary artwork. A trip to Bisbee wouldn't be complete without a stop at the quirky **The Killer Bee Guy** (✉ 15 Main St. ☎ 877/227–9338 ⊕ www.killerbeeguy.com). Killer-bee keeper Reed Booth has appeared on the Discovery Channel and the Food Network; you can sample his honey butters and mustards and pick up some killer honey recipes.

Douglas

❻ *23 mi southeast of Bisbee.*

This town on the U.S.–Mexico border was founded in 1902 by James Douglas to serve as the copper-smelting center for the mines in Bisbee. Be aware of your surroundings when wandering around this quaint little town; the area is no stranger to drug traffickers and illegal border crossings.

The must-see historic landmark in town and still the center of much of Douglas's activity is the **Gadsden Hotel** (✉ 1046 G Ave. ☎ 520/364–4481 ⊕ www.theriver.com/gadsdenhotel), built in 1907. The lobby contains a solid white Italian-marble staircase, two authentic Tiffany-vaulted skylights, and a 42-foot-long stained-glass mural. One thousand ounces of 14-karat gold leaf were used to decorate the capitals. The bar is lively all day long and still serves as a meeting place for local ranchers. However, the guest rooms are less impressive. Most of the rugs, drapes, and shower curtains look weary, and the old plumbing and fixtures aren't always well maintained. When you leave the hotel and walk out onto G Avenue, Douglas's main thoroughfare, you'll be taking a stroll back through time. A film company shooting here had to do very little to make the restaurants and shop fronts fit its 1940s plotline.

Before Douglas became the smelter for Bisbee, the site was the annual roundup ground for local ranchers, Mexican and American—among them John Slaughter, a former Texas ranger who was the sheriff of Cochise County after Wyatt Earp. The 140-acre **John Slaughter Ranch/San Bernardino Land Grant**, a National Historic Landmark, gives a glimpse of life near the border in the late 19th and early 20th centuries. The ranch once supported nearly 500 people and had vineyards, gardens, fishponds, icehouse, and a granary. You can also visit ruins of a military outpost established here in 1911 during the Mexican civil unrest. Much of the ride out to the ranch is via a graded dirt road that traverses a strikingly Western landscape of rolling hills and desert scrub. The ranch is 15 mi east of Douglas (from town, go east on 15th Street, which turns into Geronimo Trail and leads to the ranch). No dogs are permitted on the ranch grounds. ✉ *6153 Geronimo Trail* ☎ *520/558–2474* ✉ *$5* ☉ *Wed.–Sun. 10–3.*

Where to Eat

$–$$ ✕ **Grand Café.** The Marilyn Monroe tribute wall and red velvet–draped dining niche in the back may be kitschy, but the Mexican cooking here is taken very seriously. Among the soups on offer, the soothing *caldo de queso* is laced with cheese and chunks of fresh potato, and the bracing *menudo* is nicely spiced. The refried beans served on the side of such well-prepared Sonoran specialties as chiles rellenos are wonderfully flavorful. ✉ *1119 G Ave.* ☎ *520/364–2344* ▭ *MC, V* ⊘ *Closed Sun.*

Chiricahua National Monument

⓭ ❼ *58 mi northeast of Douglas on U.S. 191 to AZ 181; 36 mi southeast*
Fodor's Choice *of Willcox.*
★

Vast fields of desert grass are suddenly transformed into a landscape of forest, mountains, and striking rock formations as you enter the 12,000-acre Chiricahua National Monument. The Chiricahua Apache—who lived in the mountains for centuries and, led by Cochise and Geronimo, tried for 25 years to prevent white pioneers from settling here—dubbed it the Land of the Standing-Up Rocks. Enormous outcroppings of volcanic rock worn by erosion and fractured by uplift into strange pinnacles and spires are set in a forest where autumn and spring seem to occur at the same time. Because of the particular balance of sunshine and rain in the area, in April and May visitors will see brown, yellow, and red leaves coexisting with new green foliage. Summer in Chiricahua National Monument is exceptionally wet: from July through September there are thunderstorms nearly every afternoon. Few other areas in the United States have such a variety of plant, bird, and animal life. Deer, coati mundis, peccaries, and lizards live among the aspen, ponderosa pine, Douglas fir, oak, and cypress trees—to name just a few. Well worth the driving distance, this is a prime area for bird-watchers, and hikers have more than 17 mi of scenic trails. The admission fee is good for seven days. Some of the most beautiful and untouched camping areas in Arizona are nearby, in the Chiricahua Mountains. ✉ *AZ 181, 36 mi southeast of Willcox* ☎ *520/824–3560* ⊕ *www.nps.gov/chir* ▨ *$5* ⊘ *Visitor center open daily 8–4:30.*

off the beaten path

PEARCE – The gold camp of Pearce, 1 mi off U.S. 191, 29 mi south of Willcox, has a post office and one viable store; amid the ruins of the mill, the mine, and many old adobes. Gold was discovered here in 1894, and the town maintained a thriving population of 1,500 until the mine closed in the 1930s, turning Pearce into a ghost town.

Where to Stay

★ $$$$ ▦ **Grapevine Canyon Ranch.** This guest ranch on the west side of the Chiricahuas adjoins a working cattle ranch. Visitors get the chance to watch—and, in some cases, participate in—real day-to-day cowboy activities. Riders of all levels of experience are welcome, and hiking trails crisscross this quintessentially Western terrain. Rooms are decorated in a mix of country and Southwestern-style furnishings—and all have spacious decks and porches. Rates include meals and all activities. There is a three-night minimum. ✉ *Highland Rd.* ⊕ *Box 302, Pearce 85625*

☎ 520/826–3185 or 800/245–9202 🖨 520/826–3636 ⊕ *www.gcranch. com* ⇆ *12 rooms ⚐ Refrigerators, pool, hot tub, hiking, horseback riding, library, laundry facilities; no a/c, no room phones, no room TVs, no kids under 12* ▤ *AE, D, MC, V* ⎟◎⎟ *FAP.*

$$$$ ▦ **Sunglow Guest Ranch.** Named after the ghost town of Sunglow, this ranch consists of 9 casitas decked out in Southwestern style with cozy beds and fireplaces for chilly nights. Groomed paths wander from the casitas to the dining room and office, but you blaze your own trails down to the pond or through the grassy meadow to the barn and goat pen. Resident chef Jack Gramento serves breakfast, afternoon tea, and dinner in a dining room with a wraparound porch. You can rent mountain bikes to explore the trails in the Coronado National Forest, which surrounds the property on three sides. The ranch's naturalist leads birding expeditions on the 400-acre property, and star parties attract astronomers as this remote region offers some of the blackest skies around and perfect conditions for stargazing. ⊠ *Turkey Creek Rd.* ⌖ *HCR 1, Box 385, Pearce 85625* ☎ *520/824–3334 or 866/786–4569* 🖨 *520/824–3176* ⊕ *www.sunglowranch.com* ⇆ *4 1-room casitas, 4 2-room casitas, 1 2-bedroom casita ⚐ Café, microwaves, refrigerators, bicycles, hiking, horseshoes, library, meeting room, some pets allowed (fee); no room phones, no room TVs, no smoking* ▤ *AE, MC, V* ⎟◎⎟ *MAP.*

¢ ▦ **Portal Peak Lodge.** This barracks-style structure, just east of Chiricahua National Monument near the New Mexico border, is notable less for its rooms (clean and pleasant but nondescript) than for its winged visitors: the elegant trogon, 14 types of hummingbird and 10 species of owl are among the 330 varieties of birds that flock to nearby Cave Creek Canyon. Decks outside each room provide a good vantage point. ⊠ *1215 Main St.* ⌖ *Box 364, Portal 85632* ☎ *520/558–2223* 🖨 *520/558– 2473* ⊕ *www.portalpeaklodge.com* ⇆ *16 rooms ⚐ Restaurant, grocery, no-smoking rooms; no room phones* ▤ *AE, D, MC, V.*

CAMPING ⛺ **Bonita Canyon Campground.** Just ½ mi from the visitor center at Chir-
¢ icahua National Monument, this campground is nestled among oak and pine trees along a meandering creek. The dense vegetation gives campers a feeling of privacy and shelters an assortment of wildlife, such as javelinas, fox squirrels, and coati mundis. In spring and summer, evening naturalist programs are held at the campground's amphitheater. ⚐ *Flush toilets, drinking water, grills, picnic tables* ⇆ *24 campsites* ⊠ *Bonita Canyon Dr., Willcox* ☎ *520/824–3560* ⊕ *www.nps.gov/chir* ⚑ *Reservations not accepted* ⊙ *Open year-round.*

Fort Bowie National Historical Site

❽ *8 mi northwest of Chiricahua National Monument. Take AZ 186 east from Chiricahua National Monument; 5 mi north of junction with AZ 181, signs direct you to road leading to fort.*

It's a bit of an outing to the location of Arizona's last battle between Native Americans and U.S. troops in the Dos Cabezas (Two-Headed) Mountains. After driving down a graded but winding gravel road, you'll come to a parking lot where a challenging trail leads 1½ mi to the historic site. The fort itself is virtually in ruins, but there's a small ranger-staffed visitor center with historical displays, rest rooms, and books for sale.

Points of interest along the way, all indicated by historic markers, include the **Butterfield stage stop**, a crucial link in the journey from east to west in the mid-19th century that happened to be in the heart of Chiricahua Apache land. Chief Cochise and the stagecoach operators ignored one another until sometime in 1861, when hostilities broke out between U.S. Cavalry troops and the Apache. After an ambush by the chief's warriors at Apache Pass in 1862, U.S. troops decided a fort was desperately needed in the area, and Fort Bowie was built within weeks. There were skirmishes for the next 10 years, followed by a peaceful decade. Renewed fighting broke out in 1881. Geronimo, the new leader of the Indian warriors, finally surrendered in 1886. The fort was abandoned eight years later and fell into disrepair. ⊠ *Apache Pass Rd., 26 mi southeast of Willcox* ☎ *520/847-2500* ⊕ *www.nps.gov/fobo* ⊠ *Free* ⊙ *Daily 8–4:30.*

Willcox

❾ *26 mi northwest of Fort Bowie National Historical Site on AZ 186.*

The small town of Willcox, in the heart of Arizona ranching country, began in the late 1870s as a railroad construction camp called Maley. When the Southern Pacific Railroad line arrived in 1880, the town was renamed in honor of the highly regarded Fort Bowie commander, General Orlando B. Willcox. Once a major shipping center for cattle ranchers and mining companies, the town has preserved its rustic charm; the downtown area looks like an Old West movie set. An elevation of 4,167 feet means moderate summers and chilly winters, which is an ideal climate for growing apples, and apple pie fans from as far away as Phoenix make pilgrimages just to sample the harvest. Don't miss the mile-high apple pies and hand-pressed cider at **Stout's Cider Mill** (⊠ 1510 N. Circle I Rd. ☎ 520/384–3696).

If you visit in winter, you can see some of the more than 10,000 sandhill cranes that roost at the **Willcox Playa**, a 37,000-acre area resembling a dry lake bed 12 mi south of Willcox. They migrate in late fall and head north to nesting sites in February, and bird-watchers migrate to Willcox the third week in January for the annual Wings over Willcox birdwatching event held in their honor.

Outside Willcox is the headquarters for the **Muleshoe Ranch Cooperative Management Area** (⊠ 6502 N. Muleshoe Ranch Rd. ☎ 520/507–5229 ⊕ www.nature.org), nearly 50,000 acres of riparian desert land in the foothills of the Galiuro Mountains that are jointly owned and managed by the Nature Conservancy, the U.S. Forest Service, and the U.S. Bureau of Land Management. It's a 30-mi drive on a dirt road to the ranch—it takes about an hour to get here—but the scenery, wildlife, and hiking are well worth the bumps. Backcountry hiking and mountain-biking trips can be arranged by the ranch, and overnight accommodations are available. To reach the ranch, take Exit 340 off Interstate 10, turn right on Bisbee Avenue and continue to Airport Road, turn right again, and after

15 mi take the right fork at a junction just past a group of mailboxes and continue to the end of the road.

The **Rex Allen Arizona Cowboy Museum,** in Willcox's historic district, is a tribute to Willcox's most famous native son, cowboy singer Rex Allen. (As he requested, Allen's ashes were scattered on the grave of his horse, Koko, buried in Railroad Avenue Park across the street from the museum.) He starred in several rather average cowboy movies during the 1940s and '50s for Republic Pictures, but he's probably most famous as the friendly voice that narrated Walt Disney nature films of the 1960s. Check out the glittery suits the star wore on tour—they'd do Liberace proud. ⊠ *150 N. Railroad Ave.* ☎ *520/384–4583 or 877/234–4111* ⊕ *www.pinkbanana.com/rex* ☒ *$2* ⊙ *Daily 10–4.*

The **Willcox Commercial Store** (⊠ *180 N. Railroad Ave.* ☎ *520/384–2448*), near the Rex Allen Cowboy Museum, was established in 1881 and is the oldest retail establishment in Arizona. Locals like to boast that Geronimo used to shop here. Today it's a clothing store, with a large selection of Western wear.

The **Chiricahua Regional Museum and Research Center,** previously known as the Museum of the Southwest, is in downtown Willcox. Exhibits relating to Native American and military history and culture, including a separate Geronimo exhibit, were created by the Sulphur Springs Valley Historical Society. One oddity the museum points out is that the memoirs of Civil War general Orlando Willcox, for whom the town was named, don't even mention a visit to Arizona. ⊠ *127 E. Maley St.* ☎ *520/384–3971* ☒ *Free* ⊙ *Mon.–Sat. 10–4.*

Where to Stay & Eat

$–$$$ ✕ **Desert Rose Café.** Enjoy lunch, dinner, or the Sunday buffet with the locals at this family-owned, family-friendly restaurant in Willcox. The food is as down-home as the atmosphere—mostly burgers, chicken, steak, and seafood standards—so it's just the place to go when you want a meal that's predictable, unpretentious, but also good. ⊠ *706 S. Haskell Ave.* ☎ *520/384–0514* ▤ *AE, MC, V.*

¢–$ ✕ **Salsa Fiesta Mexican Restaurant.** You can't miss the bright neon lights of this little restaurant, just south of Interstate 10 at Exit 340 in Willcox. The interior is cheerful and clean, with tables, chairs, and walls painted in a spicy medley of hot pink, purple, turquoise, green, and orange. The menu consists of Mexican standards, and the salsa bar runs the gamut from mild to super-hot. There is a modest selection of domestic and Mexican beers, and takeout is available. ⊠ *1201 W. Rex Allen Dr.* ☎ *520/384–4233* ▤ *AE, D, MC, V.*

$–$$ ▥ **Muleshoe Ranch.** This turn-of-the-20th-century ranch is run by the Arizona chapter of the Nature Conservancy. Five casitas with linens and well-equipped kitchens sit in a pristine setting in the grassland foothills of the Galiuro Mountains. Four of the casitas are situated around a courtyard setting hacienda-style. The fifth unit, a stone cabin, is off by itself affording more privacy to its guests. There's a visitor center, 22 mi of hiking trails, a guided, ¾-mi nature walk on Saturday at 9 AM, and natural hot springs (for use by casita guests only). There's a two-night minimum from September to May, and a three-night minimum on holiday weekends. ⊠ *6502 N. Muleshoe Ranch Rd.* ⏚ *R.R. 1, Box 1542, 85643* ☎ *520/507–5229* ⊕ *www.muleshoelodging.org* ⤴ *5 units* ⏃ *Kitchens, hiking, library, piano; no a/c in some rooms, no room phones, no room TVs* ⊟ *AE, MC, V* ⊘ *Closed June–Aug.*

¢ 🖻 **Willcox Days Inn.** A clean room and good value are what you'll find here, just off the highway and close to this small town's sights. It's a handy stopping point on your way to or from the Chiricahuas, and a plentiful continental breakfast is included. ⊠ *724 N. Bisbee Ave., 85643* ☎ *520/384–4222* 🖶 *520/384–3785* ⊕ *www.daysinn.com* ⤴ *73 rooms* ⏃ *In-room data ports, some microwaves, some refrigerators, cable TV with movies, pool, laundry facilities, some pets allowed (fee)* ⊟ *AE, D, DC, MC, V* 🍽 *CP.*

Texas Canyon

❿ *16 mi west of Willcox off Interstate 10.*

Fodor'sChoice
★

A dramatic change of scenery along Interstate 10 will signal that you're entering Texas Canyon. The rock formations here are exceptional—huge boulders appear to be delicately balanced against each other.

Texas Canyon is the home of the **Amerind Foundation** (a contraction of "American" and "Indian"), founded by amateur archaeologist William Fulton in 1937 to foster understanding about Native American cultures. The research facility and museum are housed in a Spanish colonial revival–style structure designed by noted Tucson architect H. M. Starkweather. The museum's rotating displays of archaeological materials, crafts, and photographs give an overview of Native American cultures of the Southwest and Mexico. The adjacent Fulton–Hayden Memorial Art Gallery displays an assortment of art collected by William Fulton. The museum's gift shop has a superlative selection of Native American art, crafts, and jewelry. ⊠ *2100 N. Amerind Rd., 1 mi southeast of I–10 (Exit 318), Dragoon* ☎ *520/586–3666* ⊕ *www.amerind.org* ⊞ *$5* ⊘ *Oct.–May, daily 10–4; June–Sept., Wed.–Sun. 10–4.*

Benson

⓫ *12 mi west of Texas Canyon and 50 mi east of Tucson via Interstate 10.*

Even in its historic heyday as a Butterfield stagecoach station, and later as the hub of the Southern Pacific Railroad, Benson was just a place to stop on the way to somewhere else. But that role changed beginning with the 1974 discovery of a pristine cave beneath the Whetstone Mountains west of Benson and culminating 25 years later with the opening of Kartchner Caverns State Park, one of the most remarkable living cave systems in the world. Benson today is a modern boomtown, in the process of evolving into a destination to travel to instead of through.

Though the city is undergoing dramatic changes, you can see the story of Benson's past at the little **San Pedro Valley Arts and Historical Society Museum** (⊠ S. San Pedro Ave. at E. 5th St. ☎ 520/586–3070), a free museum that is closed in August.

As you pass Benson on Interstate 10, watch for Ocotillo Avenue, Exit 304. Take a left and drive about 2¼ mi, where a mailbox with a backward "SW" signals that you've come to the turnoff for **Singing Wind Bookshop.** Make a right at the mailbox and drive ¼ mi until you see a green gate. Let yourself in, close the gate, and go another ¼ mi to the shop. If you don't see the proprietor, who also runs the ranch, ring the large gong out front and she's sure to come out and welcome you. This unique bookshop-on-a-ranch has a good selection of books on Arizona wildlife, history, and geology. She doesn't take credit cards, though. ⊠ *700 W. Singing Wind Rd.* ☎ *520/586–2425* ☉ *Daily 9–5.*

Where to Stay & Eat

$–$$$ ✕ **Chute-Out Steakhouse & Saloon.** Don't be deceived by the unassuming exterior of this stucco steak house a block from Benson's main street. Once inside this warm and welcoming place, you can understand why it's one of the most popular restaurants in town. The food is excellent, and the service is efficient and friendly. Mesquite-grilled steaks, ribs, chicken, and seafood, fresh-baked breads and desserts, and salads (the house dressing is superb) make this spot well worth the visit. ⊠ *161 S. Huachuca St.* ☎ *520/586–7297* ▤ *AE, D, MC, V.*

$–$$$ ✕ **Horseshoe Steakhouse & Cantina.** For a good green-chile burrito or a patty melt, stop in at this eclectic eatery, which has graced Benson's main street for more than 60 years. You'll know you're in cowboy country when you see the neon horseshoe on the ceiling, the macramés of local cattle brands, and the large Wurlitzer jukebox with its selection of sad country-and-western ballads. ⊠ *154 E. 4th St.* ☎ *520/586–3303* ▤ *MC, V.*

$–$$ ✕ **Galleano's.** The kitchen at this upscale roadhouse, a favorite among locals, turns out traditional diner fare—including great burgers and fries—as well as pastas and salads. There's a big salad bar, too—unusual in these parts. ⊠ *601 W. 4th St.* ☎ *520/586–3523* ▤ *MC, V.*

¢–$ ✕ **Reb's Cafe & Coffee Shop.** For a more traditional take on real Southwestern food—none of that newfangled nouvelle stuff—this unpretentious spot is of the cowboy variety. It serves Mexican food and what passes for Italian, but it really prides itself on steaks and hamburgers, and a darned good breakfast. ⊠ *1020 W. 4th St.* ☎ *520/586–3856* ▤ *AE, D, DC, MC, V.*

¢ ✕ **Ruiz's Mexican Food & Cantina.** In this part of the world, the name is
Fodor's Choice pronounced "Reese." This tiny, casual spot on the main drag has been
★ in operation since 1959, accommodating a daily stream of lunch and dinner customers, hungry for green-corn tamales, chiles rellenos, *topopo* (deep-fried tortilla) salads, and other specialties. The adjoining bar serves beer, wine, and cocktails. ⊠ *687 W. 4th St.* ☎ *520/586–2707* ▤ *MC, V.*

★ $–$$ ⌂ **Holiday Inn Express.** The closest lodging to Kartchner Caverns State Park, this motel sits just off Interstate 10 at the "Kartchner Corridor," a few miles west of Benson. It has the comfort and amenities you'd expect but with a Southwestern elegance rarely found in chain motels around the area. Rooms have coffeemakers and hair dryers, and a continental breakfast is included. ⊠ *630 S. Village Loop* ⌕ *Box 2252, 85602* ☎ *520/586–8800 or 888/263–2283* 🖷 *520/586–1370* ⊕ *www.sixcontinentshotels.com* ⥰ *62 rooms* ⌔ *In-room data ports, microwaves, refrigerators, cable TV, pool, gym, laundry facilities, business services* ▤ *AE, D, DC, MC, V* ⦿ *CP.*

★ ☾ $ ⊡ **Skywatcher's Inn.** You don't have to be an astronomer to enjoy staying at this hilltop lodging on the grounds of the private Vega-Bray Observatory, but eight powerful telescopes are available for your universe-viewing pleasure. The B&B, built to accommodate sleepy stargazers, reflects the owners' delight in science: the comfortable rooms have such gadgets as lamps that simulate lightning and decorations (visible in black light) that resemble constellations painted on the ceiling. A special section in the science room is dedicated to kids. The property has a small pond and a boat for those wishing to sit back and relax or to do some bird-watching. For an additional fee, astronomers come down from Tucson on clear nights to hold stargazing sessions. ⊠ *1311 Astronomers Rd., 2 mi southeast of I–10, Exit 306* ⌖ *5655 N. Via Umbrosa, Tucson 85750* ☎ *520/615–3886* ⌗ *520/733–0600* ⊕ *www. skywatchersinn.com* ↩ *5 rooms* ⊟ *MC, V* ⫾◎⫿ *BP.*

Kartchner Caverns State Park

⑫   *9 mi south of Benson on AZ 90.*

Fodor's Choice
★

The publicity that surrounded the official opening of the Kartchner Caverns in November 1999 was in marked contrast to the secrecy that shrouded their discovery 25 years earlier and concealed their existence for 14 years. The two young men who stumbled into what is now considered one of the most spectacular cave systems anywhere recognized the significance of their find and played a fundamental role in its protection and eventual development. Great precautions have been taken to protect the wet-cave system—which comprises 13,000 feet of passages and two chambers as long as football fields—from damage by light and dryness.

The Discovery Center introduces visitors to the cave and its formations, and hour-long guided tours take small groups into the upper cave, including the large Rotunda and Throne rooms. Spectacular formations include the longest soda straw formation in the United States at 21 feet and 2 inches, and the largest column in the state reaching to an impressive height of 58 feet. The recently opened lower cave, known as the Big Room, is viewed on a separate tour. The Big Room holds the world's most extensive formation of brushite moonmilk, the first reported occurrence of turnip shields, and the first noted occurrence of birdsnest needle formations. The Big Room is also the nursery roost for female cave myotis bats from April through September, during which time the lower cave is closed in an effort to foster the cave's unique ecosystem. Kartchner Caverns is a wet, "live" cave, meaning that water still rises up from the surface to increase the multicolored calcium carbonate formations already visible.

The total cavern size is 2⅖ mi long, but the explored areas cover an area of only 1,600 feet by 1,100 feet. The average relative humidity inside is 99%, so visitors are often graced with "cave kisses," water droplets that drip from above. Because the climate outside the caves is so dry, it is estimated that if air got inside, it could deplete the annual supply of moisture in only a few days, halting the growth of the speleothems that decorate its walls. To prevent this, there are 22 environmental monitoring stations that measure air and soil temperature, relative humidity, evaporation rates, air trace gases, and airflow inside the caverns. Tour reservations are required and should be made several months in advance; hiking trails, picnic areas, and campsites are available on the park's 550 acres. ⊠ *AZ 90, 9 mi south of Exit 302 off I–10* ☎ *520/586–4100 information, 520/586–2283 tour reservations* ⊕ *www.pr.state.az.us* 🖭 *$5 per vehicle up to 4 people, $1 each additional person; Rotunda/Throne Room tours $18.95, Big Room tours $22.95* ☾ *Daily 7:30–6, cave tours (by reservation) daily 8:40–4:40.*

SOUTHWEST ARIZONA

The turbulent history of the West is writ large in this now-sleepy part of Arizona. It's home to the Tohono O'odham Indian Reservation (the largest in the country after the Navajo Nation's) and towns such as Ajo, created—and almost undone—by the copper-mining industry and Nogales, a vital entry point on the U.S.–Mexico border. Yuma, abutting the California border, was a major crossing point of the Colorado River as far back as the time of the conquistadors.

Natural attractions are a lure in this starkly scenic region: Organ Pipe Cactus National Monument provides a number of trails for desert hikers, and Buenos Aires and Imperial wildlife refuges—homes to many unusual species—are important destinations for birders and other nature watchers.

On warm weekends and especially during semester breaks, the 130-mi route from Tucson to Ajo is busy with traffic headed southwest to Puerto Penasco (Rocky Point), Mexico, the closest outlet to the sea for Arizonans. Much of the time, however, the only companions you'll have on this trek are the low-lying scrub and cactus and the mesquite, ironwood, and paloverde trees.

Nogales

🔞 *15 mi south of Tumacácori; 63 mi south of Tucson, on Interstate 19 at the Mexican border.*

Bustling Nogales can become fairly rowdy on weekend evenings, when underage Tucsonans head south of the border to drink. It has some good restaurants, however, and fine-quality crafts in addition to the usual souvenirs.

Nogales, named for the walnut trees that grew along the river here, is actually two towns: the American town and the huge Mexican city over the border. The American side was once a focal point for cattle shipping between Sonora and the United States. Today, Nogales reaps the benefits of NAFTA, with warehouses and trucking firms dedicated to the distribution of Mexican produce, making it one of the world's busiest produce ports. The American side depends on the health of the peso and the number of shoppers who cross the border from Mexico to buy American goods. The Mexican side has grown with the economic success of *maquiladoras*, factories that manufacture goods destined for the

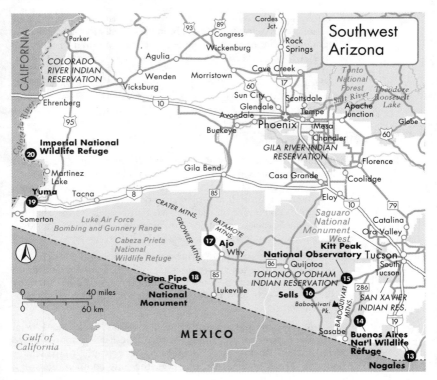

United States. There is a great deal of commerce between the two sides of Nogales.

Some of this trade is in narcotics and undocumented workers, giving this border town an edgy quality that is not representative of most other parts of Mexico. Security on the American side is very tight; don't even think about taking a firearm near the border. You'll also do better not to drive your car into Mexico: not only is there a very real possibility it may be stolen, but you'll face significant delays because of the thorough search you and your vehicle will receive upon returning. This hassle is unnecessary, though, because you can cover Nogales in a day trip, and most of the good shopping is within easy walking distance of the border crossing. Park on the Arizona side, either on the street or, better yet, in one of many guarded lots that cost about $8 for the day (use restrooms on the U.S. side before you cross).

Don't bother trading your dollars for pesos. The merchants prefer being paid with dollars and always have change on hand. You should be prepared for aggressive selling tactics and sometimes-disorienting hubbub, but locals are always glad to point you in the right direction, and almost all speak English.

Where to Stay & Eat

$–$$$ ✕ **La Roca.** East of the railroad tracks and off the beaten tourist path, La Roca is a favorite of Tucsonans. It isn't difficult to find, however; just look for the towering black sign to the east of the border entrance. The setting—a series of tiled rooms and courtyards in a stately old stone house, with a balcony overlooking a charming patio—is lovely. If you like meat, try the *carne tampiqueña,* an assortment of grilled meats that comes with chiles rellenos and an enchilada. Chicken mole (with a chocolate-chile sauce) is also a favorite. ✉ *Calle Elias 91, Nogales, Mexico* ☎ *631/312–0891* ☳ *MC, V.*

$–$$ ✕ **Elvira.** The free shot of tequila that comes with each meal will whet your appetite for Elvira's reliable fish dishes, chicken mole, and chiles rellenos. This large, friendly restaurant (divided into intimate dining areas) is at the foot of Avenida Obregón just south of the border and popular with those who visit Nogales often. Grandmother Elvira herself is no longer around, but her succulent signature dish, shrimp Elvira-style, steamed in white wine, lives on. ✉ *Avda. Obregón 1, Nogales, Mexico* ☎ *631/312–4773* ☳ *Reservations not accepted* ☳ *MC, V.*

¢–$ ✕ **Zula's.** Standard, old-fashioned border restaurant fare is served with Greek flair here on the Arizona side, with Sonoran food (tortillas, cheese, refried beans) alongside gyros and American selections, such as burgers, steaks, and seafood entrées. It makes for an interesting combination. It's not as glitzy as the south-of-the-border places, but the food is just as tasty. ✉ *982 N. Grand Ave., Nogales* ☎ *520/287–2892* ☳ *MC, V.*

¢ ⊞ **Americana Motor Hotel.** A serviceable place that has seen better days, the Americana has large, Aztec-style stone sculptures scattered around the grounds. Spacious and decorated in a Southwest motif, rooms are comfortable but worn. The restaurant and lounge are casual places to eat American food. ✉ *639 N. Grand Ave., 85621* ☎ *520/287–7211 or 800/874–8079* ☞ *97 rooms* ☳ *Restaurant, cable TV, pool, bar* ☳ *AE, MC, V.*

Shopping

The main shopping area is on the Mexican side, on Avenida Obregón, which begins a few blocks west (to your right) of the border entrance and runs north–south; just follow the crowds. You'll find handicrafts, furnishings, and jewelry here, but if you go off on some of the side streets, you might come across more interesting finds at better prices. Except at shops that indicate otherwise, bargaining is not only acceptable but expected. Playing this customary game can save you, on average, 50%, so don't be shy. The shops listed below tend to have fixed prices, so either buy here if you don't want to bargain at all, or note their prices and see if you can do better elsewhere.

Casa Bonita (✉ Avda. Obregón 134, Nogales, Mexico ☎ 631/312–3059) carries jewelry, tinwork mirrors, carved wooden chests, and household items.

El Changarro (✉ Calle Elias 93, Nogales, Mexico ☎ 631/312–0545) sells high-quality (and high-priced) furniture, antiques, pottery, and hand-woven rugs. It's next door to El Balcón de la Roca.

El Sarape (⊠ Avda. Obregón 161, Nogales, Mexico ☎ 631/312–0309) specializes in sterling silver jewelry from Taxco and women's designer clothing.

Maya de México (⊠ Avda. Obregón 150, Nogales, Mexico ☎ no phone) is the place to come for smaller folk-art items, including Day of the Dead displays, blue glass, painted dishes, and colorful clothing.

Buenos Aires National Wildlife Refuge

🔴 *66 mi southwest of Tucson; from Tucson, take AZ 86 west 22 mi to AZ 286; go south 40 mi to milepost 8, and it's another 3 mi east to the preserve headquarters.*

This remote nature preserve, in the Altar Valley and encircled by seven mountain ranges, is the only place in the United States where the Sonoran/savanna grasslands that once spread over the entire region can still be seen. The fragile ecosystem was almost completely destroyed by overgrazing, and a program to restore native grasses is currently in progress. In 1985 the U.S. Fish and Wildlife Service purchased the Buenos Aires Ranch—now headquarters for the 115,000-acre preserve—to establish a reintroduction program for the endangered masked bobwhite quail. Bird-watchers consider Buenos Aires unique because it's the only place in the United States where they can see a "grand slam" (four species) of quail: Montezuma quail, Gambel's quail, scaled quail, and masked bobwhite. If it rains, the 100-acre Aguirre Lake, 1½ mi north of the headquarters, attracts wading birds, shorebirds, and waterfowl—in all, more than 250 avian species have been spotted here. They share the turf with deer, antelope, coati mundi, badgers, bobcats, and mountain lions. Touring options include a 10-mi auto tour through the area, nature trails, a boardwalk through the marshes at Arivaca Cienega, and, by reservation only, weekend guided tours. ⊠ *AZ 286, Box 109, Sasabe 85633* ☎ *520/823–4251* 🖶 *520/823–4247* ⊕ *http://refuges.fws.gov* 🎫 *Free* ☉ *Refuge headquarters and visitor center daily sunrise–sunset.*

Where to Stay

$$$$ 🏨 **Rancho de la Osa.** This historical ranch, set on 250 eucalyptus-shaded acres near the Mexican border and Buenos Aires preserve, was built in 1889, and two adobe structures were added in the 1920s to accommodate guests, among them Lyndon Johnson and Adlai Stevenson. The rooms have modern plumbing and fixtures, wood-burning fireplaces, and porches with Adirondack chairs. Bread baked on the premises, salads made with ingredients grown in the garden, and water drawn from the well all contribute to the back-to-basics serenity. Rates include all meals and horseback riding, and guests are expected to dress for dinner. ⊠ *AZ 286* ☍ *Box 1, Sasabe 85633* ☎ *520/823–4257 or 800/872–6240* 🖶 *520/823–4238* ⊕ *www.ranchodelaosa.com* ⇆ *19 rooms* ♤ *Dining room, pool, hot tub, massage, bicycles, billiards, hiking, horseback riding, bar, lounge, library, Internet, meeting rooms; no room TVs, no kids under 6, no smoking* ⊟ *MC, V* ⊌ *FAP.*

Kitt Peak National Observatory

⓯ *56 mi southwest of Tucson; to reach Kitt Peak from Tucson, take Interstate 10 to Interstate 19 south, and then AZ 86. After 44 mi on AZ 86, turn left at AZ 386 junction and follow winding mountain road 12 mi up to observatory. (In inclement weather, contact the highway department to confirm that the road is open.)*

Funded by the National Science Foundation and managed by a group of more than 20 universities, Kitt Peak National Observatory is part of the Tohono O'odham Reservation. After much discussion back in the late 1950s, tribal leaders agreed to share a small section of their 4,400 square mi with the observatory's telescopes. Among these is the McMath, the world's largest solar telescope, which uses piped-in liquid coolant. From the visitors' gallery you can see into the telescope's light-path tunnel, which goes down hundreds of feet into the mountain. Kitt Peak scientists use these high-power telescopes to conduct vital solar research and observe distant galaxies. The scientists and staff are friendly and knowledgeable, and their enthusiasm for astronomy is contagious.

The museum's visitor center has exhibits on astronomy, information about the telescopes, and free hour-long guided tours that depart daily at 10, 11:30, and 1:30. Complimentary brochures enable you to take self-guided tours of the grounds, and there's a picnic area about 1½ mi below the observatory. The observatory buildings have vending machines, but there are no restaurants or gas stations within 20 mi of Kitt Peak. The observatory offers occasional stargazing dinner tours ($36 per person) for up to 20 people; reservations are necessary. ✉ *AZ 386, Pan Tak* ☎ *520/318–8726, 520/318–7200 recorded message* ⊕ *www.noao.edu/kpno* 💲 *$2 suggested donation* ☉ *Visitor center daily 9–3:45.*

Sells

⓰ *32 mi southwest of Kitt Peak via AZ 386 to AZ 86.*

The Tohono O'odham Reservation, the second-largest in the United States, covers 4,400 square mi between Tucson and Ajo, stretching south to the Mexican border and north almost to the city of Casa Grande. To the south of Kitt Peak, the 7,730-foot Baboquivari Peak is considered sacred by the Tohono O'odham as the home of their deity, I'itoi ("elder brother"). A little less than halfway between Tucson and Ajo, Sells—the tribal capital of the Tohono O'odham—is a good place to stop for gas or a soft drink. Much of the time there's little to see or do in Sells, but in winter an annual rodeo and fair attract thousands of visitors. If you want something more substantial than a snack, head for the Sells Shopping Center, where you'll see **Basha's Deli & Bakery** (✉ Topawa Rd. ☎ 520/383–2546). It's a good-size market and can supply all the makings for a picnic, including a picnic table near the store's entrance. For traditional Indian and Mexican food like fry bread, tacos, and chili, try the **Papago Cafe** (✉ AZ 86, near the Chevron Station ☎ 520/383–3510). The **Turquoise Turtle** (✉ AZ 86 ☎ 520/383–2411) sells baskets and other crafts made on the reservation and beyond.

en route

At **Why,** about 60 mi from Sells, AZ 86 forks off into the north and south sections of AZ 85. Originally the name of the community at this Y-shape intersection was spelled, simply and descriptively, "Y," but in 1950 the town was told that it had to have a three-letter name in order to be assigned a postal code—hence the querulous appellation that has kept travelers wondering *Why* ever since.

Ajo

⑰ *90 mi northwest of Sells.*

"Ajo" (pronounced *ah*-ho) is Spanish for garlic, and some say the town got its name from the wild garlic that grows in the area. Others claim the word is a bastardization of the Indian word *au-auho,* referring to red paint derived from a local pigment.

For many years Ajo, like Bisbee to the east, was a thriving Phelps Dodge Company town. Copper mining had been attempted in the area in the late 19th century, but it wasn't until the 1911 arrival of John Greenway, general manager of the Calumet & Arizona Mining Company, that the region began to be developed profitably. Calumet and Phelps Dodge merged in 1935, and the huge New Cornelia pit mine produced millions of tons of copper until the mine finally closed in 1985. With the town's main source of revenue gone, Ajo looked for a time as though it might shut down, but many retirees are now being lured here by the warm climate and low-cost housing.

At the center of town is a sparkling white Spanish-style plaza. The shops and restaurants that line the plaza's covered arcade today are rather modest. Unlike Bisbee, Ajo hasn't yet drawn an artistic crowd—or the upscale boutiques and eateries that tend to follow.

You get a panoramic view of Ajo's huge open-pit mine, almost 2 mi wide, from the **New Cornelia Open Pit Mine Lookout Point.** Some of the abandoned equipment remains in the pit, and various stages of mining operations are diagrammed at the covered visitors' shelters, where there's a 30-minute film about Phelps Dodge's mining operations. ⊠ *Indian Village Rd.* ☎ *520/387–7746* ☜ *$1 suggested donation* ☼ *Generally Nov.–Apr., Mon.–Sat. 10–4.*

The **Ajo Historical Society Museum** has collected a mélange of articles related to Ajo's past from local townspeople. The displays are rather disorganized, but some of the historical photographs and artifacts are fascinating, and the museum is inside the territorial-style St. Catherine's Indian Mission, built around 1942. ⊠ *160 Mission St.* ☎ *520/387–7105* ☜ *Donations requested* ☼ *Daily noon–4.*

The 860,000-acre **Cabeza Prieta National Wildlife Refuge,** about 10 minutes from Ajo, was established in 1939 as a preserve for endangered bighorn sheep and other Sonoran Desert wildlife. A permit is required to enter, and only those with four-wheel-drive vehicles, needed to traverse the rugged terrain, can obtain one from the refuge's office. ⊠ *1611 N. 2nd Ave., Ajo 85321* ☎ *520/387–6483* ⊕ *http://refuges.fws.gov* ☜ *Free* ☼ *Office weekdays 9–5, refuge daily dawn–dusk.*

Where to Stay & Eat

¢–$ ✕ **Señor Sancho.** Just about everybody in Ajo comes to this unprepossessing roadhouse at the north end of town for generous portions of Mexican food, well prepared and very reasonably priced. This friendly spot has light-wood booths and colorful murals with a Mexican motif. All the standard favorites are on the menu—hearty combination platters, tacos, enchiladas, chiles rellenos, flautas, and good chicken mole. ⊠ 663 N. 2nd Ave. ☎ 520/387–6226 ▭ No credit cards.

$ 🏠 **Guest House Inn Bed & Breakfast.** Built in 1925 to accommodate visiting Phelps Dodge VIPs, this lodging is a favorite for birders: guests can head out early to nearby Organ Pipe National Monument or just sit on the patio and watch the quail, cactus wrens, and other warblers that fly in to visit. Rooms are furnished in a range of Southwestern styles, from light Santa Fe to rich Spanish colonial. The owners speak fluent French and Spanish, and a full breakfast is served. ⊠ 700 Guest House Rd., 85321 ☎ 520/387–6133 ⊕ www.guesthouseinn.biz ⊃ 4 rooms ♿ No smoking ▭ DC, MC, V ℗ BP.

Organ Pipe Cactus National Monument

⑱ *32 mi southwest of Ajo; from Ajo, backtrack to Why and take AZ 85 south for 22 mi to reach the visitor center.*

Organ Pipe Cactus National Monument, abutting Cabeza Prieta National Wildlife Refuge but much more accessible to visitors, is the largest habitat north of the border for organ-pipe cacti. These multi-armed cousins of the saguaro are fairly common in Mexico but rare in the United States. Because they tend to grow on south-facing slopes, you won't be able to see many of them unless you take one of the two scenic loop drives: the 21-mi **Ajo Mountain Drive** or the 53-mi **Puerto Blanco Drive,** both on winding, graded one-way dirt roads.

Be aware that Organ Pipe has become an illegal border crossing hotspot. Migrant workers and drug traffickers cross from Mexico under cover of darkness. At this writing Puerto Blanco Drive was closed to the public. A two-way road that only travels 5 of the 53 mi was expected to open shortly, but the rest of the road will remain closed until further notice due to the construction of barriers along the Mexican border. Until the project is completed, there are still safety concerns at the monument. Even so, park officials emphasize that tourists have only occasionally been the victims of isolated property crimes—primarily theft of personal items from parked cars. Visitors are advised by rangers to keep valuables locked and out of plain view and not to initiate contact with groups of strangers whom they may encounter on hiking trails. A campground at the monument has 208 RV (no hookups) and tent sites. Facilities include a dump station, flush toilets, grills and picnic tables. ⊠ AZ 85 ☎ 520/387–6849 ⊕ www.nps.gov/orpi 🎟 $5 per vehicle ☺ Visitor center daily 8–5.

Yuma

⑲ *170 mi northwest of Ajo.*

Today, many people think of Yuma as a convenient stop between Phoenix or Tucson and San Diego—and this was equally true in the past. It's difficult to imagine the lower Colorado River, now dammed and bridged, as either a barrier or a means of transportation, but until the early part of the 20th century, this section of the great waterway was a force to contend with. Records show that since at least 1540 the Spanish were using Yuma (then the site of a Quechan Indian village) as a ford across a relatively shallow juncture of the Colorado.

Three centuries later, the advent of the shallow-draft steamboat made the settlement a point of entry for fortune seekers heading up through the Gulf of California to mining sites in eastern Arizona. Fort Yuma was established in 1850 to guard against Indian attacks, and by 1873 the town was a county seat, a U.S. port of entry, and an army quartermaster depot. The building of the Yuma Territorial Prison in 1876 helped stabilize the economy.

The steamboat shipping business, undermined by the completion of the Southern Pacific Railroad line in 1877, was finished off by the building of Laguna Dam in 1909, which controlled the overflow of the Colorado River and made agricultural development in the area possible. In World War II, Yuma Proving Ground was used to train bomber pilots, and General Patton readied some of his desert war forces for battle at classified areas near the city. Many who served here during the war returned to Yuma to retire, and the city's economy now relies largely on tourism. One very telling fact may shed some light on why: according to National Weather Service statistics, Yuma is the sunniest city in the United States.

Most of the interesting sights in Yuma are at the north end of town. Stop in at the **Yuma Convention and Visitors Bureau** (⌧ 377 S. Main St. ☎ 928/783–0071 or 800/293–0071 ⊕ www.visityuma.com) and pick up a walking-tour guide to the historic downtown area. The adobe-style **Arizona Historical Society Museum,** housed in the Century House, was built around 1870 by merchant E. F. Sanguinetti and exhibits artifacts from Yuma's territorial days and details the military presence in the area. ⌧ *240 S. Madison Ave.* ☎ *928/782–1841* 🎟 *Free* ⊙ *Tues.–Sat. 10–4.*

If you cross the railroad tracks at the northernmost part of town, you'll come to **Yuma Crossing National Historic Landmark,** which consists of the Quartermaster Depot and Fort Yuma, on the California side of the Colorado River. The mess hall of Fort Yuma, later used as a school for Native American children, now serves as the small **Fort Yuma Quechan Indian Museum.** Historical photographs, archaeological items, and Quechan arts and crafts are on display. ⌧ *CA 24* ☎ *760/572–0661* 🎟 *$1* ⊙ *Weekdays 8–5, Sat. 10–4.*

Ⓒ On the other side of the river from Fort Yuma, the Civil War–period quartermaster depot resupplied army posts to the north and east and served as a distribution point for steamboat freight headed overland to Arizona forts. The 1853 home of riverboat captain G. A. Johnson is the depot's earliest building and the centerpiece of the **Yuma Crossing State Historic Park.** The residence also served as a weather bureau and home for customs agents, among other functions, and the guided tour through the house provides a complete history. The complex was closed until the fall of 1997, when it reopened as a state park. The Transportation

Museum has stagecoaches, Wells Fargo wagons, and antique surreys, as well as more "modern" modes of transportation like the 1909 Model T and the 1931 Model A pickup. You can also visit a re-creation of the Commanding Officer's Quarters, complete with period furnishings and servants' quarters: you'll find the dining-room table set with antique china and linens, as if the C. O. himself were expected for dinner. ⊠ *201 N. 4th Ave., between 1st St. and the Colorado River Bridge* ☎ *928/329– 0471* ⊕ *www.pr.state.az.us* ⊡ *$4* ⊙ *Daily 9–5.*

The most notorious tourist sight in town, **Yuma Territorial Prison,** now an Arizona state historic park, was built for the most part by the convicts who were incarcerated here from 1876 until 1909, when the prison outgrew its location. The hilly site on the Colorado River, chosen for security purposes, precluded further expansion.

Visitors gazing today at the tiny cells that held six inmates each, often in 115°F heat, are likely to be appalled, but the prison—dubbed the Country Club of the Colorado by locals—was considered a model of enlightenment by turn-of-the-20th-century standards: in an era when beatings were common, the only punishments meted out here were solitary confinement and assignment to a dark cell. The complex housed a hospital as well as Yuma's only public library, where the 25¢ that visitors paid for a prison tour financed the acquisition of new books.

The 3,069 prisoners who served time at what was then the territory's only prison included men and women from 21 different countries. They came from all social classes and were sent up for everything from armed robbery and murder to violation of the Mexican Neutrality Act and polygamy. R. L. McDonald, incarcerated for forgery, had been the superintendent of the Phoenix public school system. Chosen as the prison bookkeeper, he absconded with $130 of the inmates' money when he left. Pearl Hart, convicted of stagecoach robbery, gained such notoriety for her crime that she attempted to launch a career in vaudeville after her release.

The mess hall opened as a museum in 1940, and the entire prison complex was designated a state historic park in 1961. ⊠ *1 Prison Hill Rd., near Exit 1 off I–8,* ☎ *928/783–4771* ⊕ *www.pr.state.az.us* ⊡ *$4* ⊙ *Daily 8–5; free interpretive programs at 11, 2, and 3:30.*

Where to Stay & Eat

¢–$$ ✕ **Chretin's Mexican Food.** A Yuma institution, Chretin's opened as a dance hall in the 1930s before it became one of the first Mexican restaurants in town in 1946. Don't be put off by the nondescript exterior or the entryway, which leads back past the kitchen and cashier's stand into three large dining areas. The food is all made on the premises, right down to the chips and tortillas. Try anything that features *machaca* (shredded spiced beef or chicken). ⊠ *485 S. 15th Ave.* ☎ *928/782–1291* ⊟ *D, MC, V* ⊙ *Closed Sun.*

¢–$ ✕ **Lutes Casino.** Almost always packed with locals at lunchtime, this large, funky restaurant and bar claims to be the oldest pool hall and domino parlor in Arizona. It's a great place for a burger and a brew. ⊠ *221 S. Main St.* ☎ *928/782–2192* ⊟ *No credit cards.*

☕ **$$–$$$**   🏨 **Shilo Inn.** This is an excellent family place to stay because of in-room facilities that come as close to a kitchen as you might want on a trip. Rooms are spacious, equipped with irons and ironing boards and coffeemakers, and most have views of the courtyard and pool. A full breakfast is included in the rates and served in the restaurant. This property is the only Arizona representative of this Western regional motel chain. ✉ *1550 S. Castle Dome Rd., 85365* ☎ *928/782–9511 or 800/222–2244* 📠 *928/783–1538* ⊕ *www.shiloinns.com* 🛏 *131 rooms, 15 suites* ⚖ *Restaurant, microwaves, refrigerators, cable TV with video games, pool, gym, hot tub, sauna, lounge, business services, some pets allowed (fee)* 🚭 *AE, D, DC, MC, V* ⧖ *BP.*

★ **$–$$**   🏨 **Best Western Coronado Motor Hotel.** This Spanish tile–roofed motor hotel, convenient to both the freeway and downtown historical sights, was built in 1938 and is run by the son of the original owner. Bob Hope used to stay here during World War II, when he entertained the gunnery troops training in Yuma. The rooms have such extras as irons and ironing boards and hair dryers. Yuma Landing Restaurant & Lounge is on-site with an impressive collection of historical photos. ✉ *233 4th Ave., 85364* ☎ *928/783–4453 or 800/528–1234* 📠 *928/782–7487* ⊕ *www.bestwestern.com* 🛏 *86 rooms* ⚖ *Restaurant, cable TV, in-room data ports, microwaves, refrigerators, in-room VCRs, pool, lobby lounge, laundry facilities* 🚭 *AE, D, DC, MC, V* ⧖ *BP.*

$ 🏨 **La Fuente Inn.** Keep in mind that Yuma's hotels have to compete with huge RV parks, and you begin to see why the rates are reasonable and so many extras are included. La Fuente is particularly popular with military personnel. The decor and setting may be unremarkable, but the rooms are large and very clean, and each is equipped with coffeemaker, iron, and ironing board. Room rates include continental breakfast, happy-hour drinks, and access to a nearby fitness center. ✉ *1513 E. 16th St., 85365* ☎ *928/329–1814 or 800/841–1814* 📠 *928/343–2671* ⊕ *www.lafuenteinn. com* 🛏 *96 rooms* ⚖ *BBQs, microwaves, refrigerators, cable TV, pool, hot tub, laundry facilities* 🚭 *AE, D, DC, MC, V* ⧖ *CP.*

Imperial National Wildlife Refuge

☕ **⑳**   *40 mi north of Yuma; from Yuma, take U.S. 95 north past the Proving Ground and follow the signs to the refuge.*

A guided tour is the best way to visit the 25,765-acre Imperial National Wildlife Refuge, created by backwaters formed when the Imperial Dam was built. Something of an anomaly, the refuge is home both to species indigenous to marshy rivers and to creatures that inhabit the adjacent Sonoran Desert—desert tortoises, coyotes, bobcats, and bighorn sheep. Most of all, though, this is a major bird habitat. Thousands of waterfowl and shorebirds live here year-round, and migrating flocks of swallows pass through in the spring and fall. During those seasons, expect to see everything from pelicans and cormorants to Canada geese, snowy egrets, and a variety of rarer species. Canoes can be rented at Martinez Lake Marina, 3½ mi southeast of the refuge headquarters. It's best to visit from mid-October through May, when it's cooler and the ever-present mosquitoes are least active. Kids especially enjoy the 1.3-mi

Painted Desert Nature Trail, which winds through the different levels of the Sonoran Desert. From an observation tower at the visitor center you can see the river, as well as the fields being planted with rye and millet, on which the migrating birds like to feed. ✉ *Martinez Lake Rd., Box 72217 Martinez Lake 85365* ☎ *928/783–3371* 🖷 *928/783–0652* ⊕ *http://refuges.fws.gov* ✆ *Free* ⊘ *Visitor center mid-Apr.–mid-Oct., weekdays 7:30–4; mid-Oct.–mid-Apr., weekdays 7:30–4, weekends 9–4.*

SOUTHERN ARIZONA A TO Z

To research prices, get advice from other travelers, and book travel arrangements, visit www.fodors.com.

AIR TRAVEL

America West Express has direct flights to Yuma International Airport from Phoenix. Sky West, a United subsidiary, flies nonstop from Los Angeles to Yuma.

🇫 Carriers **America West Express** ☎ 800/235-9292 ⊕ www.americawest.com **Sky West** ☎ 435/634-3000 ⊕ www.skywest.com

AIRPORTS

🇫 Airport Information **Sierra Vista Municipal Airport/Fort Huachuca** ✉ 2100 Airport Ave. ☎ 520/458-5775 ⊕ www.ci.sierra-vista.az.us/Airport/index.htm. **Yuma International Airport (YUM)** ✉ 2191 32nd St. ☎ 928/726-5882 ⊕ www.yumainternationalairport.com.

BUS TRAVEL

Greyhound Lines has service from Tucson to the stations in Benson, Willcox, and Yuma. The Ajo Stage Line offers regular shuttle van service from Tucson to Ajo.

🇫 Ajo Transportation ☎ 520/387-6467 or 800/942-1981. **Greyhound Lines** ☎ 800/454-2487 ⊕ www.greyhound.com ✉ 680 E. 4th St., Benson ☎ 520/586-3141 ✉ 622 N. Haskell Ave., Willcox ☎ 520/384-2183 ✉ 170 E. 17th Pl., Yuma ☎ 928/783-4403.

CAR RENTALS

You can rent a car from several national companies at Yuma International Airport.

🇫 Major Agencies **Avis** ☎ 928/726-5737 or 800/230-4898 ⊕ www.avis.com. **Budget** ☎ 928/344-1822 or 800/404-8033 ⊕ www.budget.com. **Dollar** ☎ 928/344-2097 or 800/800-4000 ⊕ www.dollar.com. **Hertz** ☎ 928/726-5160 or 800/654-3131 ⊕ www.hertz.com.

CAR TRAVEL

You'll need a car to tour most of southern Arizona. The best plan is to fly into Tucson, which is the hub of the area, or Phoenix, which has the most flights, and pick up a car at the airport.

SOUTHEASTERN ARIZONA From Tucson, take Interstate 10 east. When you come to Benson, take AZ 80 south to reach Tombstone, Bisbee, and Douglas. If you want to go to Sonoita and Patagonia, or just take a pretty drive, turn off Interstate 10 earlier, at the exit for AZ 83 south; you'll come to Sonoita, where this road intersects AZ 82. From here you can either continue south to Sierra Vista, head southwest on AZ 82 to Patagonia, or head east to Tombstone.

SOUTHWESTERN ARIZONA Ajo lies on AZ 85 (north–south), Yuma at the junction of Interstate 8 and U.S. 95. For a scenic route to Ajo from Tucson (126 mi), take AZ 86 west to Why and turn north on AZ 85. Yuma is 170 mi from San Diego on Interstate 8, and it is 300 mi from Las Vegas on U.S. 95.

EMERGENCIES

🔃 Emergency Services **Ambulance, Fire, or Police Emergencies** ☎ 911.
🔃 Emergency Services in Mexico **Ambulance, Fire, or Police Emergencies** ☎ 060.
🔃 Hospitals **Ajo Community Health Center** ✉ 410 Malacate St., Ajo ☎ 520/387-5651. **Benson Hospital** ✉ 350 S. Ocotillo St., Benson ☎ 520/586-2261. **Bisbee Copper Queen Hospital** ✉ 101 Cole St., Bisbee ☎ 520/432-5383. **Carondelet Health Network/ Holy Cross Hospital** ✉ 1171 W. Target Range Rd., Nogales ☎ 520/285-3000. **Northern Cochise Community Hospital** ✉ 901 W. Rex Allen Dr., Willcox ☎ 520/384-3541 or 800/696-3541. **Sierra Vista Regional Health Center** ✉ 300 El Camino Real, Sierra Vista ☎ 520/458-4641 or 800/880-0088. **Yuma Regional Medical Center** ✉ 2400 S. Ave. A, Yuma ☎ 928/344-2000.

🔃 Pharmacies **Bob's IGA Pharmacy** ✉ 900 W. Rex Allen Dr., Willcox ☎ 520/384-2502. **Medicine Shoppe Pharmacy** ✉ 795 W. 4th St., Benson ☎ 520/586-1299. **Rite Aid Pharmacy** ✉ 600 W. Catalina Dr., Yuma ☎ 928/726-7810. **Safeway Pharmacy** ✉ 101 Naco Hwy., Bisbee ☎ 520/432-3038. **Tom's Pharmacy** ✉ 40 W. Plaza St., Ajo ☎ 520/ 387-7080. **Walgreens** ✉ 1150 W. 8th St., Yuma ☎ 928/783-6834 ✉ 3121 S. 4th Ave., Yuma ☎ 928/344-0453 ✉ 21 W. Park St., Nogales ☎ 520/287-6521.

SPORTS & THE OUTDOORS

CAMPING & HIKING Douglas Ranger District and the Sierra Vista Ranger Station of the National Forest Service can give you information about camping and hiking in the Coronado National Forest, which covers most of the mountain ranges in southeastern Arizona. The Bureau of Land Management Yuma Field Office can give you details about outdoor recreational activities in that area.

🔃 **Bureau of Land Management Yuma Field Office** ✉ 2555 E. Gila Ridge Rd., Yuma 85365 ☎ 928/317-3200 ⊕ www.az.blm.gov. **Coronado National Forest** Douglas Ranger District ✉ 3081 N. Leslie Canyon Rd., Douglas ☎ 520/364-3468 ⊕ www.fs.fed.us/r3/ coronado ✉ Sierra Vista Ranger Station ✉ 5990 S. AZ 92, Hereford 85615 ☎ 520/378-0311 ⊕ www.fs.fed.us/r3/coronado.

SIGHTSEEING TOURS

BIRD-WATCHING The Southeastern Arizona Bird Observatory is a nonprofit organization that offers guided tours, educational programs, and informational materials for bird-watchers visiting, or living in, Arizona. As an aid to birders, SABO offers a map of the best bird-watching sites along the Southeastern Arizona Birding Trail, which was created in collaboration with several private and public organizations. Write to the SABO or go on their website for a copy of the map. High Lonesome Ecotours offers birding tours with lodging.

🔃 **High Lonesome Ecotours** ✉ 570 S. Little Bear Trail, Sierra Vista ☎ 520/458-9446 ⊕ www.hilonesome.com. **Southeastern Arizona Bird Observatory** ✉ Box 5521, Bisbee 85603 ☎ 520/432-1388 ⊕ www.sabo.org.

BOAT TOURS You can take a boat ride up the Colorado with Yuma River Tours. You can book 12- to 45-person jet-boat excursions through Smokey Knowlton, who has been exploring the area for more than 36 years.

🛈 **Yuma River Tours** ✉ 1920 Arizona Ave., Yuma 85364 ☎ 928/783-4400 ⊕ www.yumarivertours.com.

GUIDED TOURS Southern Arizona Adventures offers ecotours, hiking, backpacking, mountain biking, and historical/cultural expeditions from its base in Bisbee.

🛈 **Southern Arizona Adventures** ✉ 22 Main St., Bisbee ☎ 520/432-9058 or 800/319-7377 ⊕ www.arizonatour.com.

TRAIN EXCURSIONS On weekends from October through June, you can take a two-hour round-trip jaunt on the Yuma Valley Railway. The 1922 coach, pulled by one of two historic diesel engines, departs at 1 PM from the 8th Street station in Yuma and runs south alongside the Colorado River for about 11 mi. Tickets cost $10.

🛈 **Yuma Valley Railway** ✉ 2nd Ave. and 1st St., behind City Hall, Yuma ☎ 928/783-3456.

TAXIS

Benson Taxi offers transport services in the Benson area. In Sierra Vista, ABC Cab Co. provides both local and regional transport. Yuma City Cab has the best taxi service in Yuma.

🛈 **ABC Cab Co.** ☎ 520/458-8429. **Benson Taxi** ☎ 520/586-1294. **Yuma City Cab** ☎ 928/782-0111.

TRAIN TRAVEL

Amtrak trains run three times a week from Tucson east to the Benson depot and west to Yuma. Both stations are unstaffed with Amtrak personnel; however, the Benson Visitor Center is in the train depot.

🛈 **Amtrak** ☎ 800/872-7245 ⊕ www.amtrak.com. **Benson train station** ✉ 4th St. at San Pedro Ave., Benson. **Yuma train station** ✉ 281 Gila St., Yuma.

VISITOR INFORMATION

🛈 **In Southeastern Arizona Benson Railroad Depot and Visitor Center** ✉ 249 E. 4th St., Benson 85602 ☎ 520/586-4293 or 520/586-2245 ⊕ www.cityofbenson.com. **Bisbee Chamber of Commerce** ✉ 31 Subway St., Bisbee 85613 ☎ 520/432-5421 ⊕ www.bisbeearizona.com. **Douglas Visitor Center** ✉ 1125 Pan American, Douglas 85607 ☎ 520/364-2478 or 888/315-9999. **Patagonia Visitors Center** ✉ 307 McKeown Ave., Patagonia ☎ 520/394-0060 or 888/794-0060 ⊕ www.patagoniaaz.com. **Sierra Vista Convention and Visitors Bureau** ✉ 21 E. Willcox Dr., Sierra Vista 85635 ☎ 520/458-6940 or 800/288-3861 ⊕ www.visitsierravista.com. **Tombstone Chamber of Commerce and Visitor Center** ✉ 4th and Allen Sts., Tombstone 85638 ☎ 520/457-3929 or 520/457-9317 or 888/457-3929 ⊕ www.cityoftombstone.com. **Willcox Chamber of Commerce & Agriculture** ✉ 1500 N. Circle I Rd., Willcox 85643 ☎ 520/384-2272 or 800/200-2272 ⊕ www.willcoxchamber.com.

🛈 **In Southwestern Arizona Ajo Chamber of Commerce** ✉ 400 Taladro St., Ajo 85321 85321 ☎ 520/387-7742. **Nogales-Santa Cruz Chamber of Commerce** ✉ 123 W. Kino Rd., Nogales 85621 ☎ 520/287-3685 ⊕ www.nogaleschamber.com. **Yuma Convention and Visitors Bureau** ✉ 377 S. Main St., Yuma 85364 ☎ 928/783-0071 or 800/293-0071 ⊕ www.visityuma.com.

NORTHWEST ARIZONA & SOUTHEAST NEVADA

8

GET HIP TO THIS TIMELY TIP
by driving Route 66 in Kingman ⇨*p.372*

SIP A PINT
at the foot of London Bridge ⇨*p.377*

LAY YOUR BETS
in Laughlin ⇨*p.382*

SEE THE POWER BEHIND
the bright lights of Vegas
at the Hoover Dam ⇨*p.384*

WATERSKI IN THE DESERT
on Lake Mead ⇨*p.385*

Updated by
Tom Carpenter

WESTERN ARIZONA AND SOUTHEASTERN NEVADA COMPRISE a unique blend of deserts, mountains, and 1,000 mi of shoreline. From its highest elevation, Hualapai Peak at 8,417 feet, to its lowest along the Colorado River at approximately 630 feet, this wide-open region of the Southwest offers a diverse topography ranging from aspen- and pine-covered glades to the austere and soft-spoken grandeur of the Mojave Desert. Despite the superficial aridity of much of the landscape, the region bubbles with an abundance of springs and artesian wells. Without these water sources weeping from the rocks and sand, western Arizona and southeastern Nevada would never have developed into the major crossroad it is today.

The defining feature of the region is the Colorado River. Since the late Pleistocene epoch when Paleo-Indians first set foot in the river that was once described as "too thick to drink and too thin to plow," the Colorado has been a blessing and a barrier. Prehistoric traders from the Pacific Coast crossed the river at Willow Beach on their way to trade shells for pelts with the Hopi Indians and other Pueblo tribes farther east. Although the Spanish claimed the region, they showed little interest in it. Fur trappers arrived in 1826 looking for beaver. When gold was discovered in California in 1848, entrepreneurs built ferries up and down the river to accommodate the miners drawn to the area by what Cortez described as "a disease of the heart for which the only cure is gold." The influx of miners brought them in conflict with the indigenous peoples of the area, the Mojave and Hualapai tribes.

By 1883, construction of the Atchison, Topeka, and Santa Fe railroad had been completed as far as the Colorado River. No longer would the mineral wealth extracted from the area need to be shipped overland to ports in California. The precious metals could be sent back east and, along with it, cattle and hogs raised in the area. Prosperity followed, particularly for Kingman. While mining towns in the surrounding hills boomed and busted, Kingman prospered as a mercantile and distribution center.

Every spring the snowmelt of the vast Rocky Mountain watershed of the Colorado River pulsed through high basaltic canyons like water through a garden hose and washed away crops and livestock. Harnessing such a wild powerful river required no ordinary dam. In 1935, notched into the steep and narrow confines of Black Canyon on the border separating Arizona and Nevada, 727-foot high Hoover Dam took control of the Colorado River and turned its power into electricity and its floodwaters into the largest man-made reservoir in the world: Lake Mead.

The Second World War brought a different kind of boom to the region. Between the numerous mountain ranges running more or less north–south and parallel to the river, wide valleys offered the Army Air Corps an excellent location to train bomber crews. More than 36,000 airmen were trained at the Kingman Army Air Field. After the war, many of the men and women who served at the airfield, returned to the area to build lives and raise families.

Today, interstate commerce brings hundreds of thousands of vehicles through western Arizona and southeastern Nevada every day. For many who view the landscape through the glass of their air-conditioned vehicles, the landscape is a daunting vision of opaque and distant mountains shimmering in the heat rising from sun-baked pavement. For those who stop their vehicles and step into the clean open air, western Arizona and southeastern Nevada offer an enchanting blend of past and present, earth and sky, river and wind.

Exploring Northwest Arizona & Southeast Nevada

Western Arizona is a wedge of paradise for any outdoor enthusiast. The Colorado River, and the lakes that take shape along it like blue beads on a brown string, provides 1,000 mi of opportunities for fishing and water sports of all kinds. The valleys and mountains offer the curious traveler a topography replete with reasons for exploration and discovery. The three major communities of the area are Kingman, Bullhead City, and Lake Havasu City. Interstate 40, Historic Route 66, and U.S. 93 intersect in Kingman, which is also the seat of Mohave County. Bullhead City is on the Colorado River across from Laughlin, Nevada. Lake Havasu City is farther south on the Colorado River and is home to the famous London Bridge. With more than 2,100 mi of county roads in western Arizona, there are ample opportunities to strike out on your own to explore. It bears repeating that driving in the desert requires extra preparation. Make certain you are well stocked with radiator coolant, and be sure to carry plenty of water, a spare tire, a jack, and emergency supplies.

About the Restaurants

Whether you're looking for that cozy local café that smells of fresh soup and hot coffee, or the glamour of soft lighting and tablecloths complementing elegant cuisine, such dining choices are available in western Arizona. Casual dining establishments can be found in most of the communities in the region. The river communities of Lake Havasu City and Bullhead City provide the most opportunities for formal dining. Many of the finest dining establishments are in the casinos across the Colorado River from Bullhead City.

About the Hotels

A by-product of the major highways that stretch across western Arizona is the plethora of lodging choices. Most of the major chain motels and hotels have rooms available in each of the three major communities, with the added appeal of casino-hotels in Laughlin, Nevada.

WHAT IT COSTS				
	$$$$	**$$$**	**$$**	**$**	**¢**
RESTAURANTS	over $30	$20–$30	$12–$20	$8–$12	under $8
HOTELS	over $250	$175–$250	$120–$175	$70–$120	under $70

Restaurant prices are per person for a main course at dinner. Hotel prices are for two people in a standard double room in high season, excluding taxes and service charges.

GREAT ITINERARIES

If you have
3 days

Kingman ❶ ⌐ is a good place to start. Spend the morning visiting the Mohave County Museum of History and Arts and taking a walking tour of the downtown district. In the afternoon, drive out to Grand Canyon Caverns for some underground touring. Plan to spend the second day in Hualapai Mountain Park. Pack a picnic and go hiking on the trails. On your third day, take a day excursion to Chloride or Oatman. Both historic mining towns have plenty to fill your day.

If you have
5 days

Follow the suggested three-day itinerary, but make your way to Oatman rather than Chloride on the third day. You'll get there on Historic Route 66. Spend the morning visiting the shops and the Oatman Hotel, then take Route 66 west to AZ 95 and head south to Lake Havasu City ❷. Use the remainder of the day to visit the London Bridge. In the morning, make arrangements to spend the day on the lake. You'll want to relax after a day on the water, so consider taking in a dinner-theater performance at the London Arms Pub and Restaurant in the evening. In the morning, grab your binoculars and spend the a few hours looking for birds in the Havasu National Wildlife Refuge before you head back to Kingman.

8

Timing

The "H" word isn't spoken by locals. The days start "warming up" in May and grow increasingly "warm" (exceeding 100°F) until September, when things start to cool off. Mild winters see temperatures in the mid-70s along the river, low precipitation, and abundant sunshine. Lake Havasu has become a popular destination for college students on spring break, so expect crowds in and around Lake Havasu City in March. April and May are the best months for enjoying the brief and beautiful appearance of desert wild flowers. September and October are considered the perfect-weather months, with temperatures in the 70s and just a hint of autumn in the air. Generally scheduled for the first weekend in October, Andy Devine Days festivities celebrate Kingman's most famous citizen. The Route 66 Fun Run takes place the first weekend in May and starts in Seligman. Saturday morning, cars of all makes and vintages travel in a caravan to Kingman where there is a big barbecue and dance. In the morning, the caravan continues another 60 mi on "old 66" over the Black Mountains and through Oatman to Topock, where the road ends at the Colorado River.

Numbers in the text correspond to numbers in the margin and on the Northwest Arizona map.

NORTHWEST ARIZONA

Such towns as Kingman hark back to the glory days of the old Route 66, and the ghost towns of Chloride and Oatman bear testament to the mining madness that once reigned in the region. Water-sports fans, or those who just want to laze on a houseboat, will enjoy Lake Havasu, where you'll find the misplaced English icon London Bridge.

Kingman

▶ ❶ *188 mi northwest of Phoenix, 149 mi west of Flagstaff via Interstate 40*

Fodor'sChoice
★

The longest remaining stretch of **Historic Route 66** runs through Kingman. John Steinbeck called Route 66 "The Mother Road" in his novel *The Grapes of Wrath*. Established in 1926, the highway was intended to link the main streets of communities from Chicago to Los Angeles. With fewer mountains to cross and temperatures more moderate than northern highways, Route 66 appealed to travelers and interstate commerce. By 1970, the route had been replaced by the Interstate Highway system. Today, Route 66 offers travelers a nostalgic alternative to the lickety-split pace of Interstate travel, and no section of Route 66 is longer or nicer than the stretch that begins in Seligman, runs through downtown Kingman, climbs to the town of Oatman in the Black Mountains, and ends at Topock on the Colorado River.

The **Bonelli House** (✉ 430 E. Spring St. ☎ 928/753–1413), an excellent example of the Anglo-Territorial architecture popular in the early 1900s, is one of 62 buildings in the Kingman business district listed on the National Register of Historic Places. The **Kingman Area Chamber of Commerce** (✉ 333 W. Andy Devine Ave. ☎ 928/753–6106 ⊕ www. kingmanchamber.org) carries T-shirts, postcards, and the usual brochures to acquaint you with local attractions.

Western character actor Andy Devine—he played the hapless sheriff Linc Appleyard in the movie *The Man Who Shot Liberty Valance*—was from Kingman; it's obvious the moment you drive into town, as the fact is mentioned everywhere. The **Mohave County Museum of History and Arts** includes an Andy Devine Room with memorabilia from Devine's Hollywood years and, incongruously, a portrait collection of every president and first lady. There's also an exhibit of carved Kingman turquoise and a diorama depicting the expedition of Lt. Edward Beale, who led his camel-cavalry unit to the area in search of a wagon road along the 35th parallel (⇨ *General Jesup and the Camels, below*). Follow the White Cliffs Trail from downtown to see the deep ruts cut into the desert floor by the wagons that eventually came to Kingman after Beale's time. ✉ *400 W. Beale St.* ☎ *928/753–3195* ⊕ *www.ctaz.com/~mocohist/museum/index.htm* 🖾 *$3* ☺ *Weekdays 9–5, weekends 1–5.*

The highway past Kingman may seem desolate at first, but the mountains that surround the area offer outdoor activities in abundance, including those along the Kingman and Colorado rivers. Water sports play a big part in the area's recreation simply because about 1,000 mi of freshwater shoreline lies within the county along the Colorado River and around Lakes Havasu, Mohave, and Mead. Fishing and boating are very popular activities here. Kingman is only 35 mi from the river, whereas Bullhead and Lake Havasu cities are right next to water. A little exploring uncovers some scattered "ghost" towns in the area, including Chloride.

Fodor'sChoice
★

A 15-mi drive from town up Hualapai Mountain Road will take you to **Hualapai Mountain Park** (☎ 928/757–3859, 877/757–0915 for cabin reservations), where more than 2,300 wooded acres at elevations rang-

When you plan your trip to Arizona, it might not occur to you to include the western portion in your itinerary. With so many other interesting and well-known places to visit elsewhere in the state, it's easy to forget there are over 2½ million acres of land and 1,000 mi of shoreline waiting for you to discover in western Arizona. It's the best-kept secret in the state.

8

Driving
There's a lot of distance between things out here. Getting to them can require some significant windshield time. A soothing quality attends a leisurely drive to a new place, especially here in the spring. The desert air is moist with the subsiding breath of winter and the wildflowers are spilling from the earth like pastels from a tube. Roll down the windows and take it slow. Stop often. See how far you can see. Breathe in the scented desert air and you'll know forever what the desert really means.

Hiking Hualapai
You haven't truly hiked in western Arizona until you've hiked in Hualapai Mountain Park. There are dozens of fine trails throughout the region, but the trail system in the higher elevations of the park offers a striking variety of plant life such as prickly pear cactus and Arizona walnut. There are abundant species of birds and mammals such as the piñon jay and the Abert squirrel, and at the higher elevations, there are pristine stands of unmarred aspen and cool temperatures. Any of the trails can be hiked in about three hours. If you can only visit one place and do one thing in western Arizona, hiking in Hualapai Mountain Park should be it.

Water Sports
In this austere landscape, the first glimpse of water is always a thrill. A wedge of blue visible in the rough and tumble heap of basaltic mountains will lift and draw the human spirit toward itself. Out here, the roads to all water are downhill and a momentum gathers the closer you get to it. Around a bend and suddenly a big beautiful lake or a thick brown river comes into view, and all you can think about is getting in it or on it, or finding a fishing rod.

---

ing from 4,984 to 8,417 feet hold 10 mi of hiking trails as well as picnic areas, rustic cabins, and RV and tenting areas.

> **off the beaten path**

CHLORIDE – The ghost town of Chloride, Arizona's oldest silver mining camp, takes its name from a type of silver ore mined in the area. During its heyday, from 1900 to 1920, there were some 75 mines operating in the area: silver, gold, lead, zinc, molybdenum, and even turquoise were mined here. About 500 folks live in Chloride today; there are three cafés, two saloons, a grocery store, a B&B, and two RV parks. Some of the residents are artists and craftspeople who have small studios and shops in the historic buildings. Sights include the old jail, Chloride Baptist Church, Silverbelle Playhouse, and the Jim Fritz Museum. Western artist Roy Purcell painted the large murals on the rocks on the edge of town. The murals, 10 feet high

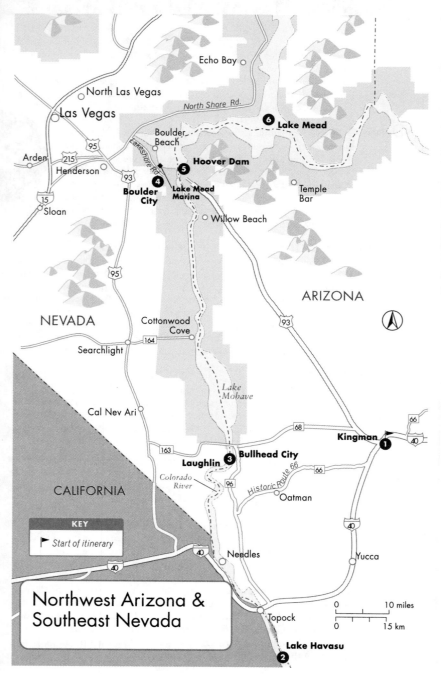

and almost 30 feet across, cover several granite boulders with depictions of a goddess figure, intertwined snakes, and numerous eastern and Native American symbols. The marked turnoff for Chloride is about 12 mi north of Kingman on U.S. 93.

★ **GRAND CANYON WEST RANCH** – This guest and working cattle ranch offers a slice of the Old West. Once the home of Tap Duncan, a member of the Hole-in-the-Wall Gang (⇨ The Man Who Died Twice box), the ranch now offers rustic cabins, home-cooked meals, horseback riding, and a stagecoach excursion. Take U.S. 93 north from Kingman 25 mi and turn right onto Pearce Ferry Road. Follow the paved road for 27 mi, then turn right onto the unpaved Diamond Bar Road. The Grand Canyon West Ranch is 7 mi farther on the right side of the road. Reservations are required. ⊠ *3785 E. Diamond Bar Ranch Rd., Meadview 86444* ☏ *702/736–8787 or 800/359–8727* ⊕ *www.grandcanyonwestranch.com.*

♻ **GRAND CANYON CAVERNS** – Nestled among rolling, juniper-covered hills 60 mi east of Kingman on Historic Route 66, the Grand Canyon Caverns and Inn have been a diversion for travelers for decades. Daily tours begin on the hour with an elevator descent to the main floor of the caverns, 210 feet below ground. These caves were formed in the limestone bed of a sea that covered northern Arizona more than 37 million years ago. The caverns are considered a dry cave, or one that no longer grows, but the full extent of the caverns is still unknown. The ¾-mi walking tour takes 45 minutes to complete. In the rodeo arena behind the 48-room hotel, area cowboys often hold calf-roping competitions that are a hoot to watch, and free to boot. ⊠ *Rte. 66* ☏ *928/422-3223* ⊒ *$11.95* ⊙ *Mar.–Oct. 8–6, Nov.–Feb. 10–5.*

Sports & Outdoor Activities

HIKING The **Hayden Peak Trail** is a branch of a 10-mi trail system within Hualapai Mountain Park. The hike begins at location No. 4, elevation 6,750 feet, shown on the trail-system map available at the ranger station. Markers along the trail coincide with the map. This is a strenuous, 5½-mi round-trip hike. A hiking stick is a valuable companion. There are benches and storm shelters along the trail. Along the way, you climb through a narrow and shallow canyon that botanists call an Interior Riparian Deciduous Forest. A forest fire scorched this part of the mountains more than 50 years ago. Today, that scar has been replaced with pristine aspens, their thick, unmarred trunks white as parchment. The ground is covered with ungrazed grasses and soft foliage called deer's ears. At the end of the trail, elevation 8,050 feet, 200 feet below the summit of Hayden Peak, there is a bench with a view to the west that includes the gleaming surface of the Colorado River, some 60 mi away.

Where to Stay & Eat

Kingman has several decent places to eat and about three dozen motels, most of them along Andy Devine Avenue. Most of the major chains are represented, including Days Inn, Motel 6, and Super 8.

CloseUp

THE MAN WHO DIED TWICE

WHEN GEORGE TAPLIN **DUNCAN WAS STRUCK** and killed by an automobile in Kingman in 1947, his obituary recorded that he was a prominent rancher in western Arizona and the owner of the Diamond Bar Ranch (now known as the Grand Canyon West Ranch). What wasn't included was any mention of his previous demise.

"Tap" Duncan was born in Texas, in 1869. He drifted from town to town throughout the Southwest. It's unknown how he came to the trade, but around the turn of the century he started robbing banks and trains as a member of the Hole-in-the-Wall Gang.

In 1904, Harvey Logan, also known as "Kid Curry," and two accomplices robbed a bank in Parachute, Colorado. A posse cornered the trio and Kid Curry was mortally wounded. When the gun smoke cleared, the posse found Kid Curry dead of a self-inflicted gunshot wound.

The posse thought they had Tap Duncan. They took the body into town and contacted the railroad agents to learn if there was a reward for Duncan. When the railroad agents saw the body, they realized it was Kid Curry, not Tap Duncan. Tap, meanwhile, was in Idaho.

There was no reward offered for Tap Duncan and the railroad agents didn't want to pay the reward for Kid Curry, so they buried a man they said was Tap Duncan and fostered the legend that Kid Curry had followed Butch Cassidy and the Sundance Kid down to Bolivia.

When the news of his demise finally reached Tap, he was already leading a respectable life in western Arizona not far from the western rim of Grand Canyon. He raised kids and cattle, and lived out the rest of his life a free man.

— Tom Carpenter

$–$$ ✕ **Hubb's Bistro.** The bustling eatery in the Brunswick Hotel caters to most tastes and does a wonderful job with everything from burgers to seafood, including some traditional French dishes. The owner is from France and very proud of his café. ✉ 315 E. Andy Devine Ave. ☏ 928/718–1800 ▭ AE, D, MC, V ✆ Closed Sun.

$ ✕ **The Fresh Tomato Margaritaville.** Out of the way but worth the effort, this casual restaurant with a Mexican motif is at the north end of town, a block north of the intersection of Bank Street and Northern Avenue. This local gem serves Mexican and American cuisine, and seafood—and the best chiles rellenos in the county. ✉ 4570 N. Bank St. ☏ 928/757–1477 ▭ AE, D, MC, V.

¢–$ ▦ **Brunswick Hotel.** This hotel opened its doors in 1909 and was the first three-story building in town. Rooms have antique furnishings. You enjoy the early-1900s ambience coupled with courtesy and today's amenities. ✉ 315 E. Andy Devine Ave., 86401 ☏ 928/718–1800 ⊕ www.hotel-brunswick.com ➘ 18 rooms, 9 with shared bath; 6 suites ♨ Restaurant, massage, bar, Internet, business services, no-smoking rooms; no TV in some rooms ▭ AE, D, MC, V ⦿| CP.

¢ ▦ **Quality Inn.** This chain motel has comfortable rooms and a small gift display with an impressive collection of Route 66 whiskey jiggers. The

complimentary Continental breakfast and in-room coffeemakers stream-
line the morning routine. ✉ *1400 E. Andy Devine Ave., 86401* ☎ *928/
753–4747 or 800/228–5151* ⊕ *www.hotelchoice.com* 📼 *98 rooms
△ Some microwaves, some refrigerators, cable TV, pool, hot tub, sauna,
no-smoking rooms* ⊟ *AE, D, DC, MC, V* �ⵔ *CP.*

> **en route**

A worthwhile stop on your way from Kingman to Lake Havasu, the
ghost town of **Oatman** is reached via old Route 66. It's a straight
shot across the Mojave Desert valley for a while, but then the road
narrows and winds precipitously for about 15 mi through the Black
Mountains. This road is public, but beyond a narrow shoulder, the
land is privately owned and heavily patrolled, thanks to still-active
gold mines throughout these low but rugged hills.

Oatman's main street is right out of the Old West; scenes from a
number of films, including *How the West Was Won,* were shot here.
It still has a remote, old-time feel: many of the natives carry side
arms, and they're not acting. You can wander into one of the three
saloons or visit the **Oatman Hotel,** where Clark Gable and Carole
Lombard honeymooned in 1939 after they were secretly married in
Kingman. The burros that often come in from nearby hills and
meander down the street, however, are the town's real draw. A
couple of stores sell hay to folks who want to feed these "wild"
beasts, which at last count numbered about a dozen and which leave
plenty of evidence of their visits in the form of "road apples"—so
watch your step. For information about the town and its attractions,
contact the **Oatman Chamber of Commerce** (☎ 928/768–6222
⊕ www.route66azlastingimpressions.com).

Two miles east of Oatman is the **Gold Road Mine,** an active
operation that dates back to 1900. A one-hour tour takes modern-
day prospectors underground for a demonstration of drilling
equipment and a visit to the "Glory Hole," where the vein
structures in the rock are highlighted with a black light to show the
gold. ✉ *AZ 66* ☎ *928/768–1600* ⊕ *goldroadmine.com* 💲 *$12*
☼ *Daily 10 AM–5 PM.*

Lake Havasu

❷ *60 mi southwest of Kingman.*

Remember the old nursery rhyme "London Bridge Is Falling Down"?
Well, it was. After about 150 years of constant use, the 294-foot-long
landmark was sinking into the Thames. When Lake Havasu City founder,
Robert McCullough, heard about this predicament, he set about actu-

Fodor's Choice
★

ally to buy **London Bridge** and have it disassembled, shipped 10,000 mi
to western Arizona, and rebuilt, stone by stone. The bridge was reconstructed on mounds of sand and took three years to complete. When it
was finished, a mile-long channel was dredged under the bridge and water
was diverted from Lake Havasu through the Bridgewater Channel.
Today, the entire city is centered on this unusual attraction.

If there's an Arizona Riviera, this is it. Lake Havasu has more than 45 mi of lake shoreline, and the area gets less than 4 inches of rain annually, which means it's almost always sunny. Spring, winter, and fall are the best times to visit. In summer, temperatures often exceed 100°F. You can rent everything from water skis to Jet Skis, small fishing boats to large houseboats. There are no fewer than 13 RV parks and campgrounds, about 125 boat-in campsites, and hundreds of hotel and motel rooms for additional creature comforts. There are golf and tennis facilities, as well as fishing guides who'll help you find, and catch, the big ones.

If you're interested in exploring nearby old mines, a wildlife sanctuary and the desert in general, join up with a four-wheel driving tour created by **Outback Adventures** (☎928/680–6151 ⊕www.outbackadventures.com).

★ The **Havasu National Wildlife Refuge** (✉ off I–40 south of Needles, CA ☎ 760/326–3853 ⊕ southwest.fws.gov), between Needles and Lake Havasu City, is a 44,371-acre refuge for wintering Canada geese and other waterfowl, such as the snowy egret and the great blue heron. The largest surviving cottonwood-willow woodland in the region is part of the **Bill Williams River National Wildlife Refuge** (✉ AZ 95, 23 mi south of Lake Havasu City ☎928/667–4144 ⊕southwest.fws.gov), south of Lake Havasu City. To reach the 6,000-acre refuge, travel south on AZ 95; the entrance is between mileposts 160 and 161.

off the beaten path

'AHAKHAV TRIBAL PRESERVE – The 2,500-acre preserve is on the Colorado Indian Tribes Reservation and is a top spot in the area for bird-watching and hiking. There are several campgrounds, parks, and recreation areas along the Colorado River. Rent a canoe ($10 an hour or $25 a day) and bird-watch along the shoreline of the backwater area branching off the Colorado River. Some 350 species of migratory and native birds live around the region or visit on their annual migrations. The 3-mi hiking trail offers exercise stations along the way, and a trail extension will lead you to the tribal historical museum and gift shop. From AZ 95 in Parker, which is at the southern end of Lake Havasu, head west on Mohave Road for about 2 mi. When you reach the PARKER INDIAN RODEO ASSOCIATION sign, continue ½ mi farther and turn left at the TRIBAL PRESERVE sign at Rodeo Drive. ✉ *25401 Rodeo Dr., Parker* ☎ *928/669–2664* 🖷 *928/ 669–8024* ⊕ *www.ahakhav.com.*

Sports & the Outdoors

GOLF The semi-private **London Bridge Golf Club** (✉ 2400 Clubhouse Dr., Lake Havasu City ☎ 928/855–2719) has two regulation 18-hole courses. Greens fees are $50 for the East course and $69 for for the West course. The West course is the championship caliber.

WATER SPORTS When construction of Parker Dam was completed in 1938, the reservoir it created to supply water to southern California and Arizona became Lake Havasu. The lake is a 45-mi-long playground for water sports of all kinds. Whether it's waterskiing, jet skiing, power boating, houseboating, swimming, fishing, you name it. If water is required, it's happening on Lake Havasu.

Lake Havasu State Park (✉ 699 London Bridge Rd. ☎ 928/855–2784 ⊕ www.pr.state.az.us) is near the London Bridge. With four boat ramps and 42 campsites, it is an extremely popular spot in summer. On the eastern shore of the lake 15 mi south of Lake Havasu City is **Cattail Cove State Park** (✛ AZ 95, 15 mi south of Lake Havasu ☎ 928/855–1223 ⊕ www.pr.state.az.us). There are 62 campsites with access to electricity and water, and public rest rooms with showers. Both parks charge $8 per vehicle for entry and are open from sunrise to 10.

If you have a boat, you have more options. You can find a quiet, secluded cove or beach to tie up and enjoy swimming or fishing or just resting. If you have a need for speed, you can plane up and down the lake with or without a skier in tow. Remember this is a lake in a desert, though. When you find a place to go ashore, don't forget that reptiles and insects live near the lake, too. So, watch where you step and shake out your shoes before you put them on.

If you don't have the equipment or the vessel necessary to enjoy your water sport, they're available for rent from a number of reputable merchants. You can rent everything from jet skis to pontoon boats, by the day or by the week, at **Sand Point Marina and RV Park** (✉ 17952 S. Sand Point Resort Rd. ☎ 928/855–0549 ⊕ www.sandpointresort.com). You can rent more than just a Jet Ski at **Arizona Jet Ski Rentals** (✉ 655 Kiowa Ave. ☎ 800/393–5558 ⊕ www.arizonawatersports.com)—jet boats, ski boats, and pontoon boats are also available.

Where to Stay & Eat
Many tourists make this stop a day trip on their way to Laughlin or Las Vegas, but there are plenty of accommodations if you'd like to stay more than a night. Of the chain hotels in town, the Best Western and the Holiday Inn are your best bets.

★ **$$-$$$** ✕ **Shugrue's.** If you've dined at the Sedona branch of this restaurant, you know what to expect here. Shugrue's features hand-cut steaks, very fresh seafood, salads, and other well-prepared American fare. The baked desserts are worth saving room for. Most tables offer good bridge views. ✉ *1425 McCulloch Blvd.* ☎ *928/453–1400* ▭ *AE, MC, V.*

★ **$-$$$** ✕ **London Arms Pub and Restaurant.** Remodeled in 2002 to present dinner theater on the weekends, this traditional-looking pub offers more than the standard fish-and-chips. Along with the salads and burgers, you can also order Cornish game hen, lobster ravioli, and prime rib. If you opt for an evening in the Theatre Banquet Room, you'll be served a four-course feast for $19.95, prior to the performances held at 5:30 and 7 on Friday and Saturday and on noon Sunday. The popular theatrical musical *I Do! I Do!* is typical of the shows performed. The cost of the show is additional and varies. ✉ *422 English Village* ☎ *928/855–8782* ▭ *AE, D, MC, V.*

$-$$ ✕ **Juicy's River Café.** This is a favorite hangout for the local folks who know good food when they taste it. The Sunday breakfast is especially popular. It's a small and cozy place (14 tables inside, 4 more outside) with a varied menu that includes such standbys as corned beef and cabbage, smoked prime rib, meat loaf, pot roast and vegetables, and homemade soups and desserts. ⊠ *25 N. Acoma Blvd.* ☎ *928/855–8429* ☐ *AE, D, MC, V.*

¢ ✗ **Chico's Tacos.** The salsa bar at this decent Mexican fast-food joint offers fresh salsa in varying degrees of spiciness. ⊠ *1641 McCulloch Blvd.* ☎ *928/680–7010* ☐ *D, MC, V.*

★ **$–$$** ☷ **London Bridge Resort.** If you want to be close to the bridge, this interesting hotel is a dependable choice. The decor is a strange mix of Tudor and Southwestern; other than that, studios are standard motel rooms with kitchenettes. One-bedroom condos have separate living and dining areas as well as full kitchens; two-bedroom condos have balconies. There's a serviceable restaurant. ⊠ *1477 Queen's Bay, 86403* ☎ *928/ 855–0888 or 800/624–7939* ☐ *928/855–9209* ⊕ *www. londonbridgeresort.com* ⇋ *4 studios, 72 1-bedroom condos, 46 2-bedroom condos* ⚑ *Restaurant, some kitchens, some kitchenettes, cable TV, golf privileges, 3 pools, beach, no-smoking rooms* ☐ *AE, D, MC, V.*

$ ☷ **Havasu Springs Resort.** On a low peninsula reaching into Lake Havasu, the four hotels of this resort maximize your options. In addition to the standard hotel rooms, the resort also offers suites and apartments. For the adventurous willing to plunk down a chunk of change for the three-night minimum (ranging from $1,035 to $1,650 depending on the size), houseboats provide a very popular Lake Havasu vacation option. These portable lodgings are good choices for large groups, as they sleep up to 12 people. ⊠ *2581 AZ 95, Parker 85344* ☎ *928/667–3361* ☐ *928/667– 1098* ⊕ *www.havasusprings.com* ⇋ *38 rooms, 4 suites, 3 apartments* ⚑ *Restaurant, cable TV, beach, lounge* ☐ *AE, D, MC, V.*

¢–$ ☷ **Island Inn.** Fido is welcome here, if he's small, that is. And together, you can walk to London Bridge and London Bridge Beach. There are 117 rooms, a pool, hot tub, and meeting rooms. Rooms are large and basic. ⊠ *1300 W. McCulloch Blvd., 86403* ☎ *928/680–0606 or 800/ 243–9955* ☐ *928/680–4218* ⇋ *117 rooms* ⚑ *Cable TV, pool, hot tub, meeting rooms, some pets allowed (fee)* ☐ *AE, D, MC, V.*

HOUSEBOATING **Club Nautical Houseboats.** What houseboats lack in speed and maneuverability, they make up for in comfort and shade. A day on the lake can be a scorching and dehydrating experience, even with the plenty of sunscreen and lots of beverages on hand. Seeing the lake, any lake, from the sheltered deck of a houseboat is a safe and enjoyable alternative to overexposure to the desert sun. ⊠ *1000 McCulloch Blvd.* ☎ *800/843– 9218* ⊕ *www.lakehavasuhouseboatrental.com.*

SOUTHEAST NEVADA

The tandem grandeur of Hoover Dam and Lake Mead will soon have another engineering marvel for company as work continues less than a ½ mi downstream on a bridge that will span the river canyon and link western Arizona to southeastern Nevada, dramatically reducing traffic across Hoover Dam. The chance to see a bridge of this size and complexity under construction is rare and makes it worth the trip to the dam if for no other reason than to stand there and watch the bridge grow. Downstream 60 mi, the casino lights of Laughlin, Nevada sparkle across the river from Bullhead City.

GENERAL JESUP & THE CAMELS

N MID-JANUARY 1858, the steamboat General Jesup stopped along the western shore of the Colorado River south of present-day Bullhead City. No steamboat had ever been so far up river. Her captain, George Johnson, needed wood for her 80-horsepower engine. He had taken the shallow-draft, 120-foot-long vessel to a point approximately 8 mi north of Davis Dam, where he turned around because he was running short of rations.

When Lt. Edward Beale saw the General Jesup, he was at the head of of a survey party on its way back from California. In addition to horses and wagons, he also had in his caravan 25 camels carrying supplies and equipment. Beale was on the return leg of an expedition to survey an all-weather wagon road from Albuquerque to Los Angeles along the 35th parallel. The road would accommodate the growing traffic of emigrants traveling to California. The camels were an experiment to test their suitability for the military in the Southwest. A North African camel driver named Hadji Ali, "Hi Jolly" to Lt. Beale and others, was in charge of the camels.

The men under Beale's command had crossed the river once already with the camels. Given the foul tempers of the beasts in the best circumstances and their obnoxious propensity to spit, no one was looking forward to forcing them across the river again. Lt. Beale asked Captain Johnson to ferry his expedition across the river. Captain Johnson was not keen on the idea. No doubt he flinched at the thought of mean-spirited camels fouling the deck of his steamboat. His mood changed, however, when Beale assured him the camels could swim across. Johnson obliged and one of the oddest intersections of fate took place on the banks of the Colorado River when Beale's camels, his "ships of the desert," swam beside the first steamboat to ply the upper reaches of the Colorado River.

The Beale Wagon Road soon became an important emigrant route and the path followed next by the railroad, and later by Route 66. Steamboats carried people and supplies up and down the Colorado River for another 50 years, until the Laguna Dam near Yuma closed the river in 1906. With the start of the Civil War, interest in the camel experiment faded. Hadji Ali stayed in the area and is buried in Quartzite. As for the 25 camels, some say their descendants still roam the region.

— Tom Carpenter

Bullhead City, Arizona & Laughlin, Nevada

❸ *35 mi northwest of Kingman.*

AZ 68 is the highway from Kingman to Bullhead City and Laughlin, Nevada. The road crosses the Sacramento Valley and climbs over the Black Mountains through Union Pass and down the other side to the Colorado River valley. At night, across the river from Bullhead City, the lights of Laughlin glitter. Bullhead City has its small-town charms, but the lights of Laughlin are difficult to ignore. Laughlin's founder, Don Laughlin, bought an eight-room motel here in 1966 and basically built the town from scratch. By the early 1980s Laughlin's Riverside Hotel-Casino was drawing gamblers and river rats from northwestern Arizona, southeastern California, and even southern Nevada, and his success attracted other casino operators. Today Laughlin is Nevada's third major resort area, attracting more than 5 million visitors annually. The city fills up, especially in winter, with retired travelers who spend at least part of the winter in Arizona and a younger resort-loving crowd. The big picture windows overlooking the Colorado River lend a bright, airy, and open feeling unique to Laughlin casinos. Take a stroll along the river walk, then make the return trip by water taxi ($3 round-trip; $2 one-way). Boating, Jet Skis, and plain old wading are other options for enjoying the water.

Across the Laughlin Bridge, ¼ mi to the north, the **Colorado River Museum** displays rich past of the tri-state region where Nevada, Arizona, and California converge. There are artifacts from the Mojave Indian Tribe, models and photographs of steamboats that once plied the river, rock and fossil specimens, and the first telephone switchboard used in neighboring Bullhead City. ⊠ *2201 AZ 68* ☎ *928/754–3399* ⊕ *www. bullheadcity.com/tourism/hismuseum.asp* ⊠ *$1* ☉ *Sept.–June, Tues.–Sun. 10 AM–4 PM.*

Where to Stay & Eat

★ ¢–$ ✗⊡ **Avi Resort & Casino.** The only tribally-owned casino in Nevada is run by the Fort Mojave Tribe. The 25,000-square-foot casino houses nearly 1,000 slot and video-poker machines; a 156-room tower with river views was opened in late 2003. The biggest draw, however, is the private white-sand beach where you can lounge or rent a watercraft. The resort has an 8-screen Brenden movie theater and plans to add a new marina, a convention facility, and a 5,000-seat showroom in 2005. Be sure to visit the **Moonshadow Grille,** preferably for the finest Sunday champagne brunch in the tri-state area. ⊠ *10000 Aha Macav Pkwy., Laughlin 89029* ☎ *702/535–5555 or 800/284–2946* ⊕ *www. avicasino.com* ⇆ *456 rooms, 29 spa suites* ♨ *5 restaurants, cable TV, 18-hole golf course, pool, gym, spa, beach, marina, bar, lounge, casino, cinema, children's programs (ages 6 weeks–12 years), no-smoking rooms* ☰ *AE, D, DC, MC, V.*

¢–$ ✗⊡ **Harrah's.** This is the classiest joint in Laughlin, and it even comes with a private sand beach. It also has two casinos (one is no smoking) and big-name entertainers perform in the Fiesta Showroom and at the 3,000-seat Rio Vista Outdoor Amphitheater. **The Range Steakhouse**

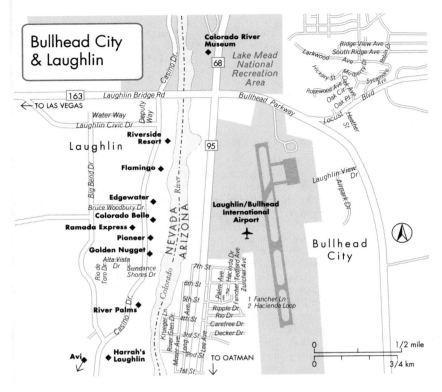

Bullhead City & Laughlin

Colorado River Museum

Lake Mead National Recreation Area

68

163

← TO LAS VEGAS

Laughlin Bridge Rd

Bullhead Parkway

Water Way

Deputy Way

Laughlin Civic Dr

Riverside Resort ◆

Laughlin

Flamingo ◆

95

Edgewater ◆

Bruce Woodbury Dr.

Colorado Belle ◆

Ramada Express ◆

Pioneer ◆

Golden Nugget ◆

Alta Vista Dr

Rio de Toro Dr

Sundance Shores Dr

River Palms ◆

Avi

Harrah's ◆ Laughlin

NEVADA

ARIZONA

Colorado River

Laughlin/Bullhead International Airport

Laughlin View Dr

Airpark Dr

Bullhead City

7th St
6th St
5th St
4th St
3rd St
2nd St
1st St

Hacienda Dr
Fancher
Tedford Ave
Zutcher Ave
Palm Ave

1 Fancher Ln
2 Hacienda Loop

Ripple Dr
Rio Dr
Carefree Dr
Decker Dr

Krueger Ln
River Glen Dr
Moser Ave
Long
Lee Ave

TO OATMAN

Ridge View Ave
South Ridge Ave
Larkwood
Hickory St
Rosewood Ave
Oak Cir
Oak Pl
Locust St
Heather St
Mulberry Dr
Sycamore Ave
Blvd

0 ————— 1/2 mile
0 ————— 3/4 km

($–$$$) serves Continental fare. ⊠ *2900 S. Casino Dr., Laughlin 89029* ☎ *702/298–4600 or 800/427–7247* ☐ *702/298–6855* ⊕ *www.harrahs.com* ⇨ *1,571 rooms* ⚭ *5 restaurants, some in-room data ports, cable TV, 2 pools, gym, hair salon, hot tub, spa, beach, 3 bars, lounge, casino, showroom, shops, meeting rooms, no-smoking floors* ☰ *AE, D, DC, MC, V.*

★ ¢–$ ✕▥ **Riverside Resort.** Town founder Don Laughlin still runs this northernmost joint himself. Check out the Loser's Lounge, with its graphic homage to famous losers, such as the *Hindenburg,* the *Titanic,* and the like. And don't pass up Don's two free classic-car showrooms with more than 80 rods, roadsters, and tin lizzies. The **Gourmet Room** restaurant serves Continental and American cuisine. ⊠ *1650 S. Casino Dr., Laughlin 89029* ☎ *702/298–2535 or 800/227–3849* ☐ *702/298–2614* ⊕ *www.riversideresort.com* ⇨ *1,440 rooms* ⚭ *6 restaurants, cable TV, 2 pools, hot tub, bowling, lounge, casino, nightclub, showroom, theater, children's programs (ages 3 months–12 years), no-smoking rooms* ☰ *AE, D, DC, MC, V.*

¢–$ ▥ **Flamingo Laughlin.** The casino at the largest resort in Laughlin has 1,500 slot and video-poker machines and a sports book. The Flamingo's 3,000-seat outdoor amphitheater, on the bank of the Colorado River, hosts big-name entertainers. Standard rooms have two double beds or a queen-size bed. Suites are larger (650 to 1,000 square feet) and equipped with coffeemakers, minibars, irons, and ironing boards. ✉ *1900 S. Casino Dr., Laughlin 89029* ☎ *702/298–5111 or 800/352–6464* 🖨 *702/298–5116* ⊕ *www.parkplace.com/flamingo/laughlin* 🛏 *1,824 rooms, 90 suites* ♻ *4 restaurants, cable TV, 3 tennis courts, pool, gym, 2 bars, lounge, casino, showroom, business services, no-smoking rooms* ▭ *AE, D, DC, MC, V.*

Boulder City, Nevada

❹ *76 mi northwest of Kingman.*

Like so many other small Western towns, Boulder City was created for the needs of a nearby construction or mining project, in this case the construction of Hoover Dam, whose builders needed to house thousands of workers and to deter them from spending their hard-earned dollars on wine, women, and Las Vegas. After the project was completed, these towns were usually left to wither and die or make it on their own, and Boulder City was no exception. Developed in the 1930s, the town once housed 5,000 construction personnel; after the dam was finished, the town lost half of its population. Slowly it began a comeback and now enjoys a pleasant standard of living; it is still home to a few of the dam builders, known locally as the "31ers." The town is 5 mi from Lake Mead and 8 mi from Hoover Dam. If you're looking for glitz and glamour, you're in the wrong place. Boulder City is the only community in Nevada where gambling is illegal. However, it is worth a brief stopover to stroll the main streets downtown and to browse the Native American and Mexican gift shops, antiques and jewelry stores, and galleries.

Built in 1932, the **Boulder Dam Hotel** (✉ 1305 Arizona St. ☎ 702/293–3510) houses a bookstore, art gallery, and restaurant. The **Boulder City/Hoover Dam Museum** (☎ 702/294–1988), which preserves and displays artifacts relating to the workers and construction of Boulder City and Hoover Dam, is in the Boulder Dam Hotel. The **Boulder City Chamber of Commerce** (☎ 702/293–2034 ⊕ www.bouldercitychamber. com) is a good place to gather information on the history of Hoover Dam and other historic sights around town.

Hoover Dam

❺ *67 mi northwest of Kingman via U.S. 93.*

Fodor'sChoice
★

Humanity's ability to reshape the natural world—for good or ill, depending on your viewpoint—is powerfully evident in the Hoover Dam. Simply put, it's incredible. Completed in 1935, the dam is 727 feet high (the equivalent of a 70-story building) and 660 feet thick at the base (more than the length of two football fields). Its construction required 4.4 million cubic yards of concrete, enough to build a two-lane highway from San Francisco to New York.

Equally amazing are the relatively minuscule construction costs. Congress authorized just $175 million to build the dam in 1928 to control floods and generate electricity.

Originally referred to as Boulder Dam, the structure was officially named Hoover Dam in recognition of President Herbert Hoover's role in the project. More than 700,000 people a year (34 million since the tours began in 1937) take tours of the dam. The Discovery Tour is a self-paced, self-guiding tour, but staff guides provide information and answer questions along the way. Talks, by the guides, are presented every 15 minutes from 9 until 4:30. You are allowed to take elevators down into the dam to visit the power-plant generators; historical exhibits on the construction of Hoover Dam and displays on the region's natural history are on the Plaza level of the visitor center. A visitor center on the Nevada side contains a theater with three revolving sections, an exhibition gallery, an observation tower, and a five-story parking garage. Due to heightened security requirements, RVs and trailers are now subject to inspection. ✉ *U.S. 93 east of Boulder City* ☎ *702/293–8321 or 702/294–3523* ⊕ *www.usbr.gov/lc/hooverdam* 🎫 *$10* ⊙ *Tours daily 9–4:30.*

Lake Mead

❻ *67 mi northwest of Kingman on U.S. 93.*

Fodor'sChoice
★

A dam as monstrous as the Hoover creates an ocean of water behind it. Lake Mead is the largest man-made reservoir in the country, covering 229 square mi. **Lakeshore Scenic Drive** (NV 166) meanders along the beautiful shore of Lake Mead. Several recreation areas and marinas are strung along the north side of the lake. **Boulder Beach,** on the Nevada side of the lake, is the closest swimming beach to Arizona and only a mile or so from the dam visitor center. **Echo Bay,** roughly 40 mi northeast of Boulder Beach, is the best place to swim in the lake because it has better sand and fewer rocks—and visitors—than the other beaches. Both Boulder Beach and Echo Bay have campsites and RV parking with public facilities and concessions. The prolonged drought in the Southwest has reduced the water level of Lake Mead. As a consequence, campsites are farther from the water's edge than in past years. Not to worry. There's still plenty of water to enjoy; it's the biggest reservoir in the world. All over the lake, anglers fish for largemouth bass, catfish, trout, and black crappie, but striped bass are the feistiest and most prevalent. Houseboating is a favorite pastime; you can rent houseboats, along with speedboats, ski boats, and Jet Skis at the marinas. Divers have a fantastic choice of underwater sights to explore, including the entire town of St. Thomas, a farming community that was inundated by the lake in the 1930s. Other activities abound, such as waterskiing, sailboarding, and snorkeling.

You can get information on the lake's history, ecology, and recreational activities, as well as driving maps and accommodations information, at the **Alan Bible Visitors Center** (✉ U.S. 93 and NV 166, Boulder City ☎ 702/293–8990), the National Park Service's visitor center for the Lake Mead area. It's just northeast of the town proper and is open daily 8:30 to 4:30.

Sports & the Outdoors

BOATING Rental options include houseboats, patio boats, fishing boats, and ski boats—pick up a list of marinas at the Alan Bible Visitors Center. Powerboats as well as houseboats are available at **Callville Bay Resort and Marina** (⊠ Callville Bay ☎ 702/565–8958 or 800/255–5561). **Echo Bay Resort** (⊠ Echo Bay ☎ 702/394–4000 or 800/752–9669) is a popular choice for Lake Mead houseboat rentals; the company also rents ski boats, fishing boats, and other personal watercraft. **Lake Mead Marina** (⊠ Boulder Beach, Boulder City ☎ 702/293–3484) has boat rentals, a beach, camping facilities, a gift shop, and a restaurant.

CRUISES **Lake Mead Cruises** (⊠ Lake Mead Marina, near Boulder Beach, Boulder City ☎ 702/293–6180 ⊕ www.lakemeadcruises.com) offers 1½-hr cruises of the Hoover Dam area on the 300-passenger *Desert Princess* every two hours from 10 AM to 4 PM daily. Also offered are breakfast-buffet cruises and early dinner and dinner-dance cruises. **Gray Line Tours** (☎ 702/384–1234 or 800/634–6579 ⊕ www.pcap.com/grayline.htm) offers a 15-mi motorized-raft trip on the Colorado from the base of Hoover Dam down Black Canyon to Willow Beach.

Where to Stay

¢–$ 🖭 **Temple Bar Resort.** This upgraded motel right on the Arizona shore of the lake is a good choice if you want a quiet room; the hotel's remote location ensures peace. The restaurant, which serves typical American fare, has outdoor seating overlooking the water. ⊠ *Temple Bar, AZ 86643* ☎ *928/767–3211 or 800/752–9669* ☞ *18 rooms, 4 cabins* ⚄ *Restaurant* ⊟ *D, MC, V.*

¢ 🖭 **Hacienda Resort.** Sitting just outside city limits, this large, Vegas-style casino eludes the Boulder City ban on gambling. Close to Lake Mead and Hoover Dam, the resort has seven restaurants, live entertainment, and more than 800 slot machines. ⊠ *U.S. 93, Boulder City, NV 89005* ☎ *702/293–5000* ⊕ *www.haciendaonline.com* ☞ *375 rooms* ⚄ *7 restaurants, casino* ⊟ *D, MC, V.*

CAMPING ⚠ **Temple Bar Campground.** Space is available on a first-come, first-
¢ served basis at this 153-site campground on the Arizona shore of the lake, but there are usually plenty of unoccupied sites on all but the busiest holiday weekends. The nightly fee is $10. ⊠ *Temple Bar, AZ 86643* ☎ *928/767–3401 or 800/752–9669* ☞ *153 sites* ⚄ *Flush toilets, dump station, running water (nonpotable), fire grates, picnic tables* ⊙ *Open year-round.*

HOUSEBOATING 🖭 **Seven Crown Resorts.** The beauty of renting a houseboat is that you
$$$$ can cruise down the lake and park where you please for as long as you like. It's an increasingly popular vacation option, especially for large groups. Seven Crown Resorts is a good resource for rentals, The boats come equipped with full kitchens and air-conditioning, and they can sleep up to 14 people. The minimum rental is for three days, two nights; you get the best rates on a one-week rental. ⬧ *Box 16247 Irvine, CA 92623* ☎ *800/752–9669 or 928/767–3211* ⊕ *www.sevencrown.com* ⚄ *Kitchens; no A/C on some boats, no room TVs* ⊟ *D, MC, V.*

NORTHWEST ARIZONA & SOUTHEAST NEVADA A TO Z

To research prices, get advice from other travelers, and book travel arrangements, visit www.fodors.com.

AIR TRAVEL

America West Express has daily flights between Kingman and Phoenix; it also flies daily between Lake Havasu City and Phoenix and Lake Havasu City and Bullhead City. Sun Country flies to Laughlin/Bullhead City from 50 cities in 18 states, including Seattle, Portland, Denver, Minneapolis/St. Paul, San Francisco, Phoenix, and Dallas/Ft. Worth. Several hotel-casinos also sponsor charter flights.

🛪 **Airlines Allegiant Charters** ☎ 800/221-1306. **America West Express** ☎ 800/235-9292. **Sun Country Airlines** ☎ 800/359-6786 ⊕ www.suncountry.com.

AIRPORTS

🛪 **Kingman Airport** ☎ 928/757-5444. **Lake Havasu City Municipal Airport** ☎ 928/764-3330. **Laughlin/Bullhead International Airport** ☎ 928/754-2134.

BUS TRAVEL

Greyhound serves Kingman, Lake Havasu City, and Bullhead City. The Bullhead City bus stops at the Airport Chevron at 600 AZ 95. To get to Laughlin, Nevada, walk to the boat dock across the highway and take a free ride to a Nevada hotel river landing.

🚌 **Greyhound** ☎ 800/231-2222 ⊕ www.greyhound.com.

CAR RENTALS

Avis, Enterprise, and Hertz have vehicles available for rent in Kingman, Lake Havasu City, and Bullhead City.

🚗 **Avis** ☎ 800/331-1212 ⊕ www.avis.com. **Enterprise** ☎ 800/261-7331 ⊕ www.enterprise.com. **Hertz** ☎ 800/654-3131 ⊕ www.hertz.com.

CAR TRAVEL

The best way to get your "kicks on Route 66" is to travel by automobile. This holds true for travel throughout western Arizona. Historic Route 66 crosses east–west and lies north of Interstate 40, which also crosses the region. U.S. 93 is the main route for north–south travel. All of these roads are in excellent condition. On Interstate 40 high winds occasionally raise enough blowing dust to restrict visibility. In winter, ice may be present on the stretch of Interstate 40 between Kingman and Seligman, as well as on sections of Route 66. When signage warns of ice ahead, heed the warnings and slow down. Most of the county roads are improved dirt roads, but washboard sections may surprise you, so take your time and drive no faster than prudence dictates. Roll down the windows and enjoy the scent of desert air.

GASOLINE Fuel up in Arizona—all grades of gasoline can be as much as 30¢ to 50¢ per gallon less in Kingman and Bullhead City than in Laughlin.

EMERGENCIES

🔏 Ambulance, Fire & Police **Emergency services** ☎ 911.

🔏 Hospitals **Havasu Regional Medical Center** ✉ 101 Civic Center La., Lake Havasu City ☎ 928/855-8185. **Kingman Regional Medical Center** ✉ 3269 Stockton Hill Rd., Kingman ☎ 928/757-2101. **Western Arizona Regional Medical Center** ✉ 2735 Silver Creek Rd., Bullhead City ☎ 928/763-2273.

TIME

The state of Nevada is in the Pacific Time Zone, whereas Arizona is in the Mountain Time Zone. However, Arizona does not use Daylight Savings Time. As a result, from late spring to early fall, Nevada and Arizona observe the same hours.

TOURS

BOATING & RAFTING TOURS There is no white water to be found on the Colorado River below Hoover Dam. Instead, the river and its lakes offer you many opportunities to explore the gorges and marshes that line the shores. If you prefer to do it yourself, look into the canoe and kayak rentals available on lakes Mead, Mohave, and Havasu. Raft adventures will take you through the Topock Gorge near Lake Havasu, or you can take a trip up river from Willow Beach 12 mi to the base of Hoover Dam. Along the way, chances are good you'll see big horn sheep moving along the steep basaltic cliffs. Expect to spend $35 to $40 for half a day, and twice that for a full-day adventure.

🔏 **Black Canyon Adventures** ☎ 800/455-3490 ⊕ www.blackcanyonadventures.com. **Desert River Outfitters** ☎ 888/529-2533 ⊕ www.desertriveroutfitters.com. **Western Arizona Canoe & Kayak Outfitter** ☎ 888/881-5038 ⊕ www.azwacko.com.

TRAIN TRAVEL

Amtrak's *Southwest Chief* stops in Kingman and in Needles, California, which is 25 mi south of Bullhead City/Laughlin. An Amtrak Thruway bus shuttles passengers to the Ramada Express in Laughlin.

🔏 **Amtrak** ☎ 800/872-7245 ⊕ www.amtrak.com.

VISITOR INFORMATION

🔏 **Boulder City Chamber of Commerce** ✉ 1305 Arizona St., Boulder City, NV 89005 ☎ 702/293-2034 ⊕ www.bouldercitychamber.com. **Bullhead City Area Chamber of Commerce** ✉ 1251 AZ 95, Bullhead City, AZ 86429 ☎ 928/754-4121 ⊕ www. bullheadchamber.com. **Kingman Area Chamber of Commerce** ✉ 120 W. Andy Devine Ave., Kingman 86402 ☎ 928/753-6106 ⊕ www.kingmanchamber.org. **Lake Havasu Tourism Bureau** ✉ 314 London Bridge Rd., Lake Havasu City 86403 ☎ 928/453-3444 or 800/242-8278 ⊕ www.golakehavasu.com. **Laughlin Chamber of Commerce** ✉ 1585 S. Casino Dr., 89029 ☎ 702/298-2214 or 800/227-5245 🖷 702/298-5708 ⊕ www. laughlinchamber.com. **Laughlin Visitors Bureau** ✉ 1555 Casino Dr., 89029 ☎ 702/298-3321 or 800/452-8445 ⊕ www.visitlaughlin.com.

UNDERSTANDING ARIZONA

ARIZONA AT A GLANCE

THE NATIVE SOUTHWEST

BOOKS & MOVIES

Fast Facts

Nickname: Grand Canyon State
Capital: Phoenix
Motto: Ditat Deus (God enriches)
State song: *Arizona*
State bird: Cactus Wren
State flower: Saguaro cactus blossom (carnegiea gigantea)
State tree: Palo verde (cercidium)
Administrative divisions: 15 counties
Entered the Union: February 14, 1912 (48th state)
Population: 5.3 million
Population density: 46.9 people per square mi
Median age: 34.2
Infant mortality rate: 6.9 deaths per 1,000 births
Literacy: 18% had trouble with basic reading. Twenty-six percent spoke a language other than English at home, usually Spanish. Forty percent reported that they did not speak English "very well."

Ethnic groups: White 62%; Latino 27%; Native American 4%; African American 3%; Asian 2%; other 2%
Religion: Unaffiliated 60%; Catholic 19%; Christian 12%; Mormon 5%; Jewish 2%; other 2%

The great pines stand at a considerable distance from each other. Each tree grows alone, murmurs alone, thinks alone. They do not intrude upon each other. The Navajos are not much in the habit of giving or of asking help. Their language is not a communicative one, and they never attempt an interchange of personality in speech. Over their forests there is the same inexorable reserve. Each tree has its exalted power to bear.
—Willa Cather (1873–1947), U.S. novelist, describing Navajo pine forests in northern Arizona.

Geography & Environment

Land area: 113,909 square mi
Terrain: Desert, with rocky mountains stretching across the southern area of the state. Erosion by rivers has formed much of the state's geography, including the Grand Canyon and the Painted Desert.
Highest point: Humphreys Peak, 12,655 feet.
Natural resources: Cement, copper (Arizona leads the nation in production), gravel, molybdenum, pine and fir forests, sand
Natural hazards: Drought, earthquakes, floods, severe storms, wildfires
Environmental issues: Air quality is bad enough that year-round monitoring is done for ground-level ozone pollution,

carbon monoxide and particulate matter, especially around Phoenix; concern over how logging should be done in Arizona's pine forests; soil erosion from overgrazing, industrial development, urbanization, and poor farming practices; most of the state suffers from limited natural fresh-water resources

Desert rains are usually so definitely demarked that the story of the man who washed his hands in the edge of an Arizona thunder shower without wetting his cuffs seems almost credible.
–Arizona: A State Guide (The WPA Guide to Arizona)

Economy

GSP: $160.6 billion
Per-capita income: $24,988
Unemployment: 5.3%
Work force: 2.7 million; financial/ management 21%; trade, transportation, and utilities 19%; government 18%; educational and health services 11%; leisure/hospitality 10%; construction 8%; manufacturing 7%; other 4%; publishing/telecom 2%
Major industries: Cattle, dairy goods, manufacturing, electronics, printing and publishing, processed foods, aerospace, transportation, high-tech research and development, communications, construction, tourism, military
Agricultural products: Broccoli, cattle, cauliflowers, cotton, dairy goods, lettuce, sorghum
Exports: $10.7 billion
Major export products: Electronic and electric equipment, fabricated metal products, industrial machinery and computers, scientific and measuring instruments, transportation equipment

Did You Know?

• Yuma, Arizona, holds the world record for most sunshine. It gets an average of 4,055 hours, or more than 90%, of the 4,456 hours of sunshine possible in a year.

• The Arizona or "Apache" Trout can only be found in the White Mountains of Arizona.

• One of Arizona's most plentiful natural resources is molybdenum, an element linked with copper production. Molybdenum is used to make steel, as well as electrodes and catalysts.

• During daylight savings, it's possible to drive in and out of time zone in Arizona in less than an hour. While the rest of the state sticks to Mountain Standard Time year-round, the state's Navajo Nation observes daylight savings.

• Cesar Chavez, who organized agricultural laborers across America, was born near Yuma, Arizona.

• Now a highly regarded public institution, the University of Arizona was started by a saloon keeper and two gamblers.

• The Hohokam, Arizona's earliest known inhabitants, were good at something crucial to Arizona today: irrigation. They built canals more than 10 mi long that channeled water to fields in the southern part of the state in about AD 300.

• More than 10% of the nation's Native Americans live in Arizona.

THE NATIVE SOUTHWEST

ONSIDERING THE ARIDITY of the Southwest, the tremendous cultural productivity of its native civilizations is a fascinating case of people turning the challenges of nature into a meaningful existence. Within the compass of the state of Arizona, Native American pottery and cliff dwellings are the most apparent evidence of this. In fact, they are isolated phenomena on a vast trade route that spanned the continent from the Pacific coast all the way to Mesoamerica, an area in which not only goods but pottery-making techniques, agricultural technologies, and spiritual beliefs were transmitted.

Some 4,000 years ago—at least 8,000 years after humans crossed the Bering Strait land bridge that once allowed passage on foot between Asia and North America—a major transition in cultures around the world saw people shifting from nomadic hunting-and-gathering lifestyles to more settled agricultural existence. In the Southwest, ancient pioneers brought the practice of cultivating corn, squash, and beans north from Mesoamerica. One group in particular, the Hohokam, is believed to have fostered this. In an area straddling the Arizona–New Mexico border, the Hohokam developed a highly productive system. Some archaeologists believe that they migrated from northwestern Mexico with knowledge of planting, growing, and irrigating. Others picture an evolution of Archaic peoples who gradually took on Mesoamerican practices. Either way, they had great success and in turn influenced their northern and eastern neighbors for more than a thousand years. Their artisans produced ritual objects, jewelry, and stone and ceramic wares with great skill. They regularly traded with Mesoamerican tribes, and Pacific-coast exchange brought in raw materials for their own and other regional artisans.

The flowering of Hohokam culture began around 2,300 years ago. The period of their growth, expansion, and eventual decline, when they began to take new ideas in from the north, lasted about 1,500 years—twice as long as the Roman Empire. During that time, they cultivated corn, beans, squash, agave, and cotton, using remarkable irrigation methods. Some of their networks of canals stretched 3 mi from the Salt and Gila rivers to planted fields. Their contact with Mesoamerican cultures periodically brought new strains of corn to the Southwest, along with religious beliefs, ritual practices, and the ball game and ball courts well known from the Maya. The Hohokam culturally fertilized the region, providing a base for the Pueblo culture that has survived into the modern era.

The Mogollon (pronounced *muh*-gee-on) were another group, occupying an area stretching from eastern-central Arizona into New Mexico from 2,000 to 500 years ago. They took on Hohokam and so-called Anasazi-cultural patterns, but they never fully embraced an agricultural lifestyle. They became skillful potters, especially those living near the Mimbres River. Their contact with the Anasazi resulted in the production of some of the Southwest's most outstanding pottery. The principle Mimbres Mogollon site is now the Gila Cliff Dwellings National Monument in New Mexico.

Romanticized, mythicized, and perhaps misunderstood, the so-called Anasazi left wondrous architectural remains, most notably at Mesa Verde in Colorado; Chaco Canyon in New Mexico; and Canyon de Chelly, Betatakin, and Keet Seel in Arizona. Composed of various groups living around the Four Corners area, they have generated the most intense interest. For centuries they lived semi-nomadically, hunting, gathering, and marginally cultivating corn, squash, and beans. They eventually settled into villages and adopted much of the Hohokam culture, more than their Mogollon neighbors did.

These various Ancestral Pueblo peoples were not pueblo dwellers yet, however. They were slow to establish year-round communities. Perhaps they weren't convinced that the Hohokam model would work in their rugged, dry canyonlands. With fewer and smaller rivers, they couldn't irrigate on the Hohokam scale. About 1,500 years ago the Pueblo-cultural pattern called Anasazi began to take shape, owing, perhaps, to the introduction of a new, more productive strain of corn.

Ancestral Pueblo peoples made a significant contribution to Southwestern culture with their architecture. Their remarkable stone masonry evolved out of a pithouse style used by Archaic peoples. A precursor of the kiva, the pithouse was constructed around a shallow, circular dugout with mud walls packed around vertical pole supports. The new stone-and-mortar houses, on the other hand, were very often rectangular in plan. In small communities they were built on a scale to house groups of a few families. These groups would have individual clan *kivas* (the Hopi word for underground ceremonial chambers) or single great kivas.

The soaring cliff dwellings of Canyon de Chelly, Betatakin, Keet Seel, and Mesa Verde represented another type of settlement, more protected from the elements and, perhaps, from raiders. Villagers cultivated the land around them. All of these communities had kivas, ritual spaces central to the lives of deeply spiritual people.

Ancestral Pueblo culture reached its height about 1,000 years ago. Hitherto Puebloans had continued to refine their use of water, not actually irrigating but using sporadic rainfall to the greatest advantage. They would line stones across slopes and cut ditches to distribute rainfall and limit erosion. Occasionally they dug canals in order to channel rainwater into planted fields. Unquestionably, they were expert dry farmers, coaxing abundance out of a harsh environment.

At the time of this climax, some people began moving from smaller, widespread communities into larger, denser settlements—perhaps like today's migrations to cities. The volume of trade in nearly all directions was tremendous, and Pueblo artisans were making superb pottery. Decorative techniques varied from region to region: black-on-white, black-on-red, black-on-orange, red-on-orange, and expressive combinations of these. People also etched petroglyphs into, and painted pictograms onto, rock faces. Rock art is found at almost all Anasazi and Sinagua sites. The quantity of artifacts that they left behind—utility and ceremonial items alike—is unparalleled among native North American groups.

* * *

AROUND 850 YEARS AGO, a cultural decline began. Drought and climatic change put pressure on the Pueblos' settled, agricultural lifestyles. Longer winters shortened growing seasons in which less rain fell. Villagers continued to move to more productive areas. By the late 1200s, Canyon de Chelly was unoccupied. Chaco Canyon had been vacant for 100 years. Settlements at Wupatki continued a little longer, into the 1300s. The Hopi Mesas, on the other hand, first built in the 1100s, were growing. They absorbed some of their migrating neighbors, and their traditions testify to their assimilation of ancient Pueblo culture.

There are also a great number of transitional settlements, many yet to be excavated, that accommodated groups leaving the immediate Four Corners area. Some of them are quite substantial. Considering these transitional settlements, what used to be a question of a culture's simply disappearing can now take a more human shape. The Anasazi didn't vanish—they chose to move. Over a couple of centuries they gradually migrated to new locations, slightly altering their lifestyles. (For some of them, that may have been part of a centuries-old practice.) In the process they passed on their knowledge to the people they joined: the Hopi, the New Mexican Zuñi, the Acoma, and other Pueblos. The Zuñi perspective on this migration is telling. As opposed to archaeologists' causes—drought, climatic change, deforestation, disease, warfare—they see it as a process of searching for "the center place," a place of spiritual rightness. And that center place is where present-day Pueblos are living.

The Sinagua, their name meaning "without water" in Spanish, belonged to a diverse group called the Hakataya, spread out across central Arizona. Wupatki, Walnut Canyon, Tuzigoot, and the inappropriately named Montezuma Castle are all Sinagua sites. These people absorbed Hohokam, Mogollon, and Anasazi cultural patterns: agriculture, village life, and the Mesoamerican ball game; stone masonry and cliff-dwelling architecture; and pottery. Situated in the middle of these three groups, they became a composite but separate culture.

As the so-called Anasazi waned, Hopi and Navajo cultures grew. The Navajo, an Apachean group from the north, gradually migrated southward along the Rocky Mountains about 5,000 years ago and settled in unoccupied places around Pueblo villages. Hunting and gathering were just about all that the land would support for them. Over time they learned farming techniques from the Pueblos and traded with them and as a result took on a character distinct from other Apachean groups, such as the 19th-century Chiracahua and Mescalero Apache. Living in small, dispersed groups, Navajos also raided Pueblo farms and villages—a practice in retrospect notoriously Apachean.

Soon after the Navajo came the Spanish, invading the Southwest early in the 16th century. Unlike Anglo-European conquerors, they allowed elements of native cultures to survive, provided that they accept a transfusion of Catholicism and alien governance. Of course, their intrusion into Southwestern life was far from cordial. Their first contact was with New Mexican Pueblos, whose understandable lack of interest in accepting Spanish rule met with the sword. Pueblo retaliation brought further hostility from the invaders, who murdered hundreds of natives and destroyed villages.

The Spanish didn't have the chance to overrun the Apacheans, whose scattered settlements were more difficult to locate than were pueblos. After the Pueblo Revolt of 1680, which drove the Spanish away, only to have them return 12 years later, the Navajo periodically housed Pueblos seeking refuge from reprisals. In return, the Pueblos taught them rituals, customs, agricultural techniques, and arts—in some of which, like weaving, they eventually surpassed their teachers. In the 1700s, drought led many Hopis to seek refuge among the Navajo in the formerly vacated Canyon de Chelly—a poignant example of the long-standing cooperative relationship of the two groups.

The Navajo also picked up European skills, some of them from the Pueblos. Directly from the Spanish they learned about silversmithing, raising cattle, and riding horses—and they became superior horsemen. Horses extended their gathering range and gave them greater mobility for trading and raiding. The Navajo were not nomadic, however. Many of them had different seasonal residences, log-and-earth hogans, as they continue to do today. These are maintained as permanent dwellings.

After independent Mexico ceded New Mexico to the United States in 1848, the Southwest's new proprietors decided to put an end to Indian raids. Over the next 16 years U.S. troops and the Navajo clashed repeatedly. The United States set up army posts within Navajo territory. They attempted to impose treaties, but U.S. agents often arranged treaties with individual headmen who had no authority that the Navajo as a whole could accept.

This misunderstanding of Navajo organization had tragic results. When raids continued, the U.S. territorial governor believed he had been betrayed. In order to safeguard the so-called frontier, he called in Colonel Kit Carson to destroy Navajo crops and livestock. Over the next few months, the People, as the Navajo call themselves, began to give themselves up. In 1864, as many as 8,000 Navajo made the forced Long Walk to captivity in Fort Sumner, 300 mi to the southeast.

The People were allowed to return to their land after four years of concentration-camp life. Fewer in number and greatly demoralized, they had to reconstruct their lives from scratch, rebuilding customs and lifestyles that had been impossible, if not forbidden, in the camps. Since then, Navajo ingenuity and an impressive ability to seize opportunities have gained them a measure of success in modern America. Their democratically governed community—Navajo Nation—numbers more than 250,000.

* * *

THE HOPI DIDN'T SUFFER SUCH BRUTAL-ITY. After conflicts with the Spanish—at the end of which they destroyed their own Christianized village of Awatovi in order to maintain the purity of Hopi ritual—their largely noncombative stance with the U.S. government afforded the Hopi more or less hands-off treatment.

In their proper observance of tradition and ritual, the Hopi are unique even among traditional Native Americans. In fact it was to Hopi spiritual leaders that many Native American traditionalists turned in the 1950s in what eventually became the Indian Unity Movement. Hopi beliefs focus on the relationship between the people, the land, and the Creator. In this strict moral order, prayer and ritual—which include the katsina rain power being dances—are necessary to keep the natural cycle in motion and to ensure the flow of life-sustaining forces. The earth is sacred, and they are its keepers.

The Hopi may well be the best dry farmers on the planet, successfully harvesting crops on a precarious 8 to 15 inches of rain per year—and no irrigation. Doubtless they manage this because they have perfected ancient Ancestral Pueblo techniques. The mesas on which they chose to live contain precious aquifers, particularly essential to life in such an arid territory. These vast water sources no doubt sustained them and their migrant guests when Pueblo peoples left places like Wupatki and Walnut Canyon and Canyon de Chelly 700 years ago. Unfortunately, the Hopi Tribal Council, which represents the progressive Christianized members of the Hopi, has sold sacred land to strip miners who in turn have destroyed parts of Black Mesa and depleted the aquifer. This is one indication of the rift between modernizers and those who continue to practice traditional ways. The traditionalists reside in the villages of Oraibi, Hotevilla, and Shungapovi. They are, understandably, intolerant of whites. They follow the Hopi Way even as contemporary life and the Tribal Council pose ever greater threats to it.

The present-day Tohono O'odham (called Papago by the Spanish) and the Pima, in central-southern Arizona, are descendants of the Hohokam. The Spanish first encountered them in the 17th century cultivating former Hohokam territory, using some of the ancient irrigation canals. Both tribes are Pimans, and both continue some Hohokam practices: living in rancherías along canals and performing costume dances and other rituals that link them to Uto-Aztecan language groups nearby in Mexico. The Pima live on the Salt River Reservation south of Phoenix, and the Tohono O'odham reservation stretches north from the Mexican border.

Like the Southwest's history, perspectives on Native American cultures are complex and fascinating—and have become confused in the clash of Euro-American and

Native American ways. Take, for example, the enchanting and mysterious word *Anasazi,* which enters into almost any discussion of native Arizonans. This Navajo word, meaning both "ancient ones" and "enemy ancestors," automatically implies a Navajo perspective. Another of equal value is that of the Hopi, whose name for the ancient culture, *Hisatsinom,* means "people of long ago." Yet another perspective is that of the New Mexican Zuñi, who prefer the word *Enote:que,* "our ancient ones, our ancestors."

To scientifically trained Euro-American archaeologists, the term Anasazi conveniently groups together a variety of ancient Pueblo peoples who had similar lifestyles but often divergent adaptations to Southwestern conditions. In past decades researchers encouraged the myth of a lost Anasazi civilization and posed virtually unanswerable questions about who the people were and how and why they "vanished" from the scene. Had they taken the beliefs and statements of the Hopi and of New Mexican Pueblos seriously—acting as both archaeologists and anthropologists—

the Hisatsinom–Enote:que–Anasazi would have fit seamlessly into the continuity of Native American life.

The perspective we can never know is that of the Ancestral Pueblos themselves—we don't even know what language they spoke. Yet we can try to get a sense of their world view by listening to contemporary Pueblos. If we project their uniquely American customs into the past, aspects of their ancestral culture come to life. And while Western tradition has its own ancient echoes, such as "know yourself" and "love your neighbor," traditional Pueblo ways speak of a life balanced in its relationship with the earth.

Sources

"What Happened to the Anasazi? Why Did They Leave? Where Did They Go?" A Panel Discussion at the Anasazi Heritage Center. Jerold G. Widdison, ed. Albuquerque: Southwest Natural and Cultural Heritage Association, 1990.

— Stephen Wolf

Stephen Wolf is a former Fodor's editor.

BOOKS & MOVIES

Books

Essays and Fiction. *Going Back to Bisbee,* by Richard Shelton, *Frog Mountain Blues,* by Charles Bowden, and *The Mountains Next Day,* by Janice Emily Bowers, are all fine personal accounts of life in southern Arizona. The hipster fiction classic *The Monkey Wrench Gang,* by Edward Abbey, details an eco-anarchist plot to blow up Glen Canyon Dam. *Stolen Gods,* a thriller by Jake Page, is set largely on Arizona's Hopi reservation and in Tucson. Three novels by Tucson-based writers skillfully evoke the interplay between Native American culture and contemporary Southwest life: *Pigs in Heaven,* by Barbara Kingsolver, *Almanac of the Dead,* by Leslie Marmon Silko, and *Yes Is Better Than No,* by Byrd Baylor. Wild West adventure, with all of the mythological glory that Hollywood has tried to capture, abounds in Zane Grey's novels—buy a new copy or look for any of the charming illustrated hardcover editions in used- or out-of-print-book stores. Tony Hillerman's mysteries will put you in an equally Southwestern mood.

General History. *Arizona: A History,* by Thomas E. Sheridan, chronicles the Anglo, Mexican, and Native American frontier and details its transformation into the modern-day Sunbelt. *Arizona Cowboys,* by Dane Coolidge, is an illustrated account of the cowboys, Native Americans, settlers, and explorers of the early 1900s. Buried-treasure hunters will be inspired by *Lost Mines of the Great Southwest,* by John D. Mitchell, which is just enough of a nibble to start you sketching maps and planning strategy. First printed back in 1891, *Some Strange Corners of Our Country,* by Charles F. Lummis, takes readers on a century-old journey to the Grand Canyon, Montezuma Castle, the Petrified Forest, and other Arizonan "strange corners." For a dip into the back roads of the past, try *Arizona Good Roads Association Illustrated Road Maps and Tour Book,* a 1913 volume, replete with hotel ads, reprinted by *Arizona Highways* magazine. *Roadside History of Arizona,* by Marshall Trimble, will bring you up-to-date on many of the same thoroughfares. *Ghost Towns of Arizona,* by James E. and Barbara H. Sherman, gives historical details on the abandoned mining towns that dot the state and provides maps to find them. For an anthology that covers the entire state's literature, consult *Named in Stone and Sky: An Arizona Anthology,* edited by Gregory McNamee.

Native American History. Two books provide excellent surveys of the ancient and more recent Native American past and cover in more depth sites mentioned in this guidebook. *Those Who Came Before: Southwestern Archaeology in the National Park System,* by Robert Lister and Florence Lister, provides a well-researched and completely accessible summary of centuries of life in the region informed by both contemporary Indian and archaeological perspectives. David G. Noble's *Ancient Ruins of the Southwest* covers similar territory more briefly and portably and includes directions for driving to sites. *Hohokam Indians of the Tucson Basin,* by Linda Gregonis, offers an in-depth look at this prehistoric tribe. In *Hopi,* by Susanne Page and Jake Page, the daily, ceremonial, and spiritual life of the tribe is explored in detail. Study up on the history of Hopi silversmithing techniques in *Hopi Silver,* by Margaret Wright. The beautifully illustrated *Hopi Indian Kachina Dolls,* by Oscar T. Branson, details the different ceremonial roles of the colorful Native American figurines. Navajo homes, ceremonies, crafts, and tribal traditions are kept alive in *The Enduring Navajo,* by Laura Gilpin. Navajo legends and trends from early days to the present are collected in *The Book of the Navajo,* by Raymond F. Locke.

A superb collection of Native American stories, songs, and poems, *Coming to Light,* edited by Brian Swann, includes material from all over the country, not only the Southwest. *Paths of Life: American Indians of the Southwest and Northern Mexico,* edited by Thomas E. Sheridan and Nancy J. Parezo, offers both contemporary and historical portraits of Native Americans.

Natural History. *The Arizona Sonora Desert Museum Book of Answers,* by David Lazaroff, covers hundreds of frequently asked natural-history questions. *Gathering the Desert,* by Gary Paul Nabhan, explores the Southwest from an ethnobotanist's viewpoint. *A Guide to Exploring Oak Creek and the Sedona Area,* by Stewart Aitchison, provides natural-history driving tours of this very scenic district. In *100 Desert Wildflowers in Natural Color,* by Natt N. Dodge, you'll find a color photo and brief description of each of the flowers included. Also written by Natt N. Dodge, *Poisonous Dwellers of the Desert* gives precise information on both venomous and nonvenomous creatures of the Southwest. *Venomous Animals of Arizona,* by Robert L. Smith, offers detailed information on venomous creatures of the Southwest. *Cacti of the Southwest,* by W. Hubert Earle, depicts some of the best-known species of the region with color photos and descriptive material. For comprehensive information on Grand Canyon geology, history, flora, and fauna, plus hiking suggestions, pick up *A Field Guide to the Grand Canyon,* by Steve Whitney. *Grand Canyon Country: Its Majesty and Lore,* by Seymour L. Fishbein, published by National Geographic Books, describes the Grand Canyon through photographs, maps, and firsthand accounts. *Common Edible and Useful Plants of the West,* by Muriel Sweet, gives the layperson descriptions of medicinal and other plants and shrubs, most of which were first discovered by Native Americans. *Roadside Geology of Arizona,* by Halka Chronic, is a good resource for finding the causes of the striking natural formations you'll see throughout the state.

Crafts. *The Traveler's Guide to American Crafts: West of the Mississippi,* by Suzanne Carmichael, gives browsers and buyers alike a useful overview of Arizona's traditional and contemporary handiwork.

General Interest. *Arizona Highways,* a monthly magazine, features exquisite color photography of this versatile state. Useful general travel information, fine pictures, and well-written historical essays all make the book *Arizona,* by Larry Cheek, a good pretrip resource.

Movies

The Arizona landscape has starred in a slew of films either as itself or as a stand-in for similar terrain—the Sahara, for instance—around the world. *The Postman* (1997), starring Kevin Costner, and *Buffalo Soldiers* (1997), starring Danny Glover, were filmed around Tucson. The Titan Missile Base near Green Valley was the locale for filming parts of *Star Trek: First Contact* (1996). Sun Devil Stadium in Tempe and Lost Dutchman State Park were featured in the blockbuster hit *Jerry Maguire* (1996). Parts of the Kevin Costner comedy *Tin Cup* (1996) were shot in Tubac. Much of director John Woo's bombastic *Broken Arrow* (1995), starring John Travolta and Christian Slater, was shot around Marble Canyon, which was also used, along with the Page–Lake Powell area, in the Mel Gibson–Jodie Foster vehicle *Maverick* (1994). Tom Hanks trotted through Monument Valley and Flagstaff in *Forrest Gump* (1994). The Tucson area served as the backdrop for much of *Boys on the Side* (1994), starring Whoopi Goldberg, Drew Barrymore, and Mary-Louise Parker. The nouveau Westerns *Tombstone* (1993), starring Val Kilmer and Kurt Russell, and Sharon Stone's *The Quick and the Dead* (1995) both made use of various sites in Mescal. Woody Harrelson and Juliette Lewis raged through Holbrook, Winslow, and other towns in *Natural Born Killers* (1994), and the Yuma area was used to otherworldly effect in the science-fiction film *Stargate*

(1994). Yuma stands in for a lot of places, including Morocco in Joseph von Sternberg's *Morocco* (1930), starring the sultry Marlene Dietrich, and the Bob Hope comedy *Road to Morocco* (1942).

The famous canyon loomed large in *Grand Canyon* (1991), starring Kevin Kline, Steve Martin, and Danny Glover. The independent cult hit *Red Rock West* (1991), directed by John Dahl and starring Nicolas Cage, was filmed in Willcox and other southeastern Arizona locales. Cage also starred, with Holly Hunter, in *Raising Arizona* (1987). Footage for the Joel Coen–directed film was shot in Scottsdale, Phoenix, and other locations. Chevy Chase frolicked through the Grand Canyon, Monument Valley, and Flagstaff in *National Lampoon's Vacation* (1983). Clint Eastwood stared down all comers in *The Outlaw Josey Wales* (1976), which showcases Patagonia and Mescal. Italian director Michelangelo Antonioni's *Zabriskie Point* (1968) includes scenes of Carefree and Phoenix. Marilyn Monroe dropped in on Phoenix in *Bus Stop* (1956). Gerd Oswald's noirish *A Kiss Before Dying* (1955), starring Robert Wagner

and Joanne Woodward, filmed in Tucson. Parts of *The Bells of St. Mary's* (1954) take place in Old Tucson. Some Arizona locations worked better than the real thing in Fred Zinnemann's *Oklahoma!* (1954). Jean Harlow whooped it up as a harried movie superstar in Victor Fleming's very funny *Bombshell* (1933), which has scenes shot in Tucson proper.

Among the many classic Westerns shot in Arizona are *The Searchers* (1956), *She Wore a Yellow Ribbon* (1949), *Fort Apache* (1948), and *Stagecoach* (1939), all directed by John Ford and starring John Wayne, both of whom spent a lot of time filming in the state over the years; *Gunfight at the OK Corral* (1957), starring Burt Lancaster and Kirk Douglas; *Johnny Guitar* (1954), director Nicholas Ray's Freudian take on the Old West that features Joan Crawford in a gender-bending performance as a tough-gal gunslinger; director Howard Hawks's moody *Red River* (1948), which stars John Wayne and Montgomery Clift; and Ford's *My Darling Clementine* (1946), in which Henry Fonda plays a reluctant sheriff.

INDEX

A

"A" Mountain (Sentinel Peak), 268
Abyss, The, 167
Actors Theatre of Phoenix, 57
Adventure tours, 325
Agate House, 260
Agave, 344
'Ahakhav Tribal Preserve, 378
Air tours, 172, 189
Air travel, F29–F31
airports, F31
with children, F34–F35
Grand Canyon, 184–185
luggage rules, F47
North-Central Arizona, 138
Northeast Arizona, 228
Northwest Arizona and Southeast Nevada, 387
Phoenix, Scottsdale, and the Valley of the Sun, 86–87
Southern Arizona, 365
Tucson, 322–323
Airport Mesa, 110
Ajo, 360–361
Ajo Historical Society Museum, 360
Alan Bible Visitors Center, 385
Alcohol and drugs, 200
Alma de Sedona ⌂ , 119
Alpine, 253–254
America West Arena, 7
Amerind Foundation, 352
Annie's Gift Shop and Tea Room ✕ , 241
Antelope Canyon, 223–224
Apache-Sitgreaves National Forest, 254
Apache Trail, F25, 80, 82–86
Arboretum, 83
Archaeology, F25, 84, 165, 249
theme trips, F51
Arcosanti, 79
Arizona Biltmore ⌂ , F23, 46
Arizona Center, 7
Arizona Historical Society Museum (Yuma), 362
Arizona Historical Society's Museum (Tucson), 275
Arizona Inn ⌂ , F23, 297–298
Arizona Opera, 56
Arizona Science Center, 7
Arizona Snowbowl, 124
Arizona-Sonora Desert Museum, F27, 283

Arizona State Museum, 275
Arizona State University, 20–21
Arizona State University Art Museum, 21
Arizona Strip, 183–184
Arizona Temple Gardens & Visitors Center Christmas Lighting, F17
Arizona Theatre Company, 57
Armory Park, 267
Art galleries and museums.
⇨ Also Museums
Eastern Arizona, 244, 249–250
Grand Canyon, 158, 174
North-Central Arizona, 104, 105, 128
Northeast Arizona, 195, 196, 201, 209, 212, 218
Northwest Arizona and Southeast Nevada, 372, 384
Phoenix, Scottsdale, and the Valley of the Sun, F26–F27, 9, 12–13, 18–19, 21, 75, 77, 84
Southern Arizona, 341, 352, 362
Tucson, 272, 275–276, 279
Art Walk, 71
Asarco Mineral Discovery Center, 319
ASU Karsten Golf Course, F26, 65
ASU Visitor Information Center, 20
ATMs, F45
Auto racing, 63
Avi Resort & Casino ✕⌂ , 382

B

Babbitt Brothers Building, 126
Bacavi, 210
Backpacking, 114–115
Ballet Arizona, 56
Balloon races, F20
Ballooning, F21
North-Central Arizona, 141
Phoenix, Scottsdale, and the Valley of the Sun, 67–68
Tucson, 310
Bank One Ballpark, 7–8
Barrio Historico (Tucson), 267
Baseball, F21, 62, 63–65, 311

Basha's Deli & Bakery, 359
Basketball, 64
Bead Museum, 13
Bed-and-breakfasts, F24, F43, 251, 338, 346
Bell Rock, 112
Benson, F25, F27–F28, 352–354
Besh-Ba-Gowah Archaeological Park, 84
Best Western Coronado Motor Hotel ⌂ , 364
Best Western Grand Canyon Squire Inn ⌂ , 154
Betatakin, 218
Bicycling, F48
Eastern Arizona, 235, 239–240, 253
Grand Canyon, 147, 153, 181, 185
North-Central Arizona, 130
Phoenix, Scottsdale, and the Valley of the Sun, 64
races, F18, F19, F20
Tucson, 311
Bill Williams River National Wildlife Refuge, 378
Biosphere 2 Center, 282
Bird Cage Theater, 341
Bird-watching, F19
Grand Canyon, 175–176
North-Central Arizona, 98
Northwest Arizona, 378
Southern Arizona, 331, 334–335, 337–338, 350, 358, 364–365, 366
Tucson, 311–312, 320
Bisbee, F18, F19, F23, F24, 343–347
Bisbee Mining and Historical Museum, 344–345
Bitter Springs, 219–220
Black Mesa, F25, 212–213
Black Theater Troupe, 57
Blue Range Primitive Area, 254
Blue Vista, 252
Boat tours, 226, 367
Boating, F21, 97–98, 225–226, 227, 380, 386
Bonelli House, 372
Boot Hill Graveyard, 340
Boulder Beach, 385
Boulder City, NV, F27, 384
Boulder City/Hoover Dam Museum, 384
Boulder Dam Hotel, 384

Boulders Resort and Golden Door Spa, The 🏨, *F23, 76*
Boyce Thompson Southwestern Arboretum, *83*
Boynton Canyon, *110*
Brewery Gulch, *345*
Briar Patch Inn 🏨, *F23, 119*
Bright Angel Lodge 🏨, *F24, 156, 161*
Bright Angel Point, *180*
Bright Angel Trailhead, *156*
Broadway Palm Dinner Theatre, *57*
Buenos Aires National Wildlife Refuge, *358*
Bullhead City, *382–384*
Burton Barr Central Library, *12*
Bus tours, *89, 189*
Bus travel, *F32*
Eastern Arizona, 261
Grand Canyon, 185
North-Central Arizona, 138
Northeast Arizona, 228
Phoenix, Scottsdale, and the Valley of the Sun, 87
Southern Arizona, 365
Tucson, 323–324
Butterfield stage stop, *350*
Butterfly Lodge Museum, *244*

C

Cabeza Prieta National Wildlife Refuge, *360*
Café Poca Cosa ✕, *F24, 288*
Café Roka ✕, *345*
Calendar of events, *F17–F20*
Callaghan Vineyards, *332–333*
Camelback Corridor, *28–30, 46–48*
Camelback Mountain and Echo Canyon Recreation Area, *66*
Camels, *381*
Cameras and photography, *F32, 200*
Cameron Trading Post ✕🏨, *F23, 174–175, 212–212*
Camp Verde, *F25, 97–98*
Camping, *F43–F44*
Eastern Arizona, 246, 251, 255–256, 258, 262
Grand Canyon, 152, 154–155, 162–163, 167, 170, 172, 174, 178, 183
North-Central Arizona, 95, 102, 105, 121, 129

Northeast Arizona, 200, 204–205, 212, 216, 218, 219, 222, 227
Northwest Arizona and Southeast Nevada, 386
Southern Arizona, 331, 336, 339, 349, 366
supplies, 186
Tucson, 312
Canyon de Chelly National Monument, *F27, 201–205*
Canyon Ranch 🏨, *301*
Canyon Rose Suites 🏨, *F23, 345–346*
Canyon Trail Rides, *182*
Canyon View Information Plaza, *156*
Canyon Wren, The 🏨, *120–121*
Cape Royal, *180*
Car rentals, *F32–33, F40*
Eastern Arizona, 262
North-Central Arizona, 138–139
Northwest Arizona and Southeast Nevada, 387
Phoenix, Scottsdale, and the Valley of the Sun, 87
Southern Arizona, 365
Tucson, 324
Car travel, *F33–F34, F40–F41*
Eastern Arizona, 262
Grand Canyon, 186–187
North-Central Arizona, 139
Northeast Arizona, 228–229
Northwest Arizona and Southeast Nevada, 373, 387
Phoenix, Scottsdale, and the Valley of the Sun, 88–89
self-drive tours, F25–F26, F51, 373
Southern Arizona, 365–366
Tucson, 324
Carefree, *F23, 73, 75–77*
Carefree-Cave Creek Chamber of Commerce, *75*
Carl Hayden Visitor Center, *224–225*
Carolina's ✕, *F25, 32*
Casa Grande Ruins National Monument, *F17, 80*
Casa Malpais Archaeological Park, *249*
Casa Tierra 🏨, *F23, 306*
Casinos, *59, 84, 310, 382–384*
Castaway shrine, *269*
Catalina Foothills, *294–295, 302–303*

Cathedral Rock Trail, *112*
Cave Creek, *73, 75–77*
Cave Creek Museum, *75*
Caverns
North-Central Arizona, 126
Northwest Arizona and Southeast Nevada, 375
Southern Arizona, 354–355
Tucson, 277, 279
Center for Creative Photography, *275–276*
Chandler, *39–40*
Chapel of the Holy Cross, *113*
Children, traveling with, *F34–F35*
Childsplay, *57*
Chinle, *F27*
Chiricahua National Monument, *F27, 348–349*
Chiricahua Regional Museum and Research Center, *351*
Chloride, *373–374*
Churches
North-Central Arizona, 113
Phoenix, 9
Tucson, F27, 271, 284
Chuska Mountains, *202*
Citrus Cafe ✕, *40*
Clarkdale, *99*
Claypool, *83*
Cliff pueblos
Canyon de Chelly National Monument, F27, 201–205
Montezuma Castle National Monument, F25, 97
Tonto National Monument, 85
Walnut Canyon National Monument, 135–136
Cliff Springs Trail, *180*
Climate, *F16*
Clothing for the trip, *F46*
Coal Canyon, *210*
Cobre Valley Center for the Arts, *84*
Coconino National Forest, *136*
Colleges and universities
Northeast Arizona, 202
Tempe, 20–21
Tucson, 272–276, 289, 297–299
Colorado River Museum, *382*
Colossal Cave Mountain Park, *277, 279*
Comfort Inn 🏨, *F24, 54*
Consulates and embassies, *F41*
Consumer protection, *F35*
Copper Queen Hotel 🏨, *345*

Copper Queen Mine Underground Tour, *343–344*
Cornville, *F24*
Coronado National Forest, *279*
Coronado National Memorial, *337*
Coronado Trail, *F26, 252*
Cottage Place ✕ , *131*
Coup Des Tartes ✕ , *30*
Courthouse Butte, *113*
Courthouse Plaza (Prescott), *103–104*
Crack-in-Rock Ruin, *137–138*
Crazy Ed's Satisfied Frog ✕ , *75*
Credit cards, *F8, F45*
Cruisers Café 66 ✕ , *F25, 150*
Cruises, *386*
Crystal Palace, *341*
Currency, *F41*
Customs and duties, *F35–F36*

D

Dahl & DiLuca ✕ , *117*
Dance
festivals and seasonal events, F17, F18, F19, 196, 197
Phoenix, 56
Tucson, 307
De Grazia's Gallery in the Sun, *279*
Dead Horse Ranch State Park, *98–99*
Deer Valley Rock Art Center, *73*
Desert Botanical Garden, *F27, 15*
Desert Caballeros Western Museum, *77*
Desert Ridge Marketplace, *69*
Desert View, *164*
Desert View Drive (Grand Canyon), *164–167*
Diamond Creek Road (Grand Canyon), *170*
Diné College, *202*
Dining, *F38*
Eastern Arizona, 234, 239, 240–241, 245, 250, 254, 255, 257, 259
Fodor's choice, F24–F25
Grand Canyon, F25, 144, 145, 150–151, 153–154, 160, 170, 172, 174, 176–177, 178, 182–183
menus in Spanish, 26

North-Central Arizona, 94, 98–99, 101, 105–106, 116–118, 126, 131–132
Northeast Arizona, 194, 203–204, 206, 209, 211, 213, 215, 217, 219, 221, 226–227
Northwest Arizona and Southeast Nevada, 370, 376, 379–380, 382–383
Phoenix, Scottsdale, and the Valley of the Sun, F24, F25, 9, 12, 14, 19, 21, 22–42, 76, 78, 80, 84
price categories, F38, 22, 94, 145, 194, 234, 288, 330, 370
Southern Arizona, 330, 333, 335, 338, 341–342, 345, 348, 350, 351, 353, 357, 359, 361, 363
Tucson, F24, F25, 270, 275, 284, 285–286, 321
Dinner theater, *57*
Dinosaur Tracks, *211*
Disabilities and accessibility, *F36–F37, 184*
Discounts and deals, *F38*
Doney Mountain, *138*
Douglas, *347–348*
Drives, *F25–F26, F51, 373*
Dude ranches, *F44, 304*
Duncan, George Taplin, *376*
Duties, *F35–F36*

E

Eastern Arizona, *F13, F25, F26, 212–263*
camping, 246, 251, 255–256, 258, 262
children, attractions for, 237–238, 243
dining, 234, 239, 240–241, 245, 250, 254, 255, 257, 259
emergencies, 262
itineraries, 233
lodging, 234, 239, 241–242, 243, 245–246, 250–251, 254, 255, 257, 258, 259
nightlife and the arts, 242, 246, 251–252
Petrified Forest and the Painted Desert, F28, 256–261
price categories, 234
shopping, 242–243, 246, 252, 259–260
sports and the outdoors, 235–236, 237–238, 239–240, 243, 244, 250, 253, 254–255, 256–257

timing the visit, 234
transportation, 261–262, 263
visitor information, 263
White Mountains, 236–256
Echo Bay, *385*
Echo Cliffs, *175, 219*
Ecotourism, *F38–F29, F51, 325*
Edna Vihel Center for the Arts, *21*
El Portal Sedona 🏨 , *118*
El Presidio Historic District (Tucson), *267*
El Tiradito, *269*
El Tour De Tucson, *F20*
El Tovar Dining Room ✕ , *F24, 160*
El Tovar Hotel 🏨 , *156, 158*
Elden Lookout Trail, *127*
Electricity, *F41*
Elephant Feet, *212*
Embassies, *F41*
Emergencies, *F41*
Eastern Arizona, 262
Grand Canyon, 187
North-Central Arizona, 140
Northeast Arizona, 229
Northwest Arizona and Southeast Nevada, 388
Phoenix, Scottsdale, and the Valley of the Sun, 89
Southern Arizona, 366
Tucson, 324–325
Encanto Park, *12*
Enchantment Resort 🏨 , *119*
Ensphere, *249*
Environmental theme trips, *F51*
Etiquette, *200*

F

Fairmont Scottsdale Princess 🏨 , *50–51*
Farrelli's Cinema Supper Club, *56*
FBR Open Golf Tournament, *F17*
Festival of Lights Boat Parade, *F20*
Festivals and seasonal events, *F17–F20*
5th Avenue (Scottsdale), *18*
Film
Grand Canyon, 153
Northeast Arizona, 223
Phoenix, Scottsdale, and the Valley of the Sun, 56–57
Film studio, *284–285*
First Mesa, *208*

Fish Creek Canyon, *85*
Fishing, *F48*
Eastern Arizona, 235, 237–238, 240, 244, 250, 253, 254–255
Grand Canyon, 149, 176
North-Central Arizona, 97–98, 113
Northeast Arizona, 197, 226
Flagstaff, *F16, F17, F19, F27, 123–135*
Flagstaff SummerFest, *F19*
Flandrau Science Center and Planetarium, *276*
Float trips, *89, 220–221*
Florence, *79–80*
Fly Exhibition Gallery, *341*
Fodor's choice, *F23–F28*
Football, *F17, 65, 249*
Fort Apache Indian Reservation, *F26, 237*
Fort Bowie National Historical Site, *349–350*
Fort Huachuca Museum, *337*
Fort Lowell Park and Museum, *279*
Fort Verde State Historic Park, *97*
Fort Yuma Quechan Indian Museum, *362*
4th Avenue (Tucson), *276*
Four Corners Monument, *216*
Four-wheeling, *64–65.*
  ⇨ *Also* Jeep tours
Fray Marcos Hotel 🏨 , *151*
Frontier Town, *75*

G

Gadsden Hotel, *347*
Gay and lesbian travelers, *F39*
Gem and mineral shows, *F17–F18*
General Jesup (steamboat), *381*
Ghost towns
Phoenix, Scottsdale, and the Valley of the Sun, 78, 82
Southern Arizona, 348
Giant Logs Trail, *260*
Gila County Historical Museum, *84*
Glen Canyon Dam, *219–227*
Glen Canyon National Recreation Area, *219–220, 224–225*
Glendale, *40–42*
Globe, *83–85*
Gold Canyon Golf Club, *F26, 65*

Gold Road Mine, *377*
Goldfield Ghost Town, *82*
Golf, *F21, F26, F48*
Eastern Arizona, 238, 240, 253, 256–257
North-Central Arizona, 114
Northeast Arizona, 221
Northwest Arizona and Southeast Nevada, 378
Phoenix, Scottsdale, and the Valley of the Sun, 5, 65–66, 75
professional tournaments, F17, F18
theme trips, F51
Tucson, 312–313
Goosenecks Region UT, *F26, 216–217*
Goulding's Trading Post, *217–218*
Governor Hunt's Tomb, *15*
Grady Gammage Auditorium, *21*
Graham Inn and Adobe Village 🏨 , *119*
Grand Canyon, *F12, 143–191*
accessibility, 184
bicycling, 147, 153, 181, 185
business hours, 188
camping, 152, 154–155, 162–163, 167, 170, 172, 174, 178, 183
camping supplies, 186
children, attractions for, 147, 149, 150, 151, 152, 154, 161, 164, 181, 182
crowds, 148
dining, F25, 144, 145, 150–151, 153–154, 160, 170, 172, 174, 176–177, 178, 182–183
emergencies, 187
fees, 187
festivals and seasonal events, F19, 163
fishing, 149, 176
free attractions, 166
guided tours, 172, 189–190
health, 187–188
hiking, 147, 156, 158–159, 165–167, 169, 181–182, 188, 189
horseback riding, 153
itineraries, 145
lodging, F23, F24, 144–145, 151–152, 154, 160–162, 170, 172, 174, 176–177, 178, 182–183
lost and found, 188

mail and shipping, 188
money matters, 188
mule rides, 159, 182
nightlife and the arts, 163
North Rim and environs, F23, F26, F28, 172–184
pets, 188–189
price categories, 145
rafting, 147, 170, 176, 189–190
shopping, 152, 163–164, 167, 186
skiing, 150, 160
South Rim, F18, F25, 146–169
sports and the outdoors, 147, 149–150, 153, 158–160, 165–167, 168, 169, 170, 176, 181–182, 188
timing the visit, 146
transportation, 184–185, 186–187
visitor information, 190–191
West Rim, 169–172
Grand Canyon Caverns, *375*
Grand Canyon Chamber Music Festival, *F19, 163*
Grand Canyon Deer Farm, *149*
Grand Canyon IMAX Theater, *153*
Grand Canyon Lodge ✕🏨 , *F23, 181, 182–183*
Grand Canyon Railway, *147, 148, 149*
Grand Canyon Village, *F24, 156–164*
Grand Canyon West, *169–170*
Grand Canyon West Ranch, *375*
Grand Hotel, The 🏨 , *154*
Grandview Point, *164*
Grapevine Canyon Ranch 🏨 , *348–349*
Grayhawk Country Club *65*
Greasewood Flats, *60*
Great Arizona Puppet Theatre, *57*
Green's Peak, *248*
Greer, *F23, F25, 244–246*
Grill at Hacienda del Sol, The ✕ , *294*
Grill at the TPC, The ✕ , *33*
Guest ranches, *F44, 304*

H

Hall of Flame, *15*
Hannagan Meadow, *254–256*
Hannagan Meadow Lodge ✕🏨 , *255*
Hano, *208*
Hassayampa Inn 🏨 , *106*

Hassayampa River Preserve,
    78
Hatathli Museum, *202*
Havasu Canyon, *171–172*
Havasu Falls, *171*
Havasu National Wildlife
    Refuge, *378*
Havasupai Tribe, *171–172*
Health concerns, *F39–F40,*
    187–188
Heard Museum, *F26–F27,*
    12–13
Heard Museum Guild Indian
    Fair and Market, *F18*
Heard Museum North, *75*
Heard Museum Shop, *71*
Helicopter tours, *172, 189*
Heritage Square, *8*
Hermit Road (Grand
    Canyon), *167–169*
Hermits Rest, *167–168*
Hermosa Inn 🖾 , *F23, 50*
Hiking, *F21–F22, F48*
Eastern Arizona, 235, 239–240,
    244, 253, 255, 257
Grand Canyon, 147, 156,
    158–159, 165–167, 169,
    181–182, 188, 189
North-Central Arizona, 95,
    97–98, 105, 112, 114–115,
    127, 129
Northeast Arizona, 197,
    202–203, 216, 219, 221, 226
Northwest Arizona and
    Southeast Nevada, 373, 375
Phoenix, Scottsdale, and the
    Valley of the Sun, 66–67
Southern Arizona, 331, 366
tours, 189
Tucson, 313–314
Historama, *340–341*
Historic Downtown District
    (Flagstaff), *126*
Historic Route *66, F26, 372*
History, *F26–F27*
Holbrook, *F19, 258–260*
Hole-in-the-Rock, *15*
Holiday Inn Express 🖾 , *353*
Holidays, *F40*
Home exchanges, *F44*
Homolovi Ruins State Park,
    F25, 257–258
Hoover Dam, *F27, 384*
Hopi ceremonies, *197, 200*
Hopi Cultural Center, *209*
Hopi House, *158, 163–164*
Hopi Mesas, *205–210*
Hopi Point, *168*
Hopi shrines, *200*

Horseback riding, *F22*
Eastern Arizona, 240
Grand Canyon, 153
North-Central Arizona, 105,
    115, 129
Northeast Arizona, 203, 216
Phoenix, Scottsdale, and the
    Valley of the Sun, 67, 75
Tucson, 314
Hostels, *F44–F45*
Hot-air ballooning. ⇨ *See*
    Ballooning
Hotel Congress 🖾 , *F24, 297*
Hotel Monte Vista 🖾 , *126*
Hotels, *F45.* ⇨ *Also* Lodging
Hotevilla, *210*
House Rock Valley, *177*
Houseboating, *227, 380, 386*
Houses, historic
Grand Canyon, 158
Northwest Arizona and
    Southeast Nevada, 372
Phoenix, Scottsdale and the
    Valley of the Sun, F27, 8, 14,
    19, 21
Southern Arizona, 362
Tucson, 269–270, 271–272
Hualapai Mountain Park, *F27,*
    372–373
Hualapai Trail, *171*
Hualapai Tribe, *171–172*
Hubbell Trading Post National
    Historic Site, *205*
Hubbell Trading Post Store,
    205

I

Imperial National Wildlife
    Refuge, *364–365*
Inn at *410* 🖾 , *132*
Inscription Rock, *204*
Insurance, *F40*
for car rentals, F33
for international travelers, F41
International Mariachi
    Conference, *F18*
International travelers,
    F40–F43
International Wildlife Museum,
    283–284
Island Trail, *135*
Itineraries, *F14–F15*

J

J. Knox Corbett House,
    269–270
Jacob Lake, *172, 174,*
    177–178
Jail Tree, *77*

Janos ✕ , *F24, 294–295*
Jasper Forest, *260*
Jazz on the Rocks Festival,
    F19
Jeep tours
Grand Canyon, 189
North-Central Arizona,
    140–141
Northeast Arizona, 203, 216
Northwest Arizona and
    Southeast Nevada, 378
Phoenix, Scottsdale, and the
    Valley of the Sun, 64–65
Southern Arizona, 345
Jerome, *95, 97, 100–102*
Jerome State Historic Park,
    100
John Slaughter Ranch/San
    Bernardino Land Grant, *347*
John Wesley Powell Memorial
    Museum, *220*
Juan Bautista de Anza
    National Historic Trail,
    321
JW Marriott's Camelback Inn
    Resort, Golf Club & Spa 🖾 ,
    50

K

Kaibab Plateau, *177*
Kaibab Plateau Visitor's
    Center, *178*
Kartchner Caverns State Park,
    F27–F28, 354–355
Kayenta, *213, 215*
KC Motel 🖾 , *239*
Keams Canyon Trading Post,
    206, 208
Keet Seel, *218*
Kingman, *F27, 372–373,*
    375–377
Kingman Area Chamber of
    Commerce, *372*
Kitt Peak National
    Observatory, *359*
Kolb Studio, *158*
Kramer's at the Manzanita
    Restaurant & Lounge ✕ ,
    F24, 98–99
Kykotsmovi, *210*

L

La Casa Vieja, *21*
La Fiesta de los Vaqueros, *F18*
La Fontanella ✕ , *27*
La Hacienda ✕ , *36*
La Posada Winslow 🖾 , *F24,*
    258
La Vuelta de Bisbee, *F18*

Lake Havasu, *F19, F27, 377–380*
Lake Mead National Recreation Area, *F28, 385–386*
Lake Powell, *F20, F23, 219–227*
Lake Powell Boulevard (Page), *220*
Lake Powell Resort ✕⚑ , *F23, 226–227*
Lakeshore Scenic Drive (Lake Mead), *385*
L'Auberge ✕, *116*
L'Auberge de Sedona ⚑ , *118*
Laughlin, NV, *382–384*
Lava Flow Trail, *136–137*
Lava River Cave, *126*
Lavender Jeep Tours, *345*
Lavender Pit Mine, *343*
Le Bistro ✕, *291*
Lees Ferry, *172, 174, 175–177*
Lenox Crater, *137*
Lipan Point, *164*
Litchfield Park, *40–42, 55*
Little America of Flagstaff ⚑ , *133*
Little House Museum, *249*
Lodge at Ventana Canyon Golf Course, *F26, 313*
Lodging, *F43–F45.* ⇨ *Also* Camping
with children, *F35*
disabilities and, *F36–F37*
Eastern Arizona, *234, 239, 241–242, 243, 245–246, 250–251, 254, 255, 257, 258, 259*
Fodor's choice, *F23–F24*
Grand Canyon, *144–145, 151–152, 154, 160–162, 170, 172, 174, 176–177, 178, 182–183*
meal plans, *F9*
North-Central Arizona, *94, 101, 106–108, 118–121, 126, 132–134*
Northeast Arizona, *194, 196, 203–204, 209, 211–212, 215, 217, 219, 221–222, 226–227*
Northwest Arizona and Southeast Nevada, *370, 376–377, 380, 382–384, 386*
Phoenix, Scottsdale, and the Valley of the Sun, *F22, 42–55, 76, 78–79, 84*
price categories, *F43, 42, 94, 145, 194, 234, 296, 330, 370*

Southern Arizona, *330, 333, 335–336, 338–339, 342, 345–346, 348–349, 351–352, 353–354, 357, 358, 361, 364*
Tucson, *296–306, 321, 322, 325*
Loews Ventana Canyon Resort ⚑ , *301–302*
London Arms Pub and Restaurant ✕, *379*
London Bridge, *F27, 377*
London Bridge Days, *F19*
London Bridge Resort ⚑ , *380*
Lon's at the Hermosa ✕, *F24, 32*
Lookout Studio, *158*
Los Dos Molinos ✕, *31–32*
Los Sombreros Mexican Cantina ✕, *37*
Lost Dutchman Mine, *81*
Lost Dutchman Gold Mine Superstition Mountain Trek, *F18*
Lowell Observatory, *126–127*
Luggage, *F47*
Lyman Lake State Park, *246, 248*

M
Madera Canyon, *319–320*
Mail and shipping, *F41–F42, 188*
Main Street (Bisbee), *345*
Main Street Arts District (Scottsdale), *18*
Marble Canyon, *175*
Marble Canyon Lodge ✕⚑ , *176–177*
Mariachi music festival, *F18*
Maria's When in Naples ✕, *36*
Maricopa Point, *168*
Mariposa Books & More, *334*
Marquesa ✕, *F24, 38*
Marshall Way Arts District (Scottsdale), *18*
Mary Elaine's ✕, *35–36*
Mather Point, *158*
Matthews Center, *21*
McFarland State Historical Park, *80*
Meal plans, *F9*
Media, *F45, 229*
Medical services. ⇨ *See* Emergencies
Mesa, *F17, 39–40*
Meteor Crater, *136*
Mexican culture, *269*
Mexican Hat, *217*

Mi Nidito ✕, *F25, 295–296*
Miami, *83*
Mine Museum, *100*
Mining operations
North-Central Arizona, *100*
Northeast Arizona, *210*
Northwest Arizona and Southeast Nevada, *377*
Phoenix, Scottsdale, and the Valley of the Sun, *73, 75, 78, 81, 82, 84*
Southern Arizona, *343–345, 360*
Tucson, *319*
Mishongnovi, *209*
Mission San Xavier del Bac, *F27, 284*
Mission tours, *325*
Mittens, *215*
Mogollon Rim, *237*
Mohave County Museum of History and Arts, *372*
Money matters, *F41, F45*
Grand Canyon, *188*
Northeast Arizona, *229*
Monti's La Casa Vieja ✕, *21*
Montezuma Castle National Monument, *F25, 97*
Montezuma Well, *97*
Monument Valley Navajo Tribal Park, *F28, 213, 215–216*
Monument Valley Visitor Center, *215–216*
Mooney Falls, *171*
Moran Point, *164–165*
Motels. ⇨ *See* Lodging
Motorcycle theme trips, *F51*
Mt. Elden Trail System, *127*
Mt. Lemmon, *279–280*
Mt. Lemmon Ski Valley, *280*
Mountain biking, *130*
Mule rides, *159, 182*
Muleshoe Ranch Cooperative Management Area, *350–351*
Museo Chicano, *9*
Museum Club, *127*
Museum of Northern Arizona, *F17, 127–128*
Museums. ⇨ *Also* Art galleries and museums
Eastern Arizona, *244, 249–250, 256, 259, 261*
Grand Canyon, *149, 158, 165*
North-Central Arizona, *F17, 100, 104–105, 127–128*

Northeast Arizona, 195–196, 201, 202, 209, 215–216, 217, 218, 220
Northwest Arizona and Southeast Nevada, 372, 382, 384
Phoenix, Scottsdale, and the Valley of the Sun, F25, F26–F27, 7, 9, 12–13, 15, 16, 18–19, 21, 73, 75, 77, 79–80, 82, 84
Southern Arizona, 337, 340, 341, 344–345, 351, 352, 360, 362, 363
Tucson, 272, 275–276, 279, 280, 283–284, 319, 321
Music, classical
festivals and seasonal events, F19, 134, 163
Grand Canyon, F19, 163
North-Central Arizona, 108, 134
Phoenix, 56
Tucson, 307, 308
Music, popular
Eastern Arizona, 251–252
festivals and seasonal events, F17, F18, F19, 108, 122
North-Central Arizona, 108, 122, 127, 134
Northeast Arizona, 223
Phoenix, Scottsdale, and the Valley of the Sun, 59, 60, 61
Tucson, 307, 309–310
Mystery Castle, 14/id

N

National Festival of the West, F18
National monuments
Grand Canyon, F27, 183
North-Central Arizona, 97, 99, 135–138
Northeast Arizona, F25, F27, 201–205, 218–219, 218–219, 225
Phoenix, Scottsdale, and the Valley of the Sun, 80, 85
Southern Arizona, 348–349, 361
National parks. ⇨ *See* Parks, national
Native American Arts & Crafts Festival, F19
Native American history theme trips, F51
Native American sites
Eastern Arizona, 237, 257–258

Grand Canyon, 158, 165, 169–170, 171–172, 174–175
North-Central Arizona, F25, 97, 110, 136–138
Northeast Arizona, 194–219, 220, 223–224, 225
Phoenix, Scottsdale, and the Valley of the Sun, 84, 85
Southern Arizona, 349–350, 352, 362
Native Americans
culture, F22, F25, F26–F27, 12–13, 15, 16, 75, 79–80, 84, 85, 95, 99, 105, 127–128, 140, 158, 165, 169–170, 171–172, 174–175, 207, 213, 214, 215–216, 217, 218, 220, 269
festivals and seasonal events, F17, F18, F19, 134, 197
petroglyph sites, 73, 137–138, 211, 235, 247, 248
Natural history theme trips, F51
Nature, F27–F28, 180
Navajo Arts and Crafts Enterprises, 174, 196, 212
Navajo Bridge, 175
Navajo Cultural Center of Kayenta, 213
Navajo Falls, 171
Navajo Nation Annual Tribal Fair, F19
Navajo Nation Council Chambers, 195–196
Navajo Nation East, 194–196, 200–205
Navajo Nation Museum, 196
Navajo Nation North, 213–219
Navajo Nation Visitor Center, 196
Navajo Nation West, 210–213
Navajo National Monument, F25, 218–219
Navajo Nations, 194–196, 200–205, 207, 210–219
Navajo Point, 165
Navajo Tribal Fairgrounds, 196
Navajo Village Heritage Center, 220
Nevada. ⇨ *See* Northwest Arizona and Southeast Nevada
New Cornelia Open Pit Mine Lookout Point, 360
Newspaper Rock, 260

Nogales, *355–358*
North-Central Arizona, F12, 92–141
camping, 95, 102, 105, 121, 129
children, attractions for, 104–105, 113–114, 126–128, 136
dining, 94, 98–99, 101, 105–106, 116–118, 126, 131–132
emergencies, 140
festivals and seasonal events, F17, 107, 108, 122, 134
Flagstaff, 123–135
Flagstaff side trips, 135–138
guided tours, 140–141
itineraries, 93
lodging, 94, 101, 106–108, 118–121, 126, 132–134
Native American culture, F25, 95, 97, 99, 105, 110, 127–128, 134, 136–138, 140
nightlife and arts, 102, 108, 121–122, 127, 134
price categories, 94
Sedona and Oak Creek Canyon, F19, F23, F25, F26, 109–123
shopping, 102, 108–109, 122–123, 134–135
sports and the outdoors, 95, 98, 105, 107, 112, 113, 114–115, 124, 127, 129–131
timing the visit, 94
transportation, 138–139, 140, 141
Verde Valley, Jerome, and Prescott, F19, F27, 95, 97–109
visitor information, 141
North Rim Drive (Canyon de Chelly), 202
Northeast Arizona, F12, 193–230
camping, 200, 204–205, 212, 216, 218, 219, 222, 227
children, attractions for, 196, 211, 215–216, 220
dining, 194, 203–204, 206, 209, 211, 213, 215, 217, 219, 221, 226–227
emergencies, 229
Glen Canyon Dam and Lake Powell, F20, F23, 219–227
guided tours, 216, 223–224, 226, 230
Hopi Mesas, 205–210
itineraries, 195

lodging, 194, 196, 203–204, 209, 211–212, 215, 217, 219, 221–222, 226–227
media, 229
money matters, 229
Navajo Nation East, 194–196, 201
Navajo Nation North and Monument Valley, 213–219
Navajo Nation West, 210–213
nightlife, 223
price categories, 194
reservation life, 207
rules, 200
shopping, 196, 197, 201, 205, 206, 208, 209, 211, 212, 223
sports and the outdoors, 197, 202–203, 216, 219, 220–221, 225–226
time zone, 229
timing the visit, 194
transportation, 228–229, 230
visitor information, 230
Northern Arizona University Observatory, *128*
Northlight Gallery, *21*
Northwest Arizona and Southeast Nevada, *F13, 369–388*
camping, 386
children, attractions for, 375
dining, 370, 376, 379–380, 382–383
emergencies, 388
guided tours, 378, 388
itineraries, 371
lodging, 370, 376–377, 380, 382–384, 386
price categories, 370
sports and the outdoors, 373, 375, 378–379, 386
time zone, 388
timing the visit, 371
transportation, 387, 388
visitor information, 388

O

Oak Creek Canyon, *F26, 109–123*
Oatman, *377*
Oatman Hotel, *377*
OK Corral (Tombstone), *340–341*
OK Corral & Stable (Apache Junction), *67*
Old Courthouse Museum, *259*
Old Oraibi, *210*
Old Town Scottsdale, *18*

Old Town Tempe Fall Festival of the Arts, *F17*
Old Tucson Studios, *284–285*
Old West Day/Bucket of Blood Races, *F19*
Old West itinerary, *F14–F15*
O'Leary Peak, *137*
O'odham Tash, *F17*
Organ Pipe Cactus National Monument, *361*
Orpheum Theatre, *9*
Outdoor activities. ⇨ *See* Sports and the outdoors

P

Package deals, *F38*
Packing, *F46–F47*
Page, *220–223*
Painted Desert, *174–175, 211, 256–261*
Painted Desert Visitor Center, *261*
Paisley Corner Bed & Breakfast 🖫 , *251*
Pancho McGillicuddy's ✕ , *150*
Papago Café ✕ , *359*
Papago Park, *15*
Papago Peaks, *66*
Papago Salado, *14–16*
Parada del Sol Rodeo and Parade, *F17*
Paradise Valley, *F23, F24, 32, 50*
Parks, national, *F46.* ⇨ *Also* Grand Canyon
Glen Canyon National Recreation Area, 219–220, 224–225
Petrified Forest National Park, F28, 256, 260–261
Saguaro National Park East, 281
Saguaro National Park West, F28, 285
Tumacácori National Historic Park, 322
Parks, state, *F49*
Eastern Arizona, F25, 246, 248, 257–258
North-Central Arizona, 97, 98–99, 100, 113–114, 128–129
Phoenix, Scottsdale, and the Valley of the Sun, 80
Southern Arizona, 334, 340, 354–355, 362–363
Tucson, 321
Passports and visas, *F42*

Patagonia, *334–336*
Patagonia Lake State Park, *334*
Patagonia-Sonoita Creek Preserve, *334*
Payson Rodeo, *F19*
Pearce, *348*
Peralta Trail, *82*
Petrified Forest National Park, *F28, 256, 260–261*
Petroglyph Trail, *248*
Petroglyphs, *73, 137–138, 211, 235, 247, 248*
Phippen Museum of Western Art, *104*
Phoenician, The 🖫 , *51–52*
Phoenician Golf Club, *66*
Phoenix, Scottsdale, and the Valley of the Sun, *F12, F27, 2–90*
Apache Trail, F25, 80, 82–86
Camelback Corridor, 28–30, 46–48
central Phoenix, 26–27, 43, 46
Chandler, 39–40
children, attractions for, 7, 8, 12–13, 14, 15–16, 21–22, 28, 29, 34, 37, 40, 48, 49, 50–51, 53–54, 57–58, 66, 69, 73, 75, 82, 84
climate, F16
cultural center of Phoenix, 9, 12–13
dining, F24, F25, 9, 12, 14, 19, 21, 22–42, 75, 76, 78, 80, 84
downtown Phoenix, 4–9, 23, 26, 42–43
east valley, 39–40, 54–55
emergencies, 89
festivals and seasonal events, F17, F18, F20
Glendale, 40–42
guided tours, 89
itineraries, 3
Litchfield Park, 40–42, 55
lodging, F23, F24, 42–55, 76, 78–79, 84
Mesa, F17, 39–40
mountains, 5
nightlife and the arts, 56–61, 78, 79, 84
north Phoenix, 48
north-central Phoenix, 30–31
Papago Salado, 14–16
Paradise Valley, F23, F24, 32, 50
price categories, 22, 42
shopping, 68–72, 76–77, 79, 85
side trips near Phoenix, 72–80

Sky Harbor Airport area, 48–49
south Phoenix, 13–14, 31–32,
49–50
sports and the outdoors, F26, 5,
61–68, 75
Tempe, F17, F26, 19–22,
39–40, 54–55
transportation, 86–89, 90
visitor information, 90
west Phoenix, 40–42
west valley, 40–42, 55
Phoenix Art Museum, 13
Phoenix Museum of History, 9
Phoenix Symphony Orchestra,
56
Phoenix Theatre, 57
Phoenix Zoo, 15–16
Photography and cameras,
F32, 200
Pima Air and Space Museum,
280
Pima County Courthouse, 271
Pima Point, 168
Pinal County Historical Society,
79–80
Pinal County Visitor's Center,
79
Pinetop-Lakeside, F19,
239–243
Pioneer Arizona Living History
Museum, 73
Pioneer Museum, 128
Pipe Spring National
Monument, F27, 183
Pizzeria Bianco ✕, 23, 26
Plane travel. ⇨ See Air travel
Planetariums and
observatories
North-Central Arizona,
126–127, 128
Southern Arizona, 359
Tucson, 276
Poetry, 308
Point Imperial, 181
Point Sublime, F26, 181
Powell Memorial, 168
Prescott, F19, F27, 95, 97,
102–109
Prescott Frontier Days and
Rodeo, F19
Prescott National Forest,
102
Price categories
dining, F38, 22, 94, 145, 194,
234, 288, 330, 370
lodging, F43, 42, 94, 145, 194,
234, 296, 330, 370
Privacy, customs, and laws,
200

Pueblo Grande Museum and
Cultural Park, F25, 16
Puerco Ruins, 260

Q

Quartzsite Pow Wow Gem and
Mineral Show, F17

R

Radio stations, 229
Rafting, F48–F49, 147, 170,
176, 189–190
Railroad Museum, 149
Railroads
Grand Canyon, 147, 148, 149
North-Central Arizona, 99
Rainbow Bridge National
Monument, 225
Rainbow Forest Museum and
Visitor Center, 261
Rainbow Trout Farm, 113
Ramsey Canyon Inn Bed &
Breakfast 🏨, 338
Ramsey Canyon Preserve, 337
Randolph Park Golf Courses,
F26, 313
Rawhide Western Town &
Steakhouse, 57
Red Rock State Park, 113
Red Setter Inn 🏨, F23, 245
Reed's Lodge 🏨, F24, 251
Reid Park Zoo, 280
Remington's Lounge, 59
Rendezvous, F18
Rendezvous Diner ✕, F25,
245
Renée Cushman Art Collection
Museum, 249–250
Restaurant Hapa ✕, F24, 37
Restaurants. ⇨ See Dining
Rex Allen Arizona Cowboy
Museum, 351
Rex Allen Days, F19
Rim Trail, 136
Riordan State Historic Park,
F27, 128–129
Ritz-Carlton 🏨, 46–47
River rafting, F48–F49, 147,
170, 176, 189–190
Riverside Resort ✕🏨, 383
Robert's ✕, 117
Rock climbing, 129
Rockhounding, F49
Rockin' R Ranch, 57–58
Rodeo of Rodeos, F17
Rodeos, F17, F18, F19, 107,
196, 314
Rose Peak, 252
Rose Tree Inn Museum, 340

Rosson House, 8
Route 66 Fun Run Weekend,
F18
Royal Palms Resort & Spa 🏨,
47
Ruiz's Mexican Food &
Cantina ✕, F25, 353

S

Sabino Canyon, 281
Saguaro National Park East,
281
Saguaro National Park West,
F28, 285
Saguaros, 282
Sailplaning, 68
St. Augustine Cathedral,
271
St. Mary's Basilica, 9
Salt River Canyon, F26,
236–237
San Bartolome Historic Site,
177
San Carlos Apache Indian
Reservation, 237
San Francisco Volcanic Field,
136–138
San Juan Inn & Trading Post
✕🏨, 217
San Pedro Riparian National
Conservation Area,
337–338
San Pedro Valley Arts and
Historical Society Museum,
352
Sanctuary on Camelback
Mountain 🏨, 50
Santa Cruz River & River Park,
271
Santa Fe Depot, 126
Schnebly Hill Scenic Drive,
110
School House Inn Bed &
Breakfast 🏨, F24, 346
Scottsdale, F17, F18, F20,
F24, F26, F27, 16–19,
32–39, 50–54. ⇨ Also
Phoenix, Scottsdale, and
the Valley of the Sun
Scottsdale Center for the Arts,
18
Scottsdale Convention and
Visitors Bureau, 18
Scottsdale Fashion Square, 70
Scottsdale Historical Museum,
18
Scottsdale Museum of
Contemporary Art, 18–19
Second Mesa, 208–209

Sedona, *F19, F23, F25,*
109–123
Sedona Golf Resort, *F26, 114*
Self-drive tours, *F25–F26,*
F51, 373
Sells, *359–360*
Senior-citizen travel, *F47*
Sentinel Peak, *268*
Sharlot Hall Museum, *F27,*
104–105
Sheridan House Inn ⬚ , *151*
Shopping, *F22, F47–F48*
Eastern Arizona, 242–243, 246,
252, 259–260
Grand Canyon, 152, 163–164,
167, 186
North-Central Arizona, 102,
108–109, 122–123, 134–135
Northeast Arizona, 196, 197,
201, 205, 206, 208, 209,
211, 212, 223
Phoenix, Scottsdale, and the
Valley of the Sun, 68–72,
76–77, 79, 85
Southern Arizona, 334, 336,
342–343, 347, 351, 353,
357–358, 359
Tucson, 315–318
Show Low, *F26, 237–239*
Shugrue's ✕ , *379*
Shungopavi, *208–209*
Sichomovi, *208*
Sierra Vista, *336–339*
Silver Creek Golf Club, *F26,*
238
Silver Dragon ✕ , *40–41*
Singing Wind Bookshop, *353*
Sipaulovi, *209*
Skiing, *F22, F49*
Eastern Arizona, 235–236, 240,
243, 244, 253, 255
Grand Canyon, 150, 160
North-Central Arizona, 124,
130–131
Tucson, 280
Skywatcher's Inn ⬚ , *354*
Slide Rock State Park,
113–114
Smoki Museum, *105*
Snoopy Rock, *114*
Snowboarding, *130–131, 240*
Snowflake-Taylor, *256–257*
Snowmobiling, *235–236,*
253, 255
Soaring, *68*
Sonoita, *331–333*
Sonoita Creek State Natural
Area, *334–335*

Sonoita Vineyards, *333*
Sonoran Desert, *283–285*
Sosa-Carillo-Frémont House,
271
South Mountain Park, *14,*
66–67
South Rim Drive (Canyon de
Chelly), *201–202*
Southeast Nevada. ⇨ *See*
Northwest Arizona and
Southeast Nevada
Southern Arizona, *F13,*
328–367
camping, 331, 336, 339, 349,
366
children, attractions for, 334,
335, 337, 340–341, 343–344,
348, 351, 354, 362–363,
364–365
dining, 330, 333, 335, 338,
341–342, 345, 348, 350,
351, 353, 357, 359, 361,
363
emergencies, 366
guided tours, 343–344, 345,
366–367
itineraries, 329
lodging, 330, 333, 335–336,
338–339, 342, 345–346,
348–349, 351–352, 353–354,
357, 358, 361, 364
nightlife, 346
price categories, 330
shopping, 334, 336, 342–343,
347, 351, 353, 357–358, 359
southeast Arizona, 330–355
southwest Arizona, 355–365
sports and the outdoors, 331,
366
timing the visit, 330
transportation, 365–366, 367
visitor information, 357
Southwest Wings Birding
Festival, *F19*
Spas, *F51, 5*
Spider Rock Overlook,
201–202
Sports and the outdoors,
F48–F49. ⇨ *Also* specific
sports
Eastern Arizona, 235–236,
237–238, 239–240, 244, 250,
253, 254–255, 256–257
Grand Canyon, 147, 149–150,
153, 158–160, 165–167, 168,
169, 170, 176, 181–182, 188
North-Central Arizona, 95, 98,
105, 107, 112, 113,
114–115, 124, 127, 129–131

Northeast Arizona, 197,
202–203, 216, 219, 220–221,
225–226
Northwest Arizona and
Southeast Nevada, 373, 375,
379–379, 386
Phoenix, Scottsdale, and the
Valley of the Sun, F26, 5,
61–68, 75
Southern Arizona, 331, 366
Tucson, F26, 269, 280,
310–315
Springerville-Eagar, *F24,*
248–252
Springerville-Eagar Regional
Chamber of Commerce, *248,*
250
Springerville Volcanic Field,
248
Standard Register PING
Tournament, *F18*
State parks. ⇨ *See* Parks,
state
Steamboat Rock, *205*
Stevens Home, *271–272*
Stinton Museum, *256*
Stout's Cider Mill, *350*
Student travel, *F49*
Submarine Rock, *114*
Summerhaven, *279–280*
Sunrise Park Resort, *243*
Sunset Crater Volcano
National Monument,
136–137
Sunset Trail, *127*
Superior, *83*
Superstition Mountain
Museum, *82*
Superstition Mountains, *82*
Surgeon's House ⬚ , *101*
Symbols, *F9*

T

T. Cook's ✕ , *29–30*
Taliesin West, *F27, 19*
Taxes, *F49*
Taxis
North-Central Arizona, 140
Phoenix, Scottsdale, and the
Valley of the Sun, 90
Southern Arizona, 367
Tucson, 325–326
Telephones, *F42–F43*
Tempe, *F17, F26, 19–22,*
39–40, 54–55
Tempe City Hall, *21*
Tempe Town Lake, *21–22*
Tennis, *68, 314–315*
Tequila, *344*

Texas Canyon, F26, 352
Thai Spices ✕, F25, 117
Theater
North-Central Arizona, 108, 134
Phoenix, Scottsdale, and the Valley of the Sun, 9, 21, 57–68
Southern Arizona, 341
Tucson, 308–309
Theme trips, F51
Theodore Roosevelt Lake Reservoir & Dam, 85
Third Mesa, 209–210
Thunderbird Hot-Air-Balloon Classic, F20
Thunderbird Lodge ✕⛫, 203–204
Time zones, F50, 229, 388
Timing the trip, F16–F20
Tipping, F50
Titan Missile Museum, 319
Tohono Chul Park, 281
Tomaso's ✕, 28
Tombstone, F19, 339–343
Tombstone Chamber of Commerce and Visitor Center, 340
Tombstone Courthouse State Historic Park, 340
Tombstone Epitaph Museum, 341
Tombstone's Helldorado Days, F19
Tonto National Monument, 85
Toroweap Overlook, 184
Tortilla Flat, 86
Tostitos Fiesta Bowl Classic, F17
Totem Pole, 215
Tournament Players Club of Scottsdale, 66
Tours and packages, F50–F51
Trailview Overlook, 168–169
Train travel, F51. ⇨ Also Railroads
Eastern Arizona, 263
North-Central Arizona, 141
Northeast Arizona, 230
Northwest Arizona and Southeast Nevada, 388
Phoenix, Scottsdale, and the Valley of the Sun, 90
Southern Arizona, 367
Tucson, 326
Transept Trail, 181, 182
Travel agencies, F51–F52
disabilities and accessibility, F37

for gay and lesbian travelers, F39
for tours and packages, F50
Trolley tours, 140
Troon North Golf Courses, F26, 66
Tuba City, F19, 211–212
Tuba City Trading Post, 211
Tubac, 320–321
Tubac Presidio State Historic Park and Museum, 321
Tubing, 68
Tucson, F13, F27, 265–326
camping, 312
Catalina foothills, 294–295, 302–303
central Tucson, the Santa Catalinas, and East, 277, 279–282, 289–292, 299–300
children, attractions for, 272, 275, 276, 277, 279, 280, 283–285
climate, F16
dining, F24, F25, 270, 275, 284, 285–296, 321
downtown, 266–272, 288–289, 296–297
eastside, 292–293, 300–301
emergencies, 324–325
festivals and seasonal events, F17–F18, 308, 314
guided tours, 325
itineraries, 267
lodging, F23, F24, 296–306, 321, 322, 325
Mexican and Native American culture, 269
nightlife and the arts, 306–310
northeast Tucson, 293, 301–302
northwest Tucson, 295, 303, 305–306
price categories, 288, 296
shopping, 315–318
side trips, 319–322
south Tucson, 295–296
sports and the outdoors, F26, 269, 280, 310–315
transportation, 322–324, 325–326
University of Arizona, 272–276, 289, 297–299
visitor information, 326
west of Tucson, 306
Westside and the Sonoran Desert, 283–285
Tucson Botanical Gardens, 281
Tucson Gem and Mineral Show, F17–F18

Tucson Marriott University Park ⛫, 298–299
Tucson Poetry Festival, 308
Tumacácori National Historic Park, 322
Turquoise Turtle, 359
Tusayan, F25, 146, 152–155
Tusayan Ruin and Museum, F25, 165
Tuzigoot National Monument, 99
Twin Knolls, 248

U

U.S. Army Intelligence Museum, 337
Uncle Bill's Place ⛫, 222
University of Arizona, 272–276, 289, 297–299
University of Arizona Museum of Art, 276
Upper Red Rock Loop, 110
Upper Ruins, 85
Utah, F26, 216–217

V

Vail Building, 126
Valley Art Theatre, 57
Valley of the Sun. ⇨ See Phoenix, Scottsdale, and the Valley of the Sun
Verde Canyon Railroad, 99
Verde Valley, 95, 97–109
Vermilion Cliffs, 175–176
Village of Elgin Winery, 333
Visas, F42
Visitor information, F52
Volcanic remains, 127, 136–138, 248, 348
Vortex tour, 111
Vulture Mine, 78

W

Wahweap, F23, 225–227
Walking tours, 325
Walnut Canyon National Monument, 135–136
Walpi, 208
Watchtower, The, 164
Water sports, F21, 373, 378–379
Weather, F16
Weaver's Needle, 82
Web sites, F52
Western Navajo Fair, F19
Westin La Paloma ⛫, 302
Whiskey Row, 105
White House Ruin, 202

White Mesa Natural Bridge, *212*
White Mountains, *236–256*
White Stallion Ranch 🏨 , *F23, 305*
Why, *360*
Wickenburg, *F18, 77–79*
Wickenburg Gold Rush Days, *F18*
Wild West shows, *57–58*
Wildlife refuges
Northwest Arizona and Southeast Nevada, 378
Phoenix, Scottsdale, and the Valley of the Sun, 78
Southern Arizona, 334–335, 337–338, 348, 358, 360, 364–365

Willcox, *350–352*
Willcox Commercial Store, *351*
Willcox Playa, *350*
Williams, *F18, 146–147, 149–152*
Williams Depot, *149*
Williams Visitor Center, *149*
Window Rock, *F19, 195–196, 201*
Window Rock Navajo Tribal Park, *196*
Wineries, *331, 332–333*
Winslow, *F24, F25*
World Championship Hoop Dance Contest, *F17*
Wupatki National Monument, *F25, 137–138*

Y

Yaki Point, *165*
Yaqui Easter, *F18*
Young's Farm, *79*
Yuma, *361–364*
Yuma Convention and Visitors Bureau, *362*
Yuma Crossing National Historic Landmark, *362*
Yuma Crossing State Historic Park, *362–363*
Yuma Territorial Prison, *363*

Z

Zoos
Phoenix, 15–16
Tucson, F27, 280, 283

FODOR'S KEY TO THE GUIDES

America's guidebook leader publishes guides for every kind of traveler.
Check out our many series and find your perfect match.

FODOR'S GOLD GUIDES
America's favorite travel-guide series offers the most detailed insider reviews of hotels, restaurants, and attractions in all price ranges, plus great background information, smart tips, and useful maps.

COMPASS AMERICAN GUIDES
Stunning guides from top local writers and photographers, with gorgeous photos, literary excerpts, and colorful anecdotes. A must-have for culture mavens, history buffs, and new residents.

FODOR'S CITYPACKS
Concise city coverage in a guide plus a foldout map. The right choice for urban travelers who want everything under one cover.

FODOR'S EXPLORING GUIDES
Hundreds of color photos bring your destination to life. Lively stories lend insight into the culture, history, and people.

FODOR'S TRAVEL HISTORIC AMERICA
For travelers who want to experience history firsthand, this series gives in-depth coverage of historic sights, plus nearby restaurants and hotels. Themes include the Thirteen Colonies, the Old West, and the Lewis and Clark Trail.

FODOR'S POCKET GUIDES
For travelers who need only the essentials. The best of Fodor's in pocket-size packages for just $9.95.

FODOR'S FLASHMAPS
Every resident's map guide, with dozens of easy-to-follow maps of public transit, restaurants, shopping, museums, and more.

FODOR'S CITYGUIDES
Sourcebooks for living in the city: thousands of in-the-know listings for restaurants, shops, sports, nightlife, and other city resources.

FODOR'S AROUND THE CITY WITH KIDS
Up to 68 great ideas for family days, recommended by resident parents. Perfect for exploring in your own backyard or on the road.

FODOR'S HOW TO GUIDES
Get tips from the pros on planning the perfect trip. Learn how to pack, fly hassle-free, plan a honeymoon or cruise, stay healthy on the road, and travel with your baby.

FODOR'S LANGUAGES FOR TRAVELERS
Practice the local language before you hit the road. Available in phrase books, cassette sets, and CD sets.

KAREN BROWN'S GUIDES
Engaging guides—many with easy-to-follow inn-to-inn itineraries—to the most charming inns and B&Bs in the U.S.A. and Europe.

SEE IT GUIDES
Illustrated guidebooks that include the practical information travelers need, in gorgeous full color. Thousands of photos, hundreds of restaurant and hotel reviews, prices, and ratings for attractions all in one indispensable package. Perfect for travelers who want the best value packed in a fresh, easy-to-use, colorful layout.

OTHER GREAT TITLES FROM FODOR'S
Baseball Vacations, The Complete Guide to the National Parks, Family Vacations, Golf Digest's Places to Play, Great American Drives of the East, Great American Drives of the West, Great American Vacations, Healthy Escapes, National Parks of the West, Skiing USA.

At bookstores everywhere.   www.fodors.com/books